Bloomsbury Rhyming Dictionary

A & C Black • London

www.acblack.com

First published in Great Britain in 2007
Reprinted 2009

A & C Black Publishers Ltd
36 Soho Square, London W1D 3QY

© A & C Black Publishers Ltd 2007

A CIP record for this book is available from the British Library.

ISBN: 978 0 7136 8192 5

This book is produced using paper that is made from wood grown in managed,
sustainable forests. It is natural, renewable and recyclable. The logging and
manufacturing processes conform to the environmental regulations of the country
of origin.

Text typeset by A & C Black
Printed in Spain by GraphyCems

Introduction

In producing this dictionary, we have pulled together over 45,000 words, names and phrases in order to provide you with as much help as possible in finding that elusive rhyme.

The easiest way to find the rhyme you need is to look up the word you are trying to rhyme with in the alphabetical index at the back of the book. Here you will see the word followed by a numerical code which indicates where you can find the entry in the main part of the book. So, for example, if you look up **cross**, you will see:

cross **13.34.7**

which means you will find words that rhyme with **cross** in section **13.34.7** of the main text.

Where a word has more than one possible pronunciation, and therefore more than one possible set of rhymes, the various possibilities are indicated in the index separated by a comma. So if you look up **liquorice**, you will see:

liquorice **10.50.12, 10.54.18**

which guides you to entries whose sounds end with *-ris* in section **10.50.12** and those whose sounds end with *-rish* in section **10.54.18**.

Where a word has more than one part of speech (for example, noun, verb) and the different parts of speech have different pronunciations, these are spelt out in the index. So if you look up **advocate**, you will see:

advocate (noun) **2.56.9**
advocate (verb) **5.47.20**

which shows you that words rhyming with the pronunciation of the noun **advocate** can be found in section **2.56.9**, while rhymes for the verb can be found in section **5.47.20**.

Within each section we have listed the words by the number of syllables they contain, and then within this by alphabetical order. The number of syllables is given in bold at the beginning of each subset of words.

You may, however, decide when you get to the relevant section in the main text that you do not want an exact rhyme with the word you looked up. In these cases it may be useful for you to know how we have split the entries in this book into groups, and therefore how the numbering system for the groups works.

We have split the entries into 22 major sections depending on the final vowel sound of the word. These sections can be distinguished using the first number(s) of the numerical code, and are as follows:

1.   *a* as in **apple**, **bad** etc
2.   ' or 'ə' as in **danger**, **station**, **accidental** etc
3.   *ah* as in **father**, **starch** etc
4.   *air* as in **chair**, **prepare** etc
5.   *ay* as in **day**, **dedicate** etc
6.   *e* as in **bed**, **head** etc
7.   *er* as in **burger**, **work** etc
8.   *ear* as in **beer**, **hear** etc
9.   *y* as in **baby**, Naomi etc
10.   *i* as in **bid**, catalyst etc
11.   *eye* as in **fly**, **guide** etc
12.   *ire* as in **dial**, **wire** etc
13.   *o* as in **cross**, **odd** etc
14.   *or* as in **core**, **fought** etc
15.   *ure* as in **cure**, **vacuous** etc
16.   *ow* as in **down**, **mouth** etc
17.   *our* as in **hour**, **tower** etc
18.   *oy* as in **destroy**, **soil** etc
19.   *oh* as in **cocoa**, radio etc
20.   *uh* as in **blood**, **trust** etc
21.   *oo* as in **book**, **put** etc
22.   *u* as in **dew**, **shoe** etc

Within each 'vowel' section, we have split the entries into groups according to the sounds and letters that follow and precede the vowel. Our aim has been to provide you with as close a match as possible to the word you are looking up, so that if there are (in general) four or more words with the same closing letter or sound, these are grouped together in a section.

So, for example, rather than providing you with a long and impenetrable list of words ending in *-ism*, we have split these into sections depending on whether they end in the sound *-dism*, *-fism*, *-kism*, and so on (see sections **2.40.45** to **2.40.89**).

If you go to the relevant section in the main text and decide you don't want to use any of the words there, you can find alternative rhymes by looking at other sections near the one you originally looked up. You can use the numerical code to navigate around similar sounding entries.

So, the first element of the numerical code (before the first full stop) indicates the final vowel sound of the word (as listed on the previous page).

The second element of the numerical code (after the first full stop) indicates a subsection within that vowel sound. This is usually caused by a change in the ending of the word, such as by a change in the final consonant. So under the vowel section **6** (words ending with the vowel sound *-e* as in bed), you will find these subsections **6.0** listing words ending with the sound *-eb*, **6.1** listing words ending with the sound *-ed*, **6.2** listing words ending with the sound *-edth*, **6.3** listing words ending with the sound *-eds* etc.

If a word ending is particularly rich in rhymes, then we have split these subsections up even further according to the sounds *before* the main vowel sound. These further subsections are indicated by the numbers after the second full stop in the numerical code. So, to continue the example from the vowel section **6**, under the subsection **6.1** (words ending in *-ed*) you will also find subsections **6.1.1** for words ending in *-bed*, **6.12** for words ending in *-abed*, **6.1.3** for words ending in *-ded*, **6.1.4** for words ending in *-head* etc.

Any time you want a wider selection of less exact rhymes, all you have to do is look at the other sections with the same prefix in the numerical code. So if you look up **frost** in the index, get to section **13.36.2** in the main text and decide you don't like any of the suggested rhymes, just look at other entries that begin with **13.36** for inspiration.

Occasionally a word simply doesn't have very many rhymes, so we have left them in short sections, mostly with cross-references to take you to other sections which will suggest possible alternative rhymes.

We have used cross-references between sections in the text to link together related word sounds (such as the variant pronunciations of grass or path), to link together common words derivations (such as linking adverbs ending in *-ly* with their 'root' adjective), or to link together related word endings (such as linking adjectives ending in *-ed* or *-ing* with their 'root' verb and vice versa). So, for example, we have given cross-references from section **3.47** (mast, vast etc) to section **1.38** (massed, bombast etc) and vice versa, from section **2.37.130** (artful, doubtful etc) to section **9.14.10** (fitfully, frightfully etc), and from section **10.42.11** (growing, rowing etc) to section **19.15.4** (borrow etc).

Finally, we have included snippets of verse from famous poets and singwriters old and new. These are dotted throughout the book so that you can see how the great and the good have used – and in some cases abused! – rhymes.

We hope you find this book useful, and good luck!

1.1: 1 Ab, dab, fab, gab, jab, Mab, nab, stab, tab; 2 Ahab, Cantab, confab, jilbab, kebab, Moab, prefab, Rajab, rehab; 3 baobab.
See also **10.42.13.**

1.1.1: 1 cab, scab; 2 vocab; 3 minicab, taxicab.

1.1.2: 1 blab, flab, lab, slab; 2 conflab.

1.1.3: 1 crab, drab, grab; 2 mihrab; 3 olive drab, smash-and-grab.

1.2: 1 abs, Babs, drabs; 2 abdabs.

1.3: 1 ad, add, cad, Chad, fad, gad, had, sad, tad; 2 Assad, cycad, dryad, dyad, gonad, jihad, maenad, monad, naiad, octad, pentad, Riyadh, triad, want ad; 3 ennead, Galahad; 4 hamadryad, Olympiad, Upanishad.
See also **1.4, 10.2.3.**

1.3.1: 1 bad, bade; 2 forbad, forbade; 3 zindabad; 4 Allahabad, Faisalabad, Hyderabad, Islamabad.

1.3.2: 1 dad; 2 Baghdad, doodad, grandad, granddad; 3 Trinidad.

1.3.3: 1 blad, clad, glad, lad, plaid; 2 ironclad, mail-clad, unclad; 3 Jack the lad.
See also **1.4.**

1.3.4: 1 mad; 2 Ahmad, nomad; 3 barking mad.

1.3.5: 1 pad; 2 footpad, gamepad, joypad, keypad, launch pad, notepad, scratchpad, touchpad; 3 helipad, lily pad.
See also **10.2.3, 10.42.14.**

1.3.6: 1 brad, rad, trad; 2 Conrad, farad, tetrad; 3 Angharad.

1.3.7: 1 grad; 2 postgrad; 3 Leningrad, Petrograd, Stalingrad, undergrad, Volgograd.

1.4: 1 adze, lads, scads; 2 gonads, small ads; 4 classified ads.
See also **1.3, 1.3.3.**

1.5: 1 cafe, caff, chaff, faff, gaff, gaffe, naff; 2 chiffchaff, decaf, Llandaff, Olaf, Piaf, pilaf, seraph.
See also **1.43, 3.23.**

1.5.1: 1 WRAF; 2 carafe, riffraff; 3 Musharraf.

1.5.2: 1 graph; 3 paragraph, phonograph, polygraph; 4 radiograph.
See also **3.23.3.**

1.6: 1 dag, fag, gag, hag, jag, mag, nag, sag, shag, snag; 2 zigzag; 3 lollygag.
See also **1.7, 10.42.34.**

1.6.1: 1 bag; 2 air bag, beanbag, cool bag, fleabag, gasbag, grab bag, growbag, handbag, ice bag, kitbag, mailbag, mixed bag, nosebag, old bag, postbag, punchbag, ragbag, ratbag, sandbag, scumbag, sleazebag, teabag, windbag; 3 carpetbag, moneybag, saddlebag; 5 diplomatic bag.
See also **1.7, 1.8.**

1.6.2: 1 blag, flag, lag, slag; 2 greylag, gulag, jet lag, old lag, red flag, white flag; 3 corner flag, yellow flag.
See also **1.7, 10.42.34.**

1.6.3: 1 brag, Bragg, crag, drag, frag, rag; 2 defrag, dishrag, Morag, toerag.
See also **1.8, 10.2.23, 10.42.34.**

1.6.4: 1 stag, tag; 2 dog tag, price tag, ragtag.

1.6.5: 1 swag, wag; 2 chinwag, wigwag; 3 scallywag.

1.7: 1 bagged, fagged, flagged, gagged, shagged; 2 debagged, jet-lagged, zigzagged.
See also **1.6, 1.6.1, 1.6.2.**

1.8: 1 bags, rags; 2 glad rags; 3 moneybags.
See also **1.6.1, 1.6.3.**

1.9: 1 badge, cadge, hadj, hajj, Madge; 2 blue badge; 3 orange badge; 5 Lailat al-Miraj.

1.10: 1 hack, shack, vac, Zac; 2 ack-ack, Dvořák, kayak, NASDAQ, Novak, Slovak, Toshack; 3 armagnac, bivouac, Kerouac, Mauriac, medevac; 4 demoniac, paranoiac.

1.10.1: 3 Bosniac, cardiac, Cluniac, iliac, kodiak, Pauillac, zodiac; 4 amnesiac, celeriac, insomniac; 5 aphrodisiac, haemophiliac, hypochondriac, paradisiac, sacroiliac.

1.10.2: 3 maniac; 5 dipsomaniac, egomaniac, kleptomaniac, mythomaniac, nymphomaniac, pyromaniac; 6 megalomaniac.

1.10.3: 1 back; 2 bareback, blowback, bounceback, buy-back, cashback, clawback, comeback, dieback, drawback, flashback, giveback, greenback, halfback, hatchback, hogback, horseback, humpback, hunchback, kickback, knockback, leaseback, loanback, pass-back, payback, playback, slingback, snapback, splashback, sweepback, switchback, talkback, throwback, wingback, zwieback; 3 money-back, piggyback.

Was none who would be foremost
To lead such dire attack;
But those behind cried 'Forward!'
And those before cried 'Back!'
(Thomas Babington Macaulay)
See also **1.12, 10.42.41.**

1.10.4: 2 aback; 3 back-to-back, centre back, paperback, quarterback.

1.10.5: 2 feedback, hardback, laid-back, redback; 4 biofeedback.

1.10.6: 2 callback, fallback, fullback, pullback, rollback, tailback; 3 saddleback, stickleback.

1.10.7: 2 cutback, fastback, fightback, outback, setback, softback, sweptback, wetback.

1.10.8: 1 jack; 2 blackjack, bootjack, carjack, cheapjack, flapjack, highjack, hijack, skipjack, skyjack; 3 applejack, crackerjack, lumberjack, natterjack, steeplejack, Union Jack; 4 Monterey Jack. *See also* **1.11, 1.12, 10.42.41.**

1.10.9: 1 yack, yak; 2 cognac, Gaillac; 4 yackety-yak.

1.10.10: 1 clack, claque, flack, flak, lack, plaque, slack; 2 Balak, shellac; 3 Cadillac. *See also* **1.11.2, 10.42.41.**

1.10.11: 1 black; 2 bootblack, eyeblack, jet-black, lampblack, pitch-black, shoeblack; 3 penny black.

1.10.12: 1 mac, Mac, smack; 2 Cormac, gobsmack, sumach, tarmac, yashmak; 3 McCormack, Potomac.

1.10.13: 1 knack, snack; 2 knick-knack, nick-nack; 3 almanac, Pasternak, Sassenach. *See also* **1.11.**

1.10.14: 1 pack; 2 backpack, cold pack, daypack, Deepak, Dipak, face pack, flatpack, ice pack, mudpack, rat pack, six-pack, unpack; 3 blister pack, bubble pack, power pack. *See also* **1.12.1, 10.42.41.**

1.10.15: 1 Braque, crack, craic, rack, wrack; 2 arrack, Barak, barmbrack, Chirac, gimcrack, hayrack, Iraq, roof rack, sérac, wisecrack; 3 anorak, Bacharach, bladder wrack, bric-a-brac, off-the-rack. *See also* **1.12.3, 10.42.42.**

1.10.16: 1 track; 2 Amtrak, backtrack, fast-track, one-track, racetrack, sheeptrack, short-track, sidetrack, soundtrack. *See also* **10.42.42.**

1.10.17: 1 sac, sack; 2 Coalsack, Cossack, Cusack, knapsack, mailsack, ransack, rucksack, sad sack, woolsack; 3 cul-de-sac, haversack; 5 amniotic sac. *See also* **1.12, 10.42.41.**

1.10.18: 1 stack, tack; 2 attack, hardtack, haystack, smokestack, thumbtack, ticktack, tie tack; 3 chimneystack; 4 counterattack. *See also* **1.12.5.**

1.10.19: 1 quack, thwack, whack; 2 bushwhack. *See also* **1.12, 10.42.41.**

1.10.20: 2 Anzac, Balzac, Barsac, dansak, Kazakh, Muzak, Prozac.

1.11: 1 axe, Bax, daks, jacks, max, pax, sax, snacks; 2 Ajax, climax, IMAX, pickaxe, Tampax; 4 anticlimax. *See also* **1.10.8, 1.10.13.**

1.11.1: 1 fax; 2 Ceefax, Fairfax; 3 Filofax, Halifax.

1.11.2: 1 flax, lax, slacks; 2 poleaxe, relax; 3 battleaxe, parallax. *See also* **1.10.10, 10.42.137.**

1.11.3: 2 anthrax, borax, hyrax, thorax.

1.11.4: 1 tax; 2 stealth tax, surtax, syntax, wealth tax; 3 overtax, supertax; 5 capital gains tax, value-added tax. *See also* **10.42.137, 10.62.3.**

1.11.5: 1 wax; 2 AWACS, beeswax, earwax. *See also* **10.42.137.**

1.12: 1 act, backed, fact, sacked, whacked; 2 enact, exact, gobsmacked, hijacked, play-act, react, transact; 3 artefact, inexact; 4 matter-of-fact, overreact; 6 Official Secrets Act. *See also* **1.10.3, 1.10.8, 1.10.17, 1.10.19, 10.42.166.**

1.12.1: 1 packed, pact; 2 close-packed; 3 Warsaw Pact; 4 suicide pact. *See also* **1.10.14.**

1.12.2: 2 compact, impact, jam-packed, Stamp Act; 3 subcompact, vacuum-packed. *See also* **10.2.70.**

1.12.3: 1 bract, cracked, wracked; 2 refract; 3 cataract, counteract, interact, overact. *See also* **1.10.15.**

1.12.4: 1 tract; 2 abstract, attract, contract, detract, distract, extract, protract, retract, subtract; 3 subcontract. *See also* **10.2.70, 10.42.166.**

1.12.5: **1** stacked, tact; **2** contact, intact.
See also **1.10.18**.

1.13: **1** Al, gal, Hal, mall, pal, sal; **2** cabal, canal, Chagall, Duval, et al.; , grand mal, halal, keypal, Laval, pen pal; **3** birth canal, chaparral, petit mal; **7** alimentary canal.
See also **3.30**.

1.13.1: **2** decal, low-cal, mescal, Pascal; **3** caracal.

1.14: **1** calk, talc; **3** catafalque.

1.15: **1** alp, palp, scalp.

1.16: **1** shalt; **2** asphalt, gestalt.

1.17: **1** salve, valve; **2** bivalve, lip salve; **3** safety valve.

1.18: **1** am, ham, mam, ma'am, Pam, sham, spam, swam, wham, yam; **2** Annam, Assam, cheongsam, East Ham, exam, iamb, Oxfam, Priam, pro-am, Siam, Vietnam, West Ham, wigwam; **3** Abraham, Mandelstam, Suriname, Uncle Sam; **4** ad nauseam, Omar Khayyam.

1.18.1: **1** dam, damn; **2** Edam, goddamn, Mesdames, Potsdam, quondam; **3** Amsterdam, cofferdam, Rotterdam.
See also **1.19, 10.42.85**.

1.18.2: **1** jam, jamb; **2** doorjamb, logjam, unjam.
See also **1.19**.

1.18.3: **1** cam, scam; **2** CAD/CAM, hakam, headcam, webcam; **3** digicam.

1.18.4: **1** clam, lam, lamb, slam; **2** flimflam, grand slam; **3** body slam.

1.18.5: **1** cram, drachm, dram, pram, ram, scram, tram; **2** Bairam, dirham, DRAM; **3** diaphragm; **4** battering ram.
See also **1.19**.

1.18.6: **1** gram; **2** diagram; **3** block diagram, cablegram, centigram, epigram, milligram, telegram, Venn diagram.

1.18.7: **3** aerogram, anagram, cryptogram, hexagram, histogram, hologram, kilogram, kissogram, mammogram, monogram, pentagram, pictogram, spidergram, strip-o-gram; **4** ideogram, organogram; **5** parallelogram; **7** electrocardiogram.

1.18.8: **2** program, programme; **3** aerogram, deprogramme, microgram, preprogram; **4** microprogram, radiogram.
See also **10.42.85**.

1.19: **1** crammed, dammed, damned, jammed.
See also **1.18.1, 1.18.2, 1.18.5**.

1.20: **1** amp, champ, cramp, damp, ramp, samp, stamp, tamp, tramp, vamp; **2** firedamp, food stamp, revamp; **3** rising damp, rubber-stamp, writer's cramp.
See also **2.54.62**.

1.20.1: **1** camp, scamp; **2** base camp, decamp, encamp; **3** aide-de-camp, prison camp; **5** concentration camp.
See also **10.42.111**.

1.20.2: **1** clamp, lamp; **2** arc lamp, blowlamp, fog lamp, headlamp, streetlamp, sunlamp, wheel clamp; **3** lava lamp, table lamp; **4** hurricane lamp.

In restless dreams I walked alone
Narrow streets of cobblestone,
'Neath the halo of a street lamp,
I turned my collar to the cold and damp
(Simon and Garfunkel)

1.21: **1** an, Anne, ban, Chan, dan, fan, Han, Jan, Juan, San, than, WAN; **2** Afghan, Cheyenne, dewan, Elsan, Hassan, Pusan, sedan, Sudan; **3** Ariane, ASEAN, Callaghan, Dalian, Mary Ann, Taliban.
See also **1.22.1, 3.34**.

1.21.1: **1** can, Cannes, scan; **2** cancan, oilcan, pecan, Spokane, tin can; **3** astrakhan, billycan, CT scan, jerrycan, overscan.

There was a young man of Japan
Whose limericks never would scan;
When they said it was so,
He replied, 'Yes, I know,
But I always try to get as many words into
the last line as ever I possibly can.'
(Limerick)
See also **1.22**.

1.21.2: **1** clan, flan, LAN; **2** Caplan, élan, Milan; **3** Catalan, gamelan, Ku Klux Klan.

1.21.3: **1** plan; **2** flight plan; **3** open-plan; **5** contingency plan.
See also **10.42.93**.

1.21.4: **1** man, Mann; **2** adman, bagman, Bergmann, binman, Bormann, caveman, conman, green man, New Man, newsman, old man, sandman, snowman, strongman, swagman, unman; **3** garbageman, Isle of Man, ladies' man, Piltdown Man, repairman; **7** Abominable Snowman.

Before the beginning of years
There came to the making of man
Time with a gift of tears,
Grief with a glass that ran.
(Algernon Charles Swinburne)
See also **1.22**.

1.21.5: **3** anchorman, Rastaman, superman, Telemann; **4** cameraman, newspaperman.

1.21.6: **2** he-man; **3** bogeyman, everyman, handyman; **4** salaryman.

1.21.7: **2** mailman, oilman; **3** middleman, muscleman; **5** Neandertal man.

1.21.8: **2** chessman, gasman, iceman, pressman, spaceman, taxman, yes man; **3** businessman; **4** Renaissance man.

1.21.9: **2** Batman, best man, straight man, stuntman; **3** minuteman.

1.21.10: **1** naan, nan; **2** Annan, Jinan.

1.21.11: **1** hardpan, pan; **2** bedpan, deadpan, dishpan, dustpan, Japan, saltpan, sampan, taipan, trepan; **3** marzipan.

1.21.12: **1** span; **2** Greenspan, lifespan, timespan, wingspan; **3** spick-and-span.
When Adam delved and Eve span,
Who was then the gentleman?
(John Ball)

1.21.13: **1** bran, gran, ran; **2** FORTRAN, Iran, outran, reran; **3** also-ran.
See also **3.34.1**.

1.21.14: **2** Oran; **3** Couperin, overran, trimaran; **4** catamaran.

1.21.15: **1** tan; **2** caftan, kaftan, Pétain, rattan, Shaitan, suntan, Wotan; **3** permatan; **4** Afghanistan, orang-utan.
See also **1.22, 3.34.2, 10.42.93**.

1.21.16: **1** van; **2** divan; **3** Aberfan, campervan, caravan, luggage van, minivan, panel van.

1.21.17: **2** Cézanne, Lausanne, Tarzan, tisane; **3** artisan, courtesan, Parmesan, partisan; **4** bipartisan, nonpartisan.

1.22: **1** and, canned, manned, NAND, sand, tanned; **2** expand, quicksand, unmanned; **3** ampersand, Samarqand, undermanned.
See also **1.21.1, 1.21.4, 1.21.15, 2.43.63, 10.2.17**.

1.22.1: **1** band, banned; **2** armband, brass band, broadband, disband, hairband, headband, jazz band, neckband, noseband, pipe band, sweatband, waistband, watchband, waveband, wristband; **3** Alice band, contraband, marching band, narrowband, one-man band; **4** elastic band.
See also **1.21, 10.2.17, 10.42.26**.

1.22.2: **1** hand; **2** backhand, cowhand, dab hand, deckhand, farmhand, firsthand, forehand, freehand, glad hand, hired hand,

left-hand, longhand, offhand, old hand, right-hand, shorthand, stagehand, unhand, whip hand; **3** beforehand, behindhand, hand-in-hand, hand-to-hand, helping hand, minute hand, overhand, underhand, upper hand.
Women are like tricks by slight of hand,
Which, to admire, we should not
understand.
(William Congreve)
See also **10.2.18**.

1.22.3: **1** bland, gland, land; **2** crashland, dreamland, dryland, farmland, fenland, flatland, gangland, grassland, heartland, homeland, Iceland, inland, Lapland, lowland, mainland, marshland, parkland, Queensland, scrubland, swampland, Thailand, unplanned, wasteland, wetland; **3** no-man's-land, promised land, tableland, thyroid gland, Zululand; **4** adrenal gland, Basutoland, cloud-cuckoo-land, endocrine gland, fat of the land, lacrimal gland, mammary gland; **5** Bechuanaland; **6** pituitary gland.
See also **2.54.77, 10.2.17, 10.42.26**.

1.22.4: **3** borderland, fatherland, hinterland, motherland, overland, wonderland; **4** Gondwanaland; **5** never-never land.

1.22.5: **2** eland; **3** Disneyland, Dixieland, fairyland, Swaziland; **4** Somaliland.

1.22.6: **1** brand, grand, rand, strand; **2** firebrand; **3** Krugerrand, operand, Rio Grande.
See also **10.2.17, 10.42.26**.

1.22.7: **1** stand; **2** bandstand, cabstand, coatstand, grandstand, handstand, hat stand, headstand, inkstand, kickstand, newsstand, nightstand, washstand, withstand; **3** music stand, one-night stand, understand; **4** Custer's Last Stand, misunderstand, umbrella stand.
Come mothers and fathers
Throughout the land
And don't criticize
What you can't understand.
(Bob Dylan)
See also **10.42.27**.

1.23: **1** Hans, manse, stance; **2** askance, expanse, finance, Penzance, romance; **3** happenstance, refinance.
See also **3.37, 10.62.3**.

1.24: **1** pants; **2** hot pants, sweatpants; **3** cargo pants, smartypants, underpants.
See also **1.25**.

1.25: 1 ant, Brandt, pant, rant; 2 extant, gallant, Levant, Rembrandt, white ant; 3 commandant, confidant, confidante, gallivant, platteland.
See also **1.24, 3.38.**

1.25.1: 1 cant, Kant, scant; 2 decant, descant, recant; 3 Tradescant.

1.26: 3 amaranth, coelacanth, perianth.

1.27: 1 banns, sans; 3 pots and pans, wedding banns.

1.28: 1 dang, fang, gang, hang, pang, sang, tang, twang, yang; 2 mustang, press-gang, Pyongyang; 3 overhang.
See also **10.42.**

1.28.1: 1 bang, bhang; 2 big bang, shebang, whiz bang; 3 charabanc.
See also **10.42.33.**

1.28.2: 1 clang, Laing, Lang, slang; 3 rhyming slang.

1.28.3: 1 prang, rang, sprang; 2 harangue, meringue, parang; 3 boomerang, Semarang, Sturm und Drang.

1.29: 2 Baudouin, Blondin, Chopin, Gauguin, Pétain, Rodin; 3 Chrétien, coq au vin, coup de main, Couperin, Limousin, Michelin; 4 au gratin.

1.30: 1 dank, drank, hank, sank, shank, spank, stank, swank, tank, thank, wank, yank; 2 Cruikshank, fishtank, scrimshank, sheepshank, think-tank; 3 petrol tank, septic tank.
See also **1.31, 1.32, 10.42.55.**

1.30.1: 1 bank; 2 blood bank, embank, fog bank, left bank, mudbank, nonbank, sandbank, seed bank, sperm bank, World Bank; 3 data bank, Jodrell Bank, merchant bank, mountebank, piggy bank, riverbank, savings bank.
See also **10.42.55.**

1.30.2: 1 blank, clank, flank, lank, Planck, plank; 2 gangplank, outflank, point-blank; 4 blankety-blank.
See also **1.32, 10.42.55.**

1.30.3: 1 crank, franc, Franck, frank, prank, rank, shrank; 2 outrank, top-rank.
See also **1.31, 1.32, 10.42.55.**

1.31: 1 Banks, Franks, Hanks, Manx, pranks, thanks; 2 Eubanks, Fairbanks, phalanx.
See also **1.30, 1.30.3.**

1.32: 1 blanked, ranked, tanked; 3 sacrosanct.
See also **1.30, 1.30.2, 1.30.3.**

1.33: 1 app, bap, chap, gap, map, pap, sap, tap, WAP, yap, zap; 2 asap, bitmap, lagniappe, mishap, road map, stopgap, trade gap, wiretap; 3 image map.
See also **1.34, 1.35.**

1.33.1: 1 cap, Capp; 2 blackcap, cloth cap, Dutch cap, flatcap, foolscap, hubcap, icecap, ink cap, kneecap, madcap, mobcap, nightcap, recap, skullcap, skycap, toecap, whitecap; 3 baseball cap, handicap, stocking cap; 4 percussion cap.
See also **1.35, 10.42.105.**

1.33.2: 1 clap, flap, lap, Lapp, slap; 2 burlap, dewlap, handclap, mudflap; 3 overlap, thunderclap.
See also **10.42.105.**

1.33.3: 1 nap, snap; 2 catnap, cold snap, dognap, kidnap.
See also **1.35, 10.42.105.**

1.33.4: 1 crap, rap, scrap, wrap; 2 enwrap, unwrap, wordwrap; 3 bubblewrap, gangsta rap.
See also **1.34, 1.35, 10.42.105.**

1.33.5: 1 trap; 2 claptrap, deathtrap, entrap, firetrap, giftwrap, satrap, speed trap, suntrap; 3 booby trap, radar trap; 4 Venus flytrap.

1.33.6: 1 strap; 2 bootstrap, chinstrap, jockstrap, mousetrap, watchstrap.
See also **1.35, 10.42.105.**

1.34: 1 apse, chaps, craps, schnapps, scraps; 2 bootstraps, perhaps, synapse, whitecaps.
See also **1.33, 1.33.4.**

1.34.1: 1 lapse; 2 collapse, elapse, prolapse, relapse.

1.35: 1 apt, capped, chapped, rapt, scrapped, strapped, wrapped; 2 adapt, cloud-capped, inapt, kidnapped, snow-capped, untapped; 3 handicapped.
See also **1.33, 1.33.1, 1.33.3, 1.33.4, 1.33.6.**

1.36: 1 ass, bass, Paz, sass; 2 ACAS, Alsace, badass, crevasse, Dias, jackass, sea bass, UCAS; 3 Caiaphas, gravitas, Phidias, vanitas; 4 Leonidas; 5 deo gratias; 6 materfamilias, paterfamilias.
See also **3.43.**

1.36.1: 1 gas; 2 coal gas, nerve gas, rare gas, tear gas, teargas; 3 biogas, laughing gas, mustard gas, noble gas; 4 natural gas.

1.36.2: 1 lass; 2 alas, Callas, Hellas, Pallas.

1.36.3: **1** mass; **2** amass, en masse, Hamas, High Mass, landmass; **3** biomass, Quatermass.
See also **1.38, 10.62.3.**

1.36.4: **1** basque, crass, Grass; **2** cuirass, damask, Gdansk, harass, Mithras, morass, Murmansk; **3** sassafras.
See also **1.38, 2.55.1, 3.43.4.**

1.37: **1** asp.
See also **3.45.**

1.38: **1** massed; **2** bombast, gymnast, harassed, lambast; **3** chloroplast; **4** enthusiast, iconoclast.
See also **1.36.3, 1.36.4, 2.54.96, 3.47.**

1.39: **1** ash, Ashe, bash, cache, cash, gash, gnash, hash, Nash, pash, sash, stash, tache; **2** abash, encash, mustache, panache, potash, rehash; **3** calabash, mountain ash, petty cash.
See also **10.42.141.**

1.39.1: **1** dash; **2** slapdash; **3** balderdash, pebbledash.
See also **1.40, 10.42.141.**

1.39.2: **1** clash, flash, lash, slash, splash; **2** backlash, backslash, eyelash, goulash, newsflash, whiplash.
See also **10.42.141.**

1.39.3: **1** mash, smash; **2** badmash, mishmash.
See also **1.40, 10.42.141.**

1.39.4: **1** brash, crash, rash, thrash, trash; **2** gatecrash, heat rash.
See also **1.40, 9.14.85, 10.42.141.**

1.40: **1** dashed, smashed, trashed; **2** abashed; **3** unabashed.
See also **1.39.1, 1.39.3, 1.39.4.**

1.41: **1** at, chat, DAT, GATT, gnat, mat, matt, Nat, sat, shat, that, twat, vat; **2** backchat, begat, chitchat, cravat, Croat, fiat, howzat, manat, resat, Sadat; **3** babysat, caveat, concordat, samizdat.

1.41.1: **1** bat; **2** brickbat, combat, dingbat, fruit bat, wombat; **3** acrobat, Ashgabat, baseball bat.
See also **1.42.**

1.41.2: **1** fat, phat; **2** low-fat, nonfat; **3** Arafat, butterfat; **4** Yawm Arafat.

1.41.3: **1** hat; **2** brass hat, old hat, straw hat, tin hat; **3** bobble hat, cowboy hat, stovepipe hat; **4** panama hat, ten-gallon hat.

1.41.4: **1** cat, scat; **2** bobcat, fat cat, hellcat, MCAT, meerkat, Muscat, polecat, tom cat, tomcat, wildcat; **3** Cheshire cat, copycat, fraidy-cat, pussycat, scaredy-cat, tabby cat.

1.41.5: **1** flat, lat, plait, slat, splat; **3** granny flat.
See also **1.42, 10.2.34.**

1.41.6: **2** bathmat, doormat, Fermat, format, placemat, prayer mat; **3** diplomat, Laundromat, reformat.

1.41.7: **1** pat, spat; **2** cowpat, expat; **3** pitapat.
See also **1.42.**

1.41.8: **1** brat, drat, frat, prat, rat, sprat; **2** Herat, mallrat, muskrat, pack rat, whereat; **3** Montserrat, ziggurat; **4** Mount Ararat.

1.41.9: **3** autocrat, bureaucrat, democrat, Eurocrat, plutocrat, technocrat; **4** aristocrat; **6** Liberal Democrat.

1.41.10: **1** tat; **2** diktat, rat-tat; **3** habitat, Photostat, thermostat, tit-for-tat; **4** ratatat-tat.

1.42: **1** flats, SATS, spats, stats; **2** combats, congrats, ersatz, mudflats.
See also **1.41.1, 1.41.5, 1.41.7.**

1.43: **1** hath, math, Plath; **3** aftermath, polymath, psychopath; **4** homeopath, naturopath, osteopath, sociopath.
See also **1.5, 3.51.**

1.44: **1** bach, batch, catch, hatch, latch, match, natch, patch, scratch, snatch, thatch; **2** attach, crosshatch, crosspatch, despatch, detach, dispatch, love match, mismatch, rematch, Sasquatch, test match; **3** purple patch, safety catch, safety match, slanging match.

Twas brillig, and the slithy toves
Did gyre and gimble in the wabe;
All mimsy were the borogoves,
And the mome raths outgrabe.
'Beware the Jabberwock, my son!
The jaws that bite, the claws that catch!'
(Lewis Carroll)
See also **1.45.**

1.45: **1** maths, patched; **2** attached, detached, mismatched, outmatched, unmatched, well-matched; **3** unattached; **4** semidetached.
See also **1.44.**

1.46: **1** chav, have, lav; **2** satnav.
See also **1.48.**

1.47: **1** Mach; **2** Cranach; **3** Sassenach.

1.48: **1** as, Chas, has, jazz, Paz, razz; **2** Diaz, La Paz, pizzazz, topaz, whereas;

3 Alcatraz, razzmatazz; **4** insofar as, insomuch as.
See also **1.46.**

2.0: **2** Freya, payer, sprayer, stayer; **3** betrayer, conveyor, doomsayer, mens rea, purveyor, ratepayer, soothsayer, surveyor, taxpayer; **4** Eritrea.

2.0.1: **2** layer, player; **3** ballplayer, bricklayer, platelayer; **4** cassette player, Himalaya.
See also **2.60, 10.42.1.**

2.1: **2** Shia, Thea; **3** Mercia, Pangaea, Phrygia, Pythia; **4** forsythia, Kampuchea, Valencia; **5** apologia.
See also **8.0.**

2.1.1: **3** Gambia, labia, Libya, Nubia, Serbia, tibia, Zambia; **4** Arabia, Colombia, Columbia, Namibia, suburbia; **5** Saudi Arabia.

2.1.2: **3** phobia; **5** claustrophobia, homophobia, hydrophobia, technophobia, xenophobia; **6** agoraphobia, arachnophobia.

2.1.3: **3** Chaldea, India, Judaea, Lydia, Medea, media, Nadia; **4** Arcadia, Cambodia, chlamydia, Grenadier; **5** hypermedia, multimedia; **6** encyclopedia.
See also **8.1.**

2.1.4: **3** Mafia, raffia, Sofia; **4** Montgolfier; **5** Philadelphia.

2.1.5: **2** skier; **3** trachea; **4** Slovakia; **6** Czechoslovakia.

2.1.6: **2** Leah; **3** buddleia, cochlea, Delia, earlier, haulier, Hialeah, Julia, nuclear; **4** Aurelia, camellia, Cecilia, chevalier, Coppelia, Cordelia, lobelia, magnolia, Mongolia, Montpellier, non-nuclear, Ophelia, peculiar, Somalia; **5** Anatolia, antinuclear, inter alia, melancholia, psychedelia, thermonuclear; **6** jacta est alea.
See also **8.4.**

2.1.7: **3** dahlia, Thalia; **4** Australia, azalea, Floralia, Mammalia, regalia, Westphalia; **5** Animalia, bacchanalia, genitalia, Lupercalia, marginalia, saturnalia; **6** paraphernalia.

2.1.8: **3** Brasília; **4** familiar, unfamiliar; **5** bougainvillea, haemophilia, necrophilia, paedophilia; **6** memorabilia, overfamiliar.

2.1.9: **3** Crimea, Grasmere, premier; **4** arrhythmia, bulimia, costumier, Mamma

Mia; **5** hypothermia, macadamia; **6** Mesopotamia.
See also **8.5.**

2.1.10: **4** anaemia, Bohemia, dysphemia, leukaemia, toxaemia, uraemia; **5** academia, septicaemia, tularaemia; **6** hyperglycaemia, hypoglycaemia; **7** pernicious anaemia, sickle-cell anaemia.

2.1.11: **3** Chechnya, cornea, hernia, hryvnia, junior, Narnia, pannier; **4** Hibernia, insignia, insomnia, petunia, Tanzania, Titania, Urania; **5** Oceania, office junior.
See also **8.6.**

2.1.12: **3** Azania; **4** Albania; **5** Lithuania, Mauritania, Pennsylvania, Transylvania.

2.1.13: **3** mania; **4** Romania, Tasmania; **5** dipsomania, kleptomania, logomania, monomania, nymphomania, pyromania; **6** erotomania, megalomania.

2.1.14: **3** senior; **4** Armenia, asthenia, gardenia, Slovenia; **5** schizophrenia.

2.1.15: **3** linear, tinea, zinnia; **4** gloxinia, Sardinia, Virginia; **5** Abyssinia, rectilinear.

2.1.16: **4** ammonia, Antonia, aphonia, begonia, Estonia, Ionia, Kolonia, pneumonia; **5** Babylonia, Caledonia, Catalonia, catatonia, Macedonia, Patagonia.

2.1.17: **2** Pia; **3** copier, croupier, Napier, rapier, rupiah, sepia; **4** Olympia; **5** Cassiopeia, pharmacopoeia, photocopier; **6** onomatopoeia.
See also **8.7.**

2.1.18: **4** dystopia, myopia, utopia; **5** cornucopia, Ethiopia.

2.1.19: **3** aria, Austria, Cambria, chorea, courier, Cumbria, Curia, destrier, diarrhoea, Ferrier, furrier, pyorrhoea, sangria, Syria, terrier, Umbria, urea, warrior, worrier; **4** acharya, Assyria, Calabria, Etruria, Manchuria, Northumbria, pro patria; **5** Alexandria, ecowarrior, hypochondria, Unknown Warrior, weekend warrior; **6** phantasmagoria.

2.1.20: **3** barrier, carrier, farrier, harrier, pariah; **4** ball-carrier, marsh harrier; **5** aircraft carrier, common carrier, people carrier, Water Carrier.

2.1.21: **3** Maria, sharia; **4** black maria, Caesarea, galleria, gonorrhoea, North Korea, pizzeria, trattoria; **5** amenorrhoea, Ave Maria.

2.1.22: **3** area; **4** Bavaria, Bulgaria, malaria, Samaria; **5** urticaria.

2.1.23: **4** Algeria, diphtheria, Iberia, inferior, Liberia, Nigeria, Siberia, superior; **6** mother superior.

2.1.24: **4** anterior, bacteria, interior, ulterior; **5** cafeteria; **7** cyanobacteria.

Wrong information always shown by the media
Negative images is the main criteria
Infecting the young minds faster than bacteria
Kids wanna act like what they see in the cinema
(Black Eyed Peas)

2.1.25: **4** exterior, hysteria, listeria, posterior, wisteria.

2.1.26: **3** Gloria; **4** euphoria, Peoria, Pretoria, Victoria; **5** Thesmophoria.

2.1.27: **3** cassia, dossier, fancier, Garcia, glacier, Hosea, Mercia, nausea, Nicaea, sightseer; **4** bilharzia, Boadicea, diglossia, dyspepsia, eclampsia, Elysia, eupepsia, financier, Nicosia, panacea, Silesia, Valencia; **5** Andalusia, pigeon fancier; **6** Dionysia, intelligentsia.
See also **8.8**.

2.1.28: **4** asphyxia, ataxia, dyslexia, dyspraxia; **5** anorexia, ataraxia.

2.1.29: **2** Tia; **3** courtier, Hestia, meteor, protea, tortilla; **4** Galatea, poinsettia.
See also **8.10**.

2.1.30: **2** via; **3** Flavia, Latvia, Silvia, trivia; **4** Batavia, Belgravia, Bolivia, Fitzrovia, Guinevere, Moldavia, Monrovia, Octavia, Olivia, Segovia; **5** Scandinavia.

2.1.31: **3** brassiere, hosier, nausea, osier; **4** Abkhazia, ambrosia, fantasia, Tunisia.

2.1.32: **2** grazier; **3** brazier, glazier; **4** aphasia, Caucasia, fantasia, Malaysia; **5** Anastasia, euthanasia, Transcaucasia.

2.1.33: **4** amnesia, ecclesia, magnesia, Silesia; **5** anaesthesia, analgesia, Indonesia, Melanesia, Micronesia, Polynesia.

2.2: **2** Boyer, coir, Goya, soya; **3** destroyer, employer, Nagoya, sequoia; **4** paranoia.

2.3: **2** Doha, mower, Noah, o'er, sewer, Shoah; **3** aloha, Genoa, lawnmower, Samoa, widower; **4** Krakatoa, Protozoa.

2.3.1: **2** boa, Boer; **3** Balboa, jerboa.

2.3.2: **2** goer; **3** churchgoer, filmgoer, foregoer, racegoer; **4** balletgoer, chapelgoer, concertgoer, moviegoer, operagoer, partygoer, theatregoer; **5** cinemagoer.

2.3.3: **2** blower, lower; **3** aloha, follower, glassblower, snowblower; **4** whistleblower.

2.3.4: **2** grower, rower; **3** borrower, flamethrower; **6** Aotearoa.

2.4: **2** brewer, doer, sewer, who're, wooer; **3** wrongdoer; **4** evildoer, kaumatua.

2.4.1: **2** ewer, sewer, skewer, viewer; **3** jaguar, Joshua, mantua, pursuer, reviewer; **4** Gargantua, interviewer.

2.5: **1** Elbe; **2** Abba, Alba, Berber, blabber, Buber, Elba, Gabba, gibber, jabber, limber, Melba, sombre, timber, Wilbur; **3** Aruba, calibre, carnauba, córdoba, Cordoba, Hecuba, marimba, peach melba, Yoruba; **4** Excalibur; **5** Addis Ababa.
See also **10.42.114**.

2.5.1: **2** arbour, barber, Barbour, dhaba, harbour; **3** indaba, Pearl Harbor.

2.5.2: **2** caber, labour, neighbour, sabre, tabor, Weber; **3** belabour, New Labour.
See also **2.33.1**.

2.5.3: **2** Chiba, Sheba; **3** amoeba, Bathsheba; **4** Curitiba.

2.5.4: **2** fibre, Khyber, Tiber; **3** dark fibre, subscriber; **4** carbon fibre, microfibre.

2.5.5: **2** clobber, cobber, jobber, robber, slobber.

2.5.6: **2** oba, sober; **3** October; **4** Manitoba; **5** ginkgo biloba.
See also **10.42.114**.

2.5.7: **2** blubber, clubber, rubber, scrubber; **3** landlubber; **4** moneygrubber.

2.5.8: **2** Cuba, scuba, tuba, tuber; **7** Santiago de Cuba.

2.5.9: **2** amber, camber, clamber, mamba, samba, timbre.

2.5.10: **2** chamber; **3** bedchamber; **4** antechamber, echo chamber.

2.5.11: **2** ember, member; **3** December, dismember, nonmember, November, remember, September.
See also **2.60**.

2.5.12: **2** Humber, lumbar, lumber, number, rumba, slumber, umber; **3** Columba, cucumber, encumber, E number, outnumber, PIN number; **5** 800 number, atomic number; **6** 0800 number.
See also **2.33.1, 2.60, 10.42.114**.

2.6: **2** adder, alder, bladder, Brenda, buddha, cheddar, dodder, elder, fielder, fodder, girder, Glenda, header, ladder, lambda, madder, Magda, Matilda, murder, plodder, purdah, shredder, solder, welder; **3** Asadha, Blackadder, Canada, do-gooder, embroider, gallbladder, Imelda, infielder, midfielder, outfielder, stepladder; **4** ambassador, Cadwaladr, Esmeralda, schadenfreude; **5** Ahura Mazda, asafoetida. *See also* **10.42.115.**

2.6.1: **2** ardour, Bader, cadre, Garda, larder, nada, RADA; **3** armada, cicada, Granada, Grenada, Jumada, lambada, Nevada; **4** autostrada, Bhadrapada, Eid al-Adha, empanada, enchilada, intifada, Torquemada; **5** aficionada, Lailat al-Qadr, pina colada, piña colada; **6** Sierra Nevada.

2.6.2: **2** Ada, raider, Seder, trader, Veda, wader; **3** crusader, Darth Vader, Grenada, invader; **4** ayurveda.

2.6.3: **2** cedar, feeder, leader, Leda; **3** Aida, cheerleader, ringleader; **5** follow-my-leader.

2.6.4: **2** breeder, Freda, Frieda, reader; **3** Derrida, mind-reader, newsreader, palmreader, proofreader, stockbreeder.

2.6.5: **2** bidder, Jiddah; **3** candida, consider, Cressida, Florida, Mérida; **4** Andromeda, primigravida, reconsider; **5** multigravida, spina bifida, unigravida. *See also* **2.33.2, 10.42.115.**

2.6.6: **2** eider, glider, Ida, rider, spider; **3** al-Qaeda, divider, hang-glider, outrider, provider; **4** paraglider. *See also* **2.60.1.**

2.6.7: **2** cider, cyder; **3** decider, insider, offsider, outsider.

2.6.8: **2** boarder, border, hoarder, order, warder; **3** disorder, keyboarder, mail order, marauder, reorder; **4** gagging order, made-to-order, pecking order; **5** herbaceous border; **6** bipolar disorder. *See also* **2.33.2, 2.60.1.**

2.6.9: **2** Cawdor; **3** camcorder, palmcorder, recorder; **4** tape recorder; **5** cassette recorder; **8** video cassette recorder.

2.6.10: **2** chowder, Gouda, howdah, powder; **3** gunpowder; **4** baking powder, curry powder, custard powder, washing powder. *See also* **2.33.2.**

2.6.11: **2** coda, Oder, odour, soda, Yoda; **3** cream soda, decoder, freeloader, off-roader, pagoda, vocoder; **4** baking soda, washing soda.

2.6.12: **2** judder, rudder, shudder, udder.

2.6.13: **2** Judah, Tudor; **3** Barbuda, Bermuda, Garuda, intruder, Neruda; **4** barracuda, Buxtehude; **7** Antigua and Barbuda.

2.6.14: **2** builder, guilder, Hilda, Kilda, tilde, Wilder; **3** bewilder, shipbuilder. *See also* **2.33.2, 10.42.115.**

2.6.15: **2** boulder, folder, moulder, older, shoulder, smoulder; **3** cold-shoulder; **4** off-the-shoulder.

2.6.16: **2** holder; **3** beholder, bondholder, cardholder, freeholder, gasholder, householder, landholder, leaseholder, potholder, shareholder, smallholder, stakeholder, stallholder, stockholder; **4** titleholder; **5** policyholder.

2.6.17: **2** goonda, launder, maunder; **3** colander, Highlander, Icelander, islander, Kaunda, lavender, rejoinder, remainder.

2.6.18: **2** Banda, candour, dander, gander, panda, pander, sander, Vanda; **3** Amanda, backhander, bystander, Leander, left-hander, Luanda, meander, Miranda, philander, pomander, red panda, right-hander, Rwanda, Uganda, veranda, Yolanda; **4** coriander, gerrymander, jacaranda, oleander, propaganda, salamander. *See also* **2.6.19, 10.42.115.**

2.6.19: **2** slander; **3** commander; **4** alexander; **6** brandy Alexander, lieutenant commander. *See also* **2.6.18.**

2.6.20: **2** bender, fender, gender, render, sender, spender, vendor; **3** agenda, defender, engender, offender, pudenda, surrender, suspender, transgender, weekender; **4** hacienda. *See also* **10.42.115.**

2.6.21: **2** blender, lender, slender, splendour; **3** calender; **4** moneylender.

2.6.22: **2** tender; **3** bartender, contender, goaltender, pretender, self-tender; **4** legal tender. *See also* **2.54.63.**

2.6.23: **2** cinder, hinder, Linda, Pindar, tinder; **3** Belinda, calendar, cylinder, Govinda, provender; **5** Chinese calendar. *See also* **2.33.2, 2.60.1.**

2.6.24: **2** binder, blinder, finder, grinder, kinda, minder; **3** bookbinder, child minder, pathfinder, reminder, sidewinder, viewfinder.

2.6.25: 2 Fonda, ponder, Rhonda, squander, Wanda, wander, yonder; 3 absconder, transponder; 4 anaconda; 5 autoresponder.

2.6.26: 2 bounder, flounder, founder; 3 all-rounder, pounder.
See also **10.42.115**.

2.6.27: 2 blunder, chunder, plunder, sunder, thunder, under, wonder; 3 asunder, rotunda, thereunder.

When I read Shakespeare I am struck with
wonder
That such trivial people should muse and
thunder
In such lovely language.
(D. H. Lawrence)
See also **10.42.115**.

2.7: 2 bather, blather, bother, breather, Crowther, either, further, gather, lather, neither, rather, slather; 3 forgather, Neruda.
See also **2.33.4, 10.42.116**.

2.7.1: 2 farther, father; 3 godfather, grandfather, Our Father, stepfather; 4 city father.

2.7.2: 2 blether, feather, heather, leather, nether, tether, weather, whether; 3 bellwether, together; 4 altogether, get-together.
See also **2.33.4**.

2.7.3: 2 dither, hither, slither, thither, whither, wither, zither.
See also **2.33.4, 2.60, 10.42.116**.

2.7.4: 2 brother, mother, other, smother; 3 another, godmother, grandmother, half-brother, queen mother, stepbrother, stepmother; 5 fairy godmother, Reverend Mother.

2.8: 1 for; 2 camphor, coffer, FIFA, gaffer, heifer, Kaffir, kafir, loofah, nakfa, Offa, offer, proffer, reefer, roofer, staffer, titfer, twofer, wafer, woofer, zephyr; 3 Recife, UEFA; 4 counteroffer; 5 opera buffa.
See also **2.33.5, 10.42.113**.

2.8.1: 3 Christopher, cockchafer, metaphor; 4 biographer, geographer, philosopher, photographer, pornographer, stenographer, typographer; 5 choreographer.

2.8.2: 2 differ, sniffer; 3 aquifer, cockchafer, conifer, Jennifer, Lucifer; 4 Apocrypha.
See also **10.42.113**.

2.8.3: 2 cipher, Haifa, lifer; 3 decipher.
See also **2.33.5**.

2.8.4: 2 chauffeur, gofer, loafer, sofa; 3 Bonhoeffer, Hanover.

2.8.5: 2 bluffer, buffer, duffer, puffer, snuffer, suffer.
See also **10.42.113**.

2.8.6: 2 alpha, Balfour, golfer, pilfer, sulphur; 3 alfalfa.

2.9: 2 alga, auger, augur, beggar, bulgur, cougar, Edgar, Eiger, Helga, Ladoga, liger, mega, mulga, Olga, sugar, tiger, Volga, vulgar; 3 beluga, bodega, Gallagher, Heidegger, MacGregor, Malaga, omega, onager; 4 Cape Trafalgar, Chattanooga, rutabaga.

There was a young lady of Riga,
Who went for a ride on a tiger;
They returned from the ride
With the lady inside,
And a smile on the face of the tiger.
(Limerick)

2.9.1: 2 blagger, bragger, dagger, Jagger, ragga, stagger, swagger; 4 carpetbagger, cloak-and-dagger.
See also **2.33.6, 10.42.117**.

2.9.2: 2 Aga, laager, lager, naga, raga, saga; 4 aga saga, Baba Yaga.

2.9.3: 2 Berger, burger, burgher; 3 beefburger, cheeseburger, hamburger; 4 Vegeburger.

2.9.4: 2 eager, meagre, Riga; 3 beleaguer; 4 overeager.
See also **2.54.63**.

2.9.5: 2 bigger, chigger, digger, jigger, ligger, nigger, snigger, vigour; 3 gravedigger, omega, vinegar; 6 balsamic vinegar.

2.9.6: 2 figure; 3 configure, disfigure, prefigure, transfigure.
See also **2.33.6**.

2.9.7: 2 rigour, trigger; 3 hair-trigger, outrigger.

2.9.8: 2 blogger, Dogger, flogger, jogger, logger; 4 pettifogger.
See also **2.60.2**.

2.9.9: 2 ogre, toga, yoga; 3 Kyoga.

2.9.10: 2 bugger, chugger, Magha, mugger, rugger; 3 debugger; 4 huggermugger.
See also **2.33.6**.

2.9.11: **2** anger, Bangor, kanga, languor, manga, panga, sanger.
See also **2.33.6.**

2.9.12: **2** finger, linger; **3** Basinger, fish finger, forefinger, malinger; **4** lady's finger.
See also **2.60.2, 10.42.117.**

2.9.13: **2** conga, donga, Tonga, wonga.

2.9.14: **2** hunger, younger; **3** fishmonger, ironmonger, warmonger; **4** costermonger, Kanchenjunga, rumourmonger, scandalmonger.

2.10: **2** badger, Borgia, cadger, dowager, dredger, forger, Georgia, ledger, puja; **3** Abuja, besieger, Elijah, procedure, Voyager; **4** astrologer, paraplegia, quadriplegia.

2.10.1: **2** charger, rajah; **3** recharger; **4** maharajah, supercharger, turbocharger.

2.10.2: **2** major, pager, wager; **3** teenager; **4** Canis Major, Ursa Major.

2.10.3: **2** merger, perjure, verdure, verger; **3** demerger.

2.10.4: **2** Major, Niger; **3** integer, manager, mortgagor, villager, voyager; **5** micromanager.

2.10.5: **2** codger, dodger, lodger, roger; **3** draft dodger; **4** Artful Dodger.

2.10.6: **2** Bolger, soldier; **3** myalgia, neuralgia, nostalgia.
See also **10.42.113.**

2.10.7: **2** conjure, ganja, grandeur, lounger, plunger, sponger; **3** avenger, messenger, phalanger, sunlounger; **4** Queen's Messenger.
See also **10.42.113.**

2.10.8: **2** danger, Grainger, manger, ranger, stranger; **3** bushranger, endanger, hydrangea, seachanger; **4** moneychanger.
See also **2.33.**

2.10.9: **2** ginger, injure, ninja, whinger; **3** challenger, derringer, harbinger, passenger, Salinger; **4** foot passenger.
See also **2.33.**

2.11: **1** yer, you, your; **2** ayah, failure, India, lawyer, saviour, sawyer; **3** behaviour, derailleur, Montesquieu, ouguiya; **4** alleluia, hallelujah, misbehaviour.

2.11.1: **2** bania, Doña, Kenya, Sonia, Tania, tenure; **3** bologna, Britannia, lasagne, Monsignor, vicuña; **4** California.

2.12: **2** burka, circa, conker, conquer, Kafka, latke, plonker, polka, Rilke, stonker, troika, vodka; **3** babushka, Kokoschka, sepulchre, tearjerker, yarmulke.

2.12.1: **2** backer, Dakar, Dhaka, hacker, knacker, lacquer, packer, slacker, smacker, Waca, yakka; **3** alpaca, attacker, backpacker, hijacker, linebacker; **5** Strait of Malacca.
See also **2.33.8.**

2.12.2: **2** cracker, tracker; **3** firecracker, maraca, nutcracker; **4** The Nutcracker.
See also **2.60.3.**

2.12.3: **3** Chanukah, Hanukkah, Ithaca, massacre, spinnaker; **5** Bandaranaike.

2.12.4: **2** Barker, Farquhar, marka, marker, markka, parka, Parker, taka, Tarka; **3** Lusaka, moussaka, Osaka, pataca, Schumacher, Vaisakha; **4** Titicaca.

2.12.5: **2** acre, baker, nacre, Quaker, shaker, taker; **3** boneshaker, broadacre, caretaker, cloaca; **4** Diefenbaker, undertaker.

2.12.6: **2** maker; **3** bookmaker, dealmaker, dressmaker, filmmaker, haymaker, homemaker, Jamaica, kingmaker, lawmaker, lossmaker, matchmaker, pacemaker, peacemaker, rainmaker, shoemaker, watchmaker; **4** automaker, mischief-maker, moneymaker, moviemaker, troublemaker, Wanamaker; **5** cabinetmaker, holidaymaker.

2.12.7: **2** breaker; **3** heartbreaker, housebreaker, icebreaker, lawbreaker, strikebreaker, tiebreaker.

2.12.8: **2** Becca, Becker, checker, chequer, lekker, Mecca, pecker, wrecker; **3** exchequer, Rebecca, Rebekah, spellchecker, woodpecker; **4** Boris Becker, double-decker, single-decker, triple-decker.
See also **2.60.3.**

2.12.9: **2** worker; **3** homeworker, outworker, pieceworker, woodworker; **4** metalworker, teleworker.
See also **2.60.3.**

2.12.10: **2** beaker, chica, pika, seeker, sneaker, speaker, streaker, tikka; **3** eureka, jobseeker, loudspeaker, paprika, Topeka; **4** Costa Rica, Dominica, Tanganyika; **5** electronica.

2.12.11: 2 bicker, dicker, picker, pika, vicar, Whicker, Wicca, wicker; 3 Boudicca, brassica, Corsica, Jessica. *See also* **10.42.113**.

2.12.12: 2 flicker, liquor, slicker; 3 replica, silica; 4 angelica, basilica.

I have seen the moment of my greatness flicker,
And I have seen the eternal Footman hold my coat, and snicker,
And in short, I was afraid.
(T. S. Eliot)

2.12.13: 2 snicker; 3 anicca, arnica, Monica, moniker; 4 Dominica, harmonica, japonica, Salonika, Veronica.

2.12.14: 3 Africa, paprika; 4 America; 6 Latin America, Middle America.

2.12.15: 2 sticker, ticker; 3 Attica, Karttika, swastika; 4 Antarctica, erotica, exotica, sciatica.

2.12.16: 2 biker, hiker, mica, Micah, striker; 3 Formica, hitchhiker; 4 balalaika.

2.12.17: 2 chocker, Cocker, docker, knocker, locker, mocha, ocker, rocker, shocker, soccer; 3 doorknocker, footlocker; 4 beta-blocker, knickerbocker; 6 Davy Jones's locker. *See also* **2.60.3**.

2.12.18: 2 corker, hawker, Lorca, orca, porker, stalker, talker; 3 deerstalker, Majorca, Mallorca, Menorca.

2.12.19: 2 walker; 3 bushwalker, shopwalker, streetwalker.

2.12.20: 2 broker, choker, coca, joker, ochre, poker, smoker, Stoker; 3 nonsmoker, pawnbroker, stockbroker; 4 Fukuoka, mediocre, tapioca.

2.12.21: 2 fucker, pucker, pukka, succour, sucker, trucker, tucker, yucca; 3 bloodsucker, seersucker; 4 motherfucker.

2.12.22: 2 Booker, cooker, hookah, hooker, looker; 3 onlooker.

2.12.23: 2 euchre, Luca, lucre, snooker; 3 bazooka, verruca.

2.12.24: 2 anchor, banker, canker, hanker, rancour, tanker, wanker; 3 Bianca, Sri Lanka; 4 Casablanca, lingua franca, Salamanca, supertanker; 5 Bullamakanka. *See also* **2.54.100, 10.42.113**.

2.12.25: 2 blinker, clinker, drinker, Inca, sinker, stinker, thinker, tinker; 3 freethinker, Soyinka.

2.12.26: 2 bunker, clunker, hunker, punka, punkah.

2.12.27: 2 busker, Oscar, Tosca, whisker; 3 Alaska, Nebraska; 4 Athabasca, Madagascar. *See also* **2.60.3**.

2.13: 2 curler, Daimler, Dervla, Fuller, Himmler, Kreisler, muffler, mullah; 3 lobola, titular.

2.13.1: 2 à la, Allah, calla, Halle, pallor, tala, valour; 3 inshallah, Valhalla; 4 Caracalla.

2.13.2: 3 Angela, bachelor, chancellor, Coppola, councillor, counsellor, cupola, embezzler, gondola, jeweller, Leveller, mandala, Pamela, pergola, puzzler, rattler, reveller, smuggler, tiddler, tippler, traveller, tricolour; 4 Agricola, alveolar, gas guzzler, hyperbola, Lord Chancellor, Methuselah, parabola, teetotaller.

2.13.3: 2 gala, Mahler, parlour; 3 Douala, impala, Kabbalah, Kampala, koala, Marsala, masala; 4 Guatemala; 5 garam masala.

2.13.4: 2 baler, jailer, kwela, mailer, sailor, scalar, tailor, Taylor, trailer, whaler; 3 blackmailer, inhaler, loudhailer, Mandela, retailer, wholesaler; 4 Venezuela. *See also* **2.33.9, 10.42.113**.

2.13.5: 2 Bella, Della, dweller, Ella, fella, feller, Heller, speller, Stella; 3 Adela, favela, Fenella, Mandela, Nigella, novella, paella; propeller, Prunella, rubella, umbrella; 4 a cappella, Arabella, Cinderella, citronella, Gabriella, mortadella, mozzarella, Rockefeller, salmonella; 5 telenovela, Valpolicella.

2.13.6: 2 cellar, seller; 3 bestseller, bookseller, saltcellar.

2.13.7: 2 stellar, teller; 3 patella; 4 fortune teller, interstellar, panatella, storyteller, tarantella.

2.13.8: 2 dealer, feeler, healer, peeler, Schiele, Scylla, sealer, sheila, vela, velar, Wheeler; 3 maxilla, tequila, three-wheeler; 4 wheeler-dealer; 5 labiovelar.

2.13.9: 2 chiller, filler, miller, pillar, Schiller, villa; 3 Anguilla, cedilla, chinchilla, Drusilla, Godzilla, Ludmila, Manila, Priscilla, similar, vanilla; 4 caterpillar, dissimilar, Manzanilla, stocking filler.

2.13.10: **2** killer; **3** giant-killer, painkiller, weedkiller; **4** lady-killer.

2.13.11: **2** thriller; **3** gorilla, guerrilla; **4** sarsaparilla.

2.13.12: **2** tiller; **3** Attila, distiller, flotilla, mantilla, scintilla.

2.13.13: **2** miler, tiler, Tyler; **3** compiler, Delilah, profiler, rottweiler; **4** decompiler.

2.13.14: **2** collar, dollar, dolour, holler, scholar, squalor, wallah; **3** ayatollah, bluecollar, white-collar; **4** petrodollar.

2.13.15: **2** caller, crawler, hauler, Orla, trawler; **3** footballer.

2.13.16: **2** Fowler, howler, prowler; **3** wildfowler.

2.13.17: **2** boiler, broiler, spoiler; **3** despoiler, potboiler; **4** double boiler.

2.13.18: **2** bowler, cola, molar, polar, solar, Zola; **3** Angola, bipolar, Ebola, granola, Loyola, payola, premolar, tombola, transpolar, viola; **4** alveolar, circumpolar, Coca-Cola, Gorgonzola, Hispaniola, Pepsi Cola, Pianola, variola.

2.13.19: **2** roller, stroller; **3** comptroller, controller, steamroller; **6** air-traffic controller.

2.13.20: **2** colour, cruller, mullah, nullah; **3** Abdullah, discolour, four-colour, medulla, off-colour, tricolour; **4** Technicolor, watercolour. *See also* **2.33.10, 10.42.113.**

2.13.21: **3** annular, cellular, copula, fistula, formula, glandular, granular, insular, modular, popular, primula, scapula, scrofula, spatula, titular, Ursula, uvula, uvular, Vistula; **4** calendula, peninsula, tarantula, unpopular; **5** multicellular, unicellular; **7** Kamchatka Peninsula.

2.13.22: **3** fibula, globular, nebula, tabular, tubular.

2.13.23: **3** angular, jugular, regular, singular; **4** arugula, Caligula, irregular, rectangular, triangular. *See also* **9.14.13.**

2.13.24: **3** circular, Dracula, jocular, macula, muscular, ocular, secular, vascular; **4** avuncular, binocular, crepuscular, molecular, oracular, spectacular, tubercular, vernacular; **5** semicircular, unspectacular; **6** cardiovascular.

2.13.25: **4** funicular, particular, testicular, vehicular; **5** perpendicular; **6** extracurricular.

2.13.26: **2** Beulah, cooler, doula, hula, moola, pula, ruler; **3** Tallulah.

2.13.27: **2** cobbler, gambler, kiblah, rambler, scrambler, scribbler, tabla, temblor, tumbler, warbler; **3** assembler; **4** disassembler; **6** enfant terrible. *See also* **2.60.**

2.13.28: **3** Adler, chandler, fiddler, handler, hurdler, idler, pedlar, saddler, toddler.

2.13.29: **2** angler, Bangla, burglar, haggler, juggler, straggler, wrangler; **4** compleat angler.

2.13.30: **2** heckler, sparkler, sprinkler, stickler; **3** chronicler, swashbuckler; **5** fin de siècle.

2.13.31: **2** Kepler, poplar, sampler, stapler; **3** Knight Templar.

2.13.32: **2** hustler, rustler, Whistler, wrestler.

2.13.33: **2** antler, butler, Hitler, settler, Tatler.

2.14: **2** asthma, bomber, Burma, comma, Cranmer, drachma, fulmar, murmur, Palma, plasma, Selma, Thelma, Wilma; **3** charisma, mahatma, miasma, sangoma; **4** terra firma.

2.14.1: **2** clamour, crammer, gamma, glamour, grammar, mama, mamma, slammer, stammer, tsamma, yammer; **3** programmer, windjammer; **4** Alabama.

2.14.2: **2** hammer; **3** jackhammer, sledgehammer, warhammer; **4** yellowhammer. *See also* **2.33.11, 10.42.113.**

2.14.3: **3** customer, Dodoma, gossamer, isomer; **4** anathema.

2.14.4: **3** cinema, enema, monomer; **4** astronomer.

2.14.5: **2** amah, armour, charmer, dharma, farmer, Gama, Kama, karma, Palmer, Parma; **4** Fujiyama, Suriname, Yokohama; **5** gentleman-farmer.

2.14.6: **2** lama, llama; **4** Dalai Lama, Panchen Lama.

2.14.7: **2** Brahma, Rama; **3** diorama; **4** panorama.

2.14.8: **2** drama; **4** costume drama, cyclorama, docudrama, melodrama, psychodrama.

2.14.9: **2** framer, gamer; **3** declaimer, disclaimer, proclaimer; **4** lion tamer.

2.14.10: **2** Emma, Gemma, lemma, tremor; **3** dilemma.

2.14.11: **2** Beemer, creamer, dreamer, FEMA, femur, lemur, Lima, schema, steamer, streamer; **3** blasphemer, daydreamer, oedema, Redeemer, Yakima; **4** emphysema, Hiroshima.

2.14.12: **2** dimmer, glimmer, shimmer, simmer, Strimmer, swimmer, trimmer; **3** anima, dulcimer, eczema, Fatima, Gordimer, Mortimer, polymer; **4** Hiroshima. *See also* **2.60.4**.

2.14.13: **2** climber, Jemima, primer, timer; **3** egg timer, two-timer; **4** Oppenheimer.

2.14.14: **2** dormer, korma, Norma, ormer, trauma.

2.14.15: **2** former; **3** informer, performer, pro forma, reformer, transformer; **4** nonconformer.

2.14.16: **2** boma, Homer, Oma, stoma; **3** aroma, diploma, lymphoma, misnomer, myeloma; **4** atheroma, carcinoma, haematoma, isangoma, melanoma, Oklahoma.

2.14.17: **2** coma; **3** beachcomber, glaucoma, sarcoma, Tacoma, trachoma.

2.14.18: **2** bummer, comer, drummer, Gummer, mummer, plumber, summer; **3** high summer, incomer, latecomer, midsummer, newcomer; **5** Indian summer.

2.14.19: **2** bloomer, boomer, Duma, rumour, Uma, umma; **3** satsuma; **4** baby boomer. *See also* **2.60.4**.

2.14.20: **2** humour, puma, tumour; **3** consumer, ill humour.

Not warped by passion, awed by rumour,
Not grave through pride, or gay through
* folly;*
An equal mixture of good humour,
And sensible soft melancholy.
(Alexander Pope)

2.14.21: **2** dogma, magma, sigma, stigma, zeugma; **3** enigma.

2.15: **2** Abner, Bremner, Brookner, Bruckner, Costner, downer, drawer, Faulkner, gonna, gunner, Heffner, joiner, Krishna, pardner, Pilsner, stunner, ulna, Wagner; **3** alumna, Arjuna, echidna, Phalguna, sundowner; **4** Hare Krishna. *See also* **14.48**.

2.15.1: **2** Anna, banner, Branagh, Hannah, manna, manner, manor, planner, scanner, spanner, tanner; **3** bandanna, Deanna, Diana, Fermanagh, Giovanna, Havana, hosanna, Montana, savanna, Savannah; **4** Indiana, Pollyanna; **5** optical scanner, Star-Spangled Banner. *See also* **2.15.7**.

2.15.2: **3** Adana, almoner, commoner, coroner, dampener, Eleanor, falconer, fastener, gardener, Helena, Kitchener, listener, Londoner, northerner, opener, Pilsner, prisoner, questioner, sharpener, softener, southerner, thickener; **4** eye-opener, tin-opener. *See also* **10.42.94**.

2.15.3: **3** pensioner, stationer; **4** confectioner, probationer, vacationer; **5** executioner; **7** Lord High Executioner.

2.15.4: **4** commissioner, conditioner, parishioner, petitioner, practitioner; **5** air conditioner, exhibitioner, High Commissioner.

2.15.5: **3** easterner, Smetana, sweetener, westerner, whitener.

2.15.6: **3** Cavanagh, governor, guvnor, Sravana, Tavener, Taverner; **6** lieutenant governor.

2.15.7: **2** garner, Ghana; **3** Alana, Astana, banana, Botswana, Guyana, iguana, mañana, mens sana, Montana, nirvana, piranha, Roxana, sultana, Tijuana, Tirana; **4** ikebana, Lippizaner, Ljubljana, marijuana, Pax Romana, Rosh Hashanah; **5** Agrahayana, fata morgana, Louisiana, Victoriana. *See also* **2.15.1**, **2.60.5**.

2.15.8: **3** Chicana, gymkhana, katana; **4** Afrikaner, katakana; **5** Americana, Pax Americana.

2.15.9: **2** Dana, drainer, eina, Gaynor, planer, strainer, trainer; **3** arcana, campaigner, complainer, container, crosstrainer, Elena, retainer; **4** entertainer, macarena. *See also* **2.60.5**.

2.15.10: **2** Brenner, henna, Jenner, senna, tenner, tenor; **3** antenna, duenna, McKenna, Siena, sienna, Vienna; **4** countertenor.

2.15.11: **2** burner, earner, learner, Turner; **3** page-turner, returner, wage earner; **4** Annapurna, CD burner.

2.15.12: **2** Dena, denar, Dvina, Gina, kina, Meena, Nina, wiener; **3** Athena, convener, demeanour, Georgina, hyena, Medina, Messina, pashmina, retsina, subpoena, verbena; **4** Cartagena, Filipina, karabiner, misdemeanour; **5** Herzegovina; **9** Bosnia and Herzegovina.

2.15.13: **2** cleaner; **3** Celina, galena, pipe cleaner, Selina; **4** semolina, St Helena, Thumbelina.
See also **2.60.5.**

2.15.14: **3** arena, czarina, farina, marina, Sabrina, Serena, tsarina; **4** ballerina; **6** prima ballerina.

2.15.15: **2** Tina; **3** cantina, Christina, fontina, Latina, Priština; **4** Argentina, concertina, scarlatina.

2.15.16: **2** Cinna, dinner, inner, pinna, sinner, Skinner, spinner, thinner, winner; **3** Asvina, beginner, breadwinner, dog's dinner, Elinor, foreigner, lamina, mariner, milliner, patina, prizewinner, retina, word-spinner; **4** money-spinner, submariner, TV dinner.

All human history attests
That happiness for man,—the hungry
sinner!—
Since Eve ate apples, much depends on
dinner.
(Lord Byron)

2.15.17: **3** stamina; **4** determiner, examiner; **5** Gewürztraminer, predeterminer.

2.15.18: **2** China, Dinah, diner, Heine, miner, minor, mynah, shiner, Steiner, whiner; **3** angina, designer, diviner, Regina, vagina; **4** Asia Minor, Canis Minor, Indochina, Ursa Minor.

2.15.19: **2** liner; **3** airliner, eyeliner, freightliner, hardliner, headliner, one-liner, onliner, recliner; **4** pantyliner; **5** North Carolina, South Carolina.

2.15.20: **2** Connor, Donna, goner, honour, wanna; **3** Bellona, dishonour, Madonna, O'Connor; **4** belladonna, prima donna, word of honour.
See also **2.33.12, 2.60.5.**

2.15.21: **2** corner, fauna, mourner, sauna, Warner; **3** Jack Horner; **4** hole-and-corner.

2.15.22: **2** boner, donor, Jonah, krona, krone, moaner, Mona, owner, Shona, toner;

3 corona, Fiona, homeowner, Iona, landowner, persona, shipowner, Verona, Winona; **4** Arizona, Desdemona, pro persona.

2.15.23: **2** loaner, loner; **3** Pamplona; **4** Barcelona.

2.15.24: **2** runner; **3** forerunner, frontrunner, gunrunner, roadrunner.

2.15.25: **2** bhuna, crooner, doona, kuna, Luna, lunar, Oonagh, schooner, sooner, tuna, tuner, Una; **3** kahuna, koruna, lacuna, lampooner, vicuna, vicuña.

2.15.26: **2** partner, Patna, vintner; **3** Mount Etna, Triratna.

2.16: **2** banger, clanger, clangour, hangar, hanger, Sanger; **3** cliffhanger, headbanger; **4** doppelganger.
See also **2.60.5.**

2.17: **2** minger, ringer, singer, springer, stringer, swinger, winger, wringer, zinger; **3** gunslinger, humdinger, Schrödinger.

2.18: **1** per; **2** chutzpah, diaper, helper, jasper, lapa, pauper, prosper, scalper, scarper, Sherpa, torpor, whisper; **4** Atahualpa, developer, mea culpa.
See also **2.33.14.**

2.18.1: **2** clapper, dapper, flapper, kappa, rapper, sapper, slapper, snapper, trapper, wrapper, zapper; **3** red snapper; **4** whippersnapper.

2.18.2: **2** caper, draper, scraper, taper, tapir, vapour; **3** escaper, skyscraper.
See also **2.33, 2.54.103, 2.60.6, 10.42.113.**

2.18.3: **2** paper; **3** art paper, flypaper, green paper, newspaper, notepaper, repaper, sandpaper, touchpaper, wallpaper, wastepaper, white paper; **4** ballot paper, blotting paper, litmus paper, tissue paper, toilet paper, wrapping paper.
See also **2.60.6.**

2.18.4: **2** leper, pepper; **3** Culpeper, high-stepper; **4** Jamaica pepper.
See also **2.33.15.**

2.18.5: **2** beeper, bleeper, Dnieper, sleeper, sweeper; **3** minesweeper.

2.18.6: **2** keeper; **3** beekeeper, bookkeeper, doorkeeper, gamekeeper, gatekeeper, goalkeeper, green keeper, greenkeeper, housekeeper, innkeeper, lockkeeper, park keeper, peacekeeper, shopkeeper, storekeeper, timekeeper, zookeeper; **4** Arequipa, lighthouse-keeper, record-keeper, wicketkeeper.

2.18.7: **2** creeper, reaper; **3** Grim Reaper, wallcreeper; **6** Virginia creeper.

2.18.8: **2** chipper, clipper, dipper, flipper, kipper, nipper, Pippa, ripper, shipper, skipper, slipper, stripper, tipper, zipper; **3** juniper, worshipper, Yom Kippur.
See also **2.60.6**.

2.18.9: **2** hyper, piper, sniper, viper, wiper; **3** Pied Piper, sandpiper.

2.18.10: **2** chopper, copper, poppa, popper, shopper, stopper, topper, whopper; **3** chart-topper, gobstopper, showstopper; **4** teenybopper.
See also **2.60.6**.

2.18.11: **2** hopper; **3** clodhopper, froghopper, grasshopper, leaf hopper, treehopper.

2.18.12: **2** cropper, dropper, proper; **3** eavesdropper, improper, sharecropper.

2.18.13: **2** moper; **3** eloper, Europa, nohoper; **4** interloper.

2.18.14: **2** cuppa, scupper, supper, upper; **3** Last Supper.

2.18.15: **2** blooper, BUPA, Cooper, Cowper, grouper, pupa, stupor, super, trooper, trouper; **3** peasouper, stormtrooper; **4** paratrooper, party-pooper, superduper.

2.18.16: **2** simper, temper, whimper; **3** distemper.
See also **2.33.16, 10.42.113**.

2.18.17: **2** camper, damper, hamper, pamper, scamper, Tampa, tamper.
See also **2.33.14**.

2.18.18: **2** bumper, dumper, jumper; **3** broad jumper, gazumper, high jumper, long jumper, tub-thumper; **4** triple jumper; **5** bumper to bumper.

2.19: **2** Basra, DEFRA, Ezra, Farrah, genre, horror, infra, Lyra, Mira, mirror, Moira, naira, para, scourer, stirrer; **3** admirer, Biafra, hegira, inquirer, shockhorror, tempura, urethra, wing mirror; **4** Isadora, rearview mirror.
See also **2.33.17**.

2.19.1: **3** agora, amphora, Ankara, cholera, conjurer, conqueror, gatherer, genera, kithara, lecturer, murderer, perjurer, plethora, sorcerer, sufferer, tessera, torturer, treasurer, usurer, viscera, wanderer; **4** adventurer, anaphora, deliverer, discoverer, malingerer, Niagara, philanderer; **5** manufacturer; **7** William the Conqueror.

2.19.2: **3** Attenborough, Canberra, Gainsborough, labourer, Marlborough, Scarborough; **4** Edinburgh, Middlesbrough.

2.19.3: **3** armourer, camera; **4** ephemera, in camera; **5** Sea of Marmara; **6** videocamera.

2.19.4: **3** corpora, emperor, opera, tempera; **4** diaspora; **7** Phantom of the Opera.

2.19.5: **3** caterer, flatterer, fruiterer, plasterer; **4** adulterer, etc, et cetera.

2.19.6: **2** Tara, Zara; **3** Asmara, Guevara, gurdwara, mascara, O'Hara, Sahara, sayonara, shikara, tiara; **4** capybara, McNamara; **5** Guadalajara.

2.19.7: **2** airer, carer, Eire, Sarah, wearer; **3** Aguilera, caldera, sierra, wayfarer; **4** capoeira, demerara, De Valera, habanera, Riviera.

2.19.8: **2** bearer; **3** cupbearer, macebearer, pallbearer, torchbearer, train-bearer; **4** standard-bearer, Water Bearer.

2.19.9: **2** error, Terra, terror; **3** holy terror, sierra; **4** cordillera, Riviera; **5** clerical error.
Of what is't fools make such vain keeping?
Sin their conception, their birth weeping,
Their life a general mist of error,
Their death a hideous storm of terror.
(John Webster)

2.19.10: **2** era, hearer, Hera, Keira, lira, sclera, sera, shearer, Vera; **3** Bagheera, chimaera, chimera, hetaera, lempira, Madeira, Shakira; **4** aloe vera, Christian Era, Common Era, rangatira.

2.19.11: **2** aura, borer, corer, flora, kora, Laura, Nora, scorer, Thora, Torah, tourer; **3** angora, Ashora, aurora, explorer, menorah, pakora, señora; **4** Leonora.
See also **2.19.13**.

2.19.12: **2** Dora; **3** Andorra, fedora, Pandora; **4** Theodora.

2.19.13: **2** Dürer, Führer, Jura, juror; **3** bravura, caesura, datura, insurer, obscura, procurer, tamboura; **4** angostura, Bujumbura; **5** coloratura; **6** acciaccatura, appoggiatura, camera obscura.
See also **2.19.11**.

2.19.14: **2** borough, burgh, burra, Curragh, thorough; **4** kookaburra.

2.19.15: **2** Barbara, cobra, Deborah, dobra, Libra, umbra, zebra; **3** algebra,

Alhambra, king cobra, macabre, penumbra, vertebra; **4** candelabra, cause célèbre; **5** abracadabra.

2.19.16: **2** Chandra, hydra, Indra, Sandra, tundra; **3** Alejandra, Cassandra, cathedra; **4** Alexandra, ex cathedra; **5** double entendre.

2.19.17: **2** Agra, bhangra, Ingres; **3** Niagara, pellagra, Viagra.

2.19.18: **2** chakra, Lycra, okra, sacra.

2.19.19: **2** Capra, copra, supra, Ypres; **4** amour-propre.

2.19.20: **2** Caitra, mantra, sutra, ultra; **4** Brahmaputra, Cleopatra.

2.19.21: **2** Chartres, Sartre; **3** Sinatra, Sumatra; **5** coup de théâtre.

2.19.22: **2** Petra, tetra; **3** belles-lettres, et cetera; **4** fête champêtre, raison d'être.

2.19.23: **2** extra; **3** orchestra; **4** aspidistra, Cosa Nostra, Zarathustra.

2.19.24: **2** Louvre, oeuvre; **3** chef-d'oeuvre, Le Havre; **4** joie de vivre.

2.20: **1** sir; **2** Ailsa, grouser, ISA, Lhasa, mouser, Scouser; **3** canvasser, Kinshasa; **4** Margasirsa.

2.20.1: **2** NASA, Nasser; **3** madrasa, Mombasa, Nyasa, trespasser; **5** antimacassar.

2.20.2: **2** acer, chaser, mesa, racer, tracer; **4** progress chaser.

2.20.3: **2** Hesse, lesser, TESSA; **3** confessor, Odessa, possessor, professor, Vanessa; **5** Edward the Confessor.

2.20.4: **2** dresser; **3** aggressor, compressor, hairdresser, oppressor, suppressor, transgressor.

2.20.5: **3** assessor, processor, successor; **4** coprocessor, food processor, intercessor, predecessor, preprocessor, word processor; **5** microprocessor, multiprocessor.

2.20.6: **2** Bursa, bursar, cursor, Mercer, purser; **3** precursor, vice versa.

2.20.7: **2** kisser, lyssa, missa; **3** Clarissa, Elissa, Larissa, mantissa, Melissa, purchaser.

2.20.8: **3** officer; **4** press officer; **5** careers officer, commissioned officer, flying officer, petty officer, police officer, traffic officer; **6** chief petty officer; **7** noncommissioned officer.

2.20.9: **2** dosser, fossa, glossa, tosser; **4** Barbarossa, double-crosser, Saragossa, Zaragoza.

2.20.10: **2** Chaucer, courser, saucer; Xhosa; **3** endorser, enforcer.

2.20.11: **2** closer, grocer; **3** Formosa, greengrocer, mimosa, samosa; **5** masala dosa; **8** anorexia nervosa.

2.20.12: **2** juicer; **3** Medusa, producer, transducer; **4** Appaloosa, Arethusa.

2.20.13: **2** boxer, coaxer, fixer, hoaxer, mixer, waxer; **3** elixir; **4** multiplexer. *See also* **2.60**.

2.20.14: **2** balsa, Elsa, salsa, Tulsa, ulcer.

2.20.15: **2** bouncer, cancer, mincer, pincer, sponsor; **3** announcer, sequencer, silencer.

2.20.16: **2** answer, chancer, dancer, lancer; **3** freelancer.

2.20.17: **2** censer, censor, fencer, Mensa, sensor, Spencer, Spenser, tensor; **3** condenser, dispenser; **4** cash dispenser.

2.20.18: **2** matzo, pizza, Schweitzer, spritzer; **3** Amritsar, howitzer, piazza, tsaritsa; **4** dopiaza, Srebrenica.

2.21: **2** Ayrshire, Berkshire, brochure, censure, Cheshire, Escher, Flintshire, fuchsia, Hampshire, kosher, Marsha, Mischa, Misha, Persia, Portia, pusher, Shropshire, tonsure, washer, Wiltshire, Yorkshire; **3** absentia, Aisha, Bedfordshire, Cambridgeshire, dementia, Derbyshire, Devonshire, dishwasher, Frobisher, Ganesha, Gloucestershire, Hertfordshire, inertia, Lancashire, Leicestershire, Lincolnshire, Lucretia, Monmouthshire, New Hampshire, Oxfordshire, Pembrokeshire, penpusher, perisher, Renfrewshire, Rhodesia, Staffordshire, St Lucia, Warwickshire, whitewasher, Worcestershire; **4** Aberdeenshire, alopecia, Austronesia, Buckinghamshire, Carmarthenshire, Clackmannanshire, Herefordshire, Northamptonshire, Nottinghamshire, Nova Scotia. *See also* **2.33**.

2.21.1: **2** Asher, flasher, masher, pasha, rasher, Sasha, slasher, smasher; **3** gatecrasher; **4** Bible-basher, haberdasher.

2.21.2: **2** Asia, fascia, geisha; **3** acacia, Croatia, Dalmatia, Eurasia, ex gratia; **4** echinacea.

2.21.3: **2** Brescia, fresher, pressure, thresher; **3** high-pressure, low-pressure, refresher; **4** acupressure. *See also* **2.33**.

2.21.4: 2 Fischer, Fisher, fissure;
3 kingfisher, militia, publisher, vanquisher, well-wisher; 4 extinguisher.

2.21.5: 2 blusher, gusher, Prussia, Russia, usher.

2.22: 2 ABTA, goitre, loiter, outer, outta, Reuter; 3 exploiter; 4 reconnoitre.

2.22.1: 2 batter, chatter, fatter, hatter, matter, natter, patter, satyr, scatter, shatter, spatter, tatter; 3 bespatter, ciabatta, end matter, front matter, Kenyatta, regatta; 4 antimatter, pitter-patter; 5 mad as a hatter, mind over matter.
See also **2.33.19, 10.42.119**.

2.22.2: 2 clatter, flatter, latter, platter, splatter.
See also **2.33.19, 10.42.119**.

2.22.3: 2 theatre; 3 Agutter, amateur, comforter, coveter, cricketer, dieter, orator, predator, proprietor, senator, stigmata; 4 amphitheatre, conservator, conspirator.

2.22.4: 2 barter, charter, data, garter, Sparta; 3 cassata, IATA, piñata, sonata, waiata; 4 Alma-Ata, chipolata, Ulaanbaatar; 6 Order of the Garter, taramasalata.
See also **2.33.20, 10.42.118**.

2.22.5: 2 Carter; 3 Jakarta, toccata; 4 Magna Carta.

2.22.6: 2 martyr; 3 stigmata; 4 alma mater, imprimatur.
See also **2.33.18**.

2.22.7: 2 strata; 3 paratha, pro rata; 5 inamorata; 6 persona non grata.

2.22.8: 2 starter, tartar, Tatar; 3 cantata, frittata, nonstarter.

2.22.9: 2 mater, pater, waiter; 3 debater, dumbwaiter, equator, peseta; 4 alma mater, animator, estimator, incubator; 5 emancipator, tergiversator.

2.22.10: 3 creator; 4 aviator, gladiator, mediator, radiator; 5 conciliator, initiator, negotiator.

2.22.11: 2 data; 3 viewdata; 4 biodata, liquidator, metadata; 5 intimidator.

2.22.12: 2 gaiter, gator; 4 aggregator, alligator, castigator, derogator, instigator, litigator, navigator, overgaiter, propagator; 5 investigator; 6 circumnavigator; 7 private investigator.
See also **2.60.7**.

2.22.13: 2 cater; 3 Mercator; 4 abdicator, applicator, duplicator, educator, fabricator,

indicator, lubricator, obfuscator; 5 adjudicator, authenticator, communicator, equivocator, pontificator, prevaricator; 8 Uniform Resource Locator.
See also **10.42.118**.

2.22.14: 2 L8R, later, Slater; 3 collator, dilator, translator; 4 escalator, legislator, oscillator, percolator, travolator, ventilator; 5 bronchodilator, defibrillator, invigilator, vasodilator.

2.22.15: 4 calculator, emulator, insulator, modulator, regulator, simulator, speculator, tabulator; 5 accumulator, dissimulator, manipulator, perambulator.

2.22.16: 4 alternator, detonator, fascinator, resonator, terminator; 5 contaminator, coordinator, denominator, exterminator, impersonator, originator, procrastinator; 7 common denominator, female impersonator.

2.22.17: 2 crater, freighter, grater; 3 curator, vibrator; 4 calibrator, integrator.

2.22.18: 3 narrator; 4 decorator, generator, liberator, moderator, numerator, operator, respirator, separator; 5 accelerator, collaborator, corroborator, enumerator, incinerator, refrigerator; 7 Boolean operator.

2.22.19: 2 traitor; 4 arbitrator, concentrator, demonstrator, illustrator, infiltrator, orchestrator, perpetrator; 5 administrator.

2.22.20: 2 tater; 3 dictator, rotator, spectator; 4 agitator, commentator, imitator; 5 facilitator; 6 prestidigitator.

2.22.21: 2 activator, cultivator, elevator, excavator, innovator, motivator, renovator.

2.22.22: 2 better, debtor, Etta, feta, fetter, sweater; 3 abettor, begetter, biretta, bruschetta, go-getter, unfetter, vendetta; 4 arietta, canzonetta, carburettor, Henrietta, operetta.
See also **2.60.7**.

2.22.23: 2 letter; 3 chain letter, French letter, love letter, newsletter, Valletta; 4 airmail letter, begging letter, open letter; 5 capital letter, covering letter, poison-pen letter.
See also **2.60.7**.

2.22.24: 2 setter; 3 pacesetter, red setter, trendsetter, typesetter; 4 English setter, Irish setter.

2.22.25: **2** Goethe, kurta; **3** Alberta, asserter, converter, deserter, frankfurter; **7** catalytic converter.

2.22.26: **2** cheater, cheetah, eater, eta, heater, teeter, theta, tweeter, vita, zeta; **3** anteater, Aouita, beefeater, defeater, Evita, fire-eater, flesh-eater, Nikita, space heater, two-seater, windcheater; **4** dolce vita, Eid al-Fitr, honeyeater, lotus-eater, Polychaeta.

2.22.27: **2** beater, beta; **3** eggbeater, wife-beater, world-beater; **4** carpet-beater.

2.22.28: **2** litre; **3** Lolita; **4** centilitre, decilitre, millilitre.

2.22.29: **2** meter, metre; **3** ammeter, Demeter, gas meter, voltmeter, wattmeter; **4** altimeter, centimetre, kilometre, millimetre, nanometre, voltammeter, water meter.

2.22.30: **3** Anita, granita, Juanita, man-eater.

2.22.31: **2** Peter, pitta; **3** repeater, saltpetre.

2.22.32: **2** greeter, praetor, Rita; **3** amrita, excreta, ureter; **4** margarita, overeater, señorita.

2.22.33: **2** hitter, skitter, titter; **3** bullshitter, catheter, marketer, picketer, pinch hitter, servitor; **4** competitor.

2.22.34: **2** bitter; **3** arbiter, embitter, orbiter, presbyter; **4** exhibitor, inhibitor.
All's over, then: does truth sound bitter As one at first believes?
Hark, 'tis the sparrows' good-night twitter About your cottage eaves!
(Robert Browning)
See also **2.54.63, 2.60.7**.

2.22.35: **3** auditor, creditor, editor; **4** subeditor.

2.22.36: **2** fitter; **3** outfitter, taffeta; **4** counterfeiter.

2.22.37: **2** flitter, glitter, litter; **4** Hippolyta.
See also **10.42.118**.

2.22.38: **3** scimitar, transmitter, trimeter; **4** altimeter, delimiter, diameter, heptameter, hexameter, octameter, parameter, pentameter, perimeter, tetrameter; **5** neurotransmitter; **7** iambic pentameter.

2.22.39: **4** barometer, chronometer, cyclometer, gasometer, geometer, hydrometer, hygrometer, kilometre,

manometer, micrometer, mileometer, milometer, Nilometer, odometer, pedometer, photometer, speedometer, swingometer, tachometer, thermometer, udometer; **5** accelerometer, anemometer, audiometer, calorimeter, electrometer, galvanometer, pluviometer, radiometer, thalassometer; **6** potentiometer.

2.22.40: **3** janitor, monitor; **5** primogenitor; **6** terra incognita.

2.22.41: **2** pitta; **3** Jupiter, trumpeter; **4** per capita.

2.22.42: **2** critter, fritter, gritter; **3** heritor, ureter; **4** apple fritter, emerita, inheritor, interpreter.

2.22.43: **2** sitter; **3** bedsitter; **4** babysitter, capacitor, solicitor.

2.22.44: **2** quitter, twitter, witter; **4** non sequitur.

2.22.45: **3** visitor; **4** compositor, depositor, expositor, health visitor, inquisitor.

2.22.46: **2** fighter, mitre, nitre; **3** firefighter, nail-biter, prizefighter, reciter; **4** ankle-biter, freedom fighter, Gastarbeiter, overnighter.

2.22.47: **2** blighter, lighter; **3** downlighter, firelighter, gauleiter, highlighter, uplighter; **5** cigarette lighter.

2.22.48: **2** raita, writer; **3** ghostwriter, screenwriter, scriptwriter, songwriter, speechwriter, typewriter; **4** CD writer, copywriter, underwriter.

2.22.49: **2** blotter, gotta, jotter, lotta, otter, plotter, potter, spotter, squatter, totter; **3** boycotter, flyswatter, pelota, ricotta, trainspotter; **4** pannacotta, teeter-totter, terracotta.
See also **10.42.118**.

2.22.50: **2** rotter, trotter; **3** foxtrotter, garrotter, globetrotter.

2.22.51: **2** daughter, mortar, slaughter; **3** aorta, goddaughter, granddaughter, manslaughter, stepdaughter; **4** bricks-and-mortar; **5** lamb to the slaughter.
See also **2.33.18**.

2.22.52: **2** Porter; **3** exporter, importer, reporter, supporter, transporter; **4** cub reporter.

2.22.53: **2** water; **3** bath water, Bayswater, dishwater, ditchwater, firewater, freshwater, groundwater, high water, holy water, hot water, ice water, limewater, low water, meltwater, rainwater, saltwater, seawater, tap water, Ullswater; **4** barley water, bread and water, Derwent Water, drinking water, in deep water, in hot water, toilet water, underwater; **5** Coniston Water, Ennerdale Water, fish out of water, like oil and water, long drink of water, mineral water; **7** like a fish out of water.

Would I could cast a sail on the water
Where many a king has gone
And many a king's daughter,
And alight at the comely trees and the
  lawn
(W.B. Yeats)

2.22.54: **2** quarter; **3** backwater, breakwater, headquarter, hindquarter; **4** Latin quarter; **5** hang draw and quarter. *See also* **2.60.8**.

2.22.55: **2** bloater, boater, chota, floater, motor, quota, rota, rotor, voter; **3** biota, Dakota, iota, promoter; **4** Minnesota, North Dakota. *See also* **2.60.7, 10.42.118**.

2.22.56: **2** butter, clutter, flutter, gutta, gutter, mutter, nutter, putter, shutter, splutter, sputter, stutter, utter; **3** dupatta; **4** bread-and-butter, peanut butter. *See also* **2.33.21, 10.42.118**.

2.22.57: **2** cutter, Qatar; **3** Calcutta, grass-cutter, Kolkata, leafcutter, woodcutter; **4** daisycutter.

2.22.58: **2** footer; **4** contributor, distributor, executor, pussyfooter; **5** interlocutor.

2.22.59: **2** hooter, looter, router, scooter, suitor; **3** accoutre, freebooter, polluter.

2.22.60: **2** neuter, pewter, tutor; **3** commuter, computer, disputer, transputer; **4** persecutor, private tutor, prosecutor; **5** microcomputer, minicomputer, neurocomputer, supercomputer, telecommuter; **6** public prosecutor. *See also* **2.33.18**.

2.22.61: **2** shooter; **3** peashooter, sharpshooter; **4** troubleshooter.

2.22.62: **2** BAFTA, crofter, EFTA, kofta, poofter.

2.22.63: **2** after, laughter, rafter; **3** hereafter, sought-after, thereafter; **4** hereinafter, thereinafter.

2.22.64: **2** drifter, grifter, lifter, snifter; **3** weightlifter.

2.22.65: **2** doctor, proctor, sphincter; **3** character, constructor, horse doctor, instructor, spin doctor, witch doctor; **4** flying doctor.

2.22.66: **2** actor, factor; **3** infractor, reactor, refractor; **4** benefactor, chiropractor, malefactor, wind-chill factor; **5** character actor; **6** highest common factor, nuclear reactor.

2.22.67: **2** tractor; **3** contractor, detractor, extractor, protractor; **4** subcontractor.

2.22.68: **2** hector, nectar, sector, vector; **3** bisector, connector, convector, defector, detector, ejector, objector, projector, protector, trifecta; **4** lie detector, private sector, public sector; **5** interconnector; **7** conscientious objector.

2.22.69: **3** collector, elector, reflector, selector; **4** debt collector.

2.22.70: **2** spectre; **3** inspector, prospector, respecter.

2.22.71: **2** rector; **3** director; **6** funeral director, managing director, musical director; **8** nonexecutive director.

2.22.72: **2** dicta, victor; **3** character, constrictor, predictor; **5** boa constrictor.

2.22.73: **3** abductor, adductor, conductor, inductor; **5** semiconductor, superconductor.

2.22.74: **2** filter, kilter, philtre, realtor, vaulter, Yalta; **4** out of kilter.

2.22.75: **2** CELTA, delta, shelter, smelter, swelter, welter; **4** helter-skelter. *See also* **2.33.18, 10.42.118**.

2.22.76: **2** Malta, Psalter, Volta, Yalta; **3** Gibraltar; **4** Upper Volta.

2.22.77: **2** altar, alter, falter, halter, Malta, psalter, Walter; **3** Gibraltar. *See also* **2.33.18, 10.42.118**.

2.22.78: **2** Gunther, junta, onto, painter, planter, pointer, quanta, saunter; **3** enchanter.

2.22.79: **2** banter, canter; **3** Atlanta, decanter, levanter, recanter; **4** Atalanta, tam-o'-shanter.

2.22.80: **2** enter, renter; **3** eventer, frequenter, inventor, magenta, polenta, presenter, re-enter, repenter, tormentor; **4** break and enter; **5** experimenter, impedimenta.

2.22.81: **2** centre; **3** dissenter, Jobcentre, off-centre, placenta, precentor; **4** epicentre. *See also* **2.33.18**.

2.22.82: 2 into, minter, Pinter, splinter, winter; 3 carpenter, midwinter; 4 Araminta, overwinter.

2.22.83: 2 printer, sprinter; 3 line printer; 4 laser printer, matrix printer, teleprinter, thermal printer; 5 bubble-jet printer, dot-matrix printer, ink-jet printer.

2.22.84: 2 counter; 3 bean counter, encounter; 4 Geiger counter; 5 over-the-counter, under-the-counter.

2.22.85: 2 Bunter, chunter, hunter, junta, punter; 3 fox-hunter, headhunter, witch-hunter; 4 bargain hunter, fortune hunter.

2.22.86: 2 copter, emptor, prompter, sculptor, tempter; 3 descriptor, diopter; 4 helicopter, Teleprompter.

2.22.87: 2 captor, chapter, raptor; 3 adapter; 5 velociraptor.

2.22.88: 2 sceptre; 3 accepter, receptor; 4 interceptor; 5 chemoreceptor.

2.22.89: 2 Auster, Baxter, bolster, booster, Brewster, Dempster, Dexter, doomster, dragster, Dumpster, fibster, Forster, fraudster, gagster, hamster, holster, keister, lobster, mobster, oldster, ouster, pollster, popster, roadster, rooster, shyster, tapster, taster, teamster, tipster, Ulster, waster, Webster, Wooster, Worcester; 3 Alastair, Alistair, baluster, shirtwaister, timewaster, upholster; 4 kappelmeister.
See also **2.33.22**.

2.22.90: 2 aster, Astor, pasta, Rasta, raster, Shasta; 3 canasta, Doncaster, Jyaistha, Lancaster, pilaster; 4 ghetto blaster, oleaster, poetaster, Zoroaster; 5 cotoneaster.
See also **2.22.91**.

2.22.91: 2 faster, pastor, plaster; 3 corn plaster, disaster; 4 alabaster, ghetto blaster, mustard plaster.
See also **2.22.90, 2.33.22**.

2.22.92: 2 caster, castor; 3 broadcaster, forecaster.

2.22.93: 2 master; 3 bandmaster, Buckmaster, bushmaster, choirmaster, drillmaster, gangmaster, grand master, hard master, headmaster, housemaster, old master, past master, paymaster, postmaster, quizmaster, remaster, ringmaster, schoolmaster, scoutmaster, taskmaster, three-master, toastmaster, webmaster; 4 lord and master, modern master, music master, overmaster, puppet master,

quartermaster, question master, stationmaster.

2.22.94: 2 Chester, ester, festa, fester, jester, Leicester, pester, quester, testa, tester, Vesta; 3 ancestor, Avesta, celesta, Esther, fiesta, investor, Manchester, northwester, podesta, protester, red leicester, semester, sequester, siesta, Silvester, sou'wester, southwester, Sylvester, trimester, Winchester; 4 arbalester, polyester.
See also **2.33.22, 10.42.118**.

2.22.95: 2 Dniester, Easter, feaster, quaestor; 3 northeaster; 4 autopista, fashionista.

2.22.96: 2 blister, glister, Lister, mister, Mr, twister, vista; 3 ballista, barista, barrister, brain-twister, Chichester, chorister, demister, forester, harvester, Manchester, register, resistor, Rochester, transistor, Winchester; 4 cash register; 5 combine harvester, parish register.
See also **2.33.22, 10.42.118**.

2.22.97: 3 banister, bannister, canister, gannister; 5 planta genista.
See also **2.60.7**.

2.22.98: 3 minister, sinister; 4 administer, bar sinister, bend sinister, first minister; 5 maladminister, prime minister; 6 cabinet minister.

2.22.99: 2 sister; 3 assister, big sister, half-sister, koeksister, night sister, stepsister, ward sister, weird sister; 4 theatre sister.

2.22.100: 2 Costa, foster, Gloucester, hosta, roster; 3 imposter, impostor; 4 double gloucester, herpes zoster, paternoster.

2.22.101: 2 cloister, oyster, roister; 4 prairie oyster; 5 native oyster.

2.22.102: 2 boaster, coaster, poster, toaster; 3 billposter, four-poster.

2.22.103: 2 Custer, duster, muster, thruster; 3 Augusta; 4 knuckle-duster.

2.22.104: 2 buster; 3 blockbuster, ghostbuster; 4 bronco-buster, bunker buster, filibuster.
See also **10.42.173**.

2.22.105: 2 bluster, cluster, fluster, lustre; 3 lacklustre.
See also **2.33.22**.

2.22.106: 2 funkster, huckster, prankster, quackster, trickster.

2.22.107: 2 minster, monster, Munster, Münster, punster, spinster; 3 Axminster, old spinster, Westminster; 4 Gila monster, green-eyed monster, Loch Ness monster.

2.22.108: 2 gangsta, gangster, songster, youngster.

2.23: 2 Arthur, author, Bertha, Eartha, ether, Luther, Martha; 3 Agatha, Golgotha, Hiawatha, Ibiza, MacArthur, Tabitha; 4 pyracantha.
See also **10.42.113**.

2.23.1: 2 anther, panther; 3 Pink Panther, Samantha.

2.24: 2 archer, betcha, butcher, clincher, cloture, creature, feature, future, gotcha, kwacha, launcher, lecher, marcher, nature, Nietzsche, nurture, poacher, preacher, rancher, scorcher, searcher, stretcher, suture, teacher, torture, voucher, wotcha; 3 birdwatcher, denature, departure, headteacher, researcher, schoolteacher; 4 Mother Nature, nomenclature, number-cruncher, true-to-nature, water feature.
See also **2.33.23, 2.60**.

2.24.1: 2 catcher, dacha, stature, Thatcher; 3 dispatcher, flycatcher, focaccia; 4 body snatcher, oystercatcher.

2.24.2: 3 aperture, armature, curvature, ligature, literature, miniature, premature, signature; 4 candidature, entablature, implicature, judicature, legislature, musculature, time signature; 5 grey literature.
See also **9.14.46**.

2.24.3: 2 pitcher, twitcher; 3 forfeiture, furniture, portraiture, signature, temperature, vestiture; 4 discomfiture, divestiture, expenditure, investiture; 5 primogeniture.

2.24.4: 2 fracture, lecture, picture, stricture; 3 conjecture, prefecture; 4 architecture, manufacture.
See also **2.33.23, 10.42.113**.

2.24.5: 2 structure; 3 restructure, substructure; 4 infrastructure, superstructure.
See also **2.33.23**.

2.24.6: 2 cincture, juncture, puncture, tincture; 4 acupuncture, lumbar puncture.

2.24.7: 2 culture, vulture; 3 subculture; 4 agriculture, aquiculture, aviculture, counterculture, floriculture, horticulture,

monoculture, pomiculture, viniculture, viticulture; 5 arboriculture.
See also **2.33.23**.

2.24.8: 2 denture, trencher, venture; 3 adventure, backbencher, coventure, debenture, indenture; 4 misadventure.

2.24.9: 2 capture, rapture, rupture, scripture, sculpture; 3 enrapture, recapture.

2.24.10: 2 fixture, gesture, mixture, moisture, pasture, posture, texture; 3 admixture, imposture; 4 dolly mixture.
See also **10.42.113**.

2.25: 2 Denver, hover, Java, mitzvah, slaver; 3 bar mitzvah, bas mitzvah, bath mitzvah, bat mitzvah, cadaver; 4 Bodhisattva.

2.25.1: 3 helluva, Kosovo, Nineveh, pareve, pavlova.

2.25.2: 2 carver, guava, Java, kava; 3 cassava; 4 Costa Brava, vena cava.

2.25.3: 2 larva, lava, laver; 3 baklava, palaver; 4 balaclava, Bratislava.

2.25.4: 2 Ava, favour, flavour, paver, raver, saver, savour, shaver, slaver; 3 disfavour, engraver, lifesaver.
See also **2.33.24, 10.42.120**.

2.25.5: 2 quaver, waiver, waver; 4 semiquaver; 6 demisemiquaver; 8 hemidemisemiquaver.
See also **10.42.120**.

2.25.6: 2 clever, ever, never, sever, Trevor; 3 best-ever, endeavour, forever, however, whatever, whenever, wherever, whichever, whoever, whomever; 4 hardly ever, never-never, overclever.

Come, my Celia, let us prove,
While we can, the sports of love,
Time will not be ours for ever,
He, at length, our good will sever.
(Ben Jonson)
See also **2.54.63**.

2.25.7: 4 howsoever, whatsoever, whensoever, wheresoever, whomsoever, whosoever.

2.25.8: 2 fervour, server; 3 file server, Minerva, observer, preserver, timeserver; 4 life preserver, superserver.

2.25.9: 2 beaver, diva, fever, Shiva, viva, weaver, weever; 3 achiever, brain-fever, deceiver, Geneva, genever, hay fever, marsh fever, receiver, retriever, transceiver, yeshiva; 4 breakbone fever, high achiever, Lassa fever, parrot fever, yellow fever; 5 glandular fever, golden retriever, underachiever; **6** Official Receiver.

2.25.10: **2** cleaver, lever; **3** believer, gear lever, school-leaver; **4** cantilever, nonbeliever, unbeliever.

2.25.11: **2** giver, quiver, shiver; **3** caregiver, gingiva, lawgiver, namegiver.

Willows whiten, aspens quiver,
Little breezes dusk and shiver.
(Alfred Tennyson)

2.25.12: **2** liver, sliver; **3** calf's liver, deliver, fast-liver, free-liver, lamb's liver, Oliver; **4** chicken liver; **5** fail to deliver.

2.25.13: **2** river; **3** downriver, Red River, upriver; **4** Old Man River, up the river, Yellow River.

2.25.14: **2** diver, fiver, Ivor, jiver, viva; **3** contriver, Godiva, saliva, survivor; **4** conjunctiva.
See also **2.60**.

2.25.15: **2** driver; **3** hell-driver, pile-driver, screwdriver, slave-driver; **4** back-seat driver, engine driver.

2.25.16: **2** drover, ova, over, Rover; **3** changeover, cutover, flyover, hangover, hungover, Jehovah, leftover, moreover, pushover, sleepover, stopover, switchover; **4** Akhmatova, carryover, going-over, half-seas over.

2.25.17: **2** Dover; **3** handover, holdover, Moldova; **4** Cliffs of Dover.

2.25.18: **3** lookover, makeover, takeover, walkover; **4** Tereshkova.

2.25.19: **2** clover; **3** all over, in clover, pavlova, pullover, rollover, spillover; **4** four-leaf clover; **5** living in clover, Navratilova.

2.25.20: **2** nova; **3** Canova, Hanover, turnover; **4** bossa nova, Casanova, maiden over, supernova.

2.25.21: **3** crossover, once-over, Passover, voiceover.

2.25.22: **2** cover; **3** air cover, cloud cover, discover, dust cover, hardcover, loose cover, recover, re-cover, uncover; **4** rediscover, undercover.
See also **2.33.24, 10.42.120**.

2.25.23: **2** glover, lover, plover; **3** dog lover, food lover, peace-lover; **4** drama-lover, live-in lover; **5** animal lover.

2.25.24: **2** groover, Hoover, louvre, mover; **3** earthmover, improver, manoeuvre, prime mover, remover,

Vancouver; **4** outmanoeuvre, people mover.
See also **10.42.120**.

2.25.25: **2** elver, salver, silver, vulva; **3** absolver, dissolver, quacksalver, quicksilver, revolver; **4** Long John Silver.

2.26: **2** aqua, fatwa, Iowa, lingua, Quechua; **3** chihuahua, Ojibwa, Ottawa, Peshawar, subaqua; **4** Kurosawa, Okinawa.

2.27: **2** buzzer, fizzer, hawser, loadsa, Pausa.

2.27.1: **2** Gaza, parser, plaza, spaza; **5** tabula rasa.

2.27.2: **2** blazer, laser, Weser; **3** stargazer, trailblazer.
See also **10.42.187**.

2.27.3: **2** Fraser, Frazer, razor; **3** appraiser, eraser, fire raiser, fund-raiser, hell-raiser; **4** curtain-raiser, Ockham's razor.

2.27.4: **2** Caesar, freezer, geezer, geyser, Giza, Pisa, squeezer, teaser, visa; **3** appeaser, brainteaser, fridge-freezer, mestiza, Teresa, Theresa; **4** Ebenezer, lemon-squeezer, Mona Lisa, Tower of Pisa.

You're the Nile,
You're the Tower of Pisa,
You're the smile
On the Mona Lisa...
But if, Baby, I'm the bottom you're the top!
(Cole Porter)

2.27.5: **2** geyser, Kaiser, miser, riser, wiser; **3** chastiser, franchiser, incisor, ioniser; **4** advertiser, appetiser, atomiser, liquidiser, merchandiser, moisturiser, nebuliser, organiser, sympathiser, synthesiser, womaniser; **5** anonymiser.

2.27.6: **4** breathalyzer, equaliser, fertiliser, stabiliser, tranquilliser; **5** immobiliser.

2.27.7: **2** visor; **3** adviser, deviser, divisor; **4** improviser, legal adviser, supervisor.

2.27.8: **2** bowser, browser, dowser, trouser, wowser; **3** espouser; **4** rabble-rouser.
See also **2.60, 10.42.190**.

2.27.9: **2** crozier, poser; **3** brown-noser, bulldozer, composer, exposer, mimosa, opposer, proposer, Spinoza; **4** decomposer, waste disposer.

2.27.10: **2** boozer, bruiser, cruiser, loser, user; **3** abuser, accuser, born loser, diffuser, excuser, refuser, yakuza; **4** battle cruiser, cabin-cruiser; **5** lollapalooza.

2.27.11: **2** bonzer, cleanser, kwanza, stanza, Windsor; **3** bonanza, cadenza, credenza, merganser, organza; **4** influenza; **5** extravaganza.

2.28: **2** Asia, azure; **3** Caucasia, embrasure, erasure, Eurasia, Malaysia; **4** Australasia, Transcaucasia.

2.29: **2** leisure, measure, pleasure, treasure; **3** displeasure; **4** countermeasure.

Drinking is the soldier's pleasure;
Rich the treasure;
Sweet the pleasure;
Sweet is pleasure after pain.
(John Dryden)
See also **2.33.27, 2.60**.

2.30: **2** freesia, seizure; **3** Rhodesia; **4** Austronesia, Indonesia, Melanesia.

2.31: **2** closure, crosier; **3** composure, disclosure, enclosure, exposure; **4** discomposure; **5** overexposure.

2.32: **2** Arab, carob, cherub, mihrab, scarab.

2.33: **2** censured, injured, leeward, mansard, method, pressured, steward, tapered, zippered; **3** endangered, Hesiod, myriad, period, unanswered.
See also **2.10.8, 2.10.9, 2.18.2, 2.21, 2.21.3**.

2.33.1: **2** cupboard, laboured, numbered, scabbard, starboard, timbered; **3** unnumbered; **4** Mother Hubbard, unencumbered.
See also **2.5.2, 2.5.12**.

2.33.2: **2** bladdered, gendered, hindered, ordered, powdered; **3** bewildered, considered, disordered, red-blooded; **4** ill-considered, simple-minded, unconsidered.
See also **2.6.5, 2.6.8, 2.6.10, 2.6.14, 2.6.23**.

2.33.3: **2** standard; **3** bog-standard, nonstandard, substandard; **4** openhanded.
See also **2.34**.

2.33.4: **2** feathered, gathered, weathered, withered.
See also **2.7, 2.7.2, 2.7.3**.

2.33.5: **2** Ashford, Bedford, Bradford, Catford, Clifford, Crawford, Deptford, Hartford, Longford, Mitford, offered, Oxford, Redford, Stamford, Stanford, Stepford, Telford, Watford, Wexford, Woodford; **3** Beresford, deciphered, eisteddfod, Hereford, Old Trafford, Rutherford, Waterford.
See also **2.8, 2.8.3**.

2.33.6: **2** angered, blackguard, buggered, haggard, laggard, niggard, sluggard, staggered; **3** beleaguered, disfigured, green-fingered, light-fingered; **4** butterfingered, nimble-fingered.
See also **2.9.1, 2.9.6, 2.9.10, 2.9.11**.

2.33.7: **2** lanyard, poniard, Spaniard, tenured, vineyard; **4** Martha's Vineyard.

2.33.8: **1** could; **2** blinkered, checkered, chequered, drunkard, knackered, stonkered, tankard; **3** bewhiskered.
See also **2.12.1**.

2.33.9: **2** ballad, pollard, salad, tailored; **3** chef's salad, fruit salad, Greek salad, mixed salad; **4** Caesar salad, Waldorf salad; **5** potato salad.
See also **2.13.4**.

2.33.10: **2** coloured, dullard; **3** discoloured; **4** multicoloured, varicoloured.
See also **2.13.20**.

2.33.11: **2** armoured, hammered, rumoured; **3** enamoured, good-humoured.
See also **2.14.2**.

2.33.12: **2** Bernard, honoured, Leonard, synod; **3** St Bernard, time-honoured; **4** concertinaed.
See also **2.15.20**.

2.33.13: **2** mannered; **3** bad-mannered, ill-mannered, mild-mannered, well-mannered.

2.33.14: **2** hampered, pampered, whispered; **3** unhampered.
See also **2.18, 2.18.17**.

2.33.15: **2** leopard, peppered, shepherd, Sheppard; **3** snow leopard; **4** German shepherd.
See also **2.18.4**.

2.33.16: **2** tempered; **3** bad-tempered, good-tempered, hot-tempered, ill-tempered, quick-tempered, short-tempered, untempered; **4** even-tempered.
See also **2.18.16**.

2.33.17: **2** Alfred, farad, Herod, hundred, kindred, Mildred, mirrored.

Half a league, half a league,
Half a league onward,
All in the valley of Death
Rode the six hundred.
(Alfred Tennyson)
See also **2.19, 2.34**.

2.33.18: **2** altered, centred, cratered, it'd, lettered, martyred, neutered, sheltered, slaughtered; **3** embittered, headquartered,

self-centred, unaltered, unfettered,
unlettered, unmetered, untutored.
See also **2.22.6, 2.22.51, 2.22.60, 2.22.75,
2.22.77.**

2.33.19: **2** battered, flattered, scattered,
shattered, tattered.
See also **2.22.1, 2.22.2.**

2.33.20: **2** bartered, chartered; **3** big-
hearted, cold-hearted, cruel-hearted,
downhearted, faint-hearted, false-hearted,
goodhearted, half-hearted, hard-hearted,
kind-hearted, lighthearted, soft-hearted,
stouthearted, unchartered, warm-hearted,
wholehearted; **4** broken-hearted, heavy-
hearted, lion-hearted, openhearted, tender-
hearted.
See also **2.22.4, 2.54.76.**

2.33.21: **2** cluttered, muttered, shuttered,
uttered; **3** uncluttered.
See also **2.22.56.**

2.33.22: **2** bastard, bustard, cloistered,
custard, dastard, flustered, mustard,
plastered; **3** blistered, registered,
sequestered, upholstered; **4** well-
upholstered.
See also **2.22.89, 2.22.91, 2.22.94, 2.22.96,
2.22.105.**

2.33.23: **2** cultured, fractured, nurtured,
orchard, pilchard, Richard, sculptured,
structured, textured, tortured; **3** enraptured,
good-natured, ill-natured, indentured,
uncultured, unstructured.
See also **2.24, 2.24.4, 2.24.5, 2.24.7.**

2.33.24: **2** covered, favoured, fevered,
flavoured, Harvard, louvred; **3** discovered,
ill-favoured, uncovered; **4** lily-livered,
undiscovered.
See also **2.25.4, 2.25.22.**

2.33.25: **2** awkward, backward,
downward, eastward, Edward, forward,
froward, Hayward, homeward, inward,
landward, leeward, leftward, northward,
onward, outward, rearward, rightward,
seaward, sideward, skyward, southward,
upward, wayward, westward, windward,
Woodward; **3** afterward, heavenward,
henceforward, northeastward,
northwestward, straightforward,
thenceforward.
See also **2.34.1.**

2.33.26: **2** blizzard, buzzard, gizzard,
hazard, lizard, wizard; **3** haphazard;
4 biohazard, geohazard.
See also **9.14.57.**

2.33.27: **2** leisured, measured, treasured;
3 unmeasured.
See also **2.29.**

2.34: **2** Harrods, hundreds, innards,
Richards, standards; **3** billiards.
See also **2.33.3, 2.33.17.**

2.34.1: **2** backwards, downwards,
earthwards, eastwards, Edwards, forwards,
inwards, leftwards, northwards, onwards,
outwards, rightwards, skywards,
southwards, upwards, westwards;
3 afterwards.
See also **2.33.25.**

2.35: **2** barrack, Braddock, bulwark,
buttock, cassock, haddock, hammock,
hassock, havoc, hummock, Isaac, mattock,
Newark, Norfolk, paddock, stomach,
Suffolk, Taoiseach, tussock; **3** elegiac,
Mubarak.
See also **2.36.**

2.35.1: **2** bollock, bullock, hillock, lilac,
pillock, pollack, pollock.
See also **2.36, 10.42.40.**

2.35.2: **2** bannock, dunnock, eunuch,
Greenock, monarch.

2.36: **2** allowance, barracks, bollocks,
buttocks, flummox, Horrocks, Isaacs,
Lennox, lummox; **5** Jobseeker's
Allowance.
See also **2.35, 2.35.1.**

2.37: **1** lethal; **2** brothel, kajal, Mitchell,
rachel, satchel, spaniel; **3** bequeathal,
betrayal, betrothal, Nathaniel, portrayal,
withdrawal; **4** nonpareil; **5** bilingual.

2.37.1: **3** axial, bestial, brachial,
bronchial, filial; **4** ambrosial, binomial,
celestial, collegial, colloquial, Ezekiel,
familial, marsupial, parochial, vestigial;
5 participial, polynomial.
See also **8.12.**

2.37.2: **3** labial; **4** adverbial, bilabial,
connubial, microbial, proverbial.

2.37.3: **3** cordial, medial, radial;
4 custodial, postprandial, primordial,
remedial; **5** noncustodial.

2.37.4: **3** corneal, cranial, finial, genial,
lineal, menial, venial; **4** baronial, colonial,
congenial; **5** ceremonial, matrilineal,
matrimonial, patrilineal, patrimonial,
testimonial.
See also **9.14.4.**

2.37.5: **4** biennial, centennial, millennial,
perennial, triennial; **5** bicentennial.

2.37.6: 2 real, riel; 3 burial, Gabriel;
4 mercurial; 5 mitochondrial;
6 entrepreneurial.

2.37.7: 3 aerial, Ariel; 5 actuarial,
adversarial, secretarial; 6 antimalarial.

2.37.8: 3 cereal, serial; 4 ethereal,
funereal, imperial, sidereal, venereal;
5 managerial.

Thy functions are ethereal,
As if within thee dwelt a glancing mind,
Organ of vision! And a Spirit aerial
Informs the cell of Hearing, dark and
blind.
(William Wordsworth)

2.37.9: 4 arterial, bacterial, material;
5 immaterial, magisterial, ministerial;
6 antibacterial.
See also **2.39**.

2.37.10: 3 boreal, Oriel; 4 arboreal,
authorial, censorial, corporeal, marmoreal,
memorial, tonsorial; 5 immemorial,
incorporeal, professorial; 6 ambassadorial.

2.37.11: 4 factorial, pictorial, sartorial,
tutorial; 5 directorial, editorial,
proprietorial; 7 extraterritorial.

2.37.12: 5 advertorial, dictatorial,
equatorial, lavatorial, piscatorial,
senatorial, territorial; 6 conspiratorial,
gladiatorial, gubernatorial, inquisitorial.

2.37.13: 3 patrial, vitriol; 4 industrial,
terrestrial; 5 postindustrial;
6 extraterrestrial.

2.37.14: 3 fluvial, jovial, trivial;
4 alluvial, convivial.

2.37.15: 2 loyal, royal; 3 disloyal, Park
Royal; 4 battle royal, pennyroyal, princess
royal.

2.37.16: 2 Sewell; 3 casual; 5 televisual;
6 audiovisual.

2.37.17: 2 jewel; 3 bejewel, gradual;
5 individual.

Thou art as tyrannous, so as thou art
As those whose beauties proudly make
them cruel;
For well thou know'st to my dear doting
heart
Thou art the fairest and most precious
jewel.
(William Shakespeare)

2.37.18: 2 dual, duel, fuel, newel;
3 annual, casual, refuel, renewal, Samuel,
sensual; 4 biofuel, Emmanuel, instinctual,
residual.
See also **2.38, 10.42.59**.

2.37.19: 2 cruel, gruel; 3 accrual,
menstrual; 4 premenstrual.

2.37.20: 3 sexual; 4 transsexual;
5 homosexual, metrosexual, psychosexual;
6 heterosexual.

2.37.21: 3 mutual, ritual, textual;
4 conceptual, contextual, eventual,
habitual, perceptual, perpetual, spiritual;
5 Lords Spiritual.
See also **9.14.3, 9.14.5**.

2.37.22: 3 actual, factual, punctual;
4 effectual; 5 ineffectual, intellectual.
See also **9.14.5**.

2.37.23: 2 barbel, bauble, feeble, foible,
garble, Keble, marble, pebble, rebel,
rouble, treble, warble; 3 enfeeble,
ensemble.
See also **2.39.1**.

2.37.24: 2 babble, dabble, drabble,
gabble, rabble, scrabble; 4 psychobabble,
technobabble.
See also **10.42.60**.

2.37.25: 3 affable, allowable, breathable,
equable, knowable, laughable, singable;
4 downloadable, ineffable, navigable,
unknowable; 5 unnavigable;
6 indefatigable.
See also **9.14.51**.

2.37.26: 3 payable, playable; 4 repayable,
unplayable.

2.37.27: 4 agreeable, foreseeable;
5 disagreeable, unforeseeable.
See also **2.37.90**.

2.37.28: 4 employable, enjoyable;
5 unemployable, unenjoyable.

2.37.29: 3 doable, viewable; 4 arguable,
renewable, unarguable, valuable;
5 invaluable.

2.37.30: 3 bribable, clubbable, probable;
4 improbable; 5 imperturbable,
indescribable.

2.37.31: 3 biddable, credible, gradable,
readable; 4 avoidable, expandable,
extrudable, formidable, incredible,
inedible, persuadable, refundable,
unreadable; 5 unavoidable,
understandable; 6 biodegradable.

2.37.32: 3 audible, laudable; 4 affordable,
inaudible; 5 unaffordable.

2.37.33: 2 bendable; 4 commendable,
dependable, expendable, extendible;
5 undependable.

2.37.34: 3 chargeable, legible; **4** eligible, illegible, knowledgeable, manageable, negligible, rechargeable, salvageable; **5** ineligible, intelligible, unmanageable; **6** unintelligible.

2.37.35: 4 corrigible, dirigible, marriageable, unbridgeable; **5** incorrigible.

2.37.36: 3 changeable, frangible, tangible; **4** exchangeable, infrangible, intangible, unchangeable; **5** interchangeable, unchallengeable.

2.37.37: 3 bankable, bookable, drinkable, likable, shockable, thinkable, workable; **4** impeccable, implacable, remarkable, undrinkable, unlikable, unsinkable, unspeakable, unthinkable, unworkable; **5** irrevocable, unremarkable. *See also* **9.14.51**.

2.37.38: 3 breakable; **4** unbreakable, unshakable; **5** unmistakable.

2.37.39: 3 clickable; **4** amicable, applicable, despicable, explicable, practicable; **5** communicable, impracticable, inapplicable, inexplicable, inextricable; **6** ineradicable.

2.37.40: 3 fallible, gullible, schoolable, syllable; **4** calculable, controllable, indelible, infallible, inviolable, recyclable; **5** incalculable, inconsolable, monosyllable, polysyllable, reconcilable, uncontrollable; **6** irreconcilable.

2.37.41: 3 saleable, scalable; **4** available, unsaleable; **5** unassailable, unavailable.

2.37.42: 3 flammable; **4** consumable, estimable, fathomable, inflammable, nonflammable, presumable, programmable, redeemable; **5** inestimable, irredeemable, unfathomable.

2.37.43: 3 damnable, tenable, trainable; **4** amenable, impregnable, untenable; **5** abominable, imaginable, indefinable, interminable, undefinable, unputdownable; **6** indeterminable, unexplainable, unimaginable.

2.37.44: 4 governable, listenable, pardonable, personable, questionable; **5** companionable, ungovernable, unpardonable, unquestionable; **6** inalienable.

2.37.45: 4 actionable, fashionable, pensionable; **5** exceptionable, impressionable, objectionable, unconscionable, unfashionable,

unmentionable; **6** unexceptionable, unobjectionable.

2.37.46: 4 reasonable, seasonable, treasonable; **5** unreasonable, unseasonable.

2.37.47: 4 attainable, obtainable, sustainable; **5** unattainable, unobtainable, unsustainable.

2.37.48: 4 discernible, returnable; **5** indiscernible, nonreturnable, undiscernible.

2.37.49: 3 capable, culpable, palpable, ropable, stoppable; **4** impalpable, incapable, inculpable, unflappable, unstoppable; **5** inescapable. *See also* **9.14.51**.

2.37.50: 3 arable, horrible, parable, terrible; **4** adorable, demonstrable, deplorable, desirable, execrable, penetrable, transferable; **5** impenetrable, nontransferable, undesirable. *See also* **9.14.51**.

2.37.51: 4 admirable, answerable, censurable, measurable, memorable, miserable, pleasurable, preferable, tolerable; **5** considerable, decipherable, immeasurable, imponderable, inexorable, innumerable, insufferable, intolerable, unalterable, unanswerable, unmemorable, unutterable; **6** inconsiderable, indecipherable. *See also* **9.14.51, 9.14.52**.

2.37.52: 4 honourable, venerable, vulnerable; **5** dishonourable, invulnerable, Right Honourable.

2.37.53: 4 comparable, operable, reparable, separable; **5** incomparable, inoperable, inseparable, insuperable, irreparable.

2.37.54: 4 favourable; **5** deliverable, manoeuvrable, recoverable, unfavourable; **6** irrecoverable, nonrecoverable.

2.37.55: 3 bearable, tearable; **4** repairable, unbearable.

2.37.56: 3 curable, durable, endurable; **4** incurable, nondurable; **5** unendurable.

2.37.57: 3 crucible, flexible, forcible, kissable, passable, peaceable, possible, taxable, traceable; **4** collapsible, impassable, impossible, inflexible, invincible, irascible, noticeable, reducible, responsible, reversible, serviceable, submersible; **5** irreducible, irreplaceable, irresponsible, irreversible, unenforceable,

unnoticeable, unpronounceable, unserviceable.
See also **9.14.53.**

2.37.58: **4** accessible, assessable, compressible, impressible; **5** inaccessible, incompressible, inexpressible, irrepressible.

2.37.59: **4** admissible, permissible, transmissible, unmissable; **5** impermissible, inadmissible.

2.37.60: **3** sensible, tensible; **4** defensible, dispensable, distensible, extensible, insensible, ostensible; **5** apprehensible, comprehensible, indefensible, indispensable, reprehensible, supersensible; **6** incomprehensible.

Had I no eyes, but ears, my ears would
*   love*
That inward beauty and invisible;
Or were I deaf, thy outward parts would
*   move*
Each part in me that were but sensible:
Though neither eyes nor ears, to hear nor
*   see,*
Yet should I be in love by touching thee.
(William Shakespeare)

2.37.61: **3** crushable, sociable, washable; **4** appreciable, insatiable, negotiable, unsociable; **5** non-negotiable; **6** inextinguishable.

2.37.62: **4** perishable, punishable; **5** distinguishable, imperishable; **6** indistinguishable.

2.37.63: **3** comfortable, portable, potable, vegetable; **4** adaptable, compatible, contemptible, corruptible, covetable, debatable, exploitable, inflatable, palatable, redoubtable, reputable, supportable, uncomfortable; **5** attributable, disreputable, incompatible, incorruptible, insupportable, unpalatable.
See also **9.14.54.**

2.37.64: **3** gettable; **4** forgettable, regrettable; **5** unforgettable.

2.37.65: **4** convertible; **5** controvertible, inconvertible, nonconvertible; **6** incontrovertible.

2.37.66: **3** eatable, treatable; **4** unbeatable, uneatable, untreatable; **5** unrepeatable.

2.37.67: **4** charitable, creditable, equitable, heritable, hospitable, irritable, marketable, predictable, profitable, transmittable, veritable; **5** discreditable,

indomitable, inequitable, inevitable, inhospitable, inimitable, uncharitable, unmarketable, unpredictable, unprofitable.
See also **9.14.54.**

2.37.68: **4** dubitable, habitable; **5** indubitable, inhabitable; **6** uninhabitable.

2.37.69: **4** excitable, ignitable, indictable, rewritable; **5** extraditable, inexcitable, unexcitable.

2.37.70: **3** notable, potable, quotable; **4** unquotable.

2.37.71: **3** mutable, scrutable, suitable; **4** commutable, computable, confutable, disputable, immutable, inscrutable, permutable, unsuitable; **5** executable, indisputable, irrefutable, substitutable.
See also **9.14.54.**

2.37.72: **3** tractable; **4** deductible, intractable, retractable; **5** indestructible, ineluctable.

2.37.73: **4** collectable, delectable, detectable, perfectible, respectable; **5** undetectable.

2.37.74: **3** printable; **4** lamentable, presentable, preventable, unprintable.

2.37.75: **3** countable; **4** accountable, uncountable; **5** insurmountable, unaccountable.
See also **9.14.54.**

2.37.76: **4** acceptable, perceptible, susceptible; **5** imperceptible, unacceptable.
See also **9.14.54.**

2.37.77: **2** Dunstable; **3** constable; **4** adjustable, combustible; **5** inexhaustible, irresistible, special constable.

2.37.78: **4** attestable, comestible, contestable, detestable, digestible, suggestible; **5** incontestable, indigestible.

2.37.79: **3** reachable, teachable, touchable, watchable; **4** approachable, detachable, impeachable, unquenchable, unreachable, unteachable, untouchable; **5** irreproachable, unapproachable, unimpeachable.

2.37.80: **3** liveable, lovable, saveable, solvable; **4** dissolvable, forgivable, insolvable, observable, resolvable, unlovable, unsolvable; **5** microwavable, unforgivable.

2.37.81: **4** achievable, believable, conceivable, perceivable, receivable, retrievable; **5** inconceivable, irretrievable, unachievable, unbelievable.

2.37.82: 3 movable; 4 immovable, provable, removable, unmovable, unprovable.

2.37.83: 3 feasible, freezable, plausible, risible; 4 disposable, implausible, unfeasible.
See also **9.14.51**.

2.37.84: 3 visible; 4 divisible, invisible; 5 indivisible.

2.37.85: 3 sizeable; 4 advisable, realisable, surmisable; 5 inadvisable, recognisable; 6 unrecognisable.

2.37.86: 3 usable; 4 accusable, excusable, reusable, unusable; 5 inexcusable.

2.37.87: 2 Abel, able, babel, cable, fable, gable, label, Mabel, sable; 3 disable, enable, unable; 4 disenable, ecolabel, Tower of Babel, web-enable.
A child should always say what's true,
And speak when he is spoken to,
And behave mannerly at table:
At least as far as he is able.
(Robert Louis Stevenson)
See also **2.38.1, 10.42.60**.

2.37.88: 2 bird table, high table, pool table, side table, stable, table; 3 card table, dining table, league table, pintable, Round Table, tide table, timetable, turntable, unstable, worktable; 4 coffee table, dressing table, picnic table, trestle table, water table; 6 operating table, periodic table.
See also **10.42.77**.

2.37.89: 2 burble, gerbil, herbal, verbal; 3 nonverbal.

2.37.90: 4 dutiable, enviable, fanciable, malleable, pitiable, variable; 5 invariable, negotiable, remediable, unenviable; 6 irremediable, non-negotiable.
See also **2.37.27**.

2.37.91: 4 amiable, permeable; 5 impermeable; 6 semipermeable.

2.37.92: 2 Cybill, dibble, dribble, kibble, nibble, nybble, quibble, scribble, sibyl; 3 cannibal, edible, Hannibal, mandible, thurible.
See also **2.38.1, 2.39.1, 10.42.60**.

2.37.93: 2 bible, libel, tribal; 4 Good News Bible, Holy Bible, King James Bible; 5 Gideon Bible, New English Bible.
See also **2.38.1, 10.42.60**.

2.37.94: 3 friable, triable, viable; 4 deniable, unviable; 5 pacifiable, undeniable, verifiable; 6 unverifiable.

2.37.95: 5 certifiable, justifiable, notifiable, quantifiable; 6 identifiable, unjustifiable; 7 unidentifiable.
See also **9.14.51**.

2.37.96: 3 liable, pliable; 4 nonliable, reliable; 5 unreliable.

2.37.97: 2 bobble, cobble, gobble, hobble, nobble, squabble, wobble; 3 Chernobyl, Grenoble.
See also **2.38.1**.

2.37.98: 2 global, noble; 3 Chernobyl, ennoble, Grenoble, ignoble.
See also **2.38.1, 9.14.50**.

2.37.99: 2 bubble, double, Hubble, rubble, stubble, trouble; 3 redouble.
Life is mostly froth and bubble;
Two things stand like stone,
Kindness in another's trouble,
Courage in your own.
(Adam Lindsay Gordon)
See also **2.38.1, 2.39.1, 9.14.50, 10.42.60**.

2.37.100: 3 chasuble, soluble, valuable, voluble; 4 insoluble; 5 indissoluble, water-soluble.

2.37.101: 2 amble, bramble, Campbell, gamble, gambol, ramble, scramble, shamble; 3 preamble, unscramble.
'Tis spring; come out to ramble
The hilly brakes around,
For under thorn and bramble
About the hollow ground
The primroses are found.
(A.E. Housman)
See also **2.38.1, 2.39.1, 10.42.78**.

2.37.102: 2 tremble; 3 assemble, dissemble, resemble; 4 disassemble, reassemble.
See also **10.42.78**.

2.37.103: 2 cymbal, gimbal, nimble, symbol, thimble, Trimble; 3 sex symbol; 4 phallic symbol; 6 fertility symbol.
See also **2.39.1**.

2.37.104: 2 bumble, crumble, fumble, grumble, humble, jumble, mumble, rumble, stumble, tumble; 4 rough-and-tumble.
See also **2.38.1, 9.14.55, 10.42.60, 10.42.78**.

2.37.105: 2 cradle, curdle, dawdle, girdle, Goodall, hurdle, ladle, modal, nodal, Rendell, yodel; 3 citadel.
See also **2.38.2, 2.39, 10.42.79**.

2.37.106: 2 addle, paddle, raddle, saddle, straddle; 3 bestraddle, packsaddle, sidesaddle, skedaddle, unsaddle.
See also **10.42.61**.

2.37.107: 2 medal, meddle, treadle; 3 bronze medal, gold medal; 4 silver medal.
See also **10.42.79**.

2.37.108: 2 pedal, peddle; 3 backpedal, soft-pedal.
See also **2.38.2, 10.42.61, 10.42.79**.

2.37.109: 2 beadle, needle, wheedle; 3 bipedal, tripedal; 4 quadrupedal; 6 Cleopatra's Needle.
See also **10.42.61**.

2.37.110: 2 diddle, fiddle, griddle, idyll, middle, piddle, riddle, twiddle, widdle; 3 infidel.
See also **2.38.2, 10.42.61**.

2.37.111: 2 bridal, bridle, idle, idol, sidle, tidal; 4 genocidal.
See also **2.54.62**.

2.37.112: 4 fratricidal, fungicidal, homicidal, pesticidal, suicidal; 5 insecticidal.

2.37.113: 2 coddle, doddle, model, noddle, swaddle, toddle, twaddle, waddle; 3 remodel; 4 mollycoddle, supermodel.
See also **2.38.2, 10.42.61**.

2.37.114: 3 colloidal, rhomboidal, spheroidal; 4 adenoidal.

2.37.115: 2 cuddle, fuddle, huddle, muddle, puddle; 3 befuddle.
See also **2.38.2**.

2.37.116: 2 doodle, feudal, noodle, poodle, strudel; 3 caboodle, canoodle.

2.37.117: 2 bundle, dirndl, fondle, Grendel, Kendall, Mendel, Oundle, roundel, trundle; 3 unbundle.

2.37.118: 2 candle, dandle, sandal, scandal, vandal.

2.37.119: 2 Handel, handle; 3 manhandle, mishandle, panhandle.
See also **10.42.79**.

2.37.120: 2 brindle, dwindle, kindle, spindle, swindle, Tyndale; 3 rekindle.
See also **10.42.79**.

2.37.121: 2 awful, baffle, bashful, careful, cheerful, Eiffel, fearful, gleeful, harmful, helpful, hopeful, joyful, lawful, offal, playful, powerful, prayerful, raffle, rifle, rueful, shameful, snaffle, stifle, tearful, TEFL, thankful, TOEFL, trifle,

vengeful, waffle, wakeful, watchful, woeful, wrongful; 3 falafel, meaningful, reproachful, sorrowful, triumphal, unhelpful, unlawful, worshipful; 4 all-powerful.
See also **2.54.80, 9.14.9, 10.42.59**.

2.37.122: 3 colourful, masterful, wonderful; 4 apocryphal, characterful.
See also **9.14.9**.

2.37.123: 2 piffle, riffle, skiffle, sniffle, whiffle; 3 fanciful, merciful.

2.37.124: 3 beautiful, bountiful, dutiful, pitiful, plentiful; 5 Lady Bountiful.

*And the heart that through danger and
    death will be dutiful,
Soul that with Cranmer in fire would
    shake hands,
With a life like a palace-home built for the
    beautiful,
Freedom of all her beloved demands.*
(Gerald Massey)
See also **9.14.9**.

2.37.125: 2 duffel, muffle, ruffle, scuffle, shuffle, snuffle, truffle; 3 kerfuffle, reshuffle.
See also **2.38**.

2.37.126: 2 dreadful, heedful, mindful, needful, prideful; 3 regardful, unmindful.

2.37.127: 2 baleful, bileful, doleful, guileful, skilful, soulful, wilful; 3 unskilful.

2.37.128: 2 baneful, gainful, manful, mournful, painful, scornful, sinful, tuneful; 3 disdainful.

2.37.129: 2 blissful, forceful, graceful, peaceful, stressful, useful; 3 disgraceful, purposeful, remorseful, resourceful, successful, suspenseful, ungraceful; 4 unremorseful, unsuccessful.
See also **2.54.80, 9.14.9**.

2.37.130: 2 artful, doubtful, fitful, fretful, fruitful, hurtful, tactful, thoughtful; 3 deceitful, eventful, forgetful, neglectful, regretful, resentful, respectful, unfruitful; 4 disrespectful, uneventful.
See also **2.54.80, 9.14.10**.

2.37.131: 2 fateful, grateful, hateful; 3 ungrateful.

2.37.132: 2 frightful, rightful, spiteful; 3 delightful, insightful.

2.37.133: 2 boastful, lustful, restful, tasteful, trustful, wasteful, wistful, zestful; 3 distasteful, distrustful, mistrustful.
See also **9.14.10**.

2.37.134: 1 healthful; 2 faithful, slothful, truthful, wrathful, youthful; 3 Old Faithful, unfaithful, untruthful.
See also **2.54.80, 9.14.9.**

2.37.135: 2 algal, bagel, Brueghel, burgle, dongle, Fingal, gargle, Gogol, gurgle, Hegel, mogul, Mongol, ogle; 3 conjugal, finagle, inveigle, Portugal.

2.37.136: 2 gaggle, haggle, straggle, waggle; 3 bedraggle.
See also **10.42.62.**

2.37.137: 2 beagle, eagle, legal, regal; 3 illegal, inveigle, spread eagle, viceregal; 4 paralegal.

2.37.138: 2 giggle, jiggle, niggle, squiggle, wiggle, wriggle; 3 madrigal, prodigal.
See also **10.42.62.**

2.37.139: 2 boggle, goggle, joggle, toggle; 3 hornswoggle.
See also **2.39.3.**

2.37.140: 2 juggle, smuggle, snuggle, struggle.
See also **10.42.62.**

2.37.141: 2 bugle, dingle, frugal, google, Mughal; 4 centrifugal.

2.37.142: 2 angle, bangle, dangle, jangle, mangle, spangle, strangle, wangle, wrangle; 3 pentangle, quadrangle, triangle, wide-angle.
See also **2.38.4, 10.42.58.**

2.37.143: 2 tangle; 3 entangle, rectangle, untangle; 4 disentangle.
See also **2.38.4.**

2.37.144: 2 ingle, jingle, mingle, shingle, single, tingle; 3 commingle, Kriss Kringle; 4 intermingle.
See also **2.38.3, 2.39.3, 10.42.62.**

2.37.145: 2 bungle, fungal, jungle; 4 antifungal.
See also **2.38.3, 10.42.58.**

2.37.146: 2 angel, brinjal, cudgel, Nigel; 3 archangel; 4 fallen angel, little angel; 5 guardian angel.

2.37.147: 2 cockle, ducal, faecal, Michael, snorkel, treacle; 3 Carmichael, cervical, maniacal, pinochle, tubercle; 4 equivocal; 5 demoniacal, paradisaical, unequivocal.
See also **2.38.5, 9.14.65, 10.42.63.**

2.37.148: 2 cackle, crackle, grackle, hackle, shackle, tackle; 3 block and tackle,

ramshackle, unshackle; 4 fishing tackle, tabernacle.
See also **2.38.5, 2.39.4, 10.42.63.**

2.37.149: 3 barnacle, binnacle, manacle, monocle, pinnacle.
See also **2.39.4.**

2.37.150: 3 coracle, miracle, oracle, spiracle; 4 reciprocal.

2.37.151: 3 obstacle, pentacle, spectacle, tentacle; 4 receptacle.
See also **2.39.4.**

2.37.152: 2 sparkle; 3 debacle, monarchal; 4 matriarchal, patriarchal.
See also **10.42.63.**

2.37.153: 2 freckle, heckle, shekel, speckle.

2.37.154: 2 circle; 3 charmed circle, crop circle, dress circle, encircle, great circle; 4 inner circle, magic circle, semicircle, social circle, traffic circle, upper circle, vicious circle.

2.37.155: 2 chicle, fickle; 3 cervical, cubicle, ethical, mythical, stoical, vehicle; 4 hierarchical, monarchical, pontifical, unethical; 5 philosophical.
See also **9.14.66.**

2.37.156: 3 medical, radical, radicle; 4 juridical, methodical; 5 paramedical, periodical.

2.37.157: 3 graphical; 4 biographical; 5 epigraphical, geographical; 6 autobiographical, lexicographical.

2.37.158: 3 logical, magical, surgical; 4 biological, illogical, liturgical; 5 pedagogical.

2.37.159: 5 astrological, chronological, cosmological, ecological, morphological, mythological, neurological, pathological, philological, phonological, psychological, seismological, technological, zoological; 6 anthropological, entomological, etymological, gynaecological, immunological, lexicological; 7 meteorological.
See also **9.14.66.**

2.37.160: 5 geological, theological; 6 archaeological, bacteriological, ideological, physiological.

2.37.161: 5 ontological, scatological, tautological; 6 dermatological, scientological.

2.37.162: 3 biblical, cyclical, follicle, helical; 4 angelical, diabolical, encyclical, umbilical; 5 evangelical.

2.37.163: 3 comical, rhythmical; 4 inimical, unrhythmical; 5 anatomical.

2.37.164: 3 chemical; 4 polemical; 5 agrochemical, biochemical, petrochemical.

2.37.165: 5 astronomical, economical, taxonomical; 6 uneconomical.

2.37.166: 2 nickel; 3 chronicle, clinical, conical, cynical, technical; 4 botanical, canonical, irenical, mechanical, pumpernickel, rabbinical, tyrannical; 5 ecumenical, puritanical.

2.37.167: 2 pickle; 3 apical, dill pickle, topical, tropical; 4 subtropical; 5 semitropical. *See also* **2.38.5**.

2.37.168: 3 typical; 4 atypical, untypical; 5 archetypical, prototypical; 6 stereotypical.

2.37.169: 2 prickle; 3 auricle, lyrical; 4 cylindrical, empirical, satirical, theatrical.

2.37.170: 3 clerical, spherical; 4 chimerical, hysterical, numerical; 5 anticlerical. *See also* **9.14.67**.

2.37.171: 4 historical, rhetorical; 5 ahistorical, allegorical, categorical, metaphorical. *See also* **9.14.67**.

2.37.172: 2 trickle; 3 metrical, ventricle; 4 electrical, symmetrical, theatrical; 5 asymmetrical, unsymmetrical. *See also* **9.14.67**.

2.37.173: 2 sickle; 3 bicycle, classical, farcical, icicle, lexical, ossicle, Popsicle, tricycle; 4 nonsensical; 5 commonsensical, neoclassical, paradoxical.

2.37.174: 2 tickle; 3 canticle, nautical, practical, tactical, vertical; 4 identical, impractical, subcortical, unpractical; 5 hypothetical, parenthetical. *See also* **2.38.5, 9.14.69**.

2.37.175: 4 fanatical, grammatical, piratical, sabbatical; 5 mathematical, problematical, ungrammatical.

2.37.176: 3 article, particle; 5 alpha particle, antiparticle, beta particle.

2.37.177: 3 heretical, metical; 4 theoretical; 5 alphabetical, antithetical, unpoetical.

2.37.178: 4 political; 5 analytical, apolitical; 7 sociopolitical.

2.37.179: 3 critical; 4 uncritical; 5 hypercritical, hypocritical, overcritical. *See also* **9.14.69**.

2.37.180: 3 cuticle; 5 cosmeceutical, nutraceutical, pharmaceutical.

2.37.181: 3 floptical, optical, sceptical; 4 elliptical.

2.37.182: 3 mystical, testicle; 4 fantastical, statistical; 5 egotistical; 6 ecclesiastical. *See also* **2.39.4**.

2.37.183: 3 musical, physical, quizzical, whimsical; 4 nonphysical, unmusical, unphysical; 5 lackadaisical, metaphysical.

2.37.184: 2 cycle; 3 life cycle, recycle, trade cycle; 4 epicycle, kilocycle, megacycle, monocycle, motorcycle, quadricycle, solar cycle, unicycle; 6 operating cycle. *See also* **2.38.5, 10.42.80**.

2.37.185: 3 focal, local, vocal, yokel; 3 bifocal.

2.37.186: 2 buckle, chuckle, knuckle, muckle, suckle, truckle; 3 Arbuckle, pinochle, unbuckle; 4 honeysuckle. *See also* **2.38.5, 10.42.63**.

2.37.187: 2 ankle, rankle, uncle; 3 carbuncle, Dutch uncle, Garfunkel, peduncle.

2.37.188: 2 crinkle, sprinkle, tinkle, twinkle, winkle, wrinkle; 4 periwinkle, Rip van Winkle. *See also* **2.38.5, 10.42.63, 10.42.80**.

2.37.189: 2 fiscal, Gaitskell, Gaskell, pascal, rascal.

2.37.190: 2 Brummell, Carmel, formal, kümmel, pommel, primal, pummel, Rommel, thermal; 3 animal, informal, minimal, optimal; 4 chromosomal, geothermal, isothermal. *See also* **9.14.14**.

2.37.191: 2 camel, mammal, trammel; 3 enamel.

2.37.192: 3 decimal, maximal; 4 centesimal; 5 duodecimal, hexadecimal; 6 infinitesimal.

2.37.193: 2 normal; 3 abnormal, subnormal; 4 paranormal, supernormal.

2.37.194: 2 dismal; 3 abysmal, baptismal, miasmal, phantasmal.

2.37.195: 2 anal, Bucknell, carnal, Cracknell, fennel, grapnel, Hucknall, hymnal, kennel, shrapnel, signal;

3 autumnal, communal, McConnell, O'Connell, tribunal.
See also **2.38.6, 2.39.5, 9.14.15, 10.42.64.**

2.37.196: 2 channel, flannel, panel; 3 empanel, impanel; 4 solar panel.
See also **2.38.6, 10.42.64.**

2.37.197: 3 arsenal, bacchanal, Juvenal, Lionel, ordinal, personal, seasonal; 4 divisional, impersonal, medicinal, occasional, provisional; 5 interpersonal.
See also **2.39.5, 9.14.16.**

2.37.198: 4 decagonal, diagonal, heptagonal, hexagonal, octagonal, orthogonal, pentagonal, polygonal.
See also **9.14.16.**

2.37.199: 3 regional; 4 original; 5 aboriginal, unoriginal.

2.37.200: 3 optional; 4 exceptional, proportional; 5 constitutional, institutional, unexceptional; 6 unconstitutional.
See also **9.14.17.**

2.37.201: 3 national, rational; 4 Grand National, irrational, transnational; 5 international, multinational, supranational; 8 Amnesty International.

2.37.202: 4 foundational, relational, sensational, vocational; 5 conversational, educational, informational, motivational, navigational, occupational, recreational, situational, unsensational; 6 denominational; 8 interdenominational.

2.37.203: 5 aberrational, aspirational, generational, inspirational, operational; 6 inoperational; 7 intergenerational.

2.37.204: 4 rotational; 5 computational, confrontational, gravitational, invitational, presentational; 6 representational.

2.37.205: 4 accessional, congressional, obsessional, processional, successional.

2.37.206: 4 confessional, professional; 5 nonprofessional, unprofessional; 6 semiprofessional.

2.37.207: 4 additional, conditional, nutritional, positional, traditional, transitional, volitional; 5 nontraditional, propositional, suppositional, unconditional.
See also **9.14.17.**

2.37.208: 3 notional; 4 devotional, emotional, promotional; 5 unemotional; 6 overemotional.

2.37.209: 3 factional, fictional, fractional, functional; 4 dysfunctional, instructional,

nonfunctional; 5 jurisdictional, multifunctional.

2.37.210: 3 sectional; 4 correctional, directional; 5 bidirectional; 6 omnidirectional.

2.37.211: 4 ascensional, conventional, dimensional, intentional; 5 fourth-dimensional, one-dimensional, three-dimensional, two-dimensional, unconventional, unintentional.
See also **9.14.17.**

2.37.212: 2 colonel, journal, kernel, vernal; 3 Avernal, diurnal, infernal, supernal; 5 lieutenant colonel.

Out of the depths of the Infinite Being
eternal,
Out of the cloud more bright than the
brightness of sun,
Out of the inmost the essence of spirit
supernal,
We issued as one.
(Ella Dietz)

2.37.213: 3 eternal, external, fraternal, internal, maternal, nocturnal, paternal; 4 coeternal, confraternal, nonexternal, sempiternal.
See also **9.14.15.**

2.37.214: 2 penal, renal, venal; 3 adrenal; 4 duodenal.

2.37.215: 3 marginal, sentinel, virginal; 4 intestinal; 5 aboriginal; 6 gastrointestinal.

2.37.216: 3 cardinal, ordinal; 5 attitudinal, longitudinal.

2.37.217: 3 criminal, germinal, seminal, terminal; 4 air terminal, subliminal.
See also **9.14.15.**

2.37.218: 3 nominal; 4 abdominal, phenomenal, prenominal, pronominal.

2.37.219: 2 final, spinal, vinyl; 3 Cup Final, doctrinal, urinal, vaginal; 4 quarterfinal, semifinal.
See also **2.39.5.**

2.37.220: 2 tonal, zonal; 3 atonal, hormonal; 4 monoclonal.

2.37.221: 2 Chunnel, funnel, gunnel, gunwale, runnel, tunnel; 4 Channel Tunnel, polytunnel.
See also **2.38.6, 10.42.64.**

2.37.222: 2 Aspell, carpal, carpel, gospel, maple, opal, papal, purple, scalpel, staple, topple; 3 disciple, Oedipal; 4 archetypal, episcopal, metacarpal, Simferopol; 5 Constantinople.

2.37.223: **2** apple, chapel, dapple, grapple; **3** Big Apple, crab apple, love apple, pineapple, Whitechapel; **4** Adam's apple, custard apple.

With death doomed to grapple,
Beneath this cold slab, he
Who lied in the chapel
Now lies in the Abbey.
(Lord Byron)

2.37.224: **2** people, sepal, steeple; **3** townspeople, tradespeople, tribespeople.

2.37.225: **2** cripple, nipple, ripple, triple; **3** maniple, principal, principle; **4** first principle, municipal, participle.
See also **2.38.7, 2.39.6, 10.42.81**.

2.37.226: **2** stipple, tipple; **3** multiple; **4** submultiple.

2.37.227: **2** chappal, couple, supple; **3** decouple, uncouple; **4** thermocouple.
See also **2.38.7, 10.42.59**.

2.37.228: **2** duple, pupal, pupil, scruple; **3** quadruple, quintuple.
See also **2.39.6**.

2.37.229: **2** ample, crumple, dimple, pimple, rumple, sample, simple, temple, trample, wimple; **3** example.
See also **2.38.7, 9.14.79**.

2.37.230: **2** April, aural, beryl, choral, Cyril, Durrell, feral, floral, mackerel, mongrel, oral, peril, scoundrel, tendril; **3** cathedral, cerebral, deferral, demurral, femoral, imperil, integral, referral, sepulchral, transferral, vertebral; **4** inaugural, polyhedral.

2.37.231: **2** Aral, barrel, carol, carrel, Carroll, Daryl, Farrell; **3** apparel.

2.37.232: **3** becquerel, cockerel, Cockerell, doggerel, federal, liberal, several, visceral; **4** behavioural, illiberal, peripheral, procedural; **5** Cape Canaveral.
See also **9.14.20**.

2.37.233: **3** admiral, numeral; **4** bicameral, ephemeral, rear-admiral, red admiral, vice-admiral; **5** unicameral.

2.37.234: **3** funeral, general, mineral; **5** consul-general, major general; **6** director-general, lieutenant general, secretary-general, Solicitor General.

2.37.235: **3** corporal, temporal, vesperal; **4** lance-corporal, Lords Temporal, puerperal; **5** Little Corporal.

2.37.236: **3** clitoral, guttural, literal, littoral, pastoral.

2.37.237: **3** lateral; **4** bilateral, collateral, trilateral; **5** equilateral, multilateral, quadrilateral, unilateral.

2.37.238: **3** doctoral, pectoral; **4** electoral, postdoctoral.

2.37.239: **3** natural, scriptural, sculptural, structural; **4** conjectural, unnatural; **5** architectural, preternatural, supernatural, supranatural.

2.37.240: **3** cultural; **4** cross-cultural; **5** agricultural, avicultural, floricultural, horticultural, multicultural, piscicultural, silvicultural, viticultural; **6** arboricultural, sociocultural.

2.37.241: **2** squirrel; **3** grey squirrel, ground squirrel, red squirrel; **4** flying squirrel.

2.37.242: **2** spiral, viral; **4** antiviral; **6** antiretroviral.
See also **2.38.8, 10.42.59**.

2.37.243: **2** coral, laurel, moral, quarrel, sorrel; **3** amoral, Balmoral, immoral.
See also **2.38.8, 2.39, 10.42.59**.

2.37.244: **2** jural, mural, neural, plural, rural, Ural; **4** epidural, extramural, intramural, photomural.

2.37.245: **2** central, neutral, petrel, petrol, spectral, ventral.

2.37.246: **2** astral, kestrel, lustral, minstrel, mistral, nostril, wastrel; **3** ancestral, orchestral, sylvestral.

2.37.247: **2** Axel, basal, dorsal, Faisal, hassle, morsel, plimsoll, pretzel, quetzal, schnitzel, sisal, tassel, vassal; **3** subdorsal.

2.37.248: **2** castle, parcel, tarsal; **3** Hardcastle, Newcastle, sandcastle; **4** bouncy castle, metatarsal, Windsor Castle.
See also **2.38, 10.42.65**.

2.37.249: **2** Cecil, nestle, pestle, trestle, vessel, wrestle.

Build me straight, O worthy Master!
Stanch and strong, a goodly vessel,
That shall laugh at all disaster,
And with wave and whirlwind wrestle!
(Henry Wadsworth Longfellow)
See also **10.42.65, 10.42.66**.

2.37.250: **3** dispersal, rehearsal, reversal; **4** dress rehearsal, universal.

2.37.251: **2** bristle, gristle, missal, missile, thistle, whistle; **3** abyssal, Burtwistle, dismissal, epistle, milk thistle,

tin whistle, wolf-whistle; **4** penny whistle; **6** Order of the Thistle.
See also **10.42.65.**

2.37.252: **2** fossil, jostle; **3** apostle, colossal.

2.37.253: **2** bustle, hustle, muscle, mussel, Russell, rustle, tussle; **3** corpuscle, Jack Russell.
See also **10.42.65, 10.42.82.**

2.37.254: **2** axle, forecastle, fo'c'sle, pixel, voxel; **4** megapixel.

2.37.255: **2** cancel, chancel, consul, Mansell, tinsel, tonsil; **3** proconsul.
See also **10.42.65.**

2.37.256: **2** mensal, pencil, stencil; **3** blue-pencil, commensal, utensil.
See also **2.39.**

2.37.257: **2** council, counsel; **3** Queen's Counsel, town council; **4** British Council, county council, parish council, Privy Council; **6** Security Council.
See also **10.42.65.**

2.37.258: **1** shall; **2** bushel, Bushell, crucial, nuptial, special; **3** especial, prenuptial, provincial; **4** antenuptial, equinoctial.

2.37.259: **2** marshal, Marshall, martial, partial; **3** air marshal, court martial, field marshal, impartial, vice-marshal; **4** air vice-marshal.
See also **2.38, 9.14.24, 10.42.59.**

2.37.260: **2** facial, glacial, racial, spacial, spatial; **3** palatial; **4** interracial, multiracial.

2.37.261: **2** Herschel; **3** commercial; **4** controversial, infomercial, uncommercial; **5** uncontroversial.

2.37.262: **3** initial, judicial; **4** interstitial, prejudicial; **5** extrajudicial.
See also **2.38, 10.42.59.**

2.37.263: **3** official; **4** artificial, beneficial, sacrificial, superficial, unofficial.
See also **9.14.24.**

2.37.264: **2** social; **3** asocial, unsocial; **4** antisocial.

2.37.265: **3** financial, substantial; **4** circumstantial, insubstantial.

2.37.266: **3** potential, sentential, sequential, tangential; **4** consequential, existential, exponential, influential, penitential, pestilential; **5** experiential, inconsequential, uninfluential.
But when he spoke of varied lore,

Paroxytones and modes potential,
She listened with a face that wore
A look half fond, half reverential.
(Harry Thurston Peck)
See also **9.14.25.**

2.37.267: **3** credential, prudential; **4** confidential, presidential, providential, residential.

2.37.268: **3** torrential; **4** deferential, differential, inferential, preferential, reverential; **5** irreverential.
See also **9.14.25.**

2.37.269: **3** essential; **4** inessential, nonessential, quintessential, unessential.
See also **2.39.**

2.37.270: **2** beetle, betel, foetal, fractal, rectal, startle, total; **3** palatal, pivotal, societal, subtotal, teetotal; **4** anecdotal, sacerdotal.
See also **2.38.9, 10.42.66.**

2.37.271: **2** battle, cattle, chattel, prattle, rattle, tattle; **3** Seattle; **4** tittle-tattle.
What passing-bells for these who die as cattle?
Only the monstrous anger of the guns.
Only the stuttering rifles' rapid rattle
Can patter out their hasty orisons.
(Wilfred Owen)
See also **2.38.9, 2.39.7, 10.42.66.**

2.37.272: **2** fatal, natal; **3** postnatal, prenatal; **4** antenatal, neonatal, parastatal, perinatal.

2.37.273: **2** fettle, kettle, nettle, petal, settle; **3** resettle, teakettle, unsettle.
See also **2.38.9, 10.42.58.**

2.37.274: **2** metal, mettle; **3** death metal, gunmetal, thrash metal; **4** heavy metal.

2.37.275: **2** hurtle, kirtle, myrtle, turtle.

2.37.276: **2** brittle, it'll, little, skittle, spittle, whittle; **3** acquittal, belittle, capital, committal, digital, genital, hospital, lickspittle, marital, orbital, skeletal, vegetal; **4** congenital, noncommittal, nondigital, premarital, suborbital; **5** extramarital, urogenital.
See also **2.39.7, 6.47.1.**

2.37.277: **2** title, vital; **3** entitle, recital, requital, subtitle.
See also **2.38.9.**

2.37.278: **2** bottle, glottal, mottle, throttle, wattle; **3** bluebottle; **4** Aristotle.
See also **2.38.9.**

2.37.279: **2** chortle, mortal, portal; **3** immortal.

Beauty is momentary in the mind—
The fitful tracing of a portal;
But in the flesh it is immortal.
The body dies; the body's beauty lives.
(Wallace Stevens)

2.37.280: 2 scuttle, shuttle, subtle; 3 rebuttal, space shuttle, unsubtle.

2.37.281: 2 brutal, footle, pootle, rootle, tootle.
See also **10.42.66.**

2.37.282: 2 frontal, lintel, quintal; 3 full-frontal; 4 contrapuntal, horizontal.
See also **9.14.26.**

2.37.283: 2 mantel, mantle; 3 dismantle, Fremantle; 4 lady's mantle.

2.37.284: 2 gentle, rental; 3 parental; 4 continental, oriental; 5 transcontinental; 6 intercontinental.

2.37.285: 2 dental; 4 accidental, incidental, occidental, transcendental; 5 coincidental, labiodental.

2.37.286: 2 mental; 3 judgmental, segmental; 4 alimental, departmental, detrimental, elemental, excremental, fundamental, governmental, incremental, instrumental, monumental, nonjudgmental, ornamental, rudimental, sacramental, sentimental, supplemental, temperamental; 5 developmental, environmental, experimental, unsentimental; 6 interdepartmental, intergovernmental, oversentimental.

2.37.287: 2 borstal, Bristol, coastal, costal, crystal, festal, hostel, pastel, pastille, pistol, postal, vestal; 3 pedestal; 4 intercostal, Pentecostal.

2.37.288: 2 chervil, grovel, hovel, naval, navel, novel, oval, shovel; 3 approval, interval, removal; 4 antinovel, disapproval.
See also **2.38.10, 10.42.67.**

2.37.289: 2 Cavell, cavil, gavel, gravel, Havel, ravel, travel; 3 time travel, unravel.
See also **2.38.10, 10.42, 10.42.67.**

2.37.290: 2 Havel, larval, marvel, Marvell; 3 rondavel.

2.37.291: 2 bevel, devil, revel; 3 bedevil, daredevil, dishevel, she-devil.
See also **2.38.11, 10.42.67.**

2.37.292: 2 level; 3 A level, eyelevel, high-level, low-level, S level, split-level, top-level; 4 AS level, entry-level, water level.
See also **2.38.11, 10.42.67.**

2.37.293: 2 evil, weevil; 3 coeval, primeval, retrieval, upheaval; 4 medieval.

2.37.294: 2 civil, drivel, shrivel, snivel, swivel; 3 aestival, carnival, festival, Percival, uncivil; 5 Harvest Festival.
See also **2.38.10, 10.42.67.**

2.37.295: 2 rival; 3 archrival, arrival, outrival, revival, survival; 4 adjectival.
See also **2.39.**

2.37.296: 2 Boswell, Cornwall, Cowell, Maxwell, Rockwell, Sewall; 3 bestowal.

2.37.297: 2 lingual; 3 bilingual, trilingual; 4 interlingual, monolingual, multilingual, unilingual.

2.37.298: 2 equal, prequel, sequel, SQL; 3 coequal, unequal.
See also **2.38.10, 10.42.59.**

2.37.299: 2 Basel, causal, damsel, groundsel, Mosel, nozzle, schnozzle; 3 bamboozle, comprisal, disposal, embezzle, noncausal, perusal, proposal, refusal, reprisal, transposal; 4 predisposal; 5 postmenopausal.

2.37.300: 2 basil, dazzle, frazzle, razzle; 3 bedazzle.
See also **2.38.12, 10.42.83.**

2.37.301: 2 hazel, nasal, phrasal; 3 appraisal; 4 reappraisal.

2.37.302: 2 diesel, easel, teasel, teazle, weasel; 4 biodiesel.

2.37.303: 2 chisel, drizzle, fizzle, frizzle, grizzle, mizzle, sizzle, swizzle.
See also **2.38.12, 10.42.83.**

2.37.304: 2 spousal, tousle; 3 arousal, carousal, espousal.
See also **2.38.12.**

2.37.305: 2 guzzle, muzzle, nuzzle, puzzle.
See also **2.38.12, 10.42.59.**

2.38: 2 fuelled, jewelled, marshalled, muffled, parcelled; 3 bejewelled, initialled, unruffled, untrammelled.
See also **2.37.18, 2.37.125, 2.37.248, 2.37.259, 2.37.262.**

2.38.1: 2 cobbled, crumbled, dribbled, fabled, gabled, garbled, humbled, jumbled, labelled, libelled, marbled, mumbled, ribald, troubled; 3 disabled, doubled, enfeebled, ennobled, redoubled, unscrambled, untroubled.
See also **2.37.87, 2.37.92, 2.37.93, 2.37.97, 2.37.98, 2.37.99, 2.37.101, 2.37.104.**

2.38.2: 2 addled, brindled, coddled, curdled, fuddled, huddled, modelled, muddled, pedalled, raddled, riddled; 3 backpedalled, befuddled, unbridled. *See also* **2.37.105, 2.37.108, 2.37.110, 2.37.113, 2.37.115.**

2.38.3: 2 bungled, mingled; 3 bedraggled, spreadeagled; 4 intermingled. *See also* **2.37.144, 2.37.145.**

2.38.4: 2 angled, mangled, spangled, strangled, tangled; 3 entangled, newfangled; 4 disentangled. *See also* **2.37.142, 2.37.143.**

2.38.5: 2 buckled, crackled, crinkled, freckled, pickled, snorkelled, speckled, tickled, wrinkled; 3 articled, recycled; 4 bespectacled. *See also* **2.37.147, 2.37.148, 2.37.167, 2.37.174, 2.37.184, 2.37.186, 2.37.188.**

2.38.6: 2 Arnold, channelled, Donald, funnelled, Ronald, signalled, tunnelled; 3 MacDonald, Reginald; 5 Benedict Arnold. *See also* **2.37.195, 2.37.196, 2.37.221.**

2.38.7: 2 coupled, crippled, crumpled, dappled, dimpled, rumpled; 3 principled; 4 unprincipled. *See also* **2.37.225, 2.37.227, 2.37.229.**

2.38.8: 2 Gerald, Harold, herald, quarrelled, spiralled; 3 emerald, Fitzgerald; 4 double-barrelled. *See also* **2.37.242, 2.37.243.**

2.38.9: 2 bottled, mottled, nettled, rattled, settled, startled, titled, totalled; 3 disgruntled, embattled, entitled, subtitled, unsettled, untitled. *See also* **2.37.270, 2.37.271, 2.37.273, 2.37.277, 2.37.278.**

2.38.10: 2 equalled, gravelled, grovelled, shovelled, shrivelled, swivelled, travelled; 3 unequalled, unravelled, unrivalled. *See also* **2.37.288, 2.37.289, 2.37.294, 2.37.298.**

2.38.11: 2 bevelled, devilled, levelled; 3 bedevilled, dishevelled. *See also* **2.37.291, 2.37.292.**

2.38.12: 2 chiselled, dazzled, frazzled, grizzled, puzzled, sozzled, tousled; 3 bedazzled. *See also* **2.37.300, 2.37.303, 2.37.304, 2.37.305.**

2.39: 2 bowels, Brussels, Daniels, Howells, hurdles, laurels, measles, morals, nuptials, oodles, Raffles, Urals; 3 arrivals, casuals, credentials, essentials, ideals, utensils; 4 German measles, inessentials, materials, pins and needles. *See also* **2.37.9, 2.37.105, 2.37.243, 2.37.256, 2.37.269, 2.37.295, 8.12, 17.4.**

2.39.1: 2 cymbals, doubles, Goebbels, marbles, nibbles, Peebles, shambles, symbols, troubles; 3 comestibles, mixed doubles, Twelve Tables, valuables, Venables; 4 collywobbles, teething troubles; 5 Augean stables, unmentionables. *See also* **2.37.23, 2.37.92, 2.37.99, 2.37.101, 2.37.103.**

2.39.2: 3 breakables, notables; 4 perishables, receivables, renewables.

2.39.3: 2 Engels, goggles, shingles, singles. *See also* **2.37.139, 2.37.144.**

2.39.4: 2 Eccles, hackles, shackles; 3 bifocals, brass knuckles, Chronicles, manacles, spectacles, testicles; 4 Tabernacles, theatricals; 5 pharmaceuticals. *See also* **2.37.148, 2.37.149, 2.37.151, 2.37.182.**

2.39.5: 2 annals, finals, signals; 3 externals, personals, virginals. *See also* **2.37.195, 2.37.197, 2.37.219.**

2.39.6: 2 Naples, scruples; 3 goose pimples, principles; 4 first principles. *See also* **2.37.225, 2.37.228.**

2.39.7: 2 Beatles, chattels, skittles, victuals, vitals; 3 genitals; 4 fundamentals. *See also* **2.37.271, 2.37.276.**

2.40: 1 am, 'em, them; 2 album, Beauchamp, Beecham, begum, Belgium, Brabham, brougham, Clapham, dodgem, fathom, Graeme, Graham, Grahame, Mitchum, Northam, ovum, phloem, sebum, sorghum, wampum; 3 amalgam, Brummagem, cardamom, Pergamum, Sheringham, stratagem, Te Deum, Walsingham; 4 jeroboam, rehoboam.

2.40.1: 3 cambium, erbium, lithium, opium, requiem, terbium; 4 alluvium, Byzantium, colloquium, effluvium, europium, niobium, promethium, seaborgium, technetium, ununbium, ytterbium; 5 mendelevium.

2.40.2: 3 idiom, indium, medium, odium, podium, rhodium, scandium, sodium, tedium; 4 compendium, rubidium; 5 rutherfordium.
Sir Humphry Davy

Abominated gravy.
He lived in the odium
Of having discovered Sodium.
(Edmund Clerihew Bentley)

2.40.3: **3** radium, stadium; **4** palladium, vanadium; **5** ununquadium.

2.40.4: **4** iridium, praesidium, presidium; **6** cryptosporidium.

2.40.5: **2** Liam; **3** allium, gallium, thallium, thulium, Valium; **4** linoleum, mausoleum, petroleum.

2.40.6: **3** helium; **4** berkelium, mycelium, nobelium; **5** epithelium.

2.40.7: **3** ileum, ilium, William; **4** beryllium, sweet william; **5** ununnilium.

2.40.8: **3** cadmium, chromium, fermium, holmium, osmium, premium; **4** encomium; **5** neodymium; **6** praseodymium.

2.40.9: **3** dubnium, hafnium, hahnium, rhenium; **4** Capernaum, einsteinium, millennium, neptunium, proscenium, ruthenium, selenium; **5** californium, unununium.

2.40.10: **3** cranium; **4** geranium, germanium, titanium, uranium; **5** Herculaneum.

2.40.11: **4** actinium, delphinium, perineum; **5** aluminium, condominium, gadolinium, protactinium.

2.40.12: **4** euphonium, harmonium, plutonium, polonium, zirconium; **5** pandemonium, pelargonium.

2.40.13: **3** atrium, curium, Miriam, yttrium; **4** delirium, opprobrium, tellurium; **5** equilibrium; **6** disequilibrium.

2.40.14: **3** barium; **4** aquarium, samarium, solarium, terrarium, vivarium; **5** columbarium, dolphinarium, honorarium, oceanarium, planetarium; **6** abecedarium.

2.40.15: **3** cerium; **4** bacterium, delirium, deuterium, imperium, meitnerium.

2.40.16: **3** bohrium, thorium; **4** emporium, nielsbohrium; **5** auditorium, crematorium, in memoriam, moratorium, oratorium, sanatorium.

2.40.17: **3** axiom, calcium, francium, hassium, Lyceum; **4** lawrencium, potassium, americium, ununhexium.

2.40.18: **3** strontium, tritium; **4** Byzantium, consortium.

2.40.19: **3** caesium, museum; **4** dysprosium, Elysium, gymnasium, magnesium, symposium, trapezium.

2.40.20: **2** boredom, dukedom, earldom, fiefdom, freedom, heirdom, kingdom, popedom, princedom, quondam, seldom, serfdom, stardom, thraldom, wisdom; **3** bishopdom, Christendom, martyrdom, subkingdom; **4** officialdom, superstardom, United Kingdom; **8** reductio ad absurdum.

2.40.21: **2** Adam, madam, Madame; **3** macadam, McAdam; **4** Tarmacadam.

2.40.22: **2** random, tandem; **3** addendum, pudendum; **4** corrigendum, memorandum, referendum; **7** quod erat demonstrandum. *See also* **9.14.70**.

2.40.23: **2** rhythm; **4** algorithm, biorhythm, logarithm.

2.40.24: **1** cwm; **2** Ascham, Beckham, bunkum, caecum, dinkum, hokum, locum, Malcolm, Newcombe, oakum, Occam, Ockham, Peckham, welcome; **3** capsicum, modicum, unwelcome; **4** Eboracum, pax vobiscum, vade mecum. *See also* **10.42.84**.

2.40.25: **2** alum, Balham, bedlam, Callum, chillum, column, emblem, golem, Gollum, Haarlem, Hallam, Harlem, hoodlum, mallam, Moslem, Muslim, phylum, problem, Salem, slalom, solemn, vallum, velum, xylem; **3** asylum, maximum, minimum, optimum, pendulum, speculum, subphylum, tantalum; **4** aspergillum, chrysanthemum, curriculum, Jerusalem, reticulum; **5** core curriculum; **7** National Curriculum. *See also* **9.14.70**.

2.40.26: **2** Pelham, vellum; **3** flagellum, post-bellum; **4** antebellum, cerebellum.

2.40.27: **2** Barnum, Bonham, Denham, Denholm, magnum, plenum, sphagnum, sternum, Tottenham, venom, Woosnam; **3** arcanum, envenom, jejunum, laburnum, lanthanum, laudanum, per annum, platinum, tympanum; **4** duodenum, interregnum, molybdenum.

2.40.28: **2** gingham, Ingham; **3** Birmingham, Buckingham, Cunningham, Nottingham, Rockingham, Sandringham.

2.40.29: **1** from; **2** ashram, Durham, Hiram, pogrom, serum, theorem, wolfram; **3** alarum, cerebrum, conundrum, marjoram, Muharram, panjandrum, pyrethrum; **4** antiserum, candelabrum, harum-scarum.

2.40.30: **2** forum, quorum; **3** decorum; **4** indecorum; **5** sanctum sanctorum, schola cantorum, victor ludorum.

2.40.31: **2** buckram, chakram, fulcrum, sacrum; **4** simulacrum.

2.40.32: **2** Bertram, nostrum, plectrum, rostrum, spectrum, tantrum, Tristram; **3** broad-spectrum, colostrum, ngultrum.

2.40.33: **1** some; **2** awesome, blossom, buxom, Epsom, fearsome, fivesome, flotsam, foursome, gladsome, gruesome, gypsum, irksome, jetsam, lissom, lithesome, loathsome, noisome, possum, threesome, tiresome, toothsome, twosome, Wrexham; **3** ad usum, alyssum, frolicsome, opossum, wearisome, worrisome.
See also **10.42.84**.

2.40.34: **3** bothersome, cumbersome, flavoursome, venturesome; **4** adventuresome.

2.40.35: **2** balsam, fulsome, toilsome, wholesome; **3** meddlesome, mettlesome, quarrelsome, troublesome, unwholesome.

2.40.36: **2** handsome, hansom, lonesome, ransom, transom, winsome; **3** burdensome.

2.40.37: **2** Grisham; **3** Havisham, Lewisham, lutetium, nasturtium.

2.40.38: **2** atom, autumn, bantam, bottom, Chatham, datum, dictum, Eltham, item, phantom, quantum, rectum, sanctum, scrotum, sputum, Streatham, symptom, Tatum, totem; **3** adytum, erratum, factotum, momentum, postmortem; **4** aconitum, ad libitum, arboretum, ultimatum; **5** ad infinitum.
So, naturalist observe, a flea
Hath smaller fleas that on him prey,
And these have smaller fleas to bite 'em.
And so proceed ad infinitum.
(Jonathan Swift)
See also **2.42**.

2.40.39: **2** stratum; **3** erratum, substratum; **4** superstratum; **5** desideratum.

2.40.40: **2** custom, system; **3** accustom, Chrysostom; **4** ecosystem.
See also **2.41, 2.42**.

2.40.41: **2** anthem, Bentham, Botham, Gotham, Grantham.

2.40.42: **2** bosom; **3** unbosom; **4** macrocosm, microcosm.

2.40.43: **2** chasm, spasm; **3** orgasm, phantasm, sarcasm; **4** pleonasm; **5** enthusiasm, iconoclasm.

2.40.44: **4** bioplasm, cytoplasm, ectoplasm, endoplasm, neoplasm, protoplasm.

2.40.45: **2** ism, schism; **3** Babism, cubism, deism, Fascism, Maoism, Sikhism, Taoism, yogism; **4** archaism, fetishism, Irishism, Judaism, Lamaism, speciesism.

2.40.46: **3** deism; **4** cronyism, toadyism, Trotskyism; **5** absenteeism, Manichaeism, presenteeism; **6** Pharisaism.

2.40.47: **3** theism; **4** atheism, pantheism; **5** McCarthyism, monotheism, polytheism.

2.40.48: **4** egoism, heroism, jingoism, Titoism; **5** albinoism.

2.40.49: **3** truism; **4** altruism, Hinduism, voodooism.

2.40.50: **3** Buddhism, dadism, faddism, nudism, sadism; **4** gourmandism, Methodism, paludism.

2.40.51: **3** dwarfism, sophism, Sufism; **4** pacifism, polymorphism; **5** philosophism; **6** anthropomorphism.

2.40.52: **2** jism; **3** ageism, magism; **4** syllogism; **5** neologism.

2.40.53: **4** anarchism, catechism, Lamarckism, masochism; **6** sadomasochism.

2.40.54: **4** botulism, cataclysm, nihilism, pointillism, populism, pugilism; **5** alcoholism, parallelism, somnambulism.

2.40.55: **4** centralism, feudalism, formalism, legalism, pluralism, vandalism, vocalism; **5** bilingualism, commensalism, evangelism, medievalism, minimalism, radicalism, regionalism, revivalism, syndicalism, triumphalism.

2.40.56: **3** realism; **4** idealism, surrealism; **6** colloquialism, colonialism, imperialism, industrialism, materialism; **7** ceremonialism; **8** neocolonialism.

2.40.57: **4** dualism; **5** mutualism, ritualism; **6** spiritualism; **7** individualism.

2.40.58: **4** embolism, herbalism, Kabbalism, symbolism, tribalism; **5** cannibalism, metabolism.

2.40.59: **4** journalism; **5** fraternalism, paternalism; **6** photojournalism.

2.40.60: **5** factionalism, functionalism, nationalism, rationalism, sectionalism; **6** conventionalism, professionalism,

sensationalism, traditionalism;
7 constitutionalism, internationalism.

2.40.61: **5** federalism, liberalism,
naturalism, structuralism;
7 multiculturalism, unilateralism.

2.40.62: **4** racialism, socialism,
specialism; **5** commercialism,
provincialism; **6** existentialism.

2.40.63: **4** brutalism, fatalism;
5 capitalism, teetotalism;
6 fundamentalism, sentimentalism.

2.40.64: **4** animism, extremism,
Islamism, optimism, short-termism;
6 overoptimism.

2.40.65: **4** atomism, dynamism,
euphemism, pessimism, totemism.

2.40.66: **3** Jainism, Zionism;
4 communism; **5** anachronism,
opportunism, revisionism.

2.40.67: **4** heathenism, humanism,
Mormonism, onanism, shamanism,
Unionism, urbanism.

2.40.68: **4** Fabianism; **5** Kantianism,
Keynesianism, Nietzscheanism;
6 Bohemianism, Cartesianism,
Hegelianism, utopianism.

2.40.69: **6** equestrianism, sectarianism;
7 epicureanism, libertarianism,
totalitarianism, vegetarianism,
Zoroastrianism; **8** authoritarianism,
egalitarianism, humanitarianism,
proletarianism, utilitarianism.

2.40.70: **4** hedonism, modernism;
5 postmodernism; **6** Mohammedanism.

2.40.71: **4** organism, paganism,
veganism; **5** antagonism, hooliganism;
6 microorganism.

2.40.72: **4** mechanism, tokenism;
5 Anglicanism; **6** Americanism,
republicanism.

2.40.73: **5** Confucianism, creationism,
expansionism, expressionism,
Impressionism, obstructionism,
perfectionism, protectionism;
6 exhibitionism, interventionism,
isolationism.

2.40.74: **4** daltonism, Platonism,
satanism, saturnism, spartanism;
5 charlatanism, Puritanism.

2.40.75: **4** albinism, Calvinism,
chauvinism, Darwinism, doctrinism,
feminism, Leninism, Stalinism;
5 determinism, Philistinism; **7** Marxism-
Leninism.

2.40.76: **3** tropism; **4** escapism, priapism;
5 malapropism.

2.40.77: **2** chrism, prism; **3** Blairism,
centrism, tourism; **4** voyeurism;
5 agritourism, ecotourism, egocentrism.

2.40.78: **4** aneurysm, aphorism,
barbarism, futurism, mannerism,
mesmerism, naturism, pauperism,
plagiarism, spoonerism, vulgarism,
welfarism; **5** adventurism, behaviourism,
consumerism, militarism, monetarism,
secularism; **6** vernacularism.

2.40.79: **4** terrorism; **6** agriterrorism,
bioterrorism, counterterrorism,
ecoterrorism.

2.40.80: **2** schism; **3** classism, Marxism,
Nazism, racism, sexism; **4** exorcism,
ostracism, paroxysm, solipsism;
6 heterosexism.

2.40.81: **4** classicism, cynicism, lyricism,
narcissism, stoicism; **5** empiricism,
laconicism; **6** egocentricism, esotericism.

2.40.82: **4** Anglicism, Gallicism,
solecism; **5** Catholicism.

2.40.83: **4** Atticism, Briticism, criticism,
Gnosticism, mysticism, scepticism,
witticism; **5** aestheticism, agnosticism,
asceticism, athleticism, eclecticism,
fanaticism, Romanticism, scholasticism,
Socraticism.

2.40.84: **4** Scotticism; **5** eroticism,
exoticism, neuroticism.

2.40.85: **3** autism, baptism, quietism;
4 defeatism, egotism, elitism, occultism,
transvestism; **5** absolutism, dilettantism,
obscurantism, Protestantism; **6** anti-
Semitism; **7** autodidactism.

2.40.86: **4** despotism, hypnotism,
magnetism, nepotism; **5** conservatism,
corporatism, favouritism, patriotism,
separatism; **7** electromagnetism.

2.40.87: **4** dogmatism, pragmatism,
rheumatism; **5** astigmatism.

2.40.88: **3** fauvism; **4** atavism,
Bolshevism; **5** recidivism.

2.40.89: **4** activism, hacktivism;
5 collectivism, negativism, positivism,
relativism.

2.41: **3** accustomed, bell-bottomed, big-
bottomed, full-bosomed; **4** unaccustomed.
See also **2.40.40**.

2.42: **2** Adams, Addams, Bottoms,
customs, diddums, doldrums, symptoms,

Williams; 3 Abrahams; 5 sweet Fanny
Adams.
See also 2.40.38, 2.40.40.

2.43: 1 an, 'n', 'un; 2 Aachen, Bronwen,
Cowan, doyen, rowan; 3 Callaghan, Don
Juan, Ghanaian, McEwen, Monaghan;
4 Eritrean, gargantuan, protozoan,
Saskatchewan; 5 Nicaraguan.

2.43.1: 2 aeon, Ian; 3 Achaean, Aegean,
Algonquian, Archaean, Fijian,
Nietzschean, pantheon, ruffian, Stygian;
4 Corinthian, Falstaffian, Hitchcockian,
Midlothian, Pecksniffian, Sisyphean,
Tartuffian, Zimbabwean; 5 Ordovician,
theologian.

2.43.2: 2 Behan, Fabian; 3 Albion,
Gambian, lesbian, Libyan, plebeian,
Zambian; 4 amphibian, Arabian,
Caribbean, Colombian, Jacobean,
Namibian.

2.43.3: 3 Andean, Freudian, guardian,
Indian, median, Odeon; 4 accordion,
Cambodian, comedian, custodian,
Edwardian, tragedian; 5 Amerindian,
antipodean.

2.43.4: 3 radian; 4 Arcadian, Barbadian,
Canadian, circadian, Palladian.

2.43.5: 3 Gideon, Lydian; 4 Dravidian,
meridian, obsidian, ophidian, quotidian,
viridian; 5 postmeridian.

2.43.6: 2 lien; 3 Bodleian, Boolean,
bullion, galleon, ganglion, Julian, scullion,
Wesleyan; 4 Aeolian, Aurelian,
chameleon, Hegelian, Herculean,
medallion, Mongolian, Napoleon,
Orwellian, parhelion, rapscallion;
5 Anatolian, Liverpudlian;
6 Machiavellian.

2.43.7: 3 alien; 4 Australian, Pygmalion;
5 bacchanalian, Daedalian; 6 Episcopalian.

2.43.8: 3 Chilean, Gillian; 4 Brazilian,
Churchillian, civilian, cotillion, gazillion,
pavilion, quadrillion, reptilian, vermilion;
5 lacertilian, Maximilian, vaudevillian.

2.43.9: 3 Damian, Permian, simian;
4 bohemian.

2.43.10: 3 Bosnian; 4 Armenian,
communion, Mancunian, Tanzanian.

2.43.11: 4 Albanian, Iranian, Jordanian,
Romanian, Ukrainian; 5 Lithuanian,
Pomeranian, Ruritanian, subterranean;
6 Mediterranean.

2.43.12: 3 Linnaean, Ninian;
4 Darwinian; 5 Abyssinian, Argentinian,
Augustinian, Palestinian.

2.43.13: 3 Etonian; 4 Devonian,
draconian, Estonian, Ionian, Newtonian,
Sheldonian; 5 Aberdonian, Amazonian,
Babylonian, Caledonian, Ciceronian.

2.43.14: 2 paean, peon; 3 Appian,
Campion, Caspian, champion, scorpion,
thespian; 4 European, Olympian,
synthespian, utopian; 5 Ethiopian.

2.43.15: 3 Adrian, Austrian, Cambrian,
carrion, Cyprian, Hadrian, Korean, Marion,
Syrian; 4 equestrian, pedestrian,
Precambrian; 5 epicurean, mitochondrion,
Pythagorean, Terpsichorean.

2.43.16: 3 Aryan; 4 agrarian, barbarian,
Bulgarian, caesarean, Caesarian,
contrarian, grammarian, Hungarian,
librarian, ovarian, Sumerian, vulgarian;
5 antiquarian, centenarian, doctrinarian,
Rastafarian, trustafarian; 6 disciplinarian,
veterinarian.

2.43.17: 6 nonagenarian, octogenarian,
sexagenarian; 7 septuagenarian.

2.43.18: 4 fruitarian, sectarian;
5 Gibraltarian, libertarian, proletarian,
vegetarian; 6 parliamentarian;
7 lactovegetarian.

2.43.19: 5 Unitarian; 6 authoritarian,
egalitarian, humanitarian, totalitarian,
utilitarian.

2.43.20: 4 Algerian, criterion, Hyperion,
Iberian, Nigerian, Nigerien,
Shakespearean, Sumerian, Valerian,
Zairean; 5 Hanoverian, presbyterian.

2.43.21: 3 Dorian, saurian; 4 Gregorian,
historian, stentorian, Victorian;
5 Ecuadorian, Singaporean, Territorian;
6 valedictorian.
See also 2.43.22.

2.43.22: 4 Arthurian, centurion, Ligurian,
Silurian, tellurian.
See also 2.43.21.

2.43.23: 3 halcyon, hessian, Messiaen;
5 Ordovician.

2.43.24: 3 bastion, Faustian, fustian,
Kantian, protean; 4 Sebastian.

2.43.25: 3 Latvian, Vivian; 4 Bolivian,
oblivion, Pavlovian, Peruvian;
5 Scandinavian; 6 antediluvian.

2.43.26: 2 Friesian; 4 Caucasian,
Dickensian, Malaysian, Parisian, Tunisian;
5 Rabelaisian.

2.43.27: **2** Alban, auburn, Bourbon, Brisbane, Cuban, gibbon, Hoban, Holborn, Lisbon, Melbourne, Oban, Osborne, ribbon, stubborn, Webern.
See also **9.14.72**.

2.43.28: **2** carbon; **4** fluorocarbon, hydrocarbon; **6** chlorofluorocarbon.

2.43.29: **2** bourbon, Durban, turban, urban; **3** suburban.

2.43.30: **2** Aidan, Camden, Croydon, Dresden, Goolden, Hampden, Jaden, Neasden, Ogden, Snowdon, sudden, Wheldon, wooden; **3** mastodon, Wimbledon.

2.43.31: **2** gladden, madden, sadden; **3** Abaddon, Ibadan.
See also **10.42.94**.

2.43.32: **2** garden, harden, pardon; **4** Berchtesgaden, Covent Garden.
See also **2.44.1, 10.42.94**.

2.43.33: **2** Aden, Baden, Hayden, laden, maiden; **3** doom-laden, germ-laden, handmaiden; **4** heavy-laden.

2.43.34: **2** deaden, leaden, redden; **4** Armageddon.
See also **2.44.1**.

2.43.35: **2** burden; **3** disburden, unburden; **4** overburden.
See also **2.44.1**.

2.43.36: **2** Eden, Sweden; **4** cotyledon; **5** dicotyledon, Garden of Eden; **6** monocotyledon.

2.43.37: **2** bidden, hidden, midden; **3** forbidden, unbidden.

2.43.38: **2** ridden, stridden; **3** bedridden, bestridden, hag-ridden, harridan, Sheridan; **4** overridden.

2.43.39: **2** Dryden, Haydn, Sidon, widen; **3** Poseidon.
See also **2.44.1**.

2.43.40: **2** modern, sodden, trodden; **3** downtrodden, gin-sodden, postmodern.

2.43.41: **2** Auden, broaden, cordon, Gordon, Jordan, Morden, warden; **3** churchwarden, dog warden; **4** traffic warden.
See also **2.44.1**.

2.43.42: **2** golden, Holden, olden; **3** beholden, embolden.

2.43.43: **2** bounden, Brendan, Hendon, linden, London, tendon; **3** abandon, Rwandan, Ugandan; **4** Greater London.
See also **2.44.1**.

2.43.44: **2** heathen, northern, southern, Swithin.

2.43.45: **2** deafen, gryphon, hyphen, often, orphan, roughen, siphon, soften, stiffen, syphon, toughen; **3** Xenophon; **6** acetaminophen.
See also **10.42.94**.

2.43.46: **2** Bergen, Coogan, Egan, jargon, Keegan, Megan, pagan, Reagan, Roentgen, Tegan, tigon, vegan; **3** McColgan, toboggan; **4** Copenhagen.

2.43.47: **2** dragon, flagon, wagon; **3** Aragon, bandwagon, snapdragon; **4** paddy wagon; **5** Komodo dragon, Uther Pendragon.

2.43.48: **3** decagon, Flannagan, heptagon, hexagon, octagon, paragon, pentagon, suffragan, tarragon.

2.43.49: **3** cardigan, hooligan, Michigan, Mulligan, Oregon, polygon, ptarmigan.

2.43.50: **2** Gorgon, Morgan, organ; **3** mouth organ.

2.43.51: **2** bogan, Hogan, Logan, slogan, Wogan.

2.43.52: **2** Belgian, bludgeon, Cajun, dudgeon, dungeon, Georgian, sojourn, Trajan, Trojan; **3** contagion, curmudgeon.

2.43.53: **3** collagen, glycogen, hydrogen, Imogen, mutagen, nitrogen, oestrogen, pathogen; **4** carcinogen, fibrinogen; **5** hallucinogen.

2.43.54: **2** burgeon, sturgeon, surgeon; **3** brain surgeon, heart surgeon, tree surgeon; **4** dental surgeon, general surgeon, neurosurgeon, plastic surgeon; **7** veterinary surgeon.
See also **10.42.94**.

2.43.55: **2** legion, region; **3** Glaswegian, Norwegian; **4** British Legion, foreign legion.

2.43.56: **2** pigeon, smidgen, widgeon; **3** antigen, Harijan, oxygen, religion, stool pigeon, wood pigeon; **4** homing pigeon; **5** carrier pigeon, passenger pigeon.

2.43.57: **2** Kenyan, Kenyon, mullion, scullion; **3** rebellion, Trevelyan.

2.43.58: **2** scallion, stallion; **3** battalion, Italian.

2.43.59: **2** billion, million, pillion, trillion, zillion; **3** carillon, cotillion; **4** multimillion.

2.43.60: **2** banyan, bunion, Bunyan, canyon, onion; **3** companion, Grand Canyon.

2.43.61: **2** minion, pinion; **3** dominion, opinion; **5** second opinion.

2.43.62: **2** union; **3** disunion, nonunion, trade union; **4** reunion, Rugby Union, students' union; **5** Holy Communion, Soviet Union; **7** European Union.

2.43.63: **1** can; **2** Aitken, beckon, Buchan, darken, falcon, hearken, liken, Lincoln, Lucan, reckon, silken, toucan, Vulcan; **3** Etruscan, Franciscan, Moroccan.
See also **1.22, 2.44.2, 10.42.95**.

2.43.64: **2** blacken, bracken, slacken, Strachan.

2.43.65: **2** bacon, shaken, waken; **3** awaken, forsaken, Jamaican, unshaken; **4** godforsaken, reawaken.
See also **10.42.95**.

2.43.66: **2** taken; **3** mistaken, partaken, retaken; **4** overtaken, undertaken.
See also **9.14.72**.

2.43.67: **2** beacon, deacon, pecan, weaken; **3** archdeacon, mohican; **4** Mozambican; **5** Belisha beacon.
See also **2.44.2**.

2.43.68: **2** Bacon, quicken, sicken, thicken; **3** Barbican, Corsican, Doonican, lexicon, Mexican, Rubicon, Vatican; **4** Dominican, pantechnicon.
See also **2.44.2, 10.42.95**.

2.43.69: **3** Anglican, Helicon, pelican, publican, silicon; **4** Republican.

2.43.70: **3** African, hurricane; **4** American; **5** all-American; **6** Native American.

2.43.71: **2** stricken; **3** fear-stricken, grief-stricken; **4** conscience-stricken, panic-stricken; **5** poverty-stricken.

2.43.72: **2** broken, token, woken; **3** awoken, betoken, foretoken, heartbroken, ryokan, unbroken.

2.43.73: **2** spoken; **3** outspoken, plain-spoken, soft-spoken, unspoken, well-spoken.

2.43.74: **2** drunken, Duncan, shrunken, sunken.
See also **2.54.82**.

2.43.75: **2** Alan, Allan, Allen, Alun, Declan, fallen, gallon, Lachlan, pollen, pylon, raglan, sullen, talon, woollen; **3** befallen, crestfallen, epsilon, pentathlon, triathlon, upsilon; **4** Guatemalan, Venezuelan; **5** Mary Magdalene.
See also **2.54.82**.

2.43.76: **2** Ellen, felon, Helen, melon; **3** Magellan; **4** watermelon; **5** honeydew melon.

2.43.77: **2** Dylan, Galen, villain, villein; **3** Babylon, Macmillan.

2.43.78: **2** Nolan, stolen, swollen; **3** Angolan.

2.43.79: **2** airman, Bergman, Boardman, Brightman, chairman, Chapman, coalman, Coleman, Colman, common, cowman, dolman, Eichmann, fireman, frogman, German, gunman, hangman, Henman, Hofmann, Kauffman, Lemmon, lemon, Newman, Perlman, ploughman, Pullman, Schumann, sermon, Sherman, Simon, summon, Wyman, Yemen; **3** acumen, Horniman, midshipman, Orangeman, patrolman, persimmon, regimen, uncommon.
See also **2.51.1**.

2.43.80: **2** gammon, Mammon, salmon; **3** backgammon.

2.43.81: **3** abdomen, alderman, Betjeman, cinnamon, cyclamen, Dobermann, fisherman, ottoman, Solomon, trawlerman, trencherman, Waterman, weatherman; **4** militiaman; **5** Song of Solomon.

2.43.82: **2** barman, Brahman, shaman, Sharman; **4** Tutankhamen.

2.43.83: **2** Bremen, Damon, Eamonn, layman, shaman, stamen; **3** duramen, highwayman.

2.43.84: **2** daemon, demon, Schliemann, seaman, semen; **3** Berryman, clergyman, ferryman, journeyman; **4** able seaman, assemblyman, nurseryman; **6** able-bodied seaman.

2.43.85: **2** freeman; **3** countryman; **4** cavalryman, infantryman, liveryman.

2.43.86: **2** Bormann, doorman, foreman, Forman, Mormon, Norman; **3** longshoreman.

2.43.87: **2** Bowman, omen, Roman, showman, yeoman; **4** Graeco-Roman.

2.43.88: **2** woman; **3** airwoman, chairwoman, charwoman, Dutchwoman, forewoman, Frenchwoman, laywoman, madwoman, old woman, stuntwoman, well-woman, Welshwoman; **4** aircraftwoman, clergywoman, countrywoman, Englishwoman, everywoman, fallen woman; **5** assemblywoman.

2.43.89: **4** alderwoman, anchorwoman, superwoman, washerwoman, weatherwoman; **5** newspaperwoman.

2.43.90: **4** councilwoman, gentlewoman, needlewoman, noblewoman.

2.43.91: **3** horsewoman, markswoman, spacewoman, spokeswoman; **4** businesswoman, congresswoman, policewoman, servicewoman; **5** ex-servicewoman.

2.43.92: **3** batswoman, craftswoman, Scotswoman, sportswoman, stateswoman, yachtswoman.

2.43.93: **3** clanswoman, kinswoman, newswoman, oarswoman, saleswoman, tribeswoman.

2.43.94: **2** crewman, human, rumen, Schuman, Trueman, Truman; **3** inhuman, subhuman; **4** superhuman.

2.43.95: **2** Bradman, Friedman, Goodman, headman, madman, Oldman; **3** husbandman.

2.43.96: **2** Eichmann, milkman, stockman, Walkman, workman.

2.43.97: **3** cattleman, councilman, gentleman, nobleman, rifleman, signalman.

2.43.98: **2** horseman, houseman, Housman, marksman, Norseman, Paxman, spokesman; **3** congressman, policeman, serviceman, talisman; **4** ex-serviceman, underclassman, upperclassman.

2.43.99: **2** batsman, craftsman, draughtsman, huntsman, Scotsman, sportsman, statesman, yachtsman.

2.43.100: **2** bushman, Flashman, freshman, Welshman; **3** Englishman.

2.43.101: **2** Altman, batman, boatman, dustman, Eastman, footman, frontman, pitman, postman, Whiteman, Whitman; **3** aircraftman, merchantman.

2.43.102: **2** churchman, coachman, Dutchman, Frenchman, henchman, watchman.

2.43.103: **2** foilsman, helmsman, oarsman, salesman, steersman, tribesman; **3** frontiersman, talisman.

2.43.104: **2** bandsman, fieldsman, groundsman, guardsman, herdsman, swordsman, tradesman, woodsman; **3** backwoodsman, ombudsman.

2.43.105: **2** clansman, kinsman, Klansman, linesman.

2.43.106: **2** Brosnan, Canaan, Conan, pennon, Ronan, tenon, Vernon; **3** Algernon, Botswanan, Lebanon; **4** Agamemnon, carrageenan, phenomenon.

2.43.107: **2** Annan, cannon, canon, Shannon; **3** Buchanan, Rhiannon.

2.43.108: **1** cap'n; **2** aspen, cheapen, dampen, deepen, happen, lumpen, ripen, saucepan, sharpen, steepen, weapon; **3** misshapen; **4** bioweapon.
See also **10.42.94**.

2.43.109: **2** open; **3** reopen, wide-open; **4** US Open.
See also **10.42.94**.

2.43.110: **2** Aaron, apron, brethren, Buren, Byron, Charon, chevron, citron, Cochran, Conran, heron, Lauren, matron, Mirren, Myron, patron, saffron, siren, sporran, warren; **3** Cameron, Dáil Éireann, Honduran, Lake Huron, Lutheran, veteran; **4** Aldebaran, Plymouth Brethren, Salvadoran.

2.43.111: **2** Aran, Arran, baron, barren, caron, Darren, Karen; **3** McLaren; **4** robber baron.

2.43.112: **2** cauldron, children, squadron; **4** decahedron, polyhedron, rhododendron, tetrahedron; **5** dodecahedron.

2.43.113: **2** Bergson, boatswain, bosun, Casson, coarsen, Dawson, Dodgson, Higson, Hodgson, Lawson, loosen, moisten, Neeson, Pearson, Simpson, Thompson, worsen; **3** MacPherson.
See also **10.42.94**.

2.43.114: **3** Acheson, Anderson, Emerson, Emmerson, Ferguson, Henderson, Jefferson, medicine, Paterson, Patterson, Peterson, Rasmussen, Sanderson, Saracen; **4** biomedicine, diocesan; **7** Ayurvedic medicine.

2.43.115: **2** arson, Carson, fasten, Larson, parson; **3** unfasten.
See also **10.42.92**.

2.43.116: **2** basin, chasten, Grayson, hasten, Jason, mason; **3** Andreessen, Freemason, handbasin, stonemason, washbasin.

2.43.117: **2** Essen, lessen, lesson; **5** delicatessen.

2.43.118: **2** person; **3** barperson, chairperson, foreperson, layperson, nonperson, salesperson, sportsperson, unperson; **4** anchorperson; **5** enlisted person; **7** person-to-person.

2.43.119: 3 craftsperson, draughtsperson, pressperson, spokesperson; 4 businessperson, congressperson, serviceperson.

2.43.120: 2 Davison, glisten, Jameson, listen; 3 Addison, Alison, Allison, Eddison, Edison, Harmison, Harrison, jettison, Maddison, madison.

2.43.121: 3 Dinesen, Tennyson, unison, venison.

2.43.122: 2 christen; 3 garrison, Morrison; 4 comparison. *See also* **10.42.94**.

2.43.123: 2 bison, Bryson, Dyson, Meissen, Tyson.

2.43.124: 2 Dobson, Gibson, Hobson, Ibsen, Robeson, Robson.

2.43.125: 2 Davidson, Hudson; 3 Amundsen, Donaldson, Richardson.

2.43.126: 2 Clarkson, Cookson, coxswain, Dixon, Hickson, oxen.

2.43.127: 2 flaxen, Jackson, klaxon, Saxon, waxen; 4 Anglo-Saxon.

2.43.128: 2 Blixen, Nixon, vixen; 3 Ericson.

2.43.129: 2 Jolson, Nelson, Nielsen, Tilson, Wilson; 3 Mendelssohn, Nicholson.

2.43.130: 2 Samson, Thomson; 3 Adamson, Williamson.

2.43.131: 2 Benson, Bunsen, Henson; 3 Berenson, Dickenson, Stephenson, Stevenson.

2.43.132: 2 Branson, chanson, Hansen, Hanson, Manson.

2.43.133: 3 Dickinson, Hopkinson, Hutchinson, Parkinson, Rawlinson, Robinson, Tomkinson, Tomlinson, Wilkinson; 4 Jack Robinson.

2.43.134: 2 Bronson, Johnson, Jonson, Swanson.

2.43.135: 2 stetson, Watson, Whitsun; 3 Bateson, Robertson.

2.43.136: 2 cushion, Laotian, Martian; 3 Andersen, pincushion; 4 Rosicrucian. *See also* **2.44.11**.

2.43.137: 2 ashen, fashion, passion, ration; 3 compassion, dispassion, refashion; 4 parrot-fashion. *See also* **2.44.12, 2.51.2**.

2.43.138: 2 Asian, Haitian; 3 Croatian, Dalmatian, summation; 4 graduation,

menstruation, retardation; 5 Serbo-Croatian.

2.43.139: 4 aviation, deviation, expiation, permeation; 5 abbreviation, alleviation, delineation.

2.43.140: 4 mediation, radiation; 5 irradiation, remediation, repudiation; 6 nonrepudiation; 7 bioremediation.

Television—the drug of the nation
Breeding ignorance and feeding
* radiation.*
(Disposable Heroes of Hiphoprisy)

2.43.141: 4 palliation, spoliation; 5 affiliation, conciliation, despoliation, humiliation, retaliation; 6 reconciliation.

2.43.142: 3 creation; 4 procreation, recreation, variation; 5 appropriation, expropriation, repatriation; 6 misappropriation.

2.43.143: 4 glaciation; 5 Annunciation, association, denunciation, pronunciation, renunciation; 6 mispronunciation, Press Association; 7 Received Pronunciation.

2.43.144: 5 appreciation, depreciation, differentiation, initiation, negotiation, propitiation, substantiation; 6 transubstantiation. *See also* **2.51.3**.

2.43.145: 4 valuation; 5 attenuation, continuation, devaluation, evacuation, evaluation, extenuation, infatuation, insinuation; 6 discontinuation, superannuation.

2.43.146: 4 fluctuation, punctuation, situation; 5 accentuation, perpetuation.

Is it worth the aggravation
To find yourself a job when there's
* nothing worth working for?*
It's a crazy situation
But all I need are cigarettes and alcohol!
(Oasis)

2.43.147: 3 libation, probation; 4 approbation, conurbation, perturbation; 5 disapprobation, exacerbation.

2.43.148: 3 gradation; 4 degradation, depredation; 5 accommodation.

2.43.149: 3 predation, sedation; 4 liquidation, oxidation, trepidation, validation; 5 consolidation, dilapidation, elucidation, intimidation, invalidation.

2.43.150: 3 foundation; 4 commendation, emendation, fecundation, inundation; 5 recommendation.

2.43.151: **4** abrogation, conjugation, elongation, expurgation, prolongation, propagation, subjugation; **5** interrogation, variegation.

2.43.152: **3** legation, negation; **4** abnegation, allegation, delegation, fumigation, navigation, obligation, relegation; **6** circumnavigation.

2.43.153: **4** congregation, segregation; **5** desegregation; **7** colonic irrigation.

2.43.154: **4** castigation, instigation, litigation, mitigation; **5** investigation.

2.43.155: **3** location, truncation, vacation, vocation; **4** allocation, altercation, avocation, collocation, colocation, confiscation, convocation, demarcation, dislocation, education, embrocation, evocation, invocation, obfuscation, provocation, relocation, revocation; **5** coeducation, echolocation, equivocation, reciprocation.

2.43.156: **4** desiccation, fornication, publication, rustication; **5** authentication, clarification, communication, intoxication, sophistication; **6** excommunication, prognostication; **7** telecommunication.
See also **2.51.3**.

2.43.157: **4** abdication, dedication, indication, medication, vindication; **5** adjudication, eradication, premedication; **6** contraindication.

2.43.158: **5** amplification, codification, edification, jollification, modification, nullification, qualification, ramification, simplification, vilification; **6** disqualification, exemplification, revivification; **11** floccinaucinihilipilification.

2.43.159: **5** magnification, signification, unification; **6** indemnification, personification, reunification.

2.43.160: **5** gentrification, glorification, purification, verification; **6** electrification, horrification.

2.43.161: **4** ossification; **5** classification, falsification, specification; **6** detoxification, diversification, intensification.

2.43.162: **5** beautification, certification, fortification, fructification, gratification, justification, mortification, mystification, notification, ratification, rectification, sanctification, stratification;

6 beatification, desertification, identification.

2.43.163: **4** application, complication, duplication, implication, replication, supplication; **5** misapplication, multiplication.

2.43.164: **4** deprecation, extrication, fabrication, imprecation, metrication; **5** prevarication.

2.43.165: **3** dilation, oblation, translation, violation; **4** annihilation, contemplation, legislation.

2.43.166: **3** collation; **4** appellation, compilation, correlation, escalation, flagellation, inhalation, percolation, revelation; **5** interpolation; **6** recapitulation.

2.43.167: **4** cancellation, consolation, constellation, desolation, exhalation, installation, isolation.

2.43.168: **3** elation, relation; **4** fibrillation, jubilation, mutilation, oscillation, titillation, vacillation, ventilation; **5** assimilation.
See also **2.51.3**.

2.43.169: **4** adulation, insulation, modulation, regulation, strangulation, tribulation, ululation, undulation; **5** coagulation, congratulation, deregulation, expostulation, perambulation, self-congratulation, triangulation; **6** tintinnabulation.
See also **2.51.3**.

2.43.170: **4** calculation, circulation, speculation; **5** articulation, ejaculation, emasculation, inoculation, matriculation, miscalculation.

2.43.171: **4** formulation, simulation, stimulation; **5** accumulation, dissimulation.

2.43.172: **4** copulation, population, stipulation; **5** depopulation, manipulation.

2.43.173: **3** deflation, inflation, reflation, stagflation; **4** disinflation; **5** hyperinflation.

2.43.174: **4** automation, consummation; **5** amalgamation.

2.43.175: **4** affirmation, confirmation, defamation, information, reformation, transformation; **5** disinformation, misinformation.

2.43.176: **4** acclamation, declamation, exclamation, inflammation, proclamation, reclamation.

2.43.177: **3** cremation; **4** animation, estimation, intimation, sublimation;

5 approximation, reanimation;
6 overestimation.

2.43.178: 3 formation; 4 back-formation, conformation, deformation, malformation.

2.43.179: 2 nation; 3 carnation, damnation, donation; 4 condemnation, incarnation, multination; 5 reincarnation.

Money, the life-blood of the nation,
Corrupts and stagnates in the veins,
Unless a proper circulation
Its motion and its heat maintains.
(Jonathan Swift)

2.43.180: 4 coronation, emanation, explanation, hibernation; 5 alienation, impersonation, miscegenation, rejuvenation.

2.43.181: 4 alternation, consternation, detonation, intonation; 5 concatenation.

2.43.182: 4 combination, divination, machination, ordination, pagination, ruination, urination; 5 coordination, imagination, indoctrination, origination, peregrination; 6 insubordination.

2.43.183: 4 declination, inclination, pollination; 5 desalination, disinclination.

2.43.184: 4 culmination, fulmination, rumination; 5 contamination, discrimination, dissemination, elimination, examination, extermination, illumination, insemination, recrimination; 6 decontamination, self-examination.

2.43.185: 4 germination, termination; 5 determination; 6 predetermination, self-determination.

2.43.186: 4 domination, nomination; 5 abomination, denomination.

2.43.187: 4 fascination, vaccination; 5 assassination, hallucination; 6 ratiocination.

2.43.188: 4 destination; 5 agglutination, predestination, procrastination.

2.43.189: 3 stagnation; 4 assignation, designation, indignation, resignation.

2.43.190: 4 exculpation, extirpation, occupation, syncopation; 5 preoccupation.

2.43.191: 4 constipation, dissipation; 5 anticipation, emancipation, participation.

2.43.192: 2 Thracian; 3 aeration, duration, Eurasian, gyration, vibration; 4 abjuration, aspiration, calibration, celebration, consecration, dehydration, execration, maturation, transpiration.

2.43.193: 3 oration, serration; 4 corporation, decoration, laceration, obscuration, perforation, peroration, saturation, ulceration; 5 commiseration, configuration, exaggeration, inauguration, incarceration, invigoration, melioration, proliferation, transfiguration; 6 amelioration, deterioration, nonproliferation; 8 interior decoration.

2.43.194: 4 aberration, liberation; 5 collaboration, corroboration, deliberation, elaboration, reverberation; 6 women's liberation.

2.43.195: 4 adoration, federation, moderation; 5 confederation, consideration, immoderation; 6 reconsideration.

2.43.196: 4 coloration, declaration, exploration, toleration; 5 acceleration, deceleration, discoloration, exhilaration.

2.43.197: 4 admiration, numeration; 5 agglomeration, commemoration, conglomeration, enumeration.

2.43.198: 3 narration; 4 veneration; 5 exoneration, remuneration.

2.43.199: 4 generation; 5 degeneration, fifth-generation, first-generation, regeneration; 6 microgeneration, second generation.

2.43.200: 4 operation, preparation, reparation, separation; 5 cooperation, evaporation, incorporation, recuperation, vituperation; 6 noncooperation.

2.43.201: 4 desperation, expiration, inspiration, perspiration, respiration; 5 exasperation.

2.43.202: 4 alteration, iteration, restoration; 5 adulteration, alliteration, obliteration, reiteration, transliteration.

2.43.203: 3 migration; 4 conflagration, denigration, emigration, immigration, integration, transmigration; 5 disintegration.

2.43.204: 3 filtration, titration; 4 arbitration, concentration, infiltration, penetration.

2.43.205: 3 castration, frustration, lustration, prostration; 4 demonstration, illustration, orchestration, registration, sequestration; 5 administration, defenestration; 6 maladministration.

2.43.206: 3 Alsatian, cessation, pulsation, sensation; 4 compensation, condensation,

conversation, dispensation;
5 tergiversation.

2.43.207: **3** fixation, taxation, vexation;
4 annexation, indexation, relaxation.

2.43.208: **3** citation, dictation, flirtation,
lactation, mutation, sortation, temptation;
4 adaptation, affectation, connotation,
delectation, dissertation, expectation,
exploitation, vegetation.

2.43.209: **4** agitation, capitation,
cogitation, gravitation, habitation,
hesitation, imitation, invitation, irritation,
levitation, limitation, meditation,
palpitation, recitation, sanitation,
visitation; **5** accreditation, cohabitation,
decapitation, delimitation, felicitation,
interpretation, precipitation, premeditation,
resuscitation, solicitation;
6 misinterpretation, prestidigitation,
rehabilitation.

2.43.210: **4** deportation, exhortation,
importation, transportation; **5** teleportation.

2.43.211: **3** flotation, notation, quotation,
rotation; **4** denotation, misquotation.

2.43.212: **4** commutation, confutation,
permutation, refutation, salutation,
transmutation.

2.43.213: **4** amputation, computation,
deputation, disputation, reputation.

2.43.214: **3** saltation; **4** consultation,
exaltation, exultation.

2.43.215: **3** plantation; **4** confrontation,
implantation, incantation, indentation,
ostentation, presentation, recantation;
5 orientation, representation.

2.43.216: **4** fragmentation, lamentation,
segmentation; **5** argumentation,
complementation, implementation.

2.43.217: **4** augmentation, fermentation,
fomentation, pigmentation;
5 documentation, instrumentation,
ornamentation, regimentation,
sedimentation; **6** experimentation.

2.43.218: **2** station; **3** crustacean, space
station, substation, workstation; **4** comfort
station, devastation, encrustation, parking
station, protestation; **5** afforestation,
deforestation, reforestation;
6 reafforestation.

2.43.219: **3** gestation; **4** attestation,
infestation, molestation; **5** manifestation.

2.43.220: **3** ovation, privation, salvation,
starvation; **4** innovation.

2.43.221: **4** aggravation, conservation,
elevation, enervation, excavation,
observation, preservation, renovation,
reservation; **5** self-preservation.

2.43.222: **4** activation, aestivation,
cultivation, deprivation, derivation,
motivation, titivation; **5** deactivation.

2.43.223: **3** causation; **4** accusation;
6 reorganisation.

2.43.224: **4** realisation; **5** aerolisation,
authorisation, improvisation, privatisation;
6 characterisation.

2.43.225: **5** civilisation, fertilisation,
globalisation, glocalisation, localisation,
socialisation, specialisation; **6** cross-
fertilisation, generalisation, rationalisation.

2.43.226: **5** Balkanisation,
modernisation, organisation, urbanisation;
6 decolonisation, disorganisation; **7** World
Health Organization, World Trade
Organization.

2.43.227: **2** freshen; **3** confession,
discretion, possession, precession,
profession; **4** dispossession, indiscretion,
self-possession.

> *Meek wifehood is no part of my*
> *profession;*
> *I am your friend, but never your*
> *possession.*
> (Vera Brittain)

2.43.228: **3** aggression, degression,
digression, progression, regression,
transgression; **4** nonaggression.

2.43.229: **3** compression, depression,
expression, impression, oppression,
repression, suppression; **4** decompression,
self-expression; **6** immunosuppression,
postnatal depression.

2.43.230: **2** session; **3** accession,
concession, obsession, procession,
recession, secession, succession;
4 intercession.

2.43.231: **2** Persian; **3** aspersion,
assertion, Cistercian, coercion, desertion,
dispersion, excursion, exertion, immersion,
incursion, insertion, submersion.

2.43.232: **2** version; **3** aversion,
conversion, diversion, inversion,
perversion, reversion, subversion;
4 introversion; **5** Authorised Version.

2.43.233: **2** Grecian; **3** accretion,
concretion, excretion, secretion, Venetian.

2.43.234: **3** completion, deletion,
depletion, Diocletian; **4** noncompletion.

2.43.235: 2 fission; 3 coition, fruition, logician, magician, suspicion, tuition; 4 intuition, Ordovician.

2.43.236: 3 ambition; 4 exhibition, inhibition, Prohibition.

2.43.237: 3 audition, edition, sedition; 4 erudition.

2.43.238: 3 addition, perdition, tradition; 4 expedition, extradition.

2.43.239: 3 condition, rendition; 4 aircondition, precondition, recondition. *See also* **2.51.4, 10.42.96.**

2.43.240: 3 volition; 4 abolition, coalition, demolition.

2.43.241: 2 mission; 3 admission, Domitian, emission, omission, remission, submission, transmission; 4 manumission.

2.43.242: 3 commission, permission; 4 decommission, High Commission, intermission; 5 academician, Royal Commission; 7 European Commission. *See also* **2.44.11.**

2.43.243: 3 clinician, cognition, ignition, munition, technician; 4 admonition, ammunition, definition, precognition, premonition, recognition; 5 low-definition.

2.43.244: 3 nutrition; 4 apparition, electrician, malnutrition, parturition, rhetorician.

2.43.245: 3 attrition, patrician; 4 obstetrician; 5 paediatrician.

2.43.246: 2 Titian; 3 beautician, dietitian, mortician, optician, partition, tactician; 4 statistician, superstition. *See also* **2.44.11.**

2.43.247: 3 petition; 4 competition, politician, repetition, theoretician; 5 mathematician.

2.43.248: 3 musician, physician, transition; 4 acquisition, disquisition, inquisition, requisition. *See also* **2.51.4.**

2.43.249: 3 position; 4 apposition, composition, deposition, disposition, exposition, imposition, opposition, preposition, proposition, supposition, transposition; 5 decomposition, indisposition, interposition, juxtaposition, predisposition, presupposition.

2.43.250: 2 caution, portion, torsion; 3 abortion, apportion, contortion,

distortion, extortion, precaution, proportion; 4 disproportion. *See also* **2.51.2.**

2.43.251: 2 lotion, notion, ocean, potion; 3 devotion.
Just like a willow,
we would cry an ocean
If we lost true love
and sweet devotion
(Elvis Presley)
See also **2.51.2.**

2.43.252: 2 motion; 3 commotion, demotion, emotion, promotion; 4 locomotion.

2.43.253: 2 Prussian, Russian; 3 concussion, discussion, percussion; 4 Belorussian, repercussion.

2.43.254: 3 Confucian; 4 attribution, contribution, diminution, distribution, Lilliputian, retribution.

2.43.255: 3 locution; 4 elocution, execution, persecution, prosecution; 5 circumlocution, electrocution, interlocution.

2.43.256: 4 constitution, destitution, institution, prostitution, restitution, substitution.

2.43.257: 3 ablution, dilution, pollution, solution; 4 absolution, air pollution, dissolution, resolution; 5 Final Solution, high-resolution, low-resolution.

2.43.258: 4 convolution, devolution, evolution, revolution; 6 counter-revolution; 8 Industrial Revolution.

2.43.259: 2 auction; 3 concoction, decoction, Dutch auction, infarction.

2.43.260: 2 action; 3 exaction, inaction, reaction, transaction; 4 counteraction, interaction.

2.43.261: 2 faction; 4 benefaction, liquefaction, putrefaction, satisfaction, stupefaction; 5 dissatisfaction.

2.43.262: 2 fraction; 3 diffraction, infraction, refraction; 4 simple fraction.

2.43.263: 2 traction; 3 abstraction, attraction, contraction, distraction, extraction, retraction, subtraction. *See also* **2.51.2.**

2.43.264: 3 connection, convection, detection, inspection, protection; 4 circumspection, disconnection, introspection, retrospection; 5 interconnection.

2.43.265: 3 affection, confection, defection, infection, perfection; 4 disaffection, disinfection, imperfection.

2.43.266: 3 dejection, ejection, injection, objection, projection, rejection, subjection; 4 interjection; 5 antirejection.

2.43.267: 3 collection, complexion, election, selection; 4 by-election, predilection, recollection.

2.43.268: 2 flection; 3 deflection, inflection, reflection; 4 genuflection.

2.43.269: 3 correction, direction, erection; 4 indirection, insurrection, resurrection; 5 hypercorrection.

2.43.270: 2 section; 3 dissection, subsection; 4 intersection, vivisection.

2.43.271: 2 friction; 3 affliction, constriction, conviction, depiction, eviction, restriction; 4 dereliction.

2.43.272: 2 diction; 3 addiction, prediction; 4 benediction, contradiction, interdiction, jurisdiction, malediction, valediction.

2.43.273: 2 fiction; 3 nonfiction, pulp fiction; 4 crucifixion, science fiction.

2.43.274: 2 suction; 3 conduction, deduction, induction, production, reduction, seduction; 4 introduction, liposuction, reproduction; 5 overproduction.

2.43.275: 3 construction, destruction, instruction, obstruction; 4 deconstruction, reconstruction; 5 microinstruction; 7 weapon of mass destruction.

2.43.276: 2 sanction; 3 distinction, extinction; 5 contradistinction. *See also* **2.51.2.**

2.43.277: 2 function, junction, unction; 3 compunction, conjunction, disjunction, dysfunction, injunction, malfunction, T-junction; 4 extreme unction; 5 spaghetti junction.

2.43.278: 3 compulsion, convulsion, emulsion, expulsion, impulsion, propulsion, repulsion, revulsion. *See also* **2.51.2.**

2.43.279: 2 mansion, scansion, stanchion; 3 expansion.

2.43.280: 2 gentian, mention, pension; 3 ascension, declension, dimension, dissension, suspension; 4 condescension. *See also* **2.51.2.**

2.43.281: 4 apprehension, comprehension, reprehension; 5 incomprehension, misapprehension.

2.43.282: 2 tension; 3 abstention, attention, contention, detention, distension, extension, intention, pretension, retention; 4 hypertension.

2.43.283: 3 convention, invention, prevention, subvention; 4 circumvention, contravention, intervention; 5 nonintervention. *See also* **2.51.2.**

2.43.284: 2 caption, option; 3 absorption, adaption, adoption, adsorption, contraption, corruption, disruption, Egyptian, exemption, redemption; 4 interruption.

2.43.285: 3 conception, deception, exception, inception, perception, reception; 4 contraception, misconception, preconception; 7 Immaculate Conception.

2.43.286: 3 conscription, description, inscription, prescription, proscription, subscription, transcription; 4 circumscription.

2.43.287: 2 gumption; 3 assumption, consumption, presumption, resumption.

2.43.288: 2 Acton, Ashton, chieftain, Clacton, gluten, Luton, newton, plankton, threaten, Troughton; 3 Tibetan, verboten; 4 hifalutin. *See also* **2.44.14, 10.42.96.**

2.43.289: 2 baton, batten, fatten, flatten, Hatton, Patten, pattern, Patton, Saturn, slattern; 3 Manhattan, Mountbatten. *See also* **2.44.14, 10.42.96.**

2.43.290: 2 quieten; 3 Anderton, Atherton, charlatan, Chesterton, Fullerton, Sheraton; 4 asyndeton, automaton.

2.43.291: 2 Barton, carton, hearten, Parton, smarten, spartan, tartan; 3 dishearten, pine marten; 4 Akhenaton, kindergarten.

2.43.292: 2 Clayton, Leighton, Leyton, phaeton, Satan, straighten.

2.43.293: 2 burton, certain, curtain, Merton; 3 drop curtain, Iron Curtain, uncertain.

2.43.294: 2 eaten, Eton, Keaton, neaten, sweeten, Teton, wheaten; 3 moth-eaten, uneaten, worm-eaten; 4 overeaten. *See also* **10.42.96.**

2.43.295: 2 beaten, Beaton, Beeton; 3 browbeaten, unbeaten; 4 weather-beaten.

2.43.296: **2** bittern, kitten, mitten, smitten; **3** flea-bitten, frostbitten, hardbitten, Honiton.

2.43.297: **3** skeleton; **5** endoskeleton, exoskeleton, metropolitan, Neapolitan; **6** cosmopolitan.

2.43.298: **2** Britain, Briton, Brittain, Britten, written; **3** ghostwritten, handwritten, puritan, rewritten, typewritten, unwritten; **4** overwritten, Samaritan, underwritten; **5** Good Samaritan.

2.43.299: **2** Blyton, brighten, Brighton, frighten, heighten, lighten, tighten, titan, whiten; **3** enlighten; **6** Admirable Crichton. *See also* **2.44.14, 10.42.96**.

2.43.300: **2** cotton, gotten, rotten; **3** forgotten, ill-gotten; **4** misbegotten.

2.43.301: **2** Laughton, Morton, Norton, Orton, shorten, tauten, Wharton; **3** foreshorten. *See also* **10.42.96**.

2.43.302: **2** button, glutton, Hutton, mutton; **3** push-button, unbutton; **4** bellybutton. *See also* **2.44.14**.

2.43.303: **2** Bolton, Carlton, Charlton, Dalton, Elton, Fulton, molten, sultan, Walton; **3** Appleton.

2.43.304: **3** Littleton, Middleton, Shackleton, simpleton, singleton, subaltern.

2.43.305: **2** Hilton, Milton, Stilton, Wilton; **3** Hamilton.

2.43.306: **2** Bunton, Clinton, Danton, lantern, Staunton, wanton, Winton; **3** badminton, Edmonton; **4** jack-o'-lantern. *See also* **2.54.82**.

2.43.307: **2** Benton, Brenton, Lenten, Trenton.

2.43.308: **3** Addington, Barrington, Bonington, Bonnington, Carrington, Eddington, Harrington, Kennington, Kensington, Lexington, Lymington, Paddington, Pilkington, Washington, Whittington, Worthington; **4** South Kensington, Stoke Newington.

2.43.309: **3** Arlington, Ellington, Islington, wellington.

2.43.310: **2** Clapton, Lipton, Repton, Shipton; **4** Mother Shipton.

2.43.311: **2** Compton, Crompton, Hampton; **3** Southampton; **4** Wolverhampton.

2.43.312: **2** Aston, Boston, capstan, Charleston, cistern, eastern, Gladstone, Heston, Houston, Huston, Johnston, Kingston, Marston, piston, Preston, Tristan, tungsten, Winston; **3** Athelstan, Ecclestone, Leytonstone, Livingstone, northeastern, Palmerston, sacristan, southeastern, Ulverstone.

2.43.313: **2** western, Weston; **3** northwestern, southwestern; **5** country and western, spaghetti Western.

2.43.314: **2** Brixton, Caxton, Hoxton, Paxton, sexton, Theakston.

2.43.315: **2** earthen, Ethan, lengthen, Nathan, python, strengthen, Swithin; **3** Jonathan, leviathan, marathon; **5** Elizabethan.

2.43.316: **2** fortune, kitchen, lichen, luncheon, stanchion, truncheon; **3** escutcheon, Hell's Kitchen, misfortune; **4** inattention.

2.43.317: **2** Christian, question; **3** combustion, exhaustion, unchristian; **5** born-again Christian. *See also* **10.42.94**.

2.43.318: **3** congestion, digestion, egestion, suggestion; **4** indigestion; **5** autosuggestion.

2.43.319: **2** Cavan, cavern, Heshvan, proven, silvan, sylvan, tavern; **3** Donovan, Sullivan, unproven.

2.43.320: **2** Avon, craven, haven, maven, raven, shaven; **3** clean-shaven, Newhaven, unshaven; **6** Stratford-upon-Avon.

2.43.321: **2** Bevan, Devon, Evan, heaven, leaven, seven, Severn; **3** eleven; **4** 7/7, 9/11; **5** 24/7; **6** AK-47.

2.43.322: **2** even, Stephen, Steven; **3** breakeven, uneven. *See also* **2.51, 2.54.82, 10.42.92**.

2.43.323: **2** driven, given, riven, Sivan, striven; **3** forgiven, God-given; **4** O'Sullivan.

2.43.324: **2** Ivan, liven, thriven, wyvern; **3** enliven.

2.43.325: **2** cloven, proven, woven; **3** Beethoven, close-woven, Eindhoven, fine-woven; **4** interwoven.

2.43.326: 2 bhavan, coven, govern, oven;
3 Dutch oven, McGovern.
See also **10.42.94.**

2.43.327: 2 chosen, cousin, crimson,
Curzon, damson, dozen, frozen, odds and
ends, poison, Susan, Tarzan; 3 Amazon,
horizon, ill-chosen, Stockhausen, well-
chosen; 4 country cousin, lazy Susan;
5 Baron Münchhausen.
See also **2.44.15.**

2.43.328: 2 blazon, brazen, raisin;
3 emblazon, liaison; 4 diapason.

2.43.329: 2 reason, season, treason;
3 peak season, preseason.
The last temptation is the greatest
treason:
To do the right deed for the wrong reason.
(T. S. Eliot)
See also **2.44.15.**

2.43.330: 2 mizzen, prison, risen;
3 arisen, citizen, denizen, imprison,
netizen, partisan.
See also **2.44.15.**

2.43.331: 2 Arjun, version; 3 corrosion,
erosion, explosion, implosion;
5 Authorised Version.

2.43.332: 2 Asian; 3 abrasion, Caucasian,
dissuasion, equation, Eurasian, evasion,
invasion, occasion, persuasion;
4 Amerasian, Australasian, British Asian,
tax evasion.

2.43.333: 2 Friesian, lesion; 3 adhesion,
cohesion; 4 Austronesian, Indonesian,
Melanesian, Polynesian.

2.43.334: 3 collision, derision, elision;
4 Elysian.

2.43.335: 2 scission; 3 concision,
decision, excision, incision, precision;
4 circumcision, imprecision, indecision.

2.43.336: 2 vision; 3 division, envision,
provision, revision; 4 subdivision,
supervision, television; 6 cable television.
See also **2.51.**

2.43.337: 3 contusion, extrusion,
intrusion, occlusion, protrusion, seclusion,
transfusion; 4 Carthusian.

2.43.338: 2 fusion; 3 confusion,
diffusion, effusion, infusion, perfusion,
profusion.

2.43.339: 3 allusion, collusion,
conclusion, delusion, exclusion, illusion,
inclusion; 4 disillusion, self-delusion.
See also **2.44.**

2.44: 2 brigand, dachshund, husband,
legend, viand; 3 househusband,
unleavened, unopened, unquestioned;
4 disillusioned.
See also **2.43.339.**

2.44.1: 2 broadened, deadened, hardened,
widened; 3 abandoned; 4 cum dividend,
overburdened.
See also **2.43.32, 2.43.34, 2.43.35, 2.43.39,
2.43.41.**

2.44.2: 2 darkened, jocund, sickened,
thickened, weakened; 3 rubicund.
See also **2.43.63, 2.43.67, 2.43.68.**

2.44.3: 2 fecund, second; 4 microsecond,
millisecond, nanosecond.
See also **2.50.**

2.44.4: 2 Cleveland, Copland, Coupland,
Dowland, eland, England, Finland,
garland, Greenland, headland, heathland,
Holland, Iceland, inland, Ireland,
moorland, Poland, Queensland, Roland,
upland, Westmoreland, woodland;
3 Maryland, Newfoundland, New Zealand;
4 Church of England, de Havilland, Hook
of Holland, Middle England, Northern
Ireland; 5 Bank of England.

2.44.5: 2 pastureland; 3 Cumberland,
Sutherland, Switzerland, timberland;
4 Northumberland.

2.44.6: 2 highland, island, Thailand;
3 Long Island; 4 desert island, Devil's
Island, floating island, Holy Island,
Pitcairn Island, traffic island; 5 Kodiak
Island, Liberty Island.

2.44.7: 2 Ackland, Auckland, Buckland,
dockland, Oakland.

2.44.8: 2 Cartland, coastland, Jutland,
Portland, Rutland, Scotland; 4 Church of
Scotland.

2.44.9: 2 almond, Desmond, diamond,
Dortmund, Drummond, Edmond, Edmund,
gourmand, Hammond, Raymond,
Redmond, Richmond; 3 ill-omened, Loch
Lomond, Rosamund.

2.44.10: 2 Bertrand, errand, gerund,
reverend; 3 fool's errand, Reverend.

2.44.11: 2 cushioned; 3 complexioned,
partitioned, proportioned; 4 air-
conditioned, decommissioned, light-
complexioned, well-proportioned.
See also **2.43.136, 2.43.242, 2.43.246.**

2.44.12: 2 fashioned, rationed;
3 impassioned, old-fashioned.
See also **2.43.137.**

2.44.13: **3** unmentioned; **4** above-mentioned, aforementioned, ill-intentioned, undermentioned, well-intentioned.

2.44.14: **2** brightened, buttoned, flattened, frightened, heightened, lightened, patterned, straitened, threatened; **3** disheartened, enlightened, foreshortened, unsweetened; **4** unenlightened.
See also **2.43.288, 2.43.289, 2.43.299, 2.43.302.**

2.44.15: **2** poisoned, reasoned, seasoned, thousand, wizened; **3** emblazoned, imprisoned, unreasoned, well-reasoned.
See also **2.43.327, 2.43.329, 2.43.330.**

2.45: **2** Clemence, conscience, patience, penance, sixpence, threepence; **3** absorbance, arrogance, disturbance, elegance, impatience, performance, repugnance, vehemence; **4** extravagance, significance; **5** insignificance.

2.45.1: **3** ambience, dalliance, deviance, prescience, sentience; **4** convenience, insouciance, omniscience, resilience, subservience; **5** inconvenience; **6** flag of convenience.

2.45.2: **3** audience, radiance; **4** expedience, obedience; **5** disobedience.

2.45.3: **3** prurience, variance; **4** experience, luxuriance; **5** inexperience.
See also **2.49.**

2.45.4: **3** affluence, confluence, congruence, continuance, effluence, influence, pursuance; **5** discontinuance.

2.45.5: **2** cadence, credence, guidance, prudence; **3** accordance, avoidance, concordance, decadence, discordance, impedance, imprudence, impudence, subsidence; **4** jurisprudence.

2.45.6: **2** riddance; **3** confidence, diffidence, evidence, providence, residence; **4** Queen's evidence, self-confidence; **5** overconfidence.

2.45.7: **3** dissidence, incidence, precedence, subsidence; **4** coincidence.

2.45.8: **3** abundance, attendance, dependence, resplendence; **4** correspondence, independence; **5** overabundance, superabundance.

2.45.9: **2** vengeance; **3** allegiance, indulgence; **4** self-indulgence; **5** overindulgence.

2.45.10: **3** convergence, divergence, emergence, insurgence, resurgence.

2.45.11: **3** diligence, indigence, negligence; **4** intelligence, intransigence; **6** counterintelligence.

2.45.12: **2** brilliance, buoyance; **3** abeyance, annoyance, clairvoyance, conveyance, flamboyance.

2.45.13: **2** parlance, semblance, silence, valance, valence, violence; **3** condolence, pestilence, resemblance, surveillance, vigilance, virulence.
See also **10.62.3.**

2.45.14: **2** balance; **3** imbalance, off-balance, unbalance; **4** counterbalance, overbalance.
See also **2.49.**

2.45.15: **3** excellence, insolence, nonchalance, nonviolence, prevalence; **4** ambivalence, benevolence, equivalence, malevolence.

2.45.16: **2** opulence; **3** ambulance, crapulence, flatulence, fraudulence, petulance, truculence, turbulence.

2.45.17: **3** assonance, consonance, dissonance, governance, ordnance, permanence, provenance, resonance.

2.45.18: **3** countenance, maintenance, sustenance; **4** high-maintenance, low-maintenance.

2.45.19: **3** abstinence, ordinance; **4** appurtenance, discountenance, impertinence, incontinence.

2.45.20: **3** dominance, eminence, prominence; **4** predominance.

2.45.21: **2** threepence, tuppence, twopence; **3** comeuppance.

2.45.22: **2** Clarence, difference, entrance, fragrance, hindrance, Terence; **3** aberrance, assurance, concurrence, deterrence, encumbrance, endurance, forbearance, indifference, occurrence, recurrence, remembrance, remonstrance; **4** recalcitrance.
See also **3.40, 10.42.139.**

2.45.23: **3** furtherance, ignorance, reverence, severance, temperance, tolerance, utterance; **4** belligerence, deliverance, exuberance, intemperance, intolerance, irreverence, nonappearance, preponderance, protuberance.

2.45.24: **3** conference, deference, inference, preference, reference, sufferance, transference; **4** circumference, cross-reference, news conference, press

conference; **5** teleconference;
6 videoconference.

2.45.25: **2** clearance; **3** adherence,
appearance, coherence; **4** disappearance,
incoherence, interference, perseverance,
reappearance.

2.45.26: **2** Florence, Lawrence, Torrance;
3 abhorrence, St Lawrence.

2.45.27: **3** insurance; **4** life assurance, life
insurance, reassurance, reinsurance, self-
assurance; **6** National Insurance.

2.45.28: **2** absence, licence, license,
nonsense, nuisance; **3** innocence, no-
nonsense, obeisance, off-licence,
renaissance; **4** reconnaissance.
See also **2.49.**

2.45.29: **2** essence; **3** quiescence,
quintessence, senescence; **4** acquiescence,
detumescence, effervescence,
evanescence, incandescence,
intumescence, luminescence.

2.45.30: **4** adolescence, coalescence,
convalescence, obsolescence.

2.45.31: **3** excrescence, florescence,
fluorescence; **4** efflorescence,
phosphorescence.

2.45.32: **3** reticence; **4** beneficence,
concupiscence, magnificence, maleficence,
munificence, reminiscence.

2.45.33: **2** sentence; **3** acceptance,
acquaintance, death sentence, importance,
impotence, reluctance, repentance;
4 nonacceptance, self-importance.

2.45.34: **2** pittance, quittance;
3 admittance, competence, penitence,
remittance; **4** capacitance, incompetence,
inheritance.

2.45.35: **2** Constance, instance,
substance; **3** circumstance, Lake
Constance.
See also **10.62.3.**

2.45.36: **2** distance; **3** long-distance,
outdistance; **4** middle-distance, spitting
distance.

2.45.37: **3** assistance, insistence,
persistence, subsistence.

2.45.38: **3** existence, resistance;
4 coexistence, nonexistence, sales
resistance; **5** passive resistance.

2.45.39: **2** grievance; **3** connivance,
contrivance, observance, relevance;
4 irrelevance, nonobservance.

2.45.40: **2** sequence; **3** consequence,
eloquence; **4** grandiloquence,
inconsequence, magniloquence.

2.45.41: **2** presence; **3** cognisance,
complaisance, malfeasance;
4 recognisance.

2.46: **2** oddments; **3** battlements,
blandishments, rudiments;
4 accoutrements, Ten Commandments.

2.47: **2** merchant, trenchant, unguent;
3 doom merchant.

2.47.1: **3** ambient, deviant, gradient,
lenient, prescient, presentient, radiant,
sapient, sentient, transient; **4** convenient,
incipient, insouciant, omniscient,
percipient, recipient, subservient;
5 inconvenient.

2.47.2: **4** expedient, ingredient, obedient;
5 disobedient.

2.47.3: **3** brilliant, salient, suppliant;
4 defoliant, ebullient, emollient,
exfoliant, resilient.

2.47.4: **3** miscreant, nutrient, orient,
prurient, recreant, variant; **4** disorient,
luxuriant.
See also **10.2.85.**

2.47.5: **2** fluent, truant; **3** affluent,
congruent, constituent, effluent, pursuant;
4 incongruent.

2.47.6: **2** lambent; **3** absorbent,
incumbent, recumbent.

2.47.7: **2** ardent, hadn't, mordant, needn't,
pedant, prudent, rodent, strident, student,
trident, verdant; **3** concordant, decadent,
discordant, imprudent, precedent;
4 antecedent, fire-retardant, flame-
retardant.

2.47.8: **2** didn't; **3** president, resident;
4 vice-president.

2.47.9: **3** confident, diffident; **4** self-
confident; **5** overconfident.

2.47.10: **3** accident, dissident, incident,
occident, oxidant, precedent; **4** coincident;
5 antioxidant.

2.47.11: **3** evident, provident;
4 improvident, self-evident.

2.47.12: **2** couldn't, shouldn't, wouldn't;
3 impudent.

2.47.13: **2** fondant; **3** abundant,
despondent, redundant, respondent;
4 correspondent; **5** superabundant.

2.47.14: **3** ascendant, defendant,
descendant, resplendent, transcendent.

2.47.15: 2 pendant, pendent; 3 dependant, dependent; 4 independent; 5 interdependent.

2.47.16: 3 attendant, intendant; 4 flight attendant; 5 superintendent.

2.47.17: 2 infant; 3 elephant, Oliphant, sycophant, triumphant.

2.47.18: 3 arrogant, elegant, litigant, termagant; 4 extravagant, inelegant. *See also* **9.14.93**.

2.47.19: 2 argent, cogent, pageant, regent, sergeant; 3 drill sergeant, indulgent; 5 overindulgent.

2.47.20: 2 agent; 3 newsagent, reagent; 4 double agent, raising agent, secret agent.

2.47.21: 2 urgent; 3 detergent, divergent, emergent, insurgent, resurgent.

2.47.22: 3 diligent, indigent, negligent; 4 intelligent, intransigent; 5 unintelligent.

2.47.23: 2 plangent, pungent, stringent, tangent; 3 astringent, contingent, cotangent.

2.47.24: 2 brilliant, buoyant, mayn't, poignant; 3 clairvoyant, flamboyant.

2.47.25: 2 bacchant, piquant, secant, vacant; 3 Tradescant.

2.47.26: 3 applicant, lubricant, mendicant, predicant, predikant, supplicant; 4 communicant, intoxicant, significant; 5 insignificant.

2.47.27: 2 coolant, sealant, silent, talent, violent; 3 appellant, assailant, inhalant, propellant, repellent, virulent; 4 monovalent, nonviolent.

2.47.28: 3 excellent, flagellant, indolent, insolent, nonchalant, redolent, somnolent; 6 anticoagulant.

2.47.29: 3 prevalent; 4 ambivalent, benevolent, equivalent, malevolent.

2.47.30: 3 jubilant, pestilent, sibilant, vigilant.

2.47.31: 3 corpulent, flatulent, fraudulent, opulent, petulant, postulant, stimulant, succulent, truculent, turbulent; 6 anticoagulant.

2.47.32: 2 clement, dormant, garment, Lamont, moment, virement; 3 embankment, employment, endearment, endowment, enjoyment, impairment, inclement, informant, interment, preferment, procurement, requirement, retirement; 4 undergarment, unemployment; 5 spur-of-the-moment.

2.47.33: 3 adamant, armament, filament, firmament, ligament, liniment, measurement, ornament, parliament, sacrament, temperament, tenement, tournament, vehement, wonderment; 4 bewilderment, disarmament, disfigurement, lineament, medicament, predicament; 6 Member of Parliament. *See also* **10.2.86**.

2.47.34: 3 betterment, testament; 4 accoutrement, New Testament, Old Testament.

2.47.35: 2 claimant, payment, raiment; 3 down payment, prepayment, repayment.

2.47.36: 3 agreement, merriment; 4 disagreement, trade agreement; 6 gentleman's agreement.

2.47.37: 3 element, regiment, sentiment; 4 presentiment; 5 accompaniment. *See also* **10.2.86**.

2.47.38: 3 condiment, pediment, rudiment; 4 embodiment, impediment, sediment.

2.47.39: 3 complement, compliment, implement, supplement.

2.47.40: 3 detriment, excrement, increment, nutriment; 4 experiment.

2.47.41: 3 argument, document, instrument, monument; 4 emolument, integument. *See also* **10.2.86**.

2.47.42: 2 oddment; 3 amendment, bombardment, commandment, secondment; 4 First Amendment.

2.47.43: 2 figment, fragment, pigment, segment. *See also* **10.2.86**.

2.47.44: 2 judgment; 3 arrangement, derangement, engagement, enlargement, estrangement, infringement, Last Judgment, misjudgment; 4 Day of Judgment, disengagement.

2.47.45: 3 abridgment, management; 4 acknowledgment, discouragement, disparagement, encouragement, mismanagement.

2.47.46: 2 ailment, concealment; 3 annulment, curtailment, enrolment, fulfilment, instalment.

2.47.47: 3 devilment, puzzlement, settlement; 4 disablement, disgruntlement, embezzlement, entanglement, entitlement.

2.47.48: **3** adjournment, adornment, atonement, cantonment, discernment, internment, postponement.

2.47.49: **3** government; **4** abandonment, apportionment, enlightenment, environment, imprisonment, self-government; **5** disillusionment, head of government.

2.47.50: **3** arraignment, attainment, containment; **4** edutainment, entertainment, infotainment.

2.47.51: **3** alignment, assignment, confinement, consignment, refinement.

2.47.52: **2** shipment; **3** encampment, entrapment, equipment, escarpment; **4** development.

2.47.53: **3** assessment, disbursement, endorsement, enforcement, enticement, harassment, inducement; **4** advertisement, embarrassment, reinforcement; **7** classified advertisement.

2.47.54: **2** basement, casement; **3** debasement, defacement; **4** bargain-basement.

I was lying in a burned out basement
With the full moon in my eyes
I was hoping for replacement
When the sun burst through the sky.
(Neil Young)

2.47.55: **2** placement; **3** displacement, emplacement, outplacement, replacement.

2.47.56: **3** advancement, announcement, commencement, enhancement, pronouncement.

2.47.57: **3** banishment, blandishment, nourishment, punishment, refreshment; **4** accomplishment, astonishment, embellishment, establishment.

2.47.58: **2** fitment; **3** abutment, allotment, apartment, assortment, commitment, compartment, comportment, department, deportment, enactment, excitement, incitement, indictment, recruitment.

2.47.59: **2** statement; **3** abatement; **4** overstatement, understatement.

2.47.60: **2** treatment; **3** ill-treatment, maltreatment, mistreatment.

2.47.61: **2** ointment; **3** appointment, contentment, enchantment, resentment; **4** disappointment, disenchantment.

2.47.62: **2** vestment; **3** adjustment, divestment, enlistment, investment; **4** disinvestment.

2.47.63: **2** catchment, parchment; **3** attachment, detachment, impeachment.

2.47.64: **2** movement, pavement; **3** achievement, bereavement, improvement, involvement.

2.47.65: **2** easement; **3** amazement, amusement, appeasement; **4** aggrandisement, enfranchisement.

2.47.66: **2** pennant, remnant; **3** complainant.

2.47.67: **3** assonant, consonant, covenant, dissonant, immanent, permanent, resonant; **4** impermanent.

2.47.68: **2** tenant, Tennant; **3** lieutenant, subtenant; **4** sitting tenant, sublieutenant.

2.47.69: **3** dominant, eminent, imminent, prominent, ruminant; **4** contaminant, determinant, predominant, pre-eminent.

2.47.70: **3** abstinent, continent, pertinent; **4** impertinent, incontinent, subcontinent.

2.47.71: **3** component, exponent, opponent, proponent.

2.47.72: **2** pregnant, stagnant; **3** indignant, malignant, repugnant.

2.47.73: **2** flippant, rampant, serpent; **3** occupant, sea serpent; **4** participant.

2.47.74: **2** different, entrant, hydrant, quadrant, torrent, tyrant, vibrant, warrant; **3** abhorrent, aspirant, celebrant, indifferent; **4** recalcitrant.
See also **10.2.82**.

2.47.75: **2** arrant, Tarrant; **3** apparent, transparent.

2.47.76: **3** colourant, cormorant, ignorant, reverent, tolerant; **4** belligerent, deodorant, expectorant, exuberant, intolerant, irreverent, itinerant, preponderant, protuberant, refrigerant; **5** antiperspirant.
See also **9.14.93**.

2.47.77: **2** parent; **3** godparent, grandparent, stepparent; **4** single parent.

2.47.78: **2** errant; **3** aberrant, deterrent, inherent, knight errant, knight-errant.

2.47.79: **3** adherent, coherent, inherent; **4** incoherent.

2.47.80: **2** currant, current; **3** blackcurrant, concurrent, crosscurrent, recurrent, redcurrant; **4** undercurrent.

2.47.81: **2** flagrant, fragrant, migrant, vagrant; **3** emigrant, immigrant.

2.47.82: **2** absent, accent, decent, docent, mustn't, nascent, recent, Vincent; **3** adjacent, complacent, conversant,

indecent, innocent, relaxant, renascent, translucent; **5** anticonvulsant.
See also **10.2.85**.

2.47.83: **3** incessant, pubescent, quiescent, senescent, tumescent; **4** acquiescent, adolescent, convalescent, effervescent, evanescent, incandescent, iridescent, obsolescent, opalescent, prepubescent, viridescent.
See also **9.14.93**.

2.47.84: **3** depressant, fluorescent, putrescent, suppressant; **4** Fertile Crescent, phosphorescent; **5** antidepressant.

2.47.85: **3** reticent; **4** beneficent, magnificent, maleficent, munificent, reminiscent.

2.47.86: **2** ancient, patient, quotient, sentient; **3** impatient, inpatient, insentient, outpatient; **4** rubefacient; **5** abortifacient.
See also **9.14.93**.

2.47.87: **3** deficient, efficient, proficient, sufficient; **4** coefficient, inefficient, insufficient, self-sufficient.
See also **9.14.93**.

2.47.88: **2** blatant, latent, mightn't, mutant, oughtn't, patent, potent; **3** accountant, adjutant, combatant, consultant, expectant, exultant, important, impotent, pollutant, reactant, reluctant, repentant, resultant; **4** disinfectant, noncombatant, omnipotent, self-important, unimportant, unrepentant.
See also **9.14.94, 10.2.82**.

2.47.89: **3** competent, hesitant, irritant, militant, penitent; **4** concomitant, exorbitant, impenitent, incompetent, inhabitant, intermittent.

2.47.90: **2** constant, instant, sextant; **3** contestant, inconstant; **4** decongestant.

2.47.91: **2** distant; **3** existent, Protestant, resistant; **4** coexistent, equidistant, nonexistent.

2.47.92: **3** assistant, consistent, insistent, persistent; **4** inconsistent; **6** personal assistant.
See also **9.14.94**.

2.47.93: **2** convent, haven't, savant, solvent; **3** insolvent, relevant; **4** irrelevant.

2.47.94: **2** fervent, servant; **3** maidservant, manservant, observant; **4** civil servant, public servant, unobservant.

2.47.95: **2** frequent; **3** consequent, delinquent, eloquent, infrequent, subsequent; **4** grandiloquent.

2.47.96: **2** doesn't, hasn't, isn't, wasn't; **3** cognisant, complaisant, recusant.

2.47.97: **2** crescent, peasant, pheasant, pleasant, present; **3** Red Crescent, unpleasant; **4** omnipresent.
See also **9.14.93, 10.2.85**.

2.48: **2** billionth, seventh, thousandth; **3** eleventh, millionth, trillionth, zillionth.

2.49: **1** canst; **2** balanced, licensed; **3** unbalanced, unlicensed, well-balanced; **4** experienced; **5** inexperienced.
See also **2.45.3, 2.45.14, 2.45.28**.

2.50: **1** viands; **2** badlands, Edmonds, Edmunds, seconds, Simmonds, thousands, wetlands; **5** hundreds-and-thousands.
See also **2.44.3**.

2.50.1: **2** Docklands, lowlands, Midlands, uplands; **3** Netherlands.

2.50.2: **2** highlands; **4** Aran Islands, Faeroe Islands, Falkland Islands, Leeward Islands, Orkney Islands, Shetland Islands, Virgin Islands, Windward Islands; **5** Canary Islands, Madeira Islands, Nicobar Islands, Ryukyu Islands; **6** Balearic Islands, Galapagos Islands, Ionian Islands, Mariana Islands, Turks and Caicos Islands; **8** Wallis and Futuna Islands.

2.51: **1** irons; **2** Athens, children's, Evans, evens, Gibbons, heavens, Lutyens, millions, mountains, Parsons, Rubens, Sirens, Stephens, Stevens, woollens; **3** environs, Gay Gordons, Kew Gardens, Orléans, provisions, St Helens, zillions; **4** Brecon Beacons, Corinthians, nether regions, New Orleans, Philippians, shenanigans; **5** Thessalonians.
See also **2.43.322, 2.43.336, 10.31.27, 12.9**.

2.51.1: **2** Clemens, commons, Simons, summons; **4** House of Commons; **6** delirium tremens.
See also **2.43.79**.

2.51.2: **2** notions, rations, ructions, sanctions; **3** ablutions, aspersions, Colossians, contractions, conventions, convulsions, dimensions, Ephesians, iron rations, precautions, proportions; **4** quarter sessions.
See also **2.43.137, 2.43.250, 2.43.251, 2.43.263, 2.43.276, 2.43.278, 2.43.280, 2.43.283**.

2.51.3: **3** Galatians; **4** Lamentations, machinations, ministrations, palpitations, regulations, relations; **5** accommodations, communications, congratulations, negotiations, United Nations; **7** telecommunications.
See also **2.43.144, 2.43.156, 2.43.168, 2.43.169.**

2.51.4: **3** conditions, munitions; **4** acquisitions; **5** working conditions.
See also **2.43.239, 2.43.248.**

2.52: **2** Aesop, bishop, catsup, hyssop, ketchup; **3** archbishop.

2.52.1: **2** gallop, Gallup, julep, scallop; **3** develop, envelop; **4** redevelop.
See also **2.53, 10.42.104.**

2.52.2: **2** dollop, lollop, scallop, trollop, Trollope, wallop; **3** codswallop.
See also **10.42.104.**

2.52.3: **2** chirrup, Europe, golden syrup, stirrup, syrup; **4** maple syrup.

2.53: **2** scalloped; **3** developed; **4** undeveloped; **5** overdeveloped, underdeveloped.
See also **2.52.1.**

2.54: **1** us; **2** Jesus, joyous, Kansas; **3** Alcaeus, Linnaeus, Matthias, rebellious, Tobias; **4** Menelaus.

2.54.1: **3** aqueous, copious, dubious, Gropius, impious, nauseous, Orpheus, scabious, Vilnius; **4** abstemious, amphibious, obsequious, Prometheus; **5** impecunious.
See also **2.54.84, 8.13.**

2.54.2: **3** odious, radius, studious, tedious, Thaddaeus; **4** commodious, melodious; **5** incommodious.

2.54.3: **3** hideous; **4** fastidious, insidious, invidious, perfidious.

2.54.4: **3** alias, bilious, Delius, malleus, nucleus; **4** Aurelius, Cornelius, punctilious, Sibelius; **5** supercilious, terra nullius.
See also **2.54.84.**

2.54.5: **3** Aeneas, igneous, ligneous, Linnaeus; **4** Arrhenius, erroneous, euphonious, Suetonius; **5** ignominious, miscellaneous.

2.54.6: **4** extraneous, spontaneous; **5** instantaneous, simultaneous, subcutaneous; **6** contemporaneous, extemporaneous.

2.54.7: **3** genius; **4** ingenious; **5** homogeneous; **6** heterogeneous.

2.54.8: **4** harmonious; **5** acrimonious, ceremonious, inharmonious, parsimonious, sanctimonious; **6** unceremonious.

2.54.9: **3** Darius, pancreas, Piraeus, Sirius, vitreous; **4** delirious, illustrious, industrious, injurious, lugubrious, salubrious; **5** insalubrious.

2.54.10: **3** various; **4** Aquarius, gregarious, hilarious, nefarious, precarious, vicarious; **5** multifarious, Sagittarius, Stradivarius.

2.54.11: **3** serious; **4** imperious, mysterious, Tiberias, Tiberius; **5** deleterious.
See also **2.54.84.**

2.54.12: **3** Boreas, glorious; **4** censorious, inglorious, laborious, notorious, uproarious, vainglorious, victorious; **5** meritorious.

2.54.13: **3** curious, furious, spurious; **4** incurious, luxurious, penurious, sulphureous.

2.54.14: **3** Cassius, Celsius, gaseous, nauseous, Perseus, Theseus; **4** Odysseus.

2.54.15: **3** beauteous, bounteous, courteous, duteous, gluteus, piteous, plenteous; **4** discourteous, Gerontius.

2.54.16: **3** devious, envious, obvious, pervious, previous; **4** impervious, lascivious, oblivious, Vesuvius.
See also **2.54.84.**

2.54.17: **3** congruous; **4** incongruous, mellifluous, superfluous.

2.54.18: **3** arduous, fatuous, sensuous, sinuous; **4** ambiguous, deciduous, incestuous; **5** discontinuous.

2.54.19: **4** innocuous, perspicuous, promiscuous; **5** inconspicuous.

2.54.20: **3** strenuous, tenuous; **4** ingenuous; **5** disingenuous.

2.54.21: **3** sumptuous, tortuous; **4** impetuous, presumptuous, tempestuous.

2.54.22: **2** bulbous, rebus; **3** arquebus, Barabbas, Barnabas, Erebus, incubus, omnibus, succubus, syllabus.

2.54.23: **2** nimbus, rhombus, thrombus; **3** Columbus; **5** cumulonimbus.

2.54.24: **2** Indus, Judas, Midas; **3** exodus, hazardous, horrendous, solidus, stupendous, tremendous.

2.54.25: **2** doofus, Dreyfus, preface, typhus; **3** amorphous; **4** polymorphous.

2.54.26: 2 Argus, bogus, Fergus, Tagus; 3 Las Vegas; 4 cunnilingus, homozygous; 5 heterozygous.

2.54.27: 4 analogous, asparagus, homologous, oesophagus, sarcophagus; 5 Areopagus.

2.54.28: 2 Angus, fungus; 3 humongous; 4 beefsteak fungus; 5 Aberdeen Angus.

2.54.29: 2 gorgeous; 3 egregious, litigious, prestigious, prodigious, religious; 4 irreligious, sacrilegious, tautologous.

2.54.30: 2 magus; 3 contagious, courageous, outrageous; 4 advantageous; 5 disadvantageous.

2.54.31: 2 Bacchus, bronchus, carcass, caucus, circus, coccus, glaucous, Gracchus, incus, raucous, ruckus; 3 abacus, Atticus, Caracas, Damascus, Spartacus; 4 Caractacus, Copernicus, flying circus, Leviticus, streptococcus, umbilicus.

2.54.32: 2 crocus, focus, locus; 3 soft focus; 4 hocus-pocus. *See also* **2.55.**

2.54.33: 2 Lucas, mucous, mucus, Sukkoth.

2.54.34: 2 discus, viscous; 3 hibiscus, meniscus.

2.54.35: 2 ageless, airless, Alice, careless, cashless, changeless, cheerless, clueless, Douglas, fearless, flawless, goalless, guileless, hairless, jealous, jobless, joyless, lawless, legless, lifeless, matchless, noiseless, parlous, peerless, powerless, scoreless, selfless, Silas, solace, soulless, speechless, starless, stylus, tireless, treeless, wireless, zealous; 3 Catullus, garrulous, Lucullus, meaningless, querulous; 4 gladiolus, overzealous. *See also* **2.54.85.**

2.54.36: 2 Callas, callous, callus, Dallas, palace, phallus.
They're changing guard at Buckingham Palace—
Christopher Robin went down with Alice.
Alice is marrying one of the guard.
'A soldier's life is terrible hard,'
Says Alice.
(A. A. Milne)
See also **2.54.85.**

2.54.37: 3 Aeschylus, colourless, featureless, frivolous, humourless, libellous, lustreless, marvellous, measureless, motherless, Nicholas, numberless, obelus, paperless, perilous,

scurrilous, Tantalus; 4 anomalous, Bucephalus, characterless, Los Angeles; 5 hydrocephalus.

2.54.38: 3 Daedalus, odourless, rudderless, scandalous.

2.54.39: 3 Angelus, bacillus, merciless, nautilus, penniless, pitiless.

2.54.40: 3 bibulous, calculus, fabulous, nebulous, populace, populous, scrupulous; 4 convolvulus, fantabulous, meticulous, miraculous, ridiculous, unscrupulous. *See also* **2.54.85.**

2.54.41: 3 credulous, pendulous, sedulous, stridulous; 4 acidulous, incredulous.

2.54.42: 3 cumulus, Romulus, stimulus, tremulous, tumulus; 5 altocumulus, cirrocumulus, stratocumulus.

2.54.43: 2 bloodless, childless, cloudless, cordless, godless, headless, heedless, needless, seedless, wordless; 3 regardless; 4 irregardless. *See also* **9.14.83.**

2.54.44: 2 boundless, endless, friendless, groundless, landless, mindless, soundless, windlass, windless. *See also* **9.14.83.**

2.54.45: 2 backless, feckless, luckless, necklace, reckless, smokeless, thankless. *See also* **2.54.85, 9.14.83.**

2.54.46: 2 charmless, dreamless, formless, gormless, harmless, homeless, rimless, seamless, timeless; 3 bottomless, fathomless, victimless.

2.54.47: 2 aimless, blameless, nameless, shameless. *See also* **2.54.85.**

2.54.48: 2 boneless, brainless, chinless, moonless, painless, sinless, skinless, spineless, stainless, sunless, toneless, tuneless. *See also* **10.31.22.**

2.54.49: 3 motionless; 4 directionless, emotionless, expressionless.

2.54.50: 2 hapless, helpless, hopeless, shapeless, sleepless, strapless, surplus, topless.

2.54.51: 2 baseless, ceaseless, classless, faceless, graceless, priceless, senseless, sexless, useless, voiceless; 3 defenceless, purposeless, remorseless, Wenceslas. *See also* **2.54.85.**

2.54.52: 2 artless, atlas, cutlass, doubtless, faultless, flightless, fruitless, guiltless, gutless, heartless, listless, restless, rootless, shiftless, sightless, spotless, stateless, tactless, tasteless, thoughtless, weightless; **3** effortless. *See also* **2.54.85, 9.14.83.**

2.54.53: **2** shitless, witless; **3** limitless, profitless, spiritless.

2.54.54: **2** countless, dauntless, pointless; **3** relentless.

2.54.55: **2** breathless, deathless, faithless, mirthless, ruthless, toothless, worthless. *See also* **2.54.85, 9.14.83.**

2.54.56: **2** loveless, nerveless, sleeveless; **3** motiveless.

2.54.57: **2** grimace, humus, litmus, Primus, Remus, Thermos, Thomas, Titmuss, Xmas; **3** Candlemas, chiasmus, enormous, Erasmus, ginormous, John Thomas, Las Palmas, Martinmas, Michaelmas, posthumous, Septimus, strabismus; **4** cantus firmus, doubting Thomas, Nicodemus, Nostradamus, Polyphemus, polysemous, Uncle Remus; **6** pontifex maximus.

2.54.58: **3** blasphemous, infamous, venomous; **4** autonomous, monogamous; **5** hippopotamus, hypothalamus.

2.54.59: **2** famous, Seamus; **3** world-famous; **4** ignoramus, Nostradamus.

2.54.60: **3** animus; **4** anonymous, eponymous, magnanimous, synonymous, unanimous; **5** pusillanimous. *See also* **9.14.81.**

2.54.61: **2** Christmas, isthmus, Xmas; **4** Father Christmas.

2.54.62: **2** Agnes, anus, clearness, closeness, coarseness, crudeness, Cygnus, dampness, deafness, Faunus, genus, glibness, heinous, Janus, menace, muchness, numbness, paleness, richness, roughness, rudeness, sharpness, smoothness, smugness, soreness, Souness, staleness, stiffness, vagueness; **3** Adonis, aloofness, Avernus, humbleness, idleness, nothingness, subtleness, uniqueness, willingness; **4** unwillingness. *See also* **1.20, 2.37.111, 3.42, 5.30.8, 6.4, 9.36.2, 10.0, 10.6.3, 10.42.73, 10.42.133, 14.42.3, 19.45, 19.52.1, 20.4.3, 20.7, 20.24, 22.17.9, 22.19.**

2.54.63: **3** baroness, bitterness, cavernous, cleverness, eagerness, gluttonous, governess, otherness, poisonous, ravenous, synchronous,

tenderness, tetanus, treasonous, Uranus, villainous, wilderness; **4** androgynous, asynchronous, autochthonous, cacophonous, diaphanous, endogenous, erogenous, indigenous, monotonous, Oceanus, togetherness. *See also* **2.6.22, 2.9.4, 2.22.34, 2.25.6, 9.16.3.**

2.54.64: **2** bareness, fairness, rareness; **3** awareness, unfairness. *See also* **4.3.**

2.54.65: **2** genus, venous, Venus; **3** canniness, edginess, glitziness, gloominess, itchiness, perkiness, quirkiness, shabbiness, showiness, stickiness, subgenus, touchiness; **4** cursoriness, intravenous, slipperiness; **5** creditworthiness, perfunctoriness. *See also* **9.6.1, 9.13.6, 9.13.8, 9.19.30, 9.24.**

2.54.66: **3** giddiness, handiness, hardiness, readiness, ruddiness, seediness, steadiness. *See also* **9.7.5, 9.7.10, 9.7.20.**

2.54.67: **3** cleanliness, friendliness, godliness, holiness, liveliness, Silenus, silliness, wiliness; **4** unfriendliness, unworldliness. *See also* **9.14.38, 9.14.61, 9.14.97.**

2.54.68: **2** penis; **3** Campinas, happiness, sleepiness; **4** unhappiness. *See also* **9.18.1, 9.18.7.**

2.54.69: **3** emptiness, frostiness, loftiness, lustiness, mistiness, scantiness. *See also* **9.22.85.**

2.54.70: **3** clumsiness, dizziness, fuzziness, haziness, nosiness, queasiness, sleaziness. *See also* **9.27.3, 9.27.4, 9.27.6, 9.27.7, 9.27.9.**

2.54.71: **2** Guinness; **3** gangrenous, glutinous, mountainous, mutinous, ominous, ruinous; **4** gelatinous, libidinous, vertiginous; **5** cartilaginous, mucilaginous, multitudinous, oleaginous. *See also* **9.14.81.**

2.54.72: **3** luminous, numinous, terminus, verminous; **4** coterminous, leguminous, voluminous.

2.54.73: **2** Highness, minus, shyness, sinus, slyness, vinous; **3** Aquinas; **4** Royal Highness. *See also* **11.5, 11.10.**

2.54.74: **2** bonus, Cronus, Jonas, onus, slowness; **3** Tithonus; **4** no claims bonus.

2.54.75: **2** badness, boldness, coldness, goodness, madness, redness, sadness, shrewdness, tiredness; **3** forwardness; **5** honest-to-goodness.
See also **19.35, 22.17.9.**

2.54.76: **3** candidness, crookedness, doggedness, vividness, wickedness, wretchedness; **4** bigheadedness, broadmindedness, cold-heartedness, farsightedness, hardheartedness, levelheadedness, long-sightedness, longwindedness, near-sightedness, preparedness, quick-wittedness, softheartedness, warm-bloodedness, warmheartedness; **5** narrow-mindedness, singlemindedness, underhandedness.
See also **2.33.20, 10.2, 10.2.23, 10.2.25, 10.2.59.**

2.54.77: **2** blandness, blindness, blondness, fondness, kindness, soundness; **3** night blindness; **4** loving kindness.
See also **1.22.3, 11.28.4, 13.23, 16.11.8.**

2.54.78: **2** blackness, darkness, likeness, sickness, thickness, weakness; **4** morning sickness, motion sickness, Prince of Darkness, sleeping sickness.

2.54.79: **2** coolness, dullness, illness, stillness, wellness.
See also **22.22.4.**

2.54.80: **2** fullness; **3** artfulness, carefulness, forcefulness, helpfulness, mindfulness, tastefulness, thoughtfulness, usefulness, watchfulness; **4** dutifulness, resourcefulness, unfaithfulness.
See also **2.37.121, 2.37.129, 2.37.130, 2.37.134.**

2.54.81: **2** calmness, dimness, firmness, sameness, Somnus; **3** alumnus; **4** quarrelsomeness.
See also **3.31, 7.18.1, 10.26.**

2.54.82: **2** cleanness, keenness, meanness, plainness; **3** barrenness, drunkenness, mundaneness, openness, stubbornness, sullenness, wantonness; **4** unevenness.
See also **2.43.74, 2.43.75, 2.43.306, 2.43.322, 5.35.5, 9.43.4, 9.43.7.**

2.54.83: **3** nervousness; **4** covetousness, lecherousness, unctuousness; **5** ingenuousness, solicitousness; **6** unambiguousness.
See also **2.54.136, 15.10.**

2.54.84: **3** seriousness; **4** biliousness; **5** lasciviousness, obliviousness, obsequiousness, uxoriousness.
See also **2.54.1, 2.54.4, 2.54.11, 2.54.16.**

2.54.85: **3** artlessness, callousness, carelessness, lawlessness, recklessness, selflessness, senselessness, shamelessness, thoughtlessness, worthlessness; **4** scrupulousness.
See also **2.54.35, 2.54.36, 2.54.40, 2.54.45, 2.54.47, 2.54.51, 2.54.52, 2.54.55.**

2.54.86: **3** preciousness, viciousness; **4** facetiousness, officiousness, salaciousness, voraciousness.
See also **2.54.116, 2.54.119, 2.54.121.**

2.54.87: **3** consciousness; **4** licentiousness, pretentiousness, selfconsciousness, unconsciousness; **5** stream of consciousness.
See also **2.54.128.**

2.54.88: **2** aptness, bluntness, brightness, deftness, faintness, fastness, greatness, softness, sweetness, wetness; **3** adroitness, astuteness, correctness, directness, politeness, promptness, quietness, remoteness, robustness, steadfastness; **4** impoliteness, incompleteness, unpleasantness.
See also **3.47.1, 5.40, 11.36.7, 11.36.16, 12.13, 13.20, 18.16, 19.47.6, 20.33, 20.44.1, 22.34.2.**

2.54.89: **2** fitness, witness; **3** eyewitness, false witness; **5** Jehovah's Witness.

2.54.90: **2** suaveness; **3** forgiveness; **4** incisiveness, offensiveness, permissiveness, persuasiveness, submissiveness.
See also **10.61.2, 10.61.7, 10.61.8, 10.61.13.**

2.54.91: **4** attentiveness, attractiveness, distinctiveness, effectiveness, inventiveness, perceptiveness, productiveness, seductiveness.
See also **10.61.39, 10.61.40, 10.61.43, 10.61.49, 10.61.51.**

2.54.92: **2** business; **3** e-business, nonbusiness, show business; **4** agribusiness, monkey business.

2.54.93: **2** carpus, corpus, lupus, opus, porpoise, tapas, trespass; **3** octopus, Oedipus, platypus; **4** magnum opus, metacarpus; **5** duck-billed platypus, habeas corpus.
See also **10.42.133.**

2.54.94: 2 purpose; 3 all-purpose, cross-purpose; 4 multipurpose; 5 general purpose.

2.54.95: 2 campus, compass, grampus, pampas, pompous, rumpus; 3 encompass, Olympus; 4 hippocampus, Mount Olympus. *See also* **2.55.**

2.54.96: 2 cirrus, Eurus, ferrous, fibrous, harass, Horace, scabrous, terrace, tigress, walrus, wondrous; 3 anhydrous, Arcturus, Carreras, chivalrous, desirous, embarrass, Honduras, ludicrous; 4 millionairess, unchivalrous. *See also* **1.38, 2.55.1, 10.42.133.**

2.54.97: 3 barbarous, Cerberus, dangerous, dolorous, Lazarus, phosphorus, rigorous, sulphurous, valorous, vigorous; 4 Epicurus, precancerous, Pythagoras, rhinoceros.

2.54.98: 3 murderous, odorous, Pandarus, ponderous, slanderous, thunderous; 4 malodorous.

2.54.99: 4 coniferous, splendiferous, vociferous; 5 carboniferous, odoriferous.

2.54.100: 3 decorous, Icarus, rancorous; 4 cantankerous, indecorous. *See also* **2.12.24.**

2.54.101: 3 amorous, clamorous, glamorous, humerus, humorous, numerous, timorous.

2.54.102: 3 generous, onerous, sonorous; 4 ungenerous.

2.54.103: 3 Bosporus, prosperous, vaporous; 4 obstreperous, viviparous. *See also* **2.18.2.**

2.54.104: 3 boisterous, dexterous, traitorous, uterus; 4 adulterous, preposterous.

2.54.105: 3 lecherous, rapturous, torturous, treacherous; 4 adventurous; 5 unadventurous.

2.54.106: 4 cadaverous, carnivorous, herbivorous, omnivorous. *See also* **14.16.**

2.54.107: 2 Cyrus, virus; 3 papyrus; 4 antivirus, retrovirus; 7 cytomegalovirus.

2.54.108: 2 chorus, Dolores, Horus, porous, Taurus; 3 dawn chorus.

2.54.109: 3 thesaurus; 4 brontosaurus, stegosaurus; 5 apatosaurus, tyrannosaurus.

2.54.110: 2 cypress, Cyprus, empress, leprous.

2.54.111: 2 actress, buttress, citrus, fortress, huntress, mattress, temptress, waitress; 3 enchantress, seductress; 4 flying buttress. *See also* **2.55.1.**

2.54.112: 2 lustrous, monstrous, oestrus, seamstress; 3 disastrous; 4 ambidextrous. *See also* **9.14.85.**

2.54.113: 2 mistress; 3 headmistress, housemistress, postmistress, schoolmistress, toastmistress.

2.54.114: 2 census, Croesus, Knossos, rhesus, tarsus, versus; 3 Caucasus, colossus, consensus, Dionysus, Ephesus, excursus, Manassas, Narcissus, Parnassus, Pegasus; 4 metatarsus, Paracelsus.

2.54.115: 2 nexus, plexus, Texas; 4 solar plexus.

2.54.116: 2 bumptious, captious, cautious, luscious, precious, scrumptious, specious, tortious; 3 atrocious, facetious, ferocious, incautious, Lucretius, precocious, Propertius; 4 semiprecious. *See also* **2.54.86.**

2.54.117: 2 spacious; 3 audacious, capacious, curvaceous, fallacious, herbaceous, loquacious, mendacious, rapacious, sagacious, salacious, sebaceous, vexatious, vivacious; 4 contumacious, efficacious, perspicacious.

2.54.118: 3 Ignatius, pugnacious, tenacious; 4 farinaceous, pertinacious. *See also* **9.14.84.**

2.54.119: 2 gracious; 3 ungracious, veracious, voracious. *See also* **2.54.86.**

2.54.120: 3 Cretaceous, flirtatious; 4 disputatious, ostentatious; 5 unostentatious. *See also* **9.14.84.**

2.54.121: 2 vicious; 3 ambitious, delicious, malicious, officious, pernicious; 5 Golden Delicious, overambitious. *See also* **2.54.86.**

2.54.122: 3 judicious, seditious; 4 expeditious, injudicious. *See also* **9.14.84.**

2.54.123: 3 auspicious, propitious, suspicious; 4 inauspicious, unpropitious.

2.54.124: 3 capricious, lubricious, Mauritius, nutritious; 4 avaricious, meretricious. *See also* **10.50.12.**

2.54.125: 3 factitious, fictitious;
4 adventitious, repetitious, superstitious,
surreptitious.
See also **9.14.84.**

2.54.126: 2 anxious, factious, fractious,
noxious; 3 infectious, obnoxious,
rambunctious.

2.54.127: 3 contentious, licentious,
pretentious, sententious, tendentious;
4 conscientious, unpretentious.

2.54.128: 2 conscious; 3 class-conscious,
self-conscious, subconscious, unconscious;
4 semiconscious, unselfconscious.
See also **2.54.87, 9.14.84.**

2.54.129: 2 Brutus, flatus, foetus, lotus,
Plautus, Plutus, POTUS, Sextus, Titus,
tortoise, Vitus; 3 arbutus, asbestos,
Augustus, boletus, covetous, detritus,
Hephaestus, Miletus, momentous,
portentous, quietus, riotous, senatus;
4 cirrostratus, eucalyptus, giant tortoise,
Herodotus, Pocahontas; 5 serendipitous;
7 coitus interruptus.

2.54.130: 2 status, stratus; 3 hiatus;
4 altostratus, apparatus.

2.54.131: 3 coitus, impetus, tinnitus;
4 calamitous, circuitous, Democritus,
emeritus, fortuitous, gratuitous, Heraclitus,
iniquitous, precipitous, ubiquitous.
See also **9.14.81.**

2.54.132: 3 Tacitus, vomitus;
4 duplicitous, felicitous, necessitous,
solicitous; 5 infelicitous.

2.54.133: 2 cactus, linctus, rictus,
Sanctus; 3 prospectus.

2.54.134: 2 Malthus; 3 acanthus,
prognathous; 4 agapanthus, amaranthus,
polyanthus.

2.54.135: 2 duchess, purchase, righteous;
3 hire purchase, rumbustious, self-
righteous.

2.54.136: 2 canvas, canvass, grievous,
naevus, nervous; 3 mischievous.
See also **2.54.83, 9.14.81.**

2.55: 1 dost, must; 2 August, ballast,
biased, breakfast, calloused, eldest, finest,
focused, greatest, highest, locust, lowest,
provost, shortest, smallest, unbiased;
3 dog's breakfast, earliest, encompassed,
unfocused; 4 English breakfast, wedding
breakfast.
See also **2.54.32, 2.54.95, 12.12.**

2.55.1: 2 buttressed, dearest, harassed,
interest, terraced; 3 disinterest,
embarrassed, self-interest.
See also **1.36.4, 2.54.96, 2.54.111.**

2.56: 1 at; 2 Ansett, Bagehot, comfort,
concert, Connacht, effort, Montfort,
Rupert, stalwart; 3 adequate, candidate,
discomfort, Don Quixote, inchoate;
4 episcopate, inadequate, precipitate;
5 intercollegiate.
See also **9.14.87, 10.2.55, 10.42.144.**

2.56.1: 2 Fiat; 3 deviate, Eliot, idiot,
Juliet, opiate, radiate, roseate, soviet;
4 affiliate, associate, collegiate, immediate,
initiate, licentiate, novitiate;
5 intermediate.
See also **10.2.38.**

2.56.2: 3 Cypriot, Herriot, laureate,
patriot; 4 appropriate, compatriot,
expatriate, inebriate; 5 baccalaureate,
commissariat, inappropriate, Poet
Laureate, proletariat, secretariat.
See also **9.14.87, 10.2.38.**

2.56.3: 3 chariot, Harriet, lariat; 6 Judas
Iscariot.

2.56.4: 2 Stewart, Stuart; 3 graduate,
postgraduate; 4 undergraduate.
See also **10.2.39.**

2.56.5: 1 but; 2 abbot, Cabot, Corbett,
Cuthbert, Herbert, Hubert, Lambert,
Robert, Schubert, sherbet, turbot;
3 celibate, halibut.

2.56.6: 2 Albert, filbert, Gilbert, Talbot;
3 Prince Albert.

2.56.7: 2 agate, argot, braggart, faggot,
ingot, legate, maggot, yoghurt;
3 conjugate, delegate, surrogate.

2.56.8: 2 bigot, frigate, spigot;
3 aggregate, congregate, profligate.

2.56.9: 2 Alcott, ducat, Eckert, Prescott,
Urquhart, wainscot; 3 advocate, collocate,
Nantucket; 5 devil's advocate.

2.56.10: 3 affricate, intricate, predicate,
syndicate; 4 certificate, Connecticut;
5 excommunicate, School Certificate,
share certificate.

2.56.11: 3 complicate, delicate, duplicate,
replicate, triplicate; 4 indelicate.
See also **10.2.43.**

2.56.12: 2 bracelet, doublet, eaglet,
gimlet, goblet, Hamlet, inlet, leaflet,
omelette, pamphlet, piglet, Pilate, ringlet,
singlet, tablet, toilet, Winslett; 3 distillate.

2.56.13: **2** ballot, palate, palette, pallet; **3** cleft palate, hard palate, soft palate; **4** secret ballot.

2.56.14: **3** correlate, coverlet, desolate, isolate; **4** disconsolate.
See also **10.2.44, 10.2.45.**

2.56.15: **2** harlot, scarlet, Scarlett, starlet, varlet; **3** Will Scarlet.

2.56.16: **2** helot, pellet, prelate, zealot.

2.56.17: **2** eyelet, islet, pilot; **3** copilot, test pilot; **4** autopilot.

2.56.18: **2** violet; **3** inviolate; **4** shrinking violet, ultraviolet; **5** African violet.

2.56.19: **3** amulet, consulate, rivulet; **4** articulate, coagulate, ejaculate, immaculate; **5** inarticulate.
See also **10.2.46.**

2.56.20: **2** anklet, booklet, chocolate, circlet, necklet; **3** hot chocolate.

2.56.21: **2** applet, caplet, chaplet, couplet, droplet, template, triplet; **3** quadruplet, quintuplet, sextuplet.

2.56.22: **2** cutlet, flatlet, gauntlet, notelet, platelet, tartlet; **3** nut cutlet.

2.56.23: **2** climate, Dermot, Diarmaid, gamut, Hammett, marmot, summat; **4** microclimate.

2.56.24: **3** animate, proximate, sublimate; **4** approximate, inanimate.
See also **10.2.47.**

2.56.25: **3** estimate, guesstimate, intimate, ultimate; **4** legitimate, penultimate; **5** illegitimate, overestimate, underestimate; **6** antepenultimate.

Farewell! thou art too dear for my possessing,
And like enough thou know'st thy estimate:
The charter of thy worth gives thee releasing;
My bonds in thee are all determinate.
(William Shakespeare)

2.56.26: **2** barnet, Barnett, bonnet, Connacht, cygnet, senate, signet; **3** alternate, designate, impregnate, incarnate; **4** importunate, pomegranate; **5** electromagnet.
See also **10.2.37.**

2.56.27: **3** baronet, definite, fortunate, sultanate; **4** affectionate, indefinite, unfortunate.

2.56.28: **3** passionate; **4** compassionate, dispassionate, extortionate, proportionate; **5** disproportionate.
See also **9.14.88.**

2.56.29: **2** linnet, minute; **3** cabinet, infinite, last minute, obstinate; **4** drinks cabinet, palatinate; **5** filing cabinet, up-to-the-minute.
See also **2.57, 9.14.88.**

2.56.30: **4** coordinate, inordinate, subordinate; **5** insubordinate, superordinate.
See also **2.57, 10.2.49.**

2.56.31: **3** laminate; **4** determinate, discriminate, effeminate; **5** indeterminate, indiscriminate.
See also **10.42.149.**

2.56.32: **2** Bharat, curate, egret, floret, Margaret, nitrate, pirate, secret; **3** aspirate, state secret, top-secret, trade secret, vertebrate; **4** invertebrate.

2.56.33: **2** Barrett, carat, caret, carrot, claret, garret, parrot.

A poet, starving in a garret,
Conning old topics like a parrot,
Invokes his mistress and his muse,
And stays at home for want of shoes.
(Jonathan Swift)

2.56.34: **3** favourite, lacerate, leveret, Margaret, perforate, saturate; **4** commensurate, degenerate, deliberate, elaborate, regenerate, triumvirate; **5** incommensurate, unregenerate; **6** overelaborate.
See also **10.2.53.**

2.56.35: **3** moderate; **4** confederate, considerate, immoderate; **5** inconsiderate.

2.56.36: **3** emirate, numerate; **4** conglomerate, innumerate.

2.56.37: **3** aspirate, corporate, desperate, disparate, separate, temperate; **4** incorporate, intemperate.
See also **2.57, 9.14.89.**

2.56.38: **3** doctorate, literate; **4** computerate, illiterate, inveterate, preliterate; **6** computer-literate.

2.56.39: **4** directorate, electorate, inspectorate, protectorate.

2.56.40: **3** accurate, obdurate; **4** barbiturate, inaccurate.
See also **9.14.89.**

2.56.41: **2** Calvert, covert, covet, culvert, divot, pivot, private, privet.
See also **2.57, 10.2.59.**

2.56.42: **2** desert; **4** Gobi Desert;
5 Mojave Desert; **6** Kalahari Desert.
See also **7.29, 10.2.57.**

2.57: **2** giblets, minutes, privates, Roberts;
3 delicates, separates, Tower Hamlets;
4 coordinates, creature comforts,
Massachusetts, particulates.
See also **2.56.29, 2.56.30, 2.56.37, 2.56.41,
5.47.45, 5.47.55, 10.56.25, 22.34.2.**

2.58: **1** hath; **2** Gareth, ha'p'orth,
Hayworth, Howarth, Kenneth, Lambeth,
penn'orth, pennyworth, Sabbath,
Wandsworth, Woolworth; **3** Goliath,
Nazareth; **4** Elisabeth, Elizabeth.

2.58.1: **3** fiftieth, fortieth, ninetieth,
sixtieth, thirtieth, twentieth; **4** seventieth.

2.58.2: **2** bismuth, Bournemouth,
mammoth, Plymouth, Portsmouth,
vermouth; **3** azimuth.

2.59: **1** of, 've; **2** would've; **3** unheard-of,
well-thought-of.

2.60: **1** Briers, pliers, wuz; **2** bathers,
bleachers, boxers, Chambers, Childers,
cobblers, dentures, divers, embers,
features, feelers, gnashers, measures,
Mellors, Messrs, numbers, players, Rivers,
Rodgers, Rogers, Sayers, scissors, Sellers,
Travers, trousers, tweezers, withers;
3 Christophers, Danvers, departures,
forefathers, hairdresser's, leftovers,
Weightwatchers; **4** binoculars,
countermeasures, Himalayas, life sciences.
See also **2.0.1, 2.5.11, 2.5.12, 2.7.3,
2.13.27, 2.20.13, 2.24, 2.25.14, 2.27.8,
2.29.**

2.60.1: **1** does; **2** Borders, cinders,
Flanders, orders, rounders, Sanders;
3 dividers, EastEnders; **4** marching orders,
Space Invaders, starter's orders.
See also **2.6.6, 2.6.8, 2.6.23, 19.4, 22.2.**

2.60.2: **2** joggers, preggers; **3** fish fingers,
green fingers, ironmonger's;
4 butterfingers.
See also **2.9.8, 2.9.12.**

2.60.3: **1** cos, cuz; **2** blinkers, bonkers,
checkers, Chequers, crackers, knickers,
knockers, mockers, starkers, Vickers,
whiskers, workers, Yonkers; **3** cat's
whiskers, French knickers, maracas,
Moluccas; **4** Americas, camiknickers,
knickerbockers.
See also **2.12.2, 2.12.8, 2.12.9, 2.12.17,
2.12.27.**

2.60.4: **1** Ms; **2** bloomers, Chalmers,
swimmers; **3** Bahamas, pyjamas.
See also **2.14.12, 2.14.19.**

2.60.5: **2** cleaners, Connors, honours,
manners, trainers; **3** bad manners, bananas,
frighteners, good manners.
See also **2.15.7, 2.15.9, 2.15.13, 2.15.20,
2.16.**

2.60.6: **2** capers, champers, choppers,
clippers, jodhpurs, papers, poppers,
rompers, vespers; **3** callipers.
See also **2.18.2, 2.18.3, 2.18.8, 2.18.10.**

2.60.7: **2** afters, bitters, fetters, gaiters,
hipsters, jitters, letters, master's, Masters,
Peters, Reuters, tatters, voters, Walters,
Winters; **3** banisters, fajitas, pig's trotters,
secateurs; **6** Angostura bitters.
See also **2.22.12, 2.22.22, 2.22.23, 2.22.34,
2.22.55.**

2.60.8: **2** quarters, Waters;
3 headquarters, headwaters, hindquarters.
See also **2.22.54.**

3.0: **1** aah, aargh, ah, are, shah, yaar, yah;
2 Iyar; **3** Aisha, entrechat, MOR, rufiyaa.
*Twinkle, twinkle, little star,
How I wonder what you are!
Up above the world so high,
Like a diamond in the sky!*
(Jane Taylor)

3.1: **2** ER, PR; **3** caviar, CPR, VCR;
5 UNHCR.

3.2: **1** baa, bah, bar, barre; **2** baba, casbah,
crossbar, crowbar, debar, disbar, Dunbar,
kasbah, Pooh-Bah, rollbar, roo bar,
sandbar, sidebar, toolbar, towbar;
3 calabar, cinnabar, handlebar, isobar,
millibar, minibar, Zanzibar; **4** hors de
combat.
See also **3.21.1, 3.43, 10.42.112.**

3.2.1: **2** Akbar, milk bar, taskbar; **3** public
bar.

3.3: **2** Adar, chadar, Dada, doodah,
Godard, radar, Sardar; **3** A&R, chowkidar,
deodar, havildar, la-di-da, lah-di-dah, objet
d'art, R and R.

3.4: **1** fa, fah, far; **2** afar, Safar, shofar.

3.5: **1** gar; **2** agar, cigar, Degas, Elgar,
gaga, nougat; **4** agar-agar, budgerigar.

3.6: **1** ha, haar, hah; **2** aha, Doha, ha-ha,
hoo-hah; **3** brouhaha, Kandahar, Omaha,
pakeha.

3.7: **1** jar; **2** ajar, jam jar, nightjar; **3** Mason
jar.
See also **10.42.112.**

3.8: **1** car, Carr, scar, ska; **2** boxcar, Dakar, fracas, hire car, in-car, markka, pushcar, railcar, Redcar, Shankar, sheika, sidecar, streetcar, tramcar; **3** advocaat, bubblecar, motorcar, trolley car; **5** Lake Titicaca.

The rich man has his motor-car,
His country and his town estate.
He smokes a fifty-cent cigar
And jeers at Fate.
(Franklin P. Adams)

3.9: **1** blah, la, lah; **2** blah-blah, éclat, galah, hoopla, Lala, mela, scalar, tolar, voilà; **3** Abelard, exemplar, Shangri-la; **5** pain au chocolat.

3.10: **1** ma, mar, Marr; **2** Armagh, Dumas, Fermat, grandma, mama, mamma, Myanmar, Omar, ouma; **3** grandmama, khansama, Panama. *See also* **3.21**.

3.11: **1** nah; **2** Bonnard, dinar, planar, sonar; **3** seminar.

3.12: **1** pa, pah, par, Parr; **2** faux pas, grandpa, oupa, papa.

3.12.1: **1** spa, spar; **2** feldspar, fluorspar.

3.13: **1** bra; **2** Accra, foie gras, hurrah, Marat, Seurat; **3** baccarat, Mardi Gras, registrar, Rivera; **5** pâté de foie gras.

3.14: **1** tzar; **2** pulsar; **4** USSR; **8** Golden Temple of Amritsar.

3.15: **1** ta, tar; **2** attar, catarrh, coal tar, guitar, Qatar, Sita, sitar, Utah; **3** avatar, Bogotá, coup d'état, steak tartare.

3.15.1: **1** star, Starr; **2** All-Star, dark star, daystar, Dog Star, dwarf star, film star, five-star, gold star, lodestar, pole star, pop star; **3** Daily Star, Eurostar, evening star, megastar, morning star, neutron star, superstar; **4** binary star.

Yesterday a child came out to wonder
Caught a dragonfly inside a jar
Fearful when the sky was full of thunder
And tearful at the falling of a star
(Joni Mitchell)

3.16: **1** cha, char; **2** achcha, cha-cha, HR. *See also* **3.21**.

3.17: **2** Navarre; **3** bolivar, Bolívar, cultivar, samovar.

3.18: **1** schwa; **2** Beauvoir, boudoir, bourgeois, pissoir, sang-froid; **3** au revoir, Chihuahua, Côte d'Ivoire, Delacroix, mutawaa, petit pois, Putonghua, reservoir; **4** je ne sais quoi, ménage à trois, petit bourgeois.

3.18.1: **1** Loire; **2** couloir, salwar, shalwar.

3.18.2: **1** moi; **2** chamois, memoir, mwah mwah; **3** aide-mémoire. *See also* **3.58, 9.15.1**.

3.18.3: **1** noir; **2** bete noire, film noir, peignoir, Renoir; **3** café noir.

3.18.4: **2** patois; **3** abattoir, escritoire, repertoire; **4** conservatoire.

3.19: **1** czar, tsar; **2** bazaar, beaux arts, bizarre, Cesar, hussar, huzzah, lazar, quasar; **3** balthazar; **4** kala-azar.

3.20: **1** barb, garb, sahib; **2** bicarb, hijab, memsahib, nawab, Punjab, rhubarb.

3.21: **1** chard, charred, Fahd, hard, marred, shard; **2** blowhard, charade, diehard, Gerard, Goddard, Hoggard, pomade, Riyadh, Stoppard, Trenchard; **3** boulevard. *See also* **3.10, 3.16, 3.22**.

3.21.1: **1** bard, barred; **2** bombard, debarred, tabard; **3** no-holds-barred, zindabad. *See also* **3.2**.

3.21.2: **1** guard; **2** Asgard, blackguard, Bogarde, chainguard, coastguard, faceguard, fireguard, Fishguard, Foot Guard, Home Guard, lifeguard, Life Guard, Midgard, mudguard, off-guard, old guard, rearguard, regard, safeguard, vanguard, Welsh Guard; **3** avant-garde, bodyguard, Coldstream Guard, disregard, Irish Guard, Kierkegaard, self-regard; **4** Grenadier Guard, national guard; **5** Praetorian Guard. *See also* **10.2.4, 10.42.14**.

3.21.3: **1** yard; **2** backyard, barnyard, boatyard, boneyard, churchyard, courtyard, dockyard, farmyard, graveyard, halyard, junkyard, poniard, schoolyard, scrapyard, shipyard, stockyard; **3** knacker's yard, timberyard.

3.21.4: **1** card; **2** court card, discard, face card, flashcard, notecard, Packard, phonecard, placard, postcard, race card, railcard, scorecard, timecard, unscarred, wildcard; **3** credit card, report card, travelcard; **4** identity card, picture-postcard. *See also* **3.22, 10.2.4**.

3.21.5: **1** lard; **2** ballade, Ballard, bollard, mallard, pollard; **3** Abelard, fusillade, interlard.

3.21.6: **2** Barnard, canard, Cunard, poignard; **3** communard, promenade.

3.21.7: **1** Sade; **2** facade, glissade, Hansard, mansard, prasad.

3.21.8: **2** Coulthard, petard, retard, ustad; **3** leotard.
See also **10.2.4.**

3.22: **1** cards, Guards; **2** charades, life guards; **3** house of cards.
See also **3.21, 3.21.4.**

3.23: **1** barf, chaff, laugh, strafe; **2** giraffe; **3** cenotaph, epitaph.
See also **1.5, 3.51.**

3.23.1: **1** half; **2** behalf, flyhalf, left half, wing half; **3** better half, centre half, half-and-half, other half.
See also **3.56.**

3.23.2: **1** calf, scarf; **2** headscarf, Metcalfe, moon-calf, veal calf; **3** golden calf.
See also **3.56.**

3.23.3: **1** graph; **2** bar graph; **3** autograph, barograph, epigraph, holograph, homograph, lithograph, monograph, paragraph, phonograph, photograph, pictograph, polygraph, seismograph, tachograph, telegraph; **4** bush telegraph, choreograph, radiograph; **7** electrocardiograph.
See also **1.5.2.**

3.23.4: **1** staff; **2** distaff, Falstaff, flagstaff, ground staff, pikestaff; **3** overstaff, quarterstaff, understaff.
See also **10.42.32.**

3.24: **1** aft, coiffed, daft, graft, raft, shaft; **2** camshaft, crankshaft, life raft, mineshaft, short-staffed, waft; **3** overstaffed, understaffed.

3.24.1: **1** draft, draught; **2** first draft, redraft; **3** overdraft.

3.24.2: **1** craft, kraft; **2** aircraft, handcraft, spacecraft, stagecraft, statecraft, witchcraft, woodcraft; **3** handicraft, hovercraft, Wollstonecraft; **4** antiaircraft.

3.25: **1** bagh, Prague, saag; **2** Camargue; **3** Nouvelle Vague.

3.26: **1** barge, hadj, large, marge, Raj, sarge; **2** enlarge; **3** overlarge.
See also **3.36.**

3.26.1: **1** charge; **2** depth charge, discharge, in charge, recharge, surcharge; **3** countercharge, free of charge, overcharge, undercharge; **6** honourable discharge.
See also **3.36.**

3.27: **1** arc, ark, Braque, dark, hark, narc, nark, quark, stark; **2** aardvark, half-dark, Iraq, Petrarch, pitch-dark, Plutarch; **3** antiquark, matriarch, Noah's ark, oligarch, patriarch, semidark.

3.27.1: **1** Bach, bark, barque; **2** debark, embark; **3** disembark, Offenbach.

3.27.2: **1** lakh, lark, plaque; **2** mudlark, skylark, titlark, woodlark; **3** meadowlark.

3.27.3: **1** Clark, Clarke, clerk; **2** bank clerk, salesclerk.

3.27.4: **1** mark, marque; **2** bench mark, benchmark, birthmark, Bismarck, black mark, bookmark, checkmark, demark, Denmark, Deutschmark, earmark, footmark, hallmark, hash mark, Kitemark, Lamarck, landmark, pockmark, postmark, remark, Remarque, tidemark, trademark, tyremark, waymark; **3** easy mark, fingermark, question mark, telemark, watermark; **4** high-water mark, low-water mark, quotation mark, strawberry mark.
See also **3.29, 10.42.40.**

3.27.5: **1** park, spark; **2** ballpark, bright spark, game park, Hyde Park; **3** Central Park, country park, double-park, Holland Park, Kempton Park, Manor Park, marine park, Regent's Park, science park, wildlife park; **4** amusement park, national park, safari park; **7** Yellowstone National Park; **8** Brecon Beacons National Park, Snowdonia National Park.
See also **3.28, 10.42.40.**

3.27.6: **1** shark; **2** blue shark, ghost shark, land shark, loan shark, nurse shark, whale shark, white shark; **3** angel shark, basking shark, great white shark, thresher shark, tiger shark; **4** hammerhead shark.

3.28: **1** Marks, Marx, sparks.
See also **3.27.5.**

3.29: **1** marked, narked; **2** earmarked, hallmarked, pockmarked, trademarked, unmarked; **3** unremarked.
See also **3.27.4.**

3.30: **1** Carl, dwaal, marl, snarl, voile; **2** banal, Bhopal, halal, locale, Mughal, real, rial, riyal, Transvaal; **3** bacchanal, Lake Baikal, rationale, Senegal; **4** Fianna Fáil.
See also **1.13.**

3.30.1: **1** Dahl, dal, dhal; **2** Heimdal, Heyerdahl, Stendhal.

3.30.2: **1** kraal; **2** chorale, corral, mistral, morale; **4** Massif Central.

3.30.3: **2** Chantal, hartal; **3** Blumenthal, emmental, femme fatale, Riefenstahl; **4** Neanderthal.

3.31: **1** arm, balm, calm, charm, farm, Guam, harm, ma'am, palm, psalm, qualm; **2** becalm, disarm, embalm, gendarme, health farm, imam, Montcalm, napalm, rearm, schoolmarm, yardarm; **3** arm-in-arm, Fleet Air Arm, funny farm.
See also **2.54.81, 3.32, 3.33, 10.42.86.**

3.31.1: **2** alarm, Islam, salaam; **4** Dar es Salaam; **5** Nation of Islam.
See also **3.32, 10.42.86.**

3.31.2: **2** Bairam, firearm, forearm, haram, ihram; **3** overarm, underarm.

3.32: **1** armed, calmed, charmed, farmed; **2** alarmed, becalmed, disarmed, embalmed, forearmed, unarmed, unharmed.
See also **3.31, 3.31.1.**

3.33: **1** alms, arms, Brahms, Psalms, qualms; **2** small arms; **3** babe in arms, coat of arms, man-at-arms, open arms.
See also **3.31.**

3.34: **1** Arne, barn, darn, Khan, Marne, naan, nan, paan, San, Sand, Sian, yarn; **2** Amman, azan, Lacan, maidan, Nisan, Oman, Sivan, Tien Shan, Vientiane, yuan; **3** Abadan, Abidjan, Autobahn, Farrakhan, Lindisfarne, Mondrian, Ramadan, Yerevan; **4** Azerbaijan.
See also **1.21, 10.42.92.**

3.34.1: **2** bodhran, Iran, Koran, Qur'an, Tehran.
See also **1.21.13.**

3.34.2: **1** tarn; **2** Bhutan, shaitan, soutane; **3** Hindustan, Kazakhstan, Rajasthan, Yucatán.
See also **1.21.15.**

3.34.3: **3** Kurdistan, Kyrgyzstan, Pakistan; **4** Afghanistan, Baluchistan, Tajikistan, Turkmenistan, Uzbekistan.

3.34.4: **2** Aswan, diwan, Don Juan, Jawan, Sichuan, Szechuan, Taiwan.

3.35: **2** command, demand, remand; **3** countermand, reprimand.
See also **10.42.26.**

3.36: **1** charged; **2** discharged, enlarged; **3** camouflaged.
See also **3.26, 3.26.1, 3.59.**

3.37: **2** advance, enhance, faience; **3** Afrikaans, circumstance.
See also **1.23, 3.40, 10.42.139, 10.62.3.**

3.37.1: **1** dance; **2** barn dance, breakdance, clog dance, folk dance, lapdance, square dance, tap dance, tea dance, war dance; **3** belly dance, Cossack dance, dinner dance, morris dance, song and dance.
> *Before the fiddlers have fled*
> *Before they ask us to pay the bill, and*
>   *while we still have that chance*
> *Let's face the music and dance*
> (Irving Berlin)
See also **10.42.139.**

3.37.2: **1** glance, lance; **2** freelance; **4** par excellence.
See also **10.42.139.**

3.37.3: **1** France, krans, prance, trance; **2** entrance.
See also **3.40, 10.42.139.**

3.37.4: **1** chance; **2** blind chance, fat chance, mischance, off chance, perchance.

3.38: **1** aren't, aunt, can't, chant, grant, Nantes, shan't, slant; **2** aslant, enchant, plainchant; **3** debutante, disenchant, maiden aunt; **4** agony aunt.
See also **1.25, 10.2.83, 10.42.168.**

3.38.1: **1** plant; **2** eggplant, houseplant, implant, supplant, transplant; **3** power plant; **4** xenotransplant.
See also **10.2.83.**

3.39: **1** blanch, Blanche, branch, ranch, tranche; **2** carte blanche; **3** avalanche, olive branch, root-and-branch, Special Branch.

3.40: **2** advanced, enhanced, entranced.
See also **2.45.22, 3.37, 3.37.3.**

3.41: **1** Blanc; **2** Sand; **3** au courant, Duchamp, Lacan, Rouen; **4** Maupassant, Mont Blanc, pension.

3.42: **1** Arp, carp, harp, scarp, sharp, Sharpe, tarp; **2** cardsharp, Jew's harp; **3** razor-sharp.
See also **2.54.62.**

3.43: **1** arse, baas, farce; **2** French farce, litas, volte-face.
See also **1.36, 3.2.**

3.43.1: **1** glass; **2** cut-glass, eyeglass, ground glass, hourglass, spyglass, stained glass, sunglass, wineglass; **3** fibreglass, isinglass, looking glass, Plexiglas, weatherglass.
See also **10.62.3.**

3.43.2: **1** class; **2** first-class, high-class, outclass, subclass, third-class, world-class; **3** cabin class, middle class, second-class,

tourist-class, underclass, upper-class, working-class.
See also **3.47.3**.

3.43.3: **1** pass, sparse; **2** bypass, impasse, railpass, surpass; **3** Khyber Pass, overpass, underpass.

A man that looks on glass,
On it may stay his eye;
Or if he pleaseth, through it pass,
And then the heaven espy.
(George Herbert)
See also **3.47.4, 10.42.132**.

3.43.4: **1** brass; **2** madras, top brass.
See also **1.36.4**.

3.43.5: **1** grass; **2** bluegrass, ryegrass, seagrass, wheatgrass; **3** coup de grâce, supergrass.

3.44: **1** ask, bask, basque, cask, flask, task; **2** hip flask.

3.44.1: **1** mask, masque; **2** death mask, facemask, gas mask, life mask, unmask; **4** oxygen mask.
See also **3.46**.

3.45: **1** clasp, gasp, grasp, hasp, rasp; **2** handclasp.
See also **10.42.104**.

3.46: **1** masked; **2** unasked, unmasked.
See also **3.44.1**.

3.47: **1** mast, vast; **2** aghast, contrast, fat-arsed, half-mast, mainmast, rat-arsed; **3** flabbergast, mizzenmast.
See also **1.38, 10.42.171**.

3.47.1: **1** fast; **2** Belfast, holdfast, steadfast; **3** colourfast, hard-and-fast.
See also **2.54.88, 10.42.171**.

3.47.2: **1** cast, caste; **2** broadcast, downcast, forecast, half-caste, miscast, newscast, outcast, outcaste, podcast, precast, recast, roughcast, sportscast, typecast, webcast, wormcast; **3** cybercast, narrowcast, opencast, open-cast, overcast, plaster cast, simulcast, targetcast, telecast, unicast.
See also **10.42.171**.

3.47.3: **1** blast, last; **2** outclassed, outlast, sandblast; **3** counterblast; **4** Elastoplast.
See also **3.43.2, 10.2.90, 10.42.171**.

3.47.4: **1** passed, past; **2** fly-past, march-past, repast; **3** unsurpassed.
Our God, our help in ages past,
Our hope for years to come,
Our shelter from the stormy blast,

And our eternal home.
(Isaac Watts)
See also **3.43.3**.

3.48: **1** harsh, marsh; **2** gouache, moustache, salt marsh, shabash, Titchmarsh.

3.49: **1** art, dart, fart, ghat, tart; **2** Bogart, Eilat, kyat, Mozart, Stuttgart; **3** Bakewell tart, work of art; **4** state of the art.
See also **3.50**.

3.49.1: **1** baht, Bart, Barthes; **2** Hobart, Rabat, Shabbat.

3.49.2: **1** hart, heart; **2** Bernhardt, Earhart, Flockhart, Reinhardt, sweetheart; **3** heart-to-heart, Purple Heart; **6** Richard the Lionheart.
Words may be false and full of art,
Sighs are the natural language of the heart.
(Thomas Shadwell)
See also **3.50**.

3.49.3: **1** cart; **2** click art, Descartes, dogcart, dustcart, go-cart, handcart, pushcart, zakat; **3** à la carte, applecart.

3.49.4: **1** mart, smart; **2** outsmart; **3** minimart.
See also **3.50**.

3.49.5: **1** part; **2** apart, depart, forepart, impart, mouthpart, op art, pop art, rampart; **3** Bonaparte, counterpart.
See also **3.50, 10.2.35, 10.42.143**.

3.49.6: **1** start; **2** deadstart, false start, fresh start, head start, restart, upstart.

3.49.7: **1** chart; **2** bar chart, flow chart, piechart, wallchart.
See also **10.2.35**.

3.50: **1** arts, darts, Ghats, Graz, hearts, parts, smarts; **2** fine arts; **3** private parts; **4** Master of Arts, performing arts; **5** Bachelor of Arts.
See also **3.49, 3.49.2, 3.49.4, 3.49.5**.

3.51: **1** Garth, hearth, lath; **2** Hogarth, McGrath.
See also **1.43, 3.23**.

3.51.1: **1** bath; **2** birdbath, bloodbath, eyebath, mudbath; **3** Turkish bath.
See also **10.42.31**.

3.51.2: **1** path; **2** flight path, footpath, towpath, warpath; **3** bridle path, garden path, primrose path.

3.52: **1** arch, larch, March, parch, starch; **2** cornstarch, frogmarch, overarch, slow march; **3** Middlemarch, wedding march.
I used to live alone before I knew ya

I've seen your flag on the marble arch
But love is not a victory march
It's a cold and it's a broken Hallelujah.
(Leonard Cohen)
See also **3.53, 10.62.5**.

3.53: 1 arched, parched, starched.
See also **3.52**.

3.54: 1 calve, carve, grave, halve, Slav, starve, suave; 3 Yugoslav.
See also **3.55, 3.56, 9.14.97, 10.42.176**.

3.55: 1 carved, halved, starved; 2 half-starved.
See also **3.54**.

3.56: 1 calves, halves, scarves.
See also **3.23.1, 3.23.2, 3.54**.

3.57: 1 ach, Bach; 2 Pesach.

3.58: 1 Mars, parse, SARS, vase; 2 memoirs, three Rs; 3 churidars, handlebars, parallel bars, vichyssoise; 4 salad niçoise.
See also **3.18.2**.

3.59: 2 barrage, collage, corsage, dressage, garage, massage, melange, ménage, mirage, triage; 3 arbitrage, badinage, camouflage, entourage, fuselage; 4 bon voyage, espionage.
See also **3.36**.

3.59.1: 2 montage, portage; 3 décolletage, reportage, sabotage; 4 photomontage.

4.0: 1 air, are, Ayer, Ayr, Cher, dare, ere, e'er, Eyre, heir, their, there, they're; 2 Adair, corsair, Daguerre, fines herbes; 3 nom de guerre; 4 surface-to-air.
Ere sin could blight or sorrow fade,
Death came with friendly care;
The opening bud to heaven conveyed,
And bade it blossom there.
(Samuel Taylor Coleridge)
See also **4.16, 4.18, 10.42.121**.

4.1: 2 Pierre; 3 derrière, premiere; 4 boutonniere, costumière, jardinière; 5 son et lumière.

4.2: 1 bare, bear; 2 ant bear, black bear, bugbear, Colbert, Flaubert, forbear, forebear, Rambert, threadbare; 3 Camembert, grizzly bear.
See also **4.18, 10.42.121**.

4.3: 1 fair, fare; 2 affair, airfare, fanfare, flat fare, funfair, horse fair, Mayfair, off-air, trade fair, unfair, warfare, welfare, workfare; 3 bill of fare, laissez-faire, savoir-faire, thoroughfare, trench warfare; 4 biowarfare, chargé d'affaires, social welfare, Vanity Fair; 5 economy fare.

I wish you'd stop ignoring me because
you're sending me to despair,
Without a sound yeh you're calling me
and I don't think it's very fair.
(Arctic Monkeys)
See also **2.54.64**.

4.4: 1 hair, hare; 2 horsehair, jugged hare, March hare, mohair; 3 camelhair, maidenhair.

4.5: 1 yeah; 2 Gruyère, Robespierre; 3 cafetière, jardinière.

4.6: 1 care, scare; 2 childcare, haircare, health care, skincare; 3 aftercare, Medicare; 4 devil-may-care.
See also **4.16, 10.42.121**.

4.7: 1 Blair, blare, Clare, flair, flare, glare, lair; 2 declare, éclair, Poor Clare, Sinclair; 3 Baudelaire, distress flare, dragon's lair.
See also **4.16.1, 10.42.121**.

4.8: 1 mare, mayor; 2 Lord Mayor, nightmare, Vermeer; 3 de la Mare, Lady Mayor; 5 Weston-super-Mare.

4.9: 1 ne'er, snare; 2 ensnare; 3 billionaire, debonair, doctrinaire, legionnaire, millionaire, open-air, questionnaire; 4 commissionaire, concessionaire, extraordinaire; 5 multimillionaire.
See also **4.16**.

4.10: 1 pair, pare, pear, spare; 2 au pair, despair, prepare, repair; 3 disrepair, prickly pear; 4 Williams pear; 5 alligator pear, avocado pear.
See also **4.16.2, 4.18, 10.42.122**.

4.10.1: 2 ampere, compare, compère, impair.
See also **4.16.2, 4.16.3**.

4.11: 1 prayer, rare; 2 confrère, Lord's Prayer; 3 au contraire, bidding prayer; 5 Book of Common Prayer.
My mother bids me bind my hair
With bands of rosy hue,
Tie up my sleeves with ribbons rare,
And lace my bodice blue.
(Anne Hunter)

4.12: 1 share; 2 A share, Bashir, job-share, ploughshare, timeshare; 3 lion's share.
See also **10.42.121**.

4.13: 1 tare, tear; 2 Altair, hectare, parterre, Voltaire; 3 solitaire; 4 pied-à-terre.
See also **8.14**.

4.13.1: 1 stair, stare; 2 Astaire, Basseterre, outstare.
See also **4.18**.

4.14: **1** chair; **2** armchair, deckchair, lounge chair, pushchair, wheelchair; **3** easy chair; **4** electric chair.

4.15: **1** ware, wear, where; **2** beachwear, beware, bridgeware, cookware, Edgware, eyewear, firmware, freeware, groupware, hardware, lapware, malware, menswear, nowhere, payware, shareware, sleepwear, somewhere, spyware, stoneware, swimwear, treeware; **3** anywhere, earthenware, everywhere, kitchenware, middleware, ovenware, tableware; **4** ready-to-wear.
See also **10.42.121**.

4.15.1: **2** aware; **3** betaware, Delaware, De La Warr, leisurewear, outerwear, silverware, Tupperware, unaware, underwear, vapourware.

4.15.2: **1** square; **2** foursquare, headsquare, Times Square, T-square.
See also **4.16**.

4.15.3: **1** swear; **2** courseware, elsewhere, forswear, glassware, sportswear.
See also **10.42.121**.

4.15.4: **2** flatware, footwear, knitwear, nightwear, software, wetware.

4.16: **1** aired, Baird, scared, squared; **2** dark-haired, ensnared, fair-haired, tow-haired, white-haired, wire-haired; **3** flaxen-haired, ginger-haired, golden-haired.
See also **4.0, 4.6, 4.9, 4.15.2**.

4.16.1: **1** flared, laird; **2** declared; **3** undeclared.
See also **4.7**.

4.16.2: **1** paired; **2** compared, prepared, repaired; **3** unprepared, well-prepared.
See also **4.10, 4.10.1**.

4.16.3: **2** impaired; **3** unimpaired; **4** hearing-impaired, vision-impaired; **5** visually impaired.
See also **4.10.1**.

4.17: **1** bairn, cairn; **2** auvergne, Sauternes.

4.18: **1** airs, Ayers, pairs, stairs, theirs, wares; **2** backstairs, downstairs, forebears, repairs, upstairs; **3** unawares; **4** current affairs, state of affairs.
See also **4.0, 4.2, 4.10, 4.13.1**.

4.19: **2** auberge; **3** concierge.

5.0: **1** a, eh, hay, hey, they, yea; **2** AA, foyer, pace, roué; **3** aka, CIA, DOA, MIA; **4** habitué, una voce.

5.1: **2** BA, Millet, PA; **3** Daumier, dossier, IPA, MBA, PDA, U3A; **4** couturier,

déshabillé, Du Maurier, YMCA; **5** RSPCA; **6** YWCA.

5.1.1: **4** atelier, escalier, espalier, hotelier, Tortelier.

5.1.2: **2** TA; **3** bustier, Cartier, metier, Poitier, quartier; **5** chocolatier.

5.2: **1** bay; **2** abbé, eBay, flambé, obey, sickbay, sorbet; **3** disobey, Hudson Bay; **4** Chesapeake Bay; **5** Guantanamo Bay.

5.3: **1** day; **2** birthday, Corday, feast day, field day, Friday, half-day, heyday, high day, mayday, May Day, midday, payday, schoolday, someday, washday, weekday, workday; **3** All Saints' Day, Anzac Day, Bastille Day, Boxing Day, démodé, girl Friday, Good Friday, Groundhog Day, holiday, Judgment Day, man Friday, name day, Pancake Day, polling day, present-day; **4** Armistice Day, bank holiday, half-holiday, Remembrance Day; **5** Independence Day, Memorial Day, public holiday.

A little rule, a little sway,
A sunbeam in a winter's day,
Is all the proud and mighty have
Between the cradle and the grave.
(John Dyer)

5.3.1: **2** g'day; **3** Labor Day, Labour Day, Muscadet, workaday; **4** Canada Day, Midsummer Day; **5** Australia Day.

5.3.2: **2** today; **3** day-to-day, latter-day, quarter day, Saturday, yesterday; **4** red-letter day.

5.3.3: **2** bidet, D-day; **3** everyday, holy day, Lady Day.

5.3.4: **2** noonday; **3** Allende, modern-day, open day, Q & A, V and A, Yaoundé.

5.3.5: **2** Monday, sundae, Sunday; **3** Palm Sunday, Whitsunday; **4** Passion Sunday; **5** Mothering Sunday, Remembrance Sunday.

Of all the days that's in the week
I dearly love but one day—
And that's the day that comes betwixt
A Saturday and Monday.
(Henry Carey)

5.3.6: **2** Doomsday, Thursday, Tuesday, Wednesday; **3** All Souls' Day, Ash Wednesday, Mother's Day, New Year's Day; **4** All Hallows' Day, April Fools' Day, Maundy Thursday, Valentine's Day; **5** St Valentine's Day.

Goodbye, Ruby Tuesday
Who could hang a name on you?

When you change with every new day
Still I'm gonna miss you...
(Rolling Stones)

5.4: **1** Faye, fey; **2** au fait, buffet, café, FA, parfait; **4** auto-da-fé, cybercafé, Morgan le Fay.

5.5: **1** gay; **2** nosegay, reggae, tenge; **3** Haringey.

5.6: **1** jay; **2** bluejay, deejay, DJ, OJ, Sanjay, veejay; **3** CCJ, popinjay.

5.7: **1** cay; **2** bouquet, decay, manqué, OK, okay, parquet, piqué, piquet, risqué, UK; **3** A-OK, appliqué, JFK, sobriquet, tourniquet; **4** 401(k), communiqué, vitamin K.
See also **5.21.1, 10.42.1.**

5.8: **1** clay, flay, lay, slay, sleigh, vlei; **2** ballet, bobsleigh, chalet, delay, franglais, inlay, L.A., melee, mislay, outlay, soufflé, valet, waylay; **3** cor anglais, relay; **4** café au lait, corps de ballet, Royal Ballet.
Yesterday, love was such an easy game to
play.
Now I need a place to hide away.
Oh, I believe in yesterday.
(John Lennon, Paul McCartney)
See also **10.42.1.**

5.8.1: **2** allay, Malay; **3** Beaujolais, cassoulet, Charolais, overlay, underlay; **4** cabriolet.

5.8.2: **2** Barclay; **3** china clay, feet of clay, potter's clay.

5.8.3: **1** play, splay; **2** airplay, byplay, child's play, display, downplay, foreplay, foul play, gameplay, horseplay, love-play, outplay, replay, screenplay, swordplay, wordplay; **3** double play, interplay, overplay, plug and play, power play, teleplay, triple play, underplay; **4** miracle play, mystery play, radio play; **5** morality play; **6** liquid-crystal display.
See also **5.21.2.**

5.9: **1** may; **2** dismay, gourmet, lamé, MA; **3** anime, consommé, Mallarmé, résumé; **5** Pouilly-Fumé.
Shall I compare thee to a summer's day?
Thou art more lovely and more
temperate.
Rough winds do shake the darling buds of
May,
And summer's lease hath all too short a
date.
(William Shakespeare)
See also **5.21.5, 10.42.1.**

5.10: **1** nay, née, neigh; **2** carnet, Corneille, Hannay, penne, pince-nez, Renée; **3** Beauharnais, Chardonnay, cloisonné, DNA, Dubonnet, Hogmanay, matinée, RNA.

5.11: **1** pay, spay; **2** back pay, coupé, épée, frappé, prepay, repay, toupee; **3** Agape, canapé, overpay, take-home pay, underpay, vin du pays.
Here lie I by the chancel door;
They put me here because I was poor.
The further in, the more you pay,
But here lie I as snug as they.
(Epitaph)

5.12: **1** brae, bray, dray, gray, grey, pray, prey, ray, spray; **2** array, beret, chambray, Fauré, foray, hombre, hooray, hurray, McCrae, moiré, purée, respray, soiree, stingray, Vouvray, X-ray; **3** cabaret, Castlereagh, cathode ray, cosmic ray, dapple-grey, de jure, Désirée, disarray, émigré, gamma ray, IRA, Maggiore; **5** Sierra Madre.
See also **5.21.8, 5.54.2.**

5.12.1: **1** fray; **2** affray, defray; **3** fromage frais.
See also **5.21.8.**

5.12.2: **1** stray, tray; **2** ashtray, astray, betray, entrée, in-tray, outré, out-tray, portray.

5.13: **1** say; **2** assay, Beyoncé, daresay, essay, gainsay, glacé, hearsay, lycée, Marseilles, naysay, passé, per se; **3** Bodensee, déclassé, fiancé, fiancée, fricassee, Nez Percé, USA; **4** MRSA; **5** Pouilly-Fuissé.
See also **10.42.1.**

5.14: **2** Boucher, cliché, crochet, O'Shea, touché; **3** Beaumarchais, Pinochet, recherché, ricochet; **4** à bon marché.

5.14.1: **2** cachet, sachet, sashay; **3** attaché, Montrachet; **5** papier-mâché.

5.15: **2** Dante, forte, jeté, latte, Loch Tay, maté, pâté, satay, sauté; **3** crudités, décolleté, velouté; **4** Aligoté, café latte, diamanté, jubilate; **5** festina lente; **6** cinema vérité.

5.15.1: **1** stay; **2** farmstay, homestay, mainstay, namaste, outstay; **3** overstay.
See also **5.54.**

5.16: **2** Ave, convey, duvet, inveigh, levee, purvey; **3** survey.

5.17: **1** qua, sway, way, weigh, whey; **2** airway, archway, byway, causeway, clearway, Conway, doorway, driveway, fairway, feng shui, Galway, gangway, halfway, hallway, hatchway, highway, Norway, one-way, parkway, pathway, railway, runway, segue, slipway, someway, stairway, Steinway, subway, throughway, thruway, tollway, tramway, two-way, walkway, Yahweh; **3** carriageway, expressway, Hemmingway, passageway, Zimbabwe; **4** companionway, superhighway.

5.17.1: **2** away, flyaway; **3** breakaway, Callaway, caraway, faraway, foldaway, Galloway, giveaway, Greenaway, hideaway, Holloway, runaway, stowaway, takeaway, tearaway, throwaway, underway.

Georgie Porgie, pudding and pie,
Kissed the girls and made them cry;
When the boys came out to play,
Georgie Porgie ran away.
(Children's Verse)

5.17.2: **3** castaway, counterweigh, cutaway, getaway, motorway, waterway.

5.17.3: **2** freeway, leeway, seaway, three-way; **3** alleyway, anyway, entryway, Milky Way, taxiway.

5.17.4: **2** Broadway, headway, midway, roadway, speedway, tideway; **3** off-Broadway; **4** off-off-Broadway.

5.17.5: **2** beltway, footway, gateway, outweigh, partway.

5.18: **2** Bizet, blasé, rosé; **3** exposé.

5.19: **3** Angers, engagé, negligee, protégé, protégée.

5.20: **1** Abe, babe; **3** astrolabe.

5.21: **1** Ade, aid, aide, fade, jade, staid, they'd; **2** Band-Aid, brigade, crusade, deaf aid, first aid, forbade; **3** hearing aid, light brigade, orangeade, palisade, renegade. *See also* **10.2.5, 10.42.15.**

5.21.1: **1** Cade; **2** arcade, blockade, brocade, cascade, cockade, decade, decayed, stockade; **3** ambuscade, barricade, cavalcade, Medicaid, motorcade; **4** penny arcade. *See also* **5.7.**

5.21.2: **1** glade, lade, laid; **2** deep-laid, displayed, inlaid, mislaid, relaid, Slade, waylaid; **3** fusillade; **4** visual aid. *See also* **5.8.3.**

5.21.3: **3** accolade, escalade, fusillade, marmalade, overlaid; **7** audiovisual aid.

5.21.4: **1** blade; **2** switchblade; **3** razor blade, Rollerblade.

5.21.5: **1** made, maid; **2** barmaid, bridesmaid, dismayed, handmade, handmaid, homemade, housemaid, ill-made, limeade, man-made, mermaid, milkmaid, nursemaid, old maid, pomade, remade, self-made, unmade, well-made; **3** chambermaid, countrymade, custom-made, dairymaid, factory-made, humanmade, kitchenmaid, machine-made, metermaid, parlourmaid, ready-made, undismayed.

Widowed wife, and married maid,
Betrothed, betrayer, and betrayed!
(Sir Walter Scott)
See also **5.9.**

5.21.6: **2** grenade, Sinead; **3** cannonade, colonnade, esplanade, hand grenade, lemonade, marinade, serenade.

5.21.7: **1** paid, spade; **2** lowpaid, postpaid, prepaid, unpaid; **3** escapade, overpaid, reply-paid, underpaid.

Ramp up my genius, be not retrograde;
But boldly nominate a spade a spade.
(Ben Jonson)

5.21.8: **1** braid, frayed, raid; **2** abrade, afraid, arrayed, comrade, parade, ram-raid, tirade, upbraid; **3** masquerade, unafraid. *See also* **5.12, 5.12.1, 10.2.5.**

5.21.9: **1** grade; **2** degrade, downgrade, upgrade; **3** centigrade, retrograde; **4** biodegrade. *See also* **10.2.5, 10.42.15.**

5.21.10: **1** trade; **2** fair trade, free trade, rag trade; **3** balustrade, stock-in-trade. *See also* **10.42.15.**

5.21.11: **1** shade; **2** eyeshade, lampshade, sunshade; **4** deadly nightshade. *See also* **5.22, 10.42.15.**

5.21.12: **2** evade, invade, Live Aid, pervade.

5.21.13: **1** Quaid, suede, wade; **2** dissuade, persuade; **4** Virginia Wade.

5.22: **1** Aids, shades; **4** jack of all trades. *See also* **5.21.11.**

5.23: **1** bathe, lathe, swathe; **2** sunbathe. *See also* **5.51, 10.42.31.**

5.24: **1** chafe, strafe, waif. *See also* **5.49.**

5.24.1: **1** safe; **2** fail-safe, unsafe, vouchsafe, wall safe.

5.25: **1** Craig, Hague, plague, vague; **2** renege.

5.26: **1** age, cage, mage, phage, sage, wage; **2** assuage, birdcage, Bronze Age, ice age, Iron Age, New Age, old age, Osage, Stone Age, teenage, third age; **3** come of age, golden age, living wage; **4** Classical Age, coming of age; **5** bacteriophage.
See also **5.38, 10.2.24, 10.62.1**.

5.26.1: **1** gage, gauge; **2** broad gauge, engage, greengage, rain gauge, wind gauge; **3** disengage, narrow gauge, pressure gauge.
See also **5.38, 10.42.37**.

5.26.2: **1** page, Paige; **2** homepage, rampage, webpage; **3** welcome page.
See also **10.42.37**.

5.26.3: **1** rage; **2** blind rage, enrage, outrage; **3** underage.
See also **5.38, 10.42.37**.

5.26.4: **1** stage; **2** backstage, downstage, forestage, offstage, onstage, upstage; **3** apron stage, landing stage, multistage.

As an unperfect actor on the stage
Who with his fear is put beside his part,
Or some fierce thing replete with too
*   much rage,*
Whose strength's abundance weakens his
*   own heart*
(William Shakespeare)
See also **10.42.37**.

5.27: **1** ache, bake, fake, hake, Jake, sake, spake; **2** clambake, forsake, headache, keepsake, namesake, opaque, sunbake, toothache; **3** bellyache, tummy ache.
See also **5.29, 10.42.43**.

5.27.1: **1** cake; **2** backache, beefcake, cheesecake, cupcake, fishcake, fruitcake, fudge cake, oatcake, oil cake, pancake, rock cake, salt cake, seedcake, shortcake, sponge cake; **3** angel cake, battercake, birthday cake, carrot cake, cattle cake, chocolate cake, Christmas cake, Eccles cake, griddlecake, layer cake, wedding cake; **4** angel food cake, devil's food cake, Madeira cake, upside-down cake.

5.27.2: **2** teacake; **3** coffee cake, Dundee cake, lardy cake.

5.27.3: **1** flake, lake, slake; **2** snowflake, Swan Lake, wine lake; **3** Great Bear Lake, Great Salt Lake, Great Slave Lake, Timberlake.

5.27.4: **1** make; **2** matchmake, remake, unmake; **3** custom-make, merrymake, tailor-make.

Every move you make

Every vow you break
Every smile you fake, every claim you
*   stake*
I'll be watching you
(The Police)
See also **10.42.44**.

5.27.5: **1** snake; **2** grass snake, sea snake; **3** flying snake, garter snake, rattlesnake, water snake.

5.27.6: **1** crake, drake, rake; **2** buckrake, corncrake, earache, firedrake, mandrake.

5.27.7: **1** brake, break; **2** air brake, daybreak, firebreak, handbrake, heartbreak, housebreak, jailbreak, leg-break, off-break, outbreak, tea break, windbreak; **3** minibreak, shooting-brake.

5.27.8: **1** shake, sheik; **2** handshake, milkshake; **4** golden handshake.
See also **5.28**.

5.27.9: **1** take; **2** gut-ache, heartache, intake, outtake, partake, retake, uptake; **3** give-and-take, overtake, undertake.
See also **10.42.46**.

5.27.10: **1** stake, steak; **2** beefsteak, grubstake, mistake, piss-take, rump steak, sweepstake; **3** fillet steak, minute steak, sirloin steak, tartar steak, T-bone steak; **4** porterhouse steak.

5.27.11: **1** quake, wake; **2** awake, earthquake; **3** half-awake, kittiwake, wide-awake.
See also **10.42.43**.

5.28: **1** Lakes, shakes; **2** bran flakes, cornflakes, soapflakes.
See also **5.27.8**.

5.29: **1** baked, caked; **2** half-baked.
See also **5.27**.

5.30: **1** ail, ale, bail, bale, fail, flail, gaol, hail, hale, jail, kale, pail, pale, shale, they'll, Yale; **2** exhale, impale, inhale.
See also **5.31, 10.42.68**.

5.30.1: **1** dale; **2** Bleasdale, Clydesdale, Drysdale, Lonsdale, Swaledale; **3** Airedale, Wensleydale; **4** Fort Lauderdale.

5.30.2: **1** gale, Gayle; **2** regale; **3** Abigail, farthingale, nightingale; **5** Florence Nightingale.

5.30.3: **1** scale; **2** descale, full-scale, greyscale, large-scale, limescale, small-scale, timescale, upscale; **3** Beaufort scale, major scale, Richter scale.

5.30.4: **1** mail, male; **2** airmail, blackmail, chain mail, email, fan mail, female,

greenmail, junk mail, voicemail; 3 direct-
mail, Royal Mail.
See also **5.31, 10.42.68.**

5.30.5: 1 nail, snail; 2 doornail, hangnail,
thumbnail, toenail; 3 coffin nail, fingernail.

5.30.6: 1 braille, frail, Grail, rail, trail;
2 contrail, derail, guardrail, handrail;
3 British Rail, dado rail, ginger ale, Holy
Grail, monorail, nonpareil.
See also **10.42.68.**

5.30.7: 1 sail, sale; 2 abseil, assail, fire
sale, foresail, headsail, mainsail, resale,
topsail, wassail, white sale, wholesale;
3 car boot sale, garage sale, jumble sale,
point-of-sale, rummage sale; 4 bring-and-
buy sale.
See also **5.32, 10.42.68.**

5.30.8: 1 stale, tail, tale; 2 cocktail,
curtail, dovetail, entail, fantail, fishtail, folk
tale, hightail, horsetail, oxtail, pigtail,
telltale, wagtail; 3 nose-to-tail, old wives'
tale, silvertail, swallowtail, yellowtail;
5 Molotov cocktail.
See also **2.54.62, 5.31, 5.32.**

5.30.9: 2 detail; 3 fairytale, ponytail,
retail.
See also **5.31, 5.32, 10.42.68.**

5.30.10: 1 vale, veil; 2 avail, prevail,
travail, unveil; 3 countervail, Maida Vale.
See also **5.31, 10.42.69.**

5.30.11: 1 quail, Quayle, wail, whale;
2 bewail, blue whale, grey whale;
3 humpback whale, killer whale.

5.31: 1 failed, jailed, veiled;
2 blackmailed, curtailed, detailed,
dovetailed, hobnailed, unveiled.
See also **5.30, 5.30.4, 5.30.8, 5.30.9,
5.30.10.**

5.32: 1 sales, tails, Wales; 2 details,
entrails; 3 hard as nails, Prince of Wales,
telesales.

> *Lovely the woods, waters, meadows,*
>   *combes, vales,*
> *All the air things wear that build this*
>   *world of Wales.*
> (Gerard Manley Hopkins)

See also **5.30.7, 5.30.8, 5.30.9.**

5.33: 1 aim, blame, dame, fame, lame,
maim, same, shame, tame; 2 defame,
selfsame; 3 aspartame, Hall of Fame.
See also **5.34.**

5.33.1: 1 game; 2 ball game, big game,
board game, card game, con game, end

game, fair game, small game, war game;
3 arcade game; 4 video game.

5.33.2: 1 flame; 2 aflame, inflame, old
flame.
See also **5.34, 10.42.84.**

5.33.3: 1 claim; 2 acclaim, declaim,
disclaim, exclaim, proclaim, reclaim;
3 counterclaim.
See also **5.34.**

5.33.4: 1 name; 2 brand name, code name,
filename, first name, forename, last name,
nickname, pen name, pet name, place
name, rename, stage name, surname, trade
name; 3 maiden name, married name,
middle name, second name, username,
whatsername, whatsisname; 4 family
name.

> *Eleanor Rigby died in the church and was*
>   *buried along with her name*
> *Nobody came*
> (John Lennon, Paul McCartney)

See also **5.34.**

5.33.5: 1 frame; 2 A-frame, cold frame,
doorframe, mainframe; 3 underframe.

5.34: 1 aimed, blamed, claimed, famed,
maimed, named; 2 acclaimed, ashamed, ill-
famed, inflamed, unclaimed, unnamed,
untamed, well-aimed; 3 aforenamed, self-
proclaimed, unashamed.
See also **5.33, 5.33.2, 5.33.3, 5.33.4.**

5.35: 1 chain, feign, gain, Jane, Jayne,
sane, Shane, Shayne, Zane; 2 again,
Hussain, inane, insane, plain Jane, profane,
regain, unchain; 3 cellophane, Mary Jane;
4 auf Wiedersehen, capital gain;
5 Calamity Jane.

> *I'm singin' in the rain, just singin' in the*
>   *rain;*
> *What a wonderful feeling, I'm happy*
>   *again.*
> (Arthur Freed)

See also **5.41.**

5.35.1: 1 bane; 2 dogbane, fleabane,
henbane, ratsbane, urbane.

5.35.2: 1 Dane, deign; 2 disdain, Great
Dane, mundane, ordain; 3 transmundane;
4 extramundane, supramundane.
See also **5.36.**

5.35.3: 1 cane, skein; 2 alkane, arcane,
chicane, cocaine, Cockaigne; 3 hurricane,
lignocaine, novocaine.

> *I was born in a cross-fire hurricane*
> *And I howled at my ma in the driving rain*
> (Rolling Stones)

See also **5.36.**

5.35.4: **1** Blain, lain, lane; **2** air lane, chilblain, Elaine, pit lane, sea lane, villein; **3** chatelaine, shipping lane, underlain; **4** Petticoat Lane.

5.35.5: **1** plain, plane; **2** airplane, biplane, complain, deplane, explain, flood plain, seaplane, tailplane, warplane; **3** aeroplane, aquaplane, hydroplane, monoplane.
See also **2.54.82, 5.36**.

5.35.6: **1** main, mane; **2** Charmaine, chow mein, demesne, domain, Germaine, germane, humane, remain, romaine; **3** Charlemagne, inhumane; **4** legerdemain; **5** top-level domain.
See also **5.41, 10.42.97**.

5.35.7: **1** pain, pane; **2** campaign, champagne, propane; **3** counterpane.
See also **5.36, 5.41**.

5.35.8: **1** crane, drain, grain, rain, reign, rein, sprain; **2** migraine, refrain, Ukraine, wholegrain; **3** acid rain.
See also **5.36.1, 5.41, 10.42.97**.

5.35.9: **2** arraign, Lorraine, moraine, terrain.

5.35.10: **1** brain; **2** birdbrain, lamebrain, membrane, peabrain; **3** scatterbrain.
See also **5.41**.

5.35.11: **1** train; **2** detrain, quatrain, retrain, road-train.
See also **5.36.1, 10.42.97**.

5.35.12: **1** strain; **2** constrain, eyestrain, restrain.
See also **5.36.3**.

5.35.13: **1** stain; **2** abstain, Beltane, bloodstain, butane, contain, detain, maintain, obtain, octane, retain, sustain; **3** Bloemfontein, high-octane, tramontane.
See also **5.36.4, 10.42.97**.

5.35.14: **2** attain, pertain; **3** appertain, ascertain, entertain.
See also **5.36.4, 10.42.97**.

5.35.15: **1** thane; **2** ethane, methane; **5** polyurethane.

5.35.16: **1** vain, vane, vein; **3** weather vane.

5.35.17: **1** swain, twain, wane; **2** coxswain, Dwayne, Gawain; **3** wax and wane.
See also **10.42.97**.

5.36: **1** caned, pained, veined; **2** explained, ordained, unfeigned; **3** preordained, unexplained.
See also **5.35.2, 5.35.3, 5.35.5, 5.35.7**.

5.36.1: **1** drained, grained, trained; **2** coarse-grained, house-trained, ingrained, untrained, well-trained; **3** potty-trained, toilet-trained.
See also **5.35.8, 5.35.11**.

5.36.2: **2** bird-brained, crackbrained, harebrained; **3** featherbrained, scatterbrained.

5.36.3: **1** strained; **2** constrained, restrained; **3** unconstrained, unrestrained.
See also **5.35.12**.

5.36.4: **2** bloodstained, contained, detained, sustained; **3** ascertained, entertained, grant-maintained, self-contained.
See also **5.35.13, 5.35.14**.

5.37: **1** change, mange; **2** exchange, loose change, shortchange; **3** chop and change, corn exchange, interchange; **4** bill of exchange, needle exchange; **5** telephone exchange.
How many special people change
How many lives are living strange
(Oasis)
See also **5.39**.

5.37.1: **1** grange, range, strange; **2** arrange, close range, estrange, free-range, long-range, outrange, short-range; **3** Cascade Range, disarrange, mountain range, prearrange, rearrange; **5** Karakoram Range.
See also **5.39**.

5.38: **1** aged, caged, waged; **2** assuaged, engaged, enraged, outraged, teenaged, unwaged; **3** disengaged, underaged.
See also **5.26, 5.26.1, 5.26.3**.

5.39: **1** changed; **2** arranged, deranged, estranged, exchanged, unchanged; **3** interchanged, prearranged.
See also **5.37, 5.37.1**.

5.40: **1** ain't, faint, feint, paint, quaint, saint, taint; **2** acquaint, complaint, constraint, greasepaint, oil paint, restraint, war paint; **3** patron saint; **4** Latter-Day Saint.
See also **2.54.88, 10.2.84, 10.42.168**.

5.41: **1** brains, gains, pains, reins; **2** cremains, remains.
See also **5.35, 5.35.6, 5.35.7, 5.35.8, 5.35.10**.

5.42: **1** ape, cape, gape, jape, nape, shape; **2** agape, misshape, reshape, shipshape; **4** Barbary ape.
See also **5.44, 10.42.104**.

5.42.1: 2 cloudscape, escape, landscape, moonscape, seascape, townscape; 3 cityscape, fire escape, riverscape. *See also* **5.44.**

5.42.2: 1 crepe, drape, grape, rape, scrape; 2 date rape, serape; 3 oilseed rape. *See also* **5.43, 5.44, 10.42.104.**

5.42.3: 1 tape; 2 great ape, red tape, Scotch tape; 3 gaffer tape, masking tape, Sellotape, sticky tape, ticker tape; 4 audiotape, videotape; 7 digital audio tape. *See also* **5.44.**

5.43: 1 drapes, traipse; 2 sour grapes. *See also* **5.42.2.**

5.44: 1 aped, draped, shaped, taped; 2 bowl-shaped, cone-shaped, egg-shaped, escaped, pear-shaped, reshaped, star-shaped, wedge-shaped. *See also* **5.42, 5.42.1, 5.42.2, 5.42.3.**

5.45: 1 ace, chase, lace, mace; 2 Candace, grimace, lactase, shoelace; 3 interlace, steeplechase, wild-goose chase.

5.45.1: 1 base, bass; 2 abase, debase, freebase, wheelbase; 3 database, double bass, drum 'n' bass, knowledge base. *See also* **5.46.**

5.45.2: 1 face; 2 coalface, deface, efface, fuckface, outface, straight face, typeface; 3 interface, pizza face; 5 face-to-face.

There is a garden in her face,
Where roses and white lilies grow;
A heav'nly paradise is that place,
Wherein all pleasant fruits do flow.
There cherries grow, which none may buy
Till 'Cherry ripe' themselves do cry.
(Thomas Campion)
See also **10.42.134.**

5.45.3: 1 case; 2 bookcase, briefcase, court case, encase, headcase, nutcase, showcase, staircase, suitcase, test case; 3 basketcase, carrycase, pillowcase, uppercase. *See also* **10.42.134.**

5.45.4: 1 place, plaice; 2 birthplace, displace, fireplace, misplace, replace, showplace, someplace, workplace; 3 anyplace, commonplace, everyplace, marketplace, meeting place; 4 watering place.

Desmond has a barrow in the market place
Molly is a singer in a band

Desmond says to Molly 'Girl I like your face'
And Molly says this as she takes him by the hand...
(The Beatles)
See also **5.46.**

5.45.5: 1 pace; 2 apace, outpace, snail's pace; 3 carapace.

5.45.6: 1 space; 2 airspace, backspace, workspace; 3 aerospace, cyberspace, hyperspace, outer space. *See also* **5.46.1, 10.42.134.**

5.45.7: 1 brace, grace, race, trace; 2 disgrace, embrace, mixed-race, rat race, retrace; 3 days of grace, master race, relay race, state of grace; 4 three-legged race.

The grave's a fine and private place,
But none, I think, do there embrace.
(Andrew Marvell)
See also **10.42.135.**

5.46: 1 baste, chaste, haste, waist, waste; 2 barefaced, debased, misplaced, po-faced, posthaste, shamefaced, shirtwaist, strait-laced, two-faced, unchaste, unplaced; 4 hazardous waste. *See also* **5.45.1, 5.45.4, 10.2.90.**

5.46.1: 1 paste, spaced; 2 toothpaste; 3 cut-and-paste. *See also* **5.45.6.**

5.46.2: 1 taste; 2 distaste, foretaste, good taste; 3 aftertaste.

I love all waste
And solitary places; where we taste
The pleasure of believing what we see
Is boundless, as we wish our souls to be.
(Percy Bysshe Shelley)

5.47: 1 8, eight, hate; 2 pet hate; 3 apartheid, graduate, menstruate; 5 individuate. *See also* **10.2.39.**

5.47.1: 2 G8; 3 expiate, nauseate, permeate; 4 delineate. *See also* **10.42.146.**

5.47.2: 3 mediate, radiate; 4 irradiate, repudiate; 5 intermediate. *See also* **10.2.38.**

5.47.3: 3 palliate; 4 affiliate, conciliate, defoliate, exfoliate, humiliate, retaliate. *See also* **10.2.38, 10.42.146.**

5.47.4: 2 create; 3 procreate, recreate, re-create; 4 appropriate, excoriate, expatriate, expropriate, inebriate, infuriate, luxuriate, repatriate; 5 misappropriate. *See also* **9.14.87, 10.2.38, 10.42.146.**

5.47.5: **3** nauseate; **4** asphyxiate, associate, dissociate, enunciate.
See also **10.2.38, 10.42.146.**

5.47.6: **3** satiate, vitiate; **4** appreciate, depreciate, expatiate, ingratiate, initiate, negotiate, officiate, propitiate, substantiate; **5** differentiate, disassociate.
See also **10.2.38, 10.42.146.**

5.47.7: **2** V8; **3** deviate, obviate; **4** abbreviate, alleviate.

5.47.8: **4** attenuate, evacuate, evaluate, extenuate, insinuate; **5** disambiguate.
See also **10.2.39.**

5.47.9: **3** actuate, fluctuate, punctuate, situate; **4** accentuate, eventuate, habituate, perpetuate.
See also **10.2.39.**

5.47.10: **1** bait; **2** abate, debate, jailbait, probate, rebate, whitebait; **3** incubate, masturbate, reprobate; **4** exacerbate.

5.47.11: **1** date; **2** backdate, blind date, mandate, postdate, predate, update; **3** antedate, double date, inundate, out-of-date, sell-by date; **4** accommodate, Julian date; **5** up-to-date.
See also **10.2.40, 10.42.145.**

5.47.12: **2** sedate; **3** candidate, fluoridate, liquidate, validate; **4** consolidate, elucidate, intimidate, invalidate.
See also **10.2.40, 10.42.145.**

5.47.13: **1** fate, fête; **2** phosphate, sulphate; **3** caliphate; **5** organophosphate.

5.47.14: **1** gait, gate; **2** Aldgate, floodgate, Highgate, lychgate, Moorgate, Newgate, Ramsgate, tailgate, tollgate; **3** Billingsgate, conjugate, elongate, Golden Gate, kissing gate, promulgate, starting gate, subjugate; **4** Brandenburg Gate.
See also **10.2.41.**

5.47.15: **3** abrogate, arrogate, delegate, derogate, propagate, relegate, Watergate; **4** interrogate.
See also **10.2.41.**

5.47.16: **2** negate; **3** fumigate, navigate; **5** circumnavigate.
See also **10.2.41.**

5.47.17: **3** aggregate, congregate, irrigate, segregate; **4** desegregate.

5.47.18: **3** castigate, instigate, litigate, mitigate; **4** investigate.
See also **10.42.145.**

5.47.19: **1** Kate; **2** locate, truncate; **3** bifurcate, defalcate, demarcate, educate,

inculcate, relocate; **4** reciprocate, re-educate.
See also **10.2.42.**

5.47.20: **2** vacate; **3** advocate, bifurcate, defecate, suffocate; **4** equivocate.
See also **10.2.42, 10.42.147.**

5.47.21: **2** placate; **3** allocate, collocate, dislocate; **4** reallocate.
See also **10.2.42.**

5.47.22: **3** desiccate; **4** authenticate, certificate, intoxicate, pontificate; **5** X-certificate.

5.47.23: **3** abdicate, dedicate, indicate, predicate, syndicate, vindicate; **4** adjudicate, eradicate.

5.47.24: **3** complicate, duplicate, explicate, implicate, replicate, silicate.
See also **10.2.43.**

5.47.25: **3** fornicate; **4** communicate; **5** excommunicate; **6** intercommunicate.

5.47.26: **3** deprecate, extricate, fabricate, lubricate; **4** prefabricate, prevaricate.
See also **10.2.42, 10.2.43, 10.42.147.**

5.47.27: **3** masticate; **4** domesticate, prognosticate, sophisticate.

5.47.28: **1** skate; **2** cheapskate, speed-skate; **3** confiscate, coruscate, figure-skate, in-line skate, obfuscate.
See also **10.2.42, 10.42.147.**

5.47.29: **1** late, slate; **2** conflate, deflate, dilate, inflate, reflate, translate, violate; **3** annihilate, legislate.

The best of men cannot suspend their fate:
The good die early, and the bad die late.
(Daniel Defoe)
See also **10.2.44, 10.2.45.**

5.47.30: **2** collate; **3** correlate, desolate, escalate, flagellate, immolate, isolate, percolate; **4** de-escalate, extrapolate, interpolate, invigilate.
See also **10.2.44, 10.2.45.**

5.47.31: **2** relate; **3** fibrillate, mutilate, oscillate, titillate, vacillate, ventilate; **4** assimilate, interrelate; **5** hyperventilate.
See also **10.2.45, 10.42.148.**

5.47.32: **3** insulate, ovulate, postulate, tabulate, ululate; **4** capitulate, encapsulate, perambulate; **5** circumambulate.
See also **10.2.46.**

5.47.33: **3** adulate, modulate, undulate; **4** demodulate.
See also **10.2.46.**

5.47.34: 3 regulate; 4 coagulate, deregulate; 5 overregulate.
See also **10.2.46.**

5.47.35: 3 calculate, circulate, speculate; 4 articulate, ejaculate, emasculate, gesticulate, inoculate, matriculate, miscalculate.
See also **10.42.148.**

5.47.36: 3 emulate, formulate, simulate, stimulate; 4 accumulate, dissimulate, reformulate.
See also **10.2.46, 10.42.148.**

5.47.37: 3 copulate, populate, stipulate; 4 depopulate, manipulate.

5.47.38: 4 congratulate, expostulate; 5 recapitulate.

5.47.39: 1 plate; 2 bookplate, breastplate, doorplate, gold plate, home plate, hot plate, L plate, nameplate, template, tin plate, tinplate; 3 boilerplate, contemplate, copperplate, fingerplate; 4 electroplate.
See also **10.42.148.**

5.47.40: 1 m8, mate; 2 checkmate, classmate, flatmate, helpmate, housemate, inmate, messmate, playmate, primate, roommate, shipmate, teammate, workmate; 3 automate, consummate; 4 amalgamate; 8 monosodium glutamate.
See also **10.2.47, 10.42.145.**

5.47.41: 2 cremate; 3 acclimate, animate, decimate, estimate, guesstimate, intimate, sublimate; 4 approximate, legitimate; 5 overestimate, underestimate.
See also **10.2.47.**

5.47.42: 2 schoolmate, soulmate, stalemate; 3 stablemate.

5.47.43: 2 donate, ornate; 3 incarnate, neonate; 4 predominate.

5.47.44: 3 alternate, cybernate, detonate, emanate, hibernate, hyphenate, pollinate, resonate; 4 alienate, concatenate, impersonate, Italianate, originate, oxygenate, proportionate, rejuvenate.
See also **10.2.48, 10.42.149.**

5.47.45: 2 innate; 3 cachinnate, desalinate, Latinate, paginate; 4 agglutinate, coordinate, procrastinate, subordinate.
See also **2.57, 10.2.49.**

5.47.46: 3 culminate, dominate, fulminate, germinate, nominate, ruminate, terminate; 4 abominate, contaminate, denominate, discriminate, disseminate,

eliminate, exterminate, illuminate, incriminate, inseminate; 5 decontaminate.
See also **10.42.149.**

5.47.47: 3 chlorinate, marinate, urinate; 4 indoctrinate.
See also **10.2.49.**

5.47.48: 3 fascinate, vaccinate; 4 assassinate, hallucinate.
See also **10.2.49, 10.42.149.**

5.47.49: 2 cognate, magnate, stagnate; 3 designate, impregnate.
See also **10.2.37.**

5.47.50: 1 pate, spate; 2 palpate, pupate; 3 dissipate, exculpate, extirpate; 4 anticipate, emancipate, participate.
See also **10.2.50.**

5.47.51: 1 crate, freight, prate, rate; 2 aerate, berate, birth rate, curate, gyrate, irate, orate, prorate, quorate, third-rate; 3 aspirate, consecrate, desecrate, inquorate, mortgage rate, second rate, zero-rate; 4 inaugurate.
See also **5.48, 10.2.51, 10.42.150.**

5.47.52: 3 decorate, federate, moderate, numerate, perforate, saturate, tolerate, underrate; 4 accelerate, acculturate, commemorate, commiserate, decelerate, enumerate, exaggerate, exhilarate, invigorate, proliferate, redecorate, refrigerate; 5 ameliorate, deteriorate.
See also **10.2.52, 10.2.53, 10.42.151.**

5.47.53: 3 liberate; 4 collaborate, corroborate, deliberate, elaborate, reverberate.
See also **10.2.52, 10.42.151.**

5.47.54: 2 narrate; 3 generate, venerate; 4 degenerate, exonerate, incinerate, regenerate, remunerate.
See also **10.2.52.**

5.47.55: 3 operate, separate; 4 cooperate, evaporate, exasperate, incorporate, recuperate; 5 reincorporate.
See also **2.57, 9.14.89, 10.42.151.**

5.47.56: 3 lacerate, macerate; 4 eviscerate, incarcerate.
See also **10.2.52.**

5.47.57: 4 adulterate, alliterate, expectorate, obliterate, reiterate, transliterate.
See also **10.2.52.**

5.47.58: 2 hydrate, vibrate; 3 adumbrate, calibrate, celebrate, dehydrate; 4 carbohydrate.
See also **10.2.51.**

5.47.59: **1** GR8, grate, great; **2** ingrate, migrate; **3** denigrate, emigrate, immigrate, integrate; **4** disintegrate, Peter the Great.
See also **10.2.51, 10.2.52, 10.42.150**.

5.47.60: **1** trait; **2** cut-rate, filtrate, nitrate; **3** arbitrate, concentrate, infiltrate, penetrate, perpetrate, self-portrait; **5** interpenetrate; **6** potassium nitrate.
See also **10.42.150**.

5.47.61: **1** straight, strait; **2** castrate, first-rate, frustrate, prostrate, substrate; **3** demonstrate, illustrate, magistrate, orchestrate, remonstrate, sequestrate.
See also **5.48, 10.42.150**.

5.47.62: **1** sate, seth; **2** pulsate; **3** compensate, insensate; **5** overcompensate.
See also **10.42.145**.

5.47.63: **1** Tate; **2** dictate, lactate, mutate, rotate, spectate; **3** acetate, amputate, annotate, commentate, potentate, vegetate; **4** facilitate, orientate; **5** disorientate.
See also **10.2.54**.

5.47.64: **3** agitate, cogitate, gravitate, hesitate, imitate, irritate, levitate, meditate, militate, palpitate; **4** debilitate, decapitate, necessitate, precipitate, premeditate, regurgitate, resuscitate; **5** incapacitate, rehabilitate.
See also **10.2.55, 10.42.145**.

5.47.65: **1** state; **2** estate, prostate, restate, rogue state, tristate, upstate, wait state; **3** apostate, city-state, frontline state, head of state, intestate, nanny state, nation-state, police state, real estate, reinstate, steady state, welfare state; **4** housing estate; **5** Minister of State; **6** Secretary of State.
Yeah I'm sorry I was late
Well I missed the train
And then the traffic was a state
And I can't be arsed to carry on in this
debate
(Arctic Monkeys)

5.47.66: **3** devastate, interstate, intrastate, member state, overstate, superstate, understate.
See also **10.2.54, 10.42.145**.

5.47.67: **3** aggravate, elevate, enervate, excavate, innovate, renovate, salivate.
See also **10.2.56, 10.42.152**.

5.47.68: **3** activate, captivate, cultivate, inactivate, motivate, titivate; **4** deactivate, demotivate, reactivate.
See also **10.2.56, 10.42.152**.

5.47.69: **1** wait, weight; **2** Braithwaite, equate, flyweight, lightweight, makeweight; **3** bantamweight, heavyweight, hundredweight, middleweight; **4** atomic weight, light heavyweight; **5** superheavyweight.
Sleight of hand and twist of fate
On a bed of nails she makes me wait
And I wait... without you.
(U2)
See also **10.2.37, 10.42.145**.

5.47.70: **2** await; **3** counterweight, featherweight, overweight, paperweight, underweight, welterweight.

5.48: **1** rates, straits, Yates; **2** dire straits, Gulf States; **3** Pearly Gates.
See also **5.47.51, 5.47.61**.

5.49: **1** faith, wraith; **2** good faith; **3** interfaith.
See also **5.24**.

5.50: **1** aitch; **2** ph; **3** ABH, GBH, HRH.

5.51: **1** cave, fave, knave, nave, pave, save, shave, stave, they've; **2** behave, concave; **3** aftershave, autosave, Fingal's Cave, misbehave; **4** Aladdin's cave.
Come not, when I am dead
To drop thy foolish tears upon my grave,
To trample round my fallen head,
And vex the unhappy dust thou wouldst
not save.
(Alfred Tennyson)
See also **5.23, 10.42.177, 10.42.178**.

5.51.1: **1** slave; **2** conclave, enclave, enslave; **3** galley slave.
See also **5.52**.

5.51.2: **1** brave, crave, grave, rave; **2** deprave, engrave, Redgrave; **3** architrave; **4** watery grave.
O! say, does that star-spangled banner
yet wave
O'er the land of the free, and the home of
the brave?
(Francis Scott Key)
See also **5.52, 9.14.97, 10.42.177**.

5.51.3: **1** waive, wave; **2** brainwave, crime wave, heatwave, New Wave; **3** microwave, tidal wave.
See also **5.52**.

5.52: **1** waived; **2** depraved, engraved, enslaved; **3** ill-behaved, well-behaved.
See also **5.51.1, 5.51.2, 5.51.3**.

5.53: **1** Graves; **2** airwaves, Bygraves.

5.54: **1** baize, chaise, daze, faze, gaze, Hayes, haze, maize, maze, phase, stays;

2 amaze, dog days, Gervais, liaise, nowadays, pj's, PJs, post-chaise; **3** cojones, hollandaise, mayonnaise, olden days, Pilates, polonaise, protease, salad days.

He would not stay for me, and who can wonder?
He would not stay for me to stand and gaze.
I shook his hand and tore my heart in sunder
And went with half my life about my ways.
(A. E. Housman)
See also **5.15.1, 5.55, 10.42.187.**

5.54.1: 1 Blaise, blaze, glaze, laze; **2** ablaze, malaise.
See also **5.55.**

5.54.2: 1 braise, craze, graze, phrase, praise, raise, raze; **2** appraise, catchphrase, erase, mores, rephrase, upraise, X-rays; **3** overpraise, paraphrase; **6** primus inter pares.
Fools may our scorn, not envy raise,
For envy is a kind of praise.
(John Gay)
See also **5.12, 5.55.**

5.54.3: 2 always, crossways, edgeways, endways, leastways, lengthways, longways, sideways, widthways; **3** anyways, wicked ways, winning ways; **4** British Airways.

5.55: 1 braised, crazed, dazed, fazed, glazed, grazed, praised, raised; **2** amazed, unfazed, upraised; **3** double-glazed.
See also **5.54, 5.54.1, 5.54.2.**

5.56: 1 beige; **2** cortège.

6.0: 1 deb, ebb, Jeb, pleb; **2** celeb, Zagreb.

6.0.1: 1 web, Webb; **2** cobweb, food web; **3** spiderweb, World Wide Web.

6.1: 1 dead, Ed, Med, Ned, said, Ted, wed, z, zed; **2** coed, gainsaid, premed, unsaid; **3** aforesaid, A to Z, newlywed.
See also **10.2.6, 10.42.16.**

6.1.1: 1 bed; **2** bunk bed, coalbed, day bed, deathbed, embed, flatbed, hotbed, imbed, raised bed, seabed, seedbed, sickbed, sunbed, twin bed; **3** bridal bed, forcing bed, marriage bed.
See also **10.42.16.**

6.1.2: 2 abed, flowerbed; **3** feather bed, lie-abed, oyster bed, riverbed, waterbed.

6.1.3: 1 fed; **2** breastfed, corn-fed, unfed, well-fed; **3** overfed, underfed.
See also **9.29.2.**

6.1.4: 1 head; **2** airhead, Bankhead, beachhead, behead, bighead, bridgehead, death's head, dopehead, egghead, forehead, Gateshead, hogshead, Holyhead, hophead, Moorehead, pisshead, railhead, slaphead, spearhead, subhead, towhead, warhead, webhead; **3** arrowhead, Beachy Head, knucklehead, petrolhead, sleepyhead.
O bed! O bed! delicious bed!
That heaven upon earth to the weary head!
(Thomas Hood)
See also **6.3, 10.2.7, 10.42.16.**

6.1.5: 2 ahead, flower head; **3** copperhead, dunderhead, figurehead, go-ahead, hammerhead, head-to-head, letterhead, loggerhead, overhead; **4** cylinder head.
See also **6.3.**

6.1.6: 2 bedhead, deadhead, godhead, hard-head, redhead, Roundhead; **3** acidhead.
See also **10.42.16.**

6.1.7: 2 blackhead, blockhead, bulkhead, cokehead, crackhead, deckhead, dickhead, thickhead.

6.1.8: 2 bonehead, pinhead, skinhead; **3** Birkenhead, fountainhead, maidenhead.

6.1.9: 2 fathead, flathead, hothead, masthead, meathead, nethead, pithead, pothead, printhead, short head, whitehead; **3** read-write head.

6.1.10: 1 bled, fled, lead, led, sled; **2** bobsled, dogsled, misled.
See also **9.14.62, 9.29.3, 10.42.18.**

6.1.11: 1 sped; **2** biped, moped, op-ed; **3** quadruped.
See also **9.29.5, 19.44.**

6.1.12: 1 cred, dread, Fred, read, red, shred, thread, tread; **2** brick-red, flame-red, Jared, retread, well-read; **3** Ethelred, infrared, Lincoln red; **4** cardinal red, pillarbox red.
See also **6.3, 10.2.6.**

6.1.13: 1 bread, bred; **2** black bread, break bread, crispbread, cross-bred, French bread, inbred, low-bred, purebred, shortbread, sweetbread, well-bred, white bread; **3** daily bread, gingerbread, interbred, laver bread, thoroughbred.
Music I heard with you was more than music,
And bread I broke with you was more than bread.
Now that I am without you, all is desolate;

All that was once beautiful is dead.
(Conrad Aiken)
See also **9.29.6.**

6.1.14: 1 spread; **2** bedspread, outspread, widespread; **3** centre spread.
See also **10.42.16.**

6.1.15: 1 shed; **2** bloodshed, cowshed, woodshed; **3** garden shed, potting shed, watershed.

6.1.16: 1 stead; **2** bedstead, bestead, farmstead, Hampstead, Hickstead, homestead, instead, Ofsted, Plumstead.

6.2: 1 breadth; **2** hair's-breadth.

6.3: 1 heads, threads; **3** loggerheads, newlyweds, overheads.
See also **6.1.4, 6.1.5, 6.1.12.**

6.4: 1 chef, clef, deaf, eff, kef, ref; **2** aleph, bass clef, Brezhnev, ganef, Kiev, Kislev, tone-deaf; **3** alto clef, IVF, MDF, Nureyev, RAF, tenor clef, treble clef, Turgenev, UNICEF; **4** Diaghilev, Mendeleyev, partially deaf, Prokofiev.
See also **2.54.62, 6.53, 10.42.32.**

6.5: 1 cleft, deft, heft, left, theft, weft; **2** bereft, grand theft; **3** autotheft.

6.6: 1 beg, egg, keg, meg; **2** bad egg, duck-egg, goose egg, nest egg, nutmeg; **3** curate's egg, powder keg; **4** chicken-and-egg situation.
See also **10.42.33.**

6.6.1: 1 leg; **2** blackleg, bootleg, dogleg, foreleg, hind leg.
See also **6.8, 10.42.33.**

6.6.2: 1 peg; **2** jpeg, mpeg; **3** Easter egg, off-the-peg, overegg, Winnipeg.

6.7: 2 barelegged, bowlegged, doglegged, long-legged, one-legged.

6.8: 1 dregs, legs; **4** daddy longlegs.
See also **6.6.1.**

6.9: 1 dredge, edge, hedge, kedge, reg, sedge, veg, wedge; **2** knife-edge, on edge; **3** cutting-edge, leading edge; **5** thin end of the wedge.
See also **6.32, 10.42.36.**

6.9.1: 1 fledge, ledge, pledge, sledge; **2** allege.
See also **6.32, 10.42.36.**

6.10: 1 fleck, heck, lek, sec; **2** Bishkek, cromlech, Dalek, exec, parsec; **3** triple sec.

6.10.1: 1 beck; **2** Birkbeck, Brubeck, pinchbeck, Purbeck, Quebec, rebec, Steinbeck, Uzbek.

6.10.2: 1 deck; **2** bedeck, flight deck, foredeck, poop deck, sun deck; **3** cassette deck, quarterdeck; **4** Melchizedek.
The boy stood on the burning deck
Whence all but he had fled;
The flame that lit the battle's wreck
Shone round him o'er the dead.
(Felicia Hemans)

6.10.3: 1 neck; **2** breakneck, crew-neck, redneck, roll-neck, roughneck, scoop neck, swan neck, V-neck, wryneck; **3** bottleneck, leatherneck, neck-and-neck, ogonek, polo-neck, rubberneck, turtleneck.

6.10.4: 1 peck, spec, speck; **2** henpeck, kopeck, OPEC.
See also **6.11.4.**

6.10.5: 1 dreck, trek, wreck; **2** shipwreck; **3** nervous wreck.
See also **6.12.8.**

6.10.6: 1 tech; **2** Aztec, BTEC, high-tech, low-tech; **3** biotech, discotheque.

6.10.7: 1 check, cheque, Czech; **2** backcheck, bad cheque, crosscheck, Dubček, forecheck, hacek, namecheck, rain check, recheck, stickcheck; **3** bodycheck, countercheck, double-check, Janáček; **4** traveller's cheque; **5** security check.
See also **6.12.**

6.11: 1 ex, hex, vex; **2** Amex, annex, annexe, convex, FX, ibex, Kleenex, Tex-Mex.
See also **6.13, 10.42.137.**

6.11.1: 2 codex, index, Spandex; **3** Rolodex; **4** FT index, Hang Seng index, Nikkei Index.

6.11.2: 1 flex; **2** ilex, reflex, Rolex, telex; **3** circumflex, retroflex.

6.11.3: 2 complex, duplex, perplex; **3** multiplex; **5** Oedipus complex.
See also **6.13, 10.42.137.**

6.11.4: 1 pecs, specs; **2** apex, Perspex, sunspecs, tippex.
See also **6.10.4.**

6.11.5: 1 Rex; **2** Durex, forex, Lurex, Pyrex.

6.11.6: 1 sex; **2** same-sex; **3** cybersex, unisex.

6.11.7: 2 cortex, latex, Semtex, vertex, vortex.

6.12: 1 checked; **2** bedecked, detect, henpecked, protect, unchecked; **3** architect.
See also **6.10.7, 10.2.76.**

6.12.1: **2** affect, defect, effect, infect, perfect, prefect; **3** disinfect, side effect, sound effect, speech defect; **4** aftereffect, snowball effect; **5** domino effect.
See also **10.2.72, 10.42.166.**

6.12.2: **2** abject, eject, inject, object, project, reject, subject; **3** interject.
See also **10.2.71.**

6.12.3: **2** collect, neglect; **3** acrolect, dialect, intellect, recollect; **4** idiolect, sociolect.
See also **10.2.73.**

6.12.4: **2** elect, select; **3** basilect, deselect; **5** president-elect.
See also **10.2.73.**

6.12.5: **1** flecked; **2** deflect, inflect, reflect; **3** genuflect.
See also **10.2.73.**

6.12.6: **2** bullnecked, connect, low-necked, stiff-necked; **3** disconnect, reconnect; **4** interconnect.
See also **10.2.74, 10.42.166.**

6.12.7: **2** aspect, expect, inspect, prospect, respect, suspect; **3** circumspect, disrespect, retrospect, self-respect.
See also **10.2.75.**

6.12.8: **1** wrecked; **2** correct, direct, erect, shipwrecked, Utrecht; **3** incorrect, indirect, misdirect, redirect, resurrect; **6** politically correct; **7** politically incorrect.
See also **6.10.5, 9.14.91, 10.2.71.**

6.12.9: **1** sect; **2** bisect, dissect, insect, trisect; **3** intersect, vivisect.
See also **10.2.71.**

6.13: **1** next, vexed; **2** perplexed; **3** oversexed, undersexed.
See also **6.11, 6.11.3.**

6.13.1: **1** Brecht, echt, text; **2** context, pretext, subtext, Utrecht; **3** hypertext, teletext; **4** videotext.
See also **10.42.170.**

6.14: **1** Elle, fell, gel, hell, jell, yell; **2** befell, Dalziel, Noel, Ravel; **3** au naturel, Cadfael, caravel, parallel, Raphael, surreal, URL; **4** materiel.

6.14.1: **1** bel, bell, belle; **2** barbell, bluebell, cowbell, doorbell, dumbbell, handbell, harebell, Nobel, rebel, snowbell; **3** Annabel, decibel, Isabel, Jezebel; **4** Liberty Bell.

6.14.2: **1** Del, dell; **2** Fidel, Rendell; **3** asphodel, citadel, infidel.

6.14.3: **1** Mel, smell; **2** pell-mell; **3** béchamel, caramel, Philomel; **4** crème caramel, HTML, SGML.

6.14.4: **1** knell; **2** Brunel, Cannelle, Parnell, quenelle.

6.14.5: **2** Chanel; **3** fontanelle, mangonel, organelle, personnel, pimpernel.

6.14.6: **2** compel, impel, lapel, propel, rappel, repel.
See also **6.15, 10.42.70.**

6.14.7: **1** spell; **2** dispel, expel, Godspell, misspell; **3** counterspell.
See also **6.15, 10.42.70.**

6.14.8: **1** cell, sell; **2** dry cell, excel, fuel cell, hard sell, nerve cell, outsell, presell, Purcell, resell, soft sell, T-cell; **3** carousel, oversell, padded cell, photocell, red blood cell, undersell; **4** ADSL.
See also **10.42.70.**

6.14.9: **1** shell; **2** bombshell, clamshell, eggshell, nutshell, seashell; **3** cockleshell, tortoiseshell; **6** Mont-Saint-Michel.
See also **10.42.70.**

6.14.10: **1** tell; **2** cartel, dentelle, foretell, hotel, motel, retell; **3** bagatelle, clientele, muscatel, Neuchatel; **4** maître d'hôtel, show-and-tell, William Tell.

A thousand tymes have I herd men telle
That ther ys joy in hevene and peyne in
*   helle,*
And I acorde wel that it ys so;
But, natheless, yet wot I wel also
That ther nis noon dwellyng in this
*   contree,*
That eyther hath in hevene or helle ybe.
(Geoffrey Chaucer)
See also **10.42.70.**

6.14.11: **1** dwell, quell, swell, well; **2** Bakewell, Blackwell, Boswell, Bridewell, Buñuel, Caldwell, Cornwell, Cromwell, farewell, groundswell, inkwell, Maxwell, Orwell, Sitwell, speedwell, stairwell, Stockwell, unwell; **3** Camberwell, Clerkenwell, Motherwell, ne'er-do-well.
See also **10.42.70.**

6.14.12: **2** gazelle, Giselle, Moselle; **4** mademoiselle, mesdemoiselles.

6.15: **1** geld, held, jelled, meld, veld, weld; **2** beheld, Danegeld, expelled, impelled, Trinkgeld, upheld, withheld; **3** jet-propelled; **4** unparallelled.
See also **6.14.6, 6.14.7, 10.42.14.**

6.16: **1** elf, self; **2** herself, himself, itself, myself, oneself, ourself, themself, thyself, yourself; **3** cyberself, inner self, outer self; **4** do-it-yourself.
See also **6.21, 6.23**.

6.16.1: **1** elk, shelf, whelk; **2** bookshelf, ice shelf; **3** mantelshelf, off-the-shelf.
My, my, at Waterloo Napoleon did
* surrender*
Oh yeah, and I have met my destiny in
* quite a similar way*
The history book on the shelf
Is always repeating itself
(Abba)
See also **6.23**.

6.17: **1** elm, helm, realm; **2** Anselm; **3** overwhelm, underwhelm.
See also **10.42.84**.

6.18: **1** help, kelp, whelp, yelp; **2** home help, self-help.
See also **10.42.104**.

6.19: **1** Celt, dealt, dwelt, knelt, melt, pelt, smelt, spelt, svelte, veldt, welt; **2** Blofeld; **3** Roosevelt.
See also **10.42.167**.

6.19.1: **1** belt; **2** black belt, brown belt, greenbelt, lifebelt, seat belt; **3** Cotton Belt, money belt, safety belt; **4** commuter belt.

6.19.2: **1** felt; **2** heartfelt; **3** Bielefeld, underfelt.

6.20: **1** belch, squelch, Welch.

6.21: **1** health, stealth, wealth; **3** commonwealth, mental health.
With what deep murmurs through time's
* silent stealth*
Doth thy transparent, cool, and watery
* wealth*
Here flowing fall
And chide and call.
(Henry Vaughan)
See also **6.16**.

6.22: **1** 12, delve, shelve, twelve.
See also **6.23, 10.42.176**.

6.23: **1** elves, selves, shelves; **2** ourselves, themselves, yourselves.
See also **6.16, 6.16.1, 6.22**.

6.24: **1** Welles, Wells; **2** Seychelles; **3** Dardanelles, wedding bells.

6.25: **1** em, gem, Jem, phlegm, stem, them; **2** ad rem, AM, a.m., brainstem, FM, IM, proem, pro tem, suprême; **3** ad finem, apophthegm; **4** Château d'Yquem, crème de la crème; **6** infra dignitatem.

6.25.1: **2** GM, pm; **3** AGM, ATM, per diem; **4** carpe diem; **6** ante meridiem.

6.25.2: **2** condemn, diadem, idem, Lib Dem, modem; **3** anadem, ibidem.
They shall grow not old, as we that are
* left grow old:*
Age shall not weary them, nor the years
* condemn.*
At the going down of the sun and in the
* morning*
We will remember them.
(Laurence Binyon)

6.25.3: **1** hem; **2** ahem, mayhem; **3** Bethlehem; **5** Star of Bethlehem.

6.26: **1** hemp, Kemp, temp.

6.27: **1** dreamt, tempt; **2** attempt, contempt, exempt, pre-empt, unkempt; **3** tax-exempt.
See also **10.2.89, 10.42.169**.

6.28: **1** Thames; **4** Old Father Thames.

6.29: **1** ben, Benn, den, en, fen, gen, glen, Glenn, hen, Jen, ken, Seine, ten, then, when, wren, yen, Zen; **2** again, Ardennes, Cayenne, Chechen, Cheyenne, doyenne, kaizen, lichen, Loren, moorhen, peahen, top-ten, UN, Verlaine; **3** allergen, born-again, CNN, halogen, ITN, mise-en-scène, Number Ten, Ségolène; **4** ibuprofen, tamoxifen.
Humpty Dumpty sat on a wall,
Humpty Dumpty had a great fall.
All the king's horses,
And all the king's men,
Couldn't put Humpty together again.
(Children's Verse)

6.29.1: **3** Adrienne, julienne; **4** comedienne, tragedienne.

6.29.2: **1** men; **2** amen, dolmen, hymen, nomen; **3** agnomen, cognomen; **4** catechumen.

6.29.3: **1** pen, Penn; **2** bullpen, Phnom Penh, pigpen, playpen; **3** EpiPen.

6.30: **1** blend, end, lend, vend, wend; **2** addend, augend, back end, bin end, bookend, Bridgend, Crouch End, dead-end, dog-end, fag end, Gravesend, high-end, Townsend, weekend, world's end; **3** apprehend, comprehend, dividend, journey's end, minuend, reprehend.
See also **10.2.19, 10.42.28**.

6.30.1: **1** bend; **2** ABEND, S-bend, unbend; **3** hairpin bend.
See also **6.39, 10.42.28**.

6.30.2: 1 fend; 2 defend, offend; 3 reoffend.
See also **10.2.19, 10.42.28.**

6.30.3: 1 mend; 2 amend, commend, emend; 3 recommend.
See also **6.39, 10.2.19, 10.42.28.**

6.30.4: 2 append, deep end, depend, stipend, upend; 4 interdepend.

6.30.5: 1 spend; 2 adspend, expend, misspend, suspend; 3 overspend, underspend.
See also **10.42.28.**

6.30.6: 1 rend, trend; 2 downtrend, uptrend; 3 bitter end.

6.30.7: 1 friend; 2 befriend, best friend, boyfriend, false friend, girlfriend, pen friend; 3 ladyfriend; 4 fair-weather friend.
Give me the avowed, erect and manly foe;
Firm I can meet, perhaps return the blow;
But of all plagues, good Heaven, thy
*   wrath can send,*
Save me, oh, save me, from the candid
*   friend.*
(George Canning)

6.30.8: 1 send; 2 ascend, descend, godsend, transcend; 3 condescend.
See also **10.42.28.**

6.30.9: 1 tend; 2 attend, contend, frontend, intend, portend, pretend, subtend; 4 superintend.
See also **10.2.20, 10.42.28.**

6.30.10: 2 best end, distend, East End, extend, Ostend, West End; 4 overextend.
See also **10.2.20.**

6.31: 1 Penge; 2 avenge, revenge, Stonehenge; 6 Montezuma's revenge.

6.32: 1 fledged, pledged, wedged; 2 alleged, gilt-edged, two-edged, unfledged; 3 double-edged, fully-fledged.
See also **6.9, 6.9.1.**

6.33: 1 dense, hence, tense, thence, whence; 2 commence, condense, immense, intense, pretence; 3 recommence.
See also **6.38, 9.14.80.**

6.33.1: 1 fence; 2 defence, offence; 3 self-defence; 6 Ministry of Defence.
See also **10.42.138.**

6.33.2: 1 pence, Spence; 2 dispense, expense, suspense; 3 recompense.

6.33.3: 1 sense; 2 horse sense, incense, sixth sense; 3 common sense, frankincense.
See also **6.38.**

6.34: 1 bent, dent, gent, Ghent, Kent, lent, spent; 2 hell-bent, ident, indent, misspent, relent, repent, Tashkent, unbent; 3 overspent, underspent; 5 semipermanent.
Who would true valour see,
Let him come hither;
One here will constant be,
Come wind, come weather
There's no discouragement
Shall make him once relent
His first avow'd intent
To be a pilgrim.
(John Bunyan)
See also **10.2.85.**

6.34.1: 1 meant; 2 augment, cement, comment, ferment, foment, fragment, lament, pigment, torment; 3 defragment, document, ornament.
See also **10.2.86.**

6.34.2: 3 complement, compliment, implement, regiment, supplement; 4 experiment.
See also **10.2.86.**

6.34.3: 1 Brent, rent, Trent; 2 rack-rent; 4 peppercorn rent.
See also **10.2.85.**

6.34.4: 1 cent, scent, sent; 2 absent, accent, ascent, assent, consent, descent, dissent, per cent; 3 heaven-sent.
In matters of commerce the fault of the
*   Dutch*
Is offering too little and asking too much;
The French are with equal advantage
*   content,*
So we'll slap on Dutch bottoms a twenty
*   per cent.*
(George Canning)
See also **10.2.85.**

6.34.5: 1 tent; 2 content, extent, intent, portent; 3 discontent, malcontent; 4 oxygen tent.
See also **10.2.85.**

6.34.6: 1 vent; 2 Advent, event, invent, prevent; 3 circumvent, nonevent, reinvent.
See also **10.2.85.**

6.34.7: 1 Gwent, went; 2 forwent, frequent; 3 underwent.

6.34.8: 2 present, resent; 3 represent; 4 misrepresent.
See also **10.2.85.**

6.35: 1 bench, blench, clench, Dench, quench, stench, tench, wench; 2 backbench, Queen's Bench, workbench.
See also **6.36.**

6.35.1: **1** drench, French, trench, wrench; **2** entrench, retrench.
See also **6.36**.

6.36: **1** clenched, drenched; **2** entrenched, sundrenched.
See also **6.35**, **6.35.1**.

6.37: **1** nth, tenth.

6.38: **2** against, condensed, incensed.
See also **6.33**, **6.33.3**.

6.39: **1** bends; **2** amends, bookends.
See also **6.30.1**, **6.30.3**.

6.40: **1** Benz, cleanse, Fens, lens; **3** contact lens, fisheye lens; **4** impatiens, locum tenens; **5** Homo sapiens.
See also **10.42.186**.

6.41: **2** Boateng, ginseng; **3** Mafikeng; **4** nasi goreng.

6.42: **1** length, strength; **2** full-length, knee-length, waist-length, wavelength; **3** feature-length, focal length, shoulder-length, tower of strength.

6.43: **1** cep, crêpe, pep, prep, rep, schlep, yep; **2** Dieppe; **4** holiday rep.
See also **6.45**.

6.43.1: **1** step, steppe; **2** doorstep, footstep, goose step, instep, lockstep, misstep, one-step, quickstep, sidestep, two-step; **3** overstep, step-by-step.
See also **6.44**, **10.42.104**.

6.44: **1** steps; **2** biceps, footsteps, forceps, triceps; **3** quadriceps.
See also **6.43.1**.

6.45: **1** crept, kept, leapt, schlepped, slept, swept, wept; **2** adept, inept, well-kept, windswept; **3** overslept.
See also **6.43**.

6.45.1: **2** accept, concept, except, precept, transept; **3** intercept.
See also **10.2.89**, **10.42.169**.

6.46: **1** depth; **2** in-depth.

6.47: **1** Bess, chess, fess, guess, Hess, Hesse, Jess, yes; **2** abbess, Black Bess, Brown Bess, BS, confess, duchesse, goddess, Jewess, largesse, outguess, possess, profess, prowess, PS, US; **3** acquiesce, bouillabaisse, deliquesce, dispossess, effervesce, NHS, repossess, SAS, second-guess, shepherdess, SOS, stewardess; **6** embarras de richesses.
See also **6.49.1**, **6.49.15**.

6.47.1: **1** bless, less; **2** unless; **3** coalesce, convalesce, nonetheless; **4** nevertheless.
That air and harmony of shape express,

Fine by degrees, and beautifully less.
(Matthew Prior)
See also **2.37.276**, **10.2.31**, **10.42.136**.

6.47.2: **1** mess; **3** HMS, PMS, SMS.

6.47.3: **1** ness; **2** finesse, lioness, Loch Ness, Sheerness; **3** deaconess, Inverness, marchioness.

6.47.4: **1** cress, stress, tress; **2** caress, distress, duress, fluoresce, heiress, mayoress, peeress, prioress; **3** murderess, sorceress, watercress; **4** manageress.
See also **6.49.5**, **10.62.3**.

6.47.5: **1** dress; **2** address, full-dress, headdress, nightdress, redress, sundress, undress; **3** battledress, cocktail dress, evening dress, readdress, wedding dress, window-dress.
To avoid complications
She never kept the same address
In conversation
She spoke just like a baroness
(Queen)
See also **6.49.7**.

6.47.6: **2** Congress, digress, egress, ingress, negress, progress, regress, transgress; **3** retrogress; **4** work in progress; **5** Trades Union Congress.

6.47.7: **1** press; **2** compress, depress, express, impress, oppress, repress, suppress; **3** decompress, gutter press; **4** Pony Express; **6** American Express, Associated Press.
See also **6.49.8**.

6.47.8: **2** abscess, assess, obsess, princess, process, recess.
See also **6.49.9**, **10.42.136**.

6.47.9: **2** process; **3** due process, preprocess, reprocess.
See also **6.49.9**, **10.42.136**.

6.47.10: **2** access, excess, success; **4** multiaccess, random-access.

6.47.11: **1** Tess; **2** giantess, priestess; **3** poetess, politesse, prophetess, viscountess.

6.48: **1** desk; **2** burlesque, cash desk, grotesque, sounddesk, sports desk; **3** arabesque, gigantesque, humoresque, Junoesque, Kafkaesque, picaresque, picturesque, Pythonesque, Ramboesque, Romanesque, statuesque.

6.49: **1** best, guest, pest; **2** beau geste, behest, Trieste; **3** Budapest, second-best, Sunday best.
See also **10.2.91**.

6.49.1: **2** confessed, gabfest, infest, professed, talkfest; **3** manifest, self-confessed; **4** Oktoberfest.
See also **6.47, 10.2.91.**

6.49.2: **1** jest; **2** digest, ingest, suggest.

6.49.3: **1** blest, lest; **2** molest, unblessed; **3** arbalest.

6.49.4: **1** nest; **2** crow's nest, love nest, wasps' nest.

6.49.5: **1** breast, Brest, crest, rest, stressed, wrest; **2** abreast, armrest, backrest, bookrest, distressed, footrest, redbreast, unrest, unstressed.
Maid of Athens, ere we part,
Give, oh give me back my heart!
Or, since that has left my breast,
Keep it now, and take the rest!
(Lord Byron)
See also **6.47.4.**

6.49.6: **2** arrest; **3** Bucharest, house arrest; **5** cardiac arrest, citizen's arrest.

6.49.7: **1** dressed; **2** headrest, undressed, well-dressed; **3** overdressed, self-addressed, underdressed.
See also **6.47.5.**

6.49.8: **1** pressed; **2** cold-pressed, compressed, depressed, hard-pressed, impressed, oppressed, repressed, suppressed; **3** unimpressed.
See also **6.47.7.**

6.49.9: **2** incest, obsessed, processed, recessed; **3** palimpsest, self-obsessed, unprocessed.
See also **6.47.8, 6.47.9.**

6.49.10: **1** test; **2** attest, contest, detest, flight-test, protest; **3** acid test, beta test, litmus test; **5** paternity test; **7** Eurovision song contest.
Keep up appearances; there lies the test
The world will give thee credit for the
rest.
(Charles Churchill)
See also **10.2.91.**

6.49.11: **1** chest; **2** hope chest, tea chest; **3** treasure chest.

6.49.12: **1** vest; **2** divest, invest, life vest; **3** disinvest, reinvest.
See also **10.2.91.**

6.49.13: **1** west; **2** Mae West, Midwest, northwest, southwest, Wild West.

6.49.14: **1** quest; **2** bequest, conquest, inquest, request; **4** Norman Conquest.

6.49.15: **1** zest; **2** possessed; **3** dispossessed, self-possessed.
See also **6.47.**

6.50: **1** crèche, flesh, mesh, thresh; **2** enmesh, gooseflesh, horseflesh; **3** Bangladesh, Marrakesh, synchromesh.

6.50.1: **1** fresh; **2** afresh, crème fraîche, refresh; **4** oven-fresh.
See also **10.42.140.**

6.51: **1** ate, debt, get, jet, met, nyet, pet, yet; **2** baguette, beget, brochette, cadet, couchette, courgette, forget, gazette, georgette, kismet, ladette, layette, nymphet, pipette, ringette, rosette, unmet, vignette; **3** crêpes suzette, epithet, marmoset, oubliette, parapet, serviette, suffragette, teacher's pet, winceyette.
See also **10.42.153.**

6.51.1: **2** duet; **3** minuet, pirouette, silhouette, statuette.

6.51.2: **1** bet; **2** abet, safe bet, Tibet; **3** alphabet; **4** aid and abet.
See also **10.42.153.**

6.51.3: **2** briquette, coquette, croquette, diskette, moquette; **3** etiquette, hic jacet, netiquette.

6.51.4: **1** let; **2** Colette, inlet, outlet, roulette, sublet, toilette, towelette; **3** epaulet, epaulette, flannelette, novelette; **4** eau de toilette, Russian roulette.
See also **10.42.153.**

6.51.5: **1** net, nett; **2** brunette, dinette, dragnet, fishnet, freenet, hairnet, Telnet, Usenet; **3** safety net; **4** mosquito net; **5** Marie Antoinette.
See also **10.42.153.**

6.51.6: **2** Burnet; **3** castanet, clarinet, Ethernet, extranet, Internet, intranet, maisonette; **4** marionette.

6.51.7: **2** spinet; **3** bassinet, kitchenette, martinet, stockinette.

6.51.8: **1** Brett, fret, threat; **2** arête, regret; **3** biothreat, Carteret, vinaigrette.
See also **6.52, 10.42.153.**

6.51.9: **2** barrette; **3** burette, cigarette, launderette, leatherette, majorette, minaret, spinneret, usherette.

6.51.10: **1** set, sett; **2** asset, beset, cassette, chipset, deep-set, earset, film set, jet set, offset, outset, preset, reset, subset, thickset, upset; **3** Exocet, heavyset, Somerset.
See also **6.52, 10.42.153.**

6.51.11: **2** dead set, handset, headset, mindset.

6.51.12: **2** inset, onset, sunset, twinset.

6.51.13: **1** stet; **2** motet, octet, quartet, quintet, septet, sextet; **3** string quartet, tête-à-tête.

6.51.14: **1** vet; **2** corvette, crevette, Tebet, Tevet.

6.51.15: **1** sweat, wet, whet; **2** cold sweat.

Hail fellow, well met,
All dirty and wet:
Find out, if you can,
Who's master, who's man.
(Jonathan Swift)
See also **6.52**.

6.52: **1** let's, sweats; **2** assets, Debrett's, Donets, regrets, rillettes; **3** castanets.
See also **6.51.8, 6.51.10, 6.51.15**.

6.53: **1** Beth, breath, death, saith, Seth; **2** Black Death, dogbreath, Gwyneth, last breath, Macbeth; **3** life-and-death, megadeath, Megadeth, shibboleth, sudden death, Velázquez; **4** Angel of Death.

No life that breathes with human breath
Has ever truly long'd for death.
(Alfred Tennyson)
See also **6.4**.

6.54: **1** etch, fetch, ketch, lech, retch, sketch, stretch, vetch, wretch; **2** outstretch; **3** overstretch, thumbnail sketch.
See also **6.55, 10.42.175**.

6.55: **1** etched, stretched; **2** far-fetched, outstretched; **3** overstretched.
See also **6.54**.

6.56: **1** Dev, lev, Neve, rev; **2** Kislev, Negev.

6.57: **1** fez; **2** Ades, Baez, Boulez, Cortés, Cortez, Gomez, Gonzalez, Inez, Márquez, Montez, oyez, Sanchez; **3** Marseillaise, Velázquez.

6.58: **2** cortege, Liège.

7.0: **1** duh, er, err, myrrh, Ur, were, whir, whirr, year; **2** à deux, aver, Ben Hur, chasseur, demur, douceur, farceur, longueur, masseur, milieu, Monsieur, poseur, Richelieu, voyeur; **3** bon viveur, connoisseur, de rigueur, force majeure, pas de deux, Schumacher; **4** entrepreneur, intrapreneur.
See also **8.14**.

7.1: **1** birr, brrr, bur, burr; **2** timber.

7.2: **1** fir, fur; **2** chauffeur, coiffeur, confer, defer, fake fur, infer, prefer, refer, transfer.
See also **7.10.3**.

7.3: **1** cur, Kerr; **2** concur, incur, occur, recur; **3** cri du coeur, reoccur.

7.4: **1** Bleu, blur, slur; **2** jongleur; **3** cordon bleu.
See also **7.10**.

7.5: **1** per, purr, spur; **2** cockspur, hotspur, larkspur.

7.6: **1** stir; **2** astir, auteur, bestir, deter, hauteur, inter, Pasteur; **3** disinter, raconteur, rapporteur, saboteur; **4** animateur, repetiteur, restaurateur; **7** agent provocateur.
See also **10.42.112**.

7.7: **1** blurb, curb, herb, kerb; **2** disturb, exurb, perturb, suburb, superb.

Dear Night! this world's defeat;
The stop to busy fools; care's check and
  curb;
The day of spirits; my soul's calm retreat
Which none disturb!
(Henry Vaughan)
See also **7.8, 7.9, 10.42.13**.

7.7.1: **1** verb; **2** adverb, proverb, reverb; **3** phrasal verb.

7.8: **2** disturbed, perturbed; **3** undisturbed, unperturbed.
See also **7.7**.

7.9: **1** burbs; **2** mixed herbs, Proverbs, suburbs.
See also **7.7**.

7.10: **1** blurred, curd, gird, Kurd, nerd, sherd, third, turd; **2** absurd, bean curd, Cape Verde, potsherd; **3** undeterred.
See also **7.4**.

7.10.1: **1** bird, Byrd; **2** blackbird, bluebird, cagebird, game bird, halberd, jailbird, jaybird, lovebird, seabird, snowbird, songbird, yardbird; **3** frigate bird, hummingbird, ladybird, mockingbird, muttonbird, whirlybird.

7.10.2: **2** lyrebird; **3** bowerbird, butcherbird, mynah bird, weaverbird.

7.10.3: **1** furred; **2** conferred, deferred, inferred, preferred; **3** tax-deferred.
See also **7.2**.

7.10.4: **1** heard, herd; **2** cowherd, goatherd, misheard, swineherd, unheard; **3** overheard.

7.10.5: **1** word; **2** buzzword, byword, catchword, code word, crossword, cuss word, foreword, headword, keyword, loanword, password, reword, swearword, watchword; **3** afterword, multiword, the f-word, weasel word; **4** four-letter word.
See also **10.2.3, 10.42.14**.

7.11: **1** kerf, serf, surf, turf; **2** boardsurf, windsurf; **3** AstroTurf.
See also **7.30, 10.42.32.**

7.12: **1** berg; **2** Goldberg, Lindbergh, Spielberg, Strindberg; **3** Heidelberg, Magdeburg; **4** lobster newburg.

7.12.2: **2** Hamburg, homburg, Limburg; **3** Luxembourg, Luxemburg, Nuremberg.

7.12.3: **2** Schoenberg; **3** Gothenburg, Gutenberg, Heisenberg, Wittenberg; **5** Yekaterinburg.

7.12.4: **2** Duisburg, iceberg, Pittsburgh, Salzburg; **3** Harrisburg; **4** Johannesburg.

7.12.5: **2** Augsburg, Duisburg, Ginsberg, Strasbourg; **3** Gettysburg, Williamsburg; **4** St Petersburg.

7.13: **1** dirge, purge, scourge, serge, splurge, surge, urge, verge; **2** asperge, converge, demiurge, diverge, upsurge; **3** dramaturge, thaumaturge.
See also **7.22.**

7.13.1: **1** merge; **2** demerge, emerge, immerge, mail merge, submerge; **3** re-emerge.
See also **7.22, 10.42.36.**

7.14: **1** cirque, dirk, irk, jerk, kirk, lurk, Merc, murk, perk, shirk, smirk, Turk, yerk; **2** berserk, Dunkirk, Falkirk, knee jerk, Selkirk; **3** Atatürk.

7.14.1: **1** berk, Bourke, burk, Burke; **2** hauberk; **3** back o'Bourke.

7.14.2: **1** quirk, work; **2** brainwork, brickwork, brushwork, clockwork, coachwork, cowork, earthwork, farmwork, firework, framework, homework, ironwork, legwork, patchwork, pipework, stonework, teamwork, witchwork; **3** openwork.
See also **7.15, 10.42.47.**

7.14.3: **3** interwork, masterwork, overwork, paperwork, plasterwork, pokerwork, timberwork, wickerwork.

7.14.4: **2** rework; **3** bodywork, busywork, donkeywork, fancywork, handiwork, journeywork.
See also **10.42.47.**

7.14.5: **2** fieldwork, groundwork, handwork, roadwork, spadework, woodwork.

7.14.6: **2** schoolwork; **3** metalwork, needlework, panelwork; **4** enamelwork.

7.14.7: **2** casework, classwork, coursework, guesswork, housework,

lacework, piecework, waxwork; **3** latticework.
See also **7.15.**

7.14.8: **2** artwork, breastwork, footwork, outwork, paintwork, shiftwork; **3** basketwork.

7.14.9: **2** fretwork, network; **4** old-boy network; **6** wide area network.
See also **10.42.47.**

7.15: **1** works; **2** brickworks, fireworks, gasworks, ironworks, roadworks, steelworks, waxworks; **3** waterworks.
See also **7.14.2, 7.14.7.**

7.16: **1** burl, churl, curl, earl, furl, hurl, Merle, pearl, perl, purl, skirl, swirl, twirl, whirl, whorl; **2** uncurl, unfurl.
See also **10.42.71.**

7.16.1: **1** girl; **2** call girl, choirgirl, cowgirl, daygirl, homegirl, It girl, new girl, old girl, salesgirl, schoolgirl, showgirl; **3** chorus girl, flower girl, papergirl, Valley Girl.

7.17: **1** world; **2** New World, Old World, old-world, real-world, Third World; **3** afterworld, netherworld, underworld.
The year's at the spring,
And day's at the morn;
Morning's at seven;
The hill-side's dew-pearled;
The lark's on the wing;
The snail's on the thorn;
God's in His heaven—
All's right with the world.
(Robert Browning)

7.18: **1** erm, germ, perm, therm; **2** wheatgerm; **3** isotherm, pachyderm, supergerm; **4** echinoderm.

7.18.1: **1** firm; **2** affirm, confirm, infirm; **3** disaffirm, reaffirm.
See also **2.54.81, 7.19, 9.14.70.**

7.18.2: **1** sperm; **3** endosperm, gymnosperm; **4** angiosperm.

7.18.3: **1** term; **2** long-term, midterm, short-term.

7.18.4: **1** squirm, worm; **2** bloodworm, bookworm, earthworm, flatworm, glowworm, hookworm, mealworm, ringworm, roundworm, silkworm, slowworm, tapeworm, woodworm.

7.19: **2** affirmed, confirmed; **3** unconfirmed.
See also **7.18.1.**

7.20: **1** churn, earn, fern, föhn, learn, spurn, urn, Verne, yearn; **2** adjourn, Ahern,

Aherne, sojourn, tree fern, unlearn, wyvern; **4** save as you earn.
See also **10.2.28, 10.42.98.**

7.20.1: **1** Bern, burn; **2** Blackburn, Coburn, Cockburn, heartburn, Hepburn, Kilburn, Shelburne, sunburn, Swinburne, windburn; **3** slash-and-burn.
See also **10.42.98.**

7.20.2: **2** concern, discern, Lucerne; **3** unconcern.
See also **7.21, 10.42.98.**

7.20.3: **1** tern, turn; **2** downturn, intern, lectern, nocturne, return, upturn, U-turn; **3** about-turn, Buggins turn, overturn, taciturn.

Oh I'm gonna buy this place and start a
  fire
Stand here until I fill all your hearts
  desire
Because I'm gonna buy this place and see
  it burn
And do back the things it did to you in
  return.
(Coldplay)
See also **7.24, 10.42.98.**

7.20.4: **1** stern, Sterne; **2** astern, pastern.

7.21: **2** concerned, unearned, upturned, well-earned, well-turned; **3** unconcerned.
See also **7.20.2.**

7.22: **1** merged, urged; **2** submerged.
See also **7.13, 7.13.1.**

7.23: **1** burnt, learnt, weren't; **2** sunburnt.

7.24: **1** Burns; **2** returns, sideburns.
See also **7.20.3.**

7.25: **1** burp, chirp, slurp, twerp; **2** Antwerp, usurp.

7.26: **1** curse, Erse, hearse, nurse, terse, worse; **2** coerce, commerce, disburse, immerse, rehearse, wet nurse; **3** reimburse.
See also **7.27, 10.42.132.**

7.26.1: **1** purse; **2** cutpurse, disperse; **3** intersperse, Privy Purse; **5** electronic purse.
See also **7.27.**

7.26.2: **1** verse; **2** adverse, averse, blank verse, converse, diverse, free verse, inverse, light verse, obverse, perverse, reverse, transverse, traverse; **3** universe; **4** chapter and verse.
It's hard to say why writing verse
Should terminate in drink or worse.
(A. P. Herbert)
See also **7.27.**

7.27: **1** cursed, first, Hearst, thirst, versed, worst; **2** Bratwurst, dispersed, headfirst, immersed, Knackwurst, Pankhurst, reversed, Sandhurst, submersed, unversed, well-versed; **3** interspersed, liverwurst, unrehearsed; **6** accursed.
See also **7.26, 7.26.1, 7.26.2.**

7.27.1: **1** burst; **2** cloudburst, downburst, outburst, starburst, sunburst.
See also **10.42.170.**

7.28: **1** Bert, blurt, Burt, dirt, flirt, girt, hurt, squirt, wert, yurt; **2** alert, desert, dessert, exert, Frankfurt, inert, ragwort, unhurt; **3** Ethelbert.
See also **7.29, 10.2.57, 10.42.154.**

7.28.1: **1** curt, skirt; **3** miniskirt, underskirt.
See also **10.42.154.**

7.28.2: **1** pert, spurt; **2** expert; **3** inexpert.

7.28.3: **1** cert; **2** assert, dead cert, insert; **3** disconcert.
See also **10.2.57, 10.42.154.**

7.28.4: **1** shirt; **2** Blackshirt, Brown Shirt, dress shirt, hair shirt, nightshirt, sweatshirt, T-shirt; **3** undershirt.

7.28.5: **2** advert, convert, covert, divert, invert, overt, pervert, revert, subvert; **4** animadvert.
See also **10.2.57, 10.42.154.**

7.28.6: **2** avert, pervert; **3** extravert, extrovert, introvert.
See also **10.2.57.**

7.29: **1** hertz; **2** deserts, outskirts; **3** gigahertz, kilohertz, megahertz.
See also **2.56.42, 7.28.**

7.30: **1** dearth, earth, firth, girth, mirth, Perth; **2** rare-earth, scorched earth, unearth; **3** down-to-earth, Middle-earth, potter's earth.
Long expected and long loved, that afar,
  God of the dim wood, you
Somewhere lay, as a child sleeping, a
  child suddenly reft from mirth,
White and wonderful yet, white in your
  youth, stretched upon foreign earth,
God, immortal and dead!
(Rupert Brooke)
See also **7.11.**

7.30.1: **1** berth, birth; **2** childbirth, rebirth, stillbirth, wide berth; **3** afterbirth, date of birth, virgin birth.

7.30.2: **1** worth; **2** Ainsworth, Hepworth, jobsworth, self-worth, Unsworth,

Wentworth, Wordsworth; **3** Butterworth, Illingworth, Kenilworth.

7.31: **1** birch, church, lurch, perch, search; **2** besmirch, Christchurch, High Church, Low Church, research, strip-search; **4** Anglican Church, Orthodox Church; **5** Episcopal Church; **6** Eastern Orthodox Church.
See also **10.42.175.**

7.32: **1** curve, derv, nerve, perv, swerve, verve; **2** hors d'oeuvre, unnerve.
See also **7.33.**

7.32.1: **1** serve; **2** conserve, listserv; **4** ready-to-serve.
See also **10.42.179.**

7.32.2: **2** deserve, observe, preserve, reserve; **3** game reserve; **5** nature reserve.
See also **7.33, 10.42.179.**

7.33: **1** curved, nerved; **2** deserved, preserved, reserved, unnerved; **3** iron-nerved, undeserved, unobserved, unreserved, well-preserved.
See also **7.32, 7.32.2.**

7.34: **1** furze, hers, Meuse; **2** berceuse, chanteuse, chartreuse, danseuse, masseuse, Messieurs.

8.0: **1** beer, bier, cheer, ear, fear, gear, jeer, kirsch, queer, rear, veer, weir, we're, year; **2** career, fakir, headgear, light-year, revere, severe, vizier, Zaire; **3** Benazir, interfere, lutetium, persevere, yesteryear; **4** Chinese New Year.
What makes all doctrines plain and
*   clear?*
About two hundred pounds a year.
And that which was prov'd true before
Prove false again? Two hundred more.
(Samuel Butler)
See also **2.1, 8.11, 8.14, 10.42.123.**

8.1: **1** dear, deer; **2** endear, idea, mandir, nadir, reindeer; **3** bombardier, brigadier, commandeer, grenadier.
See also **2.1.3, 10.42.123.**

8.2: **1** sphere; **3** atmosphere, biosphere, blogosphere, ecosphere, exosphere, hemisphere, mesosphere, stratosphere, thermosphere, troposphere; **4** ionosphere.

8.3: **1** hear, here; **2** adhere, cohere, mishear; **3** overhear.
See also **10.42.123.**

8.4: **1** clear, leer; **2** unclear; **3** Aaliyah, bandolier, cavalier, chandelier, fusilier, gondolier.
See also **2.1.6, 8.11, 10.42.123.**

8.5: **1** mere, smear; **2** Ameer, cashmere, emir, Samir; **4** cervical smear.
See also **2.1.9.**

8.6: **1** near, sneer; **2** pioneer, veneer; **3** auctioneer, buccaneer, engineer, mountaineer, mutineer, scrutineer, souvenir.
I try to say goodbye and I choke
I try to walk away and I stumble
Though I try to hide it it's clear
My world crumbles when you are not
*   near.*
(Macy Gray)
See also **2.1.11, 10.42.124, 10.42.125.**

8.7: **1** peer, pier, spear; **2** appear; **3** disappear, reappear.
See also **2.1.17, 8.11.**

8.8: **1** sear, seer; **2** sincere; **3** insincere, overseer.
See also **2.1.27, 10.42.123.**

8.9: **1** shear, sheer; **2** cashier, wind shear; **3** Renfrewshire; **4** Aberdeenshire.
See also **8.14, 10.42.123.**

8.10: **1** steer, tear, tier; **2** austere, frontier; **3** gazetteer, marketeer, muleteer, musketeer, pamphleteer, profiteer, puppeteer, racketeer, volunteer.
See also **2.1.29, 8.14, 10.42.123.**

8.11: **1** beard, cleared, feared, tiered, weird; **2** besmeared, Blackbeard, dog-eared, goatsbeard, lop-eared; **3** Aaron's beard, disappeared, old man's beard.
See also **8.0, 8.4, 8.7.**

8.12: **1** Friel, real; **2** ideal, surreal, unreal.
See also **2.37.1, 2.39.**

8.13: **1** fierce, Pearce, pierce.
O Nightingale! thou surely art
A creature of a 'fiery heart':
These notes of thine—they pierce and
*   pierce;*
Tumultuous harmony and fierce!
(William Wordsworth)
See also **2.54.1, 10.42.132.**

8.14: **1** cheers, Frears, Meares, Piers, shears, tears, years; **2** arrears, careers, three cheers; **3** donkey's years, golden years, Gondoliers, pinking shears; **4** crocodile tears.
See also **4.13, 7.0, 8.0, 8.9, 8.10.**

9.0: **1** ye; **2** Maui, Skopje; **3** employee.

9.1: **2** payee; **3** Pompeii, sae, UAE; **4** Agnus Dei.

9.2: **2** PE; **3** CBE, MBE, OBE.

9.3: **2** i.e.; **3** Hawaii; **4** PAYE, sine die.

9.4: **2** blowy, doughy, joey, showy, snowy, Zoe; **3** meadowy, shadowy, willowy, yellowy.

9.5: **2** chewy, cooee, gluey, gooey, hooey, hui, Louis, phooey, screwy; **3** Anouilh, chop suey, St Louis.

9.5.1: **2** Dewey, Dewi, dewy; **3** mildewy, sinewy; **4** evacuee, interviewee.

9.6: **1** be, bee; **2** Ashby, booby, Boothby, busby, Catesby, Cosby, Crosbie, Crosby, Dalby, Danby, Dolby, Frisbee, Gatsby, herby, Hornby, Libby, newbie, plebby, ruby, rugby; **3** Appleby, B2B, C2B, Jacobi, USB, wallaby, wannabe; **4** BYOB, Kentucky Derby; **6** mother-to-be.
Dance, then, wherever you may be;
I am the Lord of the Dance said he.
(Sydney Carter)
See also **10.62, 13.45.**

9.6.1: **2** abbey, Abby, cabbie, crabby, flabby, gabby, grabby, scabby, shabby, tabby.
See also **2.54.65.**

9.6.2: **2** barbie, derby, Rabi; **3** kohlrabi, Mugabe, Panjabi, Punjabi, Wahhabi, wasabi; **4** Abu Dhabi; **5** Mawlid al-Nabi.

9.6.3: **2** baby, maybe; **3** Achebe, bushbaby, crybaby; **4** test-tube baby.

9.6.4: **2** freebie, Hebe, Phoebe, TB; **3** honeybee, JCB, KGB.

9.6.5: **2** blobby, bobby, hobby, jobby, knobby, lobby, snobby.
See also **10.42.3.**

9.6.6: **2** dhobi, Gobi, goby, Kobe, obi, Toby; **3** adobe, Nairobi.

9.6.7: **2** chubby, clubby, grubby, hubby, scrubby, shrubby, stubby, tubby.

9.6.8: **2** Albee, bilby, trilby; **3** bumblebee, Dimbleby.

9.6.9: **2** Bambi, brumby, Formby, NIMBY, zombie; **4** Abercrombie, namby-pamby.

9.6.10: **3** Allenby, B & B, Dushanbe, R & B.

9.7: **1** Dee; **2** bawdy, broody, foodie, gaudy, Geordie, Jodie, MD, moody, OD, roadie, Sadie, shady, toady, Trudy, Verdi; **3** CJD, LSD, PhD; **4** Monteverdi, Rio Grande; **5** WMD.
See also **10.42.2.**

9.7.1: **2** baddie, baddy, caddie, caddy, daddy, faddy, laddie, laddy, Paddy; **3** big

Daddy, grandaddy, granddaddy, kabaddi, tea caddy.

9.7.2: **3** chickadee, comedy, custody, jeopardy, Lombardy, malady, melody, parody, perfidy, prosody, remedy, rhapsody, somebody, subsidy, tragedy, Zebedee; **4** black comedy, chiropody; **5** tragicomedy.
See also **9.29.1.**

9.7.3: **3** hymnody, Kennedy, monody, threnody.

9.7.4: **2** cadi, cardie, lardy, Mahdi, tardy, Yardie; **3** bacardi.

9.7.5: **2** Hardie, hardy; **3** foolhardy, half-hardy.
See also **2.54.66.**

9.7.6: **2** lady; **3** bag lady, charlady, first lady, landlady, milady, m'lady, old lady, Our Lady, pink lady, tea lady, white lady; **4** cleaning lady, dinner lady, leading lady, My Fair Lady, painted lady.
See also **10.62.**

9.7.7: **2** Eddie, eddy, Freddie, Freddy, heady, neddy, ready, steady, teddy; **3** already, rock steady, unready, unsteady; **4** combat-ready, oven-ready.
See also **9.14.39, 9.59.2.**

9.7.8: **2** birdie, birdy, nerdy, sturdy, wordy; **4** hurdy-gurdy.

9.7.9: **2** beady, didi, greedy, needy, reedy, speedy, tweedy, VD, weedy; **3** DVD, LED, STD.
See also **9.14.39.**

9.7.10: **2** CD, cedi, seedy.
See also **2.54.66.**

9.7.11: **2** biddy, bidi, giddy, kiddie, kiddy, middy, midi; **3** raggedy; **4** chickabiddy.

9.7.12: **2** Heidi, ID, tidy; **3** CID, untidy; **4** bona fide.

9.7.13: **2** shoddy, squaddie, toddy, wadi; **3** hot toddy; **4** Irrawaddy.
See also **9.14.39.**

9.7.14: **2** body, Peabody; **3** dogsbody, embody, homebody, nobody, somebody; **4** antibody, anybody, busybody, disembody, everybody.

9.7.15: **2** cloudy, dowdy, Gaudí, howdy, rowdy, Saudi.

9.7.16: **2** bloody, buddy, muddy, nuddy, ruddy, study; **3** brown study, work-study; **4** buddy-buddy, fuddy-duddy, understudy.
See also **9.29.1, 9.59.2.**

9.7.17: **2** goodie, goody, hoodie, hoody, woody; **3** Dunwoody; **4** goody-goody.
See also **9.59.2**.

9.7.18: **2** baldy, haldi, mouldy, olde, oldie; **3** unwieldy, Vivaldi; **4** Garibaldi, golden oldie, olde-worlde; **6** higgledy-piggledy.

9.7.19: **2** fundi; **3** A&E, burgundy, Burundi, Normandy, organdie, R & D.

9.7.20: **2** bandy, brandy, candy, dandy, Gandhi, grandee, handy, Mandy, randy, sandy, shandy; **3** nose candy; **6** modus operandi.
Candy
Is dandy
But liquor
Is quicker.
(Ogden Nash)
See also **2.54.66**.

9.7.21: **2** bendy, trendy; **3** attendee, effendi; **5** modus vivendi.

9.7.22: **2** bhindi, bindi, Cindy, Hindi, indie, kindy, windy; **3** Rawalpindi.

9.7.23: **2** bundy, Dundee, Sunday; **4** Easter Monday, Mrs Grundy.

9.8: **1** the, thee; **2** prithee, smithy, smoothie, smoothy, swarthy.

9.8.1: **2** worthy; **3** airworthy, blameworthy, Galsworthy, loveworthy, newsworthy, praiseworthy, roadworthy, seaworthy, unworthy; **4** unblameworthy, unroadworthy.

9.8.2: **3** noteworthy, trustworthy; **4** creditworthy, untrustworthy.

9.9: **1** fee; **2** beefy, comfy, Delphi, Dufy, Fifi, goofy, kulfi, leafy, Murphy, Sophie, Sufi, trophy, turfy, wifey; **3** Gaddafi.

9.9.1: **2** daffy, NAAFI, Taffy; **3** Gaddafi.

9.9.2: **4** calligraphy, epigraphy, lexigraphy, telegraphy.

9.9.3: **4** biography, cerography, hydrography, lithography, micrography, orthography, topography, typography; **5** anthropography, zoography; **6** autobiography, photobiography.

9.9.4: **4** geography, physiography; **5** bibliography, choreography, hagiography, palaeography, radiography, webliography; **6** historiography, phytogeography, zoogeography.

9.9.5: **4** chalcography, discography, zincography; **5** lexicography.

9.9.6: **4** holography, xylography; **5** crystallography, dactylography.

9.9.7: **4** demography, filmography, mammography, tomography.

9.9.8: **4** chronography, ethnography, hymnography, lignography, phonography, pornography, stenography; **5** iconography, oceanography.

9.9.9: **4** cartography, cryptography, glyptography, photography, phytography; **5** chromatography; **6** anaglyptography, cinematography.

9.9.10: **3** atrophy, dystrophy; **4** antistrophe, apostrophe, catastrophe, epistrophe, hypertrophy; **6** muscular dystrophy.

9.9.11: **4** gymnosophy, philosophy, theosophy; **5** anthroposophy.

9.9.12: **2** iffy, jiffy, niffy, sniffy, spiffy, squiffy, whiffy.

9.9.13: **2** coffee, offie, toffee; **3** banoffee, Greek coffee, iced coffee; **4** Irish coffee, Turkish coffee.

9.9.14: **2** Buffy, Duffy, fluffy, huffy, puffy, scruffy, stuffy, toughie.

9.10: **1** ghee, gi; **2** algae, boogie, corgi, lurgy; **3** Carnegie; **4** boogie-woogie.

9.10.1: **2** baggy, craggy, daggy, draggy, jaggy, Maggie, saggy, scraggy, shaggy.

9.10.2: **2** leggy, Peggy; **3** Carnegie.

9.10.3: **2** biggie, ciggie, ciggy, piggy, twiggy.

9.10.4: **2** boggy, doggie, doggy, foggy, froggy, groggy, moggy, soggy; **4** demagogy.

9.10.5: **2** bogey, bogie, dogie, fogy, hoagie, yogi; **3** old fogy.

9.10.6: **2** buggy, druggie, fuggy, muggy; **3** dune buggy; **4** baby buggy.

9.10.7: **2** Bangui, dengue, dinghy, dungy, lungi, pongy, twangy, zingy; **3** feringhee.

9.11: **1** he; **2** Haughey, tee-hee; **3** s/he.

9.12: **1** gee; **2** algae, bhaji, budgie, cagey, clergy, edgy, hajji, orgy, pudgy, squidgy, stagey, veggie, wedgie; **3** effigy, Mount Fuji, MSG, perigee, refugee, romaji; **4** argy-bargy.

9.12.1: **3** apogee, energy, lethargy, liturgy, mortgagee, prodigy, strategy, synergy.

9.12.2: **3** elegy, eulogy, trilogy.

9.12.3: 3 allergy; **4** analogy, metallurgy; **5** genealogy, mineralogy.

9.12.4: 3 ology; **4** algology, apology, bryology, doxology, fungology, glossology, nosology, philology, sexology, typology, zoology; **5** anthropology, methodology, reflexology; **7** otolaryngology.

9.12.5: 4 geology, neology, theology; **5** aetiology, archaeology, craniology, embryology, etiology, glaciology, gnosiology, hagiology, ichthyology, Mariology, osteology, phraseology, physiology, sociology, speleology, teleology; **6** Assyriology, astrogeology, bacteriology, ecclesiology, ontotheology, physicotheology; **7** epidemiology, phytosociology.

9.12.6: 5 audiology, cardiology, ideology, radiology.

9.12.7: 4 biology; **5** xenobiology; **6** agrobiology, astrobiology, cryobiology, ethnobiology, exobiology, marine biology, microbiology, phytobiology; **7** electrobiology, radiobiology.

9.12.8: 4 graphology, morphology, psephology; **5** ufology; **6** geomorphology.

9.12.9: 4 cacology, ecology, mycology, oncology, phycology, psychology, tocology, trichology; **5** gynaecology, lexicology, musicology, pharmacology, toxicology; **6** agroecology, bioecology, Gestalt psychology, parapsychology; **7** ethnomusicology.

9.12.10: 4 cosmology, homology, mammology, pomology, seismology; **5** entomology, enzymology, etymology, ophthalmology; **6** epistemology, folk etymology.

9.12.11: 4 ethnology, hymnology, monology, nomology, oenology; **5** arachnology, criminology, immunology, terminology; **6** endocrinology.

9.12.12: 4 chronology, phonology, phrenology; **5** campanology, demonology, iconology, lichenology, volcanology; **6** geochronology.

9.12.13: 4 technology; **5** low technology; **6** biotechnology, nanotechnology.

9.12.14: 4 agrology, andrology, astrology, dendrology, hierology, horology, hydrology, metrology, necrology, neurology, petrology, urology,

virology; **5** futurology, numerology; **6** meteorology.

9.12.15: 4 cryptology, cytology, histology, phytology, scatology, tautology; **5** deontology, Egyptology, eschatology, herpetology, olfactology; **6** dialectology, parasitology.

9.12.16: 5 climatology, dermatology, haematology, rheumatology.

9.12.17: 4 ontology; **5** gerontology, odontology; **6** palaeontology; **7** periodontology.

9.12.18: 4 anthology, mythology, pathology; **5** helminthology, ornithology; **6** psychopathology, zoopathology.

9.12.19: 2 3G, e.g., Fiji, Gigi, PG, squeegee; **3** Luigi.

9.12.20: 2 bodgie, dodgy, podgy, stodgy; **4** pedagogy.

9.12.21: 2 Angie, dingy, grungy, kanji, mangy, mingy, rangy, scungy, spongy, stingy; **3** orangey.

9.13: 1 cay, key, quay; **2** Alt key, hot key, latchkey, off-key, turnkey; **3** allen key, anarchy, Cherokee, monarchy; **4** logomachy, theomachy;

9.13.1: 2 ackee, baccy, lackey, Maquis, Paki, tackie, tacky, takkie, wacky, whacky; **3** Abnaki.

9.13.2: 2 khaki, marquee, parky, parquet, sparky; **3** autarchy, eparchy, gynarchy, hierarchy, Iraqi, malarkey, squirearchy, thearchy; **4** matriarchy, oligarchy, patriarchy, teriyaki.

9.13.3: 2 sake, sarky; **4** Kawasaki, Nagasaki.

9.13.4: 2 achy, flaky, reiki, shaky, snaky; **3** headachy.

9.13.5: 2 Becky, recce, techie, tekkie, Trekkie; **3** Mbeki.

9.13.6: 2 jerky, murky, perky, quirky, turkey; **3** cold turkey. *See also* **2.54.65.**

9.13.7: 2 beaky, cheeky, cliquey, creaky, freaky, Leakey, leaky, peaky, rekey, sneaky, squeaky, streaky; **3** Auld Reekie, dashiki, tzatziki, Waikiki; **4** cock-a-leekie; **5** Thessaloníki.

9.13.8: 2 brickie, dicky, hickey, icky, mickey, picky, quickie, Ricky, sickie, sticky, tricky, wiki; **3** colicky, doohickey, finicky, garlicky, gimmicky, panicky. *See also* **2.54.65.**

9.13.9: **2** bikie, crikey, Nike, psyche, spiky.

9.13.10: **2** choccy, cocky, hockey, jockey, rocky, stocky; **3** disc jockey, ice hockey, pondokkie.

9.13.11: **2** chalky, gawky, Gorky, pawky, porky, talkie; **3** Milwaukee; **4** walkie-talkie.

9.13.12: **2** chokey, croaky, croquet, hokey, jokey, Loki, low-key, pokey, poky, smoky, trochee; **4** Arbroath smokey, hokey cokey, karaoke.

9.13.13: **2** bakkie, ducky, mucky, yucky; **3** Kentucky.

9.13.14: **2** clucky, lucky, plucky; **3** unlucky; **5** happy-go-lucky.

9.13.15: **2** bookie, cookie, hooky, nookie, rookie; **3** play hooky.

9.13.16: **2** fluky, kooky, spooky; **3** bouzouki, kabuki.

They're creepy and they're kooky
mysterious and spooky
and not a little loopy
the Addams family.
(The Addams Family)

9.13.17: **2** bulky, Elkie, hulky, milky, silky, sulky.

9.13.18: **2** cranky, hankie, lanky, manky, swanky, Yankee; **4** hanky-panky.

9.13.19: **2** dinky, inky, kinky, pinkie, pinky, slinky, stinky; **3** Helsinki.

9.13.20: **2** donkey, honky, shonky, wonky; **4** nodding donkey.

9.13.21: **2** chunky, clunky, flunkey, flunky, funky, gunky, hunky, junkie, junky, monkey, spunky; **3** grease monkey; **4** rhesus monkey.

9.13.22: **1** ski; **2** Chomsky, dusky, Esky, husky, Jet Ski, musky, passkey, pesky, Trotsky; **3** après-ski, Kandinsky, Mussorgsky, Nijinsky, Sikorsky, Stravinsky, Tchaikovsky, waterski; **4** Brunelleschi, Dostoyevsky.
See also **10.42.2**.

9.13.23: **2** frisky, risky, whiskey, whisky; **4** Irish whiskey.

9.14: **1** lea, lee, Leigh; **2** blithely, Brierley, Buckley, coolly, Cowley, doily, gulley, gully, hourly, hugely, largely, oily, richly, smoothly, sourly, strangely, strongly, sully, wrongly; **3** Bottomley, entirely.
The Curfew tolls the knell of parting day,

The lowing herd winds slowly o'er the
lea,
The plowman homeward plods his weary
way,
And leaves the world to darkness and to
me.
(Thomas Gray)

9.14.1: **2** alley, dally, galley, Halley, mallee, pally, rally, sally, tally; **3** Aunt Sally, blind alley, doolally, Keneally, pep rally, war galley; **4** bowling alley, dilly-dally, shilly-shally, Tin Pan Alley.
See also **9.14.29, 10.42.2**.

9.14.2: **2** valley; **3** Death Valley, reveille, rift valley; **4** Happy Valley, Napa Valley; **5** Silicon Valley; **6** lily-of-the-valley.

9.14.3: **3** equally, gingerly, leisurely, majorly, perpetually, royally, soldierly.
See also **2.37.21**.

9.14.4: **2** yearly; **4** cordially, genially, peculiarly; **5** biennially, familiarly, materially; **6** ministerially.
See also **2.37.4, 9.14.36**.

9.14.5: **3** dually, usually, virtually, visually; **4** actually, annually, gradually, manually, mutually, punctually, unusually; **5** continually, eventually, habitually; **6** individually.
See also **2.37.21, 2.37.22, 15.7**.

9.14.6: **3** bubbly, neighbourly, pebbly, Stromboli, verbally; **4** hyperbole.

9.14.7: **3** cuddly, elderly, fiddly, fleur-de-lis, orderly, tiddly, twiddly; **4** disorderly.

9.14.8: **3** brotherly, fatherly, motherly, northerly, southerly.

9.14.9: **3** awfully, carefully, cheerfully, dreadfully, faithfully, fearfully, forcefully, harmfully, hopefully, manfully, painfully, thankfully, truthfully, usefully, woefully; **4** masterfully, mercifully, plentifully, powerfully, wonderfully; **5** purposefully, unsuccessfully.
See also **2.37.121, 2.37.122, 2.37.124, 2.37.129, 2.37.134**.

9.14.10: **3** fitfully, frightfully, tastefully, thoughtfully, wastefully; **4** deceitfully, regretfully, resentfully, respectfully.
See also **2.37.130, 2.37.133**.

9.14.11: **3** beggarly, giggly, legally, scraggly, straggly, wiggly.

9.14.12: **3** broccoli, crackly, crinkly, freckly, locally, rascally, sparkly, treacly; **4** melancholy.

9.14.13: **3** scholarly; **4** popularly, regularly, similarly, singularly; **5** irregularly, particularly.
See also **2.13.23**.

9.14.14: **3** family, formerly, normally, simile; **4** anomaly, facsimile, minimally, step family, stepfamily, subfamily; **5** Holy Family, superfamily.
See also **2.37.190**.

9.14.15: **3** Donnelly, finally, mannerly, signally; **4** communally, criminally, eternally, externally, internally, marginally, nominally, unmannerly; **5** subliminally.
See also **2.37.195, 2.37.213, 2.37.217**.

9.14.16: **4** personally, seasonally; **5** diagonally, occasionally, originally, provisionally.
See also **2.37.197, 2.37.198**.

9.14.17: **4** fractionally, functionally, nationally, rationally; **5** additionally, conventionally, exceptionally, professionally, proportionally, traditionally; **6** constitutionally, internationally, unconditionally.
See also **2.37.200, 2.37.207, 2.37.211**.

9.14.18: **3** properly, Tripoli; **4** duopoly, Gallipoli, monopoly, principally, Thermopylae; **5** archetypally, oligopoly.

9.14.19: **3** centrally, morally, neutrally, thoroughly; **4** summarily.

9.14.20: **4** federally, generally, literally, naturally, severally; **5** conjecturally, momentarily, unnaturally; **6** satisfactorily.
See also **2.37.232, 9.19.48**.

9.14.21: **3** merrily, verily; **4** primarily; **5** necessarily, ordinarily.

9.14.22: **4** contrarily, primarily; **5** arbitrarily, customarily, militarily, momentarily, necessarily, ordinarily, temporarily, voluntarily; **6** extraordinarily, unnecessarily.
See also **9.19.20, 9.19.31, 9.19.32, 9.19.44, 9.19.50**.

9.14.23: **3** Cecily, Cicely, Sicily, Thessaly.

9.14.24: **3** partially, racially, socially, specially; **4** commercially, especially, impartially, initially, officially; **5** artificially, controversially, prejudicially.
See also **2.37.259, 2.37.263**.

9.14.25: **4** essentially, potentially, sequentially, substantially, tangentially;

5 confidentially, consequentially, existentially, preferentially.
See also **2.37.266, 2.37.268**.

9.14.26: **3** bitterly, easterly, fatally, Italy, latterly, masterly, mortally, Natalie, painterly, prettily, quarterly, sisterly, spinsterly, totally, utterly, vitally, westerly; **4** northeasterly, northwesterly, philately, southeasterly, southwesterly; **5** accidentally, desperately, detrimentally, fundamentally, horizontally, incidentally, monumentally, sal volatile; **6** coincidentally, environmentally.
See also **2.37.282**.

9.14.27: **3** Beverley, civilly, gravelly, haveli, overly; **5** effectively.

9.14.28: **3** breezily, crazily, drizzly, lazily, miserly, snazzily.
See also **9.27, 9.27.2**.

9.14.29: **2** Ali, Bali, barley, Cali, Carly, charlie, Dali, Harley, Kali, Pali, parlay, parley, Raleigh, thali; **3** bizarrely, Divali, Diwali, finale, Kigali, Svengali.
See also **9.14.1**.

9.14.30: **2** Mali, Marley; **3** Somali, tamale.

9.14.31: **2** barely, fairly, rarely, squarely.

9.14.32: **2** bailey, ceilidh, daily, Daley, Daly, gaily, Haley, scaly; **3** Disraeli, Israeli; **4** ukelele.

9.14.33: **2** Delhi, deli, jelly, Kelly, nelly, Shelley, smelly, telly, wellie, welly; **3** New Delhi; **4** Botticelli, vermicelli; **5** Machiavelli, tagliatelle.

9.14.34: **2** belly; **3** beer belly, potbelly; **4** casus belli, Delhi belly, underbelly.

9.14.35: **2** Burghley, burly, curly, early, girlie, girly, Hurley, pearly, Shirley, surly, yearly; **3** half-yearly; **4** hurly-burly.

9.14.36: **2** Brearley, clearly, dearly, merely, nearly, really, yearly; **3** half-yearly, ideally, severely, sincerely.
See also **9.14.4**.

9.14.37: **2** Ely, freely, mealie, mealy, steely, wheelie; **3** Swahili; **4** Kiswahili, touchy-feely.

9.14.38: **2** billy, Chile, chilli, chilly, filly, frilly, gillie, hilly, Jilly, Milly, Scilly, silly, willy; **3** airily, busily, dreamily, easily, Emily, happily, heavily, hillbilly, homily, icily, jubilee, luckily; **4** rockabilly.
See also **2.54.67, 9.59.3**.

9.14.39: **3** bodily, greedily, handily, readily, shoddily, speedily, steadily; **4** unsteadily.
See also **9.7.7, 9.7.9, 9.7.13.**

9.14.40: **2** lily; **3** day lily, Galilee; **4** arum lily, gild the lily, piccalilli, water lily; **5** African lily.

9.14.41: **3** funnily, Keneally, stonily; **4** campanile, willy-nilly.

9.14.42: **3** hastily, heartily, lustily, mightily, nattily, scantily, thirstily.
See also **9.22.85, 9.22.87, 9.22.89.**

9.14.43: **2** drily, highly, Riley, slyly, smiley, wily, wryly.
See also **11.5, 11.8.**

9.14.44: **2** brolly, collie, dolly, folly, golly, holly, jolly, lolly, molly, polly, poly, trolley, volley, wally; **4** Barbirolli, Hello Dolly.

9.14.45: **2** Cawley, Crawley, Halley, poorly, Raleigh, sorely, squally, surely; **3** Bengali; **4** creepy-crawly.
See also **9.14.46.**

9.14.46: **2** poorly, purely, surely; **3** prematurely, securely.
See also **2.24.2, 9.14.45, 15.1.1.**

9.14.47: **2** coley, Foley, goalie, Holi, holy, Jolie, lowly, shoaly, slowly, solely, wholly; **3** aioli, hollowly, narrowly, unholy; **4** guacamole, ravioli, roly-poly.

9.14.48: **2** bully, fully, pulley, woolly; **3** patchouli; **5** lapis lazuli.
See also **9.59.3, 10.42.2.**

9.14.49: **2** coolie, coulis, duly, newly, truly; **3** Bernoulli, patchouli, unduly, unruly.

9.14.50: **2** ably, bubbly, Chablis, doubly, knobbly, nobly, stubbly, wobbly.
See also **2.37.98, 2.37.99.**

9.14.51: **3** audibly, capably, changeably, equably, horribly, impeccably, inaudibly, laudably, plausibly, probably, reliably, terribly, visibly; **4** arguably, demonstrably, dependably, fashionably, incredibly, miserably, presumably, reasonably, remarkably; **5** inextricably, invariably, justifiably, unquestionably, unseasonably.
See also **2.37.25, 2.37.37, 2.37.49, 2.37.50, 2.37.51, 2.37.83, 2.37.95.**

9.14.52: **4** admirably, comparably, preferably, tolerably; **5** considerably, immeasurably; **6** inconsiderably.
See also **2.37.51.**

9.14.53: **3** possibly, sensibly; **4** impossibly, noticeably, ostensibly, responsibly.
See also **2.37.57.**

9.14.54: **3** comfortably, notably, suitably; **4** acceptably, predictably, regrettably, susceptibly; **5** imperceptibly, indisputably, indubitably, inevitably, unaccountably, uncomfortably.
See also **2.37.63, 2.37.67, 2.37.71, 2.37.75, 2.37.76.**

9.14.55: **2** crumbly, humbly, Wembley; **3** assembly; **4** self-assembly.
See also **2.37.104.**

9.14.56: **2** badly, baldly, broadly, cowardly, deadly, Dudley, gladly, godly, goodly, hardly, idly, lordly, loudly, madly, medley, mildly, oddly, sadly, thirdly, widely, wildly, worldly; **3** absurdly, proudly, ungodly, unworldly; **4** otherworldly.
See also **16.6.2.**

9.14.57: **3** awkwardly, dastardly, inwardly, niggardly, outwardly, sluggardly; **4** avowedly, haphazardly, ill-naturedly.
See also **2.33.26, 16.6.**

9.14.58: **2** diddly; **3** candidly, crookedly, fixedly, hurriedly, languidly, markedly, rapidly, solidly, splendidly, timidly, vividly; **4** advisedly, allegedly, assuredly, confusedly, decidedly, deservedly, supposedly.
See also **9.29.6, 10.2.25, 10.2.26, 10.2.27, 10.2.29, 10.2.94, 10.2.95, 22.41.**

9.14.59: **4** admittedly, belatedly, expectedly, purportedly, quick-wittedly, repeatedly, reportedly, undoubtedly.
See also **10.2.64.**

9.14.60: **2** blindly, fondly, grandly, Hindley, kindly, roundly, soundly, spindly; **3** profoundly, secondly.
See also **16.11.2.**

9.14.61: **2** friendly; **3** unfriendly; **4** ecofriendly, overfriendly, ozone-friendly, user-friendly.
See also **2.54.67.**

9.14.62: **1** flea, flee; **2** briefly, chiefly, roughly, safely, stiffly, wifely.
See also **6.1.10.**

9.14.63: **1** glee; **2** Broglie, googly, ugly, vaguely.

9.14.64: **2** gangly, jangly, jungli, shingly, singly, tingly.

9.14.65: 2 Berkeley, blankly, bleakly, darkly, frankly, likely, Oakley, Shockley, weakly, weekly, wrinkly; 3 biweekly, uniquely, unlikely; 4 Annie Oakley, semiweekly; 5 reciprocally; 6 unequivocally. *See also* **2.37.147**.

9.14.66: 2 quickly, thickly; 3 ethically, graphically, musically, physically, publicly, radically, rhythmically, technically, tragically, typically; 4 intrinsically, ironically, mechanically, methodically, prolifically, specifically, sporadically, strategically, symbolically, terrifically; 5 chronologically, economically, electronically, emphatically, periodically, technologically; 6 astronomically. *See also* **2.37.155, 2.37.159, 10.12.8, 10.12.10, 10.12.13, 10.12.14, 10.12.22, 10.12.53, 10.16**.

9.14.67: 2 prickly; 4 diametrically, historically, numerically, symmetrically; 5 categorically, metaphorically, rhetorically. *See also* **2.37.170, 2.37.171, 2.37.172**.

9.14.68: 2 sickly; 3 basically, classically; 5 commonsensically, paradoxically.

9.14.69: 3 critically, erratically, practically, tactically, vertically; 4 chaotically, despotically, domestically, eccentrically, fantastically, identically, majestically, pathetically, pedantically, politically, realistically, simplistically, synthetically, theoretically; 5 alphabetically, autocratically, automatically, democratically, diplomatically, empathetically, energetically, hypocritically, hypothetically, sympathetically, systematically. *See also* **2.37.174, 2.37.179, 10.12.52, 10.12.71, 10.12.74**.

9.14.70: 2 Bromley, comely, dimly, firmly, homely, lamely, namely, seemly, termly, timely, warmly; 3 contumely, extremely, randomly, solemnly, supremely, uniformly, unseemly, untimely. *See also* **2.40.22, 2.40.25, 7.18.1, 14.33.2**.

9.14.71: 2 Darnley, finely, Henley, lonely, mainly, Manley, manly, only, plainly, Stanley, thinly, wanly; 3 evenly, heavenly, McKinley, read-only, slovenly, ungainly, unmanly; 4 genuinely, Mount McKinley.

9.14.72: 3 brokenly, certainly, maidenly, matronly, openly, slatternly, stubbornly, suddenly; 4 curmudgeonly, mistakenly. *See also* **2.43.27, 2.43.66**.

9.14.73: 3 commonly, humanly, womanly; 4 gentlemanly, uncommonly.

9.14.74: 2 cleanly, greenly, keenly, queenly; 3 obscenely, routinely.

9.14.75: 2 kingly; 3 laughingly, longingly, lovingly, mockingly, winningly; 4 annoyingly, approvingly, bewitchingly, decreasingly, frighteningly, increasingly, surprisingly, unswervingly, unthinkingly; 5 unsurprisingly. *See also* **10.42, 10.42.51, 10.42.57, 10.42.183**.

9.14.76: 3 blindingly, pleadingly, willingly; 4 accordingly, compellingly, exceedingly, outstandingly, unfeelingly, unwillingly; 5 correspondingly.

9.14.77: 3 charmingly, glaringly, screamingly, seemingly, sparingly, swimmingly; 4 alluringly, wonderingly; 5 overwhelmingly. *See also* **10.42.86**.

9.14.78: 2 Zwingli; 3 fittingly, glowingly, knowingly, wittingly; 4 insultingly, interestingly, unknowingly, unwittingly. *See also* **10.42.156, 10.42.167**.

9.14.79: 1 plea; 2 crisply, deeply, pimply, shapely, sharply, Shipley, simply; 3 panoply; 4 fait accompli. *See also* **2.37.229, 10.52**.

9.14.80: 2 Ainsley, bristly, closely, coarsely, densely, falsely, fiercely, grossly, Huxley, loosely, nicely, parsley, princely, scarcely; 3 aversely, concisely, conversely, expressly, immensely, intensely, precisely; 4 imprecisely. *See also* **6.33, 11.34, 14.29**.

9.14.81: 3 famously, nervously, purposely; 4 circuitously, dangerously, enormously, religiously; 5 anonymously, continuously, ominously; 6 contemptuously. *See also* **2.54.60, 2.54.71, 2.54.131, 2.54.136, 15.9**.

9.14.82: 4 curiously, obviously, previously, seriously, studiously, variously.

9.14.83: 3 artlessly, endlessly, faultlessly, hopelessly, jealously, needlessly,

recklessly, ruthlessly; **4** effortlessly, fabulously, perilously; **5** ridiculously.
See also **2.54.43, 2.54.44, 2.54.45, 2.54.52, 2.54.55.**

9.14.84: **3** cautiously, consciously, graciously; **4** judiciously, self-consciously, subconsciously, suspiciously, tenaciously; **5** ostentatiously, repetitiously, surreptitiously.
See also **2.54.118, 2.54.120, 2.54.122, 2.54.125, 2.54.128.**

9.14.85: **2** Ashley, fleshly, freshly, rashly; **3** fiendishly, lavishly, sheepishly, stylishly; **4** disastrously.
See also **1.39.4, 2.54.112.**

9.14.86: **2** Attlee, courtly, flatly, Hartley, hotly, motley, partly, portly, promptly, quietly, shortly, softly, stoutly, sweetly, Tetley; **3** acutely, completely, devoutly, minutely, remotely; **4** absolutely, softly-softly.
See also **13.6.**

9.14.87: **3** privately; **4** adequately, appropriately, delicately, intimately, ultimately; **5** approximately, immediately, inadequately, legitimately; **6** inappropriately.
See also **2.56, 2.56.2, 5.47.4.**

9.14.88: **4** definitely, fortunately, infinitely, obstinately, passionately; **5** indefinitely, unfortunately.
See also **2.56.28, 2.56.29.**

9.14.89: **2** greatly, lately, stately; **3** secretly; **4** accurately, moderately, separately; **5** deliberately, Johnny-come-lately.
See also **2.56.37, 2.56.40, 5.47.55.**

9.14.90: **2** knightly, lightly, nightly, rightly, slightly, sprightly, tightly, Whiteley; **3** forthrightly, fortnightly, politely, unsightly.
See also **11.36.16, 11.36.21.**

9.14.91: **2** strictly; **3** correctly, directly, distinctly, exactly, perfectly, succinctly; **4** incorrectly, indirectly.
See also **6.12.8, 10.45.**

9.14.92: **2** Bentley, bluntly, faintly, gently, Huntley, jointly, saintly.
See also **18.12.**

9.14.93: **3** absently, currently, differently, efficiently, frequently, patiently, pleasantly, presently, recently, silently, violently; **4** abundantly, apparently, confidently, elegantly, eminently, evidently, excellently, imminently,

incessantly, inherently, permanently, prominently; **5** belligerently, benevolently, conveniently, predominantly, self-confidently, significantly.
See also **2.47.18, 2.47.76, 2.47.83, 2.47.86, 2.47.87.**

9.14.94: **3** constantly, distantly, fluently, instantly, patently; **4** consequently, importantly, infrequently, persistently, reluctantly, subsequently; **5** inadvertently.
See also **2.47.88, 2.47.92.**

9.14.95: **2** beastly, Christly, costly, firstly, ghastly, ghostly, justly, lastly, mostly, Priestley, priestly, vastly; **3** honestly, modestly; **4** dishonestly, manifestly.
See also **10.53.12.**

9.14.96: **2** deathly, earthly, monthly; **3** bimonthly, unearthly.
See also **9.59.3.**

9.14.97: **2** gravely, lively, lovely; **3** naively, unlovely.
See also **2.54.67, 3.54, 5.51.2, 9.56.**

9.14.98: **4** defensively, derisively, evasively, excessively, exclusively, expansively, explosively, extensively, impressively, inclusively, intensively, offensively, progressively.
See also **10.61.2, 10.61.3, 10.61.5, 10.61.6, 10.61.8.**

9.14.99: **4** deceptively, perceptively; **5** insensitively, prohibitively, suggestively.
See also **10.61.29, 10.61.36, 10.61.51, 10.61.52.**

9.14.100: **3** actively; **4** collectively, distinctively, instinctively, objectively, positively, reactively, relatively, respectively, restrictively, secretively, selectively, sensitively; **5** alternatively, comparatively, competitively, consecutively, figuratively, imitatively, interactively, provocatively, repetitively, retroactively, speculatively, superlatively.
See also **10.61.18, 10.61.24, 10.61.38.**

9.14.101: **2** Beardsley, Dursley, grisly, Kingsley, Lesley, measly, Moseley, Mosley, muesli, paisley, Presley, Sisley, Wellesley, Wesley; **3** Hattersley.

9.15: **1** me, mi; **2** acme, Aimée, Fermi, filmi, filmy, gloomy, Lakshmi, pigmy, pygmy, stormy, wormy; **4** taxidermy.

9.15.1: **2** chamois, clammy, gammy, Grammy, hammy, jammy, mammy, Sammy, shammy, Tammy, whammy; **3** Miami.
See also **3.18.2.**

9.15.2: **3** alchemy, Bellamy, blasphemy, bosomy, enemy, infamy, Jeremy, Ptolemy, sesame, sodomy, thingummy; **4** academy, archenemy; **5** open sesame; **6** Royal Academy.

9.15.3: **3** bigamy, trigamy; **4** allogamy, endogamy, exogamy, monogamy, polygamy; **5** deuterogamy.

9.15.4: **3** bonhomie; **4** autonomy, economy, metonymy, taxonomy, zoonomy; **5** physiognomy; **6** macroeconomy.

9.15.5: **4** agronomy, astronomy, gastronomy; **5** Deuteronomy, heteronomy; **7** radio astronomy.

9.15.6: **4** anatomy, colostomy, epitome.

9.15.7: **4** dichotomy, lobotomy, phlebotomy, zootomy; **5** laparotomy, tracheotomy; **6** episiotomy.

9.15.8: **4** lumpectomy, mastectomy, vasectomy; **5** appendectomy, hysterectomy, tonsillectomy; **6** appendicectomy.

9.15.9: **2** army, balmy, barmy, palmy, Sami, smarmy, swami; **3** macramé, pastrami, Red Army, salami, tatami, tsunami; **4** origami, Sally Army; **5** Salvation Army; **7** Territorial Army.

9.15.10: **2** Amy, gamy, samey; **4** cockamamie.

9.15.11: **2** Demi, Emmy, jemmy, lemme, phlegmy, semi.

9.15.12: **2** creamy, dreamy, REME, seamy, steamy; **3** sashimi; **4** CUSeeMe.

9.15.13: **2** gimme, Jimmy, shimmy; **4** homonymy, synonymy.

9.15.14: **2** blimey, commie, grimy, limey, mommy, pommy, slimy, stymie, Tommy.

9.15.15: **2** foamy, homey, loamy; **3** Dahomey, Naomi, Salome.

9.15.16: **2** chummy, dummy, gummy, mummy, plummy, scummy, slummy, tummy, yummy; **4** gyppy tummy, tailor's dummy.

9.15.17: **2** Brummie, crummy, rummy, scrummy; **3** gin rummy.

9.15.18: **2** fumy, rheumy, roomie, roomy, spumy.

9.16: **1** knee; **2** Agni, Cagney, chimney, chunni, Daphne, Disney, Grozny, halfpenny, ha'penny, kidney, muni, Rodney, Romney, Sidney, Sigourney, Sunni, Sydney; **3** calumny.

Picture you upon my knee,
Just tea for two and two for tea.
(Irving Caesar)

9.16.1: **2** Annie, canny, cranny, fanny, granny, nanny, tannie, tranny; **3** afghani, Giovanni, uncanny.

9.16.2: **3** Albany, balcony, barony, Bethany, bryony, ebony, guaraní, Hermione, irony, larceny, peony, Saxony, tuppenny, Tuscany, twopenny, tyranny; **4** chalcedony; **5** Aborigine.

9.16.3: **3** euphony, Stephanie, symphony, Tiffany, Tisiphone; **4** cacophony, epiphany, homophony, monophony, Persephone, polyphony, telephony; **5** heterophony.
See also **2.54.63**.

9.16.4: **3** agony; **4** Antigone, cosmogony, mahogany.

9.16.5: **3** progeny; **4** ethnogeny, misogyny, ontogeny, phylogeny, polygyny; **5** anthropogeny, embryogeny.

9.16.6: **3** colony, felony, Melanie, villainy; **4** Crown Colony, miscellany; **5** Plymouth colony, prison colony, termite colony.

9.16.7: **3** Germany, harmony, hominy, Romani, Romany, simony; **4** ceremony, disharmony, hegemony, loadsamoney; **5** sea anemone; **6** civil ceremony.

9.16.8: **3** lemony, Yemeni; **4** anemone, Gethsemane, hegemony.

9.16.9: **4** acrimony, agrimony, alimony, antimony, matrimony, palimony, parsimony, patrimony, sanctimony, testimony.

9.16.10: **3** company, timpani; **4** accompany; **5** intracompany, private company, public company; **6** limited company, livery company.
See also **9.29.4**.

9.16.11: **3** Anthony, Antony, betony, botany, Brittany, cottony, destiny, dittany, gluttony, litany, mutiny; **4** monotony; **5** ethnobotany.

9.16.12: **2** barney, blarney, rani, sarnie; **3** afghani, Armani, dharani, Gianni, Guarani; **4** biryani, bouquet garni, Don Giovanni, frangipani, Hindustani, Kisangani, maharani, Modigliani, Pakistani, Rajasthani; **5** Afghanistani, Azerbaijani.

9.16.13: **2** brainy, Cheney, grainy, rainy, trainee, veni, zany; **3** Delaney, detainee, Khomeini; **4** Adar Sheni, lilangeni.

9.16.14: **2** any, Benny, Denny, fenny, Glennie, jenny, many, penny; **3** catchpenny, halfpenny, Khaman'i, Kilkenny, new penny, old penny, pinchpenny; **4** creeping jenny, Moneypenny, spinning jenny; **5** emalangeni; **6** Mary Magdalene.

9.16.15: **2** Bernie, Burney, ERNIE, gurney, journey; **3** attorney, internee; **5** District Attorney.

9.16.16: **2** beanie, genie, greeny, Heaney, meanie, teeny; **3** Athene, bikini, Eugénie, Houdini, martini, Mycenae, Puccini, Rossini, tahini, tankini, wahine, zucchini; **4** fettuccine, monokini, spaghettini.

9.16.17: **2** blini, sweeny, tweeny, weeny, wienie; **3** Bellini, Bernini, Cellini, Fellini, Helene, linguine, panini, Selene; **4** Abilene, Mussolini, Mytilene, Paganini, teeny-weeny, tortellini, Toscanini; **5** tagliolini.

9.16.18: **2** Finney, Ginny, guinea, hinny, jinni, ninny, pinny, shinny, skinny, spinney, tinnie, tinny, whinny; **3** satiny, scrutiny; **4** Mnemosyne, pickaninny; **5** aborigine, Papua New Guinea.

9.16.19: **2** mini; **3** dominee, nominee; **4** examinee, ignominy, moaning Minnie, vitamin E.

9.16.20: **2** Bonnie, bonny, briny, Johnny, Ronnie, shiny, spiny, tiny, whiny; **3** assignee, consignee, sunshiny.

9.16.21: **2** brawny, corny, horny, Pawnee, scrawny, Shawnee, tawny, thorny, tourney; **5** mulligatawny.

9.16.22: **2** brownie, browny, downy, townie; **3** box Brownie.

9.16.23: **2** bony, coney, donee, phoney, stony, Tony, yoni; **3** Marconi; **4** Berlusconi, rigatoni; **5** Antonioni, zabaglione.

9.16.24: **2** loanee, pony; **3** baloney, boloney, polony, provolone; **4** abalone, cannelloni, mascarpone, shanks's pony, Shetland pony, tortelloni.

9.16.25: **2** crony; **4** Gaborone, macaroni, minestrone, pepperoni.

Yankee Doodle came to town
Riding on a pony;
Stuck a feather in his cap

And called it Macaroni.
(Edward Bangs)

9.16.26: **2** bunny, dunny, funny, gunny, honey, loony, money, Moonie, puny, Rooney, runny, sonny, sunny, tunny, uni; **3** blood money, hot money, pin money, unfunny; **4** danger money, easy money, even money, fiat money, funny money, maundy money, pocket money, ready money.

9.16.27: **2** acne, chutney, cockney, Courtenay, Courtney, Hackney, Hockney, mockney, Putney, Whitney; **3** McCartney.

9.17: **2** hongi, Lange, slangy, tangy.

9.17.1: **2** clingy, dinghy, springy, stringy, thingy.

9.18: **1** pea, pee; **2** chickpea, chirpy, cowpea, crispy, harpy, LP, peppy, preppy, split pea, stripy, sweet pea, whoopee, wispy; **3** black-eyed pea, Euterpe, okapi, p & p, pigeon pea, RIP, VIP.

9.18.1: **2** chappie, crappy, happy, nappy, pappy, sappy, scrappy, snappy, strappy, yappy; **3** unhappy; **4** trigger-happy. *See also* **2.54.68**.

9.18.2: **3** agape, canopy, P2P, recipe, syncope; **4** apocope, Calliope, Penelope.

9.18.3: **4** endoscopy, horoscopy, microscopy, spectroscopy; **5** laparoscopy, stereoscopy.

9.18.4: **3** entropy, syrupy; **4** allotropy, misanthropy, philanthropy.

9.18.5: **3** therapy; **4** speech therapy; **5** chemotherapy, hydrotherapy, hypnotherapy, logotherapy, massotherapy, narcotherapy, phototherapy, psychotherapy, zootherapy; **6** aromatherapy, electrotherapy, osteotherapy, physiotherapy, radiotherapy, thalassotherapy.

9.18.6: **2** JP, scrapie; **3** escapee, OAP; **4** asap.

9.18.7: **2** cheapie, creepy, GP, sleepy, tepee, VP, weepie, weepy; **3** GDP, MEP, MVP, PGP, PPP, TVP; **4** RSVP. *See also* **2.54.68**.

9.18.8: **2** chippie, dippy, drippy, hippie, hippy, Lippi, lippy, nippy, slippy, snippy, yippee, zippy; **3** gossipy; **4** Mississippi.

9.18.9: **2** choppy, copy, floppy, koppie, poppy, sloppy, soppy, stroppy; **3** fair copy, jalopy; **4** photocopy.

9.18.10: **2** dopey, mopy, ropy, snow pea, soapy, topi; **3** Sinope.

9.18.11: **2** guppy, puppy, yuppie; **3** mudpuppy.

9.18.12: **2** droopy, groupie, loopy, rupee, snoopy, soupy.

9.18.13: **2** campy, MP, Pompey, scampi, skimpy, stompie, swampy; **4** Euro-MP.

9.18.14: **2** bumpy, dumpy, frumpy, grumpy, humpy, jumpy, lumpy, scrumpy, stumpy; **4** rumpy-pumpy.

9.18.15: **3** ESP, Gillespie, MSP, USP.

9.19: **1** Brie, re, Shri; **2** blurry, Cymru, debris, every, fiery, furry, Henri, henry, in re, khichri, siree, Tishri; **3** enquiry, flowery, Plaid Cymru, showery, Sri; **4** the Bowery; **5** anno Hegirae.

9.19.1: **2** Barrie, barry, carry, Garry, Gary, gharry, harry, Larry, marry, Paris, parry, tarry; **3** glengarry, miscarry, mismarry, remarry, unmarry; **4** cash and carry, intermarry; **5** Tom, Dick, and Harry. *See also* **9.29.6, 10.42.4**.

9.19.2: **3** colliery, equerry, lingerie, luxury, penury, tertiary, treasury, usury; **4** reliquary; **5** haberdashery. *See also* **9.59.10**.

9.19.3: **4** apiary, aviary, breviary, hosiery, justiciary, topiary, vespiary; **5** auxiliary, fiduciary, judiciary, pecuniary; **6** domiciliary. *See also* **9.19.62**.

9.19.4: **5** incendiary, stipendiary, subsidiary; **6** cybermediary, infomediary, intermediary.

9.19.5: **3** brewery; **4** estuary, February, January, mortuary, ossuary; **5** microbrewery.

9.19.6: **4** actuary, sanctuary, statuary; **5** obituary.

9.19.7: **3** Avebury, Banbury, blackberry, blaeberry, blubbery, blueberry, Bradbury, bribery, Cleobury, cranberry, dewberry, fibbery, gooseberry, jamboree, rubbery, Shaftesbury, shrubbery, strawberry, tayberry; **4** boysenberry, Canterbury, elderberry, loganberry.

9.19.8: **3** bilberry, Bloomsbury, Finsbury, mulberry, raspberry, robbery, Rosebery, Sainsbury, Salisbury, slobbery, snobbery; **4** armed robbery, bank robbery, corroboree, dingleberry, huckleberry, whortleberry; **5** daylight robbery, highway robbery.

9.19.9: **3** Chaudhuri, powdery, prudery, spidery; **4** dromedary, embroidery, lapidary; **5** camaraderie, hebdomadary.

9.19.10: **3** bindery, boundary, quandary, thundery; **4** legendary, secondary.

9.19.11: **3** dithery, feathery, lathery, leathery, slithery.

9.19.12: **3** porphyry, puffery, referee; **4** housewifery, midwifery, Pecksniffery, periphery, Tartuffery.

9.19.13: **3** beggary, buggery, Calgary, Diggory, Gregory, Hungary, jaggery, piggery, roguery, sugary, thuggery, vagary; **4** allegory, category, humbuggery, ironmongery, skulduggery, vinegary; **5** Devanagari, pettifoggery, subcategory.

9.19.14: **3** drudgery, forgery, gingery, injury, kedgeree, Marjorie, soldiery; **4** imagery, menagerie, orangery, savagery.

9.19.15: **3** perjury, surgery; **4** brain surgery; **5** keyhole surgery, microsurgery, neurosurgery, plastic surgery, psychosurgery; **6** cosmetic surgery, open-heart surgery.

9.19.16: **3** bakery, chicory, cookery, crockery, daiquiri, fakery, hickory, mockery, quackery, rockery, rookery, trickery, Valkyrie, Vickery; **4** Terpsichore; **5** apothecary; **6** jiggery-pokery.

9.19.17: **3** burglary, celery, cutlery, drollery, foolery, pillary, raillery, saddlery, scullery, Tuileries; **4** cajolery, chancellery, corollary, exemplary, formulary, tomfoolery, tutelary; **5** constabulary, epistolary, vocabulary.

9.19.18: **3** calorie, gallery, Mallory, Malory, salary; **4** art gallery, press gallery, rogues' gallery; **5** ladies' gallery, peanut gallery, public gallery, shooting gallery, stranger's gallery; **6** National Gallery, whispering gallery.

9.19.19: **3** Hilary, Hillary, pillory; **4** ancillary, artillery, capillary, distillery, maxillary.

9.19.20: **3** armoury, bain-marie, creamery, emery, flummery, mammary, memory, mummery, primary, rosemary, shimmery, summary, summery; **4** customary, infirmary, Montgomerie, Montgomery, perfumery. *See also* **9.14.22**.

9.19.21: **3** cannery, Connery, granary, gunnery, hymnary, joinery, nunnery, ornery, tannery; **4** buffoonery, chicanery, Quaternary.

9.19.22: **4** coronary, legionary, mercenary, ordinary, pulmonary, visionary; **5** extraordinary, illusionary, veterinary; **7** cardiopulmonary, eleemosynary.

9.19.23: **4** cautionary, missionary; **5** concessionary, discretionary, diversionary, expansionary, precautionary, seditionary; **6** evolutionary, illocutionary, revolutionary.

9.19.24: **4** stationary, stationery; **5** deflationary, inflationary, probationary, reflationary; **6** geostationary.

9.19.25: **4** dictionary, functionary; **5** confectionery, reactionary.

9.19.26: **3** venery; **4** centenary, millenary; **5** bicentenary, tercentenary, tricentenary; **6** sesquicentenary.

9.19.27: **3** deanery, greenery, plenary, scenery, venery; **4** centenary, machinery; **5** bicentenary, tercentenary; **6** quatercentenary.

9.19.28: **4** culinary, luminary, millinery, ordinary, sanguinary, seminary, urinary; **5** disciplinary, imaginary, preliminary; **7** interdisciplinary, multidisciplinary. *See also* **9.59.10**.

9.19.29: **3** binary, finery, pinery, winery; **4** refinery.

9.19.30: **3** coppery, drapery, frippery, papery, peppery, popery, slippery, trumpery; **4** extempore. *See also* **2.54.65**.

9.19.31: **3** contrary, library; **4** arbitrary, funerary, honorary, literary, temporary; **5** contemporary, extemporary, itinerary; **6** supernumerary. *See also* **9.14.22**.

9.19.32: **3** brasserie, chancery, glossary, grocery, pessary, sensory, sorcery, tracery; **4** accessory, adversary, compulsory, delusory, derisory, dispensary, illusory, incensory, lamasery, necessary, responsory; **5** extrasensory, unnecessary. *See also* **9.14.22**, **9.59.10**.

9.19.33: **3** bursary, cursory, fishery, nursery; **4** commissary, day nursery, emissary, janissary, judiciary, patisserie, precursory, promissory, rotisserie; **5** anniversary, beneficiary, penitentiary; **6** plenipotentiary.

9.19.34: **3** artery, battery, buttery, cattery, coterie, dietary, eatery, flattery, lottery, notary, pottery, psaltery, rotary, tottery, votary, watery, wintery; **4** adultery, desultory, effrontery, peremptory, proprietary.

9.19.35: **4** hortatory, offertory, prefatory, repertory, transitory; **5** accusatory, conservatory, explicatory, initiatory; **6** conciliatory, retaliatory.

9.19.36: **4** laudatory, mandatory, predatory, sudatory; **5** hereditary, validatory.

9.19.37: **4** nugatory, purgatory; **5** derogatory, obligatory.

9.19.38: **4** dilatory, solitary; **5** circulatory, consolatory, depilatory, regulatory, undulatory.

9.19.39: **4** amatory, crematory; **5** declamatory, defamatory, inflammatory, reformatory.

9.19.40: **4** minatory, signatory; **5** condemnatory, cosignatory; **6** discriminatory, hallucinatory.

9.19.41: **4** planetary, sanitary; **5** explanatory, insanitary, unsanitary; **6** interplanetary, self-explanatory.

9.19.42: **4** migratory, oratory, territory; **5** exploratory, Home Secretary, laboratory, preparatory, respiratory; **6** undersecretary.

9.19.43: **4** gyratory, migratory, placatory, rotatory; **5** accusatory, adulatory, ambulatory, celebratory, circulatory, commendatory, compensatory, deprecatory, obfuscatory, oscillatory, regulatory, revelatory; **6** anticipatory, classificatory, congratulatory, elucidatory, hallucinatory.

9.19.44: **3** glittery, jittery; **4** auditory, budgetary, military; **5** depository, expository, prohibitory, repository, suppository; **6** paramilitary. *See also* **9.14.22**.

9.19.45: **3** monitory; **4** dignitary, monetary, unitary; **5** admonitory, premonitory.

9.19.46: **4** salutary, statutory, tributary; **5** contributory; **6** circumlocutory, noncontributory.

9.19.47: **3** victory; **4** perfunctory; **5** contradictory, introductory, Pyrrhic victory, valedictory; **6** self-contradictory.

9.19.48: 4 olfactory, phylactery, refractory; 5 satisfactory; 6 dissatisfactory, unsatisfactory.
See also **9.14.20**.

9.19.49: 3 nectary, rectory; 4 directory, refectory, trajectory; 5 subdirectory.

9.19.50: 4 commentary, fragmentary, inventory, momentary, promontory, sedentary, voluntary; 5 involuntary.
See also **9.14.22**.

9.19.51: 5 complementary, complimentary, documentary, elementary, parliamentary, rockumentary, rudimentary, sedimentary, supplementary; 6 alimentary, uncomplimentary, unparliamentary; 7 drama-documentary.

9.19.52: 3 blustery, clerestory, history, mastery, mystery; 4 monastery, prehistory, upholstery.

9.19.53: 3 archery, butchery, century, hatchery, lechery, treachery, witchery; 4 bewitchery, debauchery.

9.19.54: 3 Calvary, carvery, ivory, ovary, reverie, servery, silvery, thievery; 4 discovery, recovery; 5 rediscovery.
See also **9.59.10**.

9.19.55: 3 Avery, bravery, knavery, savory, savoury, slavery; 4 unsavoury.

9.19.56: 3 livery, shivery; 4 delivery; 5 nondelivery; 6 cash on delivery.

9.19.57: 3 misery, rosary, rosery; 4 advisory; 5 supervisory.

9.19.58: 2 Bari, lari, sari, starry; 3 Campari, curare, Harare, phulkari, safari, shikari; 4 calamari, Kalahari, Mata Hari, Stradivari.

9.19.59: 2 airy, Carey, chary, Clary, dairy, faerie, fairy, hairy, lairy, Mary, nary, prairie, scary, vary, wary; 3 Azeri, canary, Hail Mary, Thierry, unwary, Virgin Mary; 4 airy-fairy, Bloody Mary, cassowary, Tipperary.
See also **9.29.6, 10.42.4**.

9.19.60: 2 Ceri, cherry, ferry, Gerry, Jerry, Kerry, merry, perry, serry, sherry, terry, very; 3 Fred Perry, Guarneri; 4 Londonderry, presbytery; 6 maraschino cherry.

9.19.61: 2 berry, bury; 4 beriberi, elderberry.
See also **9.29.6**.

9.19.62: 2 beery, bleary, cheery, dearie, deary, dreary, eerie, eyrie, leery, Peary,

teary, theory; 3 Kashmiri, Lake Erie, O'Leary, Valkyrie; 4 hara-kiri.
See also **9.19.3**.

9.19.63: 2 query, weary; 3 dog-weary, footweary, world-weary; 4 travel-weary.
See also **10.42.4**.

9.19.64: 2 diary, friary, priory, wiry; 3 expiry, inquiry, retiree.

9.19.65: 2 corrie, lorry, MORI, quarry, sorry; 3 Macquarie.

9.19.66: 2 Corey, dory, flory, glory, gory, hoary, Rory, Tori, Tory; 3 furore, john dory, Old Glory, satori, vainglory; 4 hunky-dory, Montessori, morning glory; 5 celebratory; 6 knickerbocker glory.
See also **9.19.68, 9.59.10**.

9.19.67: 2 storey, story; 3 backstory, clerestory, folk story, ghost story, life story, love story, news story, short story, sob story, tall story; 4 fairy story, horror story, multistorey; 5 cock-and-bull story; 6 never-ending story.

9.19.68: 2 Curie, Dury, fury, houri, Jewry, jury; 3 Missouri, mortuary, tandoori; 4 voluptuary.
See also **9.19.66**.

9.19.69: 2 cowrie, dowry, floury, Lowry, Maori.

9.19.70: 2 Currie, curry, dhurrie, flurry, hurry, Moray, Murray, scurry, slurry, Surrey, worry.
See also **9.29.6, 10.42.4**.

9.19.71: 2 Koori, Yuri; 3 augury, mercury, potpourri.

9.19.72: 2 Audrey, bawdry, Cowdrey, Deirdre, padre, tawdry; 3 balladry, cuckoldry, heraldry, ribaldry, wizardry.

9.19.73: 2 foundry, Hendry, laundry, sundry; 3 husbandry; 4 polyandry.

9.19.74: 1 free; 2 belfry, carefree, comfrey, dirt-free, Geoffrey, germ-free, Godfrey, Humphrey, Jeffrey, painfree, palfrey, post-free, risk-free, scot-free, smoke-free, stress-free, tax-free, Wee Free, Winfrey; 3 duty-free, fancy-free, hassle-free, trouble-free; 4 gallimaufry.
Yes, how many years can a mountain exist
Before it's washed to the sea.
Yes, how many years can some people exist
Before they're allowed to be free.
(Bob Dylan)
See also **9.29.6**.

9.19.75: 2 agree, angry, degree, hungry, puggree; 3 disagree, filigree, pedigree, verdigris.
See also **9.29.6**.

9.19.76: 1 Cree, scree; 2 decree, kukri; 3 Conakry, gimmickry, mimicry, Pitlochry.

In Xanadu did Kubla Khan
A stately pleasure-dome decree:
Where Alph, the sacred river, ran
Through caverns measureless to man
Down to a sunless sea.
(Samuel Taylor Coleridge)

9.19.77: 3 cavalry, chivalry, devilry, hostelry, jewellery, revelry, rivalry; 5 Household Cavalry.

9.19.78: 2 Henry; 3 blazonry, deaconry, falconry, heathenry, masonry, paganry, veterinary, weaponry, yeomanry; 4 archdeaconry, charlatanry, citizenry, freemasonry.

9.19.79: 1 spree; 2 Capri, osprey; 3 Grand Prix.

9.19.80: 1 tree; 2 factory, Roundtree, shoetree; 3 Babbittry, Dimitri, podiatry, psychiatry; 4 Navaratri; 5 gloria patri.

9.19.81: 3 bigotry, gadgetry, harlotry, lavatory, musketry, poetry, puppetry, secretary, signatory, zealotry; 4 idolatry, observatory, zoolatry; 6 Foreign Secretary.

9.19.82: 3 cemetery, dormitory, symmetry; 4 astrometry, asymmetry, bathometry, biometry, geometry, hydrometry, micrometry, optometry, photometry, psychometry, spectrometry, telemetry, unsymmetry, zoometry; 5 craniometry, odorimetry, olfactometry, trigonometry.

9.19.83: 2 Daltry, paltry, poultry, sultry, sweltry; 3 basketry, circuitry, coquetry, marquetry, parquetry, rocketry.

9.19.84: 2 Aintree, chantry, Daintree, gantry, pantry, Rowntree.

9.19.85: 2 wintry; 3 carpentry, Coventry, dysentery, errantry, gallantry, infantry, pageantry, peasantry, pedantry, pleasantry, tenantry.

9.19.86: 2 entry, gentry, sentry; 3 re-entry; 4 landed gentry.

9.19.87: 2 country; 3 back country, cross-country, God's country, old country, upcountry; 4 mother country.

9.19.88: 2 pastry, vestry; 3 ancestry, industry; 4 Danish pastry.

9.19.89: 3 artistry, dentistry, forestry, ministry, registry, sophistry, tapestry; 4 casuistry, Land Registry.

9.19.90: 3 chemistry, palmistry; 5 astrochemistry, biochemistry, geochemistry, phytochemistry; 6 organic chemistry; 7 inorganic chemistry.

9.19.91: 1 three; 2 A3, Guthrie, T3; 3 mp3; 5 omega-3.

9.20: 1 sea, see; 2 Boise, deep-sea, emcee, FC, fussy, hussy, mousy, North Sea, OC, pussy, Red Sea, sissy, White Sea, Yangtze; 3 ABC, BBC, D and C, Sadducee, unfussy, Yellow Sea; 4 AC/DC, Celebes Sea, Sargasso Sea.

When the stars threw down their spears,
And water'd heaven with their tears,
Did he smile his work to see?
Did he who made the Lamb make thee?
(William Blake)
See also **10.42.2**.

9.20.1: 2 brassie, Cassie, chassis, gassy, lassi, lassie, Massey, massy, sassy; 4 Tallahassee.
See also **9.20.13**.

9.20.2: 3 abbacy, embassy, odyssey, oversee, papacy, privacy, prophecy, undersea; 4 adequacy, candidacy, celibacy, controversy, idiocy, sub judice; 5 appropriacy, episcopacy, immediacy, inadequacy.

9.20.3: 3 Agassi, argosy, legacy; 4 profligacy, surrogacy.

9.20.4: 4 advocacy, delicacy, efficacy, intricacy; 5 indelicacy.

9.20.5: 3 fallacy, jealousy, policy; 5 articulacy, immaculacy.

9.20.6: 3 Christmassy, pharmacy, primacy; 4 contumacy, diplomacy, intimacy, supremacy; 5 legitimacy; 6 illegitimacy.

9.20.7: 3 lunacy, Tennessee; 4 obstinacy, Varanasi; 5 inordinacy; 6 indeterminacy.

9.20.8: 3 curacy, heresy, leprosy, piracy, secrecy; 4 accuracy, conspiracy, magistracy, obduracy; 5 biopiracy, inaccuracy; 6 idiosyncrasy.

9.20.9: 4 literacy, numeracy; 5 confederacy, degeneracy, innumeracy, inveteracy.

9.20.10: 4 adhocracy, bureaucracy, democracy, gynocracy, hierocracy, hypocrisy, isocracy, mobocracy, ochlocracy, physiocracy, quangocracy, technocracy, theocracy.

9.20.11: **4** autocracy, plutocracy, stratocracy; **5** aristocracy, gerontocracy, meritocracy.

9.20.12: **3** B2C, Battersea, courtesy, ecstasy, fantasy, phantasy; **4** apostasy, discourtesy.

9.20.13: **2** brassy, classy, Darcy, Farsi, glassy, grassy, Parcae, Parsee, quasi; **3** dalasi, IRC.
See also **9.20.1**.

9.20.14: **2** AC, Casey, desi, lacy, Macy, pace, pacy, precis, précis, racy, spacey, Stacey, Tracy; **4** Sulawesi.

9.20.15: **2** dressy, Jessie, lessee, messy, Nessie; **3** addressee, BSE; **4** GCSE, NYSE.

9.20.16: **2** Circe, mercy, Percy; **4** arsyversy, controversy.

9.20.17: **2** fleecy, greasy, PC, VC; **3** PVC; **4** Tbilisi; **5** NSPCC, WPC.

9.20.18: **2** Cissy, missy, prissy; **3** Morrissey, pharisee, pleurisy; **4** Eurydice, geodesy.

9.20.19: **2** dicey, dicy, IC, icy, pricey, pricy, spicy; **3** NYC; **4** Berenice.

9.20.20: **2** bossy, Fosse, glossy, mossy, posse.

9.20.21: **2** foresee, horsey, saucy; **3** divorcé, divorcée, Timor Sea.

9.20.22: **2** juicy, Lucy, QC; **3** Debussy, RUC, TUC; **4** WC.

9.20.23: **1** xi; **2** exe, folksy, maxi, sexy, taxi, waxy; **3** galaxy; **4** apoplexy, ataraxy, cataplexy.

9.20.24: **2** Dixie, pixie, tricksy; **3** Baltic Sea; **5** Adriatic Sea.

9.20.25: **2** Chelsea, Elsie, foxy, moxie, poxy, proxy; **3** by proxy, epoxy, plc, TLC; **4** orthodoxy; **5** heterodoxy, unorthodoxy.

9.20.26: **3** Anglesey, Aral Sea, Marshalsea, normalcy.

9.20.27: **2** bouncy, chancy, poncy, Quincy; **3** ANC, chaplaincy, C in C, De Quincey, piquancy; **4** constituency, Philippine Sea.

9.20.28: **2** Clancy, fancy, nancy; **3** unfancy; **4** astromancy, chiromancy, geomancy, hydromancy, logomancy, necromancy, psychomancy, pyromancy, sycophancy, theomancy; **5** arithmomancy, bibliomancy, ichthyomancy, oneiromancy, ophiomancy, sideromancy.

9.20.29: **3** buoyancy, flippancy, fluency, infancy, pliancy, solvency, truancy, vacancy, valency; **4** absorbency, conservancy, discrepancy, elegancy, Excellency, fraudulency, incumbency, insolvency, mendicancy, occupancy, sycophancy.

9.20.30: **3** Caspian Sea; **4** Aegean Sea, deviancy, leniency, Ligurian Sea, Tyrrhenian Sea; **5** expediency; **6** inexpediency, Mediterranean Sea.

9.20.31: **3** ardency, stridency, tendency, verdancy; **4** ascendancy, dependency, despondency, presidency, redundancy, residency; **7** chemical dependency.

9.20.32: **3** agency, clemency, cogency, dormancy, plangency, pungency, regency, stringency, Tasman Sea, urgency; **4** astringency, coagency, contingency, divergency, emergency, exigency, inclemency, insurgency; **6** Child Support Agency, counterinsurgency.
Faith is a fine invention
When gentlemen can see.
But microscopes are prudent
In an emergency.
(Emily Dickinson)

9.20.33: **3** currency, decency, flagrancy, licensee, poignancy, pregnancy, tenancy, vagrancy, vibrancy; **4** complacency, indecency, malignancy, permanency, transparency; **5** belligerency.

9.20.34: **4** deficiency, efficiency, proficiency, sufficiency; **5** inefficiency, insufficiency, self-sufficiency; **7** immunodeficiency.

9.20.35: **3** blatancy, captaincy, chieftaincy, constancy, latency, potency; **4** accountancy, consistency, consultancy, expectancy, hesitancy, inconstancy, militancy; **5** inconsistency.

9.20.36: **3** frequency; **4** delinquency, high frequency, infrequency, low frequency.

9.20.37: **2** Dempsey, gypsy, tipsy; **4** catalepsy, epilepsy, narcolepsy.

9.20.38: **2** copsy, dropsy, Topsy; **3** autopsy, biopsy, necropsy.

9.20.39: **2** antsy, artsy, chintzy, curtsy, cutesy, footsie, gutsy, Nazi, patsy, schmaltzy, tootsy, tsotsi, Yangtze; **3** Abruzzi, bankruptcy; **4** baronetcy, neoNazi, paparazzi.

9.20.40: **2** bitsy, ditsy, glitzy, ritzy; **3** Uffizi; **4** itsy-bitsy.

9.21: **1** she; **2** banshee, bolshie, bushie, bushy, chichi, cushy, fleshy, marshy, meishi, pushy, specie, squashy, sushi, Vichy; **4** Bangladeshi, prima facie, wishy-washy.

9.21.1: **2** ashy, flashy, splashy, trashy.

9.21.2: **2** dishy, fishy, gushy, mushy, plushy, slushy, squishy; **3** rubbishy; **4** maharishi.

9.22: **1** tea, tee, ti; **2** empty; **3** Alberti, AZT, BLT, EMT, GMT, inductee, PMT; **4** Don Quixote, hoity-toity, spermaceti.
Stands the Church clock at ten to three?
And is there honey still for tea?
(Rupert Brooke)
See also **9.59.13**.

9.22.1: **2** batty, catty, chatty, fatty, natty, patty, ratty, scatty, tattie, tatty; **3** chapati, Hanratty, Scarlatti; **4** Cincinnati.

9.22.2: **3** chocolatey, crotchety, deity, Flaherty, legatee, moiety, nullity; **4** O'Flaherty.

9.22.3: **3** deity, gaiety, laity; **5** spontaneity; **6** homogeneity, simultaneity; **7** contemporaneity, extemporaneity, heterogeneity.

9.22.4: **4** acuity, annuity, fatuity, gratuity, tenuity, vacuity; **5** ambiguity, assiduity, contiguity, continuity, exiguity, incongruity, ingenuity, perpetuity, perspicuity, promiscuity, superfluity; **6** discontinuity.

9.22.5: **3** liberty, probity, puberty; **4** acerbity, improbity; **6** Statue of Liberty.

9.22.6: **3** crudity, nudity, oddity; **4** absurdity, commodity, fecundity, heredity, profundity, rotundity; **5** infecundity, orotundity, rubicundity.

9.22.7: **3** Docherty, Hecate, quiddity, rackety, rickety; **4** acidity, aridity, avidity, cupidity, flaccidity, fluidity, frigidity, gelidity, gravidity, humidity, limpidity, liquidity, lucidity, morbidity, pernickety, placidity, rancidity, rapidity, rigidity, solidity, stolidity, stupidity, timidity, torpidity, turbidity, turgidity, validity, vapidity, viscidity; **5** insipidity, invalidity, pellucidity.

9.22.8: **4** credulity, fidelity, garrulity; **5** high-fidelity, incredulity, infidelity.

9.22.9: **4** causality, centrality, feudality, frugality, legality, modality, nasality, neutrality, plurality; **5** animality, illegality, principality, prodigality; **6** municipality.

9.22.10: **4** reality; **5** bestiality, cordiality, geniality, ideality, joviality, triviality, unreality; **6** conviviality, corporeality, ethereality, materiality; **7** immateriality.

9.22.11: **5** partiality, sociality, speciality; **6** impartiality, potentiality, substantiality; **7** artificiality, confidentiality, superficiality.

9.22.12: **4** duality; **5** sensuality, sexuality; **7** individuality.

9.22.13: **5** actuality, effectuality, factuality, mutuality, punctuality, virtuality; **6** eventuality, spirituality; **7** ineffectuality, intellectuality.

9.22.14: **4** locality; **5** musicality, physicality, practicality, technicality, whimsicality; **6** illogicality, impracticality, theatricality.

9.22.15: **4** formality, normality; **5** abnormality, informality.

9.22.16: **4** carnality, finality, tonality, venality; **5** criminality.

9.22.17: **4** banality; **5** functionality, nationality, personality, rationality; **6** additionality, irrationality, originality; **7** constitutionality.

9.22.18: **4** morality; **5** amorality, generality, immorality, liberality.

9.22.19: **4** brutality, fatality, mentality, mortality, totality, vitality; **5** hospitality, immortality; **6** sentimentality.

9.22.20: **4** ability, agility, anility, civility, debility, docility, facility, fragility, humility, liability, mobility, nihility, nobility, nubility, scurrility, senility, servility, sterility, tranquility, virility; **5** affability, audibility, capability, changeability, credibility, culpability, durability, fallibility, friability, gullibility, imbecility, immobility, inability, incivility, legibility, likability, pliability, probability, puerility, readability, reliability, sociability, tangibility, viability; **6** amenability, amiability, amicability, applicability, availability, dependability, desirability, eligibility, illegibility, immovability, impeccability, impregnability, inaudibility, infallibility, insatiability, intangibility, malleability, stickability, variability, vulnerability; **7** impenetrability, impermeability, inexorability, inseparability, invulnerability.
See also **9.59.13**.

9.22.21: **5** disability, flexibility, possibility, sensibility; **6** accessibility, admissibility, compressibility, impassability, impossibility, inflexibility, insensibility, invincibility, irascibility, responsibility, serviceability; **7** comprehensibility, inaccessibility, irresponsibility, learning disability.

9.22.22: **4** stability; **5** feasibility, instability, mutability, notability, plausibility, portability, scrutability, suitability, tractability, usability, visibility; **6** acceptability, accountability, adaptability, advisability, compatibility, contemptibility, convertibility, excitability, hospitability, immutability, implausibility, intractability, invisibility, irritability, palatability, perceptibility, predictability, profitability, respectability, suggestibility, susceptibility, unsuitability; **7** incompatibility, indestructibility, inevitability, noncompatibility, unacceptability, unpalatability, unpredictability, unprofitability.

9.22.23: **4** ductility, fertility, futility, gentility, hostility, motility, utility; **5** infertility, versatility, volatility. *See also* **9.59.13**.

9.22.24: **3** jollity, polity, quality; **4** equality, frivolity, high-quality, low-quality, poor-quality, star quality, top-quality; **5** inequality, letter-quality.

9.22.25: **3** amity, comity, enmity; **4** calamity, conformity, deformity, enormity, extremity, infirmity, proximity; **5** anonymity, equanimity, nonconformity, unanimity, uniformity.

9.22.26: **3** dignity, lenity; **4** amenity, indemnity, indignity, malignity, obscenity, serenity, solemnity.

9.22.27: **3** manatee, sanity, vanity; **4** humanity, inanity, insanity, profanity, urbanity; **5** Christianity, inhumanity.

9.22.28: **4** eternity, fraternity, maternity, modernity, paternity; **5** confraternity, taciturnity.

9.22.29: **3** trinity; **4** affinity, divinity, infinity, sanguinity, vicinity, virginity; **5** asininity, consanguinity, femininity, gelatinity, Holy Trinity, masculinity, saccharinity.

9.22.30: **3** unity; **4** community, disunity, immunity, impunity; **5** importunity, opportunity; **7** photo-opportunity.

9.22.31: **3** property, uppity, wapiti; **5** serendipity.

9.22.32: **3** rarity; **4** alacrity, celebrity, entirety, integrity; **5** mediocrity.

9.22.33: **3** carroty, charity, parity; **4** barbarity, disparity, imparity, vulgarity; **5** linearity, solidarity; **6** familiarity, peculiarity, subsidiarity; **7** unfamiliarity; **8** overfamiliarity.

9.22.34: **3** clarity; **4** hilarity, polarity; **5** similarity; **6** dissimilarity.

9.22.35: **5** circularity, insularity, jocularity, muscularity, popularity, regularity, singularity; **6** irregularity, particularity.

9.22.36: **3** verity; **4** asperity, austerity, celerity, dexterity, posterity, prosperity, severity, sincerity, temerity; **5** insincerity; **6** ambidexterity.

9.22.37: **4** authority, majority, minority, priority, sonority, sorority; **5** juniority, seniority; **6** inferiority, superiority.

9.22.38: **3** purity, surety; **4** futurity, impurity, insecurity, maturity, obscurity, security; **5** immaturity, prematurity; **6** biosecurity.

9.22.39: **3** falsity, nicety, paucity, scarcity, sparsity, varsity; **4** necessity, obesity.

9.22.40: **4** audacity, loquacity, mendacity, pugnacity, sagacity, tenacity, veracity, vivacity, voracity; **5** perspicacity, pertinacity.

9.22.41: **4** capacity, opacity, rapacity; **5** incapacity; **6** overcapacity.

9.22.42: **4** adversity, diversity, perversity; **5** university; **6** biodiversity.

9.22.43: **4** ethnicity, toxicity; **5** specificity, synchronicity; **6** periodicity.

9.22.44: **4** complicity, duplicity, felicity, lubricity, publicity, simplicity, sphericity; **5** eccentricity, electricity, historicity, infelicity, multiplicity; **7** hydroelectricity.

9.22.45: **4** plasticity; **5** authenticity, domesticity, elasticity; **6** inelasticity.

9.22.46: **4** globosity, pomposity, velocity, verbosity, viscosity; **5** animosity, bellicosity, curiosity, ebriosity, high-velocity, luminosity, preciosity, virtuosity; **6** impetuosity, incuriosity, religiosity.

9.22.47: **4** atrocity, ferocity, monstrosity; **5** generosity, reciprocity.

9.22.48: **3** fixity, laxity; **4** complexity, convexity, perplexity, prolixity.

9.22.49: **3** density; **4** high-density, immensity, intensity, low-density, propensity; **5** double-density, teledensity.

9.22.50: **3** chastity, entity, quantity, sanctity; **4** nonentity.

9.22.51: **3** brevity, levity, poverty, suavity, velvety; **4** longevity, naivety.

9.22.52: **3** cavity, concavity, gravity; **4** acclivity, declivity, depravity, passivity, proclivity; **5** antigravity, exclusivity, impassivity.

9.22.53: **4** captivity, festivity; **5** creativity, negativity, positivity, receptivity, relativity, sensitivity; **6** insensitivity.
See also **9.59.13**.

9.22.54: **4** activity; **5** conductivity, connectivity, inactivity, objectivity, productivity, selectivity, subjectivity; **6** overactivity; **7** radioactivity, superconductivity.

9.22.55: **3** equity; **4** antiquity, inequity, iniquity, obliquity, propinquity, ubiquity; **5** private equity.

9.22.56: **2** arty, clarty, hearty, lathi, Satie, smarty, tarty; **3** Almaty, Amati, Astarte, basmati, coati, frascati, siSwati; **4** Chakrabarti, Kiribati, Moriarty, Sarasvati; **5** Amaravati, illuminati.

9.22.57: **2** party; **3** chapati, Green Party, hen party, house party, repartee, stag party, street party, tea party, third party; **4** advance party, birthday party, cocktail party, dinner party, garden party, Labour Party, multiparty, working party; **5** fancy-dress party, Liberal Party; **6** Conservative Party, Democratic Party, Republican Party.

9.22.58: **3** karate; **4** chatterati, digerati, glitterati, Gujarati, literati.

9.22.59: **2** eighty, Haiti, matey, maty, weighty; **3** Kuwaiti, VAT.

9.22.60: **2** Betty, Etty, Getty, jetty, petty, settee, sweaty, yeti; **3** confetti, Ligeti, machete, Rossetti, spaghetti; **4** cappelletti, Donizetti, Giacometti, spermaceti.

9.22.61: **1** Qwerty; **2** Bertie, dirty, flirty, shirty, thirty.

9.22.62: **2** Beattie, ET, meaty, peaty, PT, sweetie, treaty; **3** DDT, DVT, entreaty, graffiti, OTT, Tahiti; **4** GLBT, Nefertiti.

9.22.63: **2** bitty, chitty, ditty, gritty, kitty, pity, pretty, shitty, titty, witty; **3** committee, fidgety, self-pity; **4** identity, nativity, nitty-gritty, subcommittee.
Oh, London is a fine town,
A very famous city,
Where all the streets are paved with gold,
And all the maidens pretty.
(George Colman)
See also **10.42.2**.

9.22.64: **2** city; **4** centricity, Granite City, Holy City, inner-city, intercity; **5** Mexico City, Vatican City; **6** Celestial City; **7** Open University.

9.22.65: **2** Blighty, flighty, IT, mighty, nightie, whitey; **3** almighty; **4** Aphrodite.

9.22.66: **3** piety; **4** anxiety, dubiety, impiety, satiety, society; **5** high society; **6** friendly society, humane society, pillar of society, secret society.

9.22.67: **4** ebriety, propriety, sobriety, variety; **5** contrariety, impropriety, insobriety, notoriety.

9.22.68: **2** dotty, grotty, hottie, knotty, potty, Scottie, snotty, spotty, swotty, tottie, zloty; **4** agnolotti, Buonarroti, manicotti, Pavarotti.

9.22.69: **2** forte, forty, haughty, naughty, shorty, sortie, sporty; **3** deportee; **5** pianoforte.

9.22.70: **2** doughty, gouty, pouty, shouty.

9.22.71: **2** dhoti, floaty, goatee, loti, roti, throaty; **3** Capote, coyote, devotee, maloti, MOT, peyote.

9.22.72: **2** butty, nutty, putty, rutty, smutty, suttee.

9.22.73: **2** footie, sooty; **3** amputee, bobotie, deputy.

9.22.74: **2** bootee, booty, cootie, fruity, muti, snooty; **3** bobotie, clafoutis, Djibouti; **4** Funafuti, tutti-frutti.

9.22.75: **2** beauty, cutey, cutie, duty, q.t., tutee; **3** Black Beauty, death duty, guard-duty, off duty, on duty, point duty; **4** estate duty, heavy-duty, Sleeping Beauty.

9.22.76: **2** crafty, draughty, hefty, lefty, lofty, mufti, safety, shufti, softie, softy.

9.22.77: **2** fifty, nifty, shifty, thrifty; **4** fifty-fifty.
See also **9.59.13**.

9.22.78: **2** balti, faulty, frailty, guilty, realty, salty, silty, Solti.

9.22.79: **3** cruelty, faculty, fealty, loyalty, mayoralty, novelty, penalty, royalty, specialty, subtlety; **4** Admiralty, casualty, difficulty, disloyalty.
See also **9.59.13.**

9.22.80: **2** auntie, Brontë, dainty, grantee, jaunty, Monty, ninety, pointy, runty; **3** absentee, appointee, certainty, full monty, guarantee, guaranty, seventy, warranty; **4** dilettante, suzerainty, uncertainty.
See also **9.29.**

9.22.81: **2** ante, anti, Fanti, scanty, shanty; **3** andante, Ashanti, Chianti; **4** dilettante, vigilante.

9.22.82: **2** plenty, twenty; **3** al dente, aplenty, TNT; **4** cognoscenti, horn of plenty; **5** Deo volente.

9.22.83: **2** flinty, minty, shinty; **3** sovereignty.

9.22.84: **2** bounty, county, Mountie; **3** viscounty.
See also **9.59.15.**

9.22.85: **2** beastie, bursty, chesty, feisty, frosty, frowsty, nasty, pasty, postie, sixty, testy, thirsty, toasty, yeasty, zesty; **3** bloodthirsty; **4** rhinoplasty; **5** angioplasty.
See also **2.54.69, 9.14.42.**

9.22.86: **3** amnesty, dynasty, majesty, travesty; **4** Your Majesty.

9.22.87: **2** hasty, pasty, tasty; **4** overhasty.
See also **9.14.42.**

9.22.88: **2** Christie, misty, twisty; **3** honesty, modesty, sacristy, touristy; **4** dishonesty, immodesty.

9.22.89: **2** basti, bustee, busty, crusty, dusty, fusty, gusty, lusty, musty, rusty, trustee, trusty.
See also **9.14.42.**

9.23: **2** bothy, breathy, earthy, frothy, lengthy, Lethe, mothy, mouthy, pithy, toothy; **3** Dorothy, McCarthy, Timothy; **4** Iolanthe, polymathy.

9.23.1: **3** apathy, empathy, sympathy; **4** antipathy, telepathy.

9.23.2: **4** allopathy, hydropathy; **5** homeopathy, homoeopathy, naturopathy, osteopathy, retinopathy; **11** bovine spongiform encephalopathy.

9.23.3: **2** filthy, healthy, stealthy, wealthy; **3** unhealthy.

9.24: **2** blotchy, churchy, duchy, grouchy, lychee, peachy, preachy, sketchy, stretchy, tai chi, techy, tetchy, touchy; **3** archduchy, Medici, Urumqi, Vespucci; **4** sotto voce, viva voce; **5** arrivederci.
See also **2.54.65.**

9.24.1: **2** catchy, patchy, scratchy; **3** Apache, Old Scratchy.

9.24.2: **2** nartjie, starchy; **3** Karachi, vivace; **4** mariachi.

9.24.3: **2** bitchy, itchy, kitschy, lychee, Richie, titchy, twitchy.

9.24.4: **2** Binchy, crunchy, paunchy, punchy, raunchy, scrunchie.

9.25: **2** CV, envy, Humvee, ivy, maulvi, navvy, Ravi, savvy; **3** anchovy, C of E, HGV, HIV, muscovy, Ogilvie, vis-à-vis.

9.25.1: **2** Garvey, Harvey, RV; **3** agave, peccavi.

9.25.2: **2** Davy, devi, gravy, navy, wavy; **3** agave; **4** Royal Navy.

9.25.3: **2** bevvy, bevy, Chevy, heavy, levee, Levi, levy; **3** top-heavy.

9.25.4: **2** curvy, nervy, pervy, scurvy; **4** topsy-turvy.

9.25.5: **2** TV; **3** ITV, MTV; **4** CCTV; **5** satellite TV.

9.25.6: **2** chivvy, civvy, divvy, Livy, privy, skivvy.
See also **9.59.**

9.25.7: **2** covey, lovey, luvvie; **4** lovey-dovey.

9.25.8: **2** groovy, movie; **3** B movie, SUV.
See also **9.59.**

9.26: **1** twee, we, wee, whee; **2** Bowie, Conwy, drawee, ennui, kiwi, peewee, wee-wee; **3** Malawi, ratatouille, Zimbabwe.
See also **9.29.8.**

9.26.1: **3** colloquy, obloquy, obsequy; **4** soliloquy.

9.27: **1** zee; **2** Aussie, ballsy, Coetzee, cozzie, gauzy, jazzy, jersey, Mersey, mozzy, noisy, Ozzie, palsy, pressie, prezzie, snazzy, woodsy; **3** franchisee, jalousie, New Jersey, outdoorsy, poesy; **4** palsy-walsy; **5** cerebral palsy.
See also **9.14.28.**

9.27.1: **2** khazi, Swazi; **3** Benghazi, bourgeoisie; **4** Ashkenazi, kamikaze.

9.27.2: **2** Basie, crazy, daisy, hazy, lazy; **3** jalfrezi, stir-crazy; **4** Buthelezi,

calabrese, upsadaisy, Veronese; 5 African daisy.
See also 9.14.28.

9.27.3: 2 breezy, cheesy, easy, queasy, sleazy, wheezy, Wolsey; 3 pachisi, speakeasy, uneasy, Zambezi; 4 easy-peasy, free-and-easy.
See also 2.54.70.

9.27.4: 2 busy, dizzy, fizzy, frizzy, tizzy; 3 tin lizzie; 4 busy Lizzie.
See also 2.54.70.

9.27.5: 2 blowzy, drowsy, frowzy, lousy.

9.27.6: 2 cosy, dozy, mosey, nosy, posy, prosy, rosy.
See also 2.54.70.

9.27.7: 2 fuzzy, muzzy, SCSI, scuzzy.
See also 2.54.70.

9.27.8: 2 bluesy, boozy, choosy, doozy, floozy, newsy, oozy, Uzi, woozy; 3 Brancusi, Jacuzzi.

9.27.9: 2 clumsy, flimsy, Ramsay, whimsy.
See also 2.54.70.

9.27.10: 2 frenzy, guernsey, Kinsey, Lindsay, pansy, Swansea, tansy; 3 Bermondsey, chimpanzee, Mackenzie, McKenzie; 4 teensy-weensy.

9.28: 1 dweeb, glebe, grebe; 2 Gottlieb.

9.29: 1 bead, Bede, deed, Eid, Gide, heed, he'd, mead, meed, she'd, steed; 2 bevvied, frenzied, misdeed, Rashid, Saïd; 3 propertied, title deed; 4 guaranteed.
See also 9.22.80.

9.29.1: 2 candied, indeed, studied; 3 full-bodied, parodied, unstudied; 4 able-bodied, disembodied.
See also 9.7.2, 9.7.16.

9.29.2: 1 feed; 2 breastfeed, drip-feed, force-feed, spoon-feed; 3 bottle-feed, chickenfeed.
See also 6.1.3.

9.29.3: 1 bleed, lead, Lied, plead; 2 jellied, mislead, nosebleed; 3 big-bellied, full-bellied, potbellied, unsullied; 4 yellow-bellied.
See also 6.1.10, 10.42.18.

9.29.4: 1 knead, need; 2 hackneyed, honeyed, knock-kneed, moneyed, monied, weak-kneed; 4 accompanied; 5 unaccompanied.
  When you try your best, but you don't
  succeed,

  When you get what you want, but not what
  you need,
  When you feel so tired, but you can't
  sleep,
  Stuck in reverse.
  (Coldplay)
See also 9.16.10, 10.2.8.

9.29.5: 1 speed; 2 airspeed, groundspeed, high-speed, impede, stampede, wind speed; 3 centipede, millipede; 4 velocipede.
See also 6.1.11, 10.42.17.

9.29.6: 1 breed, creed, freed, greed, read, reed, Reid, screed; 2 agreed, buried, crossbreed, curried, half-breed, harried, hurried, lip-read, married, misread, proofread, serried, Siegfried, sight-read, storied, varied, worried; 3 interbreed, liveried, salaried, unhurried, unmarried, unwearied, unworried; 4 unsalaried.
  Lord, forgive me if my need
  Sometimes shapes a human creed.
  (Countee Cullen)
See also 6.1.13, 9.14.58, 9.19.1, 9.19.59, 9.19.61, 9.19.70, 9.19.74, 9.19.75, 10.42.17.

9.29.7: 1 cede, seed; 2 accede, birdseed, concede, deseed, exceed, flaxseed, hayseed, linseed, precede, proceed, rapeseed, recede, secede, succeed, top seed; 3 aniseed, antecede, cottonseed, intercede, mustard seed, poppy seed, supersede.
See also 9.30, 10.42.17.

9.29.8: 1 swede, tweed, weed, we'd; 2 bindweed, chickweed, duckweed, harris tweed, milkweed, ragweed, seaweed; 3 tumbleweed.
See also 9.26, 9.30.

9.30: 1 Leeds, weeds; 2 proceeds; 3 widow's weeds.
See also 9.29.7, 9.29.8.

9.31: 1 breathe, seethe, sheathe, teethe, wreathe; 2 bequeath, ensheathe, unsheathe.
See also 9.56, 10.42.31.

9.32: 1 beef, chief, fief, sheaf, thief; 2 big Chief, ground beef, massif, minced beef, motif, O'Keeffe; 3 cattle thief, leitmotif, petty thief; 4 aperitif; 5 commander-in-chief, editor-in-chief.
See also 9.54, 9.58.

9.32.1: 1 leaf, lief; 2 bay leaf, belief, broadleaf, fig leaf, flyleaf, gold leaf, loose-leaf, relief, tea leaf; 3 bas-relief, bold relief, cloverleaf, comic relief, disbelief, high relief, light relief, low relief, misbelief,

nonbelief, overleaf, pain relief, poor relief, unbelief.
See also **9.58.**

9.32.2: **1** brief, grief, reef; **2** debrief; **4** barrier reef.
See also **9.33, 10.42.32.**

9.33: **1** briefs; **2** beliefs.
See also **9.32.2.**

9.34: **1** Grieg, league; **2** blitzkrieg, colleague, fatigue, intrigue, renege; **3** Football League, Ivy League, Little League, Rugby League; **4** National League; **5** American League.
See also **10.42.33.**

9.35: **1** liege, siege; **2** besiege; **3** under siege.

9.36: **1** beak, cheek, chic, eek, eke, geek, meek, seek, sheik, Sikh; **2** bezique, physique, Tajik; **3** hide-and-seek, Mozambique, stickybeak, tongue-in-cheek.

9.36.1: **1** bleak, clique, leak, leek, sleek; **2** Lalique, Malik, oblique.

9.36.2: **1** sneak; **2** technique, unique; **3** Martinique.
Other dancers may be on the floor
Dear, but my eyes will see only you,
Only you have that magic technique.
When we sway I grow weak.
(Pablo Beltrán Ruiz, Normal Gimbel)
See also **2.54.62, 10.42.48.**

9.36.3: **1** peak, peek, pique; **2** off-peak.
See also **9.37.**

9.36.4: **1** speak; **2** bespeak, netspeak, newspeak, upspeak, webspeak; **3** doublespeak, Eurospeak, technospeak; **4** computerspeak.

9.36.5: **1** creak, creek, freak, Greek, reek, shriek, streak, wreak; **2** blue streak; **3** fenugreek; **4** péripherique, téléphérique.
Heaven, I'm in heaven,
And the cares that hung around me
through the week
Seem to vanish like a gambler's lucky
streak,
When we're out together dancing cheek
to cheek.
(Irving Berlin)
See also **9.37, 10.42.48.**

9.36.6: **1** teak; **2** antique, batik, boutique, critique, mystique; **5** realpolitik.

9.36.7: **1** squeak, tweak, weak, week; **2** midweek, pipsqueak, workweek; **4** bubble and squeak.

9.37: **1** peaked, piqued, streaked; **3** hollow-cheeked, rosy-cheeked.
See also **9.36.3, 9.36.5.**

9.38: **1** deal, eel, feel, keel, Kiel, she'll, teal, veal, zeal; **2** congeal, genteel, New Deal, ordeal, reveal; **4** electric eel.
See also **9.39, 10.42.72.**

9.38.1: **1** Beale; **3** bloodmobile, bookmobile, deshabille, Dormobile, popemobile, snowmobile; **4** automobile.

9.38.2: **1** heal, heel, he'll; **2** self heal; **3** down-at-heel; **4** Achilles heel.
See also **9.39, 10.42.72.**

9.38.3: **1** meal; **2** bonemeal, cornmeal, fishmeal, oatmeal, piecemeal, schlemiel, square meal, wheatmeal, wholemeal.

9.38.4: **1** kneel, Neil; **2** anneal, chenille, O'Neill; **3** cochineal.

9.38.5: **1** creel, peal, peel, real, reel, spiel; **2** appeal, newsreel, repeal, Singspiel; **3** glockenspiel, sex appeal; **4** Court of Appeal.
See also **10.42.72.**

9.38.6: **1** seal; **2** conceal, great seal, unseal; **3** imbecile, leopard seal, Privy Seal.
See also **9.39.**

9.38.7: **1** steal, steel, Steele; **2** Castile.
Oh, there's black jack and poker and the
roulette wheel,
A fortune won and lost on ev'ry deal.
All you need's a strong heart and a nerve
of steel.
Viva Las Vegas, Viva Las Vegas.
(Elvis Presley)

9.38.8: **1** squeal, weal, we'll, wheel; **2** big wheel, cartwheel, cogwheel, fifth wheel, flywheel, freewheel, gearwheel, millwheel, pinwheel, prayer wheel, spare wheel; **3** commonweal, Ferris wheel, paddle wheel, spinning wheel, steering wheel, water wheel.
See also **10.42.72.**

9.39: **1** healed, sealed, shield, wield, yield; **2** concealed, congealed, well-heeled, windshield; **3** unconcealed.
See also **9.38, 9.38.2, 9.38.6, 10.42.14.**

9.39.1: **1** field; **2** afield, airfield, backfield, brownfield, Caulfield, coalfield, Earlsfield, Enfield, Garfield, gasfield, hayfield, infield, left field, leftfield, Mansfield, Masefield, midfield, minefield, misfield, oilfield, Oldfield, outfield, Schofield, Sheffield, snowfield, Springfield, Wakefield, wheatfield;

3 battlefield, Butterfield, chesterfield, force field.

9.40: **2** Southfields; **3** killing fields, playing fields, Spitalfields; **4** Elysian Fields.

9.41: **1** Cheam, deem, gleam, meme, theme; **2** blaspheme, grapheme, morpheme, phoneme, redeem, regime, Selim; **3** academe, Elohim, Ephraim; **5** ancien régime.

Whither is fled the visionary gleam?
Where is it now, the glory and the dream?
(William Wordsworth)
See also **9.42, 10.42.87.**

9.41.1: **1** beam; **2** crossbeam, I-beam, moonbeam, off-beam, sunbeam.
See also **10.42.87.**

9.41.2: **1** scheme; **2** hakeem, hakim, playscheme; **3** Joachim.
See also **10.42.87.**

9.41.3: **1** bream, dream, ream; **2** bireme, daydream, harem, pipe dream, Purim, supreme, trireme; **3** quinquereme; **5** American dream.
Climb ev'ry mountain, ford ev'ry stream,
Follow ev'ry rainbow, till you find your
dream.
(Oscar Hammerstein II)
See also **10.42.87.**

9.41.4: **1** cream, scream; **2** cold cream, face cream, ice cream, sour cream; **3** buttercream, clotted cream, salad cream; **4** vanishing cream.
See also **10.42.87.**

9.41.5: **1** stream; **2** airstream, bitstream, bloodstream, clickstream, Coldstream, downstream, extreme, Gulf Stream, mainstream, midstream, millstream, on-stream, slipstream, upstream.
See also **10.42.87.**

9.41.6: **1** seam, seem; **2** lexeme, Nasim, raceme.
Things are seldom what they seem,
Skim milk masquerades as cream.
(W. S. Gilbert)
See also **10.42.87.**

9.41.7: **1** steam, team, teem; **2** centime, esteem, tag-team; **3** self-esteem.
See also **10.42.87.**

9.42: **1** seamed, themed; **2** esteemed, redeemed.
See also **9.41.**

9.43: **1** e'en, sheen; **2** caffeine, ethene, morphine, poteen, tagine; **3** aubergine,

Balanchine, carragheen, Halloween, Joséphine, Medellín, Philippine, polythene.

9.43.1: **1** bean, been; **2** black bean, broad bean, Harbin, has-been, mung bean, Rabin, shebeen, soybean; **3** black-eyed bean, fava bean, jellybean, lima bean, might-have-been, pinto bean; **4** azuki bean.

9.43.2: **1** dean, dene; **2** codeine, Roedean, sardine, undine; **3** Geraldine, iodine, pethidine; **4** mujahedin.

9.43.3: **1** gene, Jean; **2** Eugene, hygiene; **3** Aberdeen, gabardine, gaberdine, grenadine.

9.43.4: **1** keen; **2** achene, Tolkien; **3** palanquin.
See also **2.54.82, 10.42.99.**

9.43.5: **1** glean, lean, spleen; **2** Aileen, Céline, colleen, Crimplene, Darlene, Eileen, Hellene, praline, scalene, Tallinn.
Jack Sprat could eat no fat,
His wife could eat no lean,
And so between them both you see,
They licked the platter clean.
(Children's Verse)
See also **10.42.99.**

9.43.6: **1** clean; **2** dry-clean, unclean; **3** Abilene, aniline, Cymbeline, gasoline, mescaline, mousseline, naphthalene, Sakhalin, squeaky-clean, trampoline, Vaseline; **4** acetylene, tetracycline; **5** polyethylene, polypropylene; **6** oxyacetylene.

9.43.7: **1** mean, mien; **2** Amin, bromine, demean, gamine, thiamine; **3** dopamine, golden mean, histamine, melamine; **4** amphetamine, glucosamine; **5** antihistamine.
See also **2.54.82, 9.46, 10.42.99.**

9.43.8: **2** Benin, quinine, strychnine; **3** mezzanine.

9.43.9: **1** preen; **2** chlorine, fluorine, Irene, latrine, Maureen, terrene, terrine, tureen; **3** Benzedrine, neoprene; **4** polystyrene.

9.43.10: **2** careen, serene; **3** figurine, glycerine, margarine, nectarine, tambourine, tangerine, wolverine.

9.43.11: **2** marine; **3** submarine; **4** aquamarine, ultramarine.
See also **9.46.**

9.43.12: **1** green, Greene; **2** gangrene; **3** Bethnal Green, bottle-green, evergreen, Golders Green, Gretna Green, Hither Green.

For there is good news yet to hear and
　fine things to be seen,
Before we go to Paradise by way of
　Kensal Green.
(G. K. Chesterton)

9.43.13: **1** screen; **2** big screen, bluescreen, on-screen, smoke screen, sunscreen, viewscreen, widescreen, windscreen.
See also **10.42.99**.

9.43.14: **1** scene, seen; **2** foreseen, Miocene, obscene, Racine, unseen, vaccine; **3** damascene, Pliocene, thyroxine, unforeseen; **5** MMR vaccine.

9.43.15: **3** kerosene, overseen, Palaeocene, plasticine.

9.43.16: **3** Eocene, Holocene, Pleistocene; **4** Oligocene.

9.43.17: **2** machine; **3** war machine; **4** Turing machine; **8** automated teller machine.

9.43.18: **1** teen; **2** eighteen, fifteen, fourteen, preteen, protein, routine, saltine, thirteen, umpteen; **3** subroutine; **4** Benedictine, lipoprotein.
See also **9.46**.

9.43.19: **3** astatine, carotene, guillotine, libertine, nicotine, velveteen.

9.43.20: **2** canteen, dentine, nineteen; **3** Byzantine.

9.43.21: **3** brigantine, brilliantine, Byzantine, clementine, quarantine, seventeen.
She was young! She was pure! She was
　new! She was nice!
She was fair! She was sweet seventeen!
He was old! He was vile and no stranger
　to vice!
He was base! He was bad! He was mean!
(Flanders and Swann)

9.43.22: **2** Christine, pristine, sixteen, Springsteen; **3** langoustine.

9.43.23: **2** convene, ravine, Slovene; **3** contravene, intervene, reconvene, supervene.
See also **10.42.99**.

9.43.24: **1** queen, 'tween, wean; **2** between, Salween; **3** beauty queen, drama queen, go-between, Hallowe'en; **4** African Queen.
She's a Killer Queen
Gunpowder, gelatine
Dynamite with a laserbeam...
(Queen)

9.43.25: **1** zine; **2** benzene, benzine, cuisine, e-zine, fanzine, webzine; **3** haute cuisine, lean cuisine, limousine, magazine; **4** nouvelle cuisine; **5** girlie magazine.
Greta Garbo, and Monroe;
Deitrich and DiMaggio;
Marlon Brando, Jimmy Dean;
On the cover of a magazine.
(Madonna)

9.44: **1** fiend.

9.45: **2** fifteenth, fourteenth, nineteenth, sixteenth, thirteenth; **3** seventeenth.

9.46: **1** Greens, jeans, means, Queens, teens; **2** baked beans, bluejeans, marines, spring greens; **3** New Orleans, Philippines, smithereens; **4** Royal Marines.
See also **9.43.7, 9.43.11, 9.43.18**.

9.47: **1** beep, bleep, cheap, cheep, creep, deep, heap, Heep, Jeep, keep, leap, peep, reap, seep, sheep, steep, Streep, sweep, veep, weep; **2** barkeep, black sheep, dirt-cheap, knee-deep, scrapheap, skin-deep, slag heap, upkeep; **3** ankle-deep, compost heap, quantum leap; **4** Uriah Heep.
The woods are lovely, dark, and deep,
But I have promises to keep,
And miles to go before I sleep,
And miles to go before I sleep.
(Robert Frost)
See also **9.48, 10.42.106, 10.42.107**.

9.47.1: **1** sleep; **2** asleep, REM sleep; **3** half-asleep, oversleep.
Now I lay me down to sleep,
I pray the Lord my soul to keep.
If I should die before I wake,
I pray the Lord my soul to take.
(Folk Verse)
See also **10.42.106**.

9.48: **1** heaps, peeps, Pepys.
See also **9.47**.

9.49: **1** cease, geese; **2** cassis, decease, Matisse, obese, pastis, premise; **3** predecease; **4** de profundis.
See also **10.62.4**.

9.49.1: **1** fleece, lease; **2** lend-lease, police, release, sublease; **3** Golden Fleece, press release, rerelease; **4** secret police; **5** military police.
Street's like a jungle
So call the police,
Following the herd
Down to Greece...
(Blur)
See also **9.50, 10.42.132**.

9.49.2: 1 Nice, niece; **2** anise, MacNeice; **4** Peloponnese.

9.49.3: 1 peace, piece; **2** codpiece, crosspiece, earpiece, eyepiece, Greenpeace, hairpiece, headpiece, mouthpiece, one-piece, showpiece, tailpiece, timepiece, two-piece; **3** chimneypiece, frontispiece, mantelpiece, War and Peace.

Come, Sleep! O Sleep, the certain knot of
peace,
The bathing-place of wit, the balm of woe,
The poor man's wealth, the prisoner's
release,
The indifferent judge between the high
and low.
(Philip Sidney)

9.49.4: 2 apiece; **3** altarpiece, centrepiece, masterpiece; **5** justice of the peace.

9.49.5: 1 crease, grease, Greece, Gris, Reece, Rhys; **2** caprice, cerise, decrease, Dumfries, increase; **3** calabrese, dentifrice, elbow grease.
See also **9.50.**

9.50: 1 beast, creased, east, feast, least, piste, priest, yeast; **2** artiste, Baptiste, beanfeast, deceased, high priest, increased, Near East, northeast, off-piste, released, southeast; **3** arriviste, brewers' yeast, east-northeast, Middle East, wildebeest; **4** movable feast.
See also **9.49.1, 9.49.5.**

9.51: 1 fiche, leash, niche, quiche; **2** baksheesh, hashish, McLeish, pastiche, unleash; **3** microfiche, nouveau riche.

9.52: 1 cheat, eat, gîte, neat, peat, teat; **2** aesthete, compete, mesquite, petite, repeat; **3** parakeet.
Thou shalt not steal; an empty feat,
When it's so lucrative to cheat.
(Arthur Hugh Clough)
See also **9.53, 10.2.58, 10.42.155.**

9.52.1: 1 beat, beet; **2** back beat, breakbeat, browbeat, deadbeat, downbeat, drumbeat, heartbeat, offbeat, upbeat; **3** sugar beet.
See also **10.42.155.**

9.52.2: 1 feat, feet; **2** cold feet, defeat, effete; **4** Château Lafite, narrow defeat.

9.52.3: 1 heat; **2** dead heat, preheat, reheat; **3** overheat, prickly heat, superheat.
See also **10.2.58, 10.42.155.**

9.52.4: 1 bleat, cleat, fleet, Lied, sleet; **2** athlete, delete, elite; **3** decathlete, heptathlete, obsolete, pentathlete, undelete.
See also **10.2.58.**

9.52.5: 1 pleat; **2** compleat, complete, deplete, French pleat, replete; **3** incomplete.
See also **10.2.58.**

9.52.6: 1 meat, meet, mete; **2** bushmeat, crabmeat, forcemeat, gamete, minced meat, mincemeat, sweetmeat; **3** easy meat, sausagemeat.
See also **10.42.155.**

9.52.7: 1 greet; **2** Magritte; **3** marguerite, overeat.
See also **10.42.155.**

9.52.8: 1 Crete; **2** concrete, discreet, discrete, excrete, secrete; **3** indiscreet.

9.52.9: 1 treat; **2** entreat, ill-treat, maltreat, retreat.

9.52.10: 1 street; **2** backstreet, Bradstreet, Fleet Street, high street, main street, mistreat, off-street, stopstreet, Wall Street; **3** civvy street, Downing Street, easy street, Harley Street, one-way street; **4** Carnaby Street, man in the street.
i'm a path of cinders (my love)
burning under your feet
you're the one who walks me (my love)
i'm your one way street
(Björk)

9.52.11: 1 seat; **2** back seat, conceit, deceit, hot seat, loveseat, mercy seat, receipt, unseat; **3** county seat; **4** ejector seat.
See also **9.53, 10.42.155.**

9.52.12: 1 sheet; **2** bedsheet, chargesheet, flow sheet, fly sheet, freesheet, newssheet, scoresheet, time sheet, worksheet; **3** datasheet.

9.52.13: 2 broadsheet, groundsheet, spreadsheet; **3** fitted sheet.

9.52.14: 1 tweet, wheat; **2** buckwheat, cracked wheat, wholewheat.

9.52.15: 1 suite, sweet; **2** en suite; **3** bittersweet, bridal suite, Nutrasweet, short and sweet, sickly-sweet; **4** honeymoon suite.
See also **9.53.**

9.53: 1 eats, Keats, sweets; **2** receipts, sweetmeats.
See also **9.52, 9.52.11, 9.52.15.**

9.54: 1 heath, Keith, Leith, neath, Reith, sheath, teeth, wreath; **2** beneath,

Blackheath; **3** dragon's teeth, laurel wreath, underneath.
See also **9.32.**

9.55: **1** beach, beech, bleach, each, leach, leech, peach, speech, teach; **2** beseech, free speech, impeach, Long Beach, Palm Beach.
See also **10.42.175.**

9.55.1: **1** breach, breech, preach, reach, screech; **2** Longreach, outreach; **3** overreach.

9.56: **1** Eve, heave, peeve, Steve, thieve, weave, we've; **2** achieve, naive, perceive, Sanjiv; **3** Christmas Eve, Genevieve, interweave, New Year's Eve, Tel Aviv; **4** recitative.
See also **9.14.97, 9.31, 9.57, 10.42.176.**

9.56.1: **1** cleave, leave, sleeve; **2** believe, French leave, relieve, shore leave, sick leave; **3** disbelieve, interleave, make-believe.
See also **10.42.176.**

9.56.2: **1** breve, grieve; **2** aggrieve, Congreve, reprieve, retrieve; **3** semibreve.
See also **9.57.**

9.56.3: **2** conceive, deceive, receive; **3** misconceive.
See also **9.57.**

9.57: **1** grieved, peeved; **2** aggrieved, believed, bereaved, broad-leaved, perceived, received, relieved; **3** disbelieved, misconceived, preconceived, unperceived, unrelieved.
See also **9.56, 9.56.2, 9.56.3.**

9.58: **1** eaves, Greaves, Jeeves, Reeves, sheaves; **2** Hargreaves, Maldives, shirtsleeves, tea leaves.
See also **9.32, 9.32.1.**

9.59: **1** ease, geez, he's, jeez, she's, these; **2** Burmese, civvies, Dives, Ganges, Hermes, marquise, movies, skivvies, species, walkies; **3** Eloise, Héloïse, Portuguese, subspecies; **4** Erinyes, Florida Keys; **5** endangered species.
See also **9.25.6, 9.25.8, 9.60.**

9.59.1: **1** bise; **2** rabies, scabies; **3** Celebes, Maccabees, Sotheby's; **4** heebie-jeebies.

9.59.2: **2** Andes, goodies, Hades, readies, studies, undies; **3** Cyclades, dolmades, East Indies, Hebrides, Sporades, West Indies; **4** Archimedes, bona fides, Eumenides,

Euripides, Parmenides, Thucydides, women's studies.
See also **9.7.7, 9.7.16, 9.7.17.**

9.59.3: **1** lees, please, sleaze; **2** Belize, displease, goolies, monthlies, smellies, Thales, willies, woollies; **3** Achilles, Hercules; **4** winter woollies; **5** holy of holies; **6** Pillars of Hercules.
See also **9.14.38, 9.14.48, 9.14.96, 9.60, 10.42.186.**

9.59.4: **2** Belize, valise; **3** Congolese, journalese, legalese, Nepalese, Singhalese, Sinhalese; **4** isosceles, Los Angeles, officialese, Praxiteles, Senegalese; **5** Mephistopheles.

9.59.5: **3** Androcles, Heracles, Pericles, Sophocles; **5** Sword of Damocles.

9.59.6: **2** camise, chemise, kameez; **3** Siamese; **4** Vietnamese.

9.59.7: **1** sneeze; **2** bee's knees, Champneys, Chinese, Guyanese, monies, sunnies, unease; **3** Pekingese.

9.59.8: **3** Cantonese, Japanese, Javanese, Lebanese, manganese, Pyrenees, Sudanese, Taiwanese; **4** Diogenes, Dodecanese; **5** Aristophanes; **7** master of ceremonies.

9.59.9: **2** appease, herpes, stapes, trapeze; **3** hush puppies.

> *O, he flies through the air with the greatest of ease,*
> *This daring young man on the flying trapeze.*
> (George Leybourne)

See also **9.60.**

9.59.10: **1** breeze; **2** Ares, Aries, caries, Ceres, Furies, reprise, series, sundries, Tories; **3** dungarees, groceries, ivories, luxuries, toiletries, Valkyries; **4** computerese, éminence grise, miniseries, necessaries; **5** preliminaries; **8** literae humaniores.
See also **9.19.2, 9.19.28, 9.19.32, 9.19.54, 9.19.66.**

9.59.11: **1** freeze, frieze; **2** deep-freeze, Humphreys; **3** antifreeze.
See also **10.42.186.**

9.59.12: **1** seize; **2** faeces, falsies, high seas, menses, Pisces, tootsies, Xerxes; **3** matrices, overseas, Ulysses; **6** Coma Berenices.
See also **10.13.10.**

9.59.13: **1** tease, Tees; **2** bootees, DTs, eighties, empties, fifties, forties, Maltese, noughties, sixties, striptease, testes;

3 diabetes, Euphrates, litotes, pyrites, royalties; 4 difficulties, facilities, festivities, hostilities, humanities; 5 Ecclesiastes.
See also **9.22, 9.22.20, 9.22.23, 9.22.53, 9.22.77, 9.22.79, 10.42.186, 10.50.30.**

9.59.14: 3 expertise, ill at ease, Socrates; 4 Hippocrates, securities.

9.59.15: 2 Mounties, nineties, panties; 3 Cervantes, Home Counties, seventies; 4 Roaring Twenties.
See also **9.22.84.**

9.59.16: 1 cheese; 2 big cheese, cream cheese, headcheese, munchies, Swiss cheese; 3 cottage cheese; 4 cauliflower cheese.

9.59.17: 1 squeeze, wheeze; 2 Louise; 3 obsequies.

9.59.18: 2 disease; 4 Hodgkin's disease; 5 Alzheimer's disease; 6 Creutzfeldt-Jakob disease, motor neuron disease.

9.60: 1 eased, pleased; 2 appeased, diseased, displeased.
See also **9.59, 9.59.3, 9.59.9.**

9.61: 2 prestige; 4 noblesse oblige.

10.0: 1 bib, fib, glib, jib, nib, squib; 2 ad lib, damp squib, sahib; 3 women's lib.
See also **2.54.62, 10.1.**

10.0.1: 1 crib, drib, rib; 2 back rib, Carib.
See also **10.1, 10.42.13.**

10.1: 1 dibs, Gibbs, nibs, ribs; 2 his nibs.
See also **10.0, 10.0.1.**

10.2: 1 hid, id, yid; 2 aphid, DFID, RFID, wretched; 3 supposed.
See also **2.54.76, 19.52.4.**

10.2.1: 2 Druid, fluid; 5 correction fluid; 6 amniotic fluid.

10.2.2: 1 bid; 2 crabbed, forbid, ibid., morbid, outbid, rabid, rebid, turbid; 3 overbid, underbid.
See also **10.42.14.**

10.2.3: 1 did; 2 added, bearded, gilded, lidded, outdid, padded, studded, worded; 3 denuded, misguided, overdid, star-studded, unguided; 4 unheralded.
See also **1.3, 1.3.5, 7.10.5, 10.18, 20.2.**

10.2.4: 2 guarded; 3 discarded, retarded, unguarded; 4 disregarded.
See also **3.21.2, 3.21.4, 3.21.8.**

10.2.5: 2 braided, faded, graded, jaded; 3 degraded, downgraded, unaided, upgraded.
See also **5.21, 5.21.8, 5.21.9.**

10.2.6: 2 breaded, dreaded, leaded, wedded; 3 unleaded, unwedded.
See also **6.1, 6.1.12.**

10.2.7: 2 headed; 3 baldheaded, bareheaded, beheaded, bigheaded, blockheaded, boneheaded, bull-headed, clear-headed, cool-headed, hardheaded, hotheaded, lightheaded, pigheaded, thickheaded, tow-headed, wrong-headed; 4 empty-headed, featherheaded, levelheaded, muddleheaded.
See also **6.1.4.**

10.2.8: 2 beaded, needed; 3 unheeded, unneeded, unseeded; 4 unimpeded.
See also **9.29.4.**

10.2.9: 3 decided, four-sided, lopsided, one-sided, three-sided; 4 double-sided, even-sided, many-sided, undecided.
See also **11.14.20.**

10.2.10: 3 divided, provided; 4 undivided, well-provided.
See also **11.14.27.**

10.2.11: 2 sordid; 3 afforded, recorded; 4 prerecorded, unrecorded, unrewarded.
See also **14.19, 14.19.5, 14.19.6.**

10.2.12: 2 crowded; 3 enshrouded, unclouded, uncrowded; 4 overclouded, overcrowded.
See also **16.6.1, 16.6.2.**

10.2.13: 2 coded, goaded, loaded; 3 decoded, encoded, eroded, exploded, outmoded; 4 overloaded, unexploded.
See also **19.23, 19.23.1, 19.23.2, 19.23.5.**

10.2.14: 2 flooded; 3 blue-blooded, cold-blooded, full-blooded, hot-blooded, warm-blooded.
See also **20.2.**

10.2.15: 2 clouded, hooded, wooded; 3 concluded, deluded, excluded, included, precluded, secluded, spring-loaded.
See also **16.6.1.**

10.2.16: 2 undid, winded, wounded; 3 longwinded; 4 underfunded.
See also **10.32.1, 11.28.6, 16.11, 22.28.**

10.2.17: 2 banded, branded, candid, landed, stranded; 3 expanded, unbranded.
See also **1.22, 1.22.1, 1.22.3, 1.22.6.**

10.2.18: 3 backhanded, barehanded, cack-handed, ham-handed, high-handed, offhanded, red-handed, short-handed, two-handed; 4 empty-handed, evenhanded, heavy-handed, openhanded, underhanded.
See also **1.22.2.**

10.2.19: 2 blended, ended, mended, splendid; 3 amended, defended, offended; 4 double-ended, open-ended, recommended, undefended.
See also **6.30, 6.30.2, 6.30.3.**

10.2.20: 3 distended, extended, intended, pretended; 4 unattended, unintended; 5 overextended.
See also **6.30.9, 6.30.10.**

10.2.21: 2 minded; 3 broad-minded, closed-minded, fair-minded, free-minded, high-minded, light-minded, like-minded, mean-minded, right-minded, small-minded, tough-minded, weak-minded; 4 absent-minded, bloody-minded, feeble-minded, narrow-minded, open-minded, party-minded, simple-minded, single-minded.
See also **11.28.5.**

10.2.22: 2 founded, grounded, rounded; 3 astounded, confounded, dumbfounded, pounded, unbounded, unfounded, well-founded, well-grounded, well-rounded.
See also **16.11, 16.11.2, 16.11.4.**

10.2.23: 2 dogged, jagged, ragged, rugged; 3 bowlegged.
See also **1.6.3, 2.54.76, 13.7.1.**

10.2.24: 2 aged, frigid, masjid, rigid, turgid; 3 nonrigid.
See also **5.26.**

10.2.25: 1 kid, skid; 2 crooked, naked, orchid, schoolkid, whiz kid, wicked; 3 buck naked, stark-naked.
See also **2.54.76, 9.14.58, 10.4, 21.4.6.**

10.2.26: 1 lid, slid; 2 Euclid, eyelid, pallid, solid, squalid, stolid, valid; 3 invalid; 4 semisolid.
See also **9.14.58.**

10.2.27: 1 mid, 'mid; 2 amid, humid, timid, tumid; 3 MacDiarmid, Mohammed, Muhammad, pyramid.
See also **9.14.58.**

10.2.28: 2 Enid, honied, horned, learned; 3 arachnid, Geminid, hominid, Leonid; 4 Oceanid.
See also **7.20, 14.35.2.**

10.2.29: 2 cupid, cuspid, limpid, lipid, rapid, stupid, tepid, torpid, vapid; 3 bicuspid, insipid, intrepid.
See also **9.14.58.**

10.2.30: 1 grid, rid; 2 acrid, arid, Astrid, florid, forehead, hatred, horrid, hybrid, Ingrid, lurid, Madrid, Modred, Mordred, putrid, sacred, torrid, Wilfred; 3 acarid, starting grid, Winifred.

10.2.31: 1 Cid; 2 blessed, cussed, flaccid, lucid, rancid, viscid; 3 pellucid.
See also **6.47.1, 20.42.**

10.2.32: 2 acid, flaccid, placid; 3 antacid, bile acid; 4 folic acid, formic acid, lactic acid, nitric acid, prussic acid, uric acid; 5 amino acid, carbolic acid, lipoic acid, nucleic acid, phosphoric acid, sulphuric acid, sulphurous acid, tartaric acid; 6 hydrochloric acid, nicotinic acid; 7 ribonucleic acid.

10.2.33: 2 fetid, gifted, gutted, rutted, tufted; 3 bigoted, handcrafted, indebted, undoubted, uplifted; 4 silhouetted; 5 multifaceted.
See also **10.7.1.**

10.2.34: 2 matted, plaited, slatted; 4 caryatid, unformatted.
See also **1.41.5.**

10.2.35: 2 charted, parted; 3 departed, uncharted; 4 dear departed.
See also **3.49.5, 3.49.7.**

10.2.36: 3 cold-hearted, downhearted, faint-hearted, flint-hearted, goodhearted, half-hearted, hard-hearted, kind-hearted, lighthearted, lionhearted, soft-hearted, stouthearted, warm-hearted, wholehearted; 4 broken-hearted, heavy-hearted, openhearted, tenderhearted.

10.2.37: 2 bated, fated, weighted; 3 fixated, ill-fated, striated; 4 antiquated, designated, long-awaited, syncopated, unabated; 5 abbreviated, reincarnated.
See also **2.56.26, 5.47.49, 5.47.69.**

10.2.38: 5 affiliated, appreciated, appropriated, associated, depreciated, dissociated, emaciated, enunciated, humiliated, inebriated, infuriated, negotiated, repudiated; 6 misappropriated, unaffiliated, uninitiated, unsubstantiated.
See also **2.56.1, 2.56.2, 5.47.2, 5.47.3, 5.47.4, 5.47.5, 5.47.6.**

10.2.39: 4 graduated, situated; 5 accentuated, attenuated, habituated, infatuated, insinuated; 6 superannuated.
See also **2.56.4, 5.47, 5.47.8, 5.47.9.**

10.2.40: 2 dated; 3 backdated, mandated, outdated, postdated; 4 antedated, inundated, liquidated; 5 dilapidated, intimidated.
See also **5.47.11, 5.47.12.**

10.2.41: 2 gated; 3 negated; 4 abrogated, castigated, corrugated, delegated, elongated, expurgated, obligated, segregated; 5 unexpurgated, unmitigated, variegated.
See also **5.47.14, 5.47.15, 5.47.16.**

10.2.42: 3 located, truncated; 4 bifurcated, deprecated, dislocated, educated, obfuscated; 5 uneducated.
See also **5.47.19, 5.47.20, 5.47.21, 5.47.26, 5.47.28.**

10.2.43: 4 complicated, dedicated, desiccated, fabricated, implicated, indicated, medicated, vindicated; 5 authenticated, certificated, domesticated, elasticated, intoxicated, prefabricated, sophisticated, uncomplicated, well-lubricated; 6 undomesticated, unsophisticated.
See also **2.56.11, 5.47.24, 5.47.26.**

10.2.44: 3 deflated, dilated, gold-plated, inflated, translated; 4 castellated, crenellated, isolated, mentholated, pixelated, tessellated; 5 etiolated.
See also **2.56.14, 5.47.29, 5.47.30.**

10.2.45: 3 belated, elated, related; 4 correlated, mutilated, unrelated, ventilated; 5 annihilated, interrelated.
See also **2.56.14, 5.47.29, 5.47.30, 5.47.31.**

10.2.46: 4 calculated, circulated, formulated, granulated, insulated, modulated, populated, postulated, regulated, simulated, strangulated; 5 accumulated, articulated, coagulated, emasculated, inoculated, manipulated, unpopulated, unregulated; 6 overpopulated, underpopulated.
See also **2.56.19, 5.47.32, 5.47.33, 5.47.34, 5.47.36.**

10.2.47: 2 mated; 3 cremated, stalemated; 4 animated, automated, decimated, estimated, guesstimated, intimated, unconsummated; 5 amalgamated; 6 underestimated.
See also **2.56.24, 5.47.40, 5.47.41.**

10.2.48: 4 carbonated; 5 alienated, hydrogenated, opinionated, oxygenated; 6 self-opinionated.
See also **5.47.44.**

10.2.49: 4 chlorinated, fascinated, geminated, laminated, marinated, nominated, terminated, vaccinated; 5 contaminated, coordinated, decaffeinated, disseminated, eliminated,

illuminated; 6 uncontaminated, uncoordinated.
See also **2.56.30, 5.47.45, 5.47.47, 5.47.48.**

10.2.50: 4 constipated, dissipated; 5 anticipated, emancipated; 6 unanticipated.
See also **5.47.50.**

10.2.51: 2 grated; 3 aerated, hydrated, top-rated, unrated, X-rated; 4 calibrated, celebrated, consecrated, dehydrated, integrated, zero-rated; 5 unconsecrated.
See also **5.47.51, 5.47.58, 5.47.59.**

10.2.52: 3 serrated; 4 decorated, hand-operated, liberated, macerated, overrated, perforated, separated, ulcerated, underrated, venerated; 5 accelerated, adulterated, confederated, corroborated, disintegrated, evaporated, exaggerated, exasperated, exhilarated, exonerated, incarcerated, incorporated, obliterated, refrigerated, undecorated; 6 unadulterated, uncorroborated; 7 computer-generated.
See also **5.47.52, 5.47.53, 5.47.54, 5.47.56, 5.47.57.**

10.2.53: 3 castrated, frustrated; 4 concentrated, demonstrated, illustrated, orchestrated, saturated; 5 unsaturated; 7 monounsaturated, polyunsaturated.
See also **2.56.34, 5.47.52.**

10.2.54: 3 unstated; 4 devastated, overstated, understated; 5 orientated; 6 disorientated.
See also **5.47.63, 5.47.66.**

10.2.55: 4 agitated, imitated, irritated; 5 debilitated, decapitated, precipitated, premeditated; 6 incapacitated, unpremeditated.
See also **2.56, 5.47.64.**

10.2.56: 4 activated, aggravated, captivated, cultivated, elevated, enervated, motivated, renovated; 5 deactivated, uncultivated, unmotivated.
See also **5.47.67, 5.47.68.**

10.2.57: 3 asserted, concerted, converted, deserted, diverted, inverted, perverted; 4 disconcerted, extroverted, introverted.
See also **2.56.42, 7.28, 7.28.3, 7.28.5, 7.28.6.**

10.2.58: 2 fetid, heated; 3 completed, conceited, deleted, depleted, repeated, untreated; 4 overheated, undefeated.
See also **9.52, 9.52.3, 9.52.4, 9.52.5.**

10.2.59: 2 fitted, pitted; 3 bracketed, carpeted, closeted, committed, corseted, coveted, edited, limited, quick-witted,

sharp-witted, targeted; **4** accredited, inhabited, inhibited, uncommitted, unlimited; **5** uninhabited, uninhibited, unsolicited.
See also **2.54.76, 2.56.41, 10.56.2, 10.56.3, 10.56.4, 10.56.5, 10.56.6, 10.56.7, 10.56.11, 10.56.22, 10.56.26, 10.56.38.**

10.2.60: **3** spirited; **4** dispirited, high-spirited, inherited, interpreted; **5** public-spirited.
See also **10.56.29, 10.56.30, 10.56.31.**

10.2.61: **2** blighted; **3** benighted, delighted, highlighted, united; **4** disunited, uninvited, unrequited.
See also **11.36.6, 11.36.14.**

10.2.62: **2** sighted; **3** clear-sighted, excited, farsighted, longsighted, nearsighted, short-sighted, unsighted; **5** overexcited.
See also **11.36.19.**

10.2.63: **2** clotted, dotted, knotted, potted, spotted; **3** besotted.
See also **13.39, 13.39.2, 13.39.4, 13.39.5, 13.39.6.**

10.2.64: **2** sorted; **3** assorted, contorted, distorted, purported, reported; **4** ill-assorted, unsupported.
See also **9.14.59, 14.44.4, 14.44.5, 14.44.8.**

10.2.65: **2** bloated, floated, moated, noted, voted; **3** demoted, devoted, full-throated, outvoted.
See also **19.47, 19.47.5, 19.47.6, 19.47.7.**

10.2.66: **3** light-footed, quick-footed, sure-footed, wing-footed; **4** distributed, heavy-footed, nimble-footed.
See also **22.34.3.**

10.2.67: **2** booted, mooted, rooted, suited; **3** deep-rooted, unsuited, uprooted, well-suited.
See also **22.34, 22.34.1, 22.34.9, 22.34.11.**

10.2.68: **2** muted; **3** disputed, reputed; **4** executed, undisputed.
See also **22.34.4, 22.34.5, 22.34.6.**

10.2.69: **2** fluted; **3** diluted, polluted; **4** convoluted, undiluted, unpolluted.
See also **22.34.7, 22.34.8.**

10.2.70: **3** abstracted, attracted, contracted, diffracted, distracted, extracted, impacted, protracted.
See also **1.12.2, 1.12.4.**

10.2.71: **3** bisected, dejected, directed, rejected.
See also **6.12.2, 6.12.8, 6.12.9.**

10.2.72: **3** affected, defected, infected; **4** disaffected, disinfected, unaffected.
See also **6.12.1.**

10.2.73: **3** collected, complected, deflected, inflected, neglected; **4** elected, unelected.
See also **6.12.3, 6.12.4, 6.12.5.**

10.2.74: **3** connected; **4** disconnected, unconnected, well-connected; **5** interconnected.
See also **6.12.6.**

10.2.75: **3** expected, respected, suspected; **4** unexpected, unsuspected.
See also **6.12.7.**

10.2.76: **3** detected, protected; **4** undetected, unprotected, write-protected.
See also **6.12.**

10.2.77: **3** addicted, afflicted, conflicted, constricted, convicted, predicted, restricted; **4** self-inflicted, unrestricted.
See also **10.14, 10.14.1, 10.14.2, 10.14.3.**

10.2.78: **3** constructed, instructed, obstructed; **4** uninstructed, unobstructed; **5** unreconstructed.
See also **20.13.**

10.2.79: **2** quilted, stilted, tilted, wilted.
See also **10.22.**

10.2.80: **2** malted, vaulted; **3** assaulted, exalted, unsalted.
See also **14.31, 14.31.2.**

10.2.81: **2** hunted, minted, mounted, stunted, tinted, wanted, wonted; **3** discounted, unwanted, unwonted.
See also **10.38.2, 10.38.4, 13.25, 16.13, 16.13.1, 20.33, 20.33.1.**

10.2.82: **3** patented, segmented, talented, warranted; **4** untenanted, unwarranted.
See also **2.47.74, 2.47.88.**

10.2.83: **2** granted, slanted; **3** enchanted, implanted, unplanted; **4** disenchanted.
See also **3.38, 3.38.1.**

10.2.84: **2** painted, sainted, tainted; **3** acquainted, unpainted, untainted; **4** unacquainted.
See also **5.40.**

10.2.85: **2** dented, rented, scented, tented; **3** accented, contented, invented, presented, unscented; **4** discontented, oriented, unfrequented; **5** disoriented, misrepresented, unprecedented; **6** underrepresented.
See also **2.47.4, 2.47.82, 2.47.97, 6.34, 6.34.3, 6.34.4, 6.34.5, 6.34.6, 6.34.8.**

10.2.86: **3** augmented, demented, fermented, fragmented, lamented, tormented; **4** documented, ornamented, regimented, unfermented, unlamented.
See also **2.47.33, 2.47.37, 2.47.41, 2.47.43, 6.34.1.**

10.2.87: **2** daunted, haunted, vaunted; **3** undaunted.
See also **14.38.**

10.2.88: **2** jointed, pointed; **3** appointed, disjointed; **4** disappointed, double-jointed, self-appointed, well-appointed.
See also **18.12.**

10.2.89: **2** scripted, sculpted; **3** accepted, adapted, adopted, attempted, corrupted, disrupted, excepted, unprompted, unscripted; **4** interrupted, unadopted, uncorrupted; **5** uninterrupted.
See also **1.35, 6.27, 6.45.1, 10.49.1, 13.33.**

10.2.90: **2** blasted, frosted, plastid, toasted, wasted, worsted; **3** exhausted, signposted; **4** flabbergasted.
See also **3.47.3, 5.46, 13.36.2, 14.43, 19.46.**

10.2.91: **2** bested, rested, tested; **3** attested, barebreasted, congested, contested, detested, flat-chested, infested, interested, invested, untested; **4** disinterested, double-breasted, predigested, rat-infested, single-breasted, uncontested, uninterested.
See also **6.49, 6.49.1, 6.49.10, 6.49.12.**

10.2.92: **2** listed, twisted; **3** blacklisted, close-fisted, enlisted, forested, ham-fisted, tightfisted, unlisted; **4** iron-fisted, unassisted.
See also **10.53.6, 10.53.27.**

10.2.93: **2** busted, crusted, dusted, trusted; **3** adjusted, disgusted, encrusted; **4** maladjusted.
See also **20.44, 20.44.1, 20.44.2, 20.44.3, 20.44.6.**

10.2.94: **1** vid; **2** avid, bovid, cervid, David, fervid, gravid, livid, Ovid, vivid; **3** beloved, Camp David; **4** Star of David.
See also **2.54.76, 9.14.58.**

10.2.95: **1** quid, squid; **2** languid, liquid; **3** illiquid.
See also **9.14.58.**

10.3: **1** didst, midst, width; **2** amidst, bandwidth.

10.4: **1** kids, SIDS; **2** rapids.
See also **10.2.25.**

10.5: **1** with; **2** forthwith, herewith, therewith.
See also **10.61.**

10.6: **1** biff, if, iff, jiff, kif, miff, niff, quiff, skiff, sniff, whiff; **2** Cardiff, Joseph, Pecksniff, Plovdiv, skewwhiff.
See also **10.58.**

10.6.1: **1** cliff, glyph, spliff; **2** bailiff, caliph, Radcliffe, Sutcliffe, Wycliffe; **3** anaglyph, hieroglyph, petroglyph.

10.6.2: **1** griff, riff; **2** midriff, serif, sheriff, tariff; **3** hippogriff, sans serif.

10.6.3: **1** stiff, tif, tiff; **2** mastiff, plaintiff, pontiff.
See also **2.54.62.**

10.6.4: **2** kerchief, mischief; **3** coverchief, handkerchief, headkerchief, neckerchief.

10.7: **1** gift, miffed, sift, swift; **2** God's gift.

10.7.1: **1** lift; **2** airlift, chair lift, facelift, forklift, shoplift, ski lift, uplift.
See also **10.2.33, 10.42.165.**

10.7.2: **1** drift, rift, shrift, thrift; **2** adrift, short shrift, snowdrift, spendthrift, spindrift.

10.7.3: **1** shift; **2** downshift, makeshift, night shift, unshift.
See also **10.42.165.**

10.8: **1** big, dig, fig, gig, jig, MIG, pig, SIG, tig; **2** Danzig, Leipzig, Mr Big, rejig, shindig; **3** guinea pig, infra dig, Irish jig, whirligig; **4** thingamajig.
See also **10.10.**

10.8.1: **1** brig, frig, prig, rig, Rigg, sprig; **2** oil rig; **3** jury-rig.
See also **10.42.33.**

10.8.2: **1** swig, twig, Whig, wig; **2** bigwig, earwig, Hedwig; **3** periwig, WYSIWYG.

10.9: **2** bewigged, square-rigged; **3** jerry-rigged, jury-rigged.

10.10: **1** Biggs, Briggs, digs.
See also **10.8.**

10.11: **2** Carthage, roughage, seepage, sewage, slippage, stoppage, stowage, visage, voyage; **3** envisage, ferriage, foliage, lineage, verbiage.

10.11.1: **2** ambage, Babbage, cabbage, cribbage, cubage, garbage; **3** red cabbage; **4** Chinese cabbage.

10.11.2: **2** adage, bandage, bondage, cordage, poundage, windage, yardage; **3** appendage.
See also **10.34.**

10.11.3: 2 baggage, luggage, mortgage;
3 remortgage; 4 second mortgage.
See also **10.34**.

10.11.4: 2 blockage, breakage, corkage,
leakage, linkage, package, shrinkage,
wreckage; 3 repackage.
See also **10.34**, **10.42.38**.

10.11.5: 2 Coolidge, haulage, mileage,
Routledge, silage, spoilage, ullage;
3 assemblage, cartilage, privilege,
sacrilege, tutelage, vassalage.

10.11.6: 2 pillage, spillage, tillage,
village; 3 mucilage, pupillage; 4 global
village, Greenwich Village, loot and
pillage.

10.11.7: 2 college, knowledge;
3 acknowledge, foreknowledge, self-
knowledge; 4 sixth-form college.
See also **10.34**.

10.11.8: 1 midge; 2 damage, homage,
plumage, rummage, scrummage; 3 brain
damage.
See also **10.34**, **10.42.38**, **10.62.1**.

10.11.9: 2 image, scrimmage;
3 pilgrimage, self-image; 4 after-image,
graven image, mental image, mirror image.

10.11.10: 2 carnage, coinage, drainage,
Greenwich, manage, spinach, tonnage;
3 mismanage, stage-manage;
4 concubinage, micromanage.
See also **10.34**.

10.11.11: 3 appanage, matronage,
orphanage, parsonage, patronage,
personage, villeinage.

10.11.12: 1 fridge, ridge; 2 borage,
cartridge, clearage, forage, partridge,
peerage, porridge, steerage, storage,
suffrage; 3 arbitrage, cold storage,
saxifrage.

10.11.13: 2 garage, marriage;
3 disparage, mixed marriage; 4 arranged
marriage, broken marriage, intermarriage.
See also **10.42.38**.

10.11.14: 2 carriage; 3 gun-carriage,
miscarriage; 4 hackney carriage,
undercarriage.
　　Love and marriage, love and marriage,
　　Go together like a horse and carriage.
　　(Sammy Cahn)

10.11.15: 3 amperage, cellarage,
Coleridge, factorage, haemorrhage,
pasturage, pilferage, sewerage, tutorage.

10.11.16: 3 acreage, anchorage,
brokerage, vicarage.

10.11.17: 3 average, beverage,
Beveridge, coverage, leverage, overage;
5 above average, batting average, blanket
coverage.

10.11.18: 2 courage; 3 discourage, Dutch
courage, encourage; 4 Mother Courage.
See also **10.42.38**.

10.11.19: 1 bridge; 2 abridge, Ambridge,
Bainbridge, Cambridge, drawbridge,
footbridge, Knightsbridge, Oxbridge, toll
bridge, Tonbridge, Trent Bridge, umbrage,
weighbridge, Woodbridge; 3 contract
bridge.

10.11.20: 2 dosage, passage, sausage,
usage; 3 back passage, misusage; 4 bird of
passage, cocktail sausage, garlic sausage,
Northeast Passage, Northwest Passage;
5 Cumberland sausage.

10.11.21: 2 message, presage; 3 off-
message, on-message, text message.
See also **10.42.38**.

10.11.22: 2 cartage, dotage, driftage,
footage, freightage, meltage, metage,
outage, portage, shortage, voltage;
3 Armitage, curettage, heritage, hermitage,
pilotage, reportage.

10.11.23: 2 cottage, potage, wattage;
3 thatched cottage; 4 country cottage,
telecottage.

10.11.24: 2 frontage, vantage, vintage;
3 advantage, parentage, percentage;
4 disadvantage.
See also **10.34**.

10.11.25: 2 hostage, postage, vestige,
wastage.
See also **10.62.1**.

10.11.26: 2 cleavage, lovage, ravage,
salvage, savage; 4 noble savage.
See also **10.62.1**.

10.11.27: 2 language, sandwich; 3 bad
language, dead language, first language;
4 body language, interlanguage,
metalanguage.

10.12: 1 chick, hick; 4 apparatchik,
Hebraic.

10.12.1: 2 laic; 3 archaic, Hebraic, Judaic,
mosaic, prosaic, spondaic, trochaic,
voltaic; 4 algebraic, formulaic, Pharisaic;
5 Ural-Altaic.

10.12.2: 2 stoic, zoic; 3 echoic, heroic;
4 Cenozoic, Mesozoic, mock-heroic,
protozoic, unheroic; 5 Palaeozoic,
Phanerozoic, Proterozoic.

10.12.3: **1** Bic; **2** cubic, pubic, rhombic; **3** acerbic, aerobic, alembic, amoebic, Arabic, cherubic, iambic, microbic; **4** anaerobic, gum arabic.

10.12.4: **3** syllabic; **4** disyllabic; **5** monosyllabic, polysyllabic.

10.12.5: **2** phobic; **4** Anglophobic, claustrophobic, Francophobic, homophobic, hydrophobic, xenophobic, zoophobic; **5** agoraphobic.

10.12.6: **1** dick; **2** Benedick, medic, medick, Nordic, syndic, Vedic; **3** acidic, clever dick, druidic, dyadic, heraldic, Icelandic, monadic, nomadic, sporadic; **4** orthopaedic, paramedic; **5** encyclopedic.

10.12.7: **3** melodic, spasmodic, threnodic; **4** episodic, periodic; **5** antispasmodic.

10.12.8: **2** fanfic, sapphic, Sufic, traffic; **3** malefic, prolific, scientific, seraphic; **4** beatific, catastrophic, geostrophic, isotrophic, unscientific.
See also **9.14.66**, **10.42.49**.

10.12.9: **2** graphic; **4** barographic, calligraphic, cryptographic, demographic, ethnographic, homographic, orthographic, photographic, pictographic, pornographic, seismographic, telegraphic, thermographic, topographic, typographic; **5** anemographic, choreographic, lexicographic, oceanographic.
See also **10.13.1**.

10.12.10: **3** horrific, terrific; **4** calorific, frigorific, honorific, soporific.
See also **9.14.66**.

10.12.11: **3** Pacific, specific; **4** nonspecific, unspecific.

10.12.12: **3** trimorphic; **4** ectomorphic, endomorphic, metamorphic, theomorphic, zoomorphic; **5** anthropomorphic, theriomorphic.

10.12.13: **2** georgic; **3** lethargic, nostalgic, strategic; **4** paraplegic, quadriplegic.
See also **9.14.66**.

10.12.14: **2** logic, magic, tragic; **3** allergic, black magic, liturgic, pelagic, white magic; **4** demagogic, dramaturgic, omophagic, pedagogic, scatologic, tautologic, thaumaturgic; **5** bathypelagic, bibliophagic.

Every little thing she does is magic;
Everything she do just turns me on.
Even though my life before was tragic

Now I know my love for her goes on.
(The Police)
See also **9.14.66**.

10.12.15: **1** kick; **2** downkick, drop kick, free kick, frog kick, goal kick, place kick, psychic, sidekick, upkick; **3** anarchic, autarchic, corner kick, flutter kick, hierarchic, monarchic, scissors kick; **4** metapsychic, oligarchic, penalty kick.
See also **10.42.49**.

10.12.16: **1** flic, flick, lick, slick; **2** bootlick, cowlick, garlic, niblick, public, relic, saltlick; **3** angelic, Catholic, hydraulic, Joe Public, republic; **4** psychedelic, Roman Catholic.
See also **10.14.2**, **10.42.49**.

10.12.17: **2** Gaelic, Gallic, phallic; **3** cephalic, italic, metallic, smart aleck, vocalic; **4** bimetallic.

10.12.18: **3** acrylic, Cyrillic, dactylic, idyllic, sibyllic; **4** imbecilic, zoophilic.

10.12.19: **2** colic, frolic, rollick; **3** Aeolic, bucolic, carbolic, diabolic, shambolic, symbolic; **4** anabolic, Anatolic, apostolic, catabolic, hyperbolic, melancholic, metabolic, parabolic, vitriolic.

10.12.20: **4** alcoholic, chocaholic, chocoholic, shopaholic, workaholic; **5** nonalcoholic.

10.12.21: **1** click; **2** cyclic, left-click, right-click; **3** double-click.

10.12.22: **1** mick; **2** filmic, gnomic, rhythmic; **3** anaemic, bulimic, ophthalmic, phonemic, systemic.
See also **9.14.66**.

10.12.23: **3** adamic, balsamic, ceramic, dynamic; **4** misogamic, panoramic; **5** aerodynamic, hydrodynamic, thermodynamic.
See also **10.13.4**.

10.12.24: **3** dysphemic, endemic, pandemic, polemic, systemic, totemic; **4** academic, epidemic.
See also **10.13.3**.

10.12.25: **4** endothermic, exothermic, hypodermic; **5** poikilothermic.

10.12.26: **2** gimmick, mimic; **3** enzymic; **4** homonymic, matronymic, patronymic.

10.12.27: **2** comic; **3** atomic, genomic; **4** palindromic, subatomic, tragicomic.

10.12.28: **4** agronomic, autonomic, bionomic, economic, ergonomic, gastronomic, metronomic, taxonomic;

5 uneconomic; **6** macroeconomic, microeconomic; **7** socioeconomic.

10.12.29: **2** cosmic, seismic; **3** miasmic, orgasmic, phantasmic, strabismic; **4** cataclysmic, cytoplasmic, ectoplasmic, endoplasmic, microcosmic, protoplasmic.

10.12.30: **1** nick, snick; **2** beatnik, clinic, cynic, ethnic, Munich, Old Nick, picnic, runic, splanchnic, sputnik, tunic; **3** arsenic, Dominic, Hellenic, Metternich; **4** multiethnic, polytechnic, schizophrenic.

10.12.31: **2** manic, panic; **3** botanic, cyanic, galvanic, Germanic, Hispanic, mechanic, organic, satanic, titanic, tympanic, volcanic; **4** Alemannic, inorganic, messianic, oceanic, puritanic; **5** sub-oceanic.
See also **10.13.6**.

10.12.32: **3** transgenic; **4** cryogenic, ethnogenic, ontogenic, pathogenic, photogenic, psychogenic, pyrogenic, telegenic; **5** anthropogenic, carcinogenic; **6** hallucinogenic, hypoallergenic.

10.12.33: **2** scenic; **3** Hellenic, hygienic, irenic; **4** unhygienic.

10.12.34: **2** chthonic; **3** bionic, carbonic, colonic, cyclonic, iconic, Ionic, laconic, sardonic, Slavonic; **4** avionic, embryonic, geoponic, histrionic, hydroponic.

10.12.35: **2** phonic; **3** aphonic, dysphonic, euphonic, symphonic; **4** homophonic, monophonic, polyphonic, quadraphonic, quadrophonic, telephonic; **5** radiophonic, stereophonic.

10.12.36: **2** chronic; **3** demonic, diachronic, harmonic, ironic, mnemonic, moronic, synchronic; **4** electronic, enharmonic, hegemonic, pandemonic, philharmonic; **5** oxymoronic.
See also **10.13.7**.

10.12.37: **2** sonic; **3** Masonic, subsonic; **4** hypersonic, supersonic, ultrasonic.

10.12.38: **2** tonic; **3** diatonic, planktonic, platonic, plutonic, protonic, subtonic, tectonic, Teutonic; **4** catatonic, gin and tonic, heptatonic, hexatonic, isotonic, supertonic; **5** architectonic, Neo-Platonic, vodka and tonic.

10.12.39: **1** pic, pick; **2** aspic, epic, hand-pick, icepick, nitpick, toothpick, unpick, Yupik; **3** biopic, cherry-pick, Olympic, philippic, priapic.
See also **10.42.49**.

10.12.40: **2** topic, tropic; **3** ectopic, myopic; **4** misanthropic, philanthropic.
See also **10.13.8**.

10.12.41: **4** microscopic, spectroscopic, telescopic; **5** kaleidoscopic, stereoscopic, submicroscopic.

10.12.42: **1** crick, rick; **2** Baldric, Cedric, Eric, hayrick, Heinrich, lyric, tugrik, Zurich; **3** Alaric, Broderick, chivalric, sulphuric; **4** panegyric.

10.12.43: **2** Garrick; **3** barbaric; **4** hyperbaric, isobaric, thermobaric.

10.12.44: **3** choleric, Frederick, limerick, maverick, rhetoric, turmeric; **4** climacteric.

10.12.45: **2** cleric, Derek, derrick, ferric, Herrick, Merrick, spheric; **3** enteric, generic, Homeric, hysteric, mesmeric, numeric; **4** atmospheric, esoteric, exoteric, mesenteric, stratospheric, tropospheric; **5** alphanumeric.

10.12.46: **2** Doric, Warwick; **3** euphoric, historic, phosphoric; **4** metaphoric, meteoric, prehistoric, semaphoric; **5** aleatoric.

10.12.47: **1** brick; **2** cambric, fabric, firebrick, gold brick, Kubrick, redbrick, rubric.

10.12.48: **1** prick; **2** cupric, pinprick; **3** bishopric; **4** archbishopric.

10.12.49: **1** trick; **2** citric, con trick, Dietrich, gastric, hat trick, old trick; **3** dioptric, dirty trick, electric, magic trick, obstetric; **5** hydroelectric.

10.12.50: **2** Patrick; **3** iatric; **4** geriatric, paediatric, psychiatric.

10.12.51: **2** metric; **3** symmetric; **4** asymmetric, bathometric, biometric, diametric, geometric, hydrometric, isometric, psychometric; **5** anthropometric.

10.12.52: **3** concentric, eccentric; **4** egocentric, ethnocentric, Eurocentric, geocentric; **5** anthropocentric, heliocentric.
See also **9.14.69**.

10.12.53: **1** sic, sick; **2** airsick, basic, carsick, classic, fossick, heartsick, homesick, lovesick, seasick, toxic; **3** dyslexic, extrinsic, forensic, intrinsic, Jurassic, thoracic, Triassic; **4** anorexic.
See also **9.14.66, 10.13.11**.

10.12.54: **1** schtick, tic, tick; **2** Baltic, Celtic, deictic, optic, rhotic; **3** authentic, cathartic; **4** inauthentic, therapeutic.
See also **10.13.12, 10.42.49**.

10.12.55: **2** attic, batik, phatic, static; **3** aquatic, ecstatic, emphatic, fanatic, hepatic, lymphatic, prelatic, sciatic; **4** acrobatic, Adriatic, aerobatic, anabatic, Asiatic, Eleatic, hydrostatic, pancreatic, subaquatic; **5** adiabatic, homeostatic.

10.12.56: **3** asthmatic, climatic, pneumatic, rheumatic, schematic, somatic, thematic, traumatic; **4** cinematic, zygomatic; **5** axiomatic, idiomatic, psychosomatic.

10.12.57: **4** diplomatic, emblematic, problematic; **5** undiplomatic, unproblematic.

10.12.58: **3** chromatic, dramatic; **4** achromatic, aromatic, programmatic, undramatic; **5** diagrammatic, epigrammatic, melodramatic, monochromatic, polychromatic.

10.12.59: **4** automatic, symptomatic, systematic; **5** asymptomatic, unsystematic; **6** semiautomatic.

10.12.60: **3** dogmatic, phlegmatic, pragmatic; **4** enigmatic; **5** paradigmatic.

10.12.61: **3** prismatic, schismatic; **4** charismatic, numismatic.

10.12.62: **3** erratic, Socratic; **4** autocratic, bureaucratic, democratic, hierocratic, Hippocratic, operatic, plutocratic, technocratic, theocratic; **5** aristocratic, meritocratic, undemocratic; **6** idiosyncratic.

10.12.63: **3** heretic, lunatic, politic; **4** arithmetic, impolitic; **5** body politic.

10.12.64: **3** ascetic, athletic, balletic, diabetic, dietetic, eidetic, poetic, prophetic; **4** copacetic, diuretic, energetic, homiletic; **5** apologetic, diaphoretic, peripatetic; **6** unapologetic.

10.12.65: **3** cosmetic, emetic, hermetic, mimetic; **4** arithmetic; **5** antiemetic.

10.12.66: **3** frenetic, genetic, kinetic, magnetic, phonetic, splenetic; **4** cybernetic; **5** psychokinetic, telekinetic; **6** electromagnetic.

10.12.67: **3** aesthetic, bathetic, pathetic, prosthetic, synthetic; **4** anaesthetic, apathetic, empathetic, nomothetic, sympathetic; **5** antipathetic, biosynthetic, photosynthetic, unsympathetic. *See also* **10.13.15**.

10.12.68: **3** bronchitic, Semitic; **4** analytic, catalytic, parasitic; **5** anti-Semitic.

10.12.69: **3** enclitic; **4** paralytic; **5** electrolytic; **6** psychoanalytic.

10.12.70: **2** critic; **3** arthritic, dendritic, diacritic, neritic; **4** sybaritic.

10.12.71: **3** biotic, chaotic, demotic, despotic, erotic, exotic, hypnotic, narcotic, neurotic, orthotic, osmotic, psychotic, quixotic, robotic, sclerotic; **4** abiotic, amniotic, idiotic, patriotic, prebiotic, probiotic, symbiotic; **5** antibiotic, antipsychotic, homoerotic, macrobiotic, monozygotic, unpatriotic. *See also* **9.14.69**, **10.13.17**.

10.12.72: **2** Arctic, hectic; **3** Antarctic, dialectic, eclectic, subarctic; **4** apoplectic.

10.12.73: **2** lactic, tactic; **3** climactic, didactic, galactic, syntactic; **4** ataractic, chiropractic, prophylactic; **5** autodidactic, extragalactic, intergalactic. *See also* **10.13.12**.

10.12.74: **2** antic, frantic, mantic; **3** Atlantic, gigantic, pedantic, romantic, semantic; **4** hierophantic, mid-Atlantic, necromantic, sycophantic, transatlantic. *See also* **9.14.69**.

10.12.75: **2** peptic, sceptic, septic; **3** aseptic, dyspeptic, eupeptic, proleptic; **4** analeptic, antiseptic, cataleptic, epileptic, Eurosceptic.

10.12.76: **2** cryptic, diptych, styptic, triptych; **3** ecliptic, elliptic; **5** apocalyptic.

10.12.77: **1** stick; **2** broomstick, caustic, chopstick, dipstick, drumstick, joss stick, joystick, lipstick, matchstick, nightstick, nonstick, rustic, slapstick, unstick, yardstick; **3** acoustic, candlestick, domestic, majestic, pogo stick; **4** carrot-and-stick. *See also* **10.13.18**.

10.12.78: **2** drastic, mastic, spastic; **3** bombastic, chiastic, dynastic, fantastic, gymnastic, monastic, sarcastic, stochastic; **4** onomastic, periphrastic, pleonastic; **5** ecclesiastic, encomiastic, enthusiastic; **6** unenthusiastic; **7** overenthusiastic.

10.12.79: **2** plastic; **3** elastic, scholastic; **4** bioplastic, inelastic, thermoplastic; **5** iconoclastic.

10.12.80: **2** cystic; **3** artistic, deistic, linguistic, logistic, sadistic, sophistic, statistic, theistic; **4** altruistic, anarchistic, atavistic, atheistic, casuistic, egoistic,

egotistic, fetishistic, jingoistic, narcissistic, solipsistic; **5** paralinguistic.
See also **10.13.19**.

10.12.81: **3** holistic, simplistic, stylistic; **5** pugilistic.

10.12.82: **3** ballistic; **4** fatalistic, formalistic, journalistic, Kabbalistic, legalistic, moralistic, realistic, socialistic; **5** animalistic, cannibalistic, idealistic, monopolistic, nationalistic, naturalistic, probabilistic, rationalistic, ritualistic, spiritualistic, surrealistic, unrealistic; **6** materialistic; **7** individualistic.

10.12.83: **2** mystic; **4** animistic, dysphemistic, euphemistic, optimistic, pessimistic, totemistic; **6** overoptimistic.

10.12.84: **4** agonistic, chauvinistic, communistic, hedonistic, Hellenistic, humanistic, mechanistic, modernistic, tokenistic; **5** antagonistic, impressionistic, opportunistic.

10.12.85: **3** heuristic, hubristic, juristic; **4** futuristic, naturistic; **5** characteristic, militaristic; **6** uncharacteristic.

10.12.86: **2** gnostic; **3** acrostic, agnostic, diagnostic, prognostic.

10.12.87: **1** thick; **2** ethic, gothic; **3** empathic; **4** telepathic; **5** homeopathic, homoeopathic.

10.12.88: **2** lithic, mythic; **4** Chalcolithic, megalithic, Mesolithic, monolithic, Neolithic; **5** Palaeolithic.

10.12.89: **2** civic, pelvic, Slavic; **3** Bolshevik, Reykjavik.

10.12.90: **1** quick, wick, Wik; **2** Bewick; **3** bailiwick, candlewick.

10.12.91: **2** music, phasic, physic; **3** amnesic, aphasic, church music, pop music, sheet music, soul music; **4** analgesic, chamber music, country music, geodesic, gospel music, Sound of Music; **5** classical music.
See also **10.13.20**.

10.13: **1** Hicks; **2** Bendix, cervix, civics, ethics; **3** aerobics, appendix, Asterix, forensics, heroics; **4** bioethics, orthopaedics.

10.13.1: **1** fix; **2** affix, graphics, prefix, suffix, transfix; **3** crucifix, specifics; **4** demographics, hieroglyphics.
See also **10.12.9, 10.15**.

10.13.2: **2** Alix, calyx, Felix, helix, Horlicks, prolix; **3** hydraulics, italics, Obelix, spondulicks.

10.13.3: **1** mix; **2** remix; **3** ceramics, genomics, intermix, phonemics, pick 'n' mix, polemics.
See also **10.12.24, 10.15**.

10.13.4: **3** dynamics; **5** aerodynamics, hydrodynamics, thermodynamics.
See also **10.12.23**.

10.13.5: **3** genomics; **4** agronomics, economics, ergonomics; **5** home economics; **6** geoeconomics, macroeconomics, microeconomics.

10.13.6: **1** nix; **2** phoenix, Unix; **3** eugenics, mechanics; **4** callisthenics, cryogenics, pyrotechnics.
See also **10.12.31**.

10.13.7: **2** onyx, phonics; **3** bionics, harmonics; **4** avionics, electronics, histrionics, hydroponics; **5** animatronics; **6** microelectronics.
See also **10.12.36**.

10.13.8: **1** pix, pyx; **2** tropics; **3** subtropics; **5** Special Olympics.
See also **10.12.40**.

10.13.9: **2** Hendrix, oryx; **3** hysterics; **4** atmospherics; **5** archaeopteryx.

10.13.10: **2** matrix; **3** bag of tricks, Beatrix, cicatrix, dot matrix, electrics, obstetrics, theatrics; **4** biometrics, dominatrix, geriatrics, isometrics, paediatrics.
See also **9.59.12**.

10.13.11: **1** six; **2** basics, classics, coccyx, Essex, Wessex; **3** MI6.
See also **10.12.53**.

10.13.12: **2** antics, optics, tactics; **3** hermeneutics, politics, semantics; **4** aeronautics, fibre optics, orthodontics, strong-arm tactics; **5** geopolitics, party politics.
See also **10.12.54, 10.12.73**.

10.13.13: **4** acrobatics, aerobatics, hydrostatics.

10.13.14: **3** dramatics, pragmatics; **4** informatics, mathematics, numismatics, telematics; **6** amateur dramatics.

10.13.15: **3** aesthetics, athletics, cosmetics, dietetics, synthetics.
See also **10.12.67**.

10.13.16: **3** genetics, kinetics, phonetics; **4** cybernetics.

10.13.17: **3** narcotics, orthotics, robotics; **4** semiotics; **5** macrobiotics.
See also **10.12.71**.

10.13.18: **1** sticks, Styx; **3** acoustics, diagnostics, fiddlesticks, gymnastics. *See also* **10.12.77**.

10.13.19: **3** ballistics, heuristics, linguistics, logistics, statistics, stylistics; **5** psycholinguistics, vital statistics. *See also* **10.12.80**.

10.13.20: **2** physics; **4** astrophysics, biophysics, geophysics, metaphysics, quantum physics. *See also* **10.12.91**.

10.14: **1** Pict; **2** convict, depict, evict, handpicked, subject. *See also* **10.2.77**.

10.14.1: **2** addict, Benedict, edict, perfect, predict, verdict; **3** contradict, drug addict, imperfect, interdict, pluperfect, word-perfect. *See also* **10.2.77**.

10.14.2: **1** licked; **2** afflict, conflict, inflict; **3** derelict. *See also* **10.2.77**, **10.12.16**.

10.14.3: **1** strict; **2** constrict, district, restrict; **3** Lake District, Peak District. *See also* **10.2.77**.

10.15: **1** fixed, mixed, twixt; **2** betwixt, transfixed. *See also* **10.13.1**, **10.13.3**.

10.16: **2** clavicle.

10.17: **1** chill, dill, gill, ill, nil, pill, sill, spill; **2** Brazil, Churchill, doorsill, windchill; **3** codicil, daffodil, overspill, windowsill.

Tis hard to say, if greater want of skill,
Appear in writing or in judging ill.
(Alexander Pope)
See also **10.18**, **10.42.73**.

10.17.1: **1** bill; **2** handbill, hornbill, Old Bill, playbill, sibyl, spoonbill, waybill; **3** double bill, Portland Bill. *See also* **10.42.73**.

10.17.2: **1** fill; **2** backfill, fulfil, infill, landfill, refill; **3** chlorophyll, overfill. *See also* **10.18**, **10.42.73**.

10.17.3: **1** hill, Jill, kill, skill; **2** anthill, deskill, downhill, dunghill, foothill, Herne Hill, Jekyll, molehill, Nob Hill, uphill, vigil, Virgil; **3** Muswell Hill, Notting Hill, overkill, Shooters Hill; **4** Capitol Hill.

Do you look for me at times,
Wistful ones?
Do you look for me at times
Strained and still?
Do you look for me at times,

When the hour for walking chimes,
On that grassy path that climbs
Up the hill?
(Thomas Hardy)

10.17.4: **1** mil, mill; **2** DeMille, sawmill, Tamil, treadmill, windmill; **4** run-of-the-mill.

10.17.5: **1** brill, drill, frill, grill, grille, krill, prill, rill, shrill, thrill, trill; **2** chargrill, Cheryl, mandrill, mixed grill, quadrille; **3** espadrille. *See also* **10.18**, **10.42.73**.

10.17.6: **1** til, till; **2** dactyl, lentil, until; **4** pterodactyl. *See also* **10.18**.

10.17.7: **1** still; **2** distil, instil, pistil, standstill, stock-still.

10.17.8: **2** anvil, cavil, devil, Grenville, Melville, Nashville, Neville, Sackville, Seville, yawnsville; **3** Baskerville, Brazzaville, Libreville, Louisville, Somerville, vaudeville.

10.17.9: **1** quill, swill, twill, will; **2** free will, goodwill, ill will, iron will, jonquil, pigswill, self-will, tranquil. *See also* **10.42.73**.

10.18: **1** billed, build, chilled, filled, gild, grilled, guild, killed, skilled, thrilled, tilled; **2** fulfilled, newbuild, rebuild, unfilled, unskilled, untilled, weak-willed, well-drilled, wergild; **3** custom-build, iron-willed, semiskilled, unfulfilled. *See also* **10.2.3**, **10.17**, **10.17.2**, **10.17.5**, **10.17.6**.

10.19: **1** bilk, ilk, milk, silk; **2** foremilk; **3** buttermilk.

10.20: **1** film; **2** clingfilm; **3** microfilm, telefilm. *See also* **10.42.84**.

10.21: **1** kiln, Milne; **2** limekiln.

10.22: **1** gilt, guilt, hilt, jilt, kilt, lilt, milt, quilt, silt, spilt, stilt, tilt, wilt. *See also* **10.2.79**.

10.22.1: **1** built; **2** in-built, rebuilt, well-built; **3** custom-built, jerry-built, purpose-built.

10.23: **1** filch, zilch.

10.24: **1** filth, tilth.

10.25: **1** Mills, Wills; **2** Catskills, foothills, no-frills; **3** Malvern Hills, Mendip Hills, Shropshire Hills; **4** Cheviot Hills.

10.26: **1** dim, gym, him, hymn, Jim, Kim, limb, limn, skim, slim, spim, swim, vim, whim; **2** maxim, passim, poem, Sikkim, victim; **3** cherubim, multigym, seraphim, sink-or-swim, verbatim.
See also **2.54.81, 10.42.84.**

10.26.1: **2** denim, minim; **3** acronym, allonym, antonym, eponym, homonym, hypernym, hyponym, metonym, paronym, pseudonym, synonym, tautonym, toponym.

10.26.2: **1** brim, crim, prim, rim, scrim, strim, trim; **2** Antrim, Purim; **3** interim; **4** Pacific Rim.
See also **10.27.**

10.26.3: **1** grim, Grimm; **2** megrim, pilgrim.

10.27: **1** trimmed; **2** clean-limbed, untrimmed; **3** semi-skimmed.
See also **10.26.2.**

10.28: **1** lymph, nymph.

10.29: **1** blimp, chimp, crimp, gimp, imp, limp, pimp, primp, scrimp, shrimp, skimp, wimp; **3** Colonel Blimp.

10.30: **1** glimpse.

10.31: **1** in, inn, shin, yin; **2** Bowen, Cohen, lie-in, Owen, Pinyin, resin, Swithin, tie-in, weigh-in, within; **3** casein, heroin, heroine, lady-in-waiting, lying-in, muezzin.

10.31.1: **2** ruin; **3** Bedouin, genuine, Menuhin, mother's ruin.
See also **10.32, 10.41.**

10.31.2: **1** bin; **2** bobbin, cabin, Corbin, dubbin, dumpbin, dustbin, Harbin, Reuben, robin; **3** wheelie bin; **4** haemoglobin, Portakabin; **5** Batman and Robin.

10.31.3: **1** din; **2** add-in, fade-in, hemmed-in, lead-in, lived-in, Odin, stand-in, trade-in; **3** almandine, Borodin, Dunedin, paladin, Saladin.

10.31.4: **1** fin, Finn; **2** boffin, coffin, dauphin, dolphin, elfin, griffin, muffin, puffin, tiffin; **3** endorphin, Mickey Finn, paraffin; **4** ragamuffin.

10.31.5: **2** bargain, begin, Beguine, login, noggin; **3** Onegin.
See also **10.42.100.**

10.31.6: **1** djinn, gin, jinn; **2** engine, gaijin, margin, pidgin, sloe gin, virgin; **3** imagine, origin, search engine; **4** vestal virgin.
See also **10.32.**

10.31.7: **1** kin; **2** akin, bodkin, break-in, bumpkin, catkin, check-in, Culkin, Deakin, firkin, Hodgkin, Larkin, look-in, munchkin, napkin, parkin, pumpkin, Pushkin, Rankin, walk-in; **3** next of kin; **4** country bumpkin.

10.31.8: **2** Burkin, gherkin, jerkin, merkin, work-in.

10.31.9: **2** chicken, pickin; **3** larrikin, manikin, mannequin, ramekin.

10.31.10: **1** skin; **2** bearskin, buckskin, buskin, calfskin, cleanskin, deerskin, doeskin, foreskin, goatskin, lambskin, moleskin, oilskin, pigskin, redskin, Ruskin, sealskin, sheepskin, snakeskin, wineskin; **4** banana skin.

10.31.11: **1** Flynn, Glynn; **2** all-in, Berlin, Boleyn, Brooklyn, Butlin, Caitlin, Catlin, Colin, Devlin, Dublin, Evelyn, Franklin, goblin, marlin, maudlin, Merlin, muslin, myelin, Palin, Stalin, Tallinn, violin; **3** hobgoblin, Llewellyn, pangolin, tarpaulin.

10.31.12: **3** chamberlain, crinoline, formalin, Jacqueline, javelin, Jocelyn, kaolin, lanolin, madeleine, mandolin, mescaline, pangolin, porcelain, zeppelin; **4** adrenalin.

10.31.13: **2** fill-in, grilling; **3** aniline, Marilyn; **4** penicillin.

10.31.14: **2** gremlin, Hamlin, Hamlyn, Kremlin; **3** globulin, insulin, masculine; **4** tuberculin; **5** gamma globulin; **6** immunoglobulin.

10.31.15: **2** chaplain, Chaplin, compline, Joplin, poplin; **3** discipline; **4** indiscipline, self-discipline.

10.31.16: **2** admin, Brahmin, carmine, cumin, ermine, famine, jasmine, lumen, thiamin, vermin, women, Yasmin; **3** albumen, albumin, Benjamin, bitumen, determine, examine, illumine, ketamine, specimen, vitamin; **4** cross-examine; **5** multivitamin.
See also **10.32, 10.42.100.**

10.31.17: **2** burn-in, Cronin, Lenin, lignin, linen, phone-in, rennin, run-in, tannin; **3** Bakunin, bedlinen, feminine, melanin; **4** melatonin, serotonin.

10.31.18: **1** pin; **2** clothespin, Crippen, Crispin, hairpin, hatpin, kingpin, linchpin, lupin, lupine, lynchpin, pippin, rapine,

stickpin, tenpin, tiepin, Turpin; **3** Dick Turpin, terrapin, underpin.
See also **10.42.100.**

10.31.19: 1 spin; **2** backspin, leg spin, off spin, side spin, tailspin, topspin.
See also **10.42.100.**

10.31.20: 1 grin; **2** Aldrin, aspirin, Catharine, Catherine, chagrin, citrine, doctrine, Erin, fibrin, florin, foreign, herein, Katherine, sarin, Sherrin, sovereign, Taryn, therein, urine, wherein; **3** Aneurin, Bukharin, Gagarin, peregrine; **4** epinephrine.
See also **10.32.**

10.31.21: 2 Turin; **3** glycerin, mandarin, Mazarin, saccharin, saccharine, warfarin; **5** nitroglycerine.

10.31.22: 1 sin; **2** niacin, pepsin, ricin, Yeltsin; **3** assassin, moccasin, Wisconsin; **4** Solzhenitsyn, streptomycin.
See also **2.54.48.**

10.31.23: 2 tocsin, toxin; **3** dioxin; **4** antitoxin, mycotoxin.

10.31.24: 1 tin; **2** biotin, built-in, captain, chitin, cretin, cut-in, Justin, marten, martin, pectin, put-in; **3** bulletin, gelatin, keratin, St Martin; **4** Benedictine, Byzantine.

10.31.25: 2 Latin, satin, statin; **3** dog Latin.

10.31.26: 2 cutin, Putin; **3** Rasputin; **4** highfalutin.

10.31.27: 2 fountain, mountain, plantain, Quentin; **4** Table Mountain.
See also **2.51.**

10.31.28: 2 Austen, Austin, Dustin, Iestyn; **3** Augustine, clandestine, intestine, predestine.

10.31.29: 1 thin; **2** Swithin; **3** paper-thin, wafer-thin.
See also **10.32, 10.42.100.**

10.31.30: 1 chin; **2** Cochin, teach-in, urchin; **3** double chin.

10.31.31: 2 Alvin, Bevin, Calvin, cave-in, drive-in, Gavin, Kelvin, live-in, Marvin, Melvin; **4** riboflavin.

10.31.32: 1 quin, Quinn, twin, win, Wynn; **2** Baldwin, Chatwin, Chegwin, Darwin, Edwin, Gershwin, Godwin, Goldwin, Goldwyn, penguin, sanguine, sequin, Tarquin; **3** harlequin.
See also **10.32, 10.41, 10.42.100.**

10.32: 1 Lind, thinned, tinned, twinned; **2** chagrined, coffined, destined, rescind,

ruined, thick-skinned, thin-skinned; **3** determined, disciplined, double-chinned, imagined, predestined, Rosalind, tamarind, wunderkind; **4** ill-disciplined, predetermined, undisciplined.
See also **10.31.1, 10.31.6, 10.31.16, 10.31.20, 10.31.29.**

10.32.1: 1 wind; **2** crosswind, downwind, headwind, ill wind, sequinned, tailwind, trade wind, upwind, whirlwind, woodwind; **3** ensanguined.
See also **10.2.16, 10.42.29.**

10.33: 1 binge, hinge, singe, tinge, twinge, whinge; **2** challenge, impinge, lozenge, scavenge, unhinge.
See also **10.35, 10.42.39.**

10.33.1: 1 cringe, fringe; **2** infringe, orange, syringe; **4** cultural cringe.
See also **10.35, 10.42.39.**

10.34: 1 bridged, ridged; **2** abridged, bandaged, damaged, managed, mortgaged, packaged; **3** acknowledged, advantaged, discouraged, encouraged, prepackaged, privileged, unabridged, undamaged; **4** disadvantaged, unacknowledged; **5** underprivileged.
See also **10.11.2, 10.11.3, 10.11.4, 10.11.7, 10.11.8, 10.11.10, 10.11.24.**

10.35: 1 fringed, hinged, tinged; **2** challenged, infringed, unhinged; **3** unchallenged.
See also **10.33, 10.33.1.**

10.36: 1 mince, prince, quince, rinse, since, wince; **2** convince, evince, Hoskins, province; **3** Port-au-Prince.
See also **10.42.138, 10.62.3.**

10.37: 1 chintz, Linz; **2** shinsplints.

10.38: 1 dint, hint, skint, squint; **2** forint, sigint; **4** Septuagint.

10.38.1: 1 flint, glint, lint, splint; **2** skinflint.

10.38.2: 1 mint; **2** catmint, humint, spearmint, varmint; **3** peppermint.
See also **10.2.81.**

10.38.3: 1 print, sprint; **2** blueprint, fine print, footprint, imprint, misprint, newsprint, offprint, reprint, screen-print, small print, thumbprint, voiceprint, woodprint; **3** fingerprint, overprint.
See also **10.42.168.**

10.38.4: 1 stint, tint; **3** aquatint, mezzotint.
See also **10.2.81.**

10.39: **1** cinch, clinch, finch, flinch, inch, lynch, pinch, winch; **2** bullfinch, chaffinch, goldfinch.

10.40: **1** plinth; **2** absinthe, Corinth, hyacinth; **3** labyrinth.

10.41: **1** twins; **2** Cribbins, gubbins, matins, muggins, ninepins, Owens, Robbins, ruins; **3** O'Higgins; **4** Siamese twins; **5** identical twins.
See also **10.31.1, 10.31.32.**

10.41.1: **2** Atkins, Butlins, Collins, Dawkins, Dickens, gremlins, Hawkins, Hopkins, Jenkins, Perkins, Tomkins, Watkins, Wilkins; **3** tom collins; **4** Tommy Atkins.

10.41.2: **3** Blue Mountains; **4** Balkan Mountains, Cairngorm Mountains, Catskill Mountains, Rocky Mountains, Smoky Mountains, Taurus Mountains, Ural Mountains; **5** Caucasus Mountains, Grampian Mountains; **7** Appalachian Mountains.

The headlong streams and fountains
Serve Thee, invisible Spirit, with untired
powers;
Cheering the wakeful tent on Syrian
mountains,
They lull perchance ten thousand
thousand flowers.
(William Wordsworth)

10.42: **2** drawing, Ewing, gnawing, hanging, longing; **3** annoying, belonging, cloying, kowtowing, practising, straphanging, travelling; **4** interlocking, soul-destroying.
See also **1.28, 2.37.289, 9.14.75, 10.50.24, 13.10.3, 13.27.1, 14.10, 14.12.1, 16.0, 18.0, 18.3.**

10.42.1: **2** saying, slaying; **3** bricklaying, decaying, dismaying, role-playing.
See also **2.0.1, 5.7, 5.8, 5.9, 5.13.**

10.42.2: **2** seeing, skiing; **3** all-seeing, bullying, dallying, dizzying, nannying, pitying, sightseeing, toadying, unseeing; **4** heliskiing, self-pitying.
See also **9.7, 9.13.22, 9.14.1, 9.14.48, 9.20.**

10.42.3: **2** being; **3** lobbying, wellbeing, well-being; **4** human being, Supreme Being.
See also **9.6.5.**

10.42.4: **3** carrying, varying, wearying, worrying; **4** card-carrying, unvarying.
See also **9.19.1, 9.19.59, 9.19.63, 9.19.70.**

10.42.5: **2** crying, dying, trying, tying, vying; **3** undying; **4** satisfying, speechifying; **5** unsatisfying.
See also **11.0, 11.3.9, 11.8, 11.11.**

10.42.6: **4** death-defying, edifying, gratifying, horrifying, mortifying, stultifying, stupefying, terrifying; **5** electrifying, unedifying.
See also **11.3.2, 11.3.5, 11.3.6, 11.3.8.**

10.42.7: **2** flying, lying; **3** high-flying, low-lying, outlying; **4** underlying.
See also **11.5, 11.5.1, 11.5.2.**

10.42.8: **2** knowing, owing, sewing, showing; **3** all-knowing, unknowing.
See also **19.0, 19.13, 19.16, 19.17.**

10.42.9: **2** going; **3** foregoing, ingoing, ongoing, outgoing, seagoing; **4** easygoing, ocean-going, thoroughgoing.
See also **19.6.**

10.42.10: **2** flowing, glowing; **3** following, mind-blowing; **4** overflowing.
See also **19.11.7, 19.11.9, 19.11.10.**

10.42.11: **2** growing, rowing; **3** borrowing, harrowing, ingrowing.
See also **19.15, 19.15.4, 19.15.6.**

10.42.12: **2** doing, viewing; **3** ensuing, undoing, wrongdoing; **4** continuing.
See also **10.46, 22.2, 22.4.9, 22.4.11, 22.4.13.**

10.42.13: **1** Bing; **2** clubbing, drubbing, jobbing, probing, ribbing, rubbing, stabbing, throbbing, tubing, webbing; **3** absorbing, backstabbing, disturbing, hobnobbing; **4** moneygrabbing, money-grubbing.
See also **1.1, 7.7, 10.0.1, 13.0, 13.0.1, 14.18, 19.22.2.**

10.42.14: **1** ding; **2** balding, bidding, bonding, budding, cladding, Fielding, flooding, funding, gelding, Harding, loading, padding, plodding, scalding, sodding, wadding, wording, yielding; **3** forbidding, foreboding, freeloading, regarding, rewording, unyielding; **4** corresponding, overcrowding.
See also **1.3.5, 3.21.2, 6.15, 7.10.5, 9.39, 10.2.2, 13.2, 13.23.1, 13.23.2, 14.28, 19.23.2, 20.2, 20.30.**

10.42.15: **2** blading, lading, shading, trading; **3** crusading, degrading, horse-trading; **4** Armatrading; **5** insider trading.
See also **5.21, 5.21.9, 5.21.10, 5.21.11.**

10.42.16: **2** bedding, golden wedding, heading, spreading, wedding; **3** beheading,

10.42.39

deadheading, subheading, white wedding;
4 diamond wedding, ruby wedding,
shotgun wedding, silver wedding.
See also **6.1, 6.1.1, 6.1.4, 4.1.6, 6.1.14.**

10.42.17: **2** beading, speeding;
3 exceeding, lip-reading, preceding,
succeeding.
See also **9.29.5, 9.29.6, 9.29.7.**

10.42.18: **2** bleeding, breeding, leading,
pleading, reading; **3** cheerleading, ill-
breeding, inbreeding, misleading, palm-
reading.
See also **6.1.10, 9.29.3.**

10.42.19: **2** gliding, hiding, riding, siding;
3 abiding, backsliding, confiding,
deciding, hangliding, horse riding,
joyriding, providing; **4** law-abiding,
overriding, paragliding.
See also **11.14, 11.14.2, 11.14.9, 11.14.17,
11.14.20.**

10.42.20: **2** hoarding; **3** marauding,
recording, rewarding; **4** unrewarding.
See also **14.19, 14.19.5, 14.19.6, 14.19.9.**

10.42.21: **2** boarding; **3** kiteboarding,
snowboarding, wakeboarding;
4 mountainboarding.
See also **14.19.1.**

10.42.22: **2** pudding; **3** black pudding,
blood pudding, eve's pudding, pease
pudding, plum pudding, rice pudding,
steamed pudding; **4** Christmas pudding,
suet pudding, summer pudding, Yorkshire
pudding; **6** bread-and-butter pudding.

10.42.23: **2** brooding; **3** concluding,
excluding, including.
See also **22.17.8, 22.17.9.**

10.42.24: **2** building; **3** outbuilding,
shipbuilding; **4** empire-building, listed
building; **5** Empire State Building.

10.42.25: **2** folding, holding, moulding;
3 cuckolding, scaffolding, smallholding.
See also **19.35, 19.35.1, 19.35.3, 19.35.4.**

10.42.26: **2** banding, branding, landing;
3 commanding, demanding;
4 undemanding.
See also **1.22.1, 1.22.3, 1.22.6, 3.35.**

10.42.27: **2** standing; **3** freestanding,
grandstanding, longstanding, outstanding,
upstanding; **4** notwithstanding,
understanding; **5** misunderstanding.
See also **1.22.7.**

10.42.28: **2** ending, mending, pending,
spending; **3** ascending, attending,
descending, heartrending, impending,

offending, unbending, unending;
4 condescending, never-ending,
parascending; **5** uncomprehending.
See also **6.30, 6.30.1, 6.30.2, 6.30.3, 6.30.5,
6.30.8, 6.30.9.**

10.42.29: **2** binding, blinding, grinding,
winding; **3** bias binding, fact-finding,
faultfinding, spellbinding.
See also **10.32.1, 11.28, 11.28.4, 11.28.6.**

10.42.30: **2** grounding, pounding,
sounding; **3** astounding, resounding,
surrounding.
See also **16.11, 16.11.4, 16.11.6, 16.11.7,
16.11.8.**

10.42.31: **2** bathing, breathing, clothing,
farthing, loathing, scathing, seething,
sheathing, soothing, Worthing; **4** penny-
farthing.
See also **3.51.1, 5.23, 9.31, 19.25, 22.18.**

10.42.32: **2** briefing, effing, golfing,
offing, Rolfing, roofing, spiffing, staffing,
stuffing, surfing; **3** debriefing, glue-
sniffing, skysurfing, windsurfing.
See also **3.23.4, 6.4, 7.11, 9.32.2, 13.5.**

10.42.33: **2** banging, begging, frigging,
legging, mugging, rigging, wigging;
3 debugging, intriguing, level pegging.
See also **1.28.1, 6.6, 6.6.1, 9.34, 10.8.1,
20.7, 20.7.1.**

10.42.34: **2** bragging, flagging, lagging,
nagging; **3** footdragging, unflagging;
4 lollygagging.
See also **1.6, 1.6.2, 1.6.3.**

10.42.35: **2** dogging, flogging, jogging,
logging; **3** footslogging; **4** pettifogging.
See also **13.7, 13.7.1, 13.7.4.**

10.42.36: **2** bulging, edging, grudging,
lodging, sledging; **3** emerging, obliging;
4 disobliging.
See also **6.9, 6.9.1, 7.13.1, 11.18, 13.9,
20.9.2, 20.18.**

10.42.37: **2** ageing, Beijing, paging,
raging, staging; **3** engaging.
See also **5.26.1, 5.26.2, 5.26.3, 5.26.4.**

10.42.38: **3** cottaging, damaging,
imaging, messaging, packaging;
4 discouraging, disparaging, encouraging.
See also **10.11.4, 10.11.8, 10.11.13,
10.11.18, 10.11.21.**

10.42.39: **2** cringing, plunging,
scrounging, sponging, swingeing;
3 challenging, unchanging, wide-ranging.
See also **10.33, 10.33.1, 20.31.**

10.42.40: 1 king; 2 Barking, fucking, hulking, marking, parking, stonking, Sun King, trucking; 3 Billie Jean King, bloodsucking, bollocking, hot-desking; 4 motherfucking, multitasking.

Friday night and the lights are low,
Looking out for the place to go,
Where they play the right music, getting
in the swing
You come in to look for a king.
(Abba)
See also **2.35.1, 3.27.4, 3.27.5, 20.10.**

10.42.41: 2 backing, lacking, packing, sacking, whacking; 3 backpacking, carjacking, hijacking, skyjacking.
See also **1.10.3, 1.10.8, 1.10.10, 1.10.14, 1.10.17.**

10.42.42: 2 cracking, racking, tracking; 3 nerve-wracking, safe-cracking.
See also **1.10.15, 1.10.16.**

10.42.43: 2 baking, waking; 3 earthshaking, muckraking.
See also **5.27, 5.27.11.**

10.42.44: 2 making; 3 haymaking, lossmaking, lovemaking, peacemaking, printmaking; 4 epoch-making, merrymaking, moneymaking, profitmaking; 5 non-profit-making.
See also **5.27.4.**

10.42.45: 3 backbreaking, groundbreaking, heartbreaking, housebreaking.

10.42.46: 2 decking, necking; 3 breathtaking, leave-taking, painstaking, risk-taking, stocktaking; 4 pony-trekking, rubbernecking, undertaking.
See also **5.27.9.**

10.42.47: 2 working; 3 hard-working, networking, reworking; 4 teleworking.
See also **7.14.2, 7.14.4, 7.14.9.**

10.42.48: 2 creaking, freaking, Peking, sneaking; 3 heat-seeking, plain-speaking, self-seeking.
See also **9.36.2, 9.36.5.**

10.42.49: 2 kicking, licking, ticking; 3 bootlicking, nitpicking, rollicking, trafficking; 4 politicking; 5 alive and kicking.
See also **10.12.8, 10.12.15, 10.12.16, 10.12.39, 10.12.54.**

10.42.50: 2 hiking, liking, striking, Viking.
See also **11.19, 11.19.1.**

10.42.51: 2 mocking, shocking, smocking, socking, stocking; 3 bluestocking.
In olden days, a glimpse of stocking
Was looked on as something shocking,
But now, Heaven knows,
Anything goes.
(Cole Porter)
See also **9.14.75, 10.46.2, 13.10, 13.10.8.**

10.42.52: 2 corking, Hawking, stalking, walking; 3 jaywalking, sleepwalking, smooth-talking, straight-talking, sweet-talking.
See also **14.24.2, 14.24.3, 14.24.4.**

10.42.53: 2 broking, joking, smoking, soaking; 4 thought-provoking.
See also **19.31.**

10.42.54: 2 booking, Brooking, cooking; 3 good-looking, nice-looking, nonsmoking; 4 forward-looking.
See also **21.4.1, 21.4.4.**

10.42.55: 2 banking, flanking, planking, ranking, spanking; 3 high-ranking, home banking; 4 private banking, telebanking.
See also **1.30, 1.30.1, 1.30.2, 1.30.3.**

10.42.56: 2 blinking, drinking, sinking, stinking; 3 unblinking.
See also **10.43, 10.43.1, 10.43.2.**

10.42.57: 2 thinking; 3 quick-thinking, right-thinking, unthinking; 4 free-thinking, wishful thinking.
See also **9.14.75.**

10.42.58: 1 fling, ling; 2 angling, boiling, bungling, changeling, cowling, darling, dialling, earthling, fledgling, gangling, halfling, hireling, howling, Rowling, ruling, schooling, starling, starveling, towelling, yearling; 3 Highland fling, potboiling, unsettling.
See also **2.37.142, 2.37.145, 2.37.273, 16.9, 17.4, 22.22.4, 22.22.6.**

10.42.59: 3 baffling, coupling, ding-a-ling, equalling, fuelling, gruelling, marshalling, piffling, puzzling, quarrelling, spiralling, stifling, ting-a-ling, trifling; 4 initialling.
See also **2.37.18, 2.37.121, 2.37.227, 2.37.242, 2.37.243, 2.37.259, 2.37.262, 2.37.298, 2.37.305.**

10.42.60: 3 babbling, humbling, labelling, libelling, marbling, quibbling, stumbling, troubling; 4 disabling, enabling.
See also **2.37.24, 2.37.87, 2.37.92, 2.37.93, 2.37.99.**

10.42.61: 3 fiddling, middling, modelling, paddling, pedalling, piddling, underling, wheedling; 4 bloodcurdling.
See also **2.37.106, 2.37.108, 2.37.109, 2.37.110, 2.37.113.**

10.42.62: 2 haggling; 3 niggling, smuggling, struggling, tingling; 4 mind-boggling, spine-tingling.
See also **2.37.136, 2.37.138, 2.37.140, 2.37.144.**

10.42.63: 3 crackling, rib-tickling, snorkelling, sparkling, suckling, twinkling; 4 swashbuckling.
See also **2.37.147, 2.37.148, 2.37.152, 2.37.186, 2.37.188.**

10.42.64: 3 channelling, funnelling, panelling, signalling, tunnelling.
See also **2.37.195, 2.37.196, 2.37.221.**

10.42.65: 2 bristling; 3 bustling, cancelling, counselling, parcelling, penciling, wrestling.
See also **2.37.248, 2.37.249, 2.37.251, 2.37.253, 2.37.255.**

10.42.66: 3 footling, hostelling, nestling, rattling, startling, totalling; 5 sabre-rattling.
See also **2.37.249, 2.37.270, 2.37.271, 2.37.281.**

10.42.67: 3 grovelling, levelling, shovelling, shrivelling, snivelling, swivelling, travelling; 4 bedevilling, unravelling.
See also **2.37.288, 2.37.289, 2.37.291, 2.37.292, 2.37.294.**

10.42.68: 2 ailing, failing, mailing, paling, railing, sailing, trailing, whaling; 3 abseiling, detailing, plain sailing, retailing, unfailing; 4 parasailing.
See also **5.30, 5.30.4, 5.30.6, 5.30.7, 5.30.9.**

10.42.69: 3 prevailing, unveiling; 4 countervailing, unavailing.
See also **5.30.10.**

10.42.70: 2 dwelling, selling, shelling, spelling, swelling, telling; 3 best-selling, compelling, foretelling, hotelling, misspelling, strong-smelling, sweet-smelling; 4 direct selling.

Love divine, all loves excelling,
Joy of heav'n to earth come down,
Fix in us thy humble dwelling,
All thy faithful mercies crown.
(Charles Wesley)
See also **6.14.6, 6.14.7, 6.14.8, 6.14.9, 6.14.10.**

10.42.71: 2 curling, hurling, sterling, Stirling.
See also **7.16.**

10.42.72: 2 ceiling, dealing, Ealing, feeling, healing; 3 appealing, Darjeeling, death-dealing, freewheeling, ill feeling, revealing, unfeeling; 4 double-dealing, unappealing; 5 insider dealing.

In Dundee and Penzance and Ealing
We're imbued with appropriate feeling:
We're British and loyal
And love every royal
And tonight we shall drink till we're
reeling.
(Wendy Cope)
See also **9.38, 9.38.2, 9.38.5, 9.38.8, 10.46.3.**

10.42.73: 2 billing, chilling, filling, killing, schilling, shilling, thrilling, willing; 3 fulfilling, mercy killing, painkilling, reskilling, unwilling, upskilling; 4 self-fulfilling.
See also **2.54.62, 10.17, 10.17.1, 10.17.2, 10.17.5.**

10.42.74: 2 filing, styling, tiling; 3 beguiling, profiling, unsmiling.
See also **11.22, 11.22.2, 11.22.6, 11.22.8.**

10.42.75: 2 calling, crawling, galling, Pauling, sprawling; 3 appalling, blackballing, enthralling, kerb crawling, name-calling.
See also **14.27.1, 14.27.5, 14.27.7, 14.27.8, 14.27.9.**

10.42.76: 2 bowling, polling, rolling; 3 controlling, logrolling, potholing.
See also **19.34.2, 19.34.4, 19.34.5, 19.34.7.**

10.42.77: 1 bling; 2 sibling, stabling.
See also **2.37.88.**

10.42.78: 2 brambling, bumbling, crumbling, gambling, rambling, rumbling, trembling.
See also **2.37.101, 2.37.102, 2.37.104.**

10.42.79: 2 dawdling, dwindling, foundling, handling, kindling, meddling, middling, seedling; 3 backpedalling.
See also **2.37.105, 2.37.107, 2.37.108, 2.37.119, 2.37.120.**

10.42.80: 1 cling; 2 cycling, duckling, inkling, sprinkling, twinkling, weakling; 3 recycling.
See also **2.37.184, 2.37.188.**

10.42.81: 2 crippling, dumpling, Kipling, sapling, stripling.
See also **2.37.225.**

10.42.82: 1 sling; 2 gin sling, nursling, rustling; 4 Singapore sling.
See also **2.37.253**.

10.42.83: 2 dazzling, gosling, quisling, Riesling, sizzling.
See also **2.37.300, 2.37.303**.

10.42.84: 1 Ming; 2 bombing, climbing, filming, flaming, Fleming, gaming, gloaming, homing, lemming, rhyming, roaming, skimming, slimming, swimming, timing; 3 blossoming, mistiming, rock climbing, two-timing, welcoming, Wyoming; 4 overwhelming, unwelcoming.
See also **2.40.24, 2.40.33, 5.33.2, 6.17, 10.20, 10.26, 11.25.1, 11.25.2, 11.25.3, 11.25.7, 13.18.1, 19.38.1, 19.38.3**.

10.42.85: 2 damning, spamming; 3 programming; 5 microprogramming.
See also **1.18.1, 1.18.8**.

10.42.86: 2 calming, charming, farming; 3 alarming, disarming, prince charming.
See also **3.31, 3.31.1, 9.14.77**.

10.42.87: 2 beaming, Dreaming, gleaming, scheming, screaming, seeming, steaming, streaming, teeming; 3 daydreaming.
See also **9.41, 9.41.1, 9.41.2, 9.41.3, 9.41.4, 9.41.5, 9.41.6, 9.41.7**.

10.42.88: 2 storming, warming; 3 barnstorming, brainstorming, conforming, heartwarming, housewarming; 4 habit-forming.
See also **14.33, 14.33.1, 14.33.4**.

10.42.89: 2 drumming, humming, numbing, plumbing; 3 mind-numbing.
See also **20.24, 20.24.3**.

10.42.90: 2 coming; 3 becoming, forthcoming, homecoming, incoming, oncoming, shortcoming, upcoming; 4 Second Coming, unbecoming, unforthcoming, up-and-coming.
See also **20.24.1**.

10.42.91: 2 blooming, booming, fuming, grooming, looming; 3 assuming, consuming; 4 all-consuming, time-consuming, unassuming.
See also **22.25, 22.25.1, 22.25.2, 22.25.3**.

10.42.92: 2 Browning, cloning, crowning, darning, Denning, droning, evening, fastening, ironing, joining, lightning, spooning, tuning, zoning; 3 adjoining, ballooning.
Why does it always rain on me?
Even when the sun is shining
I can't avoid the lightning...
(Travis)
See also **2.43.115, 2.43.322, 3.34, 12.9, 16.10.7, 18.11.1, 19.40.5, 19.40.11, 19.40.19, 22.27.3, 22.27.5, 22.27.6**.

10.42.93: 2 Canning, Channing, Manning, planning, tanning; 4 caravanning, overmanning.
See also **1.21.3, 1.21.15**.

10.42.94: 3 burgeoning, christening, deafening, eye-opening, gardening, governing, happening, maddening, opening, questioning, ravening, worsening; 4 easy listening, self-governing, unquestioning; 5 market gardening.
See also **2.15.2, 2.43.31, 2.43.32, 2.43.45, 2.43.54, 2.43.108, 2.43.109, 2.43.113, 2.43.122, 2.43.317, 2.43.326**.

10.42.95: 3 functioning, quickening, rationing, reckoning, sickening; 4 awakening, conditioning, dead reckoning; 5 air conditioning.
See also **2.43.63, 2.43.65, 2.43.68**.

10.42.96: 3 fattening, frightening, patterning, poisoning, reasoning, seasoning, shortening, sweetening, threatening; 4 disheartening, unreasoning; 5 reconditioning.
See also **2.43.239, 2.43.288, 2.43.289, 2.43.294, 2.43.299**.

10.42.97: 2 draining, training, waning; 3 abstaining, remaining; 4 entertaining, toilet training, uncomplaining.
See also **5.35.6, 5.35.8, 5.35.11, 5.35.13, 5.35.14**.

10.42.98: 2 burning, learning, turning, yearning; 3 concerning, discerning; 4 undiscerning.
See also **7.20, 7.20.1, 7.20.2, 7.20.3**.

10.42.99: 2 cleaning, greening, keening, leaning, meaning, screening; 3 demeaning, well-meaning; 4 intervening, overweening.
See also **9.43.4, 9.43.5, 9.43.7, 9.43.13, 9.43.23**.

10.42.100: 2 inning, spinning, thinning, winning; 3 beginning, designing, match-winning; 4 determining, money-spinning, underpinning.
See also **10.31.5, 10.31.16, 10.31.18, 10.31.19, 10.31.29, 10.31.32, 10.46.4, 11.27**.

10.42.101: 2 lining, mining, shining, signing, whining; 3 declining; 4 silver lining.
See also **11.27.3, 11.27.8, 11.27.11,**

11.27.15, 11.27.16.

10.42.102: 2 awning, cunning, dawning, fawning, morning, mourning, running, stunning, warning, yawning; 3 forewarning, gunrunning.
See also **14.35, 14.35.7.**

10.42.103: 2 minging, ringing, stinging, swinging; 3 mudslinging, upbringing.
See also **10.42.112, 10.42.170, 10.42.185.**

10.42.104: 1 ping; 2 coping, cupping, drooping, gaping, gasping, grasping, grouping, helping, scraping, snooping; 3 doorstepping, galloping, soft-soaping, walloping; 4 developing.
See also **2.52.1, 2.52.2, 3.45, 5.42, 5.42.2, 6.18, 6.43.1, 19.44, 20.40.2, 22.29, 22.29.2, 22.29.3.**

10.42.105: 2 capping, clapping, strapping, wrapping; 3 backslapping, bootstrapping, kidnapping.
See also **1.33.1, 1.33.2, 1.33.3, 1.33.4, 1.33.6.**

10.42.106: 2 creeping, heaping, sleeping, sweeping, weeping.
See also **9.47, 9.47.1.**

10.42.107: 2 keeping; 3 beekeeping, bookkeeping, goalkeeping, housekeeping, peacekeeping, safekeeping, stockkeeping, timekeeping; 4 record-keeping.
See also **9.47.**

10.42.108: 2 clipping, dripping, flipping, gripping, ripping, shipping, whipping; 3 fly-tipping; 4 asset-stripping, skinny-dipping.
See also **10.47.1, 10.47.4, 10.47.6, 10.47.15.**

10.42.109: 2 griping, piping, sniping, typing; 5 audiotyping.
See also **11.31, 11.31.1, 11.31.2, 11.31.3.**

10.42.110: 2 hopping, shopping, sopping, topping, whopping; 3 chart-topping, clodhopping, name-dropping, showstopping, wife swapping; 4 cybershopping, teleshopping, window-shopping.
See also **13.31.1, 13.31.7, 13.31.8.**

10.42.111: 2 camping, shrimping, thumping; 3 basejumping, showjumping, tub-thumping; 4 bungee jumping.
See also **1.20.1, 20.26.**

10.42.112: 1 bring, ring, wring; 2 barring, bullring, Goering, herring, jarring, nosering, stirring, Turing, web

ring; 3 fairy ring, red herring, unerring; 4 awe-inspiring.
See also **3.2, 3.7, 7.6, 10.42.103.**

10.42.113: 3 authoring, bickering, colouring, conjuring, differing, hammering, hankering, offering, posturing, simpering, soldiering, suffering, tailoring, tapering, texturing; 4 delayering; 5 manufacturing.
See also **2.8, 2.8.2, 2.8.5, 2.10.6, 2.10.7, 2.12.11, 2.12.24, 2.13.4, 2.13.20, 2.14.2, 2.18.2, 2.18.16, 2.23, 2.24.4, 2.24.10.**

10.42.114: 3 gibbering, jabbering, lumbering, neighbouring, sobering.
See also **2.5, 2.5.6, 2.5.12.**

10.42.115: 3 blundering, doddering, floundering, rendering, smouldering, thundering; 4 bewildering, considering, meandering, philandering; 5 gerrymandering.
See also **2.6, 2.6.5, 2.6.14, 2.6.18, 2.6.20, 2.6.26, 2.6.27.**

10.42.116: 3 blithering, dithering, gathering, withering; 4 woolgathering.
See also **2.7, 2.7.3.**

10.42.117: 3 fingering, lingering, staggering, swaggering; 4 scaremongering.
See also **2.9.1, 2.9.12.**

10.42.118: 3 bartering, blistering, catering, faltering, festering, glittering, guttering, lettering, mentoring, motoring, sweltering, tottering; 4 mouthwatering, unfaltering.
See also **2.22.4, 2.22.13, 2.22.37, 2.22.49, 2.22.55, 2.22.56, 2.22.75, 2.22.77, 2.22.94, 2.22.96.**

10.42.119: 3 battering, chattering, flattering, nattering, scattering, shattering, smattering; 4 unflattering, world-shattering.
See also **2.22.1, 2.22.2.**

10.42.120: 3 covering, flavouring, wavering; 4 manoeuvring, unwavering.
See also **2.25.4, 2.25.5, 2.25.22, 2.25.24.**

10.42.121: 2 airing, bearing, blaring, caring, daring, glaring, raring, swearing, Waring, wearing; 3 childbearing, forbearing, forswearing, hard-wearing, job-sharing, seafaring, time sharing, uncaring; 4 overbearing.
See also **4.0, 4.2, 4.6, 4.7, 4.12, 4.15, 4.15.3, 10.46.5.**

10.42.122: 2 pairing, sparing; 3 cheeseparing, despairing, unsparing.
See also **4.10.**

10.42.123: 2 clearing, earring, gearing, hearing, jeering, searing, shearing, steering; 3 endearing, God-fearing; 4 interfering, persevering, profiteering, racketeering; 5 orienteering.
See also **8.0, 8.1, 8.3, 8.4, 8.8, 8.9, 8.10**.

10.42.124: 2 sneering; 4 engineering; 6 bioengineering.
See also **8.6**.

10.42.125: 3 pioneering; 4 buccaneering, canyoneering, domineering, mountaineering, sloganeering; 5 electioneering.
See also **8.6**.

10.42.126: 2 tiring, wiring; 3 admiring, aspiring, enquiring, inquiring, inspiring, retiring, untiring; 4 uninspiring.
See also **12.0, 12.3.1, 12.5, 12.6, 12.6.1**.

10.42.127: 2 boring, flooring, roaring, soaring, warring; 3 adoring, imploring, offshoring, outpouring, rip-roaring.
See also **10.42.128, 14.1, 14.2.1, 14.8, 14.8.1, 14.12, 14.13**.

10.42.128: 2 during; 3 alluring, enduring, procuring; 4 reassuring.
See also **10.42.127, 15.1, 15.1.1, 15.4**.

10.42.129: 2 flowering, glowering, towering; 4 overpowering.
See also **17.1, 17.1.1, 17.2**.

10.42.130: 1 spring; 2 handspring, mainspring, offspring, wellspring.

10.42.131: 1 string; 2 drawstring, first-string, G-string, hamstring, shoestring; 3 second string.
See also **10.46.5**.

10.42.132: 1 sing, Singh, Synge; 2 crossing, cursing, icing, missing, nursing, passing, piercing, pricing, Sing Sing; 3 ear-piercing, engrossing, enticing, level crossing, outsourcing, policing, promising, rejoicing, resourcing, surpassing, unceasing; 4 double-crossing, unpromising.

An aged man is but a paltry thing
A tattered coat upon a stick, unless
Soul clap its hands and sing.
(W. B. Yeats)
See also **3.43.3, 7.26, 8.13, 9.49.1, 10.50.9, 11.34, 11.34.2, 13.34.7, 14.42, 14.42.4, 18.14, 19.45.2**.

10.42.133: 3 menacing, terracing, trespassing; 4 embarrassing; 5 all-encompassing; 6 antialiasing.
See also **2.54.62, 2.54.93, 2.54.96**.

10.42.134: 2 casing, facing, spacing; 4 interfacing, self-effacing.
See also **5.45.2, 5.45.3, 5.45.6**.

10.42.135: 2 bracing, racing, tracing; 3 horseracing; 4 all-embracing.
See also **5.45.7**.

10.42.136: 2 blessing, dressing, Lessing, pressing; 3 depressing, distressing, French dressing, processing, top dressing; 4 prepossessing, Russian dressing, salad dressing, window-dressing, word processing; 5 multiprocessing, teleprocessing, unprepossessing; 6 Thousand Island dressing.
See also **6.47.1, 6.47.8, 6.47.9**.

10.42.137: 2 boxing, taxing, vexing, waxing; 3 kickboxing, perplexing, price fixing, relaxing.
See also **1.11.2, 1.11.4, 1.11.5, 6.11, 6.11.3**.

10.42.138: 2 bouncing, fencing, Lansing, trouncing; 3 convincing, sequencing; 4 conferencing, conveyancing, self-financing, unconvincing; 6 teleconferencing; 7 audioconferencing, videoconferencing.
See also **6.33.1, 10.36, 16.12**.

10.42.139: 2 dancing, glancing, Lancing; 3 advancing, breakdancing, entrancing.
See also **2.45.22, 3.37, 3.37.1, 3.37.2, 3.37.3**.

10.42.140: 2 blushing, crushing, Cushing, gushing, joshing, washing; 3 onrushing, refreshing.
See also **6.50.1, 13.37, 13.37.1, 20.45, 20.45.1**.

10.42.141: 2 bashing, dashing, flashing, gnashing, smashing, thrashing; 3 earbashing, square-bashing, tongue-lashing.
See also **1.39, 1.39.1, 1.39.2, 1.39.3, 1.39.4**.

10.42.142: 2 fishing, phishing; 3 flourishing, nourishing, perishing, publishing, punishing, ravishing, skirmishing; 4 astonishing, distinguishing, overfishing; 5 apple-polishing, nanopublishing.
See also **10.54.5, 10.54.11, 10.54.13, 10.54.14, 10.54.17, 10.54.20, 10.54.22**.

10.42.143: 1 ting; 2 cutting, footing, karting, matting, outing, parting, putting, scouting, strutting, tatting; 3 first-footing, off-putting, press cutting.
See also **3.49.5, 16.16, 16.16.3, 20.47, 20.47.2, 21.14, 21.14.1**.

10.42.144: 3 comforting, dieting, disquieting, rioting, toileting, wainscoting. *See also* **2.56, 12.13.**

10.42.145: 2 dating, mating, weighting; 3 pulsating; 4 devastating, irritating, mitigating; 5 accommodating, debilitating, intimidating, unhesitating; 6 self-perpetuating. *See also* **5.47.11, 5.47.12, 5.47.18, 5.47.40, 5.47.62, 5.47.64, 5.47.66, 5.47.69.**

10.42.146: 4 nauseating; 5 excruciating, humiliating, infuriating, ingratiating. *See also* **5.47.1, 5.47.3, 5.47.4, 5.47.5, 5.47.6.**

10.42.147: 2 skating; 3 ice skating, pair-skating, speed skating; 4 deprecating, figure skating, suffocating; 5 intoxicating, prevaricating. *See also* **5.47.20, 5.47.26, 5.47.28.**

10.42.148: 2 plating; 4 calculating, scintillating, stimulating, titillating, vacillating; 5 self-regulating. *See also* **5.47.31, 5.47.35, 5.47.36, 5.47.39.**

10.42.149: 4 fascinating, hibernating; 5 discriminating, illuminating; 6 undiscriminating. *See also* **2.56.31, 5.47.44, 5.47.46, 5.47.48.**

10.42.150: 2 grating, rating; 3 frustrating; 4 able rating, penetrating; 6 ordinary rating. *See also* **5.47.51, 5.47.59, 5.47.60, 5.47.61.**

10.42.151: 4 decorating, liberating; 5 exasperating, exhilarating, invigorating; 6 deteriorating. *See also* **5.47.52, 5.47.53, 5.47.55.**

10.42.152: 4 aggravating, captivating, elevating, enervating. *See also* **5.47.67, 5.47.68.**

10.42.153: 2 betting, fretting, letting, netting, petting, setting; 3 bedwetting, bloodletting, go-getting, typesetting, upsetting, wire netting. *See also* **6.51, 6.51.2, 6.51.4, 6.51.5, 6.51.8.**

10.42.154: 2 birthing, hurting, skirting; 3 diverting, rebirthing; 4 disconcerting. *See also* **7.28, 7.28.1, 7.28.3, 7.28.5.**

10.42.155: 2 beating, cheating, fleeting, greeting, heating, Keating, meeting, seating, sheeting; 3 competing, man-eating, world-beating; 5 general meeting, self-defeating. *See also* **9.52, 9.52.1, 9.52.3, 9.52.6, 9.52.7.**

10.42.156: 2 fitting, knitting, sitting; 3 bullshitting, carpeting, close-fitting,

editing, hard-hitting, limiting, marketing, riveting, shopfitting, ticketing, unwitting; 4 dispiriting, soliciting, unremitting; 5 telemarketing. *See also* **9.14.78, 10.46.6, 10.56.4, 10.56.6, 10.56.13, 10.56.22, 10.56.23, 10.56.26, 10.56.32, 10.56.33, 10.56.34, 10.56.35.**

10.42.157: 2 splitting; 3 earsplitting, hairsplitting, sidesplitting. *See also* **10.56.19.**

10.42.158: 2 biting, lighting, sighting, slighting, whiting, writing; 3 backbiting, exciting, handwriting, inviting, moonlighting, skywriting; 4 unexciting, uninviting. *See also* **11.36, 11.36.1, 11.36.6, 11.36.10, 11.36.16.**

10.42.159: 2 fighting; 3 firefighting, infighting, warfighting. *See also* **11.36.4.**

10.42.160: 2 rotting, spotting, yachting; 3 trainspotting; 4 cybersquatting. *See also* **13.39.6, 13.39.7.**

10.42.161: 2 courting, sporting; 3 reporting, supporting, unsporting. *See also* **14.44.1, 14.44.4, 14.44.5, 14.44.6.**

10.42.162: 2 boating, coating, doting, floating; 3 free-floating, showboating. *See also* **19.47.2, 19.47.4, 19.47.5.**

10.42.163: 2 suiting, Tooting; 3 computing; 5 telecomputing. *See also* **22.34.6, 22.34.11.**

10.42.164: 2 shooting; 3 sharpshooting, trapshooting; 4 parachuting, troubleshooting. *See also* **22.34.13.**

10.42.165: 2 crofting, rafting, shifting; 3 shoplifting, uplifting, weightlifting; 5 whitewater rafting. *See also* **10.7.1, 10.7.3.**

10.42.166: 2 acting, ducting; 3 affecting, connecting, distracting, exacting, fast-acting; 4 unsuspecting. *See also* **1.12, 1.12.4, 6.12.1, 6.12.6.**

10.42.167: 2 halting, lilting, melting, quilting, vaulting; 3 consulting, insulting, revolting. *See also* **6.19, 9.14.78, 14.31, 19.36, 20.22.**

10.42.168: 2 Banting, bunting, daunting, haunting, hunting, mounting, painting, pointing, Ponting, printing, wanting; 3 accounting, enchanting, eventing, foxhunting, oil painting, parenting,

screenprinting, unstinting; **4** cost accounting, disappointing, unrelenting.
See also **3.38, 5.40, 10.38.3, 13.25, 14.38, 16.13, 16.13.1, 18.12, 20.33.1.**

10.42.169: **2** prompting, tempting; **3** accepting, excepting.
See also **6.27, 6.45.1, 13.20.**

10.42.170: **1** sting; **2** bursting, costing, frosting, listing, texting; **3** arm-twisting, exhausting, existing.
See also **6.13.1, 7.27.1, 10.42.103, 10.53, 10.53.6, 13.36.1, 13.36.2, 14.43.**

10.42.171: **2** casting, fasting, jesting, lasting, pasting, resting, tasting, testing, wasting; **3** arresting, broadcasting, contrasting, interesting, long-lasting, strong-tasting, time-wasting, webcasting; **4** everlasting, multicasting, uninteresting.
See also **3.47, 3.47.1, 3.47.2, 3.47.3.**

10.42.172: **2** boasting, ghosting, posting, roasting; **3** flyposting.
See also **19.46, 19.46.3.**

10.42.173: **2** dusting, trusting; **3** blockbusting, disgusting; **4** bunker busting.
See also **2.22.104, 20.44, 20.44.2, 20.44.6.**

10.42.174: **1** thing; **2** nothing, plaything, something; **3** anything, everything; **4** good-for-nothing, thirtysomething.
See also **10.46.**

10.42.175: **2** catching, coaching, etching, fetching, I Ching, lynching, matching, ranching, scorching, searching, stitching, teaching, touching, wenching; **3** backscratching, beseeching, bewitching, bird-watching, eye-catching, far-reaching, heart-searching, soul-searching, unflinching, weight-watching; **4** overarching, penny-pinching.
See also **6.54, 7.31, 9.55, 10.59.1, 14.47, 19.50, 20.49.**

10.42.176: **2** carving, heaving, living, loving, roving, shelving, starving, thieving; **3** clean-living, disbelieving, fun-loving, peace-loving, revolving, woodcarving; **4** cost of living.
See also **3.54, 6.22, 9.56, 9.56.1, 10.61.1, 11.38, 13.15, 19.51.1, 20.51.1.**

10.42.177: **2** caving, craving, paving, raving, shaving; **3** engraving, flag-waving.
See also **5.51, 5.51.2.**

10.42.178: **2** saving; **3** face-saving, lifesaving, timesaving; **4** labour-saving.
See also **5.51, 10.46.7.**

10.42.179: **2** Irving, serving; **3** deserving, self-serving, time-serving, unswerving; **4** undeserving.
See also **7.32.1, 7.32.2.**

10.42.180: **2** giving; **3** alms-giving, forgiving, misgiving, Thanksgiving; **4** unforgiving.
See also **10.61.**

10.42.181: **2** driving, thriving; **3** conniving, drink-driving, surviving.
See also **11.38, 11.38.3.**

10.42.182: **2** diving; **3** freediving, skin diving, skydiving.
See also **11.38.1.**

10.42.183: **2** moving; **3** approving, reproving; **4** disapproving.
See also **9.14.75, 22.38, 22.38.1.**

10.42.184: **1** wing; **2** brewing, lapwing, left-wing, right-wing.
Speed, bonny boat, like a bird on the wing;
'Onward', the sailors cry;
Carry the lad that's born to be king
Over the sea to Skye.
(Harold Edwin Boulton)
See also **13.8, 22.10.**

10.42.185: **1** swing; **2** backswing, downswing, upswing.
See also **10.42.103.**

10.42.186: **1** zing; **2** buzzing, cleansing, freezing, pleasing, teasing; **3** displeasing.
See also **6.40, 9.59.3, 9.59.11, 9.59.13, 20.53.**

10.42.187: **2** blazing, glazing, phrasing; **3** amazing, fundraising, hair-raising, self-raising, stargazing, trailblazing; **4** double-glazing, navel-gazing.
See also **2.27.2, 5.54.**

10.42.188: **2** rising; **4** advertising, agonising, appetising, civilising, compromising, merchandising, mesmerising, patronising, tantalising, womanising; **5** unappetising, uncompromising.
See also **11.42.1, 11.42.4, 11.42.13, 11.42.15, 11.42.19, 11.42.21, 11.42.25, 11.42.33.**

10.42.189: **3** surprising, uprising; **4** enterprising, unsurprising.
See also **11.42.28.**

10.42.190: **2** browsing, housing, rousing; **3** warehousing; **4** rabble-rousing.
See also **2.27.8, 16.14.1, 16.21, 16.21.1.**

10.42.191: **2** bruising, closing;
3 accusing, amusing, brown-nosing,
confusing, imposing, opposing, supposing.
See also **19.45, 19.52.1, 19.52.2, 19.52.4,
19.52.5.**

10.43: **1** chink, fink, ink, jink, kink, mink,
sink, skink, stink, sync, wink, zinc;
2 Haitink, hoodwink, lip-sync; **3** kitchen
sink, rinky-dink.
See also **10.42.56.**

10.43.1: **1** blink, clink, link, pink, slink;
2 airlink, cufflink, hotlink, rose-pink,
uplink, weblink; **3** baby pink, hyperlink,
interlink, shocking pink, tickled pink;
5 invisible ink.
See also **10.42.56, 10.44, 10.45.**

10.43.2: **1** brink, drink, rink, shrink, think;
2 ice rink, outthink, preshrink, rethink, soft
drink; **3** doublethink, fizzy drink,
overdrink.
Water, water, every where,
And all the boards did shrink;
Water, water, every where,
Nor any drop to drink.
(Samuel Taylor Coleridge)
See also **10.42.56, 10.44.**

10.44: **1** drinks, jinx, links, lynx, minx,
sphinx; **2** high jinks, larynx, methinks,
pharynx; **3** forty winks; **4** tiddlywinks.
See also **10.43.1, 10.43.2.**

10.45: **1** linked; **2** precinct, succinct;
3 index-linked.
See also **9.14.91, 10.43.1.**

10.45.1: **2** distinct, extinct, instinct;
3 indistinct.

10.46: **1** things; **2** chippings, cummings,
diggings, doings, droppings, earnings,
fixings, gleanings, Hemmings, lashings,
leggings, scratchings, trappings,
trimmings; **3** belongings, furnishings,
outgoings, waterwings; **5** comings and
goings.
See also **10.42.12, 10.42.174.**

10.46.1: **2** findings, tidings;
3 landholdings, proceedings, surroundings.

10.46.2: **2** pickings, stockings, takings,
workings; **3** King of Kings; **4** easy
pickings.
See also **10.42.51.**

10.46.3: **2** dealings, feelings, filings,
peelings, ramblings; **3** chitterlings, hard
feelings; **4** dirty dealings.
See also **10.42.72.**

10.46.4: **2** innings, winnings;
3 beginnings; **4** imaginings.
See also **10.42.100.**

10.46.5: **1** strings; **2** bearings,
heartstrings, Palm Springs; **3** wanderings.
See also **10.42.121, 10.42.131.**

10.46.6: **2** beestings, fittings, Hastings,
hustings, jottings.
See also **10.42.156.**

10.46.7: **2** leavings, ravings, savings,
shavings.
See also **10.42.178.**

10.47: **1** dip, gyp, hip, kip, pip, sip, skip,
zip; **2** bunyip, gossip, rosehip, sheep-dip,
unzip; **3** skinny-dip.
See also **10.48, 10.49.**

10.47.1: **1** blip, clip, flip, lip; **2** Dilip,
fillip, harelip, Philip, Phillip, polyp, tie clip,
tulip; **3** mint julep, paperclip; **4** stiff upper
lip.
See also **10.42.108, 10.49.**

10.47.2: **1** slip; **2** cowslip, gymslip, half-
slip, landslip, nonslip, payslip, pink slip,
sideslip; **4** Freudian slip.

10.47.3: **1** nip, snip; **2** catnip, parsnip,
turnip.

10.47.4: **1** drip, grip, rip, scrip, trip;
2 death grip, hairgrip, key grip, round trip.
See also **10.42.108, 10.49.**

10.47.5: **1** strip; **2** airstrip, filmstrip,
outstrip; **3** comic strip, Gaza Strip, rumble
strip; **4** median strip.
See also **10.49.**

10.47.6: **1** ship; **2** airship, flagship,
kingship, lightship, longship, mateship,
spaceship, starship, steamship, troopship,
warship, worship; **3** battleship, fellowship,
Ladyship, premiership, trusteeship;
4 apprenticeship, connoisseurship,
generalship, hero worship.
See also **10.42.108.**

10.47.7: **3** authorship, censorship,
dealership, leadership, lectureship,
membership, mother ship, ownership,
partnership, readership, scholarship,
sponsorship, tutorship, weather ship;
4 dictatorship, directorship, editorship,
governorship, premiership, professorship,
receivership.

10.47.8: **2** friendship, hardship, headship,
lordship, wardship; **3** comradeship,
stewardship.

10.47.9: **2** gunship, kinship, township;
3 internship; **4** partisanship.

10.47.10: 4 championship, citizenship, companionship, guardianship, musicianship, relationship; 6 interrelationship.

10.47.11: 3 brinkmanship, chairmanship, gamesmanship, penmanship, salesmanship, seamanship, showmanship, swordsmanship, workmanship; 4 one-upmanship.

10.47.12: 3 craftsmanship, draughtsmanship, horsemanship, marksmanship, sportsmanship, statesmanship.

10.47.13: 1 tip; 2 felt tip, wingtip; 3 filter-tip, fingertip.

10.47.14: 1 chip; 2 blue-chip, corn chip, courtship; 3 microchip, poker chip; 4 silicon chip, tortilla chip.
See also **10.49**.

10.47.15: 1 quip, whip; 2 bullwhip, chief whip, equip, horsewhip; 3 pistol-whip, three-line whip.
See also **10.42.108, 10.49**.

10.48: 1 CHIPS, pips; 2 eclipse, ellipse, Phillips; 3 amidships, fish and chips; 4 apocalypse, lunar eclipse, solar eclipse.
See also **10.47**.

10.49: 1 chipped, clipped, dipped, gripped, stripped, whipped, zipped; 2 Egypt, equipped, tight-lipped; 3 ill-equipped.
See also **10.47, 10.47.1, 10.47.4, 10.47.5, 10.47.14**.

10.49.1: 1 crypt, script; 2 conscript, decrypt, encrypt, postscript, subscript, transcript, typescript; 3 manuscript, nondescript, superscript.
See also **10.2.89**.

10.50: 1 hiss, kiss, Swiss, this; 2 aegis, Burgess, dais, duchess, French kiss, haggis, Lewis, marquess, marquis, Menzies, Powys; 3 Anaïs, archduchess, Judas kiss, St Louis.

You must remember this;
A kiss is still a kiss,
A sigh is just a sigh—
The fundamental things apply
As time goes by.
(Herman Hupfeld)

10.50.1: 1 bis; 2 abyss, ibis, pubis; 3 Anubis, cannabis.

10.50.2: 1 Dis, diss; 2 bodice, caddis, cowardice, Gladys, jaundice, Sardis, Tardis; 3 Charybdis, prejudice.
See also **10.53.2**.

10.50.3: 2 Memphis, office, surface; 3 box office, head office, Home Office, Oval Office, post office, resurface, War Office, work surface; 4 Foreign Office, Holy Office; 5 left-luggage office.

10.50.4: 3 artifice, benefice, edifice, orifice.

10.50.5: 1 bliss; 2 Allis, Ellis, Gillies, surplice, trellis, Wallace, Willis; 3 accomplice, Cornwallis, Marsalis, portcullis; 4 amaryllis; 6 annus mirabilis, aurora australis; 7 aurora borealis.

10.50.6: 2 chalice, malice, Tallis, tallith; 5 Buckingham Palace.

10.50.7: 3 Aeolis, chrysalis, syphilis; 4 Annapolis, Persepolis; 5 Minneapolis; 6 Indianapolis.

10.50.8: 4 acropolis, metropolis, necropolis; 5 Heliopolis, megalopolis.

10.50.9: 1 miss; 2 Amis, amiss, dermis, dismiss, near miss, premise, premiss, promise, pumice, remiss; 3 Artemis, hit-and-miss, hit-or-miss; 4 epidermis, in extremis.
See also **10.42.132, 10.53.10, 10.62.4**.

10.50.10: 2 cornice, Denis, Dennis, furnace, Glenys, harness, penis, tennis, Tunis, Venice; 3 Adonis, real tennis, reminisce; 4 table tennis.
See also **10.53.12**.

10.50.11: 1 piss; 2 auspice, coppice, hospice, Thespis; 3 precipice.
See also **10.53.15**.

10.50.12: 1 kris; 2 Boris, Cerys, Doris, Eris, Harries, Harris, hubris, iris, Morris, Norris, ogress, Paris, Tigris; 3 avarice, Charteris, clitoris, liquorice, Osiris, Polaris; 4 Cader Idris; 5 plaster of Paris.
See also **2.54.124**.

10.50.13: 1 cis, sis; 2 crisis, deixis, Frances, Francis, Isis, lexis; 3 Alexis, catharsis, pertussis, proboscis; 4 autolysis, peristalsis; 5 amanuensis.

10.50.14: 3 emphasis, genesis, nemesis; 4 diaeresis, hydrolysis, metastasis, periphrasis; 5 electrolysis, metamorphosis, overemphasis; 6 parthenogenesis.

10.50.15: 4 analysis, dialysis, paralysis; 5 self-analysis; 6 psychoanalysis.

10.50.16: 3 synthesis; 4 antithesis, hypothesis, parenthesis; 5 biosynthesis, photosynthesis.

10.50.17: 2 basis, stasis; 3 oasis; 5 homeostasis.

Temperature's dropping at the rotten oasis
Stealing kisses from the leperous faces...
(Beck)

10.50.18: 2 thesis; 3 mimesis, prosthesis; 4 exegesis; 5 psychokinesis, telekinesis; 6 amniocentesis.

10.50.19: 2 diocese; 3 archdiocese, psoriasis; 4 giardiasis; 5 elephantiasis.

10.50.20: 3 diagnosis, hypnosis, meiosis, mitosis, narcosis, osmosis, prognosis, psychosis, thrombosis; 4 halitosis, psittacosis, silicosis, symbiosis; 5 apotheosis, myxomatosis, tuberculosis; 6 mononucleosis; 7 coronary thrombosis.

10.50.21: 3 cirrhosis, necrosis, neurosis, sclerosis; 5 cystic fibrosis, leptospirosis; 6 atherosclerosis, multiple sclerosis, osteoporosis; 7 arteriosclerosis.

10.50.22: 2 axis, praxis; 3 x-axis, y-axis, z-axis; 4 prophylaxis; 5 anaphylaxis.

10.50.23: 2 sepsis; 3 asepsis, ellipsis, synopsis; 4 antisepsis.

10.50.24: 2 Curtis, glottis, gratis, lattice, lettuce, mortice, mortise, notice, Otis, poultice, practice, practise, Thetis; 3 clematis, malpractice, sharp practice; 4 epiglottis, Nunc Dimittis, rigor mortis. *See also* **10.42, 10.53.22**.

10.50.25: 3 bronchitis, bursitis, phlebitis, rhinitis; 4 gingivitis, laryngitis, meningitis, pharyngitis, sinusitis, tendinitis; 5 appendicitis, conjunctivitis, peritonitis; 6 tenosinovitis.

10.50.26: 3 colitis; 4 tonsillitis; 5 encephalitis; 6 diverticulitis; 7 poliomyelitis.

10.50.27: 3 arthritis, gastritis, nephritis; 4 enteritis; 6 gastroenteritis, osteoarthritis, rheumatoid arthritis.

10.50.28: 3 cystitis, mastitis, otitis; 4 dermatitis, hepatitis.

10.50.29: 2 countess, mantis, Prentice; 3 apprentice, Atlantis; 4 compos mentis; 5 non compos mentis; 6 in loco parentis.

10.50.30: 2 hostess, justice, solstice, testis; 3 air hostess, armistice, injustice,

interstice; 4 court of justice, winter solstice; 5 poetic justice. *See also* **9.59.13**.

10.50.31: 2 Alvis, Avis, Clovis, crevice, Davies, Davis, Elvis, Jarvis, Leavis, mavis, novice, pelvis, Travis; 3 Ben Nevis; 5 St Kitts and Nevis.

10.50.32: 2 service; 3 disservice, ex-service, in-service, lip service, self-service, wire service, World Service; 4 civil service, secret service, shuttle service; 5 national service, order of service, Special Air Service, Special Boat Service; 6 diplomatic service, National Health Service; 7 Crown Prosecution Service. *See also* **10.62.4**.

10.51: 1 bisque, fisc, whisk; 2 egg whisk; 3 basilisk, obelisk, odalisque.

10.51.1: 1 disc, disk; 2 hard disk; 3 compact disc, floppy disk, minidisc.

10.51.2: 1 brisk, frisk, RISC, risk; 3 asterisk, tamarisk.

10.52: 1 crisp, lisp, wisp; 4 potato crisp, will-o'-the-wisp. *See also* **9.14.79**.

10.53: 1 fist, schist; 2 cubist, desist, driest, druggist, dryest, exist, farthest, fascist, furthest, Maoist, resist, sophist; 3 altruist, amethyst, casuist, coexist, egoist, essayist, fetishist, jingoist, pacifist, soloist, tattooist. *See also* **10.42.170**.

10.53.1: 3 atheist, copyist, hobbyist, lobbyist, Trotskyist.

10.53.2: 2 damnedest, jaundiced, modest, nudist, sadist; 3 immodest, keyboardist, Methodist, prejudiced; 4 chiropodist, orthopaedist, propagandist. *See also* **10.50.2**.

10.53.3: 1 gist; 2 ageist; 3 elegist, strategist, suffragist.

10.53.4: 4 apologist, biologist, cosmologist, ecologist, geologist, pathologist, psychologist, technologist, zoologist; 5 archaeologist, cardiologist, climatologist, dermatologist, embryologist, escapologist, gynaecologist, ideologist, immunologist, numerologist, ophthalmologist, ornithologist.

10.53.5: 2 stockist, sun-kissed; 3 anarchist, masochist, monarchist.

10.53.6: 1 list, Liszt; 2 A-list, backlist, blacklist, B-list, cellist, checklist, cyclist, enlist, hotlist, playlist, price list, realist, shitlist, shortlist, stylist, waitlist, word list,

Z-list; **3** civil list, Honours List, idealist, nihilist, oculist, populist, pugilist, shopping list, waiting list; **4** somnambulist.
See also **10.2.92, 10.42.170.**

10.53.7: **3** analyst, finalist, herbalist, journalist, Kabbalist, loyalist, medallist, moralist, novelist, panellist, royalist, socialist, specialist, vocalist; **4** evangelist, generalist, minimalist, monopolist, naturalist, removalist, revivalist; **5** colonialist, existentialist, imperialist, industrialist, psychoanalyst, semifinalist, televangelist; **6** individualist.

10.53.8: **4** nationalist, rationalist; **5** traditionalist; **6** conversationalist, educationalist.

10.53.9: **3** catalyst; **4** capitalist; **5** fundamentalist, instrumentalist, orientalist, Pentecostalist; **6** environmentalist.

10.53.10: **1** mist; **2** chemist, dismissed, palmist, promised, psalmist, Scotch mist; **3** alarmist, animist, conformist, extremist, optimist, reformist; **4** biochemist, nonconformist.
See also **10.50.9.**

10.53.11: **3** alchemist, bigamist, Islamist, pessimist; **4** economist, polygamist, Soroptimist.

10.53.12: **2** earnest, Ernest, harnessed, honest; **3** alpinist, bassoonist, Calvinist, cartoonist, columnist, communist, dishonest, humanist, hygienist, internist, lampoonist, Leninist, machinist; **4** opportunist.
See also **9.14.95, 10.50.10.**

10.53.13: **3** arsonist, botanist, chauvinist, colonist, feminist, hedonist, modernist, organist, pianist, Satanist, timpanist, Unionist; **4** accompanist, antagonist, illusionist, misogynist, protagonist, revisionist, saxophonist, telephonist, tobacconist; **5** coreligionist.

10.53.14: **4** abortionist, contortionist, expansionist, extortionist, Impressionist, nutritionist, obstructionist, percussionist, perfectionist, projectionist, receptionist; **5** abolitionist, conservationist, devolutionist, educationist, evolutionist, exhibitionist, isolationist, preservationist, prohibitionist.

10.53.15: **1** pissed; **2** papist, rapist, tempest, Trappist, typist; **3** escapist,

therapist; **4** philanthropist; **5** audiotypist, psychotherapist; **6** physiotherapist.
See also **10.50.11.**

10.53.16: **1** grist, tryst, wrist; **2** centrist, tourist; **3** careerist, psychiatrist; **4** optometrist.

10.53.17: **2** diarist, theorist; **3** Eucharist, Everest, futurist, humorist, motorist, naturist, plagiarist, satirist, terrorist; **4** miniaturist, monetarist; **5** bioterrorist, caricaturist, cyberterrorist, ecoterrorist, horticulturist.

10.53.18: **2** florist, forest, Forrest; **3** afforest, deforest, New Forest, rainforest.

10.53.19: **2** jurist, purist, tourist; **4** manicurist, pedicurist.

10.53.20: **1** cyst; **2** assist, bassist, consist, insist, Marxist, persist, racist, sexist, subsist; **3** exorcist, pharmacist; **4** supremacist.

10.53.21: **3** classicist, lyricist, narcissist, physicist, publicist; **4** empiricist, geneticist, polemicist; **5** astrophysicist, geophysicist.

10.53.22: **2** Baptist, flautist, latest, leftist, occultist, practised, rightist; **3** defeatist, egotist, elitist, librettist, unnoticed, unpractised; **4** absolutist, Anabaptist, John the Baptist, parachutist.
See also **10.50.24.**

10.53.23: **3** dogmatist, dramatist, hypnotist, pragmatist; **4** anaesthetist, diplomatist, numismatist, separatist.

10.53.24: **2** artist; **3** con artist, drag artist, trapeze artist; **4** escape artist; **6** variety artist.

10.53.25: **2** dentist, faintest, scientist; **4** orthodontist; **5** Christian Scientist; **6** Seventh-Day Adventist.

10.53.26: **2** harvest; **3** activist, archivist, reservist; **4** collectivist, positivist, recidivist.

10.53.27: **1** twist, whist; **2** linguist; **4** Oliver Twist, ventriloquist.
See also **10.2.92.**

10.54: **1** ish; **2** bluish, boyish, hashish, Jewish, knavish, largish, longish, shrewish, youngish; **3** babyish, toadyish, yellowish.

10.54.1: **2** rubbish, snobbish, yobbish; **3** refurbish.

10.54.2: **1** dish; **2** childish, cloddish, coldish, deep-dish, goodish, Kurdish, modish, oldish, prudish, reddish, side dish, Swedish, Yiddish; **3** Petri dish.
See also **10.62.**

10.54.3: **2** caddish, faddish, laddish, radish; **3** horseradish.

10.54.4: **2** blandish, brandish, fiendish; **3** Cavendish, outlandish.

10.54.5: **1** fish, phish; **2** blowfish, codfish, crawfish, crayfish, dogfish, flyfish, goldfish, monkfish, oafish, raffish, sawfish, selfish, shellfish, starfish, sunfish, swordfish, wolfish; **3** cuttlefish, jellyfish, overfish, silverfish, standoffish, unselfish. *See also* **10.42.142.**

10.54.6: **2** catfish, flatfish, wet fish, whitefish; **3** parrotfish, pilot fish.

10.54.7: **2** aguish, doggish, piggish, priggish, roguish, sluggish, thuggish, voguish, waggish.

10.54.8: **2** blokeish, bookish, brackish, cliquish, darkish, freakish, gawkish, hawkish, mawkish, peckish, pinkish, puckish, quackish, rakish, Turkish.

10.54.9: **2** Ailish, bullish, churlish, coolish, foolish, ghoulish, girlish, hellish, Japlish, mulish, owlish, Polish, relish, smallish, stylish; **3** accomplish, devilish, embellish, purplish, ticklish, unstylish. *See also* **10.55.1.**

10.54.10: **2** polish; **3** abolish, demolish, French polish, nail polish, shoe polish; **4** spit and polish. *See also* **10.55.**

10.54.11: **2** publish, weblish; **3** establish, republish; **4** disestablish, reestablish. *See also* **10.42.142, 10.55.1.**

10.54.12: **2** English, Spanglish; **3** Old English, Queen's English.

10.54.13: **2** Amish, Beamish, blemish, famish, Flemish, Hamish, skirmish, squeamish. *See also* **10.42.142.**

10.54.14: **2** brownish, burnish, clownish, Cornish, Danish, donnish, finish, Finnish, furnish, greenish, punish; **3** admonish, astonish, diminish, kittenish, replenish, womanish; **4** photo finish. *See also* **10.42.142, 10.55.2, 10.55.3.**

10.54.15: **2** banish, clannish, garnish, mannish, Spanish, tarnish, vanish, varnish; **3** nail varnish. *See also* **10.55.2.**

10.54.16: **2** apish, foppish, frumpish, impish, lumpish, popish, sharpish, sheepish, snappish, waspish, wimpish.

10.54.17: **2** boorish, cherish, flourish, Irish, Moorish, moreish, nourish, parish, Parrish, perish, whorish; **4** Anglo-Irish. *See also* **10.42.142, 10.55.4.**

10.54.18: **2** bearish, garish, squarish; **3** feverish, gibberish, jibberish, lickerish, liquorice, liverish, nightmarish, spinsterish; **4** amateurish, impoverish. *See also* **10.55.4.**

10.54.19: **2** British, brutish, coltish, doltish, fetish, loutish, pettish, Scottish, skittish, sluttish, smartish, sweetish, wheatish, whitish; **3** coquettish.

10.54.20: **2** dervish, dovish, lavish, peevish, ravish, slavish. *See also* **10.42.142.**

10.54.21: **1** squish, swish, wish; **2** vanquish; **3** relinquish.

10.54.22: **2** anguish, languish; **3** distinguish, extinguish. *See also* **10.42.142, 10.55.**

10.55: **2** anguished, famished, furbished, polished; **3** distinguished, unblemished; **4** undistinguished. *See also* **10.54.10, 10.54.22.**

10.55.1: **2** published; **3** accomplished, embellished, established, unpolished, unpublished; **4** long-established, well-established. *See also* **10.54.9, 10.54.11.**

10.55.2: **2** banished, furnished, varnished; **3** astonished, unfurnished, unpunished, untarnished, unvarnished. *See also* **10.54.14, 10.54.15.**

10.55.3: **2** finished; **3** diminished, half-finished, unfinished; **4** undiminished. *See also* **10.54.14.**

10.55.4: **2** cherished, perished; **3** malnourished; **4** impoverished, undernourished. *See also* **10.54.17, 10.54.18.**

10.56: **1** chit, hit, it, tit; **2** base hit, bluetit, crotchet, hatchet, mishit, poet, Post-it, ratchet, smash hit; **3** albeit. *See also* **10.57.**

10.56.1: **2** cruet, suet; **3** conduit, intuit, Inuit, Jesuit.

10.56.2: **1** bit; **2** ambit, Babbitt, Cobbett, cubit, debit, gambit, gibbet, gobbet, hobbit, Nesbit, obit, orbit, rarebit, Tebbitt, titbit, two-bit; **3** exhibit, gigabit, inhibit, kilobit, megabit, prohibit, Welsh rarebit; **4** direct debit. *See also* **10.2.59, 10.57.**

10.56.3: **2** habit, rabbit; **3** Brer rabbit, cohabit, inhabit, jackrabbit; **4** bunny rabbit, Peter rabbit.
See also **10.2.59**.

10.56.4: **2** adit, audit, bandit, conduit, edit, geddit, pandit, plaudit, pundit; **3** subedit; **4** copy-edit, one-armed bandit.
See also **10.2.59, 10.42.156**.

10.56.5: **2** credit; **3** accredit, discredit; **4** line of credit; **5** family credit, letter of credit, revolving credit.
See also **10.2.59, 10.57**.

10.56.6: **1** fit; **2** befit, buffet, comfit, E-FIT, forfeit, misfit, nymphet, outfit, profit, prophet, refit, surfeit, unfit; **3** benefit, counterfeit, discomfit, fighting fit, Photofit, retrofit; **4** paper profit.
One science only will one genius fit:
So vast is art, so narrow human wit.
(Alexander Pope)
See also **10.2.59, 10.42.156, 10.57**.

10.56.7: **1** git; **2** nugget, old git, ringgit, target, vulgate; **3** off-target, on-target; **4** sitting target.
See also **10.2.59**.

10.56.8: **2** budget, gadget; **3** fussbudget, low-budget; **4** tempus fugit.

10.56.9: **2** Bridget, digit, fidget, legit, midget, widget; **4** double-digit.

10.56.10: **1** kit; **2** Becket, Beckett, blanket, Blunkett, bucket, circuit, junket, toolkit, trinket; **3** ice bucket, short-circuit, wet blanket.

10.56.11: **2** bracket, packet, racket, racquet; **3** wage packet.
See also **10.2.59, 10.57**.

10.56.12: **2** jacket; **3** dust jacket, lifejacket, ski jacket, straightjacket, straitjacket; **4** dinner jacket, donkey jacket, reefer jacket, riding jacket; **5** safari jacket.

10.56.13: **2** Haymarket, market; **3** black market, downmarket, flea market, mass-market, Newmarket, stock market, street market, upmarket; **4** aftermarket, buyer's market, Common Market, covered market, farmers' market, forward market, hypermarket, money market, open market, seller's market, supermarket.
See also **10.42.156**.

10.56.14: **2** cricket, picket, thicket, ticket, wicket; **3** big-ticket, meal ticket, mid-wicket; **4** Identikit, one-way ticket.

10.56.15: **2** docket, locket, pocket, socket; **3** air pocket, pickpocket; **4** out-of-pocket.

10.56.16: **2** Crockett, rocket, sprocket; **3** skyrocket; **4** retrorocket.

10.56.17: **1** skit; **2** biscuit, brisket, gasket, musket.

10.56.18: **2** basket, casket; **3** breadbasket, wastebasket; **4** Moses basket, picnic basket.

10.56.19: **1** flit, lit, slit, split; **2** alit, backlit, bullet, Dalit, floodlit, Follett, gullet, Hazlitt, ill-lit, mallet, moonlit, mullet, pellet, pullet, scarlet, spotlit, starlit, sunlit, twilit, unlit, valet, wallet; **3** candlelit, red mullet; **4** lickety-split, plastic bullet, rubber bullet; **5** whatchamacallit.
See also **10.42.157**.

10.56.20: **2** billet, filet, fillet, millet, skillet.

10.56.21: **1** mitt; **2** admit, dammit, emmet, helmet, hermit, Kermit, Mamet, pelmet, permit, plummet, remit, submit, summit, transmit; **3** crash helmet, goddammit, Hindemith, manumit, pith helmet, readmit.

10.56.22: **2** comet, commit, emit, grommet, limit, omit, remit, vomit; **3** delimit, speed limit; **4** credit limit.
See also **10.2.59, 10.42.156**.

10.56.23: **1** knit, nit; **2** Bennett, bonnet, Burnet, close-knit, cornet, garnet, hornet, magnet, punnet, rennet, signet, sonnet, tenet, tightknit, unit; **3** bayonet, coronet, subunit, whodunit; **4** SI unit.
See also **10.42.156**.

10.56.24: **2** gannet, granite, Janet, planet; **3** red planet; **4** Lonely Planet.

10.56.25: **2** innit, linnet, minute; **3** last minute; **5** up-to-the-minute.
See also **2.57**.

10.56.26: **1** pit, Pitt, spit; **2** carpet, cesspit, cockpit, fleapit, muppet, poppet, pulpit, puppet, respite, sandpit; **3** decrepit, parapet, red carpet; **4** magic carpet.
See also **10.2.59, 10.42.156**.

10.56.27: **2** pipit, snippet, tippet, Tippett, whippet.

10.56.28: **2** armpit, crumpet, limpet, strumpet, trumpet; **3** ear trumpet.

10.56.29: **1** Brit, frit, grit, writ; **2** bowsprit, culprit, portrait, Sanskrit,

turret; **3** Holy Writ, hypocrite, interpret, preterite; **4** misinterpret.
See also **10.2.60, 10.57.1.**

10.56.30: **2** ferret, merit; **3** demerit, inherit; **4** disinherit.
See also **10.2.60.**

10.56.31: **2** spirit; **3** dispirit, free spirit, team spirit; **4** Holy Spirit, kindred spirit; **6** methylated spirit.
See also **10.2.60, 10.57.1.**

10.56.32: **1** sit; **2** basset, bedsit, corset, cosset, Dorset, dulcet, exit, facet, faucet, gusset, house-sit, Lancet, posset, resit, russet, tacit, whatsit; **3** babysit, deficit, plebiscite.
See also **10.42.156.**

10.56.33: **2** licit; **3** complicit, elicit, explicit, illicit, implicit, solicit.
See also **10.42.156.**

10.56.34: **1** shit; **2** bullshit, dipshit, horseshit.
See also **10.42.156.**

10.56.35: **2** civet, rivet, trivet, velvet; **4** affidavit.
See also **10.42.156.**

10.56.36: **1** twit, whit, wit; **2** dimwit, halfwit, nitwit, outwit, peewit; **3** native wit.
See also **10.57.**

10.56.37: **1** quit; **2** acquit, banquet, fuckwit.
See also **10.57.**

10.56.38: **1** zit; **2** closet, howzit, posit, transit; **3** apposite, composite, deposit, opposite; **4** safe-deposit, water closet.
See also **10.2.59.**

10.56.39: **2** visit; **3** exquisite, home visit, perquisite, requisite, revisit; **4** prerequisite.

10.57: **1** bits, blitz, glitz, it's, its, quits, tits, wits; **2** Auschwitz, credits, Leibniz, plaudits, profits, rackets, racquets, rickets; **3** Austerlitz, Horowitz, off-limits, slivovitz, square brackets.
See also **10.56, 10.56.2, 10.56.5, 10.56.6, 10.56.11, 10.56.36, 10.56.37.**

10.57.1: **1** grits, spritz; **2** Biarritz, spirits; **3** good spirits, high spirits, low spirits.
See also **10.56.29, 10.56.31.**

10.58: **1** fifth, Frith, kith, myth, pith; **2** Edith, Griffith, Hadith, Judith, tallith, zenith; **3** megalith, Meredith, monolith, urban myth.
See also **10.6.**

10.58.1: **1** smith; **2** blacksmith, goldsmith, gunsmith, locksmith, wordsmith; **3** Hammersmith, silversmith.

10.58.2: **1** with; **2** Asquith, forthwith, herewith.

10.59: **1** bitch, ditch, flitch, glitch, hitch, itch, kitsch, niche, pitch, rich, snitch, stitch, titch; **2** cross-stitch, Dulwich, enrich, Greenwich, Harwich, last-ditch, ostrich, Shoreditch, unhitch, whipstitch; **3** dhobi itch; **4** Milosevic, Shostakovich.
See also **10.60.**

10.59.1: **1** switch, twitch, which, witch; **2** bewitch, Prestwich, sandwich; **3** club sandwich.
See also **10.42.175, 10.60.**

10.60: **1** hitched, pitched, switched; **2** bewitched, enriched, high-pitched, low-pitched.
See also **10.59, 10.59.1.**

10.61: **1** give, spiv; **2** endive, forgive, Kharkiv; **3** corrosive; **4** self-adhesive.
See also **10.5, 10.42.180.**

10.61.1: **1** live; **2** olive, outlive, relive.
See also **10.42.176, 11.40.**

10.61.2: **1** sieve; **2** cursive, massive, passive, plosive; **3** abrasive, adhesive, allusive, coercive, cohesive, corrosive, discursive, elusive, explosive, impassive, percussive, persuasive, possessive, recursive, reflexive, subversive.
See also **2.54.90, 9.14.98.**

10.61.3: **3** evasive, invasive, pervasive; **4** noninvasive.
See also **9.14.98.**

10.61.4: **3** aggressive, progressive, regressive; **4** nonaggressive, retrogressive.

10.61.5: **3** depressive, expressive, impressive, oppressive, repressive; **4** inexpressive, unimpressive; **5** manic-depressive.
See also **9.14.98.**

10.61.6: **3** excessive, obsessive, recessive, successive.
See also **9.14.98.**

10.61.7: **2** missive; **3** dismissive, permissive, submissive.
See also **2.54.90.**

10.61.8: **3** decisive, derisive, divisive, incisive; **4** indecisive.
See also **2.54.90, 9.14.98.**

10.61.9: **3** abusive, conducive, effusive, illusive, intrusive, obtrusive; **4** unobtrusive.

10.61.10: 3 conclusive, exclusive, inclusive, reclusive; 4 all-inclusive, inconclusive.

10.61.11: 3 compulsive, convulsive, impulsive, repulsive.

10.61.12: 3 expansive, responsive; 4 apprehensive, comprehensive, unresponsive.

10.61.13: 2 pensive; 3 defensive, expensive, extensive, intensive, offensive; 4 coextensive, inexpensive, inoffensive; 5 counteroffensive; 6 capital-intensive. *See also* **2.54.90.**

10.61.14: 2 furtive, sportive; 3 abortive, assertive, contrastive, exhaustive, expletive, supportive; 4 self-assertive.

10.61.15: 3 additive, combative, fugitive, primitive, sedative, talkative; 4 affirmative, appreciative, educative, initiative, intuitive, palliative, rebarbative; 5 associative, participative.

10.61.16: 3 ergative, negative, purgative; 4 prerogative; 5 interrogative, investigative.

10.61.17: 3 fricative; 4 indicative, predicative; 5 communicative; 6 uncommunicative.

10.61.18: 3 locative, vocative; 4 evocative, provocative. *See also* **9.14.100.**

10.61.19: 3 ablative, relative; 4 contemplative, correlative, legislative, superlative.

10.61.20: 4 cumulative, speculative; 5 accumulative, manipulative.

10.61.21: 3 formative, normative; 4 informative; 5 uninformative.

10.61.22: 3 cognitive, genitive, punitive; 4 alternative.

10.61.23: 4 definitive, infinitive, nominative; 5 agglutinative, imaginative; 6 unimaginative.

10.61.24: 3 curative, lucrative, narrative, nutritive, secretive; 4 comparative, declarative, imperative, pejorative, penetrative, restorative. *See also* **9.14.100.**

10.61.25: 4 decorative, figurative, generative, iterative; 5 alliterative, collaborative, commemorative, corroborative, degenerative, deliberative, recuperative, remunerative, vituperative; 7 neurodegenerative.

10.61.26: 4 operative; 5 cooperative, inoperative, postoperative; 6 uncooperative.

10.61.27: 4 demonstrative, illustrative; 5 administrative, undemonstrative.

10.61.28: 3 fixative, laxative, transitive; 4 ditransitive, intransitive.

10.61.29: 3 sensitive; 4 insensitive; 5 hypersensitive, oversensitive, photosensitive. *See also* **9.14.99.**

10.61.30: 3 partitive, putative; 4 competitive, consultative, exploitative, repetitive, vegetative; 5 noncompetitive, uncompetitive; 6 anticompetitive, hypercompetitive.

10.61.31: 4 imitative, meditative, qualitative, quantitative; 5 authoritative, interpretative.

10.61.32: 3 tentative; 4 frequentative, preventative; 5 argumentative, representative; 6 unrepresentative.

10.61.33: 4 conservative, derivative, innovative, preservative; 6 neoconservative.

10.61.34: 3 causative, positive; 4 accusative, acquisitive, inquisitive; 6 HIV-positive.

10.61.35: 2 dative, native, stative; 3 creative; 4 innovative.

10.61.36: 3 fugitive, sensitive; 4 interpretive, intransitive, precognitive, prohibitive; 6 counterintuitive. *See also* **9.14.99.**

10.61.37: 2 motive, votive; 3 emotive; 4 automotive, locomotive.

10.61.38: 4 attributive, consecutive, diminutive, distributive, executive; 5 chief executive. *See also* **9.14.100.**

10.61.39: 2 octave; 3 conjunctive, disjunctive, distinctive, instinctive, subjunctive. *See also* **2.54.91.**

10.61.40: 2 active; 3 attractive, inactive, reactive; 4 hyperactive, interactive, overactive, unattractive. *See also* **2.54.91.**

10.61.41: 3 proactive; 4 psychoactive, retroactive; 5 radioactive.

10.61.42: 3 affective, connective, corrective, detective, directive, invective,

objective, protective, subjective;
5 overprotective, private detective.

10.61.43: **3** defective, effective; **4** cost-effective, ineffective.
See also **2.54.91**.

10.61.44: **3** collective, elective, reflective, selective.

10.61.45: **3** perspective, prospective, respective; **4** introspective, irrespective, retrospective.

10.61.46: **2** fictive; **3** addictive, adjective, predictive, restrictive, vindictive; **4** nonrestrictive.

10.61.47: **3** conductive, deductive, inductive, productive, reductive, seductive; **4** reproductive, unproductive; **5** counterproductive.

10.61.48: **3** constructive, destructive, instructive, obstructive.

10.61.49: **2** plaintive; **3** attentive, incentive, inventive, preventive, retentive, substantive; **4** disincentive, inattentive; **5** anal-retentive.
See also **2.54.91**.

10.61.50: **2** captive; **3** adaptive, adoptive, consumptive, descriptive, disruptive, preemptive, prescriptive, presumptive, redemptive; **4** heir presumptive.

10.61.51: **3** deceptive, perceptive, receptive; **4** contraceptive, unreceptive.
See also **2.54.91, 9.14.99**.

10.61.52: **2** festive, restive; **3** digestive, suggestive.
See also **9.14.99**.

10.62: **1** biz, fizz, his, is, 'tis, viz; **2** Ashes, Cadiz, dishes, Kyrgyz, ladies, Moses, Rockies, showbiz, Suez, treatise; **3** galoshes.
See also **9.6, 9.7.6, 10.54.2**.

10.62.1: **2** Bridges, Hodges, Judges, wages; **3** damages, ravages, vestiges; **4** Rock of Ages, Yellow Pages.
See also **5.26, 10.11.8, 10.11.25, 10.11.26**.

10.62.2: **1** frizz; **2** Humphries, Jeffreys; **3** Benares, vagaries; **4** Buenos Aires.

10.62.3: **2** braces, glasses, Graces, masses, pulses, races, taxes, tresses; **3** bootlaces, finances, molasses, provinces, resources, sunglasses; **4** airs and graces, circumstances, condolences, false pretences, greenhouse gases, social graces; **5** human resources.
Men seldom make passes

At girls who wear glasses.
(Dorothy Parker)
See also **1.11.4, 1.23, 1.36.3, 2.45.13, 2.45.35, 3.37, 3.43.1, 6.47.4, 10.36, 14.42, 14.42.4, 20.21**.

10.62.4: **2** missis, missus, Mrs; **3** auspices, good offices, premises, services; **5** social services.
See also **9.49, 10.50.9, 10.50.32**.

10.62.5: **2** breeches, britches, clutches, haunches, Marches, riches.
See also **3.52, 14.39, 20.49**.

10.62.6: **1** quiz, squiz, swizz, whiz, wiz.

10.62.7: **2** Joneses, Menzies; **3** assizes; **4** bed of roses, elevenses.

11.0: **1** aye, chai, die, dye, eye, guy, I, my, sky, tchai, thigh, thy, vie, why; **2** AI, Birdseye, bull's eye, Karzai, Magi, zaikai; **3** DIY, do-or-die, DUI, naked eye; **6** DWI.
Abide with me from morn till eve,
For without Thee I cannot live;
Abide with me when night is nigh,
For without Thee I dare not die.
(John Keble)
See also **10.42.5**.

11.1: **2** GI; **3** DTI, FBI, radii; **4** minutiae.

11.2: **1** bai, bhai, bi, buy, by, bye; **2** drive-by, Dubai, goodbye, hereby, lay-by, nearby, rabbi, standby, swing-by, thereby, whereby; **3** alibi, bring-and-buy, lullaby, passer-by.
Two roads diverged in a wood, and I—
I took the one less traveled by,
And that has made all the difference.
(Robert Frost)

11.3: **2** hi-fi, sci-fi; **3** PFI.

11.3.1: **3** deify, Frenchify, liquefy, mummify, stupefy, typify, yuppify; **4** revivify.
See also **11.14.2**.

11.3.2: **2** defy; **3** codify, edify, modify, trendify; **4** acidify, humidify, solidify; **5** dehumidify.
See also **10.42.6, 11.14.2**.

11.3.3: **3** amplify, mollify, nullify, qualify, simplify, vilify; **4** disqualify, exemplify; **5** oversimplify.
See also **11.14.3**.

11.3.4: **3** dignify, magnify, signify, unify; **4** indemnify, personify, reunify.
See also **11.14.4**.

11.3.5: **3** clarify, glorify, horrify, purify, scarify, terrify, verify; **4** transmogrify.
See also **10.42.6, 11.14.2, 11.14.5**.

11.3.6: **3** gentrify, nitrify, petrify, putrefy, vitrify; **4** devitrify, electrify.
See also **10.42.6, 11.14.5.**

11.3.7: **3** calcify, classify, crucify, falsify, ossify, pacify, specify, versify; **4** declassify, detoxify, diversify, emulsify, intensify, reclassify.
See also **11.14.6.**

11.3.8: **3** beautify, certify, fortify, fructify, gratify, mortify, notify, prettify, quantify, ratify, rectify, sanctify; **4** beatify, identify, objectify.
See also **10.42.6, 11.14.7.**

11.3.9: **3** justify, mystify, satisfy, testify; **4** demystify, dissatisfy.
See also **10.42.5, 11.14.7.**

11.4: **1** hi, high; **2** Baha'i, chest-high, knee-high, sky-high, thigh-high, waist-high.

11.5: **1** Bligh, Bly, lie, sly; **2** Adlai, ally, Eli, July, outlie, white lie; **3** barefaced lie, E. coli; **4** RNLI.
See also **2.54.73, 9.14.43, 10.42.7, 11.14.10, 11.42.3.**

11.5.1: **2** belie, rely; **3** alkali, evil eye, overlie, underlie.
See also **10.42.7.**

11.5.2: **1** fly; **2** barfly, blackfly, blowfly, crane fly, dry fly, firefly, fruit fly, gadfly, greenfly, horsefly, housefly, mayfly, sandfly, wet fly, whitefly; **3** butterfly, damselfly, dragonfly, overfly, tsetse fly; **4** ichneumon fly; **5** Madam Butterfly.
'Will you walk into my parlour?' said a
spider to a fly:
''Tis the prettiest little parlour that ever
you did spy.'
(Mary Howitt)
See also **10.42.7, 11.42.3.**

11.5.3: **1** ply; **2** apply, comply, imply, reply, supply, three-ply, two-ply; **3** misapply, multiply, reapply; **4** oversupply, power supply, undersupply.
See also **11.14.10, 11.42.3.**

11.6: **1** nigh; **2** Brunei, deny, well-nigh; **3** Gemini; **5** anno domini; **6** dramatis personae.
Now I've laid me down to die
I pray my neighbors not to pry
Too deeply into sins that I
Not only cannot here deny
But much enjoyed as life flew by.
(Preston Sturges)
See also **11.14.12.**

11.7: **1** pi, pie, spy; **2** espy, magpie, mince pie, Popeye, pork pie; **3** apple pie, cottage pie, custard pie, humble pie, key lime pie, occupy, pecan pie, pumpkin pie; **4** preoccupy; **5** lemon meringue pie; **6** Mississippi mud pie.
See also **11.14.13.**

11.8: **1** braai, cry, dry, fry, pry, rai, rye, spry, try, wry; **2** awry, decry, deep-fry, lamb's fry, outcry, retry, stir-fry, war cry, wind-dry; **3** high and dry, hue and cry, samurai; **4** a priori, penalty try, rallying cry; **5** a fortiori, Alpha centauri, caravanserai; **6** a posteriori.
See also **9.14.43, 10.42.5, 11.14.15, 11.14.16.**

11.9: **1** sigh; **2** bonsai, Catseye; **3** prophesy; **4** decree nisi.

11.10: **1** shy; **2** cockshy, gun-shy, workshy; **4** camera-shy.
See also **2.54.73.**

11.11: **1** sty, Thai, tie; **2** black tie, bow tie, club tie, necktie, pigsty, untie, white tie; **3** old school tie; **6** curriculum vitae.
See also **10.42.5, 11.14.26.**

11.12: **1** gibe, jibe, vibe; **2** imbibe.

11.12.1: **1** bribe, scribe, tribe; **2** ascribe, describe, diatribe, inscribe, prescribe, proscribe, subscribe, transcribe; **3** circumscribe, unsubscribe.
See also **11.13.**

11.13: **1** bribed; **2** prescribed; **3** circumscribed; **4** oversubscribed.
See also **11.12.1.**

11.14: **1** bide, chide, I'd; **2** abide, collide, dry-eyed, hawk-eyed, pie-eyed, preside, reside, wide-eyed, wild-eyed; **3** goggle-eyed.
See also **10.42.19.**

11.14.1: **3** dewy-eyed, glassy-eyed, heavy-eyed, misty-eyed, starry-eyed.

11.14.2: **2** confide, sulphide; **3** codified, countrified, deified, modified, mummified, stupefied, terrified; **7** genetically modified.
See also **10.42.19, 11.3.1, 11.3.2, 11.3.5.**

11.14.3: **3** mollified, qualified; **4** disqualified, unqualified; **5** overqualified.
See also **11.3.3.**

11.14.4: **3** dignified, magnified, unified; **4** undignified.
See also **11.3.4.**

11.14.5: 3 clarified, glorified, horrified, petrified, rarefied, verified; 4 electrified. *See also* **11.3.5, 11.3.6.**

11.14.6: 3 classified, falsified; 4 declassified, diversified, unclassified, unspecified. *See also* **11.3.7.**

11.14.7: 3 beautified, certified, fortified, gratified, justified, mortified, mystified, satisfied, stratified; 4 dissatisfied, unfortified, unjustified, unsatisfied; 5 unidentified. *See also* **11.3.8, 11.3.9.**

11.14.8: 1 guide; 2 bug-eyed, Girl Guide, misguide.
Everyman, I will go with thee, and be thy guide,
In thy most need to go by thy side.
(Anonymous)

11.14.9: 1 hide, Hyde; 2 cowhide, horsehide, oxhide, pighide, rawhide; 3 aldehyde; 4 formaldehyde, Jekyll and Hyde. *See also* **10.42.19.**

11.14.10: 1 glide, slide; 2 allied, applied, elide, hang glide, implied, landslide, mudslide, nuclide; 3 misapplied, waterslide. *See also* **11.5, 11.5.3.**

11.14.11: 2 amide, bromide; 4 polyamide, thalidomide.

11.14.12: 1 snide; 2 cyanide, denied, green-eyed; 3 actinide, open-eyed. *See also* **11.6.**

11.14.13: 1 pied; 2 sharp-eyed; 3 occupied; 4 preoccupied, unoccupied. *See also* **11.7.**

11.14.14: 1 bride, cried, fried, pride, ride; 2 chloride, deep-fried, deride, fluoride, joy-ride, McBride, war bride; 3 override, park-and-ride.

11.14.15: 1 dried; 2 freeze-dried, sun-dried; 3 cut-and-dried. *See also* **11.8.**

11.14.16: 1 stride, tried; 2 astride, bestride, untried, well-tried. *See also* **11.8, 11.15.**

11.14.17: 1 side; 2 airside, backside, boss-eyed, cross-eyed, fireside, graveside, hillside, kerbside, lakeside, nearside, offside, outside, poolside, ringside, stateside, subside, topside, upside, wayside; 3 alongside, Argus-eyed. *See also* **10.42.19.**

11.14.18: 2 aside; 3 five-a-side, genocide, riverside, set-aside, underside, waterside.
Lost inside
Adorable illusion and I cannot hide;
I'm the one you're using, please don't push me aside;
We coulda made it cruising, yeah...
(Blondie)

11.14.19: 2 B side, quayside, seaside; 3 countryside, Merseyside.

11.14.20: 2 beside, decide; 3 fungicide, germicide, herbicide, homicide, regicide, spermicide, suicide, vermicide; 4 tyrannicide. *See also* **10.2.9, 10.42.19.**

11.14.21: 3 fratricide, matricide, parricide, patricide; 4 bactericide, uxoricide.

11.14.22: 3 pesticide; 4 infanticide, insecticide; 5 parasiticide.

11.14.23: 2 bedside, blindside, broadside, landside, roadside.

11.14.24: 2 dockside, oxide; 3 hydroxide, monoxide, peroxide; 4 nitrous oxide; 5 carbon dioxide, carbon monoxide; 6 hydrogen peroxide.

11.14.25: 2 downside, inside, onside, Tyneside; 3 coincide, Ironside, mountainside; 5 Edmund Ironside.

11.14.26: 1 tide, tied; 2 ebb tide, high tide, low tide, neap tide, noontide, peptide, red tide, riptide, tongue-tied, untied, Yuletide; 3 Eastertide, eventide, Whitsuntide, wintertide. *See also* **11.11.**

11.14.27: 2 divide, provide; 3 Great Divide, subdivide; 4 North-South divide. *See also* **10.2.10, 10.42.19.**

11.14.28: 1 wide; 2 statewide, worldwide; 3 citywide, countrywide, nationwide.

11.15: 1 Ides, strides; 2 besides, Ironsides. *See also* **11.14.16.**

11.16: 1 blithe, lithe, scythe, tithe, writhe. *See also* **11.38.**

11.17: 1 fife, rife, strife.

11.17.1: 1 life; 2 birdlife, half-life, highlife, long-life, love life, lowlife, nightlife, real-life, true-life, wildlife; 3 afterlife, Country Life, double life, facts of life, private life, true-to-life; 4 larger-than-life, water of life; 5 artificial life.
Surgeons must be very careful
When they take the knife!

Underneath their fine incisions
Stirs the culprit—Life!
(Emily Dickinson)
See also **11.40**.

11.17.2: **1** knife; **2** bread knife, clasp knife, craft knife, drawknife, fish knife, flick knife, jackknife, penknife; **3** bowie knife, butter knife, carving knife, palette knife, Stanley knife.

11.17.3: **1** wife; **2** alewife, ex-wife, fishwife, goodwife, housewife, midwife; **4** common-law wife.
See also **11.40**.

11.18: **2** oblige; **3** disoblige.
See also **10.42.36**.

11.19: **1** bike, dyke, hike, Ike, mike, psych, tyke; **2** bulldyke, hitchhike, klondike, push-bike, trailbike, Van Dyke; **3** minibike, motorbike, mountain bike, superbike.
See also **10.42.50, 11.21**.

11.19.1: **1** like; **2** alike, bell-like, birdlike, catlike, chalklike, childlike, Christlike, corpse-like, crablike, deathlike, dislike, dreamlike, ghostlike, godlike, lifelike, mislike, mouselike, rocklike, saintlike, sheep-like, snail-like, springlike, starlike, suchlike, sylphlike, unlike, vicelike, warlike, worm-like, wraithlike; **3** businesslike, insect-like, ladylike, lookalike, mirror-like, ostrich-like, parrot-like, soundalike, spider-like, spinsterlike, sportsmanlike, statesmanlike, unalike, unwarlike, workmanlike; **4** unbusinesslike, unladylike, unsportsmanlike.
See also **10.42.50, 11.21**.

11.19.2: **1** pike, shrike, spike, strike, trike; **2** bird strike, handspike, turnpike; **3** counterstrike, general strike, hunger strike, lightning strike, lucky strike, marlinespike, Scafell Pike.

11.20: **1** yikes.

11.21: **1** liked, psyched; **2** disliked, well-liked.
See also **11.19, 11.19.1**.

11.22: **1** aisle, guile, I'll, isle, vile; **2** aedile, agile, argyle, beguile, Carlisle, Carlyle, fragile, revile, servile; **3** crocodile; **4** Emerald Isle.
What's the use of worrying?
It never was worth while,
So, pack up your troubles in your old kit-bag,

And smile, smile, smile.
(George Asaf)
See also **10.42.74**.

11.22.1: **1** bile; **2** mobile, nubile; **3** immobile.

11.22.2: **1** file, mile, smile; **2** air mile, anile, defile, nail file, penile, profile, senile, zip file; **3** anglophile, camomile, cinephile, high profile, homophile, juvenile, logophile, low profile, paedophile, zoophile; **4** bibliophile.
See also **10.42.74, 11.23**.

11.22.3: **1** pile; **2** compile, stockpile, woodpile.

11.22.4: **1** rile; **2** Fair Isle, febrile, puerile, sterile, virile; **3** nonsterile; **4** antifebrile.

11.22.5: **2** decile, docile, exile, facile, fissile, missile, tensile; **3** domicile, prehensile, reconcile.
See also **11.23**.

11.22.6: **1** tile; **2** fertile, futile, motile, quartile, reptile; **3** infertile, versatile, volatile; **4** nonvolatile.
See also **10.42.74, 11.23**.

11.22.7: **2** ductile, gentile, tactile; **3** erectile, infantile, mercantile, percentile, projectile, trajectile.

11.22.8: **1** stile, style; **2** freestyle, hairstyle, hostile, lifestyle, restyle, textile, turnstile; **3** peristyle.
See also **10.42.74**.

11.22.9: **1** while; **2** awhile, erstwhile, meanwhile, worthwhile.

11.23: **1** filed, mild, tiled, wild; **2** defiled, exiled, self-styled; **3** domiciled, undefiled; **4** reconciled.
See also **11.22.2, 11.22.5, 11.22.6**.

11.23.1: **1** child; **2** brainchild, godchild, grandchild, love child, schoolchild, stepchild; **3** great-grandchild, inner child, latchkey child, only child; **6** Château Mouton-Rothschild.

11.24: **1** Giles, wiles; **3** Northern Isles, Western Isles.

11.25: **1** chime, dime, I'm, mime; **2** Sondheim; **3** five-and-dime, Guggenheim, pantomime, paradigm.

11.25.1: **1** climb, clime, lime, slime; **2** birdlime, quicklime, slaked lime, sublime.
See also **10.42.84**.

11.25.2: **1** crime, grime, prime, rhyme, rime; **3** cybercrime.
See also **10.42.84**.

11.25.3: **1** thyme, time; **2** darktime, daytime, Dreamtime, drivetime, half-time, lifetime, lunchtime, Maytime, nighttime, part-time, playtime, ragtime, sometime, springtime, teatime, two-time, uptime, wartime; **3** aforetime, anytime, flexitime, maritime.

I was promised on a time
To have reason for my rhyme;
From that time unto this season,
I received nor rhyme nor reason.
(Edmund Spenser)
See also **10.42.84**, **11.26**.

11.25.4: **2** bedtime, dead time, glide time, old-time, seedtime; **3** dinnertime, Father Time, overtime, summertime, suppertime, wintertime.

11.25.5: **2** all-time, full-time, mealtime, real-time, small-time.

11.25.6: **2** downtime, meantime, noontime, one-time; **3** just-in-time, question time; **4** Greenwich Mean Time.

11.25.7: **2** enzyme, mistime, pastime, peacetime, space-time; **3** Christmastime, lysozyme; **4** apoenzyme, holoenzyme.
See also **10.42.84**.

11.26: **1** times; **2** betimes, hard times, sometimes; **3** oftentimes.
See also **11.25.3**.

11.27: **1** chine, dine, Jain, thine; **2** design, resign; **3** anodyne, auld lang syne, wine and dine; **4** amaranthine, incarnadine, labyrinthine.
See also **10.42.100, 11.28**.

11.27.1: **2** carbine, combine, Holbein, turbine, woodbine; **3** columbine, concubine.

11.27.2: **1** fine; **2** confine, define, refine; **3** superfine.

So I'll just pretend that I know which way
to bend
And I'm gonna tell the whole world that
you're mine.
Just please understand, when I see you
clap your hands
If you stick around I'm sure that you'll be
fine.
(Scissor Sisters)
See also **11.28.1, 11.30**.

11.27.3: **1** line; **2** airline, A-line, baseline, by-line, careline, eyeline, fall line,

Fraulein, hairline, helpline, jawline, lifeline, mainline, offline, online, pipeline, punchline, saline, scoreline, shoreline, skyline, touchline; **3** aquiline, contour line, Empire-line, firing line, Plimsoll line, princess-line, service line, sibylline, Ursuline; **4** finishing line; **5** production line.
See also **10.42.101, 11.28.3, 11.30**.

11.27.4: **2** align, malign; **3** alkaline, borderline, Caroline, crystalline, power line, realign, underline, waterline.
See also **11.28.3**.

11.27.5: **2** beeline, feline, tree line; **3** party line, storyline; **4** assembly line, poverty line.

11.27.6: **2** bowline, snow line, towline; **3** yellow line; **4** Maginot Line.

11.27.7: **2** bloodline, breadline, Childline, deadline, guideline, hardline, headline, landline, redline, sideline, tideline.

11.27.8: **1** cline; **2** decline, incline, neckline, recline.
See also **10.42.101, 11.28.3**.

11.27.9: **2** hemline, plumb line, rhumb line, slimline, streamline, timeline, tramline.

11.27.10: **2** chat line, coastline, dateline, faultline, flatline, outline, sightline, waistline; **3** picket line; **7** International Date Line.

11.27.11: **1** mine; **2** carmine, coalmine, goldmine, landmine; **3** undermine.

'Dark is the hour!' 'Ay, and cold.'
'Lone is my house.' 'Ah, but mine?'
'Sight, touch, lips, eyes yearned in vain.'
'Long dead these to thine.'
(Walter de la Mare)
See also **10.42.101**.

11.27.12: **1** nine; **2** benign, canine, cloud nine, Pennine; **3** 999, asinine, leonine, saturnine.

11.27.13: **1** pine, spine; **2** alpine, opine, Scots pine, supine; **3** porcupine, subalpine, transalpine; **4** Proserpine; **5** Kenneth MacAlpine.

11.27.14: **1** brine, shrine, Strine; **2** enshrine; **3** anserine, passerine, uterine; **4** alexandrine; **5** intrauterine.

11.27.15: **1** sign, sine; **2** assign, consign, cosign, cosine, ensign, Euxine, piscine, porcine, ursine, V-sign; **3** countersign, Red Ensign; **4** internecine.
See also **10.42.101**.

11.27.16: **1** shine; **2** moonshine, outshine, shoeshine, sunshine.
See also **10.42.101**.

11.27.17: **1** tine; **2** tontine; **3** Argentine, byzantine, clementine, Constantine, eglantine, Heseltine, serpentine, turpentine, valentine; **4** adamantine, elephantine; **6** Newcastle upon Tyne.

11.27.18: **1** stein; **2** Bernstein, Eppstein, Holstein; **3** clandestine, Hammerstein, philistine, Rubinstein.

11.27.19: **1** vine; **2** bovine, divine, gluhwein, grapevine.

11.27.20: **1** swine, twine, whine, wine; **2** entwine, equine, mulled wine; **3** dessert wine, intertwine.
For truth is precious and divine,
Too rich a pearl for carnal swine.
(Samuel Butler)
See also **10.42.101, 11.28.6**.

11.28: **1** bind, dined, grind, hind, rind; **2** behind, combined, resigned, unbind; **3** daily grind, uncombined, undersigned.
See also **10.42.29, 11.27**.

11.28.1: **1** find, fined; **2** confined, defined, fact-find, refined; **3** ill-defined, predefined, unconfined, undefined, unrefined, well-defined.
See also **11.27.2**.

11.28.2: **1** kind; **2** mankind, unkind; **3** humankind, womankind.

11.28.3: **1** lined; **2** fur-lined, inclined, unlined; **3** disinclined, nonaligned, underlined.
See also **11.27.3, 11.27.4, 11.27.8**.

11.28.4: **1** blind; **2** purblind, sun blind; **3** colour-blind, eff and blind.
See also **2.54.77, 10.42.29**.

11.28.5: **1** mind; **2** closed mind, remind; **3** frame of mind, mastermind, open mind.
Georgia, Georgia, no peace I find,
Just an old sweet song keeps Georgia on
my mind.
(Stuart Gorrell)
See also **10.2.21**.

11.28.6: **1** twined, wind; **2** rewind, unwind; **3** intertwined.
See also **10.2.16, 10.42.29, 11.27.20**.

11.29: **1** pint; **2** Geraint, half-pint.

11.30: **1** Fiennes, Hines, lines; **2** confines, guidelines, Pennines, tramlines.
See also **11.27.2, 11.27.3**.

11.31: **1** hype, Skype, snipe, swipe, wipe; **2** arsewipe, sideswipe.
See also **10.42.109, 11.33**.

11.31.1: **1** pipe; **2** blowpipe, downpipe, drainpipe, hornpipe, hosepipe, peace pipe, pitch pipe, standpipe, tailpipe, windpipe; **3** exhaust pipe, water pipe.
See also **10.42.109**.

11.31.2: **1** gripe, ripe, stripe, tripe; **2** pinstripe, unripe; **3** overripe; **4** magnetic stripe.
See also **10.42.109**.

11.31.3: **1** type; **2** touch-type; **3** archetype, logotype, phenotype.
See also **10.42.109**.

11.31.4: **3** genotype, prototype, true-to-type; **4** daguerreotype, stereotype.
See also **11.33**.

11.32: **1** cripes; **2** bagpipes; **3** Stars and Stripes.

11.33: **1** hyped, striped; **3** candy-striped; **4** stereotyped.
See also **11.31, 11.31.4**.

11.34: **1** dice, gneiss, ice, lice, nice, slice, spice, splice, twice, vice; **2** advice, allspice, black ice, concise, de-ice, device, drift ice, entice, pack ice, precise, sheet ice, suffice, thin ice; **3** imprecise, paradise, sacrifice; **4** fool's paradise, self-sacrifice; **5** bird of paradise.
I vow to thee, my country—all earthly
things above—
Entire and whole and perfect, the service
of my love,
The love that asks no question: the love
that stands the test,
That lays upon the altar the dearest and
the best:
The love that never falters, the love that
pays the price,
The love that makes undaunted the final
sacrifice.
(Cecil Arthur Spring-Rice)
See also **9.14.80, 10.42.132, 11.35**.

11.34.1: **1** Brice, rice, thrice, trice; **2** fried rice; **3** cockatrice.

11.34.2: **1** price; **2** bride price, cut-price, half-price, list price, low-price; **3** asking price, market price, retail price, ticket price, underprice.
See also **10.42.132**.

11.35: **1** Christ, heist, iced; **2** unpriced, zeitgeist; **3** Jesus Christ, overpriced, poltergeist.
See also **11.34**.

11.36: **1** kite, shite, spite; **2** Cronkite, despite, gobshite, invite, respite, Shiite; **3** Muscovite.
See also **10.42.158**.

11.36.1: **1** bight, bite, byte; **2** fleabite, frostbite, snakebite, soundbite.
See also **10.42.158**.

11.36.2: **3** gigabyte, Jacobite, kilobyte, megabyte, overbite, petabyte, terabyte.

11.36.3: **2** cordite, indict, Luddite; **3** erudite, expedite, extradite, recondite, troglodyte; **4** hermaphrodite.

11.36.4: **1** fight; **2** bullfight, bunfight, cockfight, dogfight, firefight, graphite, gunfight, prize fight, saprophyte, stage fright, street fight; **3** epiphyte, neophyte.
And we are here as on a darkling plain
Swept with confused alarms of struggle and flight,
Where ignorant armies clash by night.
(Matthew Arnold)
See also **10.42.159**.

11.36.5: **1** height; **3** apartheid, Fahrenheit, gesundheit.
How do I love thee? Let me count the ways.
I love thee to the depth and breadth and height
My soul can reach, when feeling out of sight
For the ends of Being and ideal Grace.
(Elizabeth Barrett Browning)
See also **11.37**.

11.36.6: **1** blight, light, lite, sleight, slight; **2** brake light, daylight, delight, firelight, flashlight, gaslight, highlight, limelight, searchlight, skylight, starlight, torchlight, twilight; **3** candlelight, cellulite, guiding light, leading light, microlight, parking light, traffic light; **4** Turkish delight, vermiculite.
There was a young lady named Bright,
Whose speed was far faster than light;
She set out one day
In a relative way,
And returned home the previous night.
(Arthur Henry Reginald Buller)
See also **10.2.61, 10.42.158**.

11.36.7: **2** alight, polite; **3** acolyte, ArmaLite, Bakelite, Carmelite, impolite, proselyte, satellite, socialite; **4** electrolyte, metabolite, Pre-Raphaelite, theodolite.
See also **2.54.88**.

11.36.8: **2** floodlight, headlight, red light, sidelight.

11.36.9: **1** flight; **2** half-light, in-flight, spaceflight, test flight, white flight; **3** maiden flight.

11.36.10: **2** downlight, fanlight, greenlight, moonlight, penlight, sunlight; **3** neon light.
See also **10.42.158**.

11.36.11: **1** plight; **2** lamplight, stoplight, strip light.

11.36.12: **2** first light, nightlight, spotlight, streetlight; **3** pilot light.

11.36.13: **1** might, mite, smite; **2** Marmite, Semite, termite; **3** Adamite, Benthamite, dynamite, sodomite, stalagmite, Vegemite; **4** anti-Semite.

11.36.14: **1** knight, night, nite; **2** black knight, finite, first night, fortnight, goodnight, ignite, lignite, midnight, Twelfth Night, unite, weeknight, white knight; **3** Bonfire Night, fly-by-night, gelignite, Guy Fawkes Night, reunite; **5** lady of the night.
See also **10.2.61**.

11.36.15: **2** tonight; **3** ammonite, overnight, urbanite; **4** suburbanite.

11.36.16: **1** bright, fright, right, rite, sprite, write; **2** affright, all right, alright, Arkwright, birthright, contrite, dead right, downright, forthright, Fulbright, playwright, rewrite, upright, Wainwright, wheelwright; **3** copyright.
'You are old, Father William,' the young man said,
'And your hair has become very white;
And yet you incessantly stand on your head—
Do you think at your age, it is right?'
(Lewis Carroll)
See also **2.54.88, 9.14.90, 10.42.158, 11.37**.

11.36.17: **2** aright; **3** overwrite, sybarite, underwrite; **4** meteorite.

11.36.18: **1** trite; **2** Cartwright, ghostwrite, outright.

11.36.19: **1** cite, sight, site; **2** bauxite, campsite, excite, eyesight, foresight, gunsight, hindsight, incite, insight, recite, website; **3** brownfield site, phagocyte, plebiscite, second sight; **5** World Heritage Site.
The reason no man knows; let it suffice,
What we behold is censured by our eyes
Where both deliberate, the love is slight;

Who ever loved that loved not at first sight?
(Christopher Marlowe)
See also **10.2.62, 10.42.158.**

11.36.20: 3 anthracite, leucocyte, lymphocyte, marcasite, oversight, parasite.

11.36.21: 1 tight; **2** airtight, uptight; **3** appetite, bipartite, haematite, stalactite, steatite, transvestite, tripartite, watertight.
See also **9.14.90.**

11.36.22: 1 Dwight, quite, white; **2** off-white, snow-white; **3** black-and-white, lily-white.
See also **11.37.**

11.37: 1 brights, heights, rights, rites, Smuts, tights, whites; **2** last rites; **3** squatters' rights; **4** Wuthering Heights.
See also **11.36.5, 11.36.16, 11.36.22.**

11.37.1: 2 daylights, footlights, house lights, lowlights; **3** northern lights, southern lights; **5** Festival of Lights.

11.38: 1 chive, hive, I've, jive, live, skive; **2** alive, archive, beehive, connive, revive, survive; **3** unarchive; **4** Clive.
See also **10.42.176, 10.42.181, 11.16, 11.40.**

11.38.1: 1 dive; **2** crash dive, nose dive, skydive, swan dive; **3** duck and dive.
See also **10.42.182.**

11.38.2: 1 five; **2** A5, high-five; **3** .45, forty-five, MI5, nine-to-five; **4** P45.

11.38.3: 1 strive, thrive; **2** arrive, contrive, deprive, derive.
See also **10.42.181, 11.39.**

11.38.4: 2 self-drive, test drive, whist drive; **3** four-wheel drive, overdrive; **4** Rodeo Drive.

11.39: 2 arrived, contrived, deprived, derived; **3** ill-contrived, uncontrived.
See also **11.38.3.**

11.40: 1 chives, hives, lives, wives; **2** Maldives.
See also **10.61.1, 11.17.1, 11.17.3, 11.38.**

11.41: 1 reich; **2** Third Reich; **3** Österreich.

11.42: 1 guise; **2** despise, disguise, franchise, surmise, thigh-highs; **3** empathise, enfranchise, ghettoise, sympathise; **4** disenfranchise, philosophise.
See also **11.43.**

11.42.1: 2 iodise; **3** anodise, gourmandise, hybridise, jeopardise,

liquidise, merchandise, oxidise, rhapsodise, standardise, subsidise; **4** propagandise.
See also **10.42.188.**

11.42.2: 3 energise, eulogise; **4** apologise, mythologise.

11.42.3: 1 flies, lies; **2** supplies; **3** butterflies, tranquillise; **4** Lord of the Flies.
See also **11.5, 11.5.2, 11.5.3.**

11.42.4: 3 breathalyse, civilise, equalise, fossilise, idolise, legalise, localise, nasalise, scandalise, vandalise, visualise, vocalise; **4** contextualise, evangelise, monopolise, radicalise.
See also **10.42.188, 11.43.1.**

11.42.5: 2 realise; **3** idealise; **4** serialise, trivialise; **5** dematerialise, industrialise, materialise; **6** deindustrialise, editorialise, reindustrialise.
See also **11.43.1.**

11.42.6: 4 actualise, mutualise; **5** conceptualise, demutualise, desexualise; **6** individualise, intellectualise.

11.42.7: 3 globalise, mobilise, stabilise, symbolise, verbalise; **4** cannibalise, demobilise, destabilise, immobilise, metabolise.
See also **11.43.1.**

11.42.8: 3 formalise, normalise; **4** caramelise, decimalise.

11.42.9: 3 analyse, finalise, penalise; **4** criminalise, externalise, internalise, marginalise, nominalise, personalise; **5** decriminalise, depersonalise, psychoanalyse.
See also **11.43.1.**

11.42.10: 4 fictionalise, nationalise, rationalise; **5** denationalise, professionalise, sensationalise; **6** institutionalise, internationalise.
See also **11.43.1.**

11.42.11: 3 centralise, moralise, neutralise, paralyse, sterilise; **4** decentralise, demoralise, generalise, liberalise, naturalise.
See also **11.43.1.**

11.42.12: 3 socialise, specialise; **4** commercialise, initialise.
See also **11.43.1.**

11.42.13: 3 brutalise, crystallise, fertilise, tantalise, utilise; **4** immortalise, palatalise,

revitalise; 5 compartmentalise, departmentalise, sentimentalise.
See also **10.42.188, 11.43.1.**

11.42.14: 4 capitalise, hospitalise; 5 recapitalise; 6 undercapitalise.
See also **11.43.1.**

11.42.15: 2 surmise; 3 compromise, randomise; 4 economise.
See also **10.42.188.**

11.42.16: 3 atomise, customise, itemise; 4 anatomise, epitomise, lobotomise.

11.42.17: 2 demise; 3 maximise, minimise, optimise, victimise; 4 legitimise.

11.42.18: 3 immunise, recognise, scrutinise, solemnise.

11.42.19: 3 agonise, canonise, carbonise, colonise, fraternise, galvanise, ionise, lionise, mechanise, modernise, organise, patronise, synchronise, tyrannise, unionise, urbanise, vulcanise, weaponise; 4 antagonise, decolonise, homogenise, reorganise; 5 Americanise, pedestrianise, revolutionise.
See also **10.42.188, 11.43.2.**

11.42.20: 3 demonise, feminise, harmonise, humanise, sermonise; 4 dehumanise.

11.42.21: 1 fries, rise; 2 French fries, high-rise, low-rise, payrise, sunrise, theorise; 5 tequila sunrise.
See also **10.42.188.**

11.42.22: 2 arise; 3 authorise, moisturise, pasteurise, plagiarise, pressurise, pulverise, tenderise, terrorise; 4 accessorise, categorise, containerise, deodorise; 5 familiarise.
See also **11.43.4.**

11.42.23: 3 bowdlerise, burglarise, polarise.

11.42.24: 4 circularise, popularise, regularise, secularise; 5 particularise.

11.42.25: 3 glamorise, memorise, mesmerise, summarise.
Leave the road and memorize this life that pass before my eyes. Nothing is going my way.
(R.E.M.)
See also **10.42.188.**

11.42.26: 3 pauperise, temporise, vaporise; 4 extemporise.

11.42.27: 3 cauterise, factorise, satirise; 4 catheterise, characterise, computerise, militarise; 5 demilitarise.
See also **11.43.4.**

11.42.28: 1 prise, prize; 2 apprise, comprise, first prize, surprise; 3 Booker Prize, enterprise, Nobel Prize; 4 Pulitzer Prize.
Not all that tempts your wand'ring eyes And heedless hearts, is lawful prize; Nor all that glisters, gold.
(Thomas Gray)
See also **10.42.189, 11.43.3.**

11.42.29: 1 size; 2 capsize, downsize, excise, full-size, incise, king-size, life-size, midsize, outsize, queen-size, resize, right-size; 3 circumcise, exorcise, pocket-size; 4 family-size; 5 economy-size.

11.42.30: 3 boxercise, emphasise, exercise, fantasise, ostracise, oversize, supersize, synthesise; 4 hypothesise; 5 overemphasise.
See also **11.43.5.**

11.42.31: 3 anglicise, criticise, publicise; 4 italicise, politicise, romanticise.

11.42.32: 2 baptise, chastise; 3 amortise, deputise; 4 alphabetise.

11.42.33: 3 advertise, hypnotise, magnetise, privatise; 4 anaesthetise, demagnetise, democratise, proselytise, reprivatise.
See also **10.42.188.**

11.42.34: 3 dramatise, schematise, stigmatise, traumatise; 4 acclimatise, systematise.
See also **11.43.**

11.42.35: 3 digitise, sanitise, sensitise, unitise; 4 desensitise, prioritise.

11.42.36: 2 advise, devise, Levi's, revise; 3 improvise, passivise, supervise, televise; 4 incentivise.
See also **11.43.6.**

11.42.37: 1 wise; 2 clockwise, crabwise, crosswise, endwise, leastwise, lengthwise, likewise, nowise, sidewise, streetwise, unwise; 3 otherwise, penny-wise, weather-wise; 4 anticlockwise, contrariwise, counterclockwise.

11.43: 2 despised, disguised, stylised; 3 bastardised, enfranchised, traumatised, undisguised; 4 disenfranchised, unrecognised; 5 underutilised.
See also **11.42, 11.42.34.**

11.43.1: 3 civilised, crystallised, fossilised, globalised, localised, paralysed, specialised; 4 annualised, caramelised, commercialised, generalised, naturalised, personalised, ritualised, uncivilised,

unrealised; **5** industrialised;
6 institutionalised, undercapitalised,
unindustrialised.
See also **11.42.4, 11.42.5, 11.42.7, 11.42.9,
11.42.10, 11.42.11, 11.42.12, 11.42.13,
11.42.14.**

11.43.2: **3** agonised, carbonised,
galvanised, mechanised, organised,
unionised, urbanised, westernised;
4 disorganised, homogenised, unorganised.
See also **11.42.19.**

11.43.3: **1** prized; **2** comprised, surprised;
3 unsurprised.
See also **11.42.28.**

11.43.4: **3** motorised, notarised,
pasteurised, pressurised; **4** computerised,
militarised, miniaturised, transistorised,
unauthorised.
See also **11.42.22, 11.42.27.**

11.43.5: **2** fair-sized, good-sized, man-
sized, outsized, pint-sized; **3** exercised,
middle-sized, oversized, undersized;
4 unexercised.
See also **11.42.30.**

11.43.6: **2** advised, devised, revised; **3** ill-
advised, improvised, well-advised.
See also **11.42.36.**

12.0: **1** buyer, byre, dire, Dyer, higher,
hire, hiya, ire, mire, shire, sire, via;
2 admire, desire, homebuyer, Isaiah,
Josiah, messiah, quagmire; **3** Hezekiah,
Jeremiah, Messiah, Zedekiah, Zephaniah;
4 Nehemiah.
See also **10.42.126, 12.7.**

12.1: **1** fire; **2** afire, backfire, bonfire,
campfire, ceasefire, crossfire, Greek fire,
gunfire, hang fire, hellfire, misfire,
sapphire, shellfire, spitfire, sure-fire,
wildfire; **3** purifier, rapid-fire, ratifier;
5 baptism of fire.
*Blessed Cecilia, appear in visions
To all musicians, appear and inspire.
Translated daughter, come down and
　startle
Composing mortals with immortal fire.*
(W.H. Auden)
See also **12.7.**

12.1.1: **3** amplifier, certifier, magnifier,
qualifier, quantifier, testifier; **4** clarifier,
identifier.

12.1.2: **3** modifier; **4** humidifier,
postmodifier, premodifier; **5** dehumidifier.

12.1.3: **3** pacifier, versifier; **4** emulsifier,
falsifier, intensifier.

12.2: **1** flier, flyer, liar, lyre; **2** high-flier,
outlier, supplier; **3** jambalaya, multiplier.

12.3: **1** pyre; **2** empire, papaya, umpire,
vampire; **3** occupier; **4** British Empire,
Roman Empire; **5** owner-occupier; **6** Holy
Roman Empire.
*The time to hesitate is through;
No time to wallow in the mire;
Try now we can only lose;
And our love become a funeral pyre.*
(The Doors)

12.3.1: **1** spire; **2** aspire, conspire, expire,
inspire, perspire, respire, transpire.
See also **10.42.126, 12.7.**

12.4: **1** briar, brier, drier, dryer, friar, fryer,
prior, trier; **2** decrier, Grey Friar, hairdryer,
pariah, town crier, Uriah, White Friar;
3 washer-dryer, Zechariah.

12.5: **1** tire, tyre; **2** attire, entire, retire,
satire.
See also **10.42.126, 12.7.1.**

12.6: **1** wire; **2** barbed wire, hardwire,
haywire, hot-wire, newswire, rewire,
tripwire; **3** fly-by-wire, razor wire.
*Like a bird on the wire,
Like a drunk in a midnight choir
I have tried in my way to be free.*
(Leonard Cohen)
See also **10.42.126, 12.7.**

12.6.1: **1** choir, quire, squire; **2** acquire,
enquire, inquire, require.
See also **10.42.126, 12.7.**

12.7: **1** fired, hired, mired, wired;
2 admired, coal-fired, desired, expired,
gas-fired, inspired, oil-fired, required;
3 jeremiad, underwired, uninspired.
See also **12.0, 12.1, 12.3.1, 12.6, 12.6.1.**

12.7.1: **1** tired; **2** attired, dog-tired,
retired; **3** overtired.
See also **12.5.**

12.8: **1** dial, phial, trial, vial, viol; **2** denial,
misdial, mistrial, redial, retrial, sundial;
3 decrial, field trial, self-denial.

12.9: **1** Brian, Bryan, cyan, ion, iron, lion,
Ryan, scion, Zion; **2** anion, cast-iron,
cation, gridiron, Orion, O'Brien, wrought
iron; **3** dandelion, Paraguayan, Uruguayan;
4 soldering iron.
See also **2.51, 10.42.92.**

12.10: **2** alliance, appliance, compliance,
defiance, reliance; **3** misalliance; **4** self-
reliance.

12.10.1: **1** science; **3** bioscience,
Christian Science, life science,

neuroscience, pseudoscience; **4** Master of Science, natural science, social science; **5** Bachelor of Science.

12.11: **1** client, giant, pliant; **2** Bryant, compliant, defiant, reliant; **3** noncompliant, red giant.

12.12: **1** bias, pious, Pius; **2** Caius, Gaius, impious; **3** Elias. *See also* **2.55**.

12.13: **1** diet, quiet, riot; **2** disquiet, panchayat, unquiet. *See also* **2.54.88, 10.42.144**.

13.0: **1** blob, bob, cob, dob, fob, glob, gob, hob, job, lob, mob, rob, slob, sob, swab, throb, yob; **2** bag job, boob job, corncob, demob, heartthrob, Jacob, nabob, nose job, odd job; **3** inside job, put-up job; **4** thingumabob. *See also* **10.42.13**.

13.0.1: **1** knob, nob, snob; **2** doorknob, hobnob. *See also* **10.42.13**.

13.1: **1** Dobbs, Hobbes, Jobs; **3** bits and bobs.

13.2: **1** bod, clod, cod, hod, mod, nod, odd, plod, shod, sod, tod, Todd, yod; **2** Cape Cod, odd bod, roughshod, slipshod; **3** land of Nod.

And this is good old Boston,
The home of the bean and the cod,
Where the Lowells talk only to Cabots,
And the Cabots talk only to God.
(John Collins Bossidy)
See also **10.42.14**.

13.2.1: **1** god; **2** tin god; **3** demigod; **4** honest to God. *See also* **13.3**.

13.2.2: **1** pod; **2** bipod, iPod, tripod; **3** arthropod, gastropod; **4** cephalopod.

13.2.3: **1** prod, rod, trod; **2** Black Rod, hotrod, Nimrod, ramrod; **3** Aaron's rod, dowsing rod, goldenrod; **4** divining rod.

13.2.4: **1** quad, quod, squad, wad; **2** tightwad. *See also* **13.3**.

13.3: **1** gods, odds, wads; **3** odds and sods. *See also* **13.2.1, 13.2.4**.

13.4: **2** sideboards. *See also* **14.19.5, 14.19.6**.

13.5: **1** Gough, off, quaff; **2** bogof, brushoff, drop-off, face-off, falloff, hands-off, jump-off, Khrushchev, layoff, Pavlov, payoff, play-off, rip-off, showoff, time-off, tip-off, waveoff, well-off; **3** Asimov,

falling-off, Gorbachev, telling-off, ticking-off; **4** Atanasoff. *See also* **10.42.32, 13.41**.

13.5.1: **1** doff; **2** cheesed off, handoff, mid-off, sendoff, standoff.

13.5.2: **1** cough, scoff; **2** Berkoff, Chekhov, kickoff, Kraków, rake-off, takeoff; **3** Bulgakov, Nabokov, whooping cough; **4** Baryshnikov; **5** Kalashnikov.

13.5.3: **2** in-off, one-off, on-off, runoff, spin-off, turn-off; **3** Godunov, Ustinov; **4** Rachmaninov; **5** Boris Godunov.

13.5.4: **1** prof, shroff, trough; **2** far-off, tear-off; **3** Kasparov. *See also* **13.41.2**.

13.5.5: **1** toff; **2** blastoff, castoff, cutoff, Flintoff, let-off, liftoff, shut-off, write-off.

13.6: **1** croft, loft, oft, soft; **2** aloft, Ashcroft, Bancroft, choir loft, Cockcroft, hayloft, Moorcroft; **3** Lowestoft. *See also* **9.14.86**.

13.7: **1** bog, cog, fog, jog, mog, smog, snog, tog, wog, Zog; **2** befog, biog, eggnog, Hertzog, peat bog, phizog; **3** golliwog, pettifog, polliwog. *See also* **10.42.35, 13.8**.

13.7.1: **1** dog; **2** bulldog, Cadog, corn dog, guard dog, guide dog, gundog, hangdog, hot dog, lame dog, lapdog, mad dog, old dog, sheepdog, top dog, watchdog; **3** dog-eat-dog, prairie dog, tracker dog, underdog; **4** British bulldog, hair of the dog.

It's been a hard day's night
And I've been working like a dog;
It's been a hard day's night
I should be sleeping like a log.
(The Beatles)
See also **10.2.23, 10.42.35**.

13.7.2: **2** agog; **3** demagogue, pedagogue, synagogue.

13.7.3: **1** hog; **2** groundhog, hedgehog, quahog, warthog, whole hog.

The Cat, the Rat, and Lovell our dog
Rule all England under a hog.
(William Collingbourne)

13.7.4: **1** blog, clog, flog, glogg, log, slog, splog, vlog; **2** backlog, dialogue, moblog, prologue, unclog, weblog, Yule log; **3** eclogue, epilogue, waterlog. *See also* **10.42.35**.

13.7.5: **3** analogue, catalogue, monologue, travelogue; **4** ideologue.

13.7.6: **1** frog, grog, sprog; **2** bullfrog, leapfrog, tree frog; **4** goliath frog.

13.8: **1** togs, wings; **2** Joe Bloggs; **3** clever clogs.
See also **10.42.184, 13.7.**

13.9: **1** bodge, dodge, Hodge, lodge, splodge, stodge, wodge; **2** dislodge, hodgepodge; **3** horologe.
See also **10.42.36.**

13.10: **1** choc, chock, hock, jock, knock, mock, shock, smock, sock, Spock, toque, wok; **2** ad hoc, amok, Bartók, Enoch, epoch, foreshock, kapok, post hoc, shell shock, sjambok, springbok, windsock; **3** aftershock, antiknock, hollyhock, manioc; **4** electroshock.
See also **10.42.51, 13.12.**

13.10.1: **1** doc, dock; **2** burdock, Médoc, Murdoch; **3** Caradoc, Languedoc.
See also **13.12.**

13.10.2: **1** cock; **2** Adcock, Alcock, ballcock, Bangkok, gamecock, Hancock, Hickok, Hitchcock, Moorcock, peacock, stopcock, woodcock; **3** billycock, poppycock, shuttlecock, weathercock.

13.10.3: **1** flock, Glock, loch, lock, Locke, lough, schlock; **2** airlock, armlock, Belloc, caps lock, fetlock, flintlock, forelock, Havelock, hemlock, moloch, Num Lock, oarlock, rowlock, Shylock, unlock, warlock, wheel lock, Yale lock; **3** interlock.
See also **10.42.**

13.10.4: **1** bloc, Bloch, block; **2** breeze block, cellblock, Chubb lock, en bloc, roadblock, sunblock, tower block, unblock, woodblock; **3** chock-a-block, mental block, stumbling block, writer's block.

13.10.5: **2** deadlock, gridlock, headlock, padlock, wedlock.

13.10.6: **1** clock; **2** o'clock, picklock, stopclock; **3** alarm clock, cuckoo clock; **4** grandfather clock; **6** biological clock.
Hickory, dickory, dock,
The mouse ran up the clock.
The clock struck one,
The mouse ran down,
Hickory, dickory, dock.
(Children's Verse)

13.10.7: **1** croc, crock, frock, rock; **2** auroch, Ayers Rock, baroque, bedrock, defrock, shamrock.
Let's rock! Let's rock!
Ev'rybody in the whole cell block
was a dancin' to the Jailhouse Rock.
(Jerry Lieber, with Mike Stoller)

13.10.8: **1** stock; **2** bloodstock, fatstock, gunstock, joint stock, livestock, restock, rootstock, Rostock, Vostok, Woodstock; **3** Birkenstock, laughing stock, overstock, rolling stock; **4** Vladivostok.
See also **10.42.51, 13.11.**

13.11: **1** cox, fox, Knox, lox, ox, phlox, stocks; **2** Botox, detox, dreadlocks, outfox, Wilcox, Xerox; **3** equinox.
See also **13.10.8.**

13.11.1: **1** box; **2** check box, coolbox, gearbox, horsebox, icebox, inbox, jukebox, lunchbox, mailbox, matchbox, pillbox, sandbox, shoebox, snuffbox, soapbox, squeezebox, strongbox; **3** chatterbox, letterbox, moneybox, tinderbox; **4** jack-in-the-box, Pandora's box.
See also **10.42.137.**

13.11.2: **2** outbox, paintbox, postbox, saltbox; **3** chocolate-box.

13.11.3: **3** orthodox, paradox; **4** heterodox, unorthodox.

13.11.4: **1** pox; **2** cowpox, smallpox; **3** chickenpox.

13.12: **1** blocked, docked, locked, pocked, shocked; **2** concoct, deadlocked, gridlocked, half-cocked, landlocked, unlocked, well-stocked.
See also **13.10, 13.10.1.**

13.13: **1** col, doll, jol, loll, moll, pol, troll; **2** atoll, AWOL, Gogol, googol, menthol, obol, podzol, Shawwal, sterol; **3** alcohol, baby doll, Balliol, bannerol, capitol, protocol, sorbitol; **4** cholesterol; **5** paracetamol.

13.13.1: **2** phenol; **3** ethanol, Grand Guignol, Interpol, methanol, Rohypnol, Tylenol; **4** Sebastopol.

13.13.2: **1** sol; **3** aerosol, nuevo sol, parasol; **4** Costa del Sol.

13.14: **1** golf; **2** Adolf, Randolph, Rolf, Rudolf.

13.15: **1** solve; **2** absolve, devolve, dissolve, evolve, involve, resolve, revolve.
See also **10.42.176, 13.16.**

13.16: **2** absolved, dissolved, involved, resolved, unsolved; **3** uninvolved, unresolved.
See also **13.15.**

13.17: **1** hols; **2** consols; **3** Guys and Dolls.

13.18: **1** mom, Om, pom, Somme, tom; **2** condom, pompom; **3** femidom, Peeping Tom, poppadom, Uncle Tom.

13.18.1: 1 bomb; 2 A-bomb, dive-bomb, dumb bomb, firebomb, H-bomb; 3 carpet-bomb, logic bomb.
See also **10.42.84.**

13.18.2: 1 com; 2 dotcom, Ofcom, sitcom; 3 intercom.

13.18.3: 1 glom; 2 aplomb, coulomb, shalom; 3 Absalom.

13.18.4: 1 from, prom; 2 angstrom, maelstrom; 3 CD-ROM; 4 DVD-ROM.

13.19: 1 chomp, clomp, comp, pomp, romp, stomp, swamp, yomp.
See also **13.20.**

13.20: 1 prompt, swamped; 3 teleprompt.
See also **2.54.88, 10.42.169, 13.19.**

13.21: 2 begotten.

13.22: 1 Bonn, on, swan, wan, won, yon; 2 Avon, bang-on, bonbon, bouillon, Caedmon, come-on, crayon, Dion, Gabon, Inchon, muon, rayon, Yvonne; 3 carry-on, etymon, looker-on, Philemon, telethon; 5 spermatozoon.

13.22.1: 2 eon, neon, prion; 3 baryon, nucleon, tachyon; 4 Anacreon, Asunción; 5 Ceredigion; 6 Richard Coeur de Lion.

13.22.2: 1 don; 2 add-on, head-on, radon; 3 Avedon, mastodon.

13.22.3: 2 chiffon, griffon; 3 antiphon, colophon; 4 Bellerophon.

13.22.4: 1 gone, john, Jon; 2 argon, Argonne, begone, bygone, doggone, foregone, forgone, logon, Saigon, Yangon; 3 demijohn, Littlejohn, Little John, nonagon, polygon, undergone, woebegone.

13.22.5: 2 chignon, pinyon; 3 champignon; 4 boeuf bourgignon, filet mignon; 6 cabernet sauvignon.

13.22.6: 1 con, scone; 2 icon, ikon, walk-on, Yukon, zircon; 3 neocon, technikon; 4 emoticon.

13.22.7: 2 colon, Marlon, nylon, salon, Solon, Teflon; 3 Avalon, biathlon, decathlon, echelon, heptathlon; 4 beauty salon, semicolon.

13.22.8: 2 Ceylon; 3 Babylon, epsilon, upsilon.

13.22.9: 2 anon, run-on, turn-on, xenon; 4 Agamemnon, sine qua non.
The Worldly Hope men set their Hearts upon
Turns Ashes—or it prospers; and anon,
Like Snow upon the Desert's dusty Face,

Lighting a little Hour or two—is gone.
(Edward FitzGerald)

13.22.10: 2 capon, clip-on, coupon, crampon, Nippon, tampon.

13.22.11: 2 upon; 3 hereupon, put-upon, thereupon, whereupon.

13.22.12: 1 Ron; 2 boron, hadron, macron, micron, moron, neuron, neutron, thereon, whereon; 3 Acheron, chaperon, electron, Oberon, omicron, positron; 4 interferon, oxymoron.

13.22.13: 2 Perón, Sharon; 3 aileron, hanger-on.

13.22.14: 2 frisson, garçon, Oxon, soupçon, Tucson.

13.22.15: 1 shone; 2 outshone; 3 cabochon, reblochon; 4 Adar Rishon.

13.22.16: 2 baton, canton, crouton, futon, krypton, lepton, photon, piton, proton, spot-on, Teton, Triton.

13.22.17: 2 blouson, boson, hands-on, meson, odds-on; 3 always-on, Brabazon, goings-on.

13.23: 1 fond, frond, wand; 2 abscond, au fond, beau monde, beyond, haut monde; 3 tout le monde.
See also **2.54.77.**

13.23.1: 1 blond, blonde, bond; 2 ash-blond, junk bond; 3 baby bond, bearer bond, honey-blond, triple bond, vagabond; 4 platinum-blond, Premium Bond, treasury bond.
See also **10.42.14.**

13.23.2: 1 pond; 2 blancmange, despond, millpond, respond; 3 correspond; 4 bureau de change.
See also **10.42.14.**

13.24: 1 bonce, nonce, ponce, sconce; 2 ensconce, nuance, response, seance.

13.25: 1 font, Quant, want; 2 Beaumont, détente, Egmont, entente, Stormont, Vermont; 3 Hellespont, poste restante, restaurant.
See also **10.2.81, 10.42.168.**

13.26: 1 bronze, Hons, Johns; 2 bygones, long johns, mod cons, St John's; 3 pros and cons.

13.27: 1 bong, dong, gong, pong, thong, Tong, Wong; 2 bettong, biltong, ding-dong, diphthong, Hong Kong, kampong, King Kong, mahjong, mahjongg, Mekong, Ping-Pong; 3 billabong, Chittagong; 4 lapsang souchong.

13.27.1: **1** long; **2** belong, chaise longue, daylong, furlong, headlong, lifelong, livelong, nightlong, oblong, sidelong, weeklong, yearlong.

Bluebirds
Singing a song;
Nothing but bluebirds
All day long...
(Irving Berlin)
See also **10.42**.

13.27.2: **2** along, prolong; **3** hopalong, overlong, singalong.

13.27.3: **1** prong, strong, throng, wrong; **2** Armstrong, headstrong, sarong.

America, it is to thee, Thou boasted land
of liberty,
—It is to thee I raise my song,
Thou land of blood, and crime, and
wrong.
(James M. Whitfield)

13.27.4: **1** song; **2** birdsong, folksong, part song, plainsong, pop song, singsong, swan song, swansong, torch song; **3** drinking song, evensong, siren song.

13.28: **2** Caen, Longchamps; **3** bouffant, Breton, croissant, Dijon, élan, Gabon, Lyons, Mâcon, vol-au-vent; **4** arondissement, Avignon, contretemps, Danton, denouement, Maupassant, Messiaen, rapprochement, Simenon; **5** bon vivant, en passant.

13.29: **1** bonk, conch, conk, honk, plonk, wonk; **3** honky-tonk.

13.30: **1** Bronx, yonks.

13.31: **1** bop, chop, cop, dop, fop, kop, mop, op, sop; **2** bebop, chop-chop, chump chop, co-op, milksop, rollmop, sysop; **3** Mrs Mop, traffic cop.
See also **13.32**, **13.33**.

13.31.1: **1** hop; **2** bellhop, carhop, hip-hop, trip-hop; **3** bunny hop, Channel-hop.
See also **10.42.110**.

13.31.2: **1** clop, lop, plop, slop; **2** clip-clop, Dunlop, Hislop; **3** escalope.
See also **13.32**, **13.33**.

13.31.3: **1** flop; **2** flip-flop; **3** bellyflop, gigaflop, teraflop; **4** Fosbury flop.
See also **13.32**.

13.31.4: **1** pop; **2** britpop, vox pop; **3** alcopop, bodypop, lollipop.

13.31.5: **1** crop, prop, strop; **2** caltrop, cash crop, outcrop, sharecrop; **3** agitprop, Ribbentrop, turboprop.
See also **13.33**.

13.31.6: **1** drop; **2** airdrop, backdrop, dewdrop, eavesdrop, gumdrop, mail drop, raindrop, snowdrop, teardrop.
See also **13.32**.

13.31.7: **1** shop, shoppe; **2** bookshop, closed shop, pawnshop, sex shop, sweatshop, sweetshop, tuck shop, workshop; **3** barbershop, Body Shop, bucket shop, coffee shop, corner shop, knocking shop, machine shop, talking shop, window-shop; **4** charity shop.
See also **10.42.110**.

13.31.8: **1** top; **2** atop, big top, blacktop, crop top, desktop, flattop, hardtop, hilltop, laptop, palmtop, red-top, rooftop, screw top, soft top, tank top, tiptop, treetop, worktop; **3** carrot-top, countertop, mountaintop, spinning top, tabletop; **4** over-the-top.
See also **10.42.110**, **13.32**.

13.31.9: **1** stop; **2** backstop, doorstop, nonstop, one-stop, pit stop, shortstop, unstop; **3** glottal stop, whistle stop.

13.31.10: **1** swap, whop, wop; **2** doo-wop.

13.32: **1** chops, copse, flops, ops, slops, tops; **2** Cheops, cyclops, raindrops, treetops; **3** muttonchops; **4** triceratops.
See also **13.31**, **13.31.2**, **13.31.3**, **13.31.6**, **13.31.8**.

13.33: **1** chopped, cropped, lopped, opt; **2** adopt, close-cropped, co-opt.
See also **10.2.89**, **13.31**, **13.31.2**, **13.31.5**.

13.34: **1** Cos, fosse, goss, joss, toss; **2** chaos, Cronos, Eos, Hypnos, Lagos, logos, Marcos, Minos, Santos; **3** adios, Helios, Hephaistos, Thanatos; **5** inter alios.
See also **19.6.4**.

13.34.1: **1** boss; **2** emboss, Lesbos, Phobos, rooibos.

13.34.2: **1** DOS, doss; **2** kudos; **3** Abydos, Barbados, calvados, MS-DOS, reredos, tournedos.

13.34.3: **1** floss, gloss, loss, Schloss; **2** blood loss, Delos, tax loss; **3** candyfloss, fairyfloss, hearing loss, omphalos; **4** Mill on the Floss.

If you can make one heap of all your
winnings
And risk it on one turn of pitch-and-toss,
And lose, and start again at your
beginnings

And never breathe a word about your
　loss.
(Rudyard Kipling)
See also **13.36.**

13.34.4: **1** moss; **2** Amos, cosmos, demos; **3** Irish moss.
See also **19.12.**

13.34.5: **1** poss; **2** Campos, epos, topos.

13.34.6: **1** dross, Ross; **2** Eros, kaross, pharos; **3** albatross.

13.34.7: **1** cross; **2** across, Blue Cross, crisscross, George Cross, Iron Cross, Kings Cross, lacrosse, Red Cross, tau cross, uncross; **3** autocross, Celtic cross, Charing Cross, double-cross, Maltese cross, motocross, Southern Cross; **4** Military Cross; **5** Victoria Cross.

Still falls the Rain—
Dark as the world of man, black as our
　loss—
Blind as the nineteen hundred and forty
　nails
Upon the cross.
(Edith Sitwell)
See also **10.42.132, 13.36.**

13.34.8: **2** Athos, bathos, ethos, pathos.

13.35: **1** mosque; **2** Blue Mosque, kiosk; **3** abelmosk, faience, Provence, seance; **7** pièce de résistance.

13.36: **1** crossed, glossed, lost, wast; **2** compost, embossed, glasnost, long-lost, riposte.
See also **13.34.3, 13.34.7.**

13.36.1: **1** cost; **2** accost, low-cost, oncost; **3** Pentecost.
See also **10.42.170.**

13.36.2: **1** frost; **2** defrost, hoar frost, Jack Frost; **3** permafrost.
See also **10.2.90, 10.42.170.**

13.37: **1** Bosch, bosh, cloche, cosh, dosh, gosh, josh, mosh, nosh, posh, slosh, splosh, tosh; **2** brioche, kibosh; **3** mackintosh.
See also **10.42.140, 13.38.**

13.37.1: **1** quash, squash, wash; **2** awash, backwash, brainwash, car wash, eyewash, greenwash, hogwash, mouthwash, whitewash; **3** butternut squash, orange squash.
See also **10.42.140, 13.38.**

13.38: **1** sloshed, squashed; **2** brainwashed, stonewashed, unwashed, whitewashed.
See also **13.37, 13.37.1.**

13.39: **1** bot, dot, got, hot, jot, sot, tot, yacht; **2** begot, gavotte, red-hot, robot, Shevat, white-hot; **3** bergamot, cancelbot, guillemot, microdot, Shavuot.
See also **10.2.63.**

13.39.1: **1** cot, Scot, Scott; **2** Ascot, boycott, mascot, wainscot; **3** apricot, carrycot.
See also **13.40.**

13.39.2: **1** blot, clot, lot, plot, slot; **2** blood clot, inkblot, subplot; **3** monoglot, polyglot; **4** Gunpowder Plot.

They paved paradise
And put up a parking lot
With a pink hotel, a boutique
And a swinging hot spot.
(Joni Mitchell)
See also **10.2.63, 13.40.**

13.39.3: **2** allot, shallot; **3** Camelot, Lancelot, ocelot.

13.39.4: **1** knot, not, snot; **2** cannot, french knot, love knot, reef knot, slipknot, topknot, unknot, whatnot; **3** granny knot; **4** forget-me-not, Gordian knot.
See also **10.2.63.**

13.39.5: **1** pot; **2** compote, crackpot, flowerpot, hotpot, jackpot, teapot, tinpot; **3** chamber pot, coffeepot, honeypot, melting pot.
See also **10.2.63.**

13.39.6: **1** spot; **2** blind spot, despot, fusspot, hot spot, nightspot, pisspot, sexpot, soft spot, sore spot, sunspot, tight spot, weak spot; **4** penalty spot.
See also **10.2.63, 10.42.160.**

13.39.7: **1** rot, trot; **2** dogtrot, foxtrot, garrotte, globetrot, linkrot; **3** tommyrot, turkey trot.
See also **10.42.160.**

13.39.8: **1** shot; **2** big shot, bloodshot, buckshot, crack shot, dead shot, drop shot, earshot, gunshot, hotshot, long shot, mailshot, moonshot, mugshot, potshot, screenshot, slingshot, snapshot, upshot; **3** overshot, parting shot, scattershot; **4** Parthian shot.

13.39.9: **1** squat, swat, swot, twat, watt, what, wot; **2** kumquat, paraquat, somewhat; **3** aliquot, Angkor Wat, kilowatt, megawatt, milliwatt.

13.40: **1** lots, Scots, Watts, what's; **2** culottes, fleshpots, have-nots.
See also **13.39.1, 13.39.2.**

13.41: 1 goth, moth; **3** behemoth.
See also **13.5.**

13.41.1: 1 cloth; **2** backcloth, breechcloth, broadcloth, cheesecloth, dishcloth, dropcloth, facecloth, loincloth, oilcloth, sackcloth, sailcloth, washcloth; **3** saddlecloth, tablecloth, terry cloth.

13.41.2: 1 broth, froth, Roth, wrath; **2** Scotch broth.
See also **13.5.4.**

13.42: 1 blotch, botch, crotch, notch, scotch, splotch; **2** hopscotch, hotchpotch, topnotch; **3** butterscotch.

13.42.1: 1 swatch, watch; **2** night watch, stopwatch, wristwatch; **4** neighbourhood watch, suicide watch.

I am a sundial, and I make a botch
Of what is done far better by a watch.
(Hilaire Belloc)

13.43: 1 of; **2** Rostov; **3** undreamed-of; **4** Sea of Azov.

13.43.1: 2 hereof, thereof, whereof; **3** Sakharov.

13.44: 1 loch, lough, och; **2** Van Gogh.

13.45: 1 Oz, Ros, 'twas, was; **2** because.
See also **9.6.**

14.0: 1 aw, awe, chore, oar, or, ore, Orr, thaw, Thor; **2** Cahors; **3** meteor.
See also **15.0.**

14.1: 1 boar, Boer, Bohr, bore; **2** forbore; **3** hellebore.
See also **10.42.127, 14.19.1.**

14.2: 1 door; **2** backdoor, chador, closed-door, condor, Fodor, four-door, indoor, jackdaw, landau, next-door, outdoor, stridor, trapdoor, two-door; **3** corridor, cuspidor, humidor, louis d'or, Thermidor.

One, two,
Buckle my shoe;
Three, four,
Knock at the door.
(Children's Verse)

14.2.1: 2 adore; **3** commodore, Ecuador, Labrador, matador, mirador, picador, pompadour, Salvador, stevedore, troubador; **4** air commodore, conquistador, El Salvador, San Salvador, toreador; **5** door to door.

I pray thee leave, love me no more,
Call home the heart you gave me
I but in vain the saint adore,
That can, but will not, save me.
(Michael Drayton)
See also **10.42.127.**

14.3: 1 4, for, fore, four; **2** A4, Balfour, before, longed-for, therefore, wherefore; **3** four-by-four, heretofore, uncalled-for, uncared-for, unhoped-for, unlooked-for.

14.3.1: 2 guffaw; **3** metaphor, pinafore, semaphore; **4** mixed metaphor.

14.4: 1 gore; **2** Bogor, gewgaw, Igor, Tagore.

14.5: 1 haw, jaw, whore; **2** abhor, glass jaw, heehaw, Lahore, lockjaw; **3** hem and haw, lantern jaw, Lord Haw-haw.

14.6: 1 yaw, yore, your, you're; **2** Eeyore, senhor, señor, signor.
See also **14.48, 15.1.**

14.7: 1 caw, cor, core, corps; **2** air corps, Angkor, decor, drum corps, encore, hard-core, ichor, macaw, soft-core; **3** army corps, flying corps, manticore, Marine Corps; **4** esprit de corps, kwashiorkor, medical corps; **5** diplomatic corps.

14.7.1: 1 score; **2** fourscore, outscore, Peace Corps, threescore; **3** underscore.
See also **14.48.**

14.8: 1 claw, law, lore, slaw; **2** bylaw, calor, coleslaw, deplore, explore, folklore, galore, implore, lynch law, mob law, outlaw, Sod's Law; **3** Bangalore, canon law, civil law, common-law, court of law, cyberlaw, martial law, rule of law; **4** criminal law, natural law.
See also **10.42.127, 14.48.**

14.8.1: 1 flaw, floor; **2** dance floor, scofflaw, shop floor; **3** fatal flaw, tragic flaw, underfloor.
See also **10.42.127.**

14.8.2: 2 in-law; **3** son-in-law; **4** brother-in-law, daughter-in-law, father-in-law, mother-in-law, sister-in-law.

14.9: 1 maw, moor, Moore, more; **2** Amor, Blackmore, Broadmoor, claymore, Dartmoor, Exmoor, Hawksmoor, Seymour, Timor; **3** any more, Barrymore, Collymore, East Timor, Mount Rushmore; **7** omnia vincit amor.
See also **15.2.**

14.9.1: 2 Scudamore; **3** Baltimore, evermore, furthermore, nevermore, sophomore, sycamore; **4** forevermore.

14.10: 1 gnaw, nor, snore; **2** ignore; **3** Mackinaw.
See also **10.42.**

14.11: 1 paw, poor, pore, pour, spoor, spore; **2** cat's-paw, dirt-poor, downpour, pawpaw, rapport, southpaw; **3** Singapore.

Oozing charm from every pore,
He oiled his way around the floor.
(Alan Jay Lerner)
See also **15.3.**

14.12: **1** braw, craw, crore, raw, roar, straw; **2** cheese straw, furor, last straw, uproar.
See also **10.42.127.**

14.12.1: **1** draw, drawer; **2** outdraw, redraw, withdraw; **3** overdraw, top drawer.
See also **10.42, 14.48.**

14.13: **1** saw, soar, sore; **2** bedsore, buzz saw, chain saw, cold sore, Esau, eyesore, footsore, foresaw, fretsaw, hacksaw, handsaw, jigsaw, lessor, Mysore, Nassau, seesaw, Warsaw; **3** Arkansas, running sore, saddle sore.
See also **10.42.127.**

14.13.1: **3** dinosaur, hadrosaur, oversaw, plesiosaur, pterosaur; **4** circular saw, ichthyosaur, tyrannosaur.

14.14: **1** pshaw, Shaw, shore, sure; **2** ashore, assure, Bradshaw, cocksure, Crawshaw, Crenshaw, Earnshaw, ensure, foreshore, inshore, offshore, onshore, rickshaw, seashore; **4** cycle-rickshaw.
See also **14.19, 15.4.**

14.15: **1** tau, tor, tore; **2** cantor, centaur, Choctaw, mentor, Stentor, Utah; **3** guarantor, Minotaur; **5** caveat emptor.
See also **15.5.**

14.15.1: **1** store; **2** bookstore, chain store, dime-store, drugstore, feedstore, in-store, Nestor, restore; **3** alastor, discount store, megastore, superstore; **4** department store; **5** convenience store.
See also **14.19, 14.48.**

14.16: **2** Cavour; **3** carnivore, frugivore, herbivore, omnivore; **4** insectivore.
See also **2.54.106.**

14.17: **1** phwoah, squaw, swore, war, Waugh, wore; **2** forswore, Gulf War, netwar, postwar, prewar; **3** First World War, interwar, man-of-war, Trojan War, tug of war, twilight war; **4** Second World War, Vietnam War; **5** Iran-Iraq War; **6** Portuguese man-of-war.
See also **14.48.**

14.18: **1** daub, orb; **2** absorb, adsorb, bedaub.
See also **10.42.13.**

14.19: **1** ford, gawd, hoard, horde, Maud, sword, toward; **2** afford, assured, fjord, restored; **3** self-assured.
See also **10.2.11, 10.42.20, 14.14, 14.15.1, 15.6.**

14.19.1: **1** baud, board, bored; **2** billboard, cheeseboard, chessboard, dashboard, floorboard, inboard, larboard, pegboard, sailboard, scoreboard, signboard, snowboard, springboard, surfboard, switchboard, tailboard, washboard; **3** aboveboard, bed and board, chopping board, diving board, draining board, noticeboard, shuffleboard, smorgasbord; **4** bulletin board.

Society is now one polish'd horde,
Form'd of two mighty tribes, the Bores
and Bored.
(Lord Byron)
See also **10.42.21, 14.1.**

14.19.2: **2** aboard; **3** centreboard, checkerboard, clapperboard, daughterboard, fibreboard, fingerboard, mortarboard, motherboard, overboard, plasterboard, weatherboard; **4** across-the-board.

14.19.3: **2** backboard, blackboard, breadboard, buckboard, cardboard, chalkboard, chipboard, clapboard, clipboard, duckboard, hardboard, headboard, keyboard, mopboard, reboard, seaboard, shipboard, sideboard, talkboard; **3** bodyboard, storyboard; **4** emery board; **5** Admiralty Board.

14.19.4: **2** dartboard, draughtboard, footboard, lightboard, outboard, pasteboard, skateboard, whiteboard; **4** idiot board.

14.19.5: **1** chord, cord; **2** accord, concord, concorde, discord, record, ripcord, whipcord; **3** needlecord, track record; **5** umbilical cord.

Now I've heard there was a secret chord
That David played, and it pleased the
Lord
But you don't really care for music, do
you?
(Leonard Cohen)
See also **10.2.11, 10.42.20, 13.4, 14.20.**

14.19.6: **2** record; **3** clavichord, harpsichord, prerecord, tape-record; **4** misericord.
See also **10.2.11, 10.42.20, 13.4, 14.20.**

14.19.7: **1** flawed, laud, lord; **2** applaud, Gaylord, landlord, M'Lord, slumlord, warlord; **3** overlord, unexplored.

*Mine eyes have seen the glory of the
coming of the Lord:
He is trampling out the vintage where the
grapes of wrath are stored.*
(Julia Ward Howe)

14.19.8: **1** broad, fraud; **2** abroad, defraud, maraud; **3** cyberfraud, overawed.

14.19.9: **1** sward, ward; **2** award, reward, toward; **3** untoward; **6** Academy Award.
See also **10.42.20**.

14.20: **1** Broads, cords, Lords; **2** duckboards, Law Lords, records, towards; **3** House of Lords, vocal chords.
See also **14.19.5, 14.19.6**.

14.21: **1** dwarf, morph, Orff, swarf, wharf; **2** waldorf; **3** allomorph, Düsseldorf, ectomorph, endomorph, mesomorph, polymorph.
See also **14.46**.

14.22: **1** Borg, morgue, org; **2** cyborg.

14.23: **1** forge, George, gorge; **2** disgorge, engorge, Lloyd George.
See also **14.37**.

14.24: **1** auk, chalk, dork, fork, gawk, pork, Salk, York, Yorke; **2** fish fork, New York, O'Rourke, pitchfork, salt pork; **3** belly pork.
*I don't drink coffee I take tea my dear;
I like my toast done on the side;
And you can hear it in my accent when I
talk;
I'm an Englishman in New York.*
(The Police)
See also **14.26**.

14.24.1: **1** hawk, Hawke; **2** fish hawk, goshawk, mohawk, newshawk, nighthawk; **3** sparrowhawk, tomahawk; **4** mosquito hawk.

14.24.2: **1** calk, caulk, cork; **2** uncork.
See also **10.42.52, 14.26**.

14.24.3: **1** stalk, stork, talk, torque; **2** back talk, beanstalk, deerstalk, leafstalk, pep talk, sales talk, small talk, sweet-talk, uptalk; **3** baby talk, double talk, pillow talk.
See also **10.42.52, 14.25**.

14.24.4: **1** squawk, walk; **2** boardwalk, cakewalk, catwalk, crabwalk, crosswalk, jaywalk, sidewalk, sleepwalk, spacewalk, streetwalk; **3** Lambeth Walk; **4** cock of the walk.
See also **10.42.52**.

14.25: **1** Fawkes, Hawkes, Hawks, talks; **2** Guy Fawkes, peace talks.
See also **14.24.3**.

14.26: **1** corked, forked, yorked.
See also **14.24, 14.24.2**.

14.27: **1** all, awl, mall, maul, Saul, shawl, small, tall, yawl, y'all; **2** bradawl, catchall, holdall, know-all, withal; **3** carryall, Montreal, wherewithal.
*All things bright and beautiful,
All creatures great and small,
All things wise and wonderful,
The Lord God made them all.*
(C. F. Alexander)
See also **15.7**.

14.27.1: **1** ball, bawl; **2** baseball, blackball, cornball, curveball, eyeball, fireball, goofball, handball, hardball, highball, korfball, mothball, no-ball, oddball, pinball, puffball, punchball, screwball, slimeball, snowball, speedball, stickball, trackball; **3** cannonball, crystal ball, rollerball, tennis ball, volleyball; **5** eyeball-to-eyeball.
See also **10.42.75, 14.28, 14.32**.

14.27.2: **2** football, meatball, netball, paintball, softball, spitball; **3** basketball, racquetball; **6** American football; **7** Association Football.

14.27.3: **1** fall; **2** befall, deadfall, dewfall, downfall, free-fall, icefall, landfall, rainfall, snowfall, windfall; **3** waterfall.
*Then join hand in hand, brave Americans
all!
By uniting we stand, by dividing we fall.*
(John Dickinson)
See also **14.32**.

14.27.4: **2** footfall, nightfall, outfall, pitfall, pratfall, shortfall.

14.27.5: **1** gall, Gaul; **2** Bengal; **3** Donegal, Senegal.
See also **10.42.75**.

14.27.6: **1** hall, haul; **2** dancehall, food hall, guildhall, keelhaul, long haul, mess hall, short-haul, town hall, Whitehall; **3** concert hall, dining hall, entrance hall, lecture hall, music hall, overhaul; **4** assembly hall.

14.27.7: **1** call; **2** catcall, jackal, recall; **3** photocall.
See also **10.42.75**.

14.27.8: **1** pall, Paul; **2** appal, Naipaul, Nepal, St Paul.
See also **10.42.75, 14.28**.

14.27.9: **1** brawl, crawl, drawl, scrawl, sprawl, thrall, trawl; **2** cure-all, enthral, front crawl, pub-crawl; **3** free-for-all, overall.
See also **10.42.75, 14.28, 14.32.**

14.27.10: **1** stall; **2** bookstall, forestall, install; **3** fingerstall, uninstall.
See also **14.32.**

14.27.11: **1** squall, wall; **2** Cornwall, firewall, sea wall, stonewall, whitewall; **3** Berlin Wall, caterwaul, off-the-wall, Wailing Wall, wall-to-wall; **4** Hadrian's Wall.

You think you're a genius – you drive me up the wall
You're a regular original, a know-it-all.
(Shania Twain)
See also **14.28.**

14.28: **1** bald, baulk, scald, sprawled, SWALK, volk, walled; **2** appalled, blackballed, enthralled, mothballed, Oswald, piebald, so-called; **3** Archibald, Theobald.
See also **10.42.14, 14.27.1, 14.27.8, 14.27.9, 14.27.11.**

14.29: **1** false.
See also **9.14.80.**

14.30: **1** salts, schmaltz, waltz; **3** smelling salts.
See also **14.31.2.**

14.31: **1** halt, malt, vault; **2** cobalt, exalt, pole-vault.
See also **10.2.80, 10.42.167.**

14.31.1: **1** fault; **2** asphalt, default, footfault; **3** double fault.

14.31.2: **1** salt; **2** assault, basalt, rock salt; **3** somersault; **4** pepper-and-salt; **5** indecent assault.
See also **10.2.80, 14.30.**

14.32: **1** balls, falls, smalls, stalls; **2** overalls; **3** Chinese walls, coveralls; **4** Niagara Falls; **5** Yosemite Falls.
See also **14.27.1, 14.27.3, 14.27.9, 14.27.10.**

14.33: **1** corm, dorm, Maugham, norm, shawm, swarm, warm; **2** lukewarm, meerschaum.
See also **10.42.88.**

14.33.1: **1** form; **2** conform, freeform, inform, landform, malform, perform, re-form, transform, waveform; **3** chloroform, microform, misinform, outperform; **4** underperform.

God moves in a mysterious way
His wonders to perform;
He plants his footsteps in the sea,
And rides upon the storm.
(William Cowper)
See also **10.42.88, 14.34.**

14.33.2: **2** deform, reform; **3** auriform, cruciform, cuneiform, ensiform, fungiform, multiform, uniform, vermiform; **4** anseriform, bacilliform, passeriform.
See also **9.14.70, 14.34.**

14.33.3: **2** platform; **3** cross-platform; **4** drilling platform, multiplatform.

14.33.4: **1** storm; **2** barnstorm, brainstorm, dust storm, firestorm, hailstorm, rainstorm, sandstorm, snowstorm, windstorm; **3** thunderstorm.
See also **10.42.88.**

14.34: **2** back-formed, deformed, informed, malformed, reformed, transformed, unformed, well-formed; **3** ill-informed, misinformed, ready-formed, uniformed, uninformed, unreformed, well-informed.
See also **14.33.1, 14.33.2.**

14.35: **1** dawn, faun, fawn, lawn, morn, mourn, sawn, Sean, shorn, torn, Vaughan, yawn; **2** adorn, forlorn, lovelorn, Siobhan, war-torn.
See also **10.42.102, 14.36.**

14.35.1: **1** born, borne; **2** airborne, Ayckbourn, Broxbourne, Eastbourne, first-born, forborne, freeborn, Glyndebourne, highborn, inborn, lowborn, newborn, Osborne, reborn, seaborne, stillborn, suborn, unborn, wellborn; **3** waterborne.

14.35.2: **1** horn; **2** bighorn, bullhorn, Cape Horn, crumhorn, foghorn, greenhorn, shoehorn; **3** English horn, flugelhorn, Matterhorn.
See also **10.2.28, 14.36.**

14.35.3: **1** corn, scorn; **2** acorn, popcorn, sweetcorn, tricorn; **3** barleycorn, Capricorn, leprechaun, peppercorn, unicorn.

14.35.4: **1** pawn, porn, spawn; **2** frogspawn.

14.35.5: **1** brawn, drawn, prawn; **2** fine-drawn, indrawn, kingprawn, redrawn, withdrawn; **3** overdrawn.

14.35.6: **1** thorn; **2** blackthorn, hawthorn, Hawthorne.

14.35.7: **1** Quorn, sworn, warn, Warne, worn; **2** careworn, forewarn, forsworn,

outworn, shopworn, timeworn, well-worn;
3 weatherworn.
See also **10.42.102.**

14.36: 1 horned; 2 adorned; 3 unadorned.
See also **14.35, 14.35.2.**

14.37: 1 forged, gorged; 2 engorged.
See also **14.23.**

14.38: 1 daunt, flaunt, gaunt, haunt, jaunt,
taunt.
See also **10.2.87, 10.42.168.**

14.39: 1 haunch, launch, paunch, staunch;
2 relaunch.
See also **10.62.5.**

14.40: 1 dorp, gawp, Thorpe, warp; 2 time
warp.

14.41: 1 corpse; 2 Cleethorpes.

14.42: 1 Bourse, gorse, Morse, Norse;
2 divorce, endorse, remorse, resource;
3 boerewors.
See also **10.42.132, 10.62.3, 14.43.**

14.42.1: 1 force; 2 air force, brute force,
down-force, enforce, G-force, life force,
perforce, task force, workforce; 3 driving
force, reinforce, tour de force, vital force,
Wilberforce; 4 Royal Air Force.
See also **14.43.**

14.42.2: 1 hoarse, horse; 2 carthorse,
clotheshorse, dark horse, draughthorse,
drayhorse, iron horse, one-horse,
packhorse, racehorse, sea horse, warhorse,
Whitehorse, workhorse; 3 hobbyhorse,
quarter horse, stalking horse, Trojan Horse.

14.42.3: 1 coarse, course; 2 concourse,
dampcourse, discourse, first course, golf
course, racecourse, recourse; 3 intercourse,
watercourse; 4 collision course; 6 sexual
intercourse.
See also **2.54.62.**

14.42.4: 1 sauce, source; 2 mint sauce,
outsource, resource, soy sauce, white
sauce; 3 béarnaise sauce, Worcester sauce;
4 béchamel sauce, tomato sauce.
See also **10.42.132, 10.62.3.**

14.43: 1 forced; 2 divorced, endorsed,
enforced, exhaust, outsourced, unforced,
unsourced; 3 holocaust, hypocaust,
reinforced; 4 underresourced.
See also **10.2.90, 10.42.170, 14.42,
14.42.1.**

14.44: 1 aught, bought, fort, forte, fought,
ought, quart, short, thwart, wart; 2 abort,
cavort, cohort, exhort, onslaught, resort,
store-bought; 3 last resort.

So let us love, dear Love, like as we ought,
Love is the lesson which the Lord us
taught.
(Edmund Spenser)
See also **14.45.**

14.44.1: 1 caught, court; 2 Crown Court,
Earl's Court, escort, forecourt, High Court,
squash court; 3 out-of-court, tennis court;
4 family court, kangaroo court.
See also **10.42.161.**

14.44.2: 1 naught, nought, snort;
2 Connacht, dreadnought.

14.44.3: 3 aeronaut, Argonaut, astronaut,
cosmonaut, cybernaut, juggernaut.

14.44.4: 1 port; 2 airport, carport,
comport, deport, import, Newport, purport,
report, seaport; 3 davenport, heliport,
misreport, multiport, reimport, teleport.
See also **10.2.64, 10.42.161.**

14.44.5: 2 purport, support; 3 dataport;
4 income support, moral support.
See also **10.2.64, 10.42.161.**

14.44.6: 1 sport; 2 disport, export,
passport, spoilsport, transport;
3 motorsport.
See also **10.42.161, 14.45.**

14.44.7: 1 fraught, rort, sort, wrought;
2 besought, consort, distraught, re-sort;
3 overwrought.

14.44.8: 1 taught, taut, tort; 2 contort,
distort, extort, retort, self-taught.
See also **10.2.64.**

14.44.9: 1 thought; 2 forethought,
rethought; 3 aforethought, afterthought,
second thought; 5 malice aforethought.
Treason was in her thought,
And cunningly to yield herself she sought.
Seeming not won, yet won she was at
length;
In such wars women use but half their
strength.
(Christopher Marlowe)
See also **14.45.**

14.45: 1 quartz, shorts, sports, thoughts;
2 blood sports; 3 jockey shorts, second
thoughts, undershorts.
See also **14.44, 14.44.6, 14.44.9.**

14.46: 1 forth, fourth, north; 2 henceforth,
thenceforth; 3 back-and-forth, Firth of
Forth.
See also **14.21.**

14.47: 1 porch, scorch, torch;
2 blowtorch, debauch.
See also **10.42.175.**

14.48: 1 cause, clause, Dawes, drawers, gauze, laws, Moors, Mors, pause, scores, stores, wars, yaws, yours; 2 applause, Azores, indoors, outdoors, plus fours, Star Wars; 3 chest of drawers, menopause, out-of-doors, Santa Claus, tropopause.
See also **2.15, 14.6, 14.7.1, 14.8, 14.12.1, 14.15.1, 14.17, 15.2.**

15.0: 1 boor, dour, gur, Ruhr; 2 abjure, adjure, bonjour, Cavour, du jour, velour, velours; 3 petit four, plat du jour, pompadour, troubadour.
See also **14.0.**

15.1: 1 lure, Muir, pure, Ure; 2 allure, coiffure, demure, endure, immure, impure, manure, ordure, valuer; 3 Côte d'Azur.
See also **10.42.128, 14.6.**

15.1.1: 1 cure; 2 liqueur, obscure, procure, secure; 3 epicure, insecure, manicure, pedicure, sinecure.
See also **9.14.46, 10.42.128, 15.6.**

15.1.2: 2 cloture, couture, mature; 3 haute couture, immature, overture; 4 caricature.
See also **15.6.**

15.2: 1 Moor, Moore; 2 amour, Amur, Hawksmoor; 3 paramour.
See also **14.9, 14.48.**

15.3: 1 poor, spoor; 2 Kanpur, Nagpur; 3 Yom Kippur; 4 Kuala Lumpur.
See also **14.11.**

15.4: 1 sure; 2 insure, unsure; 3 embouchure, reassure.
See also **10.42.128, 14.14, 15.6.**

15.5: 1 tour, Tours; 2 contour, detour, grand tour; 4 Château Latour, mystery tour, whistle-stop tour.
See also **14.15.**

15.6: 1 cured, gourd, Lourdes; 2 coiffured, contoured, insured, inured, matured, obscured; 3 manicured, unsecured.
See also **14.19, 15.1.1, 15.1.2, 15.4.**

15.7: 2 Lowell, manual, usual, virtual, visual; 3 asexual, biannual, bisexual, consensual, continual, contractual, unusual.
See also **9.14.5, 14.27.**

15.8: 2 vacuum; 3 continuum; 4 residuum.

15.9: 2 vacuous; 3 assiduous, conspicuous, contemptuous, contiguous, continuous, exiguous; 4 unambiguous.
See also **9.14.81.**

15.10: 2 unctuous, virtuous; 3 tumultuous, unvirtuous, voluptuous.
See also **2.54.83.**

16.0: 1 bough, bow, chow, ciao, miaow, now, ow, sough, sow, Tao, tau, thou, vow, wow; 2 avow, Bilbao, bow-wow, Callao, Davao, kowtow, Lucknow, powwow; 3 Curaçao, disavow, Krakatau; 5 holier-than-thou.
See also **10.42, 16.6, 19.23.**

16.1: 1 dhow, dow, Tao; 2 endow, the Dow.
See also **16.6.**

16.2: 1 how, Howe; 2 know-how, somehow; 3 anyhow.
Why for fifty-three years I've put up with it now.
I must stop Christmas from coming, but how?
(Dr. Seuss)

16.3: 1 cow; 2 cacao, cash cow, Kraków, Macau, milch cow.
See also **16.6.**

16.4: 1 plough, slough; 2 allow, Palau, pilau, snowplough; 3 disallow.
Come, friendly bombs, and fall on Slough
To get it ready for the plough.
The cabbages are coming now:
The earth exhales.
(John Betjeman)

16.5: 1 brow, prow, row; 2 eyebrow, gherao, highbrow, Jungfrau, lowbrow.
See also **10.42.11.**

16.6: 1 bowed, cowed, loud, Saud; 2 allowed, aloud, avowed, endowed, unbowed; 3 disallowed, well-endowed.
You used to laugh about,
Everybody that was hangin' out.
Now you don't talk so loud,
Now you don't seem so proud
About having to be scrounging for your next meal.
(Bob Dylan)
See also **9.14.57, 16.0, 16.1, 16.3.**

16.6.1: 1 cloud; 2 MacLeod, war cloud; 3 funnel cloud, mushroom cloud, overcloud, thundercloud.
See also **10.2.12, 10.2.15.**

16.6.2: 1 crowd, proud, shroud; 2 enshroud, houseproud; 3 overcrowd, overproud.
See also **9.14.56, 10.2.12.**

16.7: 1 Louth, mouth; 2 bad-mouth.

16.8: 2 big-mouthed, closemouthed, loudmouthed; 3 mealy-mouthed, open-mouthed.

16.9: **1** cowl, growl, howl, jowl, owl, prowl, scowl, yowl; **2** night owl; **3** cheek-by-jowl.
See also **10.42.58**.

16.9.1: **1** foul, fowl; **2** befoul, peafowl, wildfowl; **3** guinea fowl, waterfowl.

16.10: **1** clown, noun; **2** pronoun, renown.

16.10.1: **1** down; **2** Ashdown, clampdown, closedown, comedown, drawdown, facedown, lie-down, pull-down, pushdown, rubdown, stand-down, step-down, swansdown, top-down, touchdown; **3** dressing-down, eiderdown, thistledown, tumbledown, watered-down.
No time to marry, no time to settle down,
I'm a young woman, and I ain't done
runnin' aroun'.
(Bessie Smith)

16.10.2: **2** godown, hoedown, lowdown, showdown, slowdown.

16.10.3: **2** breakdown, crackdown, knockdown, markdown, shakedown.

16.10.4: **2** run-down, sundown, turndown; **3** broken-down, button-down.

16.10.5: **2** countdown, letdown, meltdown, putdown, shutdown.

16.10.6: **1** gown; **2** ballgown, bedgown, nightgown; **3** dinner gown, evening gown, town-and-gown.

16.10.7: **1** Braun, brown, crown, drown, frown.
See also **10.42.92, 16.11.5**.

16.10.8: **1** town; **2** cross-town, downtown, Freetown, Georgetown, hick town, midtown, Motown, toytown, uptown; **3** Chinatown, Kentish Town, out-of-town, Tinseltown.

16.11: **1** mound, wound; **2** astound, redound, renowned, resound, rewound.
See also **10.2.16, 10.2.22, 10.42.30**.

16.11.1: **1** bound; **2** abound, deskbound, earthbound, eastbound, fogbound, hardbound, hidebound, homebound, housebound, icebound, inbound, northbound, outbound, pot-bound, rebound, snowbound, southbound, spellbound, unbound, westbound; **3** duty-bound, inward-bound, musclebound, outward-bound, weatherbound.

16.11.2: **1** found; **2** confound, dumbfound, newfound, profound.
All that noise, and all that sound,
All those places I got found.
And birds go flying at the speed of sound,

to show you how it all began.
(Coldplay)
See also **9.14.60, 10.2.22**.

16.11.3: **1** hound; **2** bloodhound, deerhound, elkhound, foxhound, greyhound, hellhound, horehound, newshound, wolfhound; **3** Afghan hound, basset hound, otterhound; **4** Irish wolfhound.

16.11.4: **1** pound; **2** compound, expound, green pound, impound, propound.
See also **10.2.22, 10.42.30**.

16.11.5: **1** browned, crowned, drowned, round; **2** milk round, turnround, uncrowned, whip-round; **3** all-round, baton round, daily round; **4** merry-go-round.
See also **16.10.7**.

16.11.6: **2** around, surround; **3** all-around, runaround, turnaround, workaround, wraparound.
See also **10.42.30**.

16.11.7: **1** ground; **2** aground, background, campground, fairground, foreground, high ground, home ground, playground, showground, stoneground; **3** battleground, breeding ground, common ground, middle ground, overground, underground; **4** burial ground; **5** happy hunting ground.
The stars grew bright in the winter sky,
The wind came keen with a tang of frost,
The brook was troubled for new things
lost,
The copse was happy for old things found,
The fox came home and he went to
ground.
(John Masefield)
See also **10.42.30**.

16.11.8: **1** lounge, scrounge, sound; **2** unsound; **3** cocktail lounge, infrasound, Plymouth Sound, ultrasound.
See also **2.54.77, 10.42.30**.

16.12: **1** bounce, flounce, ounce, pounce, trounce.
See also **10.42.138**.

16.12.1: **2** announce, denounce, pronounce, renounce; **3** mispronounce.

16.13: **1** count, fount; **2** account, discount, headcount, miscount, recount, re-count, viscount; **5** unit of account.
See also **10.2.81, 10.42.168**.

16.13.1: **1** mount; **2** amount, dismount, remount, surmount; **3** paramount, tantamount.
See also **10.2.81, 10.42.168**.

16.14: **1** douse, dowse, grouse, nous, Scouse, souse, spouse, Strauss; **2** Manaus. *See also* **16.15**.

16.14.1: **1** house; **2** almshouse, bathhouse, Bauhaus, clubhouse, doghouse, doll's house, dosshouse, farmhouse, flophouse, glasshouse, playhouse, poorhouse, powerhouse, roughhouse, safe house, storehouse, teahouse, warehouse, whorehouse; **3** bawdyhouse, coffeehouse, lazar-house, meeting house, Wendy house.

Twas the night before Christmas, when
all through the house
Not a creature was stirring—not even a
mouse;
The stockings were hung by the chimney
with care,
In hopes that St. Nicholas soon would be
there.
(Clement Moore)
See also **10.42.190**.

16.14.2: **3** chapterhouse, Charterhouse, house-to-house, manor house, picture house, Porterhouse, slaughterhouse, summerhouse, treasure house, Waterhouse; **4** opera house.

16.14.3: **2** birdhouse, guardhouse, madhouse, roadhouse, roundhouse, Wodehouse, Woodhouse; **4** Holyrood House.

16.14.4: **2** bakehouse, blockhouse, bunkhouse, cookhouse, crackhouse, Monkhouse, steakhouse, workhouse; **3** public house.

16.14.5: **2** alehouse, dollhouse, full house, jailhouse, schoolhouse, wheelhouse; **3** charnel house.

16.14.6: **2** greenhouse, henhouse, in-house, Stonehouse, Winehouse; **3** Mansion House, open house.

16.14.7: **2** boathouse, cathouse, courthouse, gatehouse, guest house, guesthouse, hothouse, lighthouse, nuthouse, oasthouse, outhouse, penthouse, shithouse, statehouse, White House; **4** Mary Whitehouse.

16.14.8: **1** Laos, louse; **2** booklouse, delouse, woodlouse.

16.14.9: **1** mouse; **2** dormouse, fieldmouse, titmouse; **3** cat-and-mouse, flying mouse, Mickey Mouse; **4** optical mouse.

There was a crooked man, and he walked
a crooked mile,

He found a crooked sixpence against a
crooked stile:
He bought a crooked cat, which caught a
crooked mouse,
And they all lived together in a little
crooked house.
(Children's Verse)

16.15: **1** Faust, joust, oust, roust, soused. *See also* **16.14**.

16.16: **1** bout, gout, out, shout; **2** blowout, clear-out, closeout, devout, dugout, far-out, hangout, lights out, logout, mahout, throughout, timeout, washout, without; **3** falling-out. *See also* **10.42.143**.

16.16.1: **2** about; **3** gadabout, knockabout, layabout, roundabout, roustabout, runabout, turnabout, walkabout; **5** mini roundabout.

16.16.2: **1** doubt; **2** buyout, fade-out, handout, hideout, layout, payout, read-out, self-doubt, sold-out, tryout, way-out; **3** carryout, foldout, inside-out.

Attempt the end, and never stand to
doubt;
Nothing's so hard but search will find it
out.
(Robert Herrick)

16.16.3: **1** scout; **2** blackout, boy scout, checkout, cookout, Cub Scout, girl scout, knockout, lockout, lookout, strikeout, walkout, workout; **3** talent scout. *See also* **10.42.143**.

16.16.4: **2** breakout, shake-out, stakeout, takeout.

16.16.5: **1** clout, flout, lout; **2** all-out, bailout, chillout, fallout, pullout, rollout, sellout, umlaut.

16.16.6: **1** nowt, snout; **2** brownout, burnout, drawn-out, line-out, turnout, worn-out; **3** down-and-out, long-drawn-out, out-and-out.

16.16.7: **1** pout, spout; **2** cop-out, downspout, dropout, sleep-out, wipeout; **3** waterspout.

16.16.8: **1** drought, grout, Kraut, rout, sprout, trout; **2** bean sprout, sauerkraut; **3** Brussels sprout.

16.16.9: **1** stout, tout; **2** clapped-out, cutout, flat-out, get-out, hit out, let-out, opt-out, printout, shoot-out, shoutout, shutout, washed-out, whiteout; **3** well-thought-out.

16.17: **3** hereabouts, ins and outs, thereabouts, whereabouts.

16.18: **1** mouth, south; **2** badmouth, bigmouth, goalmouth, loudmouth; **3** blabbermouth, foot-and-mouth, hand-to-mouth, motormouth, word of mouth; **5** mouth-to-mouth.

16.19: **1** couch, crouch, grouch, ouch, pouch, slouch, vouch; **2** debouch.

16.20: **2** closemouthed; **3** mealy-mouthed; **5** foul-mouthed.

16.21: **1** blouse, dowse, house; **2** espouse, rehouse.
See also **10.42.190**.

16.21.1: **1** browse, drowse, rouse; **2** arouse, carouse.
See also **10.42.190**.

17.0: **1** Bauer, bower, cower, dour, dower, Gower, hour, our, scour, shower, sour; **2** devour, half-hour, man-hour; **3** Adenauer, Schopenhauer, sweet-and-sour, whiskey sour, witching hour, zero hour; **4** meteor shower.
See also **17.5**.

17.1: **1** glower, lour, lower.
See also **10.42.129**.

17.1.1: **1** flour, flower; **2** bellflower, coneflower, cornflour, cornflower, deflower, moonflower, pasqueflower, safflower, sunflower, wallflower, white flour; **3** cauliflower, monkeyflower, passionflower.
Since brass, nor stone, nor earth, nor boundless sea,
But sad mortality o'ersways their power,
How with this rage shall beauty hold a plea,
Whose action is no stronger than a flower?
(William Shakespeare)
See also **10.42.129, 17.3**.

17.2: **1** power, tower; **2** Black power, brainpower, clock tower, empower, firepower, horsepower, kowtower, manpower, watchtower, wave power, willpower, wind power; **3** bell tower, Blackpool Tower, Bloody Tower, control tower, cooling tower, disempower, Eiffel Tower, ivory tower, micropower, overpower, superpower, tidal power; **4** Martello tower, nuclear power.
See also **10.42.129, 17.3**.

17.3: **1** coward, flowered, Howard; **2** empowered, high-powered.
See also **17.1.1, 17.2**.

17.4: **1** bowel, dowel, Powell, towel, trowel, vowel; **2** avowal, dishtowel, tea towel; **3** disavowal, disembowel.
See also **2.39, 10.42.58**.

17.5: **1** hours, ours; **3** working hours.
See also **17.0**.

18.0: **1** goy, oi, soy, toy; **2** ahoy, annoy, borzoi, convoy, envoi, envoy, Tannoy.
'And hast thou slain the Jabberwock?
Come to my arms, my beamish boy!
O frabjous day! Callooh! Callay!'
He chortled in his joy.
(Lewis Carroll)
See also **10.42, 18.5.2**.

18.1: **1** boy, buoy, joy; **2** ball boy, bellboy, busboy, choirboy, cowboy, doughboy, enjoy, hautboy, head boy, highboy, homeboy, houseboy, killjoy, lifebuoy, new boy, old boy, pageboy, playboy, po-boy, rent boy, schoolboy, tallboy, tomboy, toyboy; **3** barrow boy, blue-eyed boy, bovver boy, bully boy, errand boy, lover boy, mummy's boy, pride and joy, whipping boy; **4** principal boy.

18.2: **1** coy, koi; **2** decoy, McCoy.

18.3: **1** cloy, ploy; **2** alloy, auloi, deploy, employ; **3** disemploy, hoi polloi, kumbaloi, redeploy, trompe l'oeil.
For he lives twice who can at once employ
The present well, and e'en the past enjoy.
(Alexander Pope)
See also **10.42, 18.5.1**.

18.4: **2** Delroy, destroy, Fitzroy, Leroy, viceroy; **3** corduroy; **4** Helen of Troy.
See also **18.5.3**.

18.5: **2** cuboid, factoid, mastoid, rhomboid, schizoid, typhoid; **3** anthropoid, overjoyed, planetoid, trapezoid.

18.5.1: **1** Floyd, Lloyd; **2** colloid, employed, tabloid; **3** alkaloid, celluloid, metalloid, self-employed, unalloyed, unemployed; **4** underemployed.
See also **18.3**.

18.5.2: **2** annoyed; **3** arachnoid, humanoid, paranoid; **4** carotenoid.
See also **18.0**.

18.5.3: **2** Ackroyd, android, Boothroyd, choroid, dendroid, destroyed, negroid, steroid, thyroid; **3** aneroid, asteroid, Polaroid; **5** corticosteroid; **6** anabolic steroid.
See also **18.4**.

18.5.4: **1** void; **2** avoid, devoid, ovoid;
3 null and void.

18.6: **1** Lloyd's; **3** adenoids,
haemorrhoids.

18.7: **1** Hawick, hoick, oik.

18.8: **1** boil, broil, coil, moil, oil, roil,
spoil, toil, voile; **2** bespoil, charbroil, crude
oil, despoil, gargoyle, gumboil, hardboil,
palm oil, parboil, recoil, snake oil, turmoil,
uncoil; **3** castor oil, fuel oil, olive oil,
sunflower oil; **4** cod-liver oil, essential oil;
5 vegetable oil.
See also **18.9, 18.10.**

18.8.1: **1** foil, soil; **2** cinquefoil, jetfoil,
milfoil, subsoil, tinfoil, topsoil, trefoil;
3 aerofoil, counterfoil, hydrofoil,
undersoil; **4** Fianna Fáil.
See also **18.9.**

18.9: **1** boiled, coiled, foiled, oiled,
spoiled; **2** embroiled, hard-boiled, soft-
boiled, unspoiled, well-oiled; **3** unsoiled.
See also **18.8, 18.8.1.**

18.10: **1** spoils, toils.
See also **18.8.**

18.11: **1** coin, groin, groyne, loin;
2 Gascoigne, purloin, sirloin; **3** tenderloin.

18.11.1: **1** join; **2** adjoin, conjoin, enjoin,
rejoin.
See also **10.42.92.**

18.12: **1** joint, point; **2** anoint, appoint,
ballpoint, breakpoint, cashpoint,
checkpoint, choke point, dew point,
flashpoint, gunpoint, low point, midpoint,
pinpoint, standpoint, viewpoint; **3** breaking
point, counterpoint, disappoint, floating-
point, needlepoint, selling point.
See also **9.14.92, 10.2.88, 10.42.168.**

18.13: **1** boink, oink.

18.14: **1** Boyce, choice, voice; **2** devoice,
first choice, invoice, pro-choice, rejoice,
Rolls-Royce, tortoise; **3** Hobson's choice;
4 multiple-choice.
See also **10.42.132, 18.15.**

18.15: **1** foist, hoist, joist, moist, voiced;
2 unvoiced.
See also **18.14.**

18.16: **2** adroit, dacoit, exploit;
3 maladroit.
See also **2.54.88.**

18.17: **1** noise, poise; **2** big noise,
turquoise, white noise; **3** Anglepoise,
counterpoise; **4** avoirdupois.
*Secrets with girls, like loaded guns with
  boys,*

Are never valued till they make a noise.
(George Crabbe)

19.0: **1** o, oh, owe, tho', though, whoa,
woe, Yeo; **2** although, boyo, duo, Fuzhou,
Io, Rouault; **3** arroyo, BYO, Ohio, quid pro
quo, status quo; **4** continuo.
Monday's child is fair of face,
Tuesday's child is full of grace,
Wednesday's child is full of woe,
Thursday's child has far to go,
Friday's child is loving and giving,
*Saturday's child works hard for his
  living,*
*And the child that is born on the Sabbath
  day*
Is bonny and blithe, and good and gay.
(Children's Verse)
See also **10.42.8, 19.23.**

19.1: **2** KO, mayo; **3** Orfeo, rodeo;
5 Idomineo, Jubilate Deo.

19.2: **2** BO; **3** bagnio, Borneo, cambio,
cameo, CEO, nuncio, patio, physio, PTO,
romeo, Scipio, Scorpio; **4** Antonio,
arpeggio, Di Maggio, D'Annunzio,
Pinocchio; **5** Caravaggio.

19.2.1: **3** audio, radio, rodeo, studio,
video; **4** Palladio; **5** straight-to-video.

19.2.2: **2** Cleo, Leo; **3** Clio, folio, polio;
4 Fidelio, imbroglio, intaglio, portfolio,
seraglio.

19.2.3: **2** brio, griot, Rio, trio; **3** barrio,
Blériot, cheerio, con brio, curio, embryo,
Mario, stereo; **4** Lothario, scenario;
5 impresario, oratorio.

19.2.4: **3** ratio; **4** fellatio, mustachio,
pistachio; **5** ab initio, ex officio.

19.2.5: **4** Boccaccio, capriccio, Carpaccio,
pasticcio, radicchio; **5** braggadocio.

19.3: **1** beau, beaux, bow; **2** Asbo, bilbo,
bubo, combo, crossbow, elbow, Garbo,
hobo, longbow, Mabo, oboe, oxbow,
rainbow, turbo, yobbo; **3** dicky bow,
gazebo, placebo, theorbo; **5** Maracaibo.
Oranges and lemons,
Say the bell of St Clement's.
You owe me five farthings,
Say the bells of St Martin's.
When will you pay me?
Say the bells of Old Bailey.
When I grow rich,
Say the bells of Shoreditch.
When will that be?
Say the bells of Stepney.
I'm sure I don't know,

Says the great bell at Bow.
(Children's Verse)
See also **19.23.**

19.3.1: 2 flambeau, mambo, Rambo, Rimbaud.

19.3.2: 2 bimbo, Crimbo, limbo; **3** akimbo.

19.3.3: 2 dumbo, gumbo, jumbo; **3** Colombo; **4** mumbo jumbo.

19.4: 1 doe, doh, dough, d'oh; **2** Bordeaux, Credo, dado, dildo, dodo, Fido, kiddo, meadow, Murdo, saddo, sourdough, Waldo, weirdo, widow; **3** Ronaldo, tornado. *See also* **2.60.1, 20.53.**

19.4.1: 2 shadow; **3** eye-shadow, foreshadow; **4** overshadow; **5** five o'clock shadow.

19.4.2: 2 Bardot, Prado; **3** Barnardo, bravado, Mikado; **4** avocado, bastinado, Colorado, desperado, El Dorado, muscovado; **5** Amontillado; **6** aficionado, incommunicado.

19.4.3: 2 comedo, credo, lido; **3** aikido, libido, torpedo, tuxedo.

19.4.4: 2 judo, ludo, pseudo, Trudeau; **3** escudo, testudo.

19.4.5: 2 condo, rondeau, window; **3** commando.

19.4.6: 2 bandeau, Brando, Dando; **3** Hernando, Orlando; **4** rallentando; **5** accelerando.

19.4.7: 2 kendo; **3** crescendo; **4** decrescendo, innuendo; **5** diminuendo.

19.5: 1 faux, foe; **2** info, mofo, nympho, Sappho, Truffaut; **3** comme il faut, UFO; **5** Tel Aviv-Yafo.

19.6: 1 go; **2** ago, doggo, ergo, forego, forgo, GIGO, Glasgow, Hugo, Lego, outgo, stop-go, Virgo; **3** touch-and-go, undergo; **4** pay-as-you-go; **5** archipelago. *See also* **10.42.9.**

19.6.1: 2 Argo, argot, cargo, Fargo, largo; **3** Chicago, embargo, escargots, farrago, Iago, imago, Key Largo, virago; **4** Santiago.

19.6.2: 2 dago, sago; **3** Diego, lumbago, manchego, plumbago; **4** Winnebago.

19.6.3: 2 ego; **3** amigo, indigo, Inigo, lentigo, vertigo; **4** alter ego, impetigo, superego.

19.6.4: 2 logo, no-go, pogo, Togo; **3** a gogo. *See also* **13.34.**

19.6.5: 2 mango, quango, tango; **3** contango, fandango.

19.6.6: 2 bingo, dingo, gringo, jingo, lingo; **3** flamingo.

19.7: 1 ho, hoe; **2** backhoe, Dutch hoe, gung ho, oho; **3** Lake Tahoe, Navajo.

19.8: 1 jo, Joe; **2** banjo, dojo, Guangzhou, Hangzhou, Lanzhou, mojo, rego; **3** adagio.

19.9: 1 yo; **2** maillot, yo-yo; **3** El Niño, seraglio; **4** jalapeño.

19.10: 1 Coe; **2** Biko, Bilko, chico, Foucault, psycho, Rothko, stucco, telco; **3** Bamako, Monaco, Morocco, Nabucco, sirocco; **4** Acapulco, Puerto Rico.

19.10.1: 2 Kraków, taco, wacko; **3** tobacco.

19.10.2: 2 dekko, echo, Eco, gecko, Greco; **3** art deco, re-echo, zydeco.

19.10.3: 2 sicko, thicko; **3** calico, haricot, Mexico, New Mexico, portico; **4** politico, simpatico; **5** Fra Angelico.

19.10.4: 2 choko, cocoa, loco; **3** rococo.

19.10.5: 2 blanco, bronco, bunco, Franco; **3** flamenco, pachinko; **4** Yevtushenko.

19.10.6: 2 disco, fresco, Moscow; **3** alfresco, fiasco, Lambrusco, Tabasco, UNESCO; **4** Ionesco, Kosciusko.

19.11: 1 lo, low, Lowe, sloe, slow; **2** bolo, filo, furlough, go-slow, halo, Hounslow, kilo, Lilo, merlot, Milo, Oslo, polo, silo, solo; **3** São Paulo; **4** Marco Polo.
The flower-fed buffaloes of the spring
In the days of long ago,
Ranged where the locomotives sing
And the prairie flowers lie low.
(Vachel Lindsay)

19.11.1: 2 aloe, callow, fallow, hallow, mallow, sallow, shallow, tallow; **3** marshmallow.

19.11.2: 2 hallo, hello, hullo; **3** beefalo, Bigelow, buffalo, bungalow, gigolo, pedalo, piccolo, tangelo, tremolo; **5** Michelangelo.

19.11.3: 2 Barlow, Carlow, Harlow, Kahlo, Malo, Marlowe; **3** Giancarlo; **4** Monte Carlo.

19.11.4: 2 bellow, cello, mellow, rello, yellow; **3** bordello, Costello, Novello, Othello; **4** Donatello; **5** violoncello. *See also* **19.52.1.**

19.11.5: 2 felloe, fellow; 3 bedfellow, Longfellow, playfellow, Stringfellow.

19.11.6: 2 below, billow, gweilo, pillow, willow; 3 Manilow, Portillo; 4 armadillo, cigarillo, peccadillo.

19.11.7: 2 follow, hollow, Rollo, swallow, wallow; 3 Apollo, Barolo. *See also* **10.42.10**.

19.11.8: 1 blow; 2 deathblow, Pablo, pueblo, tableau.

19.11.9: 1 floe, flow; 2 airflow, backflow, cash flow, inflow, outflow, workflow; 3 autoflow, contraflow, ebb and flow, overflow. *See also* **10.42.10**.

19.11.10: 1 glow; 2 aglow, Anglo, Day-Glo; 3 afterglow. *See also* **10.42.10**.

19.12: 1 mo, mot, mow, schmo; 2 ammo, chemo, Como, demo, Elmo, homo, Malmö, memo, MO, promo, sumo; 3 bon mot, duomo, dynamo, Giacomo, Palermo, supremo. *See also* **13.34.4**.

19.12.1: 2 limo; 3 Eskimo; 4 fortissimo, Geronimo, prestissimo; 5 duodecimo, pianissimo.

19.12.2: 2 Cosmo, gismo, gizmo; 3 machismo.

19.13: 1 know, no, snow; 2 Benaud, Bruno, dunno, Gounod, Juno, lino, minnow, mono, porno, Renault, rhino, steno, techno, winnow, wino; 3 domino, Huguenot, Llandudno, piano, volcano.

I don't really want to stop the show,
But I thought that you might like to know,
That the singer's going to sing a song,
And he wants you all to sing along.
(John Lennon, Paul McCartney)
See also **10.42.8, 19.52.2**.

19.13.1: 2 Arno, guano, piano; 3 Chicano, Lugano, Meccano, Pisano, soprano, Sukarno; 4 oregano; 5 americano, boliviano.

19.13.2: 2 Brno, journo; 3 Averno, Falerno, inferno, Salerno.

19.13.3: 2 beano, Fino, vino, Zeno; 3 albino, bambino, casino; 4 Angeleno, Filipino, maraschino, palomino, Trasimeno.

19.13.4: 2 chino, Reno; 3 Latino, merino, neutrino; 4 andantino, cappuccino,

concertino, Frappuccino, mochaccino, pecorino, San Marino, Valentino.

19.13.5: 2 Bono, no-no, Ono; 3 de Bono, kimono, pro bono.

19.14: 1 Po, Poe; 2 campo, capo, cheapo, depot, expo, hippo, oppo, tempo, typo; 3 Aleppo, apropos, da capo, downtempo, Gestapo, uptempo; 4 Fernando Po, malapropos.

19.15: 1 bro, fro, pro, rho, roe, row; 2 Afro, Biro, burro, burrow, cornrow, dobro, Ebro, fibro, furrow, gyro, hedgerow, hydro, Miró, Monroe, Munro, per pro, Pierrot, repro, taro, tiro, tyro, windrow; 3 bolero, Diderot, McEnroe, Pissarro, Pizarro, Sapporo, to and fro; 4 Avogadro; 6 Mount Kilimanjaro.

In Flanders fields the poppies blow
Between the crosses, row on row,
That mark our place; and in the sky
The larks, still bravely singing, fly
Scarce heard amid the guns below.
(John McCrae)
See also **10.42.11, 19.23.5**.

19.15.1: 2 arrow, barrow, farrow, harrow, marrow, narrow, sparrow, tarot, yarrow; 3 Figaro, wheelbarrow. *See also* **19.52.7**.

19.15.2: 2 pharaoh; 3 bolero, dinero, ranchero, sombrero; 4 caballero.

19.15.3: 2 hero, zero; 3 De Niro, ground zero; 4 antihero, superhero; 5 absolute zero; 6 Rio de Janeiro.

19.15.4: 2 borrow, Corot, morrow, sorrow; 3 tomorrow. *See also* **10.42.11**.

19.15.5: 2 bureau, Douro, euro; 4 Politburo; 5 chiaroscuro.

19.15.6: 1 grow; 2 aggro, negro, outgrow; 3 allegro, Babygro, overgrow; 4 Montenegro. *See also* **10.42.11**.

19.15.7: 1 crow, Crowe; 2 cockcrow, escrow, macro, scarecrow, Velcro.

19.15.8: 2 bistro, Castro, cointreau, de trop, intro, maestro, metro, retro; 3 cilantro, electro, in vitro.

19.15.9: 1 throe, throw; 2 death row, Jethro, misthrow; 3 overthrow.

Death be not proud, though some have
*   called thee*
Mighty and dreadful, for, thou art not so,
For, those, whom thou think'st, thou dost
*   overthrow,*

Die not, poor death, nor yet canst thou
kill me.
(John Donne)

19.16: **1** sew, so, soh, sow; **2** also, dipso,
fatso, mezzo, miso, peso, Rousseau, say-so,
scherzo, torso, trousseau, verso; **3** calypso,
Caruso, Curaçao, espresso, maestoso, so-
and-so; **4** intermezzo, mafioso, virtuoso;
5 Burkina Faso.
See also **10.42.8.**

19.17: **1** show; **2** chat show, dumb show,
floor show, foreshow, game show, light
show, no-show, peepshow, poor show, quiz
show, roadshow, sideshow; **3** county show,
laser show, Lord Mayor's show; **4** talent
show; **5** Punch-and-Judy show, reality
show, variety show.
See also **10.42.8.**

19.18: **1** toe, tow; **2** auto, Baotou, ditto,
Otto, Pashto, photo, Pluto, Porto, pronto,
putto, quarto, righto, Shinto, tiptoe;
3 concerto, in toto, Lesotho, Maputo,
prosciutto, Toronto, undertow.

19.18.1: **2** chateau, gateau, plateau;
3 mulatto.

19.18.2: **3** castrato, Erato, esparto, legato,
staccato, Suharto, tomato, vibrato;
4 macchiato, obbligato, pizzicato; **5** loco
citato.

19.18.3: **2** Cato, NATO, Plato; **3** potato;
4 hot potato.

19.18.4: **2** ghetto; **3** falsetto, libretto,
Soweto, stiletto; **4** allegretto, Canaletto,
lazaretto.

19.18.5: **2** Quito, Tito, veto; **3** bonito,
burrito, graffito, magneto, mosquito;
4 Akihito, Hirohito, incognito.

19.18.6: **2** blotto, Giotto, grotto, lotto,
motto, Watteau; **3** risotto.

19.18.7: **2** Cocteau, recto; **3** Allecto, de
facto; **4** ipso facto; **7** in flagrante delicto.

19.18.8: **2** alto, molto; **3** contralto, little
toe, mistletoe.

19.18.9: **2** canto, panto; **3** bel canto,
portmanteau; **4** Esperanto.

19.18.10: **2** lento; **3** memento, pimento;
4 Sacramento; **5** divertimento.

19.18.11: **1** stow, Stowe; **2** Bairstow,
bestow, Bristow, Cousteau, gusto,
Mephisto, pesto, presto; **3** aristo, Callisto,
impasto, Walthamstow; **4** antipasto,
Ariosto, manifesto.
See also **19.23.6.**

19.19: **2** gaucho, honcho, macho, nacho,
poncho; **3** gazpacho.

19.20: **2** bravo, nouveau, Provo, salvo;
3 ab ovo, art nouveau, in vivo, Kosovo,
octavo; **5** alto relievo, basso relievo;
6 Antananarivo.

19.21: **2** bozo, Enzo, garbanzo, gonzo,
muso, ouzo; **3** Alfonso, Alonzo, chorizo,
Lorenzo, mestizo, proviso.

19.22: **1** daube, globe, Job, lobe, Loeb;
2 earlobe.

19.22.1: **3** Anglophobe, Francophobe,
homophobe, technophobe; **4** xenophobe.

19.22.2: **1** probe, robe; **2** aerobe,
bathrobe, disrobe, microbe, wardrobe;
3 anaerobe, garderobe.
See also **10.42.13.**

19.23: **1** bode, bowed, goad, ode, owed,
Spode, woad; **2** abode, cathode, epode,
forebode, geode, widowed; **3** episode;
4 moustachioed.
See also **10.2.13, 16.0, 19.0, 19.3.**

19.23.1: **1** code; **2** decode, encode, Morse
code, postcode, zip code; **3** colour-code,
country code, Highway Code, moral code,
penal code; **6** Napoleonic code.
See also **10.2.13.**

19.23.2: **1** load, lode; **2** boatload, busload,
carload, cartload, caseload, coachload,
download, explode, freeload, front-load,
hallowed, implode, offload, payload,
planeload, reload, shipload, trainload,
truckload, unload, upload, workload;
3 mother lode, overload.
See also **10.2.13, 10.42.14, 19.24.**

19.23.3: **1** mode; **2** commode; **3** à la
mode, discommode.

19.23.4: **1** node; **2** anode, lymph node;
3 palinode.

19.23.5: **1** road, rode, strode; **2** A-road,
bestrode, B-road, byroad, corrode, erode,
furrowed, inroad, off-road, railroad;
3 electrode, overrode; **5** Portobello Road.
See also **10.2.13, 19.15.**

19.23.6: **1** toad; **2** bestowed; **3** nematode,
pigeon-toed, trematode.
See also **19.18.11.**

19.24: **1** loads, Rhodes; **2** crossroads,
shedloads.
See also **19.23.2.**

19.25: **1** clothe, loathe; **2** reclothe,
unclothe.
See also **10.42.31, 19.26, 19.27.**

19.26: 1 clothed, loathed; **2** betrothed, unclothed.
See also **19.25.**

19.27: 1 clothes; **2** bedclothes, nightclothes; **3** underclothes.
See also **19.25.**

19.28: 1 loaf, oaf; **2** meat loaf, milk loaf; **3** cottage loaf.
See also **19.49.**

19.29: 1 brogue, drogue, rogue, vogue; **2** Minogue.

19.30: 1 doge; **2** gamboge, Limoges.

19.31: 1 bloke, choke, cloak, coke, hoke, joke, moke, oak, smoke, soak, soke, stoke, toke, woke, yoke, yolk; **2** awoke, chainsmoke, decoke, uncloak; **3** artichoke, Holyoake, okey-doke, poison oak.
My life has been one great big joke,
A dance that's walked
A song that's spoke,
I laugh so hard I almost choke
When I think about myself.
(Maya Angelou)
See also **10.42.53, 19.33.**

19.31.1: 1 broke, croak, folk, poke, Polk, spoke; **2** bespoke, dead broke, menfolk, slowpoke, stone-broke, townsfolk; **3** fisherfolk, gentlefolk, stony-broke, womenfolk.

19.31.2: 1 stroke; **2** backstroke, breaststroke, brushstroke, four-stroke, heatstroke, keystroke, sidestroke, sunstroke, two-stroke; **3** counterstroke, masterstroke; **4** penalty stroke.

19.31.3: 2 convoke, evoke, invoke, provoke, revoke.
Why with such earnest pains dost thou provoke
The years to bring the inevitable yoke.
(William Wordsworth)
See also **19.33.**

19.32: 1 coax, folks, hoax, Stokes.

19.33: 1 choked, cloaked, smoked, soaked, stoked, yoked; **2** provoked; **3** unprovoked.
See also **19.31, 19.31.3.**

19.34: 1 coal, dole, foal, goal, Joel, knoll, kohl, mole, shoal, stole, toll, vole; **2** cajole, charcoal, condole, extol, own goal; **3** vacuole.

19.34.1: 2 creole; **3** aureole, bronchiole, cabriole, gloriole, oriole, petiole.

19.34.2: 1 bole, boll, bowl; **2** dust bowl, fishbowl, punchbowl, Rose Bowl,

washbowl; **3** Cotton Bowl, goldfish bowl, Orange Bowl, Sugar Bowl, Super Bowl.
See also **10.42.76, 19.37.**

19.34.3: 1 hole, whole; **2** armhole, arsehole, blowhole, bolthole, borehole, cakehole, coal hole, eyehole, foxhole, hellhole, keyhole, loophole, lughole, manhole, mousehole, mudhole, peephole, pinhole, plughole, porthole, pothole, spyhole, Warhol, wormhole; **3** buttonhole, cubbyhole, glory hole, hidey-hole, pigeonhole, rabbithole, waterhole; **4** toad-in-the-hole.

19.34.4: 1 pole, poll; **2** bargepole, beanpole, flagpole, maypole, north pole, south pole, straw poll, tadpole, Walpole; **3** Gallup poll, MORI poll, totem pole; **4** opinion poll.
See also **10.42.76.**

19.34.5: 1 droll, prole, role, roll, scroll; **2** bankroll, bedroll, egg roll, enrol, logroll, payroll, spring roll, Swiss roll, unroll; **3** rock'n'roll, sausage roll; **4** cinnamon roll, Eskimo roll; **5** electoral roll.
Beauties in vain their pretty eyes may roll;
Charms strike the sight, but merit wins the soul.
(Alexander Pope)
See also **10.42.76.**

19.34.6: 2 parole; **3** banderole, casserole, escarole, rigmarole; **4** profiterole.

19.34.7: 1 stroll, troll; **2** control, patrol; **3** decontrol, self-control.
See also **10.42.76, 19.35, 19.37.**

19.34.8: 1 Seoul, sole, soul; **2** console, insole, rissole; **3** camisole, Dover sole, lemon sole.

19.35: 1 bold, mould, old, olde, wold; **2** age-old, controlled, remould; **3** uncontrolled; **5** radio-controlled.
Far over misty mountains cold,
To dungeons deep and caverns old,
We must away, ere break of day,
To seek the pale enchanted gold!
(J. R. R. Tolkien)
See also **2.54.75, 10.42.25, 19.34.7.**

19.35.1: 1 fold; **2** bifold, billfold, blindfold, enfold, fourfold, gatefold, ninefold, scaffold, sheepfold, sixfold, tenfold, threefold, trifold, twofold, unfold; **3** centrefold, hundredfold, manifold, multifold, thousandfold.
See also **10.42.25.**

19.35.2: **1** gold; **2** white gold; **3** marigold, pot of gold; **5** Acapulco gold.

19.35.3: **1** hold; **2** ahold, behold, foothold, freehold, handhold, household, leasehold, stronghold, threshold, toehold, uphold, withhold; **3** stranglehold.
See also **10.42.25**.

19.35.4: **1** cold, scold; **2** cuckold, head cold, ice-cold.
See also **10.42.25**.

19.35.5: **1** sold; **2** outsold, presold, resold, unsold; **3** oversold.

19.35.6: **1** told; **2** foretold, retold, twicetold, untold.

19.36: **1** bolt, colt, dolt, jolt, moult, volt; **2** deadbolt, revolt, unbolt; **3** thunderbolt.
See also **10.42.167**.

19.37: **1** bowls, Rolls, Scholes; **2** controls; **5** Master of the Rolls.
See also **19.34.2, 19.34.7**.

19.38: **1** dome, foam, holm, loam, ohm, som, tome; **2** biome, rhizome; **3** chromosome, microohm, Styrofoam.

19.38.1: **1** home; **2** rest home, Stockholm; **3** mental home, mobile home, nursing home, stately home, stay-at-home.
Mid pleasures and palaces though we may roam,
Be it ever so humble, there's no place like home.
(John Howard Payne)
See also **10.42.84**.

19.38.2: **1** comb, gnome; **2** backcomb, cockscomb, coxcomb, genome; **3** catacomb, fine-tooth comb, gastronome, honeycomb, metronome.

19.38.3: **1** chrome, roam, Rom, Rome; **2** Jerome, syndrome; **3** aerodrome, Hippodrome, monochrome, palindrome, polychrome, velodrome.
See also **10.42.84**.

19.39: **1** Holmes; **3** Sherlock Holmes.

19.40: **1** hone, Joan, own, sewn, shown, sown; **2** agon, condone, disown, leone; **3** methadone; **4** Darby and Joan.
See also **19.41**.

19.40.1: **1** Beaune, bone; **2** backbone, breastbone, cheekbone, jawbone, shinbone, tailbone, T-bone, thighbone, trombone, whalebone, wishbone; **3** collarbone, dog and bone, herringbone, marrowbone, Marylebone.
Stop all the clocks, cut off the telephone,

Prevent the dog from barking with a juicy bone,
Silence the pianos and with muffled drum
Bring out the coffin, let the mourners come.
(W. H. Auden)
See also **19.41**.

19.40.2: **1** phone; **2** car phone, earphone, Freefone, netphone, payphone, webphone; **3** entryphone, mobile phone; **4** videophone.

19.40.3: **3** allophone, Anglophone, answerphone, Dictaphone, francophone, gramophone, homophone, lusophone, megaphone, microphone, saxophone, speakerphone, telephone, vibraphone, xylophone; **4** cameraphone.

19.40.4: **1** cone, scone; **2** nose cone, pine cone; **3** silicone.

19.40.5: **1** clone, flown, loan, lone, Sloane; **2** colón, cyclone, high-flown; **3** overflown; **4** anticyclone.
See also **10.42.92, 19.41**.

19.40.6: **2** alone, Cologne, Stallone; **3** stand-alone; **4** eau de cologne.

19.40.7: **1** blown; **2** flyblown, full-blown; **3** overblown.

19.40.8: **1** moan, mown; **2** bemoan, hormone, Simone; **3** pheromone.

19.40.9: **1** known; **2** unknown, well-known; **3** unbeknown.

19.40.10: **2** Capone, corn pone, postpone, prepone.
See also **19.41**.

19.40.11: **1** crone, drone, prone, Rhône, roan; **2** neurone, Tyrone; **3** chaperone, Côtes-du-Rhône; **4** accident-prone, progesterone, testosterone.
See also **10.42.92**.

19.40.12: **1** groan, grown; **2** homegrown, outgrown; **3** fully-grown, overgrown.

19.40.13: **1** throne, thrown; **2** dethrone, enthrone; **3** overthrown.

19.40.14: **1** tone; **2** halftone, intone, ringtone, two-tone; **3** baritone, dulcitone, semitone; **5** phenobarbitone.
See also **19.41**.

19.40.15: **2** atone; **3** acetone, monotone, overtone, undertone.

19.40.16: **1** stone; **2** birthstone, Blackstone, brownstone, capstone, flagstone, footstone, gravestone, hearthstone, keystone, moonstone, rhinestone, soapstone, touchstone, whetstone; **3** Blarney stone, cornerstone, Silverstone, steppingstone, Yellowstone; **4** Rosetta stone.

How does it feel
To be without a home;
Like a complete unknown
Like a rolling stone?
(Bob Dylan)
See also **19.41**.

19.40.17: **2** bloodstone, grindstone, headstone, loadstone, lodestone, sandstone.

19.40.18: **2** brimstone, gallstone, gemstone, hailstone, limestone, milestone, millstone, tombstone; **3** cobblestone.

19.40.19: **1** zone; **2** ozone; **3** cortisone, Eurozone; **5** hydrocortisone.
See also **10.42.92, 19.41**.

19.41: **1** boned, cloned, honed, owned, stoned, toned, zoned; **2** deep-toned, disowned, postponed, pre-owned, rawboned, well-honed, whaleboned.
See also **19.40, 19.40.1, 19.40.5, 19.40.10, 19.40.14, 19.40.16, 19.40.19**.

19.42: **1** don't, won't, wont.

19.43: **1** Crohn's, Jones, Nones; **2** earphones, headphones, Tom Jones; **3** cobblestones, stepping stones.

19.43.1: **2** bare bones, barebones, crossbones, sawbones; **3** bag of bones, lazybones; **4** skull and crossbones.

19.44: **1** cope, dope, hope, mope, nope, pope, taupe; **3** isotope; **4** Cape of Good Hope.
See also **6.1.11, 10.42.104**.

19.44.1: **1** scope; **3** endoscope, gyroscope, horoscope, microscope, periscope, stethoscope, stroboscope, telescope; **4** kaleidoscope, oscilloscope.

19.44.2: **1** lope, slope; **2** elope; **3** antelope, envelope, ROMvelope.

19.44.3: **1** grope, rope, soap, trope; **2** Joe Soap, soft-soap, tightrope, towrope; **3** docusoap, misanthrope; **4** heliotrope.

19.45: **1** Bose, close, dose; **2** globose, verbose; **3** adipose, cellulose, grandiose, lachrymose, megadose, otiose, overdose.
See also **2.54.62, 10.42.191, 19.53.1**.

19.45.1: **2** jocose, Sukkoth, viscose; **3** bellicose.

19.45.2: **1** gross; **2** engross, morose, sucrose; **3** saccharose.
See also **10.42.132, 19.46**.

19.45.3: **2** fructose, lactose, maltose; **3** comatose, galactose.

19.46: **1** boast, coast, ghost, host, roast, toast; **2** engrossed, French toast, Gold Coast, nut roast, pot roast; **3** coast-to-coast, Holy Ghost, Melba toast; **4** Malabar Coast.

Tender is the ghost
The ghost I love the most,
Hiding from the sun
Waiting for the night to come.
(Blur)
See also **10.2.90, 10.42.172, 19.45.2**.

19.46.1: **1** most; **2** almost, foremost, hindmost, inmost, midmost, rearmost, topmost, utmost; **3** bottommost, easternmost, northernmost, southernmost, westernmost.

19.46.2: **3** furthermost, innermost, outermost, uppermost, uttermost.

19.46.3: **1** post; **2** bedpost, doorpost, freepost, gatepost, goalpost, lamppost, last post, milepost, outpost, signpost; **3** parcel post, winning post.

Go on, fair science, soon to thee
Shall nature yield her idle boast;
Her vulgar fingers formed a tree,
But thou hast trained it to a post.
(Oliver Wendell Holmes)
See also **10.2.90, 10.42.172**.

19.47: **1** oat, quote, stoat, tote, vote; **2** compote, devote, misquote, outvote, unquote; **3** creosote.
See also **10.2.65**.

19.47.1: **1** boat; **2** dreamboat, gunboat, houseboat, lifeboat, longboat, powerboat, rowboat, showboat, speedboat, steamboat, tugboat, U-boat; **3** motorboat, narrowboat, paddleboat, rowing boat; **4** banana-boat.

19.47.2: **1** dote; **2** wild oat; **3** anecdote, antidote, table d'hôte.
See also **10.42.162**.

19.47.3: **1** goat; **2** scapegoat, she-goat, zygote; **3** billy goat, nanny goat.

19.47.4: **1** coat; **2** dovecote, frock coat, greatcoat, housecoat, raincoat, redcoat, Sukkoth, surcoat, tail coat, topcoat, turncoat, waistcoat; **3** duffel coat, entrecote, morning coat, overcoat, petticoat, sugar-coat, undercoat.
See also **10.42.162**.

19.47.5: **1** bloat, float, gloat; **2** afloat.
See also **10.2.65, 10.42.162**.

19.47.6: **1** moat, mote, smote; **2** demote, emote, promote, remote.
See also **2.54.88, 10.2.65.**

19.47.7: **1** note; **2** banknote, connote, denote, footnote, grace note, keynote; **3** advice note, cover note, leading note; **4** treasury note.

The Owl and the Pussy-Cat went to sea
In a beautiful pea-green boat,
They took some honey, and plenty of
*   money,*
Wrapped up in a five-pound note.
(Edward Lear)
See also **10.2.65, 19.48.**

19.47.8: **1** groat, rote, throat, wrote; **2** cutthroat, ghostwrote, rewrote, sore throat; **3** overwrote, underwrote.

19.48: **1** Coates, notes, Oates, oats.
See also **19.47.7.**

19.49: **1** both, loath, loth, oath, quoth, sloth, troth; **2** Sukkoth; **3** Shavuoth; **5** Hippocratic oath.
See also **19.28.**

19.49.1: **1** growth; **2** outgrowth; **3** antigrowth, overgrowth, undergrowth.

19.50: **1** broach, brooch, coach, poach, roach; **2** approach, cockroach, encroach, reproach, slowcoach, stagecoach.
See also **10.42.175.**

19.51: **1** clove, cove, drove, hove, Jove, mauve, stove, wove; **2** alcove, behove; **3** interwove.

19.51.1: **1** grove, rove, strove, throve, trove; **2** Bromsgrove, mangrove; **3** treasure-trove.
See also **10.42.176.**

19.52: **1** beaux, chose, doze, hose, those; **2** bongos, bulldoze, death throes, glucose, nachos; **3** Barnardo's, Berlioz, pantyhose, small potatoes; **4** metamorphose.

19.52.1: **1** close; **2** bellows, disclose, enclose, foreclose, gallows, shallows.
See also **2.54.62, 10.42.191, 19.11.4, 19.53.1.**

19.52.2: **1** noes, nose; **2** brown-nose, chinos, diagnose, hard-nose; **3** misdiagnose, parson's nose, runny nose, toffeenose.

Rudolph the Red-Nosed Reindeer
Had a very shiny nose,
And if you ever saw it,
You would even say it glows.
(Johnny Marks)
See also **10.42.191, 19.13.**

19.52.3: **1** pose; **2** depose, repose.

19.52.4: **1** oppose, propose, suppose; **3** interpose, juxtapose, presuppose.
See also **10.2, 10.42.191, 19.53.2.**

19.52.5: **2** compose, impose; **3** decompose, discompose; **4** superimpose.
See also **10.42.191, 19.53.3.**

19.52.6: **2** dispose, expose, transpose; **3** indispose, predispose; **4** overexpose, underexpose.
See also **19.53.4.**

19.52.7: **1** prose, rose, throes; **2** Ambrose, arose, Burroughs, Burrowes, dextrose, dog rose, narrows, primrose; **3** Comoros, damask rose, tuberose, Tudor rose; **4** evening primrose.
See also **19.15.1.**

19.53: **2** hard-nosed, pug-nosed, red-nosed, snub-nosed; **3** home and hosed, toffee-nosed.

19.53.1: **1** closed; **2** disclosed, enclosed; **3** undisclosed.
See also **19.45, 19.52.1.**

19.53.2: **2** opposed, proposed, supposed; **3** juxtaposed, unopposed.
See also **19.52.4.**

19.53.3: **2** composed; **3** decomposed, discomposed, self-imposed.
See also **19.52.5.**

19.53.4: **2** disposed, exposed; **3** ill-disposed, indisposed, predisposed, well-disposed; **4** overexposed, underexposed.
See also **19.52.6.**

19.54: **1** doge, loge, Vosges.

20.0: **1** chub, cub, dub, hub, nub, pub, snub, sub; **2** hubbub; **3** gastropub, syllabub; **4** Beelzebub.

20.0.1: **1** blub, club, flub; **2** fan club, nightclub; **3** country club, Jockey Club, private club.
See also **20.1.**

20.0.2: **1** drub, grub, rub, scrub, shrub.
See also **20.1.**

20.0.3: **1** stub, tub; **2** bathtub, hot tub, twin-tub, washtub.

20.1: **1** clubs, scrubs, Stubbs; **3** Wormwood Scrubs.
See also **20.0.1, 20.0.2.**

20.2: **1** blood, bud, crud, cud, dud, flood, Hudd, mud, scud, spud, stud, thud; **2** debud, lifeblood, M'Lud, rosebud, taste bud; **3** chew the cud; **4** stick-in-the-mud.

Roses have thorns, and silver fountains
　mud;
Clouds and eclipses stain both moon and
　sun,
And loathsome canker lives in sweetest
　bud.
All men make faults.
(William Shakespeare)
See also **10.2.3, 10.2.14, 10.42.14, 20.3.**

20.3: **1** duds, suds; **2** soapsuds, taste buds.
See also **20.2.**

20.4: **1** buff, chough, duff, guff, huff, muff, puff, snuff; **2** cream puff, earmuff, enough, rebuff; **3** powder puff.
See also **20.6.**

20.4.1: **1** cuff, scuff; **2** earcuff, handcuff; **3** off-the-cuff.
See also **20.5, 20.6.**

20.4.2: **1** bluff, Clough, fluff, luff, slough.

20.4.3: **1** gruff, rough, ruff, scruff, stuff, tough; **2** dandruff, dyestuff, feedstuff, foodstuff, greenstuff, hot stuff, kid's stuff, lodestuff.
See also **2.54.62.**

20.5: **2** earmuffs, golden handcuffs, handcuffs; **3** fisticuffs.
See also **20.4.1.**

20.6: **1** chuffed, puffed, scuffed, stuffed, tuft.
See also **20.4, 20.4.1.**

20.7: **1** chug, dug, fug, hug, jug, mug, pug, smug, snug, thug, tug, ugh; **2** bear hug; **3** toby jug.
See also **2.54.62, 10.42.33.**

20.7.1: **1** bug; **2** bedbug, debug, firebug, humbug, web bug; **3** doodlebug, jitterbug, ladybug, litterbug, mealybug, superbug.
See also **10.42.33.**

20.7.2: **1** glug, lug, plug, slug; **2** earplug, unplug; **3** chug-a-lug.
See also **20.8.**

20.7.3: **1** drug, rug, shrug, trug; **2** hearthrug.
See also **20.8.**

20.8: **1** drugged, plugged; **2** unplugged.
See also **20.7.2, 20.7.3.**

20.9: **1** bludge, budge, fudge, nudge, sludge, smudge.

20.9.1: **1** judge; **2** adjudge, forejudge, line judge, misjudge, prejudge; **3** hanging judge.

20.9.2: **1** drudge, grudge, trudge; **2** begrudge.
See also **10.42.36.**

20.10: **1** chuck, duck, fuck, guck, puck, ruck, shuck, snuck, stuck, suck, truck, tuck, yuck, yuk; **2** shelduck, unstuck, woodchuck.
See also **10.42.40, 20.11.**

20.10.1: **1** buck; **2** nubuck, sawbuck, young buck.

20.10.2: **1** cluck, luck, pluck; **2** blind luck, mukluk, potluck, tough luck; **3** lady luck; **4** beginner's luck.

20.10.3: **1** muck, schmuck; **2** amuck, Lord Muck; **3** Lady Muck; **4** high muck-a-muck.

20.10.4: **1** struck; **2** awestruck, dumbstruck, moonstruck, stagestruck, starstruck; **3** horror-struck, terror-struck, thunderstruck.

20.11: **1** Bucks., crux, flux, shucks, tux; **2** big bucks, deluxe, influx, Linux; **3** Benelux, megabucks.
See also **20.10.**

20.12: **1** duct; **2** abduct, deduct, product, tear duct, viaduct; **3** aqueduct, by-product, end product, oviduct, waste product.

20.12.2: **2** conduct, induct; **3** misconduct, safe-conduct; **4** code of conduct.

20.13: **2** construct, instruct, obstruct; **3** deconstruct, reconstruct, self-destruct.
See also **10.2.78.**

20.14: **1** dull, gull, hull, lull, mull, null; **2** annul, seagull; **3** herring gull.

20.14.1: **1** cull, scull, skull; **2** numbskull, numskull.

20.15: **1** bulb; **2** flashbulb.

20.16: **1** gulf; **2** engulf; **3** Persian Gulf.

20.17: **1** bulk, hulk, skulk, sulk.

20.18: **1** bulge; **2** divulge, indulge; **4** overindulge.
See also **10.42.36.**

20.19: **1** gulp, pulp.
See also **20.20.**

20.20: **1** gulped, pulped, sculpt.
See also **10.2.89, 20.19.**

20.21: **1** Hulse, pulse; **2** convulse, impulse, repulse.
See also **10.62.3.**

20.22: **1** cult; **2** adult, consult, exult, insult, kidult, occult, result, tumult; **3** catapult, end result.
See also **10.42.167.**

20.23: **1** gulch, mulch.

20.24: **1** bum, chum, dumb, glum, gum, hum, mum, numb, plum, plumb, slum, sum, swum, thumb, tum, um, yum; **2** benumb, checksum, dim sum, dum-dum, Tom Thumb; **3** bubblegum, chewing gum. *See also* **2.54.62, 10.42.89, 20.28.**

20.24.1: **1** come, cum, scum; **2** become, income, outcome, pond scum, succumb; **3** overcome. *See also* **10.42.90.**

20.24.2: **1** crumb, rum, scrum, strum, thrum; **2** breadcrumb, therefrom. *See also* **20.28.**

20.24.3: **1** drum; **2** eardrum, humdrum, Red Rum; **3** kettledrum.
It's in the world I become
Content in the hum
Between voice and drum
(Faithless)
See also **10.42.89.**

20.25: **1** bumf, humph; **2** galumph, triumph.

20.26: **1** bump, chump, dump, hump, stump, sump, thump, ump; **2** core dump, gazump, mugwump, speed bump, tree stump, tub-thump; **3** rubbish dump. *See also* **10.42.111, 20.27.**

20.26.1: **1** jump; **2** high jump, long jump, queue-jump, ski jump, star jump; **3** bungee jump, triple jump, water jump. *See also* **20.27.**

20.26.2: **1** clump, lump, plump, slump; **3** sugar lump.

20.26.3: **1** pump; **3** parish pump, petrol pump, stomach pump, vacuum pump.

20.26.4: **1** frump, grump, rump, trump. *See also* **20.27.**

20.27: **1** dumps, jumps, mumps, stumps, trumps; **2** goose bumps. *See also* **20.26, 20.26.1, 20.26.4.**

20.28: **1** crumbs, sums; **2** breadcrumbs. *See also* **20.24, 20.24.2.**

20.29: **1** bun, fun, Hun, none, nun, pun, shun, spun; **2** finespun, homespun; **3** Chelsea bun.
You've taken the fun
Out of everything;
You're making me run
When I don't want to think.
(Blur)

20.29.1: **1** done, Donne, dun; **2** half-done, outdone, redone, undone, Verdun, well-done; **3** overdone, underdone.

20.29.2: **1** gun; **2** begun, big gun, flashgun, handgun, outgun, popgun, shogun, shotgun; **3** Tommy gun; **4** submachine gun.

20.29.3: **1** run; **2** close-run, forerun, outrun, rerun; **3** Cresta Run, overrun, underrun. *See also* **20.32.**

20.29.4: **1** son, sun; **2** godson, grandson, stepson; **3** Rising Sun.
Mad dogs and Englishmen
Go out in the mid-day sun;
The Japanese don't care to, the Chinese
* wouldn't dare to;*
Hindus and Argentines sleep firmly from
* twelve to one,*
But Englishmen detest a siesta.
(Noël Coward)

20.29.5: **1** stun, ton, tonne, tun; **2** short ton; **3** megaton. *See also* **20.30.**

20.29.6: **1** 1, one, won; **2** 2.1, A1, someone, square one, T1; **3** all-in-one, anyone, everyone, number one, one-to-one, World War I; **4** Formula One.

20.30: **1** bund, fund, stunned; **2** refund, rotund; **3** cummerbund, moribund, orotund. *See also* **10.42.14, 20.29.5.**

20.31: **1** grunge, gunge, lunge, plunge, sponge; **2** expunge; **3** muskellunge. *See also* **10.42.39.**

20.32: **1** dunce, once, runs. *See also* **20.29.3.**

20.33: **1** blunt, bunt, cunt, dunt, punt, shunt, stunt; **3** exeunt. *See also* **2.54.88, 10.2.81.**

20.33.1: **1** hunt; **2** draghunt, fox hunt, headhunt, manhunt, witch-hunt; **4** National Hunt. *See also* **10.2.81, 10.42.168.**

20.33.2: **1** brunt, front, grunt, runt; **2** affront, beachfront, cold front, confront, forefront, seafront, shirtfront, shopfront, storefront, upfront, warm front; **3** back-to-front, oceanfront, riverfront, waterfront, Western Front; **4** National Front, popular front; **5** back to front.

20.34: **1** brunch, bunch, crunch, hunch, lunch, munch, punch, scrunch; **3** number-crunch, ploughman's lunch, Sunday lunch.

20.35: **1** month; **2** twelvemonth.

20.36: **1** bung, dung, hung, sung, swung, young; **2** among, unsung; **3** overhung.

If all the world and love were young,
And truth in every shepherd's tongue,
These pretty pleasures might me move
To live with thee, and be thy love.
(Walter Raleigh)

20.36.1: **1** clung, flung, lung, slung; **2** far-flung, low-slung; **3** aqualung.

20.36.2: **1** rung, sprung, strung, wrung; **2** hamstrung; **3** highly-strung.

20.36.3: **1** stung, tongue; **2** forked tongue; **3** mother tongue.

20.37: **2** sharp-tongued; **3** double-tongued, honey-tongued, silver-tongued.

20.38: **1** bunk, chunk, clunk, dunk, flunk, funk, gunk, hunk, junk, Monck, monk, plunk, punk, skunk, slunk, spunk, stunk, sunk; **2** blue funk, chipmunk, cowpunk, debunk, jazz-funk, Podunk, slam dunk; **3** cyberpunk.

20.38.1: **1** drunk, shrunk, trunk; **2** preshrunk, punch-drunk.

20.39: **1** flunked; **2** adjunct, defunct.

20.40: **1** up, yup; **2** blowup, frame-up, fry-up, hang-up, higher-up, hung-up, leg-up, punch-up, screw-up, tie-up, warm-up; **3** follow-up, pick-me-up, shoot-'em-up, washing-up.

I guess now it's time for me to give up;
I feel it's time.
Got a picture of you beside me
Got your lipstick mark still on your coffee
* cup...*
(Take That)

20.40.1: **2** buildup, clued-up, foldup, holdup, made-up, mixed-up, paid-up, round-up, sendup, souped-up, standup, worked-up; **4** sunny-side up.

20.40.2: **1** cup; **2** backup, checkup, crack-up, eggcup, hiccup, hookup, linkup, look-up, markup, pick-up, stuck-up, teacup, workup, World Cup; **3** buttercup, Davis Cup, loving cup, Melbourne Cup, Stanley Cup, stirrup cup, Wightman Cup; **5** Americas Cup, European Cup.
See also **10.42.104**.

20.40.3: **2** breakup, makeup, shake-up, take-up; **3** FA Cup.

The moment I wake up
Before I put on my makeup
I say a little prayer for you.
(Burt Bacharach, Hal David)

20.40.4: **2** cockup, knock-up, lockup, mock-up.

20.40.5: **2** call-up, dial-up, foul-up, pile-up, roll-up, snarl-up.

20.40.6: **2** cleanup, lineup, pin-up, sunup, tune-up.

20.40.7: **1** pup; **2** slap-up, slip-up, step-up, top-up, zip-up.

20.40.8: **2** clear-up, flare-up; **3** cover-up, runner-up.

20.40.9: **1** sup; **2** close-up, lace-up, mix-up, press-up, toss-up.

20.40.10: **2** nosh-up, push-up, smash-up, wash-up.

20.40.11: **1** tup; **2** built-up, bust-up, dust-up, fit-up, getup, jumped-up, let-up, paste-up, pent-up, puffed-up, setup, sit-up, split-up, startup, washed-up, write-up, wrought-up.

20.40.12: **2** balls-up, booze-up, close-up, knees-up.

20.41: **2** abrupt, bankrupt, corrupt, disrupt, erupt, irrupt; **3** interrupt.

20.42: **1** cuss, fuss, Gus, Huss, muss, pus, suss, thus, truss, us; **2** concuss, discuss, villus.
See also **10.2.31, 20.44**.

20.42.1: **1** bus; **2** Airbus; **3** blunderbuss, minibus, trolleybus.

20.42.2: **1** plus; **2** cost-plus, nonplus; **4** eleven-plus.

20.43: **1** busk, dusk, husk, musk, rusk, tusk, Usk; **2** cornhusk.

20.44: **1** fussed, gust, must, sussed; **2** august, concussed, disgust.
See also **10.2.93, 10.42.173, 20.42**.

20.44.1: **1** bust; **2** combust, robust; **3** boom and bust.
See also **2.54.88, 10.2.93**.

20.44.2: **1** dost, dust; **2** sawdust, stardust.
Only the actions of the just
Smell sweet, and blossom in their dust.
(James Shirley)
See also **10.2.93, 10.42.173**.

20.44.3: **1** just; **2** adjust, unjust; **3** readjust.
See also **10.2.93**.

20.44.4: **1** lust; **2** bloodlust, nonplussed; **3** wanderlust.

20.44.5: **1** crust, rust, thrust; **2** piecrust, shortcrust, upthrust; **3** upper crust.

20.44.6: **1** trust; **2** brains trust, distrust, entrust, mistrust; **3** antitrust; **4** National Trust.
See also **10.2.93, 10.42.173**.

20.45: **1** gush, hush, mush; **2** hush-hush.
See also **10.42.140, 20.46.**

20.45.1: **1** blush, flush, lush, plush, slush; **2** four-flush, straight flush; **3** royal flush.
See also **10.42.140, 20.46.**

20.45.2: **1** crush, rush, thrush; **2** bulrush, gold rush, inrush, onrush, uprush; **3** mistle thrush.
See also **10.42.140, 20.46.**

20.45.3: **1** brush; **2** airbrush, broad-brush, hairbrush, nailbrush, paintbrush, sagebrush, toothbrush; **3** underbrush.
See also **20.46.**

20.46: **1** brushed, crushed, flushed, hushed, rushed.
See also **20.45, 20.45.1, 20.45.2, 20.45.3.**

20.47: **1** glut, hut, jut, mutt, phut, putt, rut, shut, slut, smut, strut, tut; **2** izzat, tut-tut; **3** Nissen hut; **4** open-and-shut.
See also **10.42.143.**

20.47.1: **1** but, butt, gut; **2** abut, beergut, catgut, rebut, rotgut; **3** scuttlebutt; **4** cigarette butt.

20.47.2: **1** cut; **2** clean-cut, clear-cut, crew cut, haircut, half-cut, low-cut, offcut, price cut, uncut, woodcut; **3** intercut, linocut, undercut, uppercut.
See also **10.42.143.**

20.47.3: **1** Cnut, nut; **2** betel nut, chestnut, cobnut, donut, doughnut, groundnut, peanut, walnut; **3** Brazil nut, coconut, cola nut, hazelnut, monkey nut, old chestnut, sweet chestnut; **4** water chestnut.
See also **20.48.**

20.48: **1** guts, klutz, nuts, Smuts; **2** peanuts; **3** greedy guts.
See also **20.47.3.**

20.49: **1** clutch, crutch, Dutch, hutch, much, such, touch; **2** Cape Dutch, nonesuch, retouch; **3** double Dutch, Midas touch, overmuch.
See also **10.42.175, 10.62.5, 20.50.**

20.50: **1** touched; **2** untouched.
See also **20.49.**

20.51: **1** dove, gov, guv, shove; **2** above; **3** turtledove.

20.51.1: **1** love, luv; **2** calf love, free love; **3** cupboard love, puppy love; **4** Dr Strangelove.

White in the moon the long road lies,
The moon stands blank above;
White in the moon the long road lies
That leads me from my love.
(A. E. Housman)
See also **10.42.176, 20.52.**

20.51.2: **1** glove; **2** foxglove, kid glove; **3** boxing glove, dataglove, hand-in-glove.

20.52: **1** gloved, loved; **2** much-loved, unloved.
See also **20.51.1.**

20.53: **1** buzz, does, fuzz, 'cause; **2** abuzz.
See also **10.42.186, 19.4, 22.2.**

21.0: **1** pud, should; **2** diode, Talmud.

21.0.1: **1** good; **2** feel-good, Gielgud; **3** common good; **5** finger-lickin' good.

21.0.2: **1** hood; **2** boyhood, childhood, falsehood, girlhood, godhood, manhood, selfhood, smoke hood; **3** babyhood, likelihood, livelihood, maidenhood, nationhood, victimhood, widowhood, womanhood.

21.0.3: **3** bachelorhood, brotherhood, fatherhood, motherhood, neighbourhood, sisterhood.

21.0.4: **2** knighthood, priesthood, sainthood, statehood; **3** adulthood, parenthood.

21.0.5: **1** stood; **2** withstood; **3** understood; **4** misunderstood.

21.0.6: **1** wood, would; **2** Attwood, Blackwood, Broadwood, brushwood, deadwood, dogwood, driftwood, Eastwood, firewood, Fleetwood, Goodwood, Greenwood, hardwood, heartwood, Hogwood, matchwood, Norwood, plywood, pulpwood, redwood, rosewood, softwood, Wedgwood, Westwood, wormwood; **3** Bollywood, Collingwood, cottonwood, Cricklewood, Hollywood, Isherwood, Littlewood, sandalwood, satinwood, Underwood.

One impulse from a vernal wood
May teach you more of man,
Of moral evil and of good,
Than all the sages can.
(William Wordsworth)
See also **21.2.**

21.1: **1** couldst, shouldst, wouldst.

21.2: **1** goods, woods; **2** backwoods, white goods; **3** worldly goods; **4** babe in the woods, neck of the woods.
See also **21.0.6.**

21.3: **1** poof, woof.

21.4: **1** chook, nook, shook; **2** forsook; **3** inglenook.

21.4.1: 1 book; **2** bankbook, casebook, cashbook, chequebook, closed book, cookbook, coursebook, daybook, e-book, Good Book, guidebook, handbook, logbook, matchbook, passbook, phone book, prayer book, rulebook, Schoenberg, schoolbook, scrapbook, sketchbook, songbook, studbook, wordbook, workbook, yearbook; **3** address book, comic book, copybook, double-book, open book, overbook, storybook; **4** cookery book; **5** coffee-table book.
See also **10.42.54, 21.6.**

21.4.2: 2 datebook, notebook, textbook; **3** pocketbook, statute book, subnotebook.

21.4.3: 1 hook, Hooke; **2** billhook, boathook, fishhook, unhook, Windhoek; **3** tenterhook.
See also **21.6.**

21.4.4: 1 cook, Cooke; **3** overcook, pastrycook; **4** ready-to-cook.
See also **10.42.54, 21.6.**

21.4.5: 1 look; **2** New Look, outlook, wet-look; **3** overlook.

That later we, though parted then,
May still recall these evenings when
Fear gave his watch no look;
The lion griefs loped from the shade
And on our knees their muzzles laid
And Death put down his book.
(W. H. Auden)
See also **21.6.**

21.4.6: 1 brook, Brooke, Bruch, crook, rook; **2** Innsbruck; **3** Beaverbrook, Bolingbroke.
See also **10.2.25.**

21.4.7: 1 schtuck, took; **2** mistook, retook; **3** undertook.

21.5: 1 Fuchs; **3** tenterhooks.

Come live with me, and be my love,
And we will some new pleasures prove
Of golden sands, and crystal brooks,
With silken lines, and silver hooks.
(John Donne)

21.6: 1 booked, cooked, hooked; **2** half-cooked, precooked, uncooked; **3** overcooked, overlooked, undercooked.
See also **21.4.1, 21.4.3, 21.4.4, 21.4.5.**

21.7: 1 bull, pull; **2** Abdul, John Bull, Kabul, ring-pull; **3** Istanbul, karakul, Sitting Bull.

21.7.1: 1 full; **2** armful, bagful, bowlful, boxful, brimful, chock-full, cupful, earful, eyeful, glassful, handful, houseful,

mouthful, roomful, sackful, skinful, spoonful, tankful, tubful; **3** bellyful, flavourful, overfull, revengeful, shovelful, thimbleful.

21.7.2: 2 fistful, plateful, potful; **3** bucketful, pocketful.

21.7.3: 1 wool; **2** glass wool, lambswool; **4** dyed-in-the-wool.
Baa, baa, black sheep,
Have you any wool?
Yes, sir, yes, sir,
Three bags full;
One for the master,
And one for the dame,
And one for the little boy
Who lives down the lane.
(Children's Verse)

21.8: 1 wolf, Wolfe, Woolf; **2** aardwolf, cry wolf, lone wolf, werewolf; **3** Ethelwulf, prairie wolf, timber wolf.

21.9: 1 schtum, shtoom; **2** kumkum.

21.10: 1 Jung; **2** Bandung; **3** Nibelung; **5** Götterdämmerung.

21.11: 1 oops, whoops.
See also **22.29.**

21.12: 1 brusque, puss, wuss; **2** hummus, humus, Irkutsk, sourpuss.

21.13: 1 bush, push, shush, tush, whoosh; **2** ambush, cost-push, swoosh; **3** Hindu Kush, Shepherds Bush.

21.14: 1 foot, soot; **2** afoot, barefoot, Bigfoot, crow's foot, cubic foot, forefoot, hotfoot, trench foot, wrong-foot; **3** athlete's foot, pussyfoot, tenderfoot, underfoot.
See also **10.42.143.**

21.14.1: 1 put; **2** input, kaput, output, throughput.
See also **10.42.143.**

21.15: 2 kibbutz, Vaduz.

21.16: 1 butch, putsch.

22.0: 1 goo, Jew, jus, ooh, woo; **2** bayou, bijou, Corfu, juju, kung fu, Manju, ragout, tofu; **3** Anjou, déjà vu, rendezvous; **4** Ouagadougou, tu-whit tu-whoo.

22.1: 1 boo; **2** babu, bamboo, boo-boo, taboo, zebu; **3** bugaboo, caribou, marabou, marabout, peekaboo.

22.2: 1 do, du; **2** ado, Chengdu, hairdo, Hindu, hoodoo, kudu, outdo, redo, saddhu, sadhu, to-do, undo, Urdu, voodoo; **3** billet-doux, derring-do, Kathmandu, overdo, skean-dhu, well-to-do; **4** didgeridoo, Tamil Nadu; **5** cock-a-doodle-doo.

Knowing me, knowing you
There is nothing we can do;
Knowing me, knowing you
We just have to face it
This time we're through.
(Benny Andersson)
See also **2.60.1, 10.42.12, 20.53.**

22.3: 1 who; 2 boohoo, yahoo, yoo-hoo; 3 ballyhoo, Oahu; 4 Netanyahu.

22.4: 1 ewe, pew, spew, u, U, yew; 2 ague, argue, curlew, debut, EU, imbue, leu, Matthew, purlieu; 3 ICU, IOU, Montagu, VDU.
See also **22.17.2.**

22.4.1: 1 dew, due; 2 adieu, fondue, mildew, subdue, undue; 3 honeydew, mountain dew, overdue, residue.
See also **22.17.2, 22.40.1.**

22.4.2: 1 few, phew, whew; 2 Corfu, curfew, nephew.

Nor is the People's Judgment always
true:
The Most may err as grossly as the Few.
(John Dryden)

22.4.3: 1 hew, hue, Hugh; 2 Goodhew; 3 clerihew.

22.4.4: 1 cue, Kew, kyu, queue; 2 HQ, IQ, thank you; 3 Autocue, barbecue, curlicue, FAQ, pdq; 4 GCHQ.
See also **22.17.2.**

22.4.5: 1 skew; 2 askew, fescue, miscue, rescue; 3 Montesquieu.
See also **22.17.2.**

22.4.6: 2 value; 3 devalue, face value, par value, revalue, street value; 4 overvalue, undervalue; 5 nominal value.
See also **22.17.2.**

22.4.7: 5 lbw, POW; 9 W3, WWW.

22.4.8: 1 mew, mu; 2 emu; 4 Bartholomew.

22.4.9: 1 knew, new, nu; 2 Agnew, anew, brand new, brand-new, cum new, menu, non-U, renew, sinew, venue; 3 continue, ingenue, ingénue, retinue; 4 discontinue.
See also **10.42.12, 22.17.3.**

22.4.10: 3 avenue, parvenu, revenue; 4 Fifth Avenue; 5 Inland Revenue; 6 Madison Avenue.

22.4.11: 1 sue; 2 ensue, issue, pursue, tissue.
See also **10.42.12.**

22.4.12: 1 stew; 3 impromptu, in situ, Irish stew.
See also **22.17.4.**

22.4.13: 1 view; 2 preview, purview, review, revue; 3 bird's-eye view, interview, overview, pay-per-view, peer review, point of view, rave review.
See also **10.42.12.**

22.5: 1 coo, coup; 2 Baku, cuckoo, haiku; 3 bill and coo, Ceaușescu, seppuku, sudoku.

22.6: 1 clue, glue, lieu, loo, Lou, slew; 2 aloo, halloo, igloo, Lulu, unglue, Zulu; 3 superglue, Tuvalu; 4 Honolulu.
See also **22.17.7.**

22.6.1: 3 Angelou, ormolu, Portaloo, vindaloo, Waterloo; 4 hullabaloo.

22.6.2: 1 blew, blue; 2 true-blue; 3 black-and-blue, Danish blue.

Rain falling on my shoes
Heading out for the East Coast;
Lord knows I've paid some dues getting
through
Tangled up in blue.
(Bob Dylan)
See also **22.40.**

22.6.3: 1 flew, flu, flue; 3 overflew.

22.7: 1 moo, moue; 2 Camus, muumuu.

22.8: 1 gnu; 2 canoe, Vishnu; 3 entre nous, Martinů.

22.9: 1 poo, pooh; 2 coypu, hapu, pooh-pooh, shampoo.

22.10: 1 brew, grew, roo, roux, rue, shrew; 2 Carew, guru, Hebrew, home-brew, Nehru, outgrew; 3 Nauru.
See also **10.42.184, 22.40.3.**

22.10.1: 2 Peru; 3 buckaroo, jackaroo, kangaroo, Uluru, wallaroo.

22.10.2: 1 drew; 2 Andrew, redrew, withdrew.

22.10.3: 1 crew; 2 accrue, aircrew, ecru; 3 cabin crew.

22.10.4: 1 screw; 2 corkscrew, jackscrew, loose screw, thumbscrew, unscrew; 3 Phillips screw; 5 Archimedes' screw.

22.10.5: 1 strew, true; 2 construe, untrue; 3 misconstrue.
See also **22.17.10.**

22.10.6: 1 threw, thro', through, thru; 2 breakthrough, clickthrough, drive-through, readthrough, run-through, see-through, walkthrough; 3 follow-through, overthrew.

22.11: 1 Sioux, sou, sue; 2 lasso; 3 aperçu; 4 pari passu, tiramisu.

22.11.1: 3 jujitsu, keiretsu, shiatsu, zaibatsu.

22.12: 1 shoe, shoo; 2 cashew, gumshoe, Honshu, horseshoe, Kyushu, sandshoe, snowshoe; 3 overshoe; 4 Kitakyushu. *See also* **22.40**.

22.12.1: 2 issue, tissue; 3 atishoo, reissue; 4 Mogadishu.

22.13: 1 2, to, too, two; 2 2.2, et tu, Fitou, hereto, K2, mangetout, set-to, tattoo, thereto, tutu, vatu, whereto; 3 cockatoo, hitherto, manitou, talking-to, World War II; 4 catch-22, Tombouctou, Vanuatu; 6 mirabile dictu.

Daisy, Daisy, give me your answer, do!
I'm half crazy, all for the love of you!
It won't be a stylish marriage,
I can't afford a carriage,
But you'll look sweet upon the seat
Of a bicycle made for two!
(Harry Dacre)

22.13.1: 2 Bantu, into, lean-to, one-two, Sintu, unto; 3 ubuntu.

22.14: 1 chew; 2 achoo, choo choo, eschew, statue, virtue; 3 Jimmy Choo; 4 easy virtue, Machu Picchu; 5 cardinal virtue.

22.15: 1 zoo; 2 kazoo, razoo, wazoo.

22.16: 1 boob, lube, rube; 2 jujube.

22.16.1: 1 cube, tube; 2 Danube, test-tube; 4 cathode ray tube, Eustachian tube; 5 fallopian tube.

22.17: 1 dude, Jude, mood, who'd; 2 Mahmoud, Saud.

22.17.1: 1 food; 2 junk food, seafood, wholefood; 3 Frankenfood, frozen food, fusion food, rabbit food, superfood; 5 convenience food.

22.17.2: 1 feud, pseud, skewed, you'd; 2 devalued, exude, imbued, prelude, subdued, valued; 3 barbecued, multihued; 4 undervalued.
See also **22.4, 22.4.1, 22.4.4, 22.4.5, 22.4.6**.

22.17.3: 1 nude; 2 denude, renewed; 3 continued; 4 discontinued.
See also **22.4.9**.

22.17.4: 1 stewed; 2 étude, quietude; 3 consuetude, hebetude, inquietude; 4 desuetude.
See also **22.4.12**.

22.17.5: 3 amplitude, lassitude, longitude, magnitude, plenitude, pulchritude, servitude, solitude, turpitude;

4 decrepitude, infinitude, solicitude, vicissitude; 6 verisimilitude.

22.17.6: 3 altitude, aptitude, attitude, certitude, fortitude, gratitude, latitude, multitude, platitude, rectitude; 4 beatitude, correctitude, exactitude, inaptitude, incertitude, ineptitude, ingratitude; 5 inexactitude; 11 terminological inexactitude.

22.17.7: 1 glued, lewd; 2 allude, collude, delude, elude, unglued; 3 interlude.
See also **22.6**.

22.17.8: 2 conclude, exclude, include, occlude, preclude, seclude.
See also **10.42.23**.

22.17.9: 1 brood, crude, prude, rood, rude, shrewd; 2 uncrewed.
See also **2.54.62, 2.54.75, 10.42.23**.

22.17.10: 1 strewed; 2 extrude, intrude, obtrude, protrude; 3 Gertrude.
See also **22.10.5**.

22.18: 1 booth, smooth, soothe.
See also **10.42.31, 22.38**.

22.19: 1 goof, hoof, kloof, pouf, roof, spoof, yoof; 2 aloof, sunroof; 3 cloven hoof; 4 opéra bouffe.
See also **2.54.62, 10.42.32, 22.36**.

22.19.1: 1 fugue, Moog, proof; 2 bombproof, childproof, dampproof, draughtproof, fireproof, flameproof, foolproof, heatproof, leakproof, lightproof, rainproof, reproof, rustproof, shockproof, showerproof, soundproof; 3 bulletproof, ovenproof, overproof, shatterproof, waterproof, weatherproof; 4 burden of proof.

Limb by limb and tooth by tooth
Tearing up inside of me
Every day every hour
I wish that I was bullet proof.
(Radiohead)

22.20: 1 huge, kludge, scrooge, stooge; 2 deluge, refuge; 3 centrifuge, febrifuge, subterfuge, vermifuge; 4 wildlife refuge.

22.21: 1 fluke, gook, kook, Luke, snook, souk, spook, spruik; 2 chinook, Farouk, Seljuk; 3 Mameluke; 4 gobbledegook.

22.21.1: 1 duke, nuke, puke; 2 archduke, rebuke.

22.22: 1 Boole, boules, fool, ghoul, joule, who'll; 2 Banjul, cagoule, Elul, Raoul, tomfool, virgule; 3 April fool.

22.22.1: **1** mewl, mule, tulle, you'll, Yule; **2** barbule, capsule, globule, granule, ovule, plumule, pustule; **3** vestibule.

22.22.2: **2** module, nodule, schedule; **3** reschedule.
See also **22.23**.

22.22.3: **2** bascule, reticule; **3** majuscule, minuscule, molecule, ridicule; **4** animalcule.

22.22.4: **1** cool, school; **2** air-cool, art school, choir school, day school, faith school, film school, first school, high school, homeschool, law school, night school, old-school, play school, playschool, prep school, preschool, state school, uncool; **3** ballet school, boarding school, driving school, grammar school, infant school, junior school, music school, reform school, riding school, special school, summer school, Sunday school, ultracool; **4** medical school, nursery school; **5** comprehensive school, secondary school.

A wise man poor
Is like a sacred book that's never read,
To himself he lives, and to all else seems
  dead.
This age thinks better of a gilded fool
Than of a threadbare saint in wisdom's
  school.
(Thomas Dekker)
See also **2.54.79, 10.42.58, 22.23**.

22.22.5: **1** pool, spool; **2** ampoule, Blackpool, cesspool, fixed-spool, whirlpool; **3** Liverpool, swimming pool.
See also **22.23**.

22.22.6: **1** drool, rule; **2** ferrule, home rule, misrule, mob rule, self-rule, slide rule; **3** overrule, work-to-rule.
See also **10.42.58, 22.23, 22.24**.

22.22.7: **1** stool, tool; **2** footstool, kickstool, O'Toole, retool, toadstool; **3** cucking stool, ducking stool, machine tool, milking stool.
See also **22.23, 22.24**.

22.23: **1** Gould, pooled, ruled, tooled; **2** air-cooled, cooled, scheduled, unschooled; **3** unscheduled, water-cooled.
See also **22.22.2, 22.22.4, 22.22.5, 22.22.6, 22.22.7**.

22.24: **1** rules, tools; **4** Queensberry rules.
See also **22.22.6, 22.22.7**.

22.25: **1** boom, doom, tomb, whom, womb, zoom; **2** entomb, Khartoum; **3** baby boom, catacomb, sonic boom, va va voom.
See also **10.42.91, 22.26**.

22.25.1: **1** fume, Hulme, Hume, spume; **2** assume, consume, costume, exhume, legume, perfume, presume, resume, subsume, volume; **3** Douglas-Home; **4** swimming costume.
See also **10.42.91, 22.26**.

22.25.2: **1** bloom, flume, gloom, loom, plume; **2** broadloom, Goldblum, heirloom; **3** nom de plume.
See also **10.42.91**.

22.25.3: **1** broom, brougham, groom, rheum, room, vroom; **2** bathroom, boxroom, bridegroom, classroom, formroom, greenroom, guestroom, gunroom, houseroom, legroom, men's room, mushroom, newsroom, playroom, showroom, staffroom, storeroom, tearoom, washroom; **3** anteroom, boiler room, common room, elbowroom, ladies' room, powder room; **4** little boys' room, reception room; **5** utility room.

Fake Tales of San Francisco
Echo through the room;
More point to a wedding disco
Without a bride or groom.
(Arctic Monkeys)
See also **10.42.91, 22.26**.

22.25.4: **2** boardroom, guardroom, headroom, wardroom; **3** bedroom.

22.25.5: **2** backroom, cloakroom, darkroom, sickroom, stockroom, workroom.

22.25.6: **2** ballroom, mailroom, poolroom, saleroom, schoolroom, strongroom; **3** dining room, drawing room, dressing room, living room, sitting room, waiting room, weighing room.

22.25.7: **2** chat room, courtroom, guestroom, restroom, stateroom.

22.26: **1** doomed, groomed, plumed; **2** assumed, consumed, costumed, perfumed, well-groomed.
See also **22.25, 22.25.1, 22.25.3**.

22.27: **1** boon, June, moon, noon, swoon; **2** baboon, buffoon, forenoon, harpoon, jejune, lampoon, Muldoon, typhoon; **3** afternoon, Brigadoon, honeymoon, hunter's moon, Mills & Boon.

Hey diddle diddle,
The cat and the fiddle,
The cow jumped over the moon;

The little dog laughed
To see such sport,
And the dish ran away with the spoon.
(Children's Verse)

22.27.1: **1** goon; **2** dragoon, lagoon, Rangoon.

22.27.2: **1** dune; **2** commune, immune, impugn, rough-hewn, sand dune, tribune; **4** autoimmune.

22.27.3: **1** tune; **2** attune, fine-tune, Neptune; **3** importune, opportune; **4** inopportune.

My luve's like a red red rose
That's newly sprung in June:
My luve's like the melodie
That's sweetly play'd in tune.
(Robert Burns)
See also **10.42.92, 22.28.**

22.27.4: **2** Cancún, cocoon, raccoon, tycoon.

22.27.5: **1** loon; **2** balloon, doubloon, Kowloon, saloon; **4** hot-air balloon.
See also **10.42.92.**

22.27.6: **1** spoon; **2** teaspoon; **3** dessertspoon, tablespoon, Witherspoon.
See also **10.42.92.**

22.27.7: **1** croon, kroon, prune, rune, strewn; **2** maroon, poltroon; **3** Cameroon, macaroon.

22.27.8: **1** soon; **2** bassoon, monsoon, Sassoon.

22.27.9: **2** cartoon, festoon, platoon, pontoon, spittoon.

22.28: **1** tuned, wound; **2** attuned, marooned.
See also **10.2.16, 22.27.3.**

22.29: **1** coop, coupe, dupe, hoop, poop, scoop, snoop, soup, stoep, stoop, stoup, swoop, whoop; **2** pea soup, recoup; **3** cock-a-hoop, nincompoop, oxtail soup; **5** primordial soup.
See also **10.42.104, 21.11.**

22.29.1: **1** gloop, loop, sloop; **3** cantaloupe, Guadeloupe; **4** infinite loop.

22.29.2: **1** croup, droop, drupe, troop, troupe.
See also **10.42.104, 22.30.**

22.29.3: **1** group; **2** in-group, newsgroup, peer group, playgroup, pop group, regroup, subgroup; **3** pressure group, splinter group, supergroup, working group.
See also **10.42.104.**

22.30: **1** oops, troops; **3** paratroops.
See also **22.29.2.**

22.31: **1** goose, juice, moose, mousse, noose; **2** Århus, caboose, couscous, fruit juice, mongoose, papoose, vamoose; **3** apple juice, Betelgeuse, gastric juice, orange juice; **4** barnacle goose, tomato juice.

22.31.1: **1** puce, Seuss, use, Zeus; **2** abuse, disuse, excuse, misuse, obtuse, reuse; **3** overuse, single-use.
See also **22.41.**

22.31.2: **1** deuce; **2** conduce, deduce, induce, produce, reduce, seduce.

22.31.3: **2** adduce, produce, traduce; **3** introduce, mass-produce, reproduce; **4** overproduce, reintroduce.

I'm g-not a Camel or a Kangaroo
So let me introduce,
I'm g-neither man nor moose
Oh g-no g-no g-no I'm a Gnu.
(Flanders and Swann)

22.31.4: **2** diffuse, Morpheus, Orpheus, profuse, refuse.
See also **22.41.**

22.31.5: **1** loose, sluice; **2** footloose, recluse, unloose.

22.31.6: **1** Bruce, spruce, truce; **2** abstruse; **3** Belarus; **4** Robert the Bruce.

22.32: **1** boost, juiced, Proust, roost; **2** mot juste; **3** self-induced.

22.33: **1** douche, louche, swoosh.

22.34: **1** coot, hoot, jute, moot, scoot, snoot, toot; **3** bandicoot, Nunavut.
See also **10.2.67.**

22.34.1: **1** boot; **2** coldboot, gumboot, hardboot, jackboot, reboot, ski boot, warmboot; **3** cowboy boot, Denver boot, desert boot, football boot, riding boot.
See also **10.2.67.**

22.34.2: **1** beaut, butte, newt, ute; **2** astute, confute, hirsute, minute, pursuit, refute, solute; **4** Argyll and Bute.
See also **2.54.88, 2.57.**

22.34.3: **2** tribute; **3** attribute, contribute, distribute; **4** redistribute.
See also **10.2.66.**

22.34.4: **1** cute; **2** acute; **3** execute, persecute, prosecute; **4** electrocute.
See also **10.2.68.**

22.34.5: **1** mute; **2** commute, deaf-mute, transmute; **4** telecommute.
See also **10.2.68.**

22.34.6: **2** compute, depute, dispute, impute, repute, statute; **3** constitute, destitute, disrepute, ill-repute, institute, prostitute, substitute; **4** reconstitute; **5** Women's Institute.
See also **10.2.68, 10.42.163**.

22.34.7: **1** flute, loot, lute; **2** dilute; **3** champagne flute, Magic Flute.
It is the little rift within the lute,
That by and by will make the music mute,
And ever widening slowly silence all.
(Alfred Tennyson)
See also **10.2.69**.

22.34.8: **2** pollute, salute; **3** absolute, dissolute, resolute; **4** irresolute; **5** decree absolute.
See also **10.2.69**.

22.34.9: **1** brute, root, route; **2** beetroot, Beirut, cheroot, cube root, en route, recruit, square root, taproot, uproot; **3** arrowroot, autoroute.
Yet what I sowed and what the orchard
yields
My brother's sons are gathering stalk and
root,
Small wonder then my children glean in
fields
They have not sown, and feed on bitter
fruit.
(Arna Bontemps)
See also **10.2.67**.

22.34.10: **1** fruit; **2** breadfruit, dried fruit, grapefruit, jackfruit, soft fruit, starfruit; **3** passion fruit; **4** forbidden fruit, low-hanging fruit.

22.34.11: **1** suit; **2** dress suit, jumpsuit, lawsuit, lounge suit, shell suit, spacesuit, strong suit, swimsuit, tracksuit; **3** bathing suit, birthday suit, bodysuit, boiler suit, diving suit, Hatshepsut, monkey suit, morning suit.
See also **10.2.67, 10.42.163**.

22.34.12: **2** catsuit, pantsuit, sweatsuit, wetsuit, zoot suit.

22.34.13: **1** chute, shoot; **2** crapshoot, offshoot; **3** overshoot, parachute.
See also **10.42.164**.

22.35: **1** Coutts; **2** cahoots, grassroots, jack boots.

22.36: **1** sleuth, youth; **2** Duluth, forsooth, tollbooth, uncouth; **4** eternal youth.
Just at the age 'twixt boy and youth,

When thought is speech, and speech is
truth.
(Sir Walter Scott)
See also **22.19**.

22.36.1: **1** Ruth, strewth, truth; **2** half-truth, untruth.

22.36.2: **1** tooth; **2** Bluetooth, bucktooth, dog's tooth, eyetooth, milk tooth, sweet tooth.

22.37: **1** Gooch, hooch, Lodz, mooch, pooch, smooch.

22.38: **1** groove, move, who've, you've; **2** false move, remove.
See also **10.42.183, 22.18, 22.39**.

22.38.1: **1** prove; **2** approve, disprove, improve, reprove; **3** disapprove.
See also **10.42.183**.

22.39: **1** grooved, moved, proved; **2** approved, disproved, improved, removed, unmoved; **3** unapproved.
See also **22.38**.

22.40: **1** blues, booze, choose, lose, ooze, Ouse, schmooze, snooze, who's, whose; **2** horseshoes, Toulouse.
See also **22.6.2, 22.12**.

22.40.1: **1** dues, Hughes, mews, muse, news, thews, use; **2** abuse, accuse, amuse, enthuse, excuse, ill-use, Matthews, misuse, perfuse, purlieus, reuse; **3** disabuse, overuse, Syracuse; **4** hypotenuse.
About binomial theorems I'm teeming
with a lot of news,
With many cheerful facts about the
square on the hypoteneuse.
(W. S. Gilbert)
See also **22.4.1, 22.41**.

22.40.2: **1** fuse; **2** confuse, defuse, diffuse, infuse, refuse, suffuse, transfuse.
See also **22.41**.

22.40.3: **1** bruise, cruise, ruse, trews; **2** Andrews, Hebrews, peruse; **3** Santa Cruz, Socceroos, Veracruz.
See also **22.10**.

22.41: **1** fused, used; **2** accused, amused, bemused, confused, diffused, disused, excused, misused, refused, unused, well-used; **3** overused, underused.
See also **9.14.58, 22.31.1, 22.31.4, 22.40.1, 22.40.2**.

22.42: **1** Bruges, luge, rouge; **3** Baton Rouge.

Alphabetical Index

adept **6.45**
adequacy **9.20.2**
adequate **2.56**
adequately **9.14.87**
Ades **6.57**
à deux **7.0**
ad finem **6.25**
adhere **8.3**
adherence **2.45.25**
adherent **2.47.79**
adhesion **2.43.333**
adhesive **10.61.2**
ad hoc **13.10**
adhocracy **9.20.10**
adieu **22.4.1**
ad infinitum **2.40.38**
adios **13.34**
adipose **19.45**
adit **10.56.4**
adjacent **2.47.82**
adjectival **2.37.295**
adjective **10.61.46**
adjoin **18.11.1**
adjoining **10.42.92**
adjourn **7.20**
adjournment **2.47.48**
adjudge **20.9.1**
adjudicate **5.47.23**
adjudication **2.43.157**
adjudicator **2.22.13**
adjunct **20.39**
adjure **15.0**
adjust **20.44.3**
adjustable **2.37.77**
adjusted **10.2.93**
adjustment **2.47.62**
adjutant **2.47.88**
Adlai **11.5**
Adler **2.13.28**
ad lib **10.0**
ad libitum **2.40.38**
adman **1.21.4**
admin **10.31.16**
administer **2.22.98**
administration **2.43.205**
administrative **10.61.27**
administrator **2.22.19**
admirable **2.37.51**
Admirable Crichton **2.43.299**
admirably **9.14.52**
admiral **2.37.233**
Admiralty **9.22.79**
Admiralty Board **14.19.3**
admiration **2.43.197**
admire **12.0**
admired **12.7**
admirer **2.19**
admiring **10.42.126**
admissibility **9.22.21**

admissible **2.37.59**
admission **2.43.241**
admit **10.56.21**
admittance **2.45.34**
admittedly **9.14.59**
admixture **2.24.10**
admonish **10.54.14**
admonition **2.43.243**
admonitory **9.19.45**
ad nauseam **1.18**
ado **22.2**
adobe **9.6.6**
adolescence **2.45.30**
adolescent **2.47.83**
Adolf **13.14**
Adonis **2.54.62, 10.50.10**
adopt **13.33**
adopted **10.2.89**
adoption **2.43.284**
adoptive **10.61.50**
adorable **2.37.50**
adoration **2.43.195**
adore **14.2.1**
adoring **10.42.127**
adorn **14.35**
adorned **14.36**
adornment **2.47.48**
ad rem **6.25**
adrenal **2.37.214**
adrenal gland **1.22.3**
adrenalin **10.31.12**
Adrian **2.43.15**
Adriatic **10.12.55**
Adriatic Sea **9.20.24**
Adrienne **6.29.1**
adrift **10.7.2**
adroit **18.16**
adroitness **2.54.88**
ADSL **6.14.8**
adsorb **14.18**
adsorption **2.43.284**
adspend **6.30.5**
adulate **5.47.33**
adulation **2.43.169**
adult **20.22**
adulterate **5.47.57**
adulterated **10.2.52**
adulteration **2.43.202**
adulterer **2.19.5**
adulterous **2.54.104**
adultery **9.19.34**
adulthood **21.0.4**
adumbrate **5.47.58**
ad usum **2.40.33**
advance **3.37**
advanced **3.40**
advancement **2.47.56**
advance party **9.22.57**
advancing **10.42.139**
advantage **10.11.24**
advantaged **10.34**
advantageous **2.54.30**

Advent **6.34.6**
adventitious **2.54.125**
adventure **2.24.8**
adventurer **2.19.1**
adventuresome **2.40.34**
adventurism **2.40.78**
adventurous **2.54.105**
adverb **7.7.1**
adverbial **2.37.2**
adversarial **2.37.7**
adversary **9.19.32**
adverse **7.26.2**
adversity **9.22.42**
advert **7.28.5**
advertise **11.42.33**
advertisement **2.47.53**
advertiser **2.27.5**
advertising **10.42.188**
advertorial **2.37.12**
advice **11.34**
advice note **19.47.7**
advisable **2.37.85**
advise **11.42.36**
advised **11.43.6**
advisedly **9.14.58**
adviser **2.27.7**
advisory **9.19.57**
advocaat **3.8**
advocacy **9.20.4**
advocate (noun) **2.56.9**
advocate (verb) **5.47.20**
adytum **2.40.38**
adze **1.4**
aedile **11.22**
Aegean **2.43.1**
Aegean Sea **9.20.30**
aegis **10.50**
Aeneas **2.54.5**
Aeolian **2.43.6**
Aeolic **10.12.19**
Aeolis **10.50.7**
aeon **2.43.1**
aerate **5.47.51**
aerated **10.2.51**
aeration **2.43.192**
aerial **2.37.7**
aerobatics **10.13.13**
aerobe **19.22.2**
aerobic **10.12.3**
aerobics **10.13**
aerodrome **19.38.3**
aerodynamic **10.12.23**
aerodynamics **10.13.4**
aerofoil **18.8.1**
aerogram **1.18.7, 1.18.8**
aerolisation **2.43.224**
aeronaut **14.44.3**
aeronautics **10.13.12**
aeroplane **5.35.5**
aerosol **13.13.2**

aerospace **5.45.6**
Aeschylus **2.54.37**
Aesop **2.52**
aesthete **9.52**
aesthetic **10.12.67**
aestheticism **2.40.83**
aesthetics **10.13.15**
aestival **2.37.294**
aestivation **2.43.222**
aetiology **9.12.5**
afar **3.4**
affable **2.37.25**
affair **4.3**
affect **6.12.1**
affectation **2.43.208**
affected **10.2.72**
affecting **10.42.166**
affection **2.43.265**
affectionate **2.56.27**
affective **10.61.42**
affidavit **10.56.35**
affiliate (noun) **2.56.1**
affiliate (verb) **5.47.3**
affiliated **10.2.38**
affiliation **2.43.141**
affinity **9.22.29**
affirm **7.18.1**
affirmation **2.43.175**
affirmative **10.61.15**
affirmed **7.19**
affix **10.13.1**
afflict **10.14.2**
afflicted **10.2.77**
affliction **2.43.271**
affluence **2.45.4**
affluent **2.47.5**
afford **14.19**
affordable **2.37.32**
afforded **10.2.11**
afforest **10.53.18**
afforestation **2.43.218**
affray **5.12.1**
affricate **2.56.10**
affright **11.36.16**
affront **20.33.2**
Afghan **1.21**
Afghan hound **16.11.3**
afghani **9.16.1, 9.16.12**
Afghanistan **1.21.15, 3.34.3**
Afghanistani **9.16.12**
aficionada **2.6.1**
aficionado **19.4.2**
afield **9.39.1**
afire **12.1**
aflame **5.33.2**
afloat **19.47.5**
afoot **21.14**
aforementioned **2.44.13**
aforenamed **5.34**
aforesaid **6.1**
aforethought **14.44.9**

aka **5.0**
Akbar **3.2.1**
Akhenaton **2.43.291**
Akhmatova **2.25.16**
Akihito **19.18.5**
akimbo **19.3.2**
akin **10.31.7**
Al **1.13**
à la **2.13.1**
Alabama **2.14.1**
alabaster **2.22.91**
à la carte **3.49.3**
alacrity **9.22.32**
Aladdin's cave **5.51**
à la mode **19.23.3**
Alan **2.43.75**
Alana **2.15.7**
Alaric **10.12.42**
alarm **3.31.1**
alarm clock **13.10.6**
alarmed **3.32**
alarming **10.42.86**
alarmist **10.53.10**
alarum **2.40.29**
alas **1.36.2**
Alaska **2.12.27**
Alastair **2.22.89**
alastor **14.15.1**
Alba **2.5**
Alban **2.43.27**
Albania **2.1.12**
Albanian **2.43.11**
Albany **9.16.2**
albatross **13.34.6**
Albee **9.6.8**
albeit **10.56**
Albert **2.56.6**
Alberta **2.22.25**
Alberti **9.22**
albinism **2.40.75**
albino **19.13.3**
albinoism **2.40.48**
Albion **2.43.2**
album **2.40**
albumen **10.31.16**
albumin **10.31.16**
Alcaeus **2.54**
Alcatraz **1.48**
alchemist **10.53.11**
alchemy **9.15.2**
Alcock **13.10.2**
alcohol **13.13**
alcoholic **10.12.20**
alcoholism **2.40.54**
alcopop **13.31.4**
Alcott **2.56.9**
alcove **19.51**
Aldebaran **2.43.110**
aldehyde **11.14.9**
al dente **9.22.82**
alder **2.6**
alderman **2.43.81**
alderwoman **2.43.89**

Aldgate **5.47.14**
Aldrin **10.31.20**
ale **5.30**
aleatoric **10.12.46**
alehouse **16.14.5**
Alejandra **2.19.16**
Alemannic **10.12.31**
alembic **10.12.3**
aleph **6.4**
Aleppo **19.14**
alert **7.28**
A level **2.37.292**
alewife **11.17.3**
alexander **2.6.19**
Alexandra **2.19.16**
Alexandria **2.1.19**
alexandrine **11.27.14**
Alexis **10.50.13**
alfalfa **2.8.6**
Alfonso **19.21**
Alfred **2.33.17**
alfresco **19.10.6**
alga **2.9**
algae **9.10, 9.12**
algal **2.37.135**
algebra **2.19.15**
algebraic **10.12.1**
Algeria **2.1.23**
Algerian **2.43.20**
Algernon **2.43.106**
algology **9.12.4**
Algonquian **2.43.1**
algorithm **2.40.23**
Alhambra **2.19.15**
Ali **9.14.29**
alias **2.54.4**
alibi **11.2**
Alice **2.54.35**
Alice band **1.22.1**
alien **2.43.7**
alienate **5.47.44**
alienated **10.2.48**
alienation **2.43.180**
alight **11.36.7**
align **11.27.4**
alignment **2.47.51**
Aligoté **5.15**
alimental **2.37.286**
alimentary **9.19.51**
alimentary canal **1.13**
alimony **9.16.9**
A-line **11.27.3**
aliquot **13.39.9**
Alison **2.43.120**
A-list **10.53.6**
Alistair **2.22.89**
alit **10.56.19**
alive **11.38**
alive and kicking
 10.42.49
Alix **10.13.2**
alkali **11.5.1**
alkaline **11.27.4**

alkaloid **18.5.1**
alkane **5.35.3**
all **14.27**
Allah **2.13.1**
Allahabad **1.3.1**
all-American **2.43.70**
Allan **2.43.75**
all-around **16.11.6**
allay **5.8.1**
all-consuming
 10.42.91
Allecto **19.18.7**
allegation **2.43.152**
allege **6.9.1**
alleged **6.32**
allegedly **9.14.58**
allegiance **2.45.9**
allegorical **2.37.171**
allegory **9.19.13**
allegretto **19.18.4**
allegro **19.15.6**
alleluia **2.11**
all-embracing
 10.42.135
Allen **2.43.75**
Allenby **9.6.10**
all-encompassing
 10.42.133
Allende **5.3.4**
allen key **9.13**
allergen **6.29**
allergy **9.12.3**
alleviate **5.47.7**
alleviation **2.43.139**
alley **9.14.1**
alleyway **5.17.3**
All Hallows' Day
 5.3.6
alliance **12.10**
allied **11.14.10**
alligator **2.22.12**
alligator pear **4.10**
all-in **10.31.11**
all-inclusive **10.61.10**
all-in-one **20.29.6**
Allis **10.50.5**
Allison **2.43.120**
alliterate **5.47.57**
alliteration **2.43.202**
alliterative **10.61.25**
allium **2.40.5**
all-knowing **10.42.8**
allocate **5.47.21**
allocation **2.43.155**
allogamy **9.15.3**
allonym **10.26.1**
allopathy **9.23.2**
allophone **19.40.3**
allot **13.39.3**
allotment **2.47.58**
allotropy **9.18.4**
all-out **16.16.5**
all over **2.25.19**

allow **16.4**
allowable **2.37.25**
allowance **2.36**
alloy **18.3**
all-powerful **2.37.121**
all-purpose **2.54.94**
all right **11.36.16**
all-round **16.11.5**
all-rounder **2.6.26**
All Saints' Day **5.3**
all-seeing **10.42.2**
All Souls' Day **5.3.6**
allspice **11.34**
All-Star **3.15.1**
all-time **11.25.5**
allude **22.17.7**
allure **15.1**
alluring **10.42.128**
allusion **2.43.339**
allusive **10.61.2**
alluvial **2.37.14**
alluvium **2.40.1**
ally **11.5**
Alma-Ata **2.22.4**
alma mater **2.22.6,
 2.22.9**
almanac **1.10.13**
almandine **10.31.3**
almighty **9.22.65**
almond **2.44.9**
almoner **2.15.2**
almost **19.46.1**
alms **3.33**
alms-giving **10.42.180**
almshouse **16.14.1**
aloe **19.11.1**
aloe vera **2.19.10**
aloft **13.6**
aloha **2.3, 2.3.3**
alone **19.40.6**
along **13.27.2**
alongside **11.14.17**
Alonzo **19.21**
aloo **22.6**
aloof **22.19**
aloofness **2.54.62**
alopecia **2.21**
alp **1.15**
alpaca **2.12.1**
alpha **2.8.6**
alphabet **6.51.2**
alphabetical **2.37.177**
alphabetise **11.42.32**
Alpha centauri **11.8**
alpha particle **2.37.176**
alpine **11.27.13**
alpinist **10.53.12**
al-Qaeda **2.6.6**
already **9.7.7**
alright **11.36.16**
Alsace **1.36**
Alsatian **2.43.206**
also **19.16**

also-ran 1.21.13
Altair 4.13
altar 2.22.77
altarpiece 9.49.4
alter 2.22.77
alteration 2.43.202
altercation 2.43.155
altered 2.33.18
alter ego 19.6.3
alternate 2.56.26,
5.47.44
alternation 2.43.181
alternative 10.61.22
alternatively 9.14.100
alternator 2.22.16
although 19.0
altimeter 2.22.29,
2.22.38
altitude 22.17.6
Alt key 9.13
Altman 2.43.101
alto 19.18.8
alto clef 6.4
altocumulus 2.54.42
altogether 2.7.2
alto relievo 19.20
altostratus 2.54.130
altruism 2.40.49
altruist 10.53
altruistic 10.12.80
alum 2.40.25
aluminium 2.40.11
alumna 2.15
alumnus 2.54.81
Alun 2.43.75
alveolar 2.13.2,
2.13.18
Alvis 10.50.31
always 5.54.3
always-on 13.22.17
alyssum 2.40.33
Alzheimer's disease
9.59.18
AM 6.25
am 1.18, 2.40
amah 2.14.5
amalgam 2.40
amalgamate 5.47.40
amalgamated 10.2.47
amalgamation
2.43.174
Amanda 2.6.18
amanuensis 10.50.13
amaranth 1.26
amaranthine 11.27
amaranthus 2.54.134
Amaravati 9.22.56
amaryllis 10.50.5
amass 1.36.3
amateur 2.22.3
amateur dramatics
10.13.14
amateurish 10.54.18

amatory 9.19.39
amaze 5.54
amazed 5.55
amazement 2.47.65
amazing 10.42.187
Amazon 2.43.327
Amazonian 2.43.13
ambage 10.11.1
ambassador 2.6
ambassadorial 2.37.10
amber 2.5.9
ambidexterity 9.22.36
ambidextrous 2.54.112
ambience 2.45.1
ambient 2.47.1
ambiguity 9.22.4
ambiguous 2.54.18
ambit 10.56.2
ambition 2.43.236
ambitious 2.54.121
ambivalence 2.45.15
ambivalent 2.47.29
amble 2.37.101
Ambridge 10.11.19
Ambrose 19.52.7
ambrosia 2.1.31
ambrosial 2.37.1
ambulance 2.45.16
ambuscade 5.21.1
ambush 21.13
Ameer 8.5
ameliorate 5.47.52
amelioration 2.43.193
amen 6.29.2
amenable 2.37.43
amend 6.30.3
amended 10.2.19
amendment 2.47.42
amends 6.39
amenity 9.22.26
amenorrhoea 2.1.21
Amerasian 2.43.332
America 2.12.14
American 2.43.70
Americana 2.15.8
American dream
9.41.3
American Express
6.47.7
American football
14.27.2
Americanise 11.42.19
Americanism 2.40.72
americano 19.13.1
Americas 2.60.3
Americas Cup 20.40.2
americium 2.40.17
Amerindian 2.43.3
amethyst 10.53
Amex 6.11
amiable 2.37.91
amicable 2.37.39
amid 10.2.27

amide 11.14.11
amidships 10.48
amigo 19.6.3
Amin 9.43.7
amino acid 10.2.32
Amis 10.50.9
Amish 10.54.13
amiss 10.50.9
amity 9.22.25
Amman 3.34
ammeter 2.22.29
ammo 19.12
ammonia 2.1.16
ammonite 11.36.15
ammunition 2.43.243
amnesia 2.1.33
amnesiac 1.10.1
amnesic 10.12.91
amnesty 9.22.86
Amnesty International
2.37.201
amniocentesis
10.50.18
amniotic fluid 10.2.1
amniotic sac 1.10.17
amoeba 2.5.3
amoebic 10.12.3
amok 13.10
among 20.36
Amontillado 19.4.2
Amor 14.9
amoral 2.37.243
amorality 9.22.18
amorous 2.54.101
amorphous 2.54.25
amortise 11.42.32
Amos 13.34.4
amount 16.13.1
amour 15.2
amour-propre 2.19.19
amp 1.20
amperage 10.11.15
ampere 4.10.1
ampersand 1.22
amphetamine 9.43.7
amphibian 2.43.2
amphibious 2.54.1
amphitheatre 2.22.3
amphora 2.19.1
ample 2.37.229
amplification 2.43.158
amplifier 12.1.1
amplitude 22.17.5
ampoule 22.22.5
amputate 5.47.63
amputation 2.43.213
amputee 9.22.73
amrita 2.22.32
Amritsar 2.20.18
Amsterdam 1.18.1
Amtrak 1.10.16
amuck 20.10.3
amulet 2.56.19

Amundsen 2.43.125
Amur 15.2
amuse 22.40.1
amused 22.41
amusement 2.47.65
amusement park
3.27.5
Amy 9.15.10
an 1.21, 2.43
Anabaptist 10.53.22
anabolic steroid 18.5.3
anachronism 2.40.66
anaconda 2.6.25
Anacreon 13.22.1
anadem 6.25.2
anaemia 2.1.10
anaemic 10.12.22
anaerobe 19.22.2
anaerobic 10.12.3
anaesthesia 2.1.33
anaesthetic 10.12.67
anaesthetise 11.42.33
anaesthetist 10.53.23
anaglyph 10.6.1
anaglyptography 9.9.9
anagram 1.18.7
Anaïs 10.50
anal 2.37.195
analeptic 10.12.75
analgesia 2.1.33
analgesic 10.12.91
analogous 2.54.27
analogue 13.7.5
analogy 9.12.3
anal-retentive 10.61.49
analyse 11.42.9
analysis 10.50.15
analytic 10.12.68
analytical 2.37.178
anaphora 2.19.1
anaphylaxis 10.50.22
anarchism 2.40.53
anarchist 10.53.5
anarchistic 10.12.80
anarchy 9.13
Anastasia 2.1.32
anathema 2.14.3
Anatolia 2.1.6
Anatolian 2.43.6
Anatolic 10.12.19
anatomical 2.37.163
anatomise 11.42.16
anatomy 9.15.6
ANC 9.20.27
ancestor 2.22.94
ancestral 2.37.246
ancestry 9.19.88
anchor 2.12.24
anchorage 10.11.16
anchorman 1.21.5
anchorperson 2.43.118
anchorwoman 2.43.89
anchovy 9.25

ancien régime **9.41**
ancient **2.47.86**
ancillary **9.19.19**
and **1.22**
Andalusia **2.1.27**
andante **9.22.81**
Andean **2.43.3**
Andersen **2.43.136**
Anderson **2.43.114**
Anderton **2.43.290**
Andorra **2.19.12**
Andreessen **2.43.116**
Andrew **22.10.2**
Andrews **22.40.3**
Androcles **9.59.5**
androgynous **2.54.63**
android **18.5.3**
andrology **9.12.14**
Andromeda **2.6.5**
anecdotal **2.37.270**
anecdote **19.47.2**
anemographic **10.12.9**
anemometer **2.22.39**
anemone **9.16.8**
aneroid **18.5.3**
Aneurin **10.31.20**
aneurysm **2.40.78**
anew **22.4.9**
angel **2.37.146**
Angela **2.13.2**
angel cake **5.27.1**
Angeleno **19.13.3**
angel food cake **5.27.1**
angelic **10.12.16**
angelica **2.12.12**
angelical **2.37.162**
Angel of Death **6.53**
Angelou **22.6.1**
angel shark **3.27.6**
Angelus **2.54.39**
anger **2.9.11**
angered **2.33.6**
Angers **5.19**
Angharad **1.3.6**
Angie **9.12.21**
angina **2.15.18**
angioplasty **9.22.85**
angiosperm **7.18.2**
Angkor **14.7**
Angkor Wat **13.39.9**
angle **2.37.142**
angled **2.38.4**
Anglepoise **18.17**
angler **2.13.29**
Anglesey **9.20.26**
Anglican **2.43.69**
Anglican Church **7.31**
Anglicanism **2.40.72**
anglicise **11.42.31**
Anglicism **2.40.82**
angling **10.42.58**
Anglo **19.11.10**
Anglo-Irish **10.54.17**

anglophile **11.22.2**
Anglophobe **19.22.1**
Anglophobic **10.12.5**
Anglophone **19.40.3**
Anglo-Saxon **2.43.127**
Angola **2.13.18**
Angolan **2.43.78**
angora **2.19.11**
angostura **2.19.13**
Angostura bitters
2.60.7
angry **9.19.75**
angstrom **13.18.4**
Anguilla **2.13.9**
anguish **10.54.22**
anguished **10.55**
angular **2.13.23**
Angus **2.54.28**
anhydrous **2.54.96**
anicca **2.12.13**
aniline **9.43.6,**
10.31.13
anility **9.22.20**
anima **2.14.12**
animadvert **7.28.5**
animal **2.37.190**
animalcule **22.22.3**
Animalia **2.1.7**
animalistic **10.12.82**
animality **9.22.9**
animal lover **2.25.23**
animate (adj) **2.56.24**
animate (verb) **5.47.41**
animated **10.2.47**
animateur **7.6**
animation **2.43.177**
animator **2.22.9**
animatronics **10.13.7**
anime **5.9**
animism **2.40.64**
animist **10.53.10**
animistic **10.12.83**
animosity **9.22.46**
animus **2.54.60**
anion **12.9**
anise **9.49.2**
aniseed **9.29.7**
Anita **2.22.30**
Anjou **22.0**
Ankara **2.19.1**
ankle **2.37.187**
ankle-biter **2.22.46**
anklet **2.56.20**
Anna **2.15.1**
Annabel **6.14.1**
annals **2.39.5**
Annam **1.18**
Annan **1.21.10,**
2.43.107
Annapolis **10.50.7**
Annapurna **2.15.11**
Anne **1.21**
anneal **9.38.4**

annex **6.11**
annexation **2.43.207**
annexe **6.11**
Annie **9.16.1**
Annie Oakley **9.14.65**
annihilate **5.47.29**
annihilated **10.2.45**
annihilation **2.43.165**
anniversary **9.19.33**
anno domini **11.6**
anno Hegirae **9.19**
annotate **5.47.63**
announce **16.12.1**
announcement **2.47.56**
announcer **2.20.15**
annoy **18.0**
annoyance **2.45.12**
annoyed **18.5.2**
annoying **10.42**
annoyingly **9.14.75**
annual **2.37.18**
annualised **11.43.1**
annually **9.14.5**
annul **20.14**
annular **2.13.21**
annulment **2.47.46**
Annunciation **2.43.143**
annus mirabilis
10.50.5
anode **19.23.4**
anodise **11.42.1**
anodyne **11.27**
anoint **18.12**
anomalous **2.54.37**
anomaly **9.14.14**
anon **13.22.9**
anonymiser **2.27.5**
anonymity **9.22.25**
anonymous **2.54.60**
anonymously **9.14.81**
anorak **1.10.15**
anorexia **2.1.28**
anorexia nervosa
2.20.11
anorexic **10.12.53**
another **2.7.4**
Anouilh **9.5**
Anselm **6.17**
anseriform **14.33.2**
anserine **11.27.14**
Ansett **2.56**
answer **2.20.16**
answerable **2.37.51**
answerphone **19.40.3**
ant **1.25**
antacid **10.2.32**
antagonise **11.42.19**
antagonism **2.40.71**
antagonist **10.53.13**
antagonistic **10.12.84**
Antananarivo **19.20**
Antarctic **10.12.72**
Antarctica **2.12.15**

ant bear **4.2**
ante **9.22.81**
anteater **2.22.26**
antebellum **2.40.26**
antecede **9.29.7**
antecedent **2.47.7**
antechamber **2.5.10**
antedate **5.47.11**
antedated **10.2.40**
antediluvian **2.43.25**
antelope **19.44.2**
ante meridiem **6.25.1**
antenatal **2.37.272**
antenna **2.15.10**
antenuptial **2.37.258**
antepenultimate
2.56.25
anterior **2.1.24**
anteroom **22.25.3**
anthem **2.40.41**
anther **2.23.1**
anthill **10.17.3**
anthology **9.12.18**
Anthony **9.16.11**
anthracite **11.36.20**
anthrax **1.11.3**
anthropocentric
10.12.52
anthropogenic
10.12.32
anthropogeny **9.16.5**
anthropography **9.9.3**
anthropoid **18.5**
anthropological
2.37.159
anthropology **9.12.4**
anthropometric
10.12.51
anthropomorphic
10.12.12
anthropomorphism
2.40.51
anthroposophy **9.9.11**
anti **9.22.81**
antiaircraft **3.24.2**
antialiasing **10.42.133**
antibacterial **2.37.9**
antibody **9.7.14**
antic **10.12.74**
anticipate **5.47.50**
anticipated **10.2.50**
anticipation **2.43.191**
anticipatory **9.19.43**
anticlerical **2.37.170**
anticlimax **1.11**
anticlockwise **11.42.37**
anticoagulant **2.47.28,**
2.47.31
anticonvulsant **2.47.82**
antics **10.13.12**
anticyclone **19.40.5**
antidepressant **2.47.84**
antidote **19.47.2**

antiemetic 10.12.65
antifebrile 11.22.4
antifreeze 9.59.11
antifungal 2.37.145
antigen 2.43.56
Antigone 9.16.4
antigravity 9.22.52
antigrowth 19.49.1
Antigua and Barbuda
  2.6.13
antihero 19.15.3
antihistamine 9.43.7
antiknock 13.10
antimacassar 2.20.1
antimalarial 2.37.7
antimatter 2.22.1
antimony 9.16.9
antinovel 2.37.288
antinuclear 2.1.6
antioxidant 2.47.10
antiparticle 2.37.176
antipasto 19.18.11
antipathetic 10.12.67
antipathy 9.23.1
antiperspirant 2.47.76
antiphon 13.22.3
antipodean 2.43.3
antipsychotic 10.12.71
antiquarian 2.43.16
antiquark 3.27
antiquated 10.2.37
antique 9.36.6
antiquity 9.22.55
antirejection 2.43.266
antiretroviral 2.37.242
anti-Semite 11.36.13
anti-Semitic 10.12.68
anti-Semitism 2.40.85
antisepsis 10.50.23
antiseptic 10.12.75
antiserum 2.40.29
antisocial 2.37.264
antispasmodic 10.12.7
antistrophe 9.9.10
antithesis 10.50.16
antithetical 2.37.177
antitoxin 10.31.23
antitrust 20.44.6
antiviral 2.37.242
antivirus 2.54.107
antler 2.13.33
Antonia 2.1.16
Antonio 19.2
Antonioni 9.16.23
Antony 9.16.11
antonym 10.26.1
Antrim 10.26.2
antsy 9.20.39
Antwerp 7.25
Anubis 10.50.1
anus 2.54.62
anvil 10.17.8
anxiety 9.22.66

anxious 2.54.126
any 9.16.14
anybody 9.7.14
anyhow 16.2
any more 14.9
anyone 20.29.6
anyplace 5.45.4
anything 10.42.174
anytime 11.25.3
anyway 5.17.3
anyways 5.54.3
anywhere 4.15
Anzac 1.10.20
Anzac Day 5.3
A-OK 5.7
aorta 2.22.51
Aotearoa 2.3.4
Aouita 2.22.26
apace 5.45.5
Apache 9.24.1
apart 3.49.5
apartheid 5.47, 11.36.5
apartment 2.47.58
apathetic 10.12.67
apathy 9.23.1
apatosaurus 2.54.109
ape 5.42
aped 5.44
aperçu 22.11
aperitif 9.32
aperture 2.24.2
apex 6.11.4
aphasia 2.1.32
aphasic 10.12.91
aphid 10.2
aphonia 2.1.16
aphonic 10.12.35
aphorism 2.40.78
aphrodisiac 1.10.1
Aphrodite 9.22.65
apiary 9.19.3
apical 2.37.167
apiece 9.49.4
apish 10.54.16
aplenty 9.22.82
aplomb 13.18.3
apocalypse 10.48
apocalyptic 10.12.76
apocope 9.18.2
Apocrypha 2.8.2
apocryphal 2.37.122
apogee 9.12.1
apolitical 2.37.178
Apollo 19.11.7
apologetic 10.12.64
apologia 2.1
apologise 11.42.2
apologist 10.53.4
apology 9.12.4
apophthegm 6.25
apoplectic 10.12.72
apostasy 9.20.12
apostate 5.47.65

a posteriori 11.8
apostle 2.37.252
apostolic 10.12.19
apostrophe 9.9.10
apothecary 9.19.16
apotheosis 10.50.20
app 1.33
appal 14.27.8
Appalachian
  Mountains 10.41.2
appalled 14.28
appalling 10.42.75
Appaloosa 2.20.12
appanage 10.11.11
apparatchik 10.12
apparatus 2.54.130
apparel 2.37.231
apparent 2.47.75
apparition 2.43.244
appeal 9.38.5
appealing 10.42.72
appear 8.7
appearance 2.45.25
appease 9.59.9
appeased 9.60
appeasement 2.47.65
appeaser 2.27.4
appellant 2.47.27
appellation 2.43.166
append 6.30.4
appendage 10.11.2
appendectomy 9.15.8
appendicectomy
  9.15.8
appendicitis 10.50.25
appendix 10.13
appertain 5.35.14
appetiser 2.27.5
appetising 10.42.188
appetite 11.36.21
Appian 2.43.14
applaud 14.19.7
applause 14.48
apple 2.37.223
Appleby 9.6
applecart 3.49.3
apple fritter 2.22.42
applejack 1.10.8
apple pie 11.7
apple-polishing
  10.42.142
applet 2.56.21
Appleton 2.43.303
appliance 12.10
applicable 2.37.39
applicant 2.47.26
application 2.43.163
applicator 2.22.13
applied 11.14.10
appliqué 5.7
apply 11.5.3
appoggiatura 2.19.13
appoint 18.12

appointed 10.2.88
appointee 9.22.80
appointment 2.47.61
apportion 2.43.250
apportionment 2.47.49
apposite 10.56.38
apposition 2.43.249
appraisal 2.37.301
appraise 5.54.2
appraiser 2.27.3
appreciable 2.37.61
appreciate 5.47.6
appreciation 2.43.144
appreciative 10.61.15
apprehend 6.30
apprehensible 2.37.60
apprehension 2.43.281
apprehensive 10.61.12
apprentice 10.50.29
apprenticeship 10.47.6
apprise 11.42.28
approachable 2.37.79
approbation 2.43.147
appropriacy 9.20.2
appropriate (adj)
  2.56.2
appropriate (verb)
  5.47.4
appropriated 10.2.38
appropriately 9.14.87
appropriation 2.43.142
approval 2.37.288
approve 22.38.1
approving 10.42.183
approvingly 9.14.75
approximate (adj)
  2.56.24
approximate (verb)
  5.47.41
approximation
  2.43.177
appurtenance 2.45.19
après-ski 9.13.22
apricot 13.39.1
April 2.37.230
April fool 22.22
April Fools' Day 5.3.6
a priori 11.8
apron 2.43.110
apron stage 5.26.4
apropos 19.14
apse 1.34
apt 1.35
aptitude 22.17.6
aptness 2.54.88
aqua 2.26
aqualung 20.36.1
aquamarine 9.43.11
aquaplane 5.35.5
aquarium 2.40.14
Aquarius 2.54.10
aquatic 10.12.55
aquatint 10.38.4

aqueduct 20.12
aqueous 2.54.1
aquiculture 2.24.7
aquifer 2.8.2
aquiline 11.27.3
Aquinas 2.54.73
Arab 2.32
Arabella 2.13.5
arabesque 6.48
Arabia 2.1.1
Arabian 2.43.2
Arabic 10.12.3
arable 2.37.50
arachnid 10.2.28
arachnoid 18.5.2
arachnology 9.12.11
arachnophobia 2.1.2
Arafat 1.41.2
Aragon 2.43.47
Aral 2.37.231
Aral Sea 9.20.26
Araminta 2.22.82
Aran 2.43.111
Aran Islands 2.50.2
arbalest 6.49.3
arbalester 2.22.94
arbiter 2.22.34
arbitrage 3.59,
  10.11.12
arbitrarily 9.14.22
arbitrary 9.19.31
arbitrate 5.47.60
arbitration 2.43.204
arbitrator 2.22.19
arboreal 2.37.10
arboretum 2.40.38
arboricultural 2.37.240
arboriculture 2.24.7
arbour 2.5.1
Arbroath smokey
  9.13.12
Arbuckle 2.37.186
arbutus 2.54.129
arc 3.27
arcade 5.21.1
arcade game 5.33.1
Arcadia 2.1.3
Arcadian 2.43.4
arcana 2.15.9
arcane 5.35.3
arcanum 2.40.27
arch 3.52
Archaean 2.43.1
archaeological
  2.37.160
archaeologist 10.53.4
archaeology 9.12.5
archaeopteryx 10.13.9
archaic 10.12.1
archaism 2.40.45
archangel 2.37.146
archbishop 2.52
archbishopric 10.12.48

archdeacon 2.43.67
archdeaconry 9.19.78
archdiocese 10.50.19
archduchess 10.50
archduchy 9.24
archduke 22.21.1
arched 3.53
archenemy 9.15.2
archer 2.24
archery 9.19.53
archetypal 2.37.222
archetypally 9.14.18
archetype 11.31.3
archetypical 2.37.168
Archibald 14.28
Archimedes 9.59.2
Archimedes' screw
  22.10.4
archipelago 19.6
architect 6.12
architectonic 10.12.38
architectural 2.37.239
architecture 2.24.4
architrave 5.51.2
archive 11.38
archivist 10.53.26
archrival 2.37.295
archway 5.17
arc lamp 1.20.2
Arctic 10.12.72
Arcturus 2.54.96
ardency 9.20.31
Ardennes 6.29
ardent 2.47.7
ardour 2.6.1
arduous 2.54.18
are 3.0, 4.0
area 2.1.22
arena 2.15.14
aren't 3.38
Areopagus 2.54.27
Arequipa 2.18.6
Ares 9.59.10
arête 6.51.8
Arethusa 2.20.12
argent 2.47.19
Argentina 2.15.15
Argentine 11.27.17
Argentinian 2.43.12
Argo 19.6.1
argon 13.22.4
Argonaut 14.44.3
Argonne 13.22.4
argosy 9.20.3
argot 2.56.7, 19.6.1
arguable 2.37.29
arguably 9.14.51
argue 22.4
argument 2.47.41
argumentation
  2.43.216
argumentative
  10.61.32

Argus 2.54.26
Argus-eyed 11.14.17
argy-bargy 9.12
argyle 11.22
Argyll and Bute
  22.34.2
Århus 22.31
aria 2.1.19
Ariane 1.21
arid 10.2.30
aridity 9.22.7
Ariel 2.37.7
Aries 9.59.10
arietta 2.22.22
aright 11.36.17
Ariosto 19.18.11
arise 11.42.22
arisen 2.43.330
aristo 19.18.11
aristocracy 9.20.11
aristocrat 1.41.9
aristocratic 10.12.62
Aristophanes 9.59.8
Aristotle 2.37.278
arithmetic (noun)
  10.12.63
arithmetic (noun, adj)
  10.12.65
Arizona 2.15.22
Arjun 2.43.331
Arjuna 2.15
ark 3.27
Arkansas 14.13
Arkwright 11.36.16
Arlington 2.43.309
arm 3.31
armada 2.6.1
armadillo 19.11.6
Armageddon 2.43.34
Armagh 3.10
armagnac 1.10
ArmaLite 11.36.7
armament 2.47.33
Armani 9.16.12
Armatrading 10.42.15
armature 2.24.2
armband 1.22.1
armchair 4.14
armed 3.32
armed robbery 9.19.8
Armenia 2.1.14
Armenian 2.43.10
armful 21.7.1
armhole 19.34.3
arm-in-arm 3.31
armistice 10.50.30
Armistice Day 5.3
Armitage 10.11.22
armlock 13.10.3
armour 2.14.5
armoured 2.33.11
armourer 2.19.3
armoury 9.19.20

armpit 10.56.28
armrest 6.49.5
arms 3.33
Armstrong 13.27.3
arm-twisting
  10.42.170
army 9.15.9
army corps 14.7
Arne 3.34
arnica 2.12.13
Arno 19.13.1
Arnold 2.38.6
A-road 19.23.5
aroma 2.14.16
aromatherapy 9.18.5
aromatic 10.12.58
arondissement 13.28
arose 19.52.7
around 16.11.6
arousal 2.37.304
arouse 16.21.1
Arp 3.42
arpeggio 19.2
arquebus 2.54.22
arrack 1.10.15
arraign 5.35.9
arraignment 2.47.50
Arran 2.43.111
arrange 5.37.1
arranged 5.39
arranged marriage
  10.11.13
arrangement 2.47.44
arrant 2.47.75
array 5.12
arrayed 5.21.8
arrears 8.14
arrest 6.49.6
Arrhenius 2.54.5
arrhythmia 2.1.9
arrival 2.37.295
arrivals 2.39
arrive 11.38.3
arrived 11.39
arrivederci 9.24
arriviste 9.50
arrogance 2.45
arrogant 2.47.18
arrogate 5.47.15
arrow 19.15.1
arrowhead 6.1.4
arrowroot 22.34.9
arroyo 19.0
arse 3.43
arsehole 19.34.3
arsenal 2.37.197
arsenic 10.12.30
arsewipe 11.31
arson 2.43.115
arsonist 10.53.13
arsy-versy 9.20.16
art 3.49
art deco 19.10.2

autocross 13.34.7
Autocue 22.4.4
auto-da-fé 5.4
autodidactic 10.12.73
autodidactism 2.40.85
autoflow 19.11.9
autograph 3.23.3
autoimmune 22.27.2
autolysis 10.50.13
automaker 2.12.6
automate 5.47.40
automated 10.2.47
automated teller
    machine 9.43.17
automatic 10.12.59
automation 2.43.174
automaton 2.43.290
automobile 9.38.1
automotive 10.61.37
autonomic 10.12.28
autonomous 2.54.58
autonomy 9.15.4
autopilot 2.56.17
autopista 2.22.95
autopsy 9.20.38
autoresponder 2.6.25
autoroute 22.34.9
autosave 5.51
autostrada 2.6.1
autosuggestion
    2.43.318
autotheft 6.5
autumn 2.40.38
autumnal 2.37.195
auvergne 4.17
auxiliary 9.19.3
Ava 2.25.4
avail 5.30.10
available 2.37.41
avalanche 3.39
Avalon 13.22.7
avant-garde 3.21.2
avarice 10.50.12
avaricious 2.54.124
avatar 3.15
Ave 5.16
Avebury 9.19.7
Avedon 13.22.2
Ave Maria 2.1.21
avenge 6.31
avenger 2.10.7
avenue 22.4.10
aver 7.0
average 10.11.17
Avernal 2.37.212
Averno 19.13.2
Avernus 2.54.62
averse 7.26.2
aversely 9.14.80
aversion 2.43.232
avert 7.28.6
Avery 9.19.55
Avesta 2.22.94

aviary 9.19.3
aviation 2.43.139
aviator 2.22.10
avicultural 2.37.240
aviculture 2.24.7
avid 10.2.94
avidity 9.22.7
Avignon 13.28
avionic 10.12.34
avionics 10.13.7
Avis 10.50.31
avocado 19.4.2
avocado pear 4.10
avocation 2.43.155
Avogadro 19.15
avoid 18.5.4
avoidable 2.37.31
avoidance 2.45.5
avoirdupois 18.17
Avon 2.43.320, 13.22
avow 16.0
avowal 17.4
avowed 16.6
avowedly 9.14.57
avuncular 2.13.24
aw 14.0
AWACS 1.11.5
await 5.47.70
awake 5.27.11
awaken 2.43.65
awakening 10.42.95
award 14.19.9
aware 4.15.1
awareness 2.54.64
awash 13.37.1
away 5.17.1
awe 14.0
awe-inspiring
    10.42.112
awesome 2.40.33
awestruck 20.10.4
awful 2.37.121
awfully 9.14.9
awhile 11.22.9
awkward 2.33.25
awkwardly 9.14.57
awl 14.27
awning 10.42.102
awoke 19.31
awoken 2.43.72
AWOL 13.13
awry 11.8
axe 1.11
Axel 2.37.247
axial 2.37.1
axiom 2.40.17
axiomatic 10.12.56
axis 10.50.22
axle 2.37.254
Axminster 2.22.107
ayah 2.11
ayatollah 2.13.14
Ayckbourn 14.35.1

aye 11.0
Ayer 4.0
Ayers 4.18
Ayers Rock 13.10.7
Ayr 4.0
Ayrshire 2.21
ayurveda 2.6.2
Ayurvedic medicine
    2.43.114
azalea 2.1.7
azan 3.34
Azania 2.1.12
Azerbaijan 3.34
Azerbaijani 9.16.12
Azeri 9.19.59
azimuth 2.58.2
Azores 14.48
AZT 9.22
Aztec 6.10.6
azuki bean 9.43.1
azure 2.28
B & B 9.6.10
B2B 9.6
B2C 9.20.12
BA 5.1
baa 3.2
baas 3.43
baba 3.2
Baba Yaga 2.9.2
Babbage 10.11.1
Babbitt 10.56.2
Babbittry 9.19.80
babble 2.37.24
babbling 10.42.60
babe 5.20
babe in arms 3.33
babe in the woods 21.2
babel 2.37.87
Babism 2.40.45
baboon 22.27
Babs 1.2
babu 22.1
babushka 2.12
baby 9.6.3
baby bond 13.23.1
baby boom 22.25
baby boomer 2.14.19
baby buggy 9.10.6
baby doll 13.13
Babygro 19.15.6
babyhood 21.0.2
babyish 10.54
Babylon 2.43.77,
    13.22.8
Babylonia 2.1.16
Babylonian 2.43.13
babysat 1.41
babysit 10.56.32
babysitter 2.22.43
baby talk 14.24.3
bacardi 9.7.4
baccalaureate 2.56.2
baccarat 3.13

bacchanal 2.37.197,
    3.30
bacchanalia 2.1.7
bacchanalian 2.43.7
bacchant 2.47.25
Bacchus 2.54.31
baccy 9.13.1
Bach 3.27.1, 3.57
bach 1.44
Bacharach 1.10.15
bachelor 2.13.2
bachelorhood 21.0.3
Bachelor of Arts 3.50
Bachelor of Science
    12.10.1
bacilliform 14.33.2
bacillus 2.54.39
back 1.10.3
backache 5.27.1
back-and-forth 14.46
back beat 9.52.1
backbench 6.35
backbencher 2.24.8
backbiting 10.42.158
backbone 19.40.1
backbreaking 10.42.45
backchat 1.41
backcheck 6.10.7
backcloth 13.41.1
backcomb 19.38.2
back country 9.19.87
backdate 5.47.11
backdated 10.2.40
backdoor 14.2
backdrop 13.31.6
backed 1.12
back end 6.30
backer 2.12.1
backfield 9.39.1
backfill 10.17.2
backfire 12.1
backflow 19.11.9
back-formation
    2.43.178
back-formed 14.34
backgammon 2.43.80
background 16.11.7
backhand 1.22.2
backhanded 10.2.18
backhander 2.6.18
backhoe 19.7
backing 10.42.41
backlash 1.39.2
backless 2.54.45
backlist 10.53.6
backlit 10.56.19
backlog 13.7.4
back o'Bourke 7.14.1
backpack 1.10.14
backpacker 2.12.1
backpacking 10.42.41
back passage 10.11.20
back pay 5.11

backpedal 2.37.108
backpedalled 2.38.2
backpedalling 10.42.79
backrest 6.49.5
back rib 10.0.1
backroom 22.25.5
back seat 9.52.11
back-seat driver 2.25.15
backside 11.14.17
backslapping 10.42.105
backslash 1.39.2
backspace 5.45.6
backspin 10.31.19
backstabbing 10.42.13
backstage 5.26.4
backstairs 4.18
backstop 13.31.9
backstory 9.19.67
backstreet 9.52.10
backstroke 19.31.2
backswing 10.42.185
back talk 14.24.3
back-to-back 1.10.4
back to front 20.33.2
back-to-front 20.33.2
backtrack 1.10.16
backup 20.40.2
backward 2.33.25
backwards 2.34.1
backwash 13.37.1
backwater 2.22.54
backwoods 21.2
backwoodsman 2.43.104
backyard 3.21.3
Bacon 2.43.68
bacon 2.43.65
bacteria 2.1.24
bacterial 2.37.9
bactericide 11.14.21
bacteriological 2.37.160
bacteriology 9.12.5
bacteriophage 5.26
bacterium 2.40.15
bad 1.3.1
badass 1.36
bad cheque 6.10.7
baddie 9.7.1
baddy 9.7.1
bade 1.3.1
bad egg 6.6
Baden 2.43.33
Bader 2.6.1
badge 1.9
badger 2.10
badinage 3.59
badlands 2.50
bad language 10.11.27
badly 9.14.56

bad-mannered 2.33.13
bad manners 2.60.5
badmash 1.39.3
badminton 2.43.306
badmouth 16.18
bad-mouth 16.7
badness 2.54.75
bad-tempered 2.33.16
Baez 6.57
baffle 2.37.121
baffling 10.42.59
BAFTA 2.22.62
bag 1.6.1
bagatelle 6.14.10
Bagehot 2.56
bagel 2.37.135
bagful 21.7.1
baggage 10.11.3
bagged 1.7
baggy 9.10.1
bagh 3.25
Baghdad 1.3.2
Bagheera 2.19.10
bag lady 9.7.6
bagman 1.21.4
bagnio 19.2
bag of bones 19.43.1
bag of tricks 10.13.10
bagpipes 11.32
bags 1.8
baguette 6.51
bah 3.2
Baha'i 11.4
Bahamas 2.60.4
baht 3.49.1
bai 11.2
bail 5.30
bailey 9.14.32
bailiff 10.6.1
bailiwick 10.12.90
bailout 16.16.5
Bainbridge 10.11.19
bain-marie 9.19.20
Bairam 1.18.5, 3.31.2
Baird 4.16
bairn 4.17
Bairstow 19.18.11
bait 5.47.10
baize 5.54
bake 5.27
baked 5.29
baked beans 9.46
bakehouse 16.14.4
Bakelite 11.36.7
baker 2.12.5
bakery 9.19.16
Bakewell 6.14.11
Bakewell tart 3.49
baking 10.42.43
baking powder 2.6.10
baking soda 2.6.11
bakkie 9.13.13
baklava 2.25.3

baksheesh 9.51
Baku 22.5
Bakunin 10.31.17
balaclava 2.25.3
Balak 1.10.10
balalaika 2.12.16
balance 2.45.14
balanced 2.49
Balanchine 9.43
Balboa 2.3.1
balcony 9.16.2
bald 14.28
balderdash 1.39.1
baldheaded 10.2.7
balding 10.42.14
baldly 9.14.56
Baldric 10.12.42
baldy 9.7.18
bale 5.30
Balearic Islands 2.50.2
baleful 2.37.127
baler 2.13.4
Balfour 2.8.6, 14.3
Balham 2.40.25
Bali 9.14.29
Balkanisation 2.43.226
Balkan Mountains 10.41.2
ball 14.27.1
ballad 2.33.9
ballade 3.21.5
balladry 9.19.72
Ballard 3.21.5
ballast 2.55
ball-carrier 2.1.20
ballcock 13.10.2
ballerina 2.15.14
ballet 5.8
balletgoer 2.3.2
balletic 10.12.64
ballet school 22.22.4
ball game 5.33.1
ballgown 16.10.6
Balliol 13.13
ballista 2.22.96
ballistics 10.13.19
balloon 22.27.5
ballooning 10.42.92
ballot 2.56.13
ballot paper 2.18.3
ballpark 3.27.5
ballplayer 2.0.1
ballpoint 18.12
ballroom 22.25.6
balls 14.32
balls-up 20.40.12
ballsy 9.27
ballyhoo 22.3
balm 3.31
Balmoral 2.37.243
balmy 9.15.9
baloney 9.16.24
balsa 2.20.14

balsam 2.40.35
balsamic 10.12.23
balsamic vinegar 2.9.5
balthazar 3.19
balti 9.22.78
Baltic 10.12.54
Baltic Sea 9.20.24
Baltimore 14.9.1
Baluchistan 3.34.3
baluster 2.22.89
balustrade 5.21.10
Balzac 1.10.20
Bamako 19.10
Bambi 9.6.9
bambino 19.13.3
bamboo 22.1
bamboozle 2.37.299
ban 1.21
banal 3.30
banality 9.22.17
banana 2.15.7
banana-boat 19.47.1
bananas 2.60.5
banana skin 10.31.10
Banbury 9.19.7
Bancroft 13.6
band 1.22.1
Banda 2.6.18
bandage 10.11.2
bandaged 10.34
Band-Aid 5.21
bandanna 2.15.1
Bandaranaike 2.12.3
bandeau 19.4.6
banded 10.2.17
banderole 19.34.6
bandicoot 22.34
banding 10.42.26
bandit 10.56.4
bandmaster 2.22.93
bandolier 8.4
bandsman 2.43.104
bandstand 1.22.7
Bandung 21.10
bandwagon 2.43.47
bandwidth 10.3
bandy 9.7.20
bane 5.35.1
baneful 2.37.128
bang 1.28.1
Bangalore 14.8
banger 2.16
banging 10.42.33
Bangkok 13.10.2
Bangla 2.13.29
Bangladesh 6.50
Bangladeshi 9.21
bangle 2.37.142
bang-on 13.22
Bangor 2.9.11
Bangui 9.10.7
bania 2.11.1
banish 10.54.15

banished 10.55.2
banishment 2.47.57
banister 2.22.97
banisters 2.60.7
banjo 19.8
Banjul 22.22
bank 1.30.1
bankable 2.37.37
bank clerk 3.27.3
banker 2.12.24
Bankhead 6.1.4
bank holiday 5.3
banking 10.42.55
banknote 19.47.7
Bank of England
2.44.4
bank robbery 9.19.8
bankroll 19.34.5
bankrupt 20.41
bankruptcy 9.20.39
Banks 1.31
banned 1.22.1
banner 2.15.1
bannerol 13.13
bannister 2.22.97
bannock 2.35.2
banns 1.27
banoffee 9.9.13
banquet 10.56.37
banshee 9.21
bantam 2.40.38
bantamweight 5.47.69
banter 2.22.79
Banting 10.42.168
Bantu 22.13.1
banyan 2.43.60
baobab 1.1
Baotou 19.18
bap 1.33
baptise 11.42.32
baptism 2.40.85
baptismal 2.37.194
baptism of fire 12.1
Baptist 10.53.22
Baptiste 9.50
bar 3.2
Barabbas 2.54.22
Barak 1.10.15
barb 3.20
Barbadian 2.43.4
Barbados 13.34.2
Barbara 2.19.15
barbarian 2.43.16
barbaric 10.12.43
barbarism 2.40.78
barbarity 9.22.33
Barbarossa 2.20.9
barbarous 2.54.97
Barbary ape 5.42
barbecue 22.4.4
barbecued 22.17.2
barbed wire 12.6
barbel 2.37.23

barbell 6.14.1
barber 2.5.1
barbershop 13.31.7
Barbican 2.43.68
barbie 9.6.2
Barbirolli 9.14.44
barbiturate 2.56.40
Barbour 2.5.1
Barbuda 2.6.13
barbule 22.22.1
Barcelona 2.15.23
bar chart 3.49.7
Barclay 5.8.2
bard 3.21.1
Bardot 19.4.2
bare 4.2
bareback 1.10.3
bare bones 19.43.1
barebones 19.43.1
barefaced 5.46
barefaced lie 11.5
barefoot 21.14
barehanded 10.2.18
bareheaded 10.2.7
barelegged 6.7
barely 9.14.31
bareness 2.54.64
barf 3.23
barfly 11.5.2
bargain 10.31.5
bargain-basement
2.47.54
bargain hunter 2.22.85
barge 3.26
bargepole 19.34.4
bar graph 3.23.3
Bari 9.19.58
barista 2.22.96
baritone 19.40.14
barium 2.40.14
bark 3.27.1
barkeep 9.47
Barker 2.12.4
Barking 10.42.40
barking mad 1.3.4
barley 9.14.29
barleycorn 14.35.3
barley water 2.22.53
Barlow 19.11.3
barmaid 5.21.5
barman 2.43.82
barmbrack 1.10.15
bar mitzvah 2.25
barmy 9.15.9
barn 3.34
Barnabas 2.54.22
barnacle 2.37.149
barnacle goose 22.31
Barnard 3.21.6
Barnardo 19.4.2
Barnardo's 19.52
barn dance 3.37.1
barnet 2.56.26

Barnett 2.56.26
barney 9.16.12
barnstorm 14.33.4
barnstorming 10.42.88
Barnum 2.40.27
barnyard 3.21.3
barograph 3.23.3
barographic 10.12.9
Barolo 19.11.7
barometer 2.22.39
baron 2.43.111
baroness 2.54.63
baronet 2.56.27
baronetcy 9.20.39
baronial 2.37.4
Baron Münchhausen
2.43.327
barony 9.16.2
baroque 13.10.7
barperson 2.43.118
barque 3.27.1
barrack 2.35
barracks 2.36
barracuda 2.6.13
barrage 3.59
barre 3.2
barred 3.21.1
barrel 2.37.231
barren 2.43.111
barrenness 2.54.82
Barrett 2.56.33
barrette 6.51.9
barricade 5.21.1
Barrie 9.19.1
barrier 2.1.20
barrier reef 9.32.2
barring 10.42.112
Barrington 2.43.308
barrio 19.2.3
barrister 2.22.96
barrow 19.15.1
barrow boy 18.1
barry 9.19.1
Barrymore 14.9
Barsac 1.10.20
bar sinister 2.22.98
Bart 3.49.1
bartender 2.6.22
barter 2.22.4
bartered 2.33.20
bartering 10.42.118
Barthes 3.49.1
Bartholomew 22.4.8
Bartók 13.10
Barton 2.43.291
baryon 13.22.1
Baryshnikov 13.5.2
basal 2.37.247
basalt 14.31.2
bascule 22.22.3
base 5.45.1
baseball 14.27.1
baseball bat 1.41.1

baseball cap 1.33.1
base camp 1.20.1
base hit 10.56
basejumping
10.42.111
Basel 2.37.299
baseless 2.54.51
baseline 11.27.3
basement 2.47.54
bash 1.39
bashful 2.37.121
bashing 10.42.141
Bashir 4.12
basic 10.12.53
basically 9.14.68
basics 10.13.11
Basie 9.27.2
basil 2.37.300
basilect 6.12.4
basilica 2.12.12
basilisk 10.51
basin 2.43.116
Basinger 2.9.12
basis 10.50.17
bask 3.44
basket 10.56.18
basketball 14.27.2
basketcase 5.45.3
basketry 9.19.83
basketwork 7.14.8
basking shark 3.27.6
bas mitzvah 2.25
basque 3.44
Basra 2.19
bass (noun) 1.36
bass (noun, adj) 5.45.1
bass clef 6.4
basset 10.56.32
Basseterre 4.13.1
basset hound 16.11.3
bassinet 6.51.7
bassist 10.53.20
bassoon 22.27.8
bassoonist 10.53.12
basso relievo 19.20
bastard 2.33.22
bastardised 11.43
baste 5.46
basti 9.22.89
Bastille Day 5.3
bastinado 19.4.2
bastion 2.43.24
Basutoland 1.22.3
bat 1.41.1
Batavia 2.1.30
batch 1.44
bated 10.2.37
Bateson 2.43.135
bath 3.51.1
bathe 5.23
bather 2.7
bathers 2.60
bathetic 10.12.67

bathhouse 16.14.1
bathing 10.42.31
bathmat 1.41.6
bath mitzvah 2.25
bathometric 10.12.51
bathos 13.34.8
bathrobe 19.22.2
bathroom 22.25.3
Bathsheba 2.5.3
bathtub 20.0.3
bath water 2.22.53
bathypelagic 10.12.14
batik 9.36.6
Batman 1.21.9
batman 2.43.101
Batman and Robin 10.31.2
bat mitzvah 2.25
baton 2.43.289, 13.22.16
Baton Rouge 22.42
baton round 16.11.5
batsman 2.43.99
batswoman 2.43.92
battalion 2.43.58
batten 2.43.289
batter 2.22.1
battercake 5.27.1
battered 2.33.19
battering 10.42.119
battering ram 1.18.5
Battersea 9.20.12
battery 9.19.34
batting average 10.11.17
battle 2.37.271
battleaxe 1.11.2
battle cruiser 2.27.10
battledress 6.47.5
battlefield 9.39.1
battleground 16.11.7
battlements 2.46
battle royal 2.37.15
battleship 10.47.6
batty 9.22.1
bauble 2.37.23
baud 14.19.1
Baudelaire 4.7
Baudouin 1.29
Bauer 17.0
Bauhaus 16.14.1
bauxite 11.36.19
Bavaria 2.1.22
bawdry 9.19.72
bawdy 9.7
bawdyhouse 16.14.1
bawl 14.27.1
Bax 1.11
Baxter 2.22.89
bay 5.2
bay leaf 9.32.1
bayonet 10.56.23
bayou 22.0

Bayswater 2.22.53
bazaar 3.19
bazooka 2.12.23
BBC 9.20
be 9.6
beach 9.55
beachcomber 2.14.17
beachfront 20.33.2
beachhead 6.1.4
beachwear 4.15
Beachy Head 6.1.4
beacon 2.43.67
bead 9.29
beaded 10.2.8
beading 10.42.17
beadle 2.37.109
beady 9.7.9
beagle 2.37.137
beak 9.36
beaker 2.12.10
beaky 9.13.7
Beale 9.38.1
beam 9.41.1
beaming 10.42.87
Beamish 10.54.13
bean 9.43.1
beanbag 1.6.1
bean counter 2.22.84
bean curd 7.10
beanfeast 9.50
beanie 9.16.16
beano 19.13.3
beanpole 19.34.4
bean sprout 16.16.8
bear 4.2
bearable 2.37.55
beard 8.11
bearded 10.2.3
Beardsley 9.14.101
bearer 2.19.8
bearer bond 13.23.1
bear hug 20.7
bearing 10.42.121
bearings 10.46.5
béarnaise sauce 14.42.4
bearskin 10.31.10
beast 9.50
beastie 9.22.85
beastly 9.14.95
beat 9.52.1
beaten 2.43.295
beater 2.22.27
beatific 10.12.8
beatification 2.43.162
beatify 11.3.8
beating 10.42.155
beatitude 22.17.6
Beatles 2.39.7
beatnik 10.12.30
Beaton 2.43.295
Beatrix 10.13.10
Beattie 9.22.62

beau 19.3
Beauchamp 2.40
Beaufort scale 5.30.3
beau geste 6.49
Beauharnais 5.10
Beaujolais 5.8.1
Beaumarchais 5.14
beau monde 13.23
Beaumont 13.25
Beaune 19.40.1
beaut 22.34.2
beauteous 2.54.15
beautician 2.43.246
beautification 2.43.162
beautified 11.14.7
beautiful 2.37.124
beautify 11.3.8
beauty 9.22.75
beauty queen 9.43.24
beauty salon 13.22.7
Beauvoir 3.18
beaux 19.3, 19.52
beaux arts 3.19
beaver 2.25.9
Beaverbrook 21.4.6
bebop 13.31
becalm 3.31
becalmed 3.32
because 13.45
Becca 2.12.8
béchamel 6.14.3
béchamel sauce 14.42.4
Bechuanaland 1.22.3
beck 6.10.1
Becker 2.12.8
Becket 10.56.10
Beckett 10.56.10
Beckham 2.40.24
beckon 2.43.63
Becky 9.13.5
become 20.24.1
becoming 10.42.90
becquerel 2.37.232
bed 6.1.1
bed and board 14.19.1
bedaub 14.18
bedazzle 2.37.300
bedazzled 2.38.12
bedbug 20.7.1
bedchamber 2.5.10
bedclothes 19.27
bedding 10.42.16
Bede 9.29
bedeck 6.10.2
bedecked 6.12
bedevil 2.37.291
bedevilled 2.38.11
bedevilling 10.42.67
bedfellow 19.11.5
Bedford 2.33.5
Bedfordshire 2.21
bedgown 16.10.6

bedhead 6.1.6
bedlam 2.40.25
bedlinen 10.31.17
bed of roses 10.62.7
Bedouin 10.31.1
bedpan 1.21.11
bedpost 19.46.3
bedraggle 2.37.136
bedraggled 2.38.3
bedridden 2.43.38
bedrock 13.10.7
bedroll 19.34.5
bedroom 22.25.4
bedsheet 9.52.12
bedside 11.14.23
bedsit 10.56.32
bedsitter 2.22.43
bedsore 14.13
bedspread 6.1.14
bedstead 6.1.16
bedwetting 10.42.153
bee 9.6
beech 9.55
Beecham 2.40
beef 9.32
beefalo 19.11.2
beefburger 2.9.3
beefcake 5.27.1
beefeater 2.22.26
beefsteak 5.27.10
beefsteak fungus 2.54.28
beefy 9.9
beehive 11.38
beekeeper 2.18.6
beekeeping 10.42.107
beeline 11.27.5
Beelzebub 20.0
Beemer 2.14.11
been 9.43.1
beep 9.47
beeper 2.18.5
beer 8.0
beer belly 9.14.34
beery 9.19.62
bee's knees 9.59.7
beestings 10.46.6
beeswax 1.11.5
beet 9.52.1
Beethoven 2.43.325
beetle 2.37.270
Beeton 2.43.295
beetroot 22.34.9
befall 14.27.3
befallen 2.43.75
befell 6.14
befit 10.56.6
befog 13.7
before 14.3
beforehand 1.22.2
befoul 16.9.1
befriend 6.30.7
befuddle 2.37.115

bionomic 10.12.28
biophysics 10.13.20
biopic 10.12.39
biopiracy 9.20.8
bioplasm 2.40.44
bioplastic 10.12.79
biopsy 9.20.38
bioremediation 2.43.140
biorhythm 2.40.23
bioscience 12.10.1
biosecurity 9.22.38
biosphere 8.2
biosynthesis 10.50.16
biosynthetic 10.12.67
biota 2.22.55
biotech 6.10.6
biotechnology 9.12.13
bioterrorism 2.40.79
bioterrorist 10.53.17
biothreat 6.51.8
biotin 10.31.24
biowarfare 4.3
bioweapon 2.43.108
bipartisan 1.21.17
bipartite 11.36.21
biped 6.1.11
bipedal 2.37.109
biplane 5.35.5
bipod 13.2.2
bipolar 2.13.18
bipolar disorder 2.6.8
birch 7.31
bird 7.10.1
birdbath 3.51.1
birdbrain 5.35.10
bird-brained 5.36.2
birdcage 5.26
birdhouse 16.14.3
birdie 9.7.8
birdlife 11.17.1
birdlike 11.19.1
birdlime 11.25.1
bird of paradise 11.34
bird of passage 10.11.20
birdseed 9.29.7
Birdseye 11.0
bird's-eye view 22.4.13
birdsong 13.27.4
bird table 2.37.88
birdwatcher 2.24
bird-watching 10.42.175
birdy 9.7.8
bireme 9.41.3
biretta 2.22.22
Birkbeck 6.10.1
Birkenhead 6.1.8
Birkenstock 13.10.8
Birmingham 2.40.28
Biro 19.15

birr 7.1
birth 7.30.1
birth canal 1.13
birthday 5.3
birthday cake 5.27.1
birthday party 9.22.57
birthday suit 22.34.11
birthing 10.42.154
birthmark 3.27.4
birthplace 5.45.4
birth rate 5.47.51
birthright 11.36.16
birthstone 19.40.16
biryani 9.16.12
bis 10.50.1
biscuit 10.56.17
bise 9.59.1
bisect 6.12.9
bisected 10.2.71
bisector 2.22.68
bisexual 15.7
Bishkek 6.10
bishop 2.52
bishopdom 2.40.20
bishopric 10.12.48
Bismarck 3.27.4
bismuth 2.58.2
bison 2.43.123
bisque 10.51
bistro 19.15.8
bit 10.56.2
bitch 10.59
bitchy 9.24.3
bite 11.36.1
biting 10.42.158
bitmap 1.33
bits 10.57
bits and bobs 13.1
bitstream 9.41.5
bitsy 9.20.40
bitter 2.22.34
bitter end 6.30.6
bitterly 9.14.26
bittern 2.43.296
bitterness 2.54.63
bitters 2.60.7
bittersweet 9.52.15
bitty 9.22.63
bitumen 10.31.16
bivalve 1.17
bivouac 1.10
biz 10.62
bizarre 3.19
bizarrely 9.14.29
Bizet 5.18
blab 1.1.2
blabber 2.5
blabbermouth 16.18
black 1.10.11
Blackadder 2.6
black-and-blue 22.6.2
black-and-white 11.36.22

blackball 14.27.1
blackballed 14.28
blackballing 10.42.75
black bean 9.43.1
black bear 4.2
Blackbeard 8.11
Black Beauty 9.22.75
black belt 6.19.1
blackberry 9.19.7
Black Bess 6.47
blackbird 7.10.1
black bread 6.1.13
Blackburn 7.20.1
blackcap 1.33.1
black comedy 9.7.2
blackcurrant 2.47.80
Black Death 6.53
blacken 2.43.64
black-eyed bean 9.43.1
black-eyed pea 9.18
blackfly 11.5.2
blackguard 2.33.6, 3.21.2
blackhead 6.1.7
Blackheath 9.54
black ice 11.34
blackjack 1.10.8
black knight 11.36.14
blackleg 6.6.1
blacklist 10.53.6
blacklisted 10.2.92
black magic 10.12.14
blackmail 5.30.4
blackmailed 5.31
blackmailer 2.13.4
black maria 2.1.21
black mark 3.27.4
black market 10.56.13
Blackmore 14.9
blackness 2.54.78
blackout 16.16.3
Blackpool 22.22.5
Black power 17.2
black pudding 10.42.22
Black Rod 13.2.3
black sheep 9.47
Blackshirt 7.28.4
blacksmith 10.58.1
Blackstone 19.40.16
blackthorn 14.35.6
black tie 11.11
Blackwell 6.14.11
Blackwood 21.0.6
blad 1.3.3
bladder 2.6
bladdered 2.33.2
bladder wrack 1.10.15
blade 5.21.4
blading 10.42.15
blaeberry 9.19.7
blag 1.6.2
blagger 2.9.1

blah 3.9
blah-blah 3.9
Blain 5.35.4
Blair 4.7
Blairism 2.40.77
Blaise 5.54.1
blame 5.33
blamed 5.34
blameless 2.54.47
blameworthy 9.8.1
Blanc 3.41
blanch 3.39
Blanche 3.39
blanco 19.10.5
bland 1.22.3
blandish 10.54.4
blandishment 2.47.57
blandishments 2.46
blandness 2.54.77
blank 1.30.2
blanked 1.32
blanket 10.56.10
blanket coverage 10.11.17
blankety-blank 1.30.2
blankly 9.14.65
blank verse 7.26.2
blare 4.7
blaring 10.42.121
blarney 9.16.12
Blarney stone 19.40.16
blasé 5.18
blaspheme 9.41
blasphemer 2.14.11
blasphemous 2.54.58
blasphemy 9.15.2
blast 3.47.3
blasted 10.2.90
blastoff 13.5.5
blatancy 9.20.35
blatant 2.47.88
blather 2.7
blaze 5.54.1
blazer 2.27.2
blazon 2.43.328
blazonry 9.19.78
bleach 9.55
bleachers 2.60
bleak 9.36.1
bleary 9.19.62
Bleasdale 5.30.1
bleat 9.52.4
bled 6.1.10
bleed 9.29.3
bleeding 10.42.18
bleep 9.47
bleeper 2.18.5
blemish 10.54.13
blench 6.35
blend 6.30
blended 10.2.19
blender 2.6.21
Blériot 19.2.3

bless 6.47.1
blessed 10.2.31
blessing 10.42.136
blest 6.49.3
blether 2.7.2
Bleu 7.4
blew 22.6.2
Bligh 11.5
blight 11.36.6
blighted 10.2.61
blighter 2.22.47
Blighty 9.22.65
blimey 9.15.14
blimp 10.29
blind 11.28.4
blind alley 9.14.1
blind chance 3.37.4
blind date 5.47.11
blinder 2.6.24
blindfold 19.35.1
blinding 10.42.29
blindingly 9.14.76
blind luck 20.10.2
blindly 9.14.60
blindness 2.54.77
blind rage 5.26.3
blindside 11.14.23
blind spot 13.39.6
bling 10.42.77
blini 9.16.17
blink 10.43.1
blinker 2.12.25
blinkered 2.33.8
blinkers 2.60.3
blinking 10.42.56
blip 10.47.1
bliss 10.50.5
blissful 2.37.129
B-list 10.53.6
blister 2.22.96
blistered 2.33.22
blistering 10.42.118
blister pack 1.10.14
blithe 11.16
blithely 9.14
blithering 10.42.116
blitz 10.57
blitzkrieg 9.34
Blixen 2.43.128
blizzard 2.33.26
bloat 19.47.5
bloated 10.2.65
bloater 2.22.55
blob 13.0
blobby 9.6.5
bloc 13.10.4
Bloch 13.10.4
block 13.10.4
blockade 5.21.1
blockage 10.11.4
block and tackle
    2.37.148
blockbuster 2.22.104

blockbusting
    10.42.173
block diagram 1.18.6
blockhead 6.1.7
blockheaded 10.2.7
blockhouse 16.14.4
Bloemfontein 5.35.13
Blofeld 6.19
blog 13.7.4
blogger 2.9.8
blogosphere 8.2
bloke 19.31
blokeish 10.54.8
Blondin 1.29
blondness 2.54.77
blood 20.2
blood bank 1.30.1
bloodbath 3.51.1
blood clot 13.39.2
bloodcurdling
    10.42.61
bloodhound 16.11.3
bloodless 2.54.43
bloodletting 10.42.153
bloodline 11.27.7
blood loss 13.34.3
bloodlust 20.44.4
bloodmobile 9.38.1
blood pudding
    10.42.22
bloodshed 6.1.15
bloodshot 13.39.8
blood sports 14.45
bloodstain 5.35.13
bloodstained 5.36.4
bloodstock 13.10.8
bloodstone 19.40.17
bloodstream 9.41.5
bloodsucker 2.12.21
bloodsucking 10.42.40
bloodthirsty 9.22.85
bloodworm 7.18.4
bloody 9.7.16
bloody-minded
    10.2.21
bloom 22.25.2
bloomer 2.14.19
bloomers 2.60.4
blooming 10.42.91
blooper 2.18.15
blossom 2.40.33
blossoming 10.42.84
blot 13.39.2
blotch 13.42
blotchy 9.24
blotter 2.22.49
blotting paper 2.18.3
blotto 19.18.6
blouse 16.21
blouson 13.22.17
blow 19.11.8
blowback 1.10.3
blower 2.3.3

blowfish 10.54.5
blowfly 11.5.2
blowhard 3.21
blowhole 19.34.3
blowlamp 1.20.2
blown 19.40.7
blowout 16.16
blowpipe 11.31.1
blowtorch 14.47
blowup 20.40
blowy 9.4
blowzy 9.27.5
BLT 9.22
blub 20.0.1
blubber 2.5.7
blubbery 9.19.7
bludge 20.9
bludgeon 2.43.52
blue 22.6.2
blue badge 1.9
bluebell 6.14.1
blueberry 9.19.7
bluebird 7.10.1
blue-blooded 10.2.14
bluebottle 2.37.278
blue-chip 10.47.14
blue-collar 2.13.14
Blue Cross 13.34.7
blue funk 20.38
bluegrass 3.43.5
bluejay 5.6
bluejeans 9.46
Blue Mountains
    10.41.2
blue-pencil 2.37.256
blueprint 10.38.3
blues 22.40
bluescreen 9.43.13
blue shark 3.27.6
bluestocking 10.42.51
blue streak 9.36.5
bluesy 9.27.8
bluetit 10.56
Bluetooth 22.36.2
blue whale 5.30.11
bluff 20.4.2
bluffer 2.8.5
bluish 10.54
Blumenthal 3.30.3
blunder 2.6.27
blunderbuss 20.42.1
blundering 10.42.115
Blunkett 10.56.10
blunt 20.33
bluntly 9.14.92
bluntness 2.54.88
blur 7.4
blurb 7.7
blurred 7.10
blurry 9.19
blurt 7.28
blush 20.45.1
blusher 2.21.5

blushing 10.42.140
bluster 2.22.105
blustery 9.19.52
Bly 11.5
Blyton 2.43.299
B movie 9.25.8
BO 19.2
boa 2.3.1
boa constrictor 2.22.72
Boadicea 2.1.27
boar 14.1
board 14.19.1
boarder 2.6.8
board game 5.33.1
boarding 10.42.21
boarding school
    22.22.4
Boardman 2.43.79
boardroom 22.25.4
boardsurf 7.11
boardwalk 14.24.4
boast 19.46
boaster 2.22.102
boastful 2.37.133
boasting 10.42.172
boat 19.47.1
Boateng 6.41
boater 2.22.55
boathook 21.4.3
boathouse 16.14.7
boating 10.42.162
boatload 19.23.2
boatman 2.43.101
boatswain 2.43.113
boatyard 3.21.3
bob 13.0
bobbin 10.31.2
bobble 2.37.97
bobble hat 1.41.3
bobby 9.6.5
bobcat 1.41.4
bobotie 9.22.73,
    9.22.74
bobsled 6.1.10
bobsleigh 5.8
Boccaccio 19.2.5
bod 13.2
bode 19.23
bodega 2.9
Bodensee 5.13
bodge 13.9
bodgie 9.12.20
Bodhisattva 2.25
bodhran 3.34.1
bodice 10.50.2
bodily 9.14.39
bodkin 10.31.7
Bodleian 2.43.6
body 9.7.14
bodyboard 14.19.3
bodycheck 6.10.7
bodyguard 3.21.2

body language 10.11.27
body politic 10.12.63
bodypop 13.31.4
Body Shop 13.31.7
body slam 1.18.4
body snatcher 2.24.1
bodysuit 22.34.11
bodywork 7.14.4
Boer 2.3.1, 14.1
boerewors 14.42
boeuf bourgignon 13.22.5
boffin 10.31.4
bog 13.7
bogan 2.43.51
Bogarde 3.21.2
Bogart 3.49
bogey 9.10.5
bogeyman 1.21.6
boggle 2.37.139
boggy 9.10.4
bogie 9.10.5
bogof 13.5
Bogor 14.4
Bogotá 3.15
bog-standard 2.33.3
bogus 2.54.26
Bohemia 2.1.10
bohemian 2.43.9
Bohemianism 2.40.68
Bohr 14.1
bohrium 2.40.16
boiled 18.9
boiler 2.13.17
boilerplate 5.47.39
boiler room 22.25.3
boiler suit 22.34.11
boiling 10.42.58
boink 18.13
Boise 9.20
boisterous 2.54.104
bold 19.35
boldness 2.54.75
bole 19.34.2
bolero 19.15, 19.15.2
boletus 2.54.129
Boleyn 10.31.11
Bolger 2.10.6
Bolingbroke 21.4.6
Bolívar 3.17
bolivar 3.17
Bolivia 2.1.30
Bolivian 2.43.25
boliviano 19.13.1
boll 19.34.2
bollard 3.21.5
bollock 2.35.1
bollocking 10.42.40
bollocks 2.36
Bollywood 21.0.6
bolo 19.11
bologna 2.11.1

boloney 9.16.24
Bolshevik 10.12.89
Bolshevism 2.40.88
bolshie 9.21
bolster 2.22.89
bolt 19.36
Bolton 2.43.303
boma 2.14.16
bomb 13.18.1
bombard 3.21.1
bombardier 8.1
bombardment 2.47.42
bombast 1.38
bombastic 10.12.78
bomber 2.14
bombing 10.42.84
bombproof 22.19.1
bombshell 6.14.9
bona fide 9.7.12
bona fides 9.59.2
bonanza 2.27.11
Bonaparte 3.49.5
bonbon 13.22
bonce 13.24
bond 13.23.1
bondage 10.11.2
bondholder 2.6.16
bonding 10.42.14
bone 19.40.1
boned 19.41
bonehead 6.1.8
boneheaded 10.2.7
boneless 2.54.48
bonemeal 9.38.3
boner 2.15.22
boneshaker 2.12.5
boneyard 3.21.3
bonfire 12.1
Bonfire Night 11.36.14
bong 13.27
bongos 19.52
Bonham 2.40.27
Bonhoeffer 2.8.4
bonhomie 9.15.4
Bonington 2.43.308
bonito 19.18.5
bonjour 15.0
bonk 13.29
bonkers 2.60.3
bon mot 19.12
Bonn 13.22
Bonnard 3.11
bonnet 2.56.26, 10.56.23
Bonnington 2.43.308
Bono 19.13.5
bonsai 11.9
bonus 2.54.74
bon vivant 13.28
bon viveur 7.0
bon voyage 3.59
bony 9.16.23
bonzer 2.27.11

boo 22.1
boob 22.16
boo-boo 22.1
booby 9.6
booby trap 1.33.5
boogie 9.10
boogie-woogie 9.10
boohoo 22.3
book 21.4.1
bookable 2.37.37
bookbinder 2.6.24
bookcase 5.45.3
booked 21.6
bookend 6.30
bookends 6.39
Booker 2.12.22
Booker Prize 11.42.28
bookie 9.13.15
booking 10.42.54
bookish 10.54.8
bookkeeper 2.18.6
bookkeeping 10.42.107
booklet 2.56.20
booklouse 16.14.8
bookmaker 2.12.6
bookmark 3.27.4
bookmobile 9.38.1
Book of Common Prayer 4.11
bookplate 5.47.39
bookrest 6.49.5
bookseller 2.13.6
bookshelf 6.16.1
bookshop 13.31.7
bookstall 14.27.10
bookstore 14.15.1
bookworm 7.18.4
Boole 22.22
Boolean 2.43.6
Boolean operator 2.22.18
boom 22.25
boom and bust 20.44.1
boomer 2.14.19
boomerang 1.28.3
booming 10.42.91
boon 22.27
boor 15.0
boorish 10.54.17
boost 22.32
booster 2.22.89
boot 22.34.1
bootblack 1.10.11
booted 10.2.67
bootee 9.22.74
bootees 9.59.13
booth 22.18
Boothby 9.6
Boothroyd 18.5.3
bootjack 1.10.8
bootleg 6.6.1
bootlick 10.12.16

bootlicking 10.42.49
bootstrap 1.33.6
bootstrapping 10.42.105
bootstraps 1.34
booty 9.22.74
booze 22.40
boozer 2.27.10
booze-up 20.40.12
boozy 9.27.8
bop 13.31
borage 10.11.12
borax 1.11.3
Bordeaux 19.4
bordello 19.11.4
border 2.6.8
borderland 1.22.4
borderline 11.27.4
Borders 2.60.1
bore 14.1
boreal 2.37.10
Boreas 2.54.12
bored 14.19.1
boredom 2.40.20
borehole 19.34.3
borer 2.19.11
Borg 14.22
Borgia 2.10
boring 10.42.127
Boris 10.50.12
Boris Becker 2.12.8
Boris Godunov 13.5.3
Bormann 1.21.4, 2.43.86
born 14.35.1
born-again 6.29
born-again Christian 2.43.317
borne 14.35.1
Borneo 19.2
born loser 2.27.10
Borodin 10.31.3
boron 13.22.12
borough 2.19.14
borrow 19.15.4
borrower 2.3.4
borrowing 10.42.11
borstal 2.37.287
borzoi 18.0
Bosch 13.37
Bose 19.45
bosh 13.37
Bosnia and Herzegovina 2.15.12
Bosniac 1.10.1
Bosnian 2.43.10
bosom 2.40.42
bosomy 9.15.2
boson 13.22.17
Bosporus 2.54.103
boss 13.34.1
bossa nova 2.25.20
boss-eyed 11.14.17

bossy 9.20.20
Boston 2.43.312
bosun 2.43.113
Boswell 2.37.296,
6.14.11
bot 13.39
botanical 2.37.166
botanist 10.53.13
botany 9.16.11
botch 13.42
both 19.49
Botham 2.40.41
bother 2.7
bothersome 2.40.34
bothy 9.23
Botox 13.11
Botswana 2.15.7
Botswanan 2.43.106
Botticelli 9.14.33
bottle 2.37.278
bottled 2.38.9
bottle-feed 9.29.2
bottle-green 9.43.12
bottleneck 6.10.3
bottom 2.40.38
bottomless 2.54.46
Bottomley 9.14
bottommost 19.46.1
Bottoms 2.42
botulism 2.40.54
Boucher 5.14
Boudicca 2.12.11
boudoir 3.18
bouffant 13.28
bougainvillea 2.1.8
bough 16.0
bought 14.44
bouillabaisse 6.47
bouillon 13.22
boulder 2.6.15
boules 22.22
boulevard 3.21
Boulez 6.57
bounce 16.12
bounceback 1.10.3
bouncer 2.20.15
bouncing 10.42.138
bouncy 9.20.27
bouncy castle 2.37.248
bound 16.11.1
boundary 9.19.10
bounden 2.43.43
bounder 2.6.26
boundless 2.54.44
bounteous 2.54.15
bountiful 2.37.124
bounty 9.22.84
bouquet 5.7
bouquet garni 9.16.12
Bourbon 2.43.27
bourbon 2.43.29
bourgeois 3.18
bourgeoisie 9.27.1

Bourke 7.14.1
Bournemouth 2.58.2
Bourse 14.42
bout 16.16
boutique 9.36.6
boutonniere 4.1
bouzouki 9.13.16
bovid 10.2.94
bovine 11.27.19
bovine spongiform
encephalopathy
9.23.2
bovver boy 18.1
bow (noun) 19.3
bow (verb, noun) 16.0
bowdlerise 11.42.23
bowed 16.6, 19.23
bowel 17.4
bowels 2.39
Bowen 10.31
bower 17.0
bowerbird 7.10.2
the Bowery 9.19
Bowie 9.26
bowie knife 11.17.2
bowl 19.34.2
bowlegged 6.7,
10.2.23
bowler 2.13.18
bowlful 21.7.1
bowline 11.27.6
bowling 10.42.76
bowling alley 9.14.1
bowls 19.37
bowl-shaped 5.44
Bowman 2.43.87
bowser 2.27.8
bowsprit 10.56.29
bow tie 11.11
bow-wow 16.0
box 13.11.1
box Brownie 9.16.22
boxcar 3.8
boxer 2.20.13
boxercise 11.42.30
boxers 2.60
boxful 21.7.1
boxing 10.42.137
Boxing Day 5.3
boxing glove 20.51.2
box office 10.50.3
boxroom 22.25.3
boy 18.1
Boyce 18.14
boycott 13.39.1
boycotter 2.22.49
Boyer 2.2
boyfriend 6.30.7
boyhood 21.0.2
boyish 10.54
boyo 19.0
boy scout 16.16.3
boysenberry 9.19.7

bozo 19.21
bra 3.13
braai 11.8
Brabazon 13.22.17
Brabham 2.40
brace 5.45.7
bracelet 2.56.12
brachial 2.37.1
bracing 10.42.135
bracken 2.43.64
bracket 10.56.11
bracketed 10.2.59
brackish 10.54.8
bract 1.12.3
brad 1.3.6
bradawl 14.27
Bradbury 9.19.7
Braddock 2.35
Bradford 2.33.5
Bradman 2.43.95
Bradshaw 14.14
Bradstreet 9.52.10
brae 5.12
brag 1.6.3
Bragg 1.6.3
braggadocio 19.2.5
braggart 2.56.7
bragger 2.9.1
bragging 10.42.34
Brahma 2.14.7
Brahman 2.43.82
Brahmaputra 2.19.20
Brahmin 10.31.16
Brahms 3.33
braid 5.21.8
braided 10.2.5
braille 5.30.6
brain 5.35.10
brainchild 11.23.1
brain damage 10.11.8
brain-fever 2.25.9
brainless 2.54.48
brainpower 17.2
brains 5.41
brainstem 6.25
brainstorm 14.33.4
brainstorming
10.42.88
brains trust 20.44.6
brain surgeon 2.43.54
brain surgery 9.19.15
brainteaser 2.27.4
brain-twister 2.22.96
brainwash 13.37.1
brainwashed 13.38
brainwave 5.51.3
brainwork 7.14.2
brainy 9.16.13
braise 5.54.2
braised 5.55
Braithwaite 5.47.69
brake 5.27.7
brake light 11.36.6

bramble 2.37.101
brambling 10.42.78
bran 1.21.13
Branagh 2.15.1
branch 3.39
Brancusi 9.27.8
brand 1.22.6
branded 10.2.17
Brandenburg Gate
5.47.14
branding 10.42.26
brandish 10.54.4
brand name 5.33.4
brand new 22.4.9
brand-new 22.4.9
Brando 19.4.6
Brandt 1.25
brandy 9.7.20
brandy Alexander
2.6.19
bran flakes 5.28
Branson 2.43.132
Braque 1.10.15, 3.27
brash 1.39.4
Brasília 2.1.8
brass 3.43.4
brass band 1.22.1
brasserie 9.19.32
brass hat 1.41.3
brassica 2.12.11
brassie 9.20.1
brassiere 2.1.31
brass knuckles 2.39.4
brassy 9.20.13
brat 1.41.8
Bratislava 2.25.3
Bratwurst 7.27
Braun 16.10.7
bravado 19.4.2
brave 5.51.2
bravery 9.19.55
bravo 19.20
bravura 2.19.13
braw 14.12
brawl 14.27.9
brawn 14.35.5
brawny 9.16.21
bray 5.12
brazen 2.43.328
brazier 2.1.32
Brazil 10.17
Brazilian 2.43.8
breach 9.55.1
bread 6.1.13
bread-and-butter
2.22.56
bread-and-butter
pudding 10.42.22
bread and water
2.22.53
breadbasket 10.56.18
breadcrumb 20.24.2
breadcrumbs 20.28

breaded 10.2.6
breadfruit 22.34.10
bread knife 11.17.2
breadline 11.27.7
breadth 6.2
breadwinner 2.15.16
break 5.27.7
breakable 2.37.38
breakables 2.39.2
breakage 10.11.4
break and enter 2.22.80
breakaway 5.17.1
breakbeat 9.52.1
breakbone fever 2.25.9
break bread 6.1.13
breakdance 3.37.1
breakdancing 10.42.139
breakdown 16.10.3
breaker 2.12.7
breakeven 2.43.322
breakfast 2.55
break-in 10.31.7
breaking point 18.12
breakneck 6.10.3
breakout 16.16.4
breakpoint 18.12
breakthrough 22.10.6
breakup 20.40.3
breakwater 2.22.54
bream 9.41.3
Brearley 9.14.36
breast 6.49.5
breastbone 19.40.1
breastfed 6.1.3
breastfeed 9.29.2
breastplate 5.47.39
breaststroke 19.31.2
breastwork 7.14.8
breath 6.53
breathable 2.37.25
breathalyse 11.42.4
breathalyzer 2.27.6
breathe 9.31
breather 2.7
breathing 10.42.31
breathless 2.54.55
breathtaking 10.42.46
breathy 9.23
Brecon Beacons 2.51
Brecon Beacons National Park 3.27.5
bred 6.1.13
breech 9.55.1
breechcloth 13.41.1
breeches 10.62.5
breed 9.29.6
breeder 2.6.4
breeding ground 16.11.7
breeze 9.59.10
breeze block 13.10.4

breezily 9.14.28
breezy 9.27.3
Bremen 2.43.83
Bremner 2.15
Brenda 2.6
Brendan 2.43.43
Brenner 2.15.10
Brent 6.34.3
Brenton 2.43.307
Brer rabbit 10.56.3
Brescia 2.21.3
Brest 6.49.5
brethren 2.43.110
Breton 13.28
Brett 6.51.8
breve 9.56.2
breviary 9.19.3
brevity 9.22.51
brew 22.10
brewer 2.4
brewers' yeast 9.50
brewery 9.19.5
brewing 10.42.184
Brewster 2.22.89
Brezhnev 6.4
Brian 12.9
briar 12.4
bribable 2.37.30
bribe 11.12.1
bribed 11.13
bribery 9.19.7
bric-a-brac 1.10.15
Brice 11.34.1
brick 10.12.47
brickbat 1.41.1
brickie 9.13.8
bricklayer 2.0.1
bricklaying 10.42.1
brick-red 6.1.12
bricks-and-mortar 2.22.51
brickwork 7.14.2
brickworks 7.15
bridal 2.37.111
bridal bed 6.1.1
bridal suite 9.52.15
bride 11.14.14
bridegroom 22.25.3
bride price 11.34.2
bridesmaid 5.21.5
Bridewell 6.14.11
bridge 10.11.19
bridgehead 6.1.4
Bridgend 6.30
Bridges 10.62.1
Bridget 10.56.9
bridgeware 4.15
bridle 2.37.111
bridle path 3.51.2
Brie 9.19
brief 9.32.2
briefcase 5.45.3
briefing 10.42.32

briefly 9.14.62
briefs 9.33
brier 12.4
Brierley 9.14
Briers 2.60
brig 10.8.1
brigade 5.21
brigadier 8.1
Brigadoon 22.27
brigand 2.44
brigantine 9.43.21
Briggs 10.10
bright 11.36.16
brighten 2.43.299
brightened 2.44.14
Brightman 2.43.79
brightness 2.54.88
Brighton 2.43.299
brights 11.37
bright spark 3.27.5
brill 10.17.5
brilliance 2.45.12
brilliant 2.47.3, 2.47.24
brilliantine 9.43.21
brim 10.26.2
brimful 21.7.1
brindle 2.37.120
brindled 2.38.2
brine 11.27.14
bring 10.42.112
bring-and-buy 11.2
bring-and-buy sale 5.30.7
brinjal 2.37.146
brink 10.43.2
brinkmanship 10.47.11
briny 9.16.20
brio 19.2.3
brioche 13.37
briquette 6.51.3
Brisbane 2.43.27
brisk 10.51.2
brisket 10.56.17
bristle 2.37.251
bristling 10.42.65
bristly 9.14.80
Bristol 2.37.287
Bristow 19.18.11
Brit 10.56.29
Britain 2.43.298
Britannia 2.11.1
britches 10.62.5
Briticism 2.40.83
British 10.54.19
British Airways 5.54.3
British Asian 2.43.332
British bulldog 13.7.1
British Council 2.37.257
British Empire 12.3
British Legion 2.43.55
British Rail 5.30.6
Briton 2.43.298

britpop 13.31.4
Brittain 2.43.298
Brittany 9.16.11
Britten 2.43.298
brittle 2.37.276
Brixton 2.43.314
Brno 19.13.2
bro 19.15
B-road 19.23.5
broad 14.19.8
broadacre 2.12.5
broadband 1.22.1
broad bean 9.43.1
broad-brush 20.45.3
broadcast 3.47.2
broadcaster 2.22.92
broadcasting 10.42.171
broadcloth 13.41.1
broaden 2.43.41
broadened 2.44.1
broad gauge 5.26.1
broad jumper 2.18.18
broadleaf 9.32.1
broadloom 22.25.2
broadly 9.14.56
broad-minded 10.2.21
broad-mindedness 2.54.76
Broadmoor 14.9
Broads 13.4, 14.20
broadsheet 9.52.13
broadside 11.14.23
broad-spectrum 2.40.32
Broadway 5.17.4
brocade 5.21.1
broccoli 9.14.12
brochette 6.51
brochure 2.21
Broderick 10.12.42
Broglie 9.14.63
brogue 19.29
broil 18.8
broiler 2.13.17
broken 2.43.72
broken-down 16.10.4
broken-hearted 2.33.20, 10.2.36
brokenly 9.14.72
broken marriage 10.11.13
broker 2.12.20
brokerage 10.11.16
broking 10.42.53
brolly 9.14.44
bromide 11.14.11
bromine 9.43.7
Bromley 9.14.70
Bromsgrove 19.51.1
bronchial 2.37.1
bronchiole 19.34.1
bronchitic 10.12.68

bungalow 19.11.2
bungee jump 20.26.1
bungee jumping
  10.42.111
bungle 2.37.145
bungled 2.38.3
bungling 10.42.58
bunion 2.43.60
bunk 20.38
bunk bed 6.1.1
bunker 2.12.26
bunker buster 2.22.104
bunker busting
  10.42.173
bunkhouse 16.14.4
bunkum 2.40.24
bunny 9.16.26
bunny hop 13.31.1
bunny rabbit 10.56.3
Bunsen 2.43.131
bunt 20.33
Bunter 2.22.85
bunting 10.42.168
Bunton 2.43.306
Buñuel 6.14.11
Bunyan 2.43.60
bunyip 10.47
Buonarroti 9.22.68
buoy 18.1
buoyance 2.45.12
buoyancy 9.20.29
buoyant 2.47.24
BUPA 2.18.15
bur 7.1
burble 2.37.89
burbs 7.9
burden 2.43.35
burden of proof
  22.19.1
burdensome 2.40.36
burdock 13.10.1
bureau 19.15.5
bureaucracy 9.20.10
bureaucrat 1.41.9
bureaucratic 10.12.62
Buren 2.43.110
burette 6.51.9
burgeon 2.43.54
burgeoning 10.42.94
burger 2.9.3
Burgess 10.50
burgh 2.19.14
burgher 2.9.3
Burghley 9.14.35
burglar 2.13.29
burglarise 11.42.23
burglary 9.19.17
burgle 2.37.135
burgundy 9.7.19
burial 2.37.6
burial ground 16.11.7
buried 9.29.6
burk 7.14.1

burka 2.12
Burke 7.14.1
Burkin 10.31.8
Burkina Faso 19.16
burl 7.16
burlap 1.33.2
burlesque 6.48
burly 9.14.35
Burma 2.14
Burmese 9.59
burn 7.20.1
burner 2.15.11
Burnet 6.51.6, 10.56.23
Burney 9.16.15
burn-in 10.31.17
burning 10.42.98
burnish 10.54.14
burnout 16.16.6
Burns 7.24
burnt 7.23
burp 7.25
burr 7.1
burra 2.19.14
burrito 19.18.5
burro 19.15
Burroughs 19.52.7
burrow 19.15
Burrowes 19.52.7
Bursa 2.20.6
bursar 2.20.6
bursary 9.19.33
bursitis 10.50.25
burst 7.27.1
bursting 10.42.170
bursty 9.22.85
Burt 7.28
burton 2.43.293
Burtwistle 2.37.251
Burundi 9.7.19
bury 9.19.61
bus 20.42.1
busboy 18.1
busby 9.6
bush 21.13
bushbaby 9.6.3
bushel 2.37.258
Bushell 2.37.258
bushie 9.21
bushman 2.43.100
bushmaster 2.22.93
bushmeat 9.52.6
bushranger 2.10.8
bush telegraph 3.23.3
bushwalker 2.12.19
bushwhack 1.10.19
bushy 9.21
busily 9.14.38
business 2.54.92
businessman 1.21.8
businessperson
  2.43.119
businesswoman
  2.43.91

busk 20.43
busker 2.12.27
buskin 10.31.10
busload 19.23.2
bust 20.44.1
bustard 2.33.22
busted 10.2.93
bustee 9.22.89
buster 2.22.104
bustier 5.1.2
bustle 2.37.253
bustling 10.42.65
bust-up 20.40.11
busty 9.22.89
busy 9.27.4
busybody 9.7.14
busy Lizzie 9.27.4
busywork 7.14.4
but 2.56.5
but (noun) 20.47.1
butane 5.35.13
butch 21.16
butcher 2.24
butcherbird 7.10.2
butchery 9.19.53
Buthelezi 9.27.2
butler 2.13.33
Butlin 10.31.11
butt 20.47.1
butte 22.34.2
butter 2.22.56
buttercream 9.41.4
buttercup 20.40.2
butterfat 1.41.2
Butterfield 9.39.1
butterfingered 2.33.6
butterfingers 2.60.2
butterflies 11.42.3
butterfly 11.5.2
butter knife 11.17.2
buttermilk 10.19
butternut squash
  13.37.1
butterscotch 13.42
Butterworth 7.30.2
buttery 9.19.34
buttock 2.35
buttocks 2.36
button 2.43.302
button-down 16.10.4
buttoned 2.44.14
buttress 2.54.111
buttressed 2.55.1
butty 9.22.72
buxom 2.40.33
Buxtehude 2.6.13
buy 11.2
buy-back 1.10.3
buyer 12.0
buyer's market
  10.56.13
buzz 20.53
buzzard 2.33.26

buzzer 2.27
buzzing 10.42.186
buzz saw 14.13
buzzword 7.10.5
by 11.2
bye 11.2
by-election 2.43.267
bygone 13.22.4
bygones 13.26
Bygraves 5.53
bylaw 14.8
by-line 11.27.3
BYO 19.0
BYOB 9.6
bypass 3.43.3
byplay 5.8.3
by-product 20.12
by proxy 9.20.25
Byrd 7.10.1
byre 12.0
byroad 19.23.5
Byron 2.43.110
bystander 2.6.18
byte 11.36.1
byway 5.17
byword 7.10.5
Byzantine 9.43.20,
  9.43.21, 10.31.24
byzantine 11.27.17
Byzantium 2.40.1,
  2.40.18
C2B 9.6
cab 1.1.1
cabal 1.13
caballero 19.15.2
cabaret 5.12
cabbage 10.11.1
cabbie 9.6.1
caber 2.5.2
cabernet sauvignon
  13.22.5
cabin 10.31.2
cabin class 3.43.2
cabin crew 22.10.3
cabin-cruiser 2.27.10
cabinet 2.56.29
cabinetmaker 2.12.6
cabinet minister
  2.22.98
cable 2.37.87
cablegram 1.18.6
cable television
  2.43.336
cabochon 13.22.15
caboodle 2.37.116
caboose 22.31
Cabot 2.56.5
cabriole 19.34.1
cabriolet 5.8.1
cabstand 1.22.7
cacao 16.3
cache 1.39
cachet 5.14.1

caught 14.44.1
cauldron 2.43.112
Caulfield 9.39.1
cauliflower 17.1.1
cauliflower cheese
9.59.16
caulk 14.24.2
causal 2.37.299
causality 9.22.9
causation 2.43.223
causative 10.61.34
cause 14.48
'cause 20.53
cause célèbre 2.19.15
causeway 5.17
caustic 10.12.77
cauterise 11.42.27
caution 2.43.250
cautionary 9.19.23
cautious 2.54.116
cautiously 9.14.84
cavalcade 5.21.1
cavalier 8.4
cavalry 9.19.77
cavalryman 2.43.85
Cavan 2.43.319
Cavanagh 2.15.6
cave 5.51
caveat 1.41
caveat emptor 14.15
cave-in 10.31.31
Cavell 2.37.289
caveman 1.21.4
Cavendish 10.54.4
cavern 2.43.319
cavernous 2.54.63
caviar 3.1
cavil 2.37.289, 10.17.8
caving 10.42.177
cavity 9.22.52
cavort 14.44
Cavour 14.16, 15.0
caw 14.7
Cawdor 2.6.9
Cawley 9.14.45
Caxton 2.43.314
cay 5.7, 9.13
Cayenne 6.29
CBE 9.2
CCJ 5.6
CCTV 9.25.5
CD 9.7.10
CD burner 2.15.11
CD-ROM 13.18.4
CD writer 2.22.48
cease 9.49
ceasefire 12.1
ceaseless 2.54.51
Ceauşescu 22.5
Cecil 2.37.249
Cecilia 2.1.6
Cecily 9.14.23
cedar 2.6.3

cede 9.29.7
cedi 9.7.10
cedilla 2.13.9
Cedric 10.12.42
Ceefax 1.11.1
ceilidh 9.14.32
ceiling 10.42.72
celeb 6.0
Celebes 9.59.1
Celebes Sea 9.20
celebrant 2.47.74
celebrate 5.47.58
celebrated 10.2.51
celebration 2.43.192
celebratory 9.19.43,
9.19.66
celebrity 9.22.32
celeriac 1.10.1
celerity 9.22.36
celery 9.19.17
celesta 2.22.94
celestial 2.37.1
Celestial City 9.22.64
celibacy 9.20.2
celibate 2.56.5
Celina 2.15.13
Céline 9.43.5
cell 6.14.8
cellar 2.13.6
cellarage 10.11.15
cellblock 13.10.4
Cellini 9.16.17
cellist 10.53.6
cello 19.11.4
cellophane 5.35
cellular 2.13.21
cellulite 11.36.6
celluloid 18.5.1
cellulose 19.45
Celsius 2.54.14
Celt 6.19
CELTA 2.22.75
Celtic 10.12.54
Celtic cross 13.34.7
cement 6.34.1
cemetery 9.19.82
cenotaph 3.23
censer 2.20.17
censor 2.20.17
censorial 2.37.10
censorious 2.54.12
censorship 10.47.7
censurable 2.37.51
censure 2.21
censured 2.33
census 2.54.114
cent 6.34.4
centenarian 2.43.16
centenary 9.19.26,
9.19.27
centennial 2.37.5
centesimal 2.37.192
centigrade 5.21.9

centigram 1.18.6
centilitre 2.22.28
centime 9.41.7
centimetre 2.22.29
centipede 9.29.5
central 2.37.245
centralise 11.42.11
centralism 2.40.55
centrality 9.22.9
centrally 9.14.19
Central Park 3.27.5
centre 2.22.81
centre back 1.10.4
centreboard 14.19.2
centred 2.33.18
centrefold 19.35.1
centre half 3.23.1
centrepiece 9.49.4
centre spread 6.1.14
centricity 9.22.64
centrifugal 2.37.141
centrifuge 22.20
centrism 2.40.77
centrist 10.53.16
centurion 2.43.22
century 9.19.53
CEO 19.2
cep 6.43
cephalic 10.12.17
cephalopod 13.2.2
ceramic 10.12.23
ceramics 10.13.3
Cerberus 2.54.97
cereal 2.37.8
cerebellum 2.40.26
cerebral 2.37.230
cerebral palsy 9.27
cerebrum 2.40.29
Ceredigion 13.22.1
ceremonial 2.37.4
ceremonialism 2.40.56
ceremonious 2.54.8
ceremony 9.16.7
Ceres 9.59.10
Ceri 9.19.60
cerise 9.49.5
cerium 2.40.15
cerography 9.9.3
cert 7.28.3
certain 2.43.293
certainly 9.14.72
certainty 9.22.80
certifiable 2.37.95
certificate 2.56.10,
5.47.22
certificated 10.2.43
certification 2.43.162
certified 11.14.7
certifier 12.1.1
certify 11.3.8
certitude 22.17.6
Cervantes 9.59.15

cervical 2.37.147,
2.37.155, 10.16
cervical smear 8.5
cervid 10.2.94
cervix 10.13
Cerys 10.50.12
Cesar 3.19
cessation 2.43.206
cesspit 10.56.26
cesspool 22.22.5
Ceylon 13.22.8
Cézanne 1.21.17
cha 3.16
Chablis 9.14.50
cha-cha 3.16
Chad 1.3
chadar 3.3
chador 14.2
chafe 5.24
chaff 1.5, 3.23
chaffinch 10.39
Chagall 1.13
chagrin 10.31.20
chagrined 10.32
chai 11.0
chain 5.35
chainguard 3.21.2
chain letter 2.22.23
chain mail 5.30.4
chain saw 14.13
chain-smoke 19.31
chain store 14.15.1
chair 4.14
chair lift 10.7.1
chairman 2.43.79
chairmanship 10.47.11
chairperson 2.43.118
chairwoman 2.43.88
chaise 5.54
chaise longue 13.27.1
chakra 2.19.18
Chakrabarti 9.22.56
chakram 2.40.31
chalcedony 9.16.2
chalcography 9.9.5
Chalcolithic 10.12.88
Chaldea 2.1.3
chalet 5.8
chalice 10.50.6
chalk 14.24
chalklike 11.19.1
chalky 9.13.11
challenge 10.33
challenged 10.35
challenger 2.10.9
challenging 10.42.39
Chalmers 2.60.4
chamber 2.5.10
chamberlain 10.31.12
chambermaid 5.21.5
chamber pot 13.39.5
Chambers 2.60
chambray 5.12

coldish **10.54.2**
coldness **2.54.75**
cold pack **1.10.14**
cold-pressed **6.49.8**
cold-shoulder **2.6.15**
cold snap **1.33.3**
cold sore **14.13**
cold storage **10.11.12**
Coldstream **9.41.5**
Coldstream Guard **3.21.2**
cold sweat **6.51.15**
cold turkey **9.13.6**
Coleman **2.43.79**
Coleridge **10.11.15**
coleslaw **14.8**
Colette **6.51.4**
coley **9.14.47**
colic **10.12.19**
colicky **9.13.8**
Colin **10.31.11**
colitis **10.50.26**
collaborate **5.47.53**
collaboration **2.43.194**
collaborative **10.61.25**
collaborator **2.22.18**
collage **3.59**
collagen **2.43.53**
collapse **1.34.1**
collapsible **2.37.57**
collar **2.13.14**
collarbone **19.40.1**
collate **5.47.30**
collateral **2.37.237**
collation **2.43.166**
collator **2.22.14**
collect **6.12.3**
collectable **2.37.73**
collected **10.2.73**
collection **2.43.267**
collective **10.61.44**
collectivism **2.40.89**
collectivist **10.53.26**
collector **2.22.69**
colleen **9.43.5**
college **10.11.7**
collegial **2.37.1**
collegiate **2.56.1**
collide **11.14**
collie **9.14.44**
colliery **9.19.2**
Collingwood **21.0.6**
collision **2.43.334**
collision course **14.42.3**
collocate (noun) **2.56.9**
collocate (verb) **5.47.21**
collocation **2.43.155**
colloid **18.5.1**
colloidal **2.37.114**
colloquial **2.37.1**
colloquialism **2.40.56**

colloquium **2.40.1**
colloquy **9.26.1**
collude **22.17.7**
collusion **2.43.339**
Collymore **14.9**
collywobbles **2.39.1**
Colman **2.43.79**
colocation **2.43.155**
Cologne **19.40.6**
Colombia **2.1.1**
Colombian **2.43.2**
Colombo **19.3.3**
colon **13.22.7**
colón **19.40.5**
colonel **2.37.212**
Colonel Blimp **10.29**
colonial **2.37.4**
colonialism **2.40.56**
colonialist **10.53.7**
colonic **10.12.34**
colonic irrigation **2.43.153**
colonise **11.42.19**
colonist **10.53.13**
colonnade **5.21.6**
colony **9.16.6**
colophon **13.22.3**
Colorado **19.4.2**
coloration **2.43.196**
coloratura **2.19.13**
colossal **2.37.252**
Colossians **2.51.2**
colossus **2.54.114**
colostomy **9.15.6**
colostrum **2.40.32**
colour **2.13.20**
colourant **2.47.76**
colour-blind **11.28.4**
colour-code **19.23.1**
coloured **2.33.10**
colourfast **3.47.1**
colourful **2.37.122**
colouring **10.42.113**
colourless **2.54.37**
colt **19.36**
coltish **10.54.19**
Columba **2.5.12**
columbarium **2.40.14**
Columbia **2.1.1**
columbine **11.27.1**
Columbus **2.54.23**
column **2.40.25**
columnist **10.53.12**
com **13.18.2**
coma **2.14.17**
Coma Berenices **9.59.12**
comatose **19.45.3**
comb **19.38.2**
combat **1.41.1**
combatant **2.47.88**
combative **10.61.15**
combat-ready **9.7.7**

combats **1.42**
combination **2.43.182**
combine **11.27.1**
combine harvester **2.22.96**
combo **19.3**
combust **20.44.1**
combustible **2.37.77**
combustion **2.43.317**
come **20.24.1**
comeback **1.10.3**
comedian **2.43.3**
comedienne **6.29.1**
comedo **19.4.3**
comedown **16.10.1**
comedy **9.7.2**
comely **9.14.70**
come of age **5.26**
come-on **13.22**
comer **2.14.18**
comestible **2.37.78**
comestibles **2.39.1**
comeuppance **2.45.21**
comfit **10.56.6**
comfort **2.56**
comfortable **2.37.63**
comfortably **9.14.54**
comforter **2.22.3**
comforting **10.42.144**
comfort station **2.43.218**
comfrey **9.19.74**
comfy **9.9**
comic **10.12.27**
comical **2.37.163**
comic strip **10.47.5**
coming **10.42.90**
coming of age **5.26**
comings and goings **10.46**
comity **9.22.25**
comma **2.14**
command **3.35**
commandant **1.25**
commandeer **8.1**
commander **2.6.19**
commander-in-chief **9.32**
commanding **10.42.26**
commandment **2.47.42**
commando **19.4.5**
comme il faut **19.5**
commemorate **5.47.52**
commemoration **2.43.197**
commemorative **10.61.25**
commence **6.33**
commencement **2.47.56**
commend **6.30.3**
commendable **2.37.33**

commendation **2.43.150**
commendatory **9.19.43**
commensal **2.37.256**
commensalism **2.40.55**
commensurate **2.56.34**
comment **6.34.1**
commentary **9.19.50**
commentate **5.47.63**
commentator **2.22.20**
commerce **7.26**
commercial **2.37.261**
commercialise **11.42.12**
commercialised **11.43.1**
commercialism **2.40.62**
commercially **9.14.24**
commingle **2.37.144**
commiserate **5.47.52**
commiseration **2.43.193**
commissariat **2.56.2**
commission **2.43.242**
commissionaire **4.9**
commissioned officer **2.20.8**
commissioner **2.15.4**
commitment **2.47.58**
committal **2.37.276**
committed **10.2.59**
committee **9.22.63**
commode **19.23.3**
commodious **2.54.2**
commodity **9.22.6**
commodore **14.2.1**
common **2.43.79**
common carrier **2.1.20**
common denominator **2.22.16**
commoner **2.15.2**
Common Era **2.19.10**
common good **21.0.1**
common ground **16.11.7**
common-law **14.8**
common-law wife **11.17.3**
commonly **9.14.73**
Common Market **10.56.13**
commonplace **5.45.4**
common room **22.25.3**
commons **2.51.1**
common sense **6.33.3**
commonsensical **2.37.173**
commonsensically **9.14.68**
commonweal **9.38.8**
commonwealth **6.21**

convulsion 2.43.278
convulsions 2.51.2
convulsive 10.61.11
Conway 5.17
Conwy 9.26
coo 22.5
cooee 9.5
Coogan 2.43.46
cook 21.4.4
Cooke 21.4.4
cooked 21.6
cooker 2.12.22
cookery 9.19.16
cookhouse 16.14.4
cookie 9.13.15
cooking 10.42.54
cookout 16.16.3
Cookson 2.43.126
cookware 4.15
cool 22.22.4
coolant 2.47.27
cool bag 1.6.1
coolbox 13.11.1
cooled 22.23
cooler 2.13.26
Coolidge 10.11.5
coolie 9.14.49
coolish 10.54.9
coolly 9.14
coolness 2.54.79
co-op 13.31
coop 22.29
Cooper 2.18.15
cooperate 5.47.55
cooperation 2.43.200
cooperative 10.61.26
co-opt 13.33
coordinate 2.56.30,
  5.47.45
coordinated 10.2.49
coordinates 2.57
coordination 2.43.182
coordinator 2.22.16
coot 22.34
cootie 9.22.74
cop 13.31
copacetic 10.12.64
cope 19.44
Copenhagen 2.43.46
Copernicus 2.54.31
copier 2.1.17
copilot 2.56.17
coping 10.42.104
copious 2.54.1
Copland 2.44.4
cop-out 16.16.7
Coppelia 2.1.6
copper 2.18.10
copperhead 6.1.5
copperplate 5.47.39
coppery 9.19.30
coppice 10.50.11
Coppola 2.13.2

copra 2.19.19
coprocessor 2.20.5
copse 13.32
copsy 9.20.38
copter 2.22.86
copula 2.13.21
copulate 5.47.37
copulation 2.43.172
copy 9.18.9
copycat 1.41.4
copy-edit 10.56.4
copyist 10.53.1
copyright 11.36.16
copywriter 2.22.48
coq au vin 1.29
coquetry 9.19.83
coquette 6.51.3
coquettish 10.54.19
cor 14.7
coracle 2.37.150
coral 2.37.243
cor anglais 5.8
Corbett 2.56.5
Corbin 10.31.2
cord 14.19.5
cordage 10.11.2
Corday 5.3
Cordelia 2.1.6
cordial 2.37.3
cordiality 9.22.10
cordially 9.14.4
cordillera 2.19.9
cordite 11.36.3
cordless 2.54.43
Cordoba 2.5
córdoba 2.5
cordon 2.43.41
cordon bleu 7.4
cords 13.4, 14.20
corduroy 18.4
core 14.7
core curriculum
  2.40.25
core dump 20.26
coreligionist 10.53.13
corer 2.19.11
Corey 9.19.66
Corfu 22.0, 22.4.2
corgi 9.10
coriander 2.6.18
Corinth 10.40
Corinthian 2.43.1
Corinthians 2.51
cork 14.24.2
corkage 10.11.4
corked 14.26
corker 2.12.18
corking 10.42.52
corkscrew 22.10.4
corm 14.33
Cormac 1.10.12
cormorant 2.47.76
corn 14.35.3

cornball 14.27.1
corn chip 10.47.14
corncob 13.0
corncrake 5.27.6
corn dog 13.7.1
cornea 2.1.11
corneal 2.37.4
Corneille 5.10
Cornelius 2.54.4
corner 2.15.21
corner flag 1.6.2
corner kick 10.12.15
corner shop 13.31.7
cornerstone 19.40.16
cornet 10.56.23
corn exchange 5.37
corn-fed 6.1.3
cornflakes 5.28
cornhusk 20.43
cornice 10.50.10
Cornish 10.54.14
cornmeal 9.38.3
corn plaster 2.22.91
corn pone 19.40.10
cornrow 19.15
cornstarch 3.52
cornucopia 2.1.18
Cornwall 2.37.296,
  14.27.11
Cornwallis 10.50.5
Cornwell 6.14.11
corny 9.16.21
corollary 9.19.17
corona 2.15.22
coronary 9.19.22
coronary thrombosis
  10.50.20
coronation 2.43.180
coroner 2.15.2
coronet 10.56.23
Corot 19.15.4
corpora 2.19.4
corporal 2.37.235
corporate 2.56.37
corporation 2.43.193
corporatism 2.40.86
corporeal 2.37.10
corporeality 9.22.10
corps 14.7
corps de ballet 5.8
corpse 14.41
corpulent 2.47.31
corpus 2.54.93
corpuscle 2.37.253
corral 3.30.2
correct 6.12.8
correction 2.43.269
correctional 2.37.210
correction fluid 10.2.1
correctitude 22.17.6
corrective 10.61.42
correctly 9.14.91
correctness 2.54.88

correlate (noun)
  2.56.14
correlate (verb)
  5.47.30
correlated 10.2.45
correlation 2.43.166
correlative 10.61.19
correspond 13.23.2
correspondence 2.45.8
correspondent 2.47.13
corresponding
  10.42.14
correspondingly
  9.14.76
corridor 14.2
corrie 9.19.65
corrigendum 2.40.22
corrigible 2.37.35
corroborate 5.47.53
corroborated 10.2.52
corroboration 2.43.194
corroborative 10.61.25
corroborator 2.22.18
corroboree 9.19.8
corrode 19.23.5
corrosion 2.43.331
corrosive 10.61,
  10.61.2
corrugated 10.2.41
corrupt 20.41
corruptible 2.37.63
corruption 2.43.284
corsage 3.59
corsair 4.0
corset 10.56.32
corseted 10.2.59
Corsica 2.12.11
Corsican 2.43.68
cortege 6.58
cortège 5.56
Cortés 6.57
cortex 6.11.7
Cortez 6.57
corticosteroid 18.5.3
cortisone 19.40.19
coruscate 5.47.28
corvette 6.51.14
Cos 13.34
cos 2.60.3
Cosa Nostra 2.19.23
Cosby 9.6
cosh 13.37
cosign 11.27.15
cosignatory 9.19.40
cosine 11.27.15
cosmeceutical
  2.37.180
cosmetic 10.12.65
cosmetics 10.13.15
cosmetic surgery
  9.19.15
cosmic 10.12.29
cosmic ray 5.12

crofting 10.42.165
Crohn's 19.43
croissant 13.28
cromlech 6.10
Crompton 2.43.311
Cromwell 6.14.11
crone 19.40.11
Cronkite 11.36
Cronos 13.34
Cronus 2.54.74
crony 9.16.25
cronyism 2.40.46
crook 21.4.6
crooked 10.2.25
crookedly 9.14.58
crookedness 2.54.76
croon 22.27.7
crooner 2.15.25
crop 13.31.5
crop circle 2.37.154
cropped 13.33
cropper 2.18.12
crop top 13.31.8
croquet 9.13.12
croquette 6.51.3
crore 14.12
Crosbie 9.6
Crosby 9.6
crosier 2.31
cross 13.34.7
crossbar 3.2
crossbeam 9.41.1
crossbones 19.43.1
crossbow 19.3
cross-bred 6.1.13
crossbreed 9.29.6
crosscheck 6.10.7
cross-country 9.19.87
cross-cultural 2.37.240
crosscurrent 2.47.80
crossed 13.36
cross-examine 10.31.16
cross-eyed 11.14.17
cross-fertilisation 2.43.225
crossfire 12.1
crosshatch 1.44
crossing 10.42.132
crossover 2.25.21
crosspatch 1.44
crosspiece 9.49.3
cross-platform 14.33.3
cross-purpose 2.54.94
cross-reference 2.45.24
crossroads 19.24
cross-town 16.10.8
crosstrainer 2.15.9
crosswalk 14.24.4
crossways 5.54.3
crosswind 10.32.1
crosswise 11.42.37

crossword 7.10.5
crotch 13.42
crotchet 10.56
crotchety 9.22.2
crouch 16.19
Crouch End 6.30
croup 22.29.2
croupier 2.1.17
crouton 13.22.16
crow 19.15.7
crowbar 3.2
crowd 16.6.2
crowded 10.2.12
Crowe 19.15.7
crown 16.10.7
Crown Colony 9.16.6
Crown Court 14.44.1
crowned 16.11.5
crowning 10.42.92
Crown Prosecution Service 10.50.32
crow's foot 21.14
crow's nest 6.49.4
Crowther 2.7
Croydon 2.43.30
crozier 2.27.9
crucial 2.37.258
crucible 2.37.57
crucifix 10.13.1
crucifixion 2.43.273
cruciform 14.33.2
crucify 11.3.7
crud 20.2
crude 22.17.9
crudeness 2.54.62
crude oil 18.8
crudités 5.15
crudity 9.22.6
cruel 2.37.19
cruel-hearted 2.33.20
cruelty 9.22.79
cruet 10.56.1
Cruikshank 1.30
cruise 22.40.3
cruiser 2.27.10
cruller 2.13.20
crumb 20.24.2
crumble 2.37.104
crumbled 2.38.1
crumbling 10.42.78
crumbly 9.14.55
crumbs 20.28
crumhorn 14.35.2
crummy 9.15.17
crumpet 10.56.28
crumple 2.37.229
crumpled 2.38.7
crunch 20.34
crunchy 9.24.4
crusade 5.21
crusader 2.6.2
crusading 10.42.15
crush 20.45.2

crushable 2.37.61
crushed 20.46
crushing 10.42.140
crust 20.44.5
crustacean 2.43.218
crusted 10.2.93
crusty 9.22.89
crutch 20.49
crux 20.11
crybaby 9.6.3
crying 10.42.5
cryobiology 9.12.7
cryogenic 10.12.32
cryogenics 10.13.6
crypt 10.49.1
cryptic 10.12.76
cryptogram 1.18.7
cryptographic 10.12.9
cryptography 9.9.9
cryptology 9.12.15
cryptosporidium 2.40.4
crystal 2.37.287
crystal ball 14.27.1
crystalline 11.27.4
crystallise 11.42.13
crystallised 11.43.1
crystallography 9.9.6
cry wolf 21.8
CT scan 1.21.1
cub 20.0
Cuba 2.5.8
cubage 10.11.1
Cuban 2.43.27
cube 22.16.1
cube root 22.34.9
cubic 10.12.3
cubic foot 21.14
cubicle 2.37.155, 10.16
cubism 2.40.45
cubist 10.53
cubit 10.56.2
cuboid 18.5
cub reporter 2.22.52
Cub Scout 16.16.3
cucking stool 22.22.7
cuckold 19.35.4
cuckolding 10.42.25
cuckoldry 9.19.72
cuckoo 22.5
cuckoo clock 13.10.6
cucumber 2.5.12
cud 20.2
cuddle 2.37.115
cuddly 9.14.7
cudgel 2.37.146
cue 22.4.4
cuff 20.4.1
cufflink 10.43.1
cuirass 1.36.4
cuisine 9.43.25
cul-de-sac 1.10.17
Culkin 10.31.7

cull 20.14.1
culminate 5.47.46
culmination 2.43.184
culottes 13.40
culpable 2.37.49
Culpeper 2.18.4
culprit 10.56.29
cult 20.22
cultivar 3.17
cultivate 5.47.68
cultivated 10.2.56
cultivation 2.43.222
cultivator 2.22.21
cultural 2.37.240
cultural cringe 10.33.1
culture 2.24.7
cultured 2.33.23
culvert 2.56.41
cum 20.24.1
Cumberland 2.44.5
Cumberland sausage 10.11.20
cumbersome 2.40.34
Cumbria 2.1.19
cum dividend 2.44.1
cumin 10.31.16
cummerbund 20.30
cummings 10.46
cum new 22.4.9
cumulative 10.61.20
cumulonimbus 2.54.23
cumulus 2.54.42
Cunard 3.21.6
cuneiform 14.33.2
cunnilingus 2.54.26
Cunningham 2.40.28
cunt 20.33
cup 20.40.2
cupbearer 2.19.8
cupboard 2.33.1
cupboard love 20.51.1
cupcake 5.27.1
Cup Final 2.37.219
cupful 21.7.1
cupid 10.2.29
cupola 2.13.2
cuppa 2.18.14
cupping 10.42.104
cupric 10.12.48
cur 7.3
curable 2.37.56
Curaçao 16.0, 19.16
curacy 9.20.8
curare 9.19.58
curate (noun) 2.56.32
curate (verb) 5.47.51
curate's egg 6.6
curative 10.61.24
curator 2.22.17
curb 7.7
curd 7.10
curdle 2.37.105
curdled 2.38.2

cure 15.1.1
cure-all 14.27.9
cured 15.6
curettage 10.11.22
curfew 22.4.2
Curia 2.1.19
Curie 9.19.68
curio 19.2.3
curious 2.54.13
curiously 9.14.82
Curitiba 2.5.3
curium 2.40.13
curl 7.16
curler 2.13
curlew 22.4
curlicue 22.4.4
curling 10.42.71
curly 9.14.35
curmudgeon 2.43.52
curmudgeonly 9.14.72
Curragh 2.19.14
currant 2.47.80
current 2.47.80
current affairs 4.18
curriculum 2.40.25
curriculum vitae 11.11
Currie 9.19.70
curried 9.29.6
curry 9.19.70
curry powder 2.6.10
curse 7.26
cursed 7.27
cursing 10.42.132
cursive 10.61.2
cursor 2.20.6
cursoriness 2.54.65
cursory 9.19.33
curt 7.28.1
curtail 5.30.8
curtailed 5.31
curtailment 2.47.46
curtain 2.43.293
curtain-raiser 2.27.3
Curtis 10.50.24
curtsy 9.20.39
curvaceous 2.54.117
curvature 2.24.2
curve 7.32
curveball 14.27.1
curved 7.33
curvy 9.25.4
Curzon 2.43.327
Cusack 1.10.17
CUSeeMe 9.15.12
Cushing 10.42.140
cushion 2.43.136
cushioned 2.44.11
cushy 9.21
cuspid 10.2.29
cuspidor 14.2
cuss 20.42
cussed 10.2.31
cuss word 7.10.5

custard 2.33.22
custard apple 2.37.223
custard pie 11.7
custard powder 2.6.10
Custer 2.22.103
Custer's Last Stand
  1.22.7
custodial 2.37.3
custodian 2.43.3
custody 9.7.2
custom 2.40.40
customarily 9.14.22
customary 9.19.20
custom-built 10.22.1
customer 2.14.3
customise 11.42.16
custom-made 5.21.5
custom-make 5.27.4
customs 2.42
cut 20.47.2
cut-and-dried 11.14.15
cut-and-paste 5.46.1
cutaway 5.17.2
cutback 1.10.7
cute 22.34.4
cutesy 9.20.39
cutey 9.22.75
cut-glass 3.43.1
Cuthbert 2.56.5
cuticle 2.37.180
cutie 9.22.75
cut-in 10.31.24
cutin 10.31.26
cutlass 2.54.52
cutlery 9.19.17
cutlet 2.56.22
cutoff 13.5.5
cutout 16.16.9
cutover 2.25.16
cut-price 11.34.2
cutpurse 7.26.1
cut-rate 5.47.60
cutter 2.22.57
cutthroat 19.47.8
cutting 10.42.143
cutting-edge 6.9
cuz 2.60.3
CV 9.25
cwm 2.40.24
cyan 12.9
cyanic 10.12.31
cyanide 11.14.12
cyanobacteria 2.1.24
cybercafé 5.4
cybercast 3.47.2
cybercrime 11.25.2
cyberfraud 14.19.8
cyberlaw 14.8
cybermediary 9.19.4
cybernate 5.47.44
cybernaut 14.44.3
cybernetic 10.12.66
cybernetics 10.13.16

cyberself 6.16
cybersex 6.11.6
cybershopping
  10.42.110
cyberspace 5.45.6
cybersquatting
  10.42.160
cyberterrorist
  10.53.17
Cybill 2.37.92
cyborg 14.22
cycad 1.3
Cyclades 9.59.2
cyclamen 2.43.81
cycle 2.37.184
cycle-rickshaw 14.14
cyclic 10.12.21
cyclical 2.37.162
cycling 10.42.80
cyclist 10.53.6
cyclometer 2.22.39
cyclone 19.40.5
cyclonic 10.12.34
cyclops 13.32
cyclorama 2.14.8
cyder 2.6.7
cygnet 2.56.26
Cygnus 2.54.62
cylinder 2.6.23
cylinder head 6.1.5
cylindrical 2.37.169
cymbal 2.37.103
cymbals 2.39.1
Cymbeline 9.43.6
Cymru 9.19
cynic 10.12.30
cynical 2.37.166
cynicism 2.40.81
cypress 2.54.110
Cyprian 2.43.15
Cypriot 2.56.2
Cyprus 2.54.110
Cyril 2.37.230
Cyrillic 10.12.18
Cyrus 2.54.107
cyst 10.53.20
cystic 10.12.80
cystic fibrosis 10.50.21
cystitis 10.50.28
cytology 9.12.15
cytomegalovirus
  2.54.107
cytoplasm 2.40.44
czar 3.19
czarina 2.15.14
Czech 6.10.7
Czechoslovakia 2.1.5
dab 1.1
dabble 2.37.24
dab hand 1.22.2
da capo 19.14
dacha 2.24.1
dachshund 2.44

dacoit 18.16
dactyl 10.17.6
dactylic 10.12.18
dactylography 9.9.6
dad 1.3.2
Dada 3.3
daddy 9.7.1
daddy longlegs 6.8
dadism 2.40.50
dado 19.4
dado rail 5.30.6
Daedalian 2.43.7
Daedalus 2.54.38
daemon 2.43.84
daffodil 10.17
daffy 9.9.1
daft 3.24
dag 1.6
dagger 2.9.1
daggy 9.10.1
dago 19.6.2
Daguerre 4.0
daguerreotype 11.31.4
Dahl 3.30.1
dahlia 2.1.7
Dahomey 9.15.15
Dáil Éireann 2.43.110
daily 9.14.32
daily bread 6.1.13
daily grind 11.28
daily round 16.11.5
Daily Star 3.15.1
Daimler 2.13
Daintree 9.19.84
dainty 9.22.80
daiquiri 9.19.16
dairy 9.19.59
dairymaid 5.21.5
dais 10.50
daisy 9.27.2
daisycutter 2.22.57
Dakar 2.12.1, 3.8
Dakota 2.22.55
daks 1.11
dal 3.30.1
Dalai Lama 2.14.6
dalasi 9.20.13
Dalby 9.6
dale 5.30.1
Dalek 6.10
Daley 9.14.32
Dali 9.14.29
Dalian 1.21
Dalit 10.56.19
Dallas 2.54.36
dalliance 2.45.1
dally 9.14.1
dallying 10.42.2
Dalmatia 2.21.2
Dalmatian 2.43.138
Dalton 2.43.303
daltonism 2.40.74
Daly 9.14.32

death grip 10.47.4
deathless 2.54.55
deathlike 11.19.1
deathly 9.14.96
death mask 3.44.1
death metal 2.37.274
death row 19.15.9
death sentence 2.45.33
death's head 6.1.4
death throes 19.52
deathtrap 1.33.5
Death Valley 9.14.2
deb 6.0
debacle 2.37.152
debagged 1.7
debar 3.2
debark 3.27.1
debarred 3.21.1
debase 5.45.1
debased 5.46
debasement 2.47.54
debatable 2.37.63
debate 5.47.10
debater 2.22.9
debauch 14.47
debauchery 9.19.53
debenture 2.24.8
debilitate 5.47.64
debilitated 10.2.55
debilitating 10.42.145
debit 10.56.2
debonair 4.9
de Bono 19.13.5
Deborah 2.19.15
debouch 16.19
Debrett's 6.52
debrief 9.32.2
debriefing 10.42.32
debris 9.19
debt 6.51
debt collector 2.22.69
debtor 2.22.22
debud 20.2
debug 20.7.1
debugger 2.9.10
debugging 10.42.33
debunk 20.38
Debussy 9.20.22
debut 22.4
debutante 3.38
decade 5.21.1
decadence 2.45.5
decadent 2.47.7
decaf 1.5
decaffeinated 10.2.49
decagon 2.43.48
decagonal 2.37.198
decahedron 2.43.112
decal 1.13.1
decamp 1.20.1
decant 1.25.1
decanter 2.22.79
decapitate 5.47.64

decapitated 10.2.55
decapitation 2.43.209
decathlete 9.52.4
decathlon 13.22.7
decay 5.7
decayed 5.21.1
decaying 10.42.1
decease 9.49
deceased 9.50
deceit 9.52.11
deceitful 2.37.130
deceitfully 9.14.10
deceive 9.56.3
deceiver 2.25.9
decelerate 5.47.52
deceleration 2.43.196
December 2.5.11
decent 2.47.82
decentralise 11.42.11
deception 2.43.285
deceptive 10.61.51
deceptively 9.14.99
decibel 6.14.1
decide 11.14.20
decided 10.2.9
decider 2.6.7
deciding 10.42.19
deciduous 2.54.18
decile 11.22.5
decilitre 2.22.28
decimal 2.37.192
decimalise 11.42.8
decimate 5.47.41
decimated 10.2.47
decipher 2.8.3
decipherable 2.37.51
deciphered 2.33.5
decision 2.43.335
decisive 10.61.8
deck 6.10.2
deckchair 4.14
deckhand 1.22.2
deckhead 6.1.7
declaim 5.33.3
declaimer 2.14.9
declamation 2.43.176
declamatory 9.19.39
Declan 2.43.75
declaration 2.43.196
declarative 10.61.24
declare 4.7
declared 4.16.1
déclassé 5.13
declassified 11.14.6
declension 2.43.280
declination 2.43.183
decline 11.27.8
declining 10.42.101
decoction 2.43.259
decode 19.23.1
decoded 10.2.13
decoder 2.6.11
decoke 19.31

décolletage 3.59.1
décolleté 5.15
decolonisation
  2.43.226
decolonise 11.42.19
decommission
  2.43.242
decommissioned
  2.44.11
decompiler 2.13.13
decompose 19.52.5
decomposed 19.53.3
decomposer 2.27.9
decomposition
  2.43.249
decompress 6.47.7
decompression
  2.43.229
decongestant 2.47.90
deconstruct 20.13
deconstruction
  2.43.275
decontaminate 5.47.46
decontamination
  2.43.184
decontrol 19.34.7
decor 14.7
decorate 5.47.52
decorated 10.2.52
decorating 10.42.151
decoration 2.43.193
decorative 10.61.25
decorator 2.22.18
decorous 2.54.100
decorum 2.40.30
decouple 2.37.227
decoy 18.2
decrease 9.49.5
decreasingly 9.14.75
decree 9.19.76
decree absolute
  22.34.8
decree nisi 11.9
decrepit 10.56.26
decrepitude 22.17.5
decrescendo 19.4.7
decrier 12.4
decriminalise 11.42.9
decrypt 10.49.1
dedicate 5.47.23
dedication 2.43.157
deduce 22.31.2
deduct 20.12
deductible 2.37.72
deduction 2.43.274
deductive 10.61.47
Dee 9.7
deed 9.29
deejay 5.6
deem 9.41
Deepak 1.10.14
deep-dish 10.54.2
deepen 2.43.108

deep end 6.30.4
deep-freeze 9.59.11
deep-fried 11.14.14
deep-laid 5.21.2
deeply 9.14.79
deep-rooted 10.2.67
deep-sea 9.20
deep-set 6.51.10
deep-toned 19.41
deer 8.1
deerhound 16.11.3
deerskin 10.31.10
deerstalker 2.12.18
de-escalate 5.47.30
deface 5.45.2
defacement 2.47.54
de facto 19.18.7
defalcate 5.47.19
defamation 2.43.175
defamatory 9.19.39
defame 5.33
default 14.31.1
defeat 9.52.2
defeater 2.22.26
defeatism 2.40.85
defeatist 10.53.22
defecate 5.47.20
defect 6.12.1
defected 10.2.72
defection 2.43.265
defective 10.61.43
defector 2.22.68
defence 6.33.1
defenceless 2.54.51
defend 6.30.2
defendant 2.47.14
defended 10.2.19
defender 2.6.20
defenestration
  2.43.205
defensible 2.37.60
defensive 10.61.13
defer 7.2
deference 2.45.24
deferential 2.37.268
deferral 2.37.230
deferred 7.10.3
defiance 12.10
defiant 12.11
defibrillator 2.22.14
deficiency 9.20.34
deficient 2.47.87
deficit 10.56.32
defile 11.22.2
defiled 11.23
define 11.27.2
defined 11.28.1
definite 2.56.27
definitely 9.14.88
definition 2.43.243
definitive 10.61.23
deflate 5.47.29
deflated 10.2.44

dentine 9.43.20
dentist 10.53.25
dentistry 9.19.89
denture 2.24.8
dentures 2.60
denude 22.17.3
denuded 10.2.3
denunciation 2.43.143
Denver 2.25
Denver boot 22.34.1
deny 11.6
deodar 3.3
deodorant 2.47.76
deodorise 11.42.22
deo gratias 1.36
deontology 9.12.15
Deo volente 9.22.82
depart 3.49.5
departed 10.2.35
department 2.47.58
departmental 2.37.286
departmentalise 11.42.13
department store 14.15.1
departure 2.24
departures 2.60
depend 6.30.4
dependable 2.37.33
dependant 2.47.15
dependence 2.45.8
dependency 9.20.31
dependent 2.47.15
depersonalise 11.42.9
depict 10.14
depiction 2.43.271
depilatory 9.19.38
deplane 5.35.5
deplete 9.52.5
depleted 10.2.58
depletion 2.43.234
deplorable 2.37.50
deplore 14.8
deploy 18.3
depopulate 5.47.37
depopulation 2.43.172
deport 14.44.4
deportation 2.43.210
deportee 9.22.69
deportment 2.47.58
depose 19.52.3
deposit 10.56.38
deposition 2.43.249
depositor 2.22.45
depository 9.19.44
depot 19.14
deprave 5.51.2
depraved 5.52
depravity 9.22.52
deprecate 5.47.26
deprecated 10.2.42
deprecating 10.42.147
deprecation 2.43.164

deprecatory 9.19.43
depreciate 5.47.6
depreciated 10.2.38
depreciation 2.43.144
depredation 2.43.148
depress 6.47.7
depressant 2.47.84
depressed 6.49.8
depression 2.43.229
depressive 10.61.5
deprivation 2.43.222
deprive 11.38.3
deprived 11.39
de profundis 9.49
deprogramme 1.18.8
Deptford 2.33.5
depth 6.46
depth charge 3.26.1
deputation 2.43.213
depute 22.34.6
deputise 11.42.32
deputy 9.22.73
De Quincey 9.20.27
derail 5.30.6
derailleur 2.11
deranged 5.39
derangement 2.47.44
derby 9.6.2
Derbyshire 2.21
deregulate 5.47.34
deregulation 2.43.169
Derek 10.12.45
derelict 10.14.2
dereliction 2.43.271
deride 11.14.14
de rigueur 7.0
derision 2.43.334
derisive 10.61.8
derisively 9.14.98
derisory 9.19.32
derivation 2.43.222
derivative 10.61.33
derive 11.38.3
derived 11.39
dermatitis 10.50.28
dermatological 2.37.161
dermatologist 10.53.4
dermatology 9.12.16
dermis 10.50.9
Dermot 2.56.23
derogate 5.47.15
derogator 2.22.12
derogatory 9.19.37
derrick 10.12.45
Derrida 2.6.4
derrière 4.1
derring-do 22.2
derringer 2.10.9
derv 7.32
dervish 10.54.20
Dervla 2.13

Derwent Water 2.22.53
desalinate 5.47.45
desalination 2.43.183
descale 5.30.3
descant 1.25.1
Descartes 3.49.3
descend 6.30.8
descendant 2.47.14
descending 10.42.28
descent 6.34.4
describe 11.12.1
description 2.43.286
descriptive 10.61.50
descriptor 2.22.86
Desdemona 2.15.22
desecrate 5.47.51
deseed 9.29.7
desegregate 5.47.17
desegregation 2.43.153
deselect 6.12.4
desensitise 11.42.35
desert 2.56.42, 7.28
desert boot 22.34.1
deserted 10.2.57
deserter 2.22.25
desertification 2.43.162
desertion 2.43.231
desert island 2.44.6
deserts 7.29
deserve 7.32.2
deserved 7.33
deservedly 9.14.58
deserving 10.42.179
desexualise 11.42.6
deshabille 9.38.1
déshabillé 5.1
desi 9.20.14
desiccate 5.47.22
desiccated 10.2.43
desiccation 2.43.156
desideratum 2.40.39
design 11.27
designate (adj) 2.56.26
designate (verb) 5.47.49
designated 10.2.37
designation 2.43.189
designer 2.15.18
designing 10.42.100
desirable 2.37.50
desire 12.0
desired 12.7
Désirée 5.12
desirous 2.54.96
desist 10.53
desk 6.48
deskbound 16.11.1
Desmond 2.44.9
desolate 2.56.14, 5.47.30

desolation 2.43.167
despair 4.10
despairing 10.42.122
despatch 1.44
desperado 19.4.2
desperate 2.56.37
desperately 9.14.26
desperation 2.43.201
despicable 2.37.39
despise 11.42
despised 11.43
despite 11.36
despoil 18.8
despoiler 2.13.17
despoliation 2.43.141
despond 13.23.2
despondency 9.20.31
despondent 2.47.13
despot 13.39.6
despotic 10.12.71
despotically 9.14.69
despotism 2.40.86
dessert 7.28
dessertspoon 22.27.6
dessert wine 11.27.20
destabilise 11.42.7
destination 2.43.188
destined 10.32
destiny 9.16.11
destitution 2.43.256
destrier 2.1.19
destroy 18.4
destroyed 18.5.3
destroyer 2.2
destruction 2.43.275
destructive 10.61.48
desuetude 22.17.4
desultory 9.19.34
detach 1.44
detachable 2.37.79
detached 1.45
detachment 2.47.63
detail 5.30.9
detailed 5.31
detailing 10.42.68
details 5.32
detain 5.35.13
detained 5.36.4
detainee 9.16.13
detect 6.12
detectable 2.37.73
detected 10.2.76
detection 2.43.264
detective 10.61.24
detector 2.22.68
détente 13.25
detention 2.43.282
deter 7.6
detergent 2.47.21
deteriorate 5.47.52
deteriorating 10.42.151
deterioration 2.43.193

dissolve 13.15
dissolved 13.16
dissolver 2.25.25
dissonance 2.45.17
dissonant 2.47.67
dissuade 5.21.13
dissuasion 2.43.332
distaff 3.23.4
distance 2.45.36
distant 2.47.91
distantly 9.14.94
distaste 5.46.2
distasteful 2.37.133
distemper 2.18.16
distend 6.30.10
distended 10.2.20
distensible 2.37.60
distension 2.43.282
distil 10.17.7
distillate 2.56.12
distiller 2.13.12
distillery 9.19.19
distinct 10.45.1
distinction 2.43.276
distinctive 10.61.39
distinctiveness 2.54.91
distinctly 9.14.91
distinguish 10.54.22
distinguishable
  2.37.62
distinguished 10.55
distinguishing
  10.42.142
distort 14.44.8
distorted 10.2.64
distortion 2.43.250
distract 1.12.4
distracted 10.2.70
distracting 10.42.166
distraction 2.43.263
distraught 14.44.7
distress 6.47.4
distressed 6.49.5
distress flare 4.7
distribute 22.34.3
distributed 10.2.66
distribution 2.43.254
distributive 10.61.38
distributor 2.22.58
district 10.14.3
District Attorney
  9.16.15
distrust 20.44.6
distrustful 2.37.133
disturb 7.7
disturbance 2.45
disturbed 7.8
disturbing 10.42.13
disunion 2.43.62
disunited 10.2.61
disunity 9.22.30
disuse 22.31.1
disused 22.41

disyllabic 10.12.4
ditch 10.59
ditchwater 2.22.53
dither 2.7.3
dithering 10.42.116
dithery 9.19.11
ditransitive 10.61.28
ditsy 9.20.40
dittany 9.16.11
ditto 19.18
ditty 9.22.63
diuretic 10.12.64
diurnal 2.37.212
diva 2.25.9
Divali 9.14.29
divan 1.21.16
dive 11.38.1
dive-bomb 13.18.1
diver 2.25.14
diverge 7.13
divergence 2.45.10
divergency 9.20.32
divergent 2.47.21
divers 2.60
diverse 7.26.2
diversification
  2.43.161
diversified 11.14.6
diversify 11.3.7
diversion 2.43.232
diversionary 9.19.23
diversity 9.22.42
divert 7.28.5
diverted 10.2.57
diverticulitis 10.50.26
divertimento 19.18.10
diverting 10.42.154
Dives 9.59
divest 6.49.12
divestiture 2.24.3
divestment 2.47.62
divide 11.14.27
divided 10.2.10
dividend 6.30
divider 2.6.6
dividers 2.60.1
divination 2.43.182
divine 11.27.19
diviner 2.15.18
diving 10.42.182
diving board 14.19.1
divining rod 13.2.3
divinity 9.22.29
divisible 2.37.84
division 2.43.336
divisional 2.37.197
divisive 10.61.8
divisor 2.27.7
divorce 14.42
divorcé 9.20.21
divorced 14.43
divorcée 9.20.21
divot 2.56.41

divulge 20.18
divvy 9.25.6
Diwali 9.14.29
diwan 3.34.4
Dixie 9.20.24
Dixieland 1.22.5
Dixon 2.43.126
DIY 11.0
dizziness 2.54.70
dizzy 9.27.4
dizzying 10.42.2
DJ 5.6
Djibouti 9.22.74
djinn 10.31.6
DNA 5.10
Dnieper 2.18.5
Dniester 2.22.95
do 22.2
DOA 5.0
doable 2.37.29
dob 13.0
Dobbs 13.1
Dobermann 2.43.81
dobra 2.19.15
dobro 19.15
Dobson 2.43.124
doc 13.10.1
docent 2.47.82
docile 11.22.5
docility 9.22.20
dock 13.10.1
docked 13.12
docker 2.12.17
docket 10.56.15
dockland 2.44.7
Docklands 2.50.1
dockside 11.14.24
dockyard 3.21.3
doctor 2.22.65
doctoral 2.37.238
doctorate 2.56.38
doctrinaire 4.9
doctrinal 2.37.219
doctrinarian 2.43.16
doctrine 10.31.20
doctrinism 2.40.75
docudrama 2.14.8
document (noun)
  2.47.41
document (verb)
  6.34.1
documentary 9.19.51
documentation
  2.43.217
documented 10.2.86
dodder 2.6
doddering 10.42.115
doddle 2.37.113
dodecahedron
  2.43.112
Dodecanese 9.59.8
dodge 13.9
dodgem 2.40

dodger 2.10.5
Dodgson 2.43.113
dodgy 9.12.20
dodo 19.4
Dodoma 2.14.3
doe 19.4
doer 2.4
does 2.60.1, 20.53
doeskin 10.31.10
doesn't 2.47.96
doff 13.5.1
dog 13.7.1
dog and bone 19.40.1
dogbane 5.35.1
dogbreath 6.53
dogcart 3.49.3
dog days 5.54
doge 19.30, 19.54
dog-eared 8.11
dog-eat-dog 13.7.1
dog-end 6.30
dogfight 11.36.4
dogfish 10.54.5
dogged 10.2.23
doggedness 2.54.76
Dogger 2.9.8
doggerel 2.37.232
doggie 9.10.4
dogging 10.42.35
doggish 10.54.7
doggo 19.6
doggone 13.22.4
doggy 9.10.4
doghouse 16.14.1
dogie 9.10.5
dog Latin 10.31.25
dogleg 6.6.1
doglegged 6.7
dog lover 2.25.23
dogma 2.14.21
dogmatic 10.12.60
dogmatism 2.40.87
dogmatist 10.53.23
dognap 1.33.3
do-gooder 2.6
dog rose 19.52.7
dogsbody 9.7.14
dog's breakfast 2.55
dog's dinner 2.15.16
dogsled 6.1.10
Dog Star 3.15.1
dog's tooth 22.36.2
dog tag 1.6.4
dog-tired 12.7.1
dogtrot 13.39.7
dog warden 2.43.41
dog-weary 9.19.63
dogwood 21.0.6
doh 19.4
d'oh 19.4
Doha 2.3, 3.6
doily 9.14
doing 10.42.12

doings **10.46**
do-it-yourself **6.16**
dojo **19.8**
Dolby **9.6**
dolce vita **2.22.26**
doldrums **2.42**
dole **19.34**
doleful **2.37.127**
doll **13.13**
dollar **2.13.14**
dollhouse **16.14.5**
dollop **2.52.2**
doll's house **16.14.1**
dolly **9.14.44**
dolly mixture **2.24.10**
dolmades **9.59.2**
dolman **2.43.79**
dolmen **6.29.2**
Dolores **2.54.108**
dolorous **2.54.97**
dolour **2.13.14**
dolphin **10.31.4**
dolphinarium **2.40.14**
dolt **19.36**
doltish **10.54.19**
domain **5.35.6**
dome **19.38**
domestic **10.12.77**
domesticate **5.47.27**
domesticity **9.22.45**
domicile **11.22.5**
domiciled **11.23**
domiciliary **9.19.3**
dominance **2.45.20**
dominant **2.47.69**
dominate **5.47.46**
domination **2.43.186**
dominatrix **10.13.10**
dominee **9.16.19**
domineering **10.42.125**
Dominic **10.12.30**
Dominica **2.12.10,
2.12.13**
Dominican **2.43.68**
dominion **2.43.61**
domino **19.13**
domino effect **6.12.1**
Domitian **2.43.241**
don **13.22.2**
Doña **2.11.1**
Donald **2.38.6**
Donaldson **2.43.125**
donate **5.47.43**
Donatello **19.11.4**
donation **2.43.179**
Doncaster **2.22.90**
done **20.29.1**
donee **9.16.23**
Donegal **14.27.5**
Donets **6.52**
dong **13.27**
donga **2.9.13**
Don Giovanni **9.16.12**

dongle **2.37.135**
Donizetti **9.22.60**
Don Juan **2.43, 3.34.4**
donkey **9.13.20**
donkey jacket **10.56.12**
donkey's years **8.14**
donkeywork **7.14.4**
Donna **2.15.20**
Donne **20.29.1**
Donnelly **9.14.15**
donnish **10.54.14**
donor **2.15.22**
Donovan **2.43.319**
Don Quixote **2.56,
9.22**
don't **19.42**
donut **20.47.3**
doodad **1.3.2**
doodah **3.3**
doodle **2.37.116**
doodlebug **20.7.1**
doofus **2.54.25**
doohickey **9.13.8**
doolally **9.14.1**
doom **22.25**
doomed **22.26**
doom-laden **2.43.33**
doom merchant **2.47**
doomsayer **2.0**
Doomsday **5.3.6**
doomster **2.22.89**
doona **2.15.25**
Doonican **2.43.68**
door **14.2**
doorbell **6.14.1**
do-or-die **11.0**
doorframe **5.33.5**
doorjamb **1.18.2**
doorkeeper **2.18.6**
doorknob **13.0.1**
doorknocker **2.12.17**
doorman **2.43.86**
doormat **1.41.6**
doornail **5.30.5**
doorplate **5.47.39**
doorpost **19.46.3**
doorsill **10.17**
doorstep **6.43.1**
doorstepping
10.42.104
doorstop **13.31.9**
door to door **14.2.1**
doorway **5.17**
doo-wop **13.31.10**
doozy **9.27.8**
dop **13.31**
dopamine **9.43.7**
dope **19.44**
dopehead **6.1.4**
dopey **9.18.10**
dopiaza **2.20.18**
doppelganger **2.16**
Dora **2.19.12**

Dorian **2.43.21**
Doric **10.12.46**
Doris **10.50.12**
dork **14.24**
dorm **14.33**
dormant **2.47.32**
dormer **2.14.14**
dormitory **9.19.82**
Dormobile **9.38.1**
dormouse **16.14.9**
Dorothy **9.23**
dorp **14.40**
dorsal **2.37.247**
Dorset **10.56.32**
Dortmund **2.44.9**
dory **9.19.66**
DOS **13.34.2**
dosage **10.11.20**
dose **19.45**
dosh **13.37**
doss **13.34.2**
dosser **2.20.9**
dosshouse **16.14.1**
dossier **2.1.27, 5.1**
dost **2.55, 20.44.2**
Dostoyevsky **9.13.22**
dot **13.39**
dotage **10.11.22**
dotcom **13.18.2**
dote **19.47.2**
doting **10.42.162**
dot matrix **10.13.10**
dot-matrix printer
2.22.83
dotted **10.2.63**
dotty **9.22.68**
Douala **2.13.3**
double **2.37.99**
double agent **2.47.20**
double-barrelled
2.38.8
double bass **5.45.1**
double bill **10.17.1**
double boiler **2.13.17**
double-book **21.4.1**
double-check **6.10.7**
double chin **10.31.30**
double-chinned **10.32**
double-click **10.12.21**
double-cross **13.34.7**
double-crosser **2.20.9**
double-crossing
10.42.132
doubled **2.38.1**
double date **5.47.11**
double-dealing
10.42.72
double-decker **2.12.8**
double-density **9.22.49**
double-digit **10.56.9**
double Dutch **20.49**
double-edged **6.32**
double-ended **10.2.19**

double entendre
2.19.16
double fault **14.31.1**
double-glazed **5.55**
double gloucester
2.22.100
double-jointed
10.2.88
double life **11.17.1**
double-park **3.27.5**
double play **5.8.3**
doubles **2.39.1**
double-sided **10.2.9**
doublespeak **9.36.4**
doublet **2.56.12**
double talk **14.24.3**
double-tongued **20.37**
doubloon **22.27.5**
doubly **9.14.50**
doubt **16.16.2**
doubtful **2.37.130**
doubting Thomas
2.54.57
doubtless **2.54.52**
douceur **7.0**
douche **22.33**
dough **19.4**
doughboy **18.1**
doughnut **20.47.3**
doughty **9.22.70**
doughy **9.4**
Douglas **2.54.35**
Douglas-Home
22.25.1
doula **2.13.26**
dour **15.0, 17.0**
Douro **19.15.5**
douse **16.14**
dove **20.51**
dovecote **19.47.4**
Dover **2.25.17**
Dover sole **19.34.8**
dovetail **5.30.8**
dovetailed **5.31**
dovish **10.54.20**
dow **16.1**
the Dow **16.1**
dowager **2.10**
dowdy **9.7.15**
dowel **17.4**
dower **17.0**
Dowland **2.44.4**
down **16.10.1**
down-and-out **16.16.6**
down-at-heel **9.38.2**
downbeat **9.52.1**
downburst **7.27.1**
downcast **3.47.2**
downer **2.25**
downfall **14.27.3**
down-force **14.42.1**
downgrade **5.21.9**
downgraded **10.2.5**

emanation 2.43.180
emancipate 5.47.50
emancipated 10.2.50
emancipation 2.43.191
emancipator 2.22.9
emasculate 5.47.35
emasculation 2.43.170
embalm 3.31
embalmed 3.32
embank 1.30.1
embankment 2.47.32
embargo 19.6.1
embark 3.27.1
embarras de richesses
6.47
embarrass 2.54.96
embarrassed 2.55.1
embarrassing
10.42.133
embarrassment
2.47.53
embassy 9.20.2
embattled 2.38.9
embed 6.1.1
embellish 10.54.9
embellished 10.55.1
embellishment 2.47.57
ember 2.5.11
embers 2.60
embezzle 2.37.299
embezzlement 2.47.47
embezzler 2.13.2
embitter 2.22.34
embittered 2.33.18
emblazon 2.43.328
emblazoned 2.44.15
emblem 2.40.25
emblematic 10.12.57
embodiment 2.47.38
embody 9.7.14
embolden 2.43.42
embolism 2.40.58
emboss 13.34.1
embossed 13.36
embouchure 15.4
embrace 5.45.7
embrasure 2.28
embrocation 2.43.155
embroider 2.6
embroidery 9.19.9
embroiled 18.9
embryo 19.2.3
embryogeny 9.16.5
embryologist 10.53.4
embryology 9.12.5
embryonic 10.12.34
emcee 9.20
emend 6.30.3
emendation 2.43.150
emerald 2.38.8
Emerald Isle 11.22
emerge 7.13.1
emergence 2.45.10

emergency 9.20.32
emergent 2.47.21
emerging 10.42.36
emerita 2.22.42
emeritus 2.54.131
Emerson 2.43.114
emery 9.19.20
emery board 14.19.3
emetic 10.12.65
emigrant 2.47.81
emigrate 5.47.59
emigration 2.43.203
émigré 5.12
Emily 9.14.38
eminence 2.45.20
éminence grise 9.59.10
eminent 2.47.69
emir 8.5
emirate 2.56.36
emission 2.43.241
emit 10.56.22
Emma 2.14.10
Emmanuel 2.37.18
emmental 3.30.3
Emmerson 2.43.114
emmet 10.56.21
Emmy 9.15.11
emollient 2.47.3
emolument 2.47.41
emote 19.47.6
emoticon 13.22.6
emotion 2.43.252
emotional 2.37.208
emotionless 2.54.49
emotive 10.61.37
empanada 2.6.1
empanel 2.37.196
empathetic 10.12.67
empathic 10.12.87
empathise 11.42
empathy 9.23.1
emperor 2.19.4
emphasis 10.50.14
emphasise 11.42.30
emphatic 10.12.55
emphatically 9.14.66
emphysema 2.14.11
empire 12.3
empire-building
10.42.24
Empire-line 11.27.3
Empire State Building
10.42.24
empirical 2.37.169
empiricism 2.40.81
empiricist 10.53.21
emplacement 2.47.55
employ 18.3
employable 2.37.28
employed 18.5.1
employee 9.0
employer 2.2
employment 2.47.32

emporium 2.40.16
empower 17.2
empowered 17.3
empress 2.54.110
empties 9.59.13
emptiness 2.54.69
emptor 2.22.86
empty 9.22
empty-handed 10.2.18
empty-headed 10.2.7
EMT 9.22
emu 22.4.8
emulate 5.47.36
emulator 2.22.15
emulsifier 12.1.3
emulsify 11.3.7
emulsion 2.43.278
en 6.29
enable 2.37.87
enabling 10.42.60
enact 1.12
enactment 2.47.58
enamel 2.37.191
enamelwork 7.14.6
enamoured 2.33.11
en bloc 13.10.4
encamp 1.20.1
encampment 2.47.52
encapsulate 5.47.32
encase 5.45.3
encash 1.39
encephalitis 10.50.26
enchant 3.38
enchanted 10.2.83
enchanter 2.22.78
enchanting 10.42.168
enchantment 2.47.61
enchantress 2.54.111
enchilada 2.6.1
encircle 2.37.154
enclave 5.51.1
enclitic 10.12.69
enclose 19.52.1
enclosed 19.53.1
enclosure 2.31
encode 19.23.1
encoded 10.2.13
encomium 2.40.8
encompass 2.54.95
encompassed 2.55
encore 14.7
encounter 2.22.84
encourage 10.11.18
encouragement
2.47.45
encouraging 10.42.38
encrustation 2.43.218
encrusted 10.2.93
encrypt 10.49.1
encumber 2.5.12
encumbrance 2.45.22
encyclical 2.37.162
encyclopedia 2.1.3

encyclopedic 10.12.6
end 6.30
endanger 2.10.8
endangered 2.33
endangered species
9.59
endear 8.1
endearing 10.42.123
endearment 2.47.32
endeavour 2.25.6
ended 10.2.19
endemic 10.12.24
end game 5.33.1
ending 10.42.28
endive 10.61
endless 2.54.44
endlessly 9.14.83
end matter 2.22.1
endocrine gland 1.22.3
endocrinology 9.12.11
endogamy 9.15.3
endogenous 2.54.63
endomorphic 10.12.12
endoplasm 2.40.44
endorphin 10.31.4
endorse 14.42
endorsed 14.43
endorsement 2.47.53
endorser 2.20.10
endoscope 19.44.1
endoscopy 9.18.3
endoskeleton 2.43.297
endosperm 7.18.2
endothermic 10.12.25
endow 16.1
endowed 16.6
endowment 2.47.32
end product 20.12
end result 20.22
endurable 2.37.56
endurance 2.45.22
endure 15.1
enduring 10.42.128
endways 5.54.3
endwise 11.42.37
enema 2.14.14
enemy 9.15.2
energetic 10.12.64
energise 11.42.2
energy 9.12.1
enervate 5.47.67
enervated 10.2.56
enervating 10.42.152
enervation 2.43.221
enfant terrible 2.13.27
enfeeble 2.37.23
enfeebled 2.38.1
Enfield 9.39.1
enfold 19.35.1
enforce 14.42.1
enforced 14.43
enforcement 2.47.53
enforcer 2.20.10

258

funnelling 10.42.64
funnily 9.14.41
funny 9.16.26
funny farm 3.31
fur 7.2
furbished 10.55
Furies 9.59.10
furious 2.54.13
furl 7.16
fur-lined 11.28.3
furlong 13.27.1
furlough 19.11
furnace 10.50.10
furnish 10.54.14
furnished 10.55.2
furnishings 10.46
furniture 2.24.3
furor 14.12
furore 9.19.66
furred 7.10.3
furrier 2.1.19
furrow 19.15
furrowed 19.23.5
furry 9.19
further 2.7
furtherance 2.45.23
furthermore 14.9.1
furthermost 19.46.2
furthest 10.53
furtive 10.61.14
fury 9.19.68
furze 7.34
fuse 22.40.2
fused 22.41
fuselage 3.59
fusilier 8.4
fusillade 3.21.5,
  5.21.2, 5.21.3
fusion 2.43.338
fusion food 22.17.1
fuss 20.42
fussbudget 10.56.8
fussed 20.44
fusspot 13.39.6
fussy 9.20
fustian 2.43.24
fusty 9.22.89
futile 11.22.6
futility 9.22.23
futon 13.22.16
future 2.24
futurism 2.40.78
futurist 10.53.17
futuristic 10.12.85
futurity 9.22.38
futurology 9.12.14
Fuzhou 19.0
fuzz 20.53
fuzziness 2.54.70
fuzzy 9.27.7
the f-word 7.10.5
FX 6.11
G8 5.47.1

gab 1.1
gabardine 9.43.3
Gabba 2.5
gabble 2.37.24
gabby 9.6.1
gaberdine 9.43.3
gabfest 6.49.1
gable 2.37.87
gabled 2.38.1
Gabon 13.22, 13.28
Gaborone 9.16.25
Gabriel 2.37.6
Gabriella 2.13.5
gad 1.3
gadabout 16.16.1
Gaddafi 9.9, 9.9.1
gadfly 11.5.2
gadget 10.56.8
gadgetry 9.19.81
gadolinium 2.40.11
Gaelic 10.12.17
gaff 1.5
gaffe 1.5
gaffer 2.8
gaffer tape 5.42.3
gag 1.6
gaga 3.5
Gagarin 10.31.20
gage 5.26.1
gagged 1.7
gagging order 2.6.8
gaggle 2.37.136
gagster 2.22.89
gaiety 9.22.3
gaijin 10.31.6
Gaillac 1.10.9
gaily 9.14.32
gain 5.35
gainful 2.37.128
gains 5.41
gainsaid 6.1
gainsay 5.13
Gainsborough 2.19.2
gait 5.47.14
gaiter 2.22.12
gaiters 2.60.7
Gaitskell 2.37.189
Gaius 12.12
gal 1.13
gala 2.13.3
galactose 19.45.3
galah 3.9
Galahad 1.3
Galapagos Islands
  2.50.2
Galatea 2.1.29
Galatians 2.51.3
galaxy 9.20.23
gale 5.30.2
Galen 2.43.77
galena 2.15.13
Galilee 9.14.40
gall 14.27.5

Gallagher 2.9
gallant 1.25
gallantry 9.19.85
gallbladder 2.6
galleon 2.43.6
galleria 2.1.21
gallery 9.19.18
galley 9.14.1
galley slave 5.51.1
Gallic 10.12.17
Gallicism 2.40.82
gallimaufry 9.19.74
galling 10.42.75
Gallipoli 9.14.18
gallium 2.40.5
gallivant 1.25
gallon 2.43.75
gallop 2.52.1
galloping 10.42.104
Galloway 5.17.1
gallows 19.52.1
gallstone 19.40.18
Gallup 2.52.1
Gallup poll 19.34.4
galore 14.8
galoshes 10.62
Galsworthy 9.8.1
galumph 20.25
galvanic 10.12.31
galvanise 11.42.19
galvanised 11.43.2
galvanometer 2.22.39
Galway 5.17
Gama 2.14.5
Gambia 2.1.1
Gambian 2.43.2
gambit 10.56.2
gamble 2.37.101
gambler 2.13.27
gambling 10.42.78
gamboge 19.30
gambol 2.37.101
game 5.33.1
game bird 7.10.1
gamecock 13.10.2
gamekeeper 2.18.6
gamelan 1.21.2
gamepad 1.3.5
game park 3.27.5
gameplay 5.8.3
gamer 2.14.9
game reserve 7.32.2
game show 19.17
gamesmanship
  10.47.11
gamete 9.52.6
gamine 9.43.7
gaming 10.42.84
gamma 2.14.1
gamma globulin
  10.31.14
gamma ray 5.12
gammon 2.43.80

gammy 9.15.1
gamut 2.56.23
gamy 9.15.10
gander 2.6.18
Gandhi 9.7.20
ganef 6.4
Ganesha 2.21
gang 1.28
Ganges 9.59
gangland 1.22.3
gangling 10.42.58
ganglion 2.43.6
gangly 9.14.64
gangmaster 2.22.93
gangplank 1.30.2
gangrene 9.43.12
gangrenous 2.54.71
gangsta 2.22.108
gangsta rap 1.33.4
gangster 2.22.108
gangway 5.17
ganja 2.10.7
gannet 10.56.24
gannister 2.22.97
gantry 9.19.84
gaol 5.30
gap 1.33
gape 5.42
gaping 10.42.104
gar 3.5
garage sale 5.30.7
garam masala 2.13.3
garb 3.20
garbage 10.11.1
garbageman 1.21.4
garbanzo 19.21
garble 2.37.23
garbled 2.38.1
Garbo 19.3
Garcia 2.1.27
garçon 13.22.14
Garda 2.6.1
garden 2.43.32
gardener 2.15.2
gardenia 2.1.14
gardening 10.42.94
Garden of Eden
  2.43.36
garden party 9.22.57
garden path 3.51.2
garden shed 6.1.15
garderobe 19.22.2
Gareth 2.58
Garfield 9.39.1
Garfunkel 2.37.187
Gargantua 2.4.1
gargantuan 2.43
gargle 2.37.135
gargoyle 18.8
Garibaldi 9.7.18
garland 2.44.4
garlic 10.12.16
garlicky 9.13.8

garlic sausage 10.11.20
garment 2.47.32
garner 2.15.7
garnet 10.56.23
garret 2.56.33
Garrick 10.12.43
garrison 2.43.122
garrotte 13.39.7
garrotter 2.22.50
garrulity 9.22.8
garrulous 2.54.35
Garry 9.19.1
garter 2.22.4
garter snake 5.27.5
Garth 3.51
Garuda 2.6.13
Garvey 9.25.1
Gary 9.19.1
gas 1.36.1
gasbag 1.6.1
Gascoigne 18.11
gaseous 2.54.14
gas-fired 12.7
gas guzzler 2.13.2
gash 1.39
gasholder 2.6.16
Gaskell 2.37.189
gasket 10.56.17
gaslight 11.36.6
gasman 1.21.8
gas mask 3.44.1
gas meter 2.22.29
gasoline 9.43.6
gasometer 2.22.39
gasp 3.45
gasping 10.42.104
gassy 9.20.1
Gastarbeiter 2.22.46
gastric 10.12.49
gastritis 10.50.27
gastroenteritis 10.50.27
gastrointestinal 2.37.215
gastronomic 10.12.28
gastronomy 9.15.5
gastropod 13.2.2
gastropub 20.0
gasworks 7.15
gate 5.47.14
gateau 19.18.1
gatecrash 1.39.4
gatecrasher 2.21.1
gated 10.2.41
gatefold 19.35.1
gatehouse 16.14.7
gatekeeper 2.18.6
gatepost 19.46.3
Gateshead 6.1.4
gateway 5.17.5
gather 2.7
gathered 2.33.4

gatherer 2.19.1
gathering 10.42.116
gator 2.22.12
Gatsby 9.6
GATT 1.41
gaucho 19.19
Gaudí 9.7.15
gaudy 9.7
gauge 5.26.1
Gauguin 1.29
Gaul 14.27.5
gauleiter 2.22.47
gaunt 14.38
gauntlet 2.56.22
gauze 14.48
gauzy 9.27
gavel 2.37.289
Gavin 10.31.31
gavotte 13.39
Gawain 5.35.17
gawd 14.19
gawk 14.24
gawkish 10.54.8
gawky 9.13.11
gawp 14.40
gay 5.5
Gay Gordons 2.51
Gayle 5.30.2
Gaylord 14.19.7
Gaynor 2.15.9
Gaza 2.27.1
Gaza Strip 10.47.5
gaze 5.54
gazebo 19.3
gazelle 6.14.12
gazette 6.51
gazetteer 8.10
gazillion 2.43.8
gazpacho 19.19
gazump 20.26
gazumper 2.18.18
GBH 5.50
GCHQ 22.4.4
GCSE 9.20.15
g'day 5.3.1
GDP 9.18.7
gear 8.0
gearbox 13.11.1
gearing 10.42.123
gear lever 2.25.10
gearwheel 9.38.8
gecko 19.10.2
geddit 10.56.4
gee 9.12
geek 9.36
geese 9.49
geez 9.59
geezer 2.27.4
Geiger counter 2.22.84
geisha 2.21.2
gel 6.14
gelatin 10.31.24
gelatinity 9.22.29

gelatinous 2.54.71
geld 6.15
gelding 10.42.14
gelignite 11.36.14
gem 6.25
Gemini 11.6
Geminid 10.2.28
Gemma 2.14.10
gen 6.29
gendarme 3.31
gender 2.6.20
gendered 2.33.2
genealogy 9.12.3
genera 2.19.1
general 2.37.234
generalisation 2.43.225
generalise 11.42.11
generalised 11.43.1
generalist 10.53.7
generality 9.22.18
generally 9.14.20
general meeting 10.42.155
general purpose 2.54.94
generalship 10.47.6
general surgeon 2.43.54
generate 5.47.54
generation 2.43.199
generational 2.37.203
generative 10.61.25
generator 2.22.18
generic 10.12.45
generosity 9.22.47
generous 2.54.102
genesis 10.50.14
genetic 10.12.66
genetically modified 11.14.2
geneticist 10.53.21
genetics 10.13.16
Geneva 2.25.9
genever 2.25.9
Genevieve 9.56
genial 2.37.4
geniality 9.22.10
genially 9.14.4
genie 9.16.16
genital 2.37.276
genitalia 2.1.7
genitals 2.39.7
genitive 10.61.22
genius 2.54.7
Genoa 2.3
genocidal 2.37.111
genocide 11.14.18
genomic 10.12.27
genomics 10.13.3, 10.13.5
genotype 11.31.4
genre 2.19

gent 6.34
genteel 9.38
gentian 2.43.280
gentility 9.22.23
gentle 2.37.284
gentlefolk 19.31.1
gentleman 2.43.97
gentleman-farmer 2.14.5
gentlemanly 9.14.73
gentleman's agreement 2.47.36
gentlewoman 2.43.90
gently 9.14.92
gentrification 2.43.160
gentrify 11.3.6
gentry 9.19.86
genuflect 6.12.5
genuflection 2.43.268
genuine 10.31.1
genuinely 9.14.71
genus 2.54.62, 2.54.65
geocentric 10.12.52
geochemistry 9.19.90
geochronology 9.12.12
geode 19.23
geodesic 10.12.91
geodesy 9.20.18
geoeconomics 10.13.5
Geoffrey 9.19.74
geographer 2.8.1
geographical 2.37.157
geography 9.9.4
geohazard 2.33.26
geological 2.37.160
geologist 10.53.4
geology 9.12.5
geometer 2.22.39
geometric 10.12.51
geomorphology 9.12.8
geophysicist 10.53.21
geophysics 10.13.20
geopolitics 10.13.12
geoponic 10.12.34
Geordie 9.7
George 14.23
George Cross 13.34.7
Georgetown 16.10.8
georgette 6.51
Georgia 2.10
Georgian 2.43.52
georgic 10.12.13
Georgina 2.15.12
geostationary 9.19.24
geostrophic 10.12.8
geothermal 2.37.190
Geraint 11.29
Gerald 2.38.8
Geraldine 9.43.2
geranium 2.40.10
Gerard 3.21
gerbil 2.37.89
geriatric 10.12.50

Gonzalez 6.57
gonzo 19.21
goo 22.0
Gooch 22.37
good 21.0.1
Goodall 2.37.105
goodbye 11.2
good faith 5.49
good-for-nothing
10.42.174
Good Friday 5.3
goodhearted 2.33.20,
10.2.36
Goodhew 22.4.3
good-humoured
2.33.11
goodie 9.7.17
goodies 9.59.2
goodish 10.54.2
good-looking 10.42.54
goodly 9.14.56
Goodman 2.43.95
good manners 2.60.5
good-natured 2.33.23
goodness 2.54.75
Good News Bible
2.37.93
goodnight 11.36.14
good offices 10.62.4
goods 21.2
Good Samaritan
2.43.298
good-sized 11.43.5
good spirits 10.57.1
good taste 5.46.2
good-tempered
2.33.16
goodwife 11.17.3
goodwill 10.17.9
goody 9.7.17
goody-goody 9.7.17
gooey 9.5
goof 22.19
goofball 14.27.1
goofy 9.9
google 2.37.141
googly 9.14.63
googol 13.13
gook 22.21
Goolden 2.43.30
goolies 9.59.3
goon 22.27.1
goonda 2.6.17
goose 22.31
gooseberry 9.19.7
goose bumps 20.27
goose egg 6.6
gooseflesh 6.50
goose pimples 2.39.6
goose step 6.43.1
Gorbachev 13.5
Gordian knot 13.39.4
Gordimer 2.14.12

Gordon 2.43.41
gore 14.4
gorge 14.23
gorged 14.37
gorgeous 2.54.29
Gorgon 2.43.50
Gorgonzola 2.13.18
gorilla 2.13.11
Gorky 9.13.11
gormless 2.54.46
gorse 14.42
gory 9.19.66
gosh 13.37
goshawk 14.24.1
gosling 10.42.83
go-slow 19.11
gospel 2.37.222
goss 13.34
gossamer 2.14.3
gossip 10.47
gossipy 9.18.8
got 13.39
gotcha 2.24
goth 13.41
Gotham 2.40.41
Gothenburg 7.12.3
gothic 10.12.87
gotta 2.22.49
gotten 2.43.300, 13.21
Götterdämmerung
21.10
Gottlieb 9.28
gouache 3.48
Gouda 2.6.10
Gough 13.5
goulash 1.39.2
Gould 22.23
Gounod 19.13
gourd 15.6
gourmand 2.44.9
gourmandise 11.42.1
gourmandism 2.40.50
gourmet 5.9
gout 16.16
gouty 9.22.70
gov 20.51
govern 2.43.326
governable 2.37.44
governance 2.45.17
governess 2.54.63
governing 10.42.94
government 2.47.49
governmental 2.37.286
governor 2.15.6
governorship 10.47.7
Govinda 2.6.23
Gower 17.0
gown 16.10.6
goy 18.0
Goya 2.2
GP 9.18.7
GR8 5.47.59
grab 1.1.3

grab bag 1.6.1
grabby 9.6.1
Gracchus 2.54.31
grace 5.45.7
graceful 2.37.129
graceless 2.54.51
grace note 19.47.7
gracious 2.54.119
graciously 9.14.84
grackle 2.37.148
grad 1.3.7
gradable 2.37.31
gradation 2.43.148
grade 5.21.9
graded 10.2.5
gradient 2.47.1
gradual 2.37.17
gradually 9.14.5
graduate (adj, noun)
2.56.4
graduate (verb) 5.47
graduated 10.2.39
graduation 2.43.138
Graeco-Roman
2.43.87
Graeme 2.40
graffiti 9.22.62
graffito 19.18.5
graft 3.24
Graham 2.40
Grahame 2.40
Grail 5.30.6
grain 5.35.8
grained 5.36.1
Grainger 2.10.8
grainy 9.16.13
gram 1.18.6
grammar 2.14.1
grammarian 2.43.16
grammar school
22.22.4
grammatical 2.37.175
Grammy 9.15.1
gramophone 19.40.3
Grampian Mountains
10.41.2
grampus 2.54.95
gran 1.21.13
Granada 2.6.1
granary 9.19.21
grand 1.22.6
grandad 1.3.2
grandaddy 9.7.1
Grand Canyon 2.43.60
grandchild 11.23.1
granddad 1.3.2
granddaddy 9.7.1
granddaughter 2.22.51
grandee 9.7.20
grandeur 2.10.7
grandfather 2.7.1
grandfather clock
13.10.6

Grand Guignol 13.13.1
grandiloquence
2.45.40
grandiloquent 2.47.95
grandiose 19.45
grandly 9.14.60
grandma 3.10
grand mal 1.13
grandmama 3.10
grand master 2.22.93
grandmother 2.7.4
Grand National
2.37.201
grandpa 3.12
grandparent 2.47.77
Grand Prix 9.19.79
grand slam 1.18.4
grandson 20.29.4
grandstand 1.22.7
grandstanding
10.42.27
grand theft 6.5
grand tour 15.5
grange 5.37.1
granita 2.22.30
granite 10.56.24
Granite City 9.22.64
granny 9.16.1
granny flat 1.41.5
granny knot 13.39.4
granola 2.13.18
grant 3.38
granted 10.2.83
grantee 9.22.80
Grantham 2.40.41
grant-maintained
5.36.4
granular 2.13.21
granulated 10.2.46
granule 2.22.1
grape 5.42.2
grapefruit 22.34.10
grapevine 11.27.19
graph 1.5.2, 3.23.3
grapheme 9.41
graphic 10.12.9
graphical 2.37.157
graphically 9.14.66
graphics 10.13.1
graphite 11.36.4
graphology 9.12.8
grapnel 2.37.195
grapple 2.37.223
Grasmere 2.1.9
grasp 3.45
grasping 10.42.104
Grass 1.36.4
grass 3.43.5
grass-cutter 2.22.57
grasshopper 2.18.11
grassland 1.22.3
grassroots 22.35
grass snake 5.27.5

grovelling 10.42.67
grow 19.15.6
growbag 1.6.1
grower 2.3.4
growing 10.42.11
growl 16.9
grown 19.40.12
growth 19.49.1
groyne 18.11
Grozny 9.16
grub 20.0.2
grubby 9.6.7
grubstake 5.27.10
grudge 20.9.2
grudging 10.42.36
gruel 2.37.19
gruelling 10.42.59
gruesome 2.40.33
gruff 20.4.3
grumble 2.37.104
grump 20.26.4
grumpy 9.18.14
grunge 20.31
grungy 9.12.21
grunt 20.33.2
Gruyère 4.5
gryphon 2.43.45
G-string 10.42.131
guacamole 9.14.47
Guadalajara 2.19.6
Guadeloupe 22.29.1
Guam 3.31
Guangzhou 19.8
guano 19.13.1
Guantanamo Bay 5.2
Guarani 9.16.12
guaraní 9.16.2
guarantee 9.22.80
guaranteed 9.29
guaranty 9.22.80
guard 3.21.2
guard dog 13.7.1
guarded 10.2.4
guardhouse 16.14.3
guardian 2.43.3
guardian angel
    2.37.146
guardianship 10.47.10
guardrail 5.30.6
guardroom 22.25.4
Guards 3.22
guardsman 2.43.104
Guarneri 9.19.60
Guatemala 2.13.3
Guatemalan 2.43.75
guava 2.25.2
gubbins 10.41
gubernatorial 2.37.12
guck 20.10
guernsey 9.27.10
guerrilla 2.13.11
guess 6.47

guesstimate 2.56.25,
    5.47.41
guesswork 7.14.7
guest 6.49
guesthouse 16.14.7
guest house 16.14.7
guestroom 22.25.3,
    22.25.7
Guevara 2.19.6
guff 20.4
guffaw 14.3.1
Guggenheim 11.25
guidance 2.45.5
guide 11.14.8
guide dog 13.7.1
guideline 11.27.7
guidelines 11.30
guiding light 11.36.6
guild 10.18
guilder 2.6.14
guildhall 14.27.6
guile 11.22
guileful 2.37.127
guileless 2.54.35
guillemot 13.39
guillotine 9.43.19
guilt 10.22
guiltless 2.54.52
guilty 9.22.78
guinea 9.16.18
guinea fowl 16.9.1
guinea pig 10.8
Guinevere 2.1.30
Guinness 2.54.71
guise 11.42
guitar 3.15
Gujarati 9.22.58
gulag 1.6.2
gulch 20.23
gulf 20.16
Gulf States 5.48
Gulf Stream 9.41.5
Gulf War 14.17
gull 20.14
gullet 10.56.19
gulley 9.14
gullible 2.37.40
gully 9.14
gulp 20.19
gulped 20.20
gum 20.24
gum arabic 10.12.3
gumbo 19.3.3
gumboot 22.34.1
gumdrop 13.31.6
Gummer 2.14.18
gummy 9.15.16
gumption 2.43.287
gumshoe 22.12
gun 20.29.2
gunboat 19.47.1
gun-carriage 10.11.14
gundog 13.7.1

gunfight 11.36.4
gunfire 12.1
gunge 20.31
gung ho 19.7
gunk 20.38
gunky 9.13.21
gunman 2.43.79
gunmetal 2.37.274
gunnel 2.37.221
gunner 2.15
gunnery 9.19.21
gunny 9.16.26
gunpoint 18.12
gunpowder 2.6.10
Gunpowder Plot
    13.39.2
gunroom 22.25.3
gunrunner 2.15.24
gunship 10.47.9
gunshot 13.39.8
gun-shy 11.10
gunsight 11.36.19
gunslinger 2.17
gunsmith 10.58.1
gunstock 13.10.8
Gunther 2.22.78
gunwale 2.37.221
guppy 9.18.11
gur 15.0
gurdwara 2.19.6
gurgle 2.37.135
gurney 9.16.15
guru 22.10
Gus 20.42
gush 20.45
gusher 2.21.5
gushing 10.42.140
gusset 10.56.32
gust 20.44
gusto 19.18.11
gusty 9.22.89
gut-ache 5.27.9
Gutenberg 7.12.3
Guthrie 9.19.91
gutless 2.54.52
guts 20.48
gutsy 9.20.39
gutta 2.22.56
gutted 10.2.33
gutter 2.22.56
guttering 10.42.118
gutter press 6.47.7
guttural 2.37.236
guv 20.51
guvnor 2.15.6
guy 11.0
Guyana 2.15.7
Guyanese 9.59.7
Guy Fawkes 14.25
Guy Fawkes Night
    11.36.14
Guys and Dolls 13.17
guzzle 2.37.305

Gwent 6.34.7
Gwyneth 6.53
gym 10.26
gymkhana 2.15.8
gymnasium 2.40.19
gymnast 1.38
gymnastic 10.12.78
gymnastics 10.13.18
gymnosophy 9.9.11
gymnosperm 7.18.2
gymslip 10.47.2
gynaecological
    2.37.159
gynaecologist 10.53.4
gynaecology 9.12.9
gynarchy 9.13.2
gynocracy 9.20.10
gyp 10.47
gyppy tummy 9.15.16
gypsum 2.40.33
gypsy 9.20.37
gyrate 5.47.51
gyration 2.43.192
gyratory 9.19.43
gyro 19.15
gyroscope 19.44.1
ha 3.6
haar 3.6
Haarlem 2.40.25
habanera 2.19.7
habeas corpus 2.54.93
haberdasher 2.21.1
haberdashery 9.19.2
habit 10.56.3
habitable 2.37.68
habitat 1.41.10
habitation 2.43.209
habit-forming
    10.42.88
habitual 2.37.21
habitually 9.14.5
habituate 5.47.9
habituated 10.2.39
habitué 5.0
hacek 6.10.7
hacienda 2.6.20
hack 1.10
hacker 2.12.1
hackle 2.37.148
hackles 2.39.4
Hackney 9.16.27
hackney carriage
    10.11.14
hackneyed 9.29.4
hacksaw 14.13
hacktivism 2.40.89
had 1.3
haddock 2.35
Hades 9.59.2
Hadith 10.58
hadj 1.9, 3.26
hadn't 2.47.7
Hadrian 2.43.15

Hadrian's Wall 14.27.11
hadron 13.22.12
hadrosaur 14.13.1
haematite 11.36.21
haematology 9.12.16
haematoma 2.14.16
haemoglobin 10.31.2
haemophilia 2.1.8
haemophiliac 1.10.1
haemorrhage 10.11.15
haemorrhoids 18.6
hafnium 2.40.9
hag 1.6
haggard 2.33.6
haggis 10.50
haggle 2.37.136
haggler 2.13.29
haggling 10.42.62
hagiography 9.9.4
hagiology 9.12.5
hag-ridden 2.43.38
Hague 5.25
hah 3.6
ha-ha 3.6
hahnium 2.40.9
Haifa 2.8.3
haiku 22.5
hail 5.30
hailstone 19.40.18
hailstorm 14.33.4
hair 4.4
hairband 1.22.1
hairbrush 20.45.3
haircare 4.6
haircut 20.47.2
hairdo 22.2
hairdresser 2.20.4
hairdresser's 2.60
hairdryer 12.4
hairgrip 10.47.4
hairless 2.54.35
hairline 11.27.3
hairnet 6.51.5
hair of the dog 13.7.1
hairpiece 9.49.3
hairpin 10.31.18
hairpin bend 6.30.1
hair's-breadth 6.2
hair shirt 7.28.4
hairsplitting 10.42.157
hairstyle 11.22.8
hair-trigger 2.9.7
hairy 9.19.59
Haiti 9.22.59
Haitian 2.43.138
Haitink 10.43
hajj 1.9
hajji 9.12
hakam 1.18.3
hake 5.27
hakeem 9.41.2
hakim 9.41.2

Hal 1.13
halal 1.13, 3.30
halberd 7.10.1
halcyon 2.43.23
haldi 9.7.18
hale 5.30
Haley 9.14.32
half 3.23.1
half-and-half 3.23.1
half-asleep 9.47.1
half-awake 5.27.11
halfback 1.10.3
half-baked 5.29
half-breed 9.29.6
half-brother 2.7.4
half-caste 3.47.2
half-cocked 13.12
half-cooked 21.6
half-cut 20.47.2
half-dark 3.27
half-day 5.3
half-done 20.29.1
half-finished 10.55.3
half-hardy 9.7.5
half-hearted 2.33.20, 10.2.36
half-holiday 5.3
half-hour 17.0
half-life 11.17.1
half-light 11.36.9
halfling 10.42.58
half-mast 3.47
halfpenny 9.16
half-pint 11.29
half-price 11.34.2
half-seas over 2.25.16
half-sister 2.22.99
half-slip 10.47.2
half-starved 3.55
half-time 11.25.3
halftone 19.40.14
half-truth 22.36.1
halfway 5.17
halfwit 10.56.36
half-yearly 9.14.35, 9.14.36
halibut 2.56.5
Halifax 1.11.1
halitosis 10.50.20
hall 14.27.6
Hallam 2.40.25
Halle 2.13.1
hallelujah 2.11
Halley 9.14.1, 9.14.45
hallmark 3.27.4
hallmarked 3.29
hallo 19.11.2
Hall of Fame 5.33
halloo 22.6
hallow 19.11.1
hallowed 19.23.2
Halloween 9.43
Hallowe'en 9.43.24

hallucinate 5.47.48
hallucination 2.43.187
hallucinatory 9.19.40, 9.19.43
hallucinogen 2.43.53
hallucinogenic 10.12.32
hallway 5.17
halo 19.11
halogen 6.29
halt 14.31
halter 2.22.77
halting 10.42.167
halve 3.54
halved 3.55
halves 3.56
halyard 3.21.3
ham 1.18
hamadryad 1.3
Hamas 1.36.3
Hamburg 7.12.2
hamburger 2.9.3
ham-fisted 10.2.92
ham-handed 10.2.18
Hamilton 2.43.305
Hamish 10.54.13
Hamlet 2.56.12
hammer 2.14.2
hammered 2.33.11
hammerhead 6.1.5
hammerhead shark 3.27.6
hammering 10.42.113
Hammersmith 10.58.1
Hammerstein 11.27.18
Hammett 2.56.23
hammock 2.35
Hammond 2.44.9
hammy 9.15.1
Hampden 2.43.30
hamper 2.18.17
hampered 2.33.14
Hampshire 2.21
Hampstead 6.1.16
Hampton 2.43.311
hamster 2.22.89
hamstring 10.42.131
hamstrung 20.36.2
Han 1.21
Hancock 13.10.2
hand 1.22.2
handbag 1.6.1
handbasin 2.43.116
handbell 6.14.1
handbill 10.17.1
handbrake 5.27.7
handcart 3.49.3
handclap 1.33.2
handclasp 3.45
handcraft 3.24.2
handcrafted 10.2.33
handcuff 20.4.1
handcuffs 20.5

Handel 2.37.119
handful 21.7.1
hand grenade 5.21.6
handgun 20.29.2
handhold 19.35.3
handicap 1.33.1
handicapped 1.35
handicraft 3.24.2
handily 9.14.39
handiness 2.54.66
hand-in-glove 20.51.2
hand-in-hand 1.22.2
handiwork 7.14.4
handkerchief 10.6.4
handle 2.37.119
handlebar 3.2
handlebars 3.58
handler 2.13.28
handling 10.42.79
handmade 5.21.5
handmaid 5.21.5
handmaiden 2.43.33
handoff 13.5.1
handout 16.16.2
handover 2.25.17
hand-pick 10.12.39
handpicked 10.14
handrail 5.30.6
handsaw 14.13
handset 6.51.11
handshake 5.27.8
hands-off 13.5
handsome 2.40.36
hands-on 13.22.17
handspike 11.19.2
handspring 10.42.130
handstand 1.22.7
hand-to-hand 1.22.2
hand-to-mouth 16.18
handwork 7.14.5
handwriting 10.42.158
handwritten 2.43.298
handy 9.7.20
handyman 1.21.6
hang 1.28
hangar 2.16
hangdog 13.7.1
hang draw and quarter 2.22.54
hanger 2.16
hanger-on 13.22.13
hang fire 12.1
hang glide 11.14.10
hang-glider 2.6.6
hanging 10.42
hanging judge 20.9.1
hangman 2.43.79
hangnail 5.30.5
hangout 16.16
hangover 2.25.16
Hang Seng index 6.11.1
hang-up 20.40

hollow 19.11.7
Holloway 5.17.1
hollow-cheeked 9.37
hollowly 9.14.47
holly 9.14.44
hollyhock 13.10
Hollywood 21.0.6
holm 19.38
Holmes 19.39
holmium 2.40.8
holocaust 14.43
Holocene 9.43.16
hologram 1.18.7
holograph 3.23.3
holography 9.9.6
hols 13.17
Holstein 11.27.18
holster 2.22.89
Holy Bible 2.37.93
Holy City 9.22.64
Holy Communion 2.43.62
holy day 5.3.3
Holy Family 9.14.14
Holy Ghost 19.46
Holy Grail 5.30.6
Holyhead 6.1.4
Holy Island 2.44.6
Holyoake 19.31
Holy Office 10.50.3
holy of holies 9.59.3
Holy Roman Empire 12.3
Holyrood House 16.14.3
Holy Spirit 10.56.31
holy terror 2.19.9
Holy Trinity 9.22.29
holy water 2.22.53
Holy Writ 10.56.29
homage 10.11.8
hombre 5.12
homburg 7.12.2
home 19.38.1
home and hosed 19.53
home banking 10.42.55
homebody 9.7.14
homebound 16.11.1
homeboy 18.1
home-brew 22.10
homebuyer 12.0
homecoming 10.42.90
Home Counties 9.59.15
home economics 10.13.5
homegirl 7.16.1
home ground 16.11.7
homegrown 19.40.12
Home Guard 3.21.2
home help 6.18
homeland 1.22.3

homeless 2.54.46
homely 9.14.70
homemade 5.21.5
homemaker 2.12.6
Home Office 10.50.3
homeopath 1.43
homeopathic 10.12.87
homeopathy 9.23.2
homeostasis 10.50.17
homeostatic 10.12.55
homeowner 2.15.22
homepage 5.26.2
home plate 5.47.39
Homer 2.14.16
home rule 22.22.6
homeschool 22.22.4
Home Secretary 9.19.42
homesick 10.12.53
homespun 20.29
homestay 5.15.1
homestead 6.1.16
home visit 10.56.39
homeward 2.33.25
homework 7.14.2
homeworker 2.12.9
homey 9.15.15
homicidal 2.37.112
homicide 11.14.20
homiletic 10.12.64
homily 9.14.38
homing 10.42.84
homing pigeon 2.43.56
hominid 10.2.28
hominy 9.16.7
homo 19.12
homoeopathic 10.12.87
homoeopathy 9.23.2
homogeneity 9.22.3
homogeneous 2.54.7
homogenise 11.42.19
homogenised 11.43.2
homograph 3.23.3
homographic 10.12.9
homologous 2.54.27
homology 9.12.10
homonym 10.26.1
homonymic 10.12.26
homonymy 9.15.13
homophile 11.22.2
homophobe 19.22.1
homophobia 2.1.2
homophobic 10.12.5
homophone 19.40.3
homophonic 10.12.35
homophony 9.16.3
Homo sapiens 6.40
homosexual 2.37.20
homozygous 2.54.26
honcho 19.19
Honduran 2.43.110
Honduras 2.54.96

hone 19.40
honed 19.41
honest 10.53.12
honestly 9.14.95
honest to God 13.2.1
honest-to-goodness 2.54.75
honesty 9.22.88
honey 9.16.26
honeybee 9.6.4
honeycomb 19.38.2
honeydew 22.4.1
honeydew melon 2.43.76
honeyeater 2.22.26
honeyed 9.29.4
honeymoon 22.27
honeymoon suite 9.52.15
honeypot 13.39.5
honeysuckle 2.37.186
honey-tongued 20.37
hongi 9.17
Hong Kong 13.27
honied 10.2.28
Honiton 2.43.296
honk 13.29
honky 9.13.20
honky-tonk 13.29
Honolulu 22.6
honorarium 2.40.14
honorary 9.19.31
honorific 10.12.10
honour 2.15.20
honourable 2.37.52
honourable discharge 3.26.1
honoured 2.33.12
honours 2.60.5
Honours List 10.53.6
Hons 13.26
Honshu 22.12
hooch 22.37
hood 21.0.2
hooded 10.2.15
hoodie 9.7.17
hoodlum 2.40.25
hoodoo 22.2
hoodwink 10.43
hoody 9.7.17
hooey 9.5
hoof 22.19
hoo-hah 3.6
hook 21.4.3
hookah 2.12.22
Hooke 21.4.3
hooked 21.6
hooker 2.12.22
Hook of Holland 2.44.4
hookup 20.40.2
hookworm 7.18.4
hooky 9.13.15

hooligan 2.43.49
hooliganism 2.40.71
hoop 22.29
hoopla 3.9
hooray 5.12
hoot 22.34
hooter 2.22.59
Hoover 2.25.24
hop 13.31.1
hopalong 13.27.2
hope 19.44
hope chest 6.49.11
hopeful 2.37.121
hopefully 9.14.9
hopeless 2.54.50
hopelessly 9.14.83
hophead 6.1.4
Hopkins 10.41.1
Hopkinson 2.43.133
hopper 2.18.11
hopping 10.42.110
hopscotch 13.42
Horace 2.54.96
horde 14.19
horehound 16.11.3
horizon 2.43.327
horizontal 2.37.282
horizontally 9.14.26
Horlicks 10.13.2
hormonal 2.37.220
hormone 19.40.8
horn 14.35.2
hornbill 10.17.1
Hornby 9.6
horned 10.2.28, 14.36
hornet 10.56.23
Horniman 2.43.79
horn of plenty 9.22.82
hornpipe 11.31.1
hornswoggle 2.37.139
horny 9.16.21
horologe 13.9
horology 9.12.14
horoscope 19.44.1
horoscopy 9.18.3
Horowitz 10.57
horrendous 2.54.24
horrible 2.37.50
horribly 9.14.51
horrid 10.2.30
horrific 10.12.10
horrification 2.43.160
horrified 11.14.5
horrify 11.3.5
horrifying 10.42.6
Horrocks 2.36
horror 2.19
horror story 9.19.67
horror-struck 20.10.4
hors de combat 3.2
hors d'oeuvre 7.32
horse 14.42.2
horseback 1.10.3

humongous 2.54.28
humoresque 6.48
humorist 10.53.17
humorous 2.54.101
humour 2.14.20
humourless 2.54.37
hump 20.26
humpback 1.10.3
humpback whale 5.30.11
humph 20.25
Humphrey 9.19.74
Humphreys 9.59.11
Humphries 10.62.2
humpy 9.18.14
humus 2.54.57, 21.12
Humvee 9.25
Hun 20.29
hunch 20.34
hunchback 1.10.3
hundred 2.33.17
hundredfold 19.35.1
hundreds 2.34
hundreds-and-thousands 2.50
hundredweight 5.47.69
hung 20.36
Hungarian 2.43.16
Hungary 9.19.13
hunger 2.9.14
hungover 2.25.16
hungry 9.19.75
hung-up 20.40
hunk 20.38
hunker 2.12.26
hunky 9.13.21
hunky-dory 9.19.66
hunt 20.33.1
hunted 10.2.81
hunter 2.22.85
hunter's moon 22.27
hunting 10.42.168
Huntley 9.14.92
huntress 2.54.111
huntsman 2.43.99
hurdle 2.37.105
hurdler 2.13.28
hurdles 2.39
hurdy-gurdy 9.7.8
hurl 7.16
Hurley 9.14.35
hurling 10.42.71
hurly-burly 9.14.35
hurrah 3.13
hurray 5.12
hurricane 2.43.70, 5.35.3
hurricane lamp 1.20.2
hurried 9.29.6
hurriedly 9.14.58
hurry 9.19.70
hurt 7.28
hurtful 2.37.130

hurting 10.42.154
hurtle 2.37.275
husband 2.44
husbandman 2.43.95
husbandry 9.19.73
hush 20.45
hushed 20.46
hush-hush 20.45
hush puppies 9.59.9
husk 20.43
husky 9.13.22
Huss 20.42
Hussain 5.35
hussar 3.19
hussy 9.20
hustings 10.46.6
hustle 2.37.253
hustler 2.13.32
Huston 2.43.312
hut 20.47
hutch 20.49
Hutchinson 2.43.133
Hutton 2.43.302
Huxley 9.14.80
huzzah 3.19
hyacinth 10.40
hybrid 10.2.30
hybridise 11.42.1
Hyde 11.14.9
Hyde Park 3.27.5
Hyderabad 1.3.1
hydra 2.19.16
hydrangea 2.10.8
hydrant 2.47.74
hydrate 5.47.58
hydrated 10.2.51
hydraulic 10.12.16
hydraulics 10.13.2
hydro 19.15
hydrocarbon 2.43.28
hydrocephalus 2.54.37
hydrochloric acid 10.2.32
hydrocortisone 19.40.19
hydrodynamic 10.12.23
hydrodynamics 10.13.4
hydroelectric 10.12.49
hydrofoil 18.8.1
hydrogen 2.43.53
hydrogenated 10.2.48
hydrogen peroxide 11.14.24
hydrography 9.9.3
hydrology 9.12.14
hydrolysis 10.50.14
hydrometer 2.22.39
hydrometric 10.12.51
hydropathy 9.23.2
hydrophobia 2.1.2
hydrophobic 10.12.5

hydroplane 5.35.5
hydroponic 10.12.34
hydroponics 10.13.7
hydrostatic 10.12.55
hydrostatics 10.13.13
hydrotherapy 9.18.5
hydroxide 11.14.24
hyena 2.15.12
hygienic 10.12.33
hygienist 10.53.12
hygrometer 2.22.39
hymen 6.29.2
hymn 10.26
hymnal 2.37.195
hymnary 9.19.21
hymnody 9.7.3
hymnography 9.9.8
hymnology 9.12.11
hype 11.31
hyped 11.33
hyper 2.18.9
hyperactive 10.61.40
hyperbaric 10.12.43
hyperbola 2.13.2
hyperbole 9.14.6
hypercorrection 2.43.269
hypercritical 2.37.179
hyperglycaemia 2.1.10
hyperinflation 2.43.173
Hyperion 2.43.20
hyperlink 10.43.1
hypermarket 10.56.13
hypermedia 2.1.3
hypernym 10.26.1
hypersensitive 10.61.29
hypersonic 10.12.37
hyperspace 5.45.6
hypertension 2.43.282
hypertext 6.13.1
hypertrophy 9.9.10
hyperventilate 5.47.31
hyphen 2.43.45
hyphenate 5.47.44
Hypnos 13.34
hypnosis 10.50.20
hypnotherapy 9.18.5
hypnotic 10.12.71
hypnotise 11.42.33
hypnotism 2.40.86
hypnotist 10.53.23
hypoallergenic 10.12.32
hypocaust 14.43
hypochondria 2.1.19
hypochondriac 1.10.1
hypocrisy 9.20.10
hypocrite 10.56.29
hypocritical 2.37.179
hypocritically 9.14.69
hypodermic 10.12.25

hypoglycaemia 2.1.10
hyponym 10.26.1
hypotenuse 22.40.1
hypothalamus 2.54.58
hypothermia 2.1.9
hypothesis 10.50.16
hypothesise 11.42.30
hypothetical 2.37.174
hyrax 1.11.3
hyssop 2.52
hysterectomy 9.15.8
hysteria 2.1.25
hysterical 2.37.170
hysterics 10.13.9
I 11.0
i.e. 9.3
Iago 19.6.1
iamb 1.18
iambic 10.12.3
iambic pentameter 2.22.38
Ian 2.43.1
IATA 2.22.4
iatric 10.12.50
Ibadan 2.43.31
I-beam 9.41.1
Iberia 2.1.23
Iberian 2.43.20
ibex 6.11
ibid. 10.2.2
ibidem 6.25.2
ibis 10.50.1
Ibiza 2.23
Ibsen 2.43.124
ibuprofen 6.29
IC 9.20.19
Icarus 2.54.100
ice 11.34
ice age 5.26
ice bag 1.6.1
iceberg 7.12.4
icebound 16.11.1
icebox 13.11.1
icebreaker 2.12.7
ice bucket 10.56.10
icecap 1.33.1
ice-cold 19.35.4
ice cream 9.41.4
iced 11.35
iced coffee 9.9.13
icefall 14.27.3
ice hockey 9.13.10
Iceland 1.22.3, 2.44.4
Icelander 2.6.17
Icelandic 10.12.6
iceman 1.21.8
ice pack 1.10.14
icepick 10.12.39
ice rink 10.43.2
ice shelf 6.16.1
ice skating 10.42.147
ice water 2.22.53
I Ching 10.42.175

inclement 2.47.32
inclination 2.43.183
incline 11.27.8
inclined 11.28.3
in clover 2.25.19
include 22.17.8
including 10.42.23
inclusion 2.43.339
inclusive 10.61.10
inclusively 9.14.98
incognito 19.18.5
incoherence 2.45.25
incoherent 2.47.79
income 20.24.1
incomer 2.14.18
income support 14.44.5
incoming 10.42.90
incommensurate 2.56.34
incommodious 2.54.2
incommunicado 19.4.2
incomparable 2.37.53
incompatibility 9.22.22
incompatible 2.37.63
incompetence 2.45.34
incompetent 2.47.89
incomplete 9.52.5
incompleteness 2.54.88
incomprehensible 2.37.60
incomprehension 2.43.281
incompressible 2.37.58
inconceivable 2.37.81
inconclusive 10.61.10
incongruent 2.47.5
incongruity 9.22.4
incongruous 2.54.17
inconsequence 2.45.40
inconsequential 2.37.266
inconsiderable 2.37.51
inconsiderably 9.14.52
inconsiderate 2.56.35
inconsistency 9.20.35
inconsistent 2.47.92
inconsolable 2.37.40
inconspicuous 2.54.19
inconstancy 9.20.35
inconstant 2.47.90
incontestable 2.37.78
incontinence 2.45.19
incontinent 2.47.70
incontrovertible 2.37.65
inconvenience 2.45.1
inconvenient 2.47.1
inconvertible 2.37.65

incorporate 2.56.37, 5.47.55
incorporation 2.43.200
incorporeal 2.37.10
incorrect 6.12.8
incorrectly 9.14.91
incorrigible 2.37.35
incorruptible 2.37.63
increase 9.49.5
increased 9.50
increasingly 9.14.75
incredible 2.37.31
incredulity 9.22.8
incredulous 2.54.41
increment 2.47.40
incremental 2.37.286
incriminate 5.47.46
incubate 5.47.10
incubator 2.22.9
incubus 2.54.22
inculcate 5.47.19
inculpable 2.37.49
incumbency 9.20.29
incumbent 2.47.6
incur 7.3
incurable 2.37.56
incurious 2.54.13
incursion 2.43.231
incus 2.54.31
indaba 2.5.1
indebted 10.2.33
indecent 2.47.82
indecent assault 14.31.2
indecipherable 2.37.51
indecision 2.43.335
indecisive 10.61.8
indecorous 2.54.100
indecorum 2.40.30
indeed 9.29.1
in deep water 2.22.53
indefatigable 2.37.25
indefensible 2.37.60
indefinable 2.37.43
indefinite 2.56.27
indefinitely 9.14.88
indelible 2.37.40
indelicacy 9.20.4
indelicate 2.56.11
indemnification 2.43.159
indemnify 11.3.4
indemnity 9.22.26
indent 6.34
indentation 2.43.215
indenture 2.24.8
indentured 2.33.23
independence 2.45.8
Independence Day 5.3
independent 2.47.15
in-depth 6.46
indescribable 2.37.30
indestructible 2.37.72

indeterminable 2.37.43
indeterminacy 9.20.7
indeterminate 2.56.31
index 6.11.1
indexation 2.43.207
index-linked 10.45
India 2.1.3, 2.11
Indian 2.43.3
Indiana 2.15.1
Indianapolis 10.50.7
Indian summer 2.14.18
indicate 5.47.23
indication 2.43.157
indicative 10.61.17
indicator 2.22.13
indict 11.36.3
indictable 2.37.69
indictment 2.47.58
indie 9.7.22
indifference 2.45.22
indifferent 2.47.74
indigence 2.45.11
indigenous 2.54.63
indigent 2.47.22
indigestible 2.37.78
indigestion 2.43.318
indignant 2.47.72
indignation 2.43.189
indignity 9.22.26
indirect 6.12.8
indirection 2.43.269
indirectly 9.14.91
indiscernible 2.37.48
indiscipline 10.31.15
indiscreet 9.52.8
indiscretion 2.43.227
indiscriminate 2.56.31
indispensable 2.37.60
indispose 19.52.6
indisposed 19.53.4
indisposition 2.43.249
indisputable 2.37.71
indisputably 9.14.54
indissoluble 2.37.100
indistinct 10.45.1
indistinguishable 2.37.62
indium 2.40.2
individual 2.37.17
individualise 11.42.6
individualism 2.40.57
individualist 10.53.7
individualistic 10.12.82
individuality 9.22.12
individually 9.14.5
individuate 5.47
indivisible 2.37.84
Indochina 2.15.18
indoctrinate 5.47.47
indoctrination 2.43.182
indolent 2.47.28

indomitable 2.37.67
Indonesia 2.1.33, 2.30
Indonesian 2.43.333
indoor 14.2
Indra 2.19.16
indrawn 14.35.5
indubitable 2.37.68
indubitably 9.14.54
induce 22.31.2
inducement 2.47.53
induct 20.12.2
inductee 9.22
induction 2.43.274
inductive 10.61.47
inductor 2.22.73
indulge 20.18
indulgence 2.45.9
indulgent 2.47.19
Indus 2.54.24
industrial 2.37.13
industrialise 11.42.5
industrialised 11.43.1
industrialism 2.40.56
industrialist 10.53.7
Industrial Revolution 2.43.258
industrious 2.54.9
industry 9.19.88
inebriate 2.56.2, 5.47.4
inebriated 10.2.38
inedible 2.37.31
ineffable 2.37.25
ineffective 10.61.43
ineffectual 2.37.22
ineffectuality 9.22.13
inefficiency 9.20.34
inefficient 2.47.87
inelastic 10.12.79
inelasticity 9.22.45
inelegant 2.47.18
ineligible 2.37.34
ineluctable 2.37.72
inept 6.45
ineptitude 22.17.6
inequality 9.22.24
inequitable 2.37.67
inequity 9.22.55
ineradicable 2.37.39
inert 7.28
inertia 2.21
inescapable 2.37.49
inessential 2.37.269
inessentials 2.39
inestimable 2.37.42
inevitability 9.22.22
inevitable 2.37.67
inevitably 9.14.54
inexact 1.12
inexactitude 22.17.6
inexcitable 2.37.69
inexcusable 2.37.86
inexhaustible 2.37.77
inexorable 2.37.51

inorganic 10.12.31
inorganic chemistry 9.19.90
inpatient 2.47.86
input 21.14.1
inquest 6.49.14
inquietude 22.17.4
inquire 12.6.1
inquirer 2.19
inquiring 10.42.126
inquiry 9.19.64
inquisition 2.43.248
inquisitive 10.61.34
inquisitor 2.22.45
inquisitorial 2.37.12
inquorate 5.47.51
in re 9.19
inroad 19.23.5
inrush 20.45.2
insalubrious 2.54.9
ins and outs 16.17
insane 5.35
insanitary 9.19.41
insanity 9.22.27
insatiable 2.37.61
inscribe 11.12.1
inscription 2.43.286
inscrutable 2.37.71
insect 6.12.9
insecticidal 2.37.112
insecticide 11.14.22
insectivore 14.16
insecure 15.1.1
insecurity 9.22.38
inseminate 5.47.46
insemination 2.43.184
insensate 5.47.62
insensibility 9.22.21
insensible 2.37.60
insensitive 10.61.29
insensitively 9.14.99
insensitivity 9.22.53
insentient 2.47.86
inseparable 2.37.53
insert 7.28.3
insertion 2.43.231
in-service 10.50.32
inset 6.51.12
inshallah 2.13.1
inside 11.14.25
inside-out 16.16.2
insider 2.6.7
insider dealing 10.42.72
insider trading 10.42.15
insidious 2.54.3
insight 11.36.19
insightful 2.37.132
insignia 2.1.11
insignificance 2.45
insignificant 2.47.26
insincere 8.8

insincerity 9.22.36
insinuate 5.47.8
insinuated 10.2.39
insinuation 2.43.145
insipid 10.2.29
insist 10.53.20
insistence 2.45.37
insistent 2.47.92
in situ 22.4.12
insobriety 9.22.67
insofar as 1.48
insole 19.34.8
insolence 2.45.15
insolent 2.47.28
insoluble 2.37.100
insolvable 2.37.80
insolvency 9.20.29
insolvent 2.47.93
insomnia 2.1.11
insomniac 1.10.1
insomuch as 1.48
insouciance 2.45.1
insouciant 2.47.1
inspect 6.12.7
inspection 2.43.264
inspector 2.22.70
inspectorate 2.56.39
inspiration 2.43.201
inspirational 2.37.203
inspire 12.3.1
inspired 12.7
inspiring 10.42.126
instability 9.22.22
install 14.27.10
installation 2.43.167
instalment 2.47.46
instance 2.45.35
instant 2.47.90
instantaneous 2.54.6
instantly 9.14.94
instead 6.1.16
instep 6.43.1
instigate 5.47.18
instigation 2.43.154
instigator 2.22.12
instil 10.17.7
instinct 10.45.1
instinctive 10.61.39
instinctual 2.37.18
institution 2.43.256
institutional 2.37.200
institutionalise 11.42.10
institutionalised 11.43.1
in-store 14.15.1
instruct 20.13
instructed 10.2.78
instruction 2.43.275
instructional 2.37.209
instructive 10.61.48
instructor 2.22.65
instrument 2.47.41

instrumental 2.37.286
instrumentalist 10.53.9
instrumentation 2.43.217
insubordinate 2.56.30
insubordination 2.43.182
insubstantial 2.37.265
insufferable 2.37.51
insufficiency 9.20.34
insufficient 2.47.87
insular 2.13.21
insularity 9.22.35
insulate 5.47.32
insulated 10.2.46
insulation 2.43.169
insulator 2.22.15
insulin 10.31.14
insult 20.22
insulting 10.42.167
insultingly 9.14.78
insuperable 2.37.53
insupportable 2.37.63
insurance 2.45.27
insure 15.4
insured 15.6
insurer 2.19.13
insurgence 2.45.10
insurgency 9.20.32
insurgent 2.47.21
insurmountable 2.37.75
insurrection 2.43.269
intact 1.12.5
intaglio 19.2.2
intake 5.27.9
intangible 2.37.36
integer 2.10.4
integral 2.37.230
integrate 5.47.59
integrated 10.2.51
integration 2.43.203
integrator 2.22.17
integrity 9.22.32
integument 2.47.41
intellect 6.12.3
intellectual 2.37.22
intellectualise 11.42.6
intellectuality 9.22.13
intelligence 2.45.11
intelligent 2.47.22
intelligentsia 2.1.27
intelligible 2.37.34
intemperance 2.45.23
intemperate 2.56.37
intend 6.30.9
intendant 2.47.16
intended 10.2.20
intense 6.33
intensely 9.14.80
intensification 2.43.161
intensifier 12.1.3

intensify 11.3.7
intensity 9.22.49
intensive 10.61.13
intent 6.34.5
intention 2.43.282
intentional 2.37.211
inter 7.6
interact 1.12.3
interaction 2.43.260
interactive 10.61.40
inter alia 2.1.6
inter alios 13.34
interbred 6.1.13
interbreed 9.29.6
intercede 9.29.7
intercept 6.45.1
interceptor 2.22.88
intercession 2.43.230
intercessor 2.20.5
interchange 5.37
interchangeable 2.37.36
interchanged 5.39
intercity 9.22.64
intercollegiate 2.56
intercom 13.18.2
intercommunicate 5.47.25
interconnect 6.12.6
interconnected 10.2.74
interconnection 2.43.264
interconnector 2.22.68
intercontinental 2.37.284
intercostal 2.37.287
intercourse 14.42.3
intercut 20.47.2
interdenominational 2.37.202
interdepartmental 2.37.286
interdepend 6.30.4
interdependent 2.47.15
interdict 10.14.1
interdiction 2.43.272
interest 2.55.1
interestingly 9.14.78
interface 5.45.2
interfacing 10.42.134
interfaith 5.49
interfere 8.0
interference 2.45.25
interfering 10.42.123
interferon 13.22.12
intergenerational 2.37.203
intergovernmental 2.37.286
interim 10.26.2
interior 2.1.24
interior decoration 2.43.193

jangly 9.14.64
janitor 2.22.40
January 9.19.5
Janus 2.54.62
Japan 1.21.11
Japanese 9.59.8
jape 5.42
Japlish 10.54.9
japonica 2.12.13
jar 3.7
jardinière 4.1, 4.5
Jared 6.1.12
jargon 2.43.46
jarring 10.42.112
Jarvis 10.50.31
jasmine 10.31.16
Jason 2.43.116
jasper 2.18
jaundice 10.50.2
jaundiced 10.53.2
jaunt 14.38
jaunty 9.22.80
Java 2.25, 2.25.2
Javanese 9.59.8
javelin 10.31.12
Jawan 3.34.4
jawbone 19.40.1
jawline 11.27.3
jay 5.6
jaybird 7.10.1
Jayne 5.35
jaywalk 14.24.4
jaywalking 10.42.52
jazz 1.48
jazz band 1.22.1
jazz-funk 20.38
jazzy 9.27
JCB 9.6.4
jealous 2.54.35
jealously 9.14.83
jealousy 9.20.5
jeans 9.46
Jeb 6.0
Jeep 9.47
jeer 8.0
jeering 10.42.123
Jeeves 9.58
jeez 9.59
Jefferson 2.43.114
Jeffrey 9.19.74
Jeffreys 10.62.2
Jehovah 2.25.16
Jehovah's Witness
2.54.89
jejune 22.27
jejunum 2.40.27
Jekyll and Hyde
11.14.9
jell 6.14
jelled 6.15
jellied 9.29.3
jelly 9.14.33
jellybean 9.43.1

jellyfish 10.54.5
Jem 6.25
Jemima 2.14.13
jemmy 9.15.11
Jen 6.29
je ne sais quoi 3.18
Jenkins 10.41.1
Jenner 2.15.10
Jennifer 2.8.2
jenny 9.16.14
jeopardise 11.42.1
jeopardy 9.7.2
jerboa 2.3.1
jeremiad 12.7
Jeremiah 12.0
Jeremy 9.15.2
jerk 7.14
jerkin 10.31.8
jerky 9.13.6
jeroboam 2.40
Jerome 19.38.3
Jerry 9.19.60
jerry-built 10.22.1
jerrycan 1.21.1
jerry-rigged 10.9
jersey 9.27
Jerusalem 2.40.25
Jess 6.47
Jessica 2.12.11
Jessie 9.20.15
jest 6.49.2
jester 2.22.94
Jesuit 10.56.1
Jesus 2.54
Jesus Christ 11.35
jet 6.51
jet-black 1.10.11
jeté 5.15
jetfoil 18.8.1
Jethro 19.15.9
jet lag 1.6.2
jet-lagged 1.7
jet-propelled 6.15
jetsam 2.40.33
jet set 6.51.10
Jet Ski 9.13.22
jettison 2.43.120
jetty 9.22.60
Jew 22.0
jewel 2.37.17
jewelled 2.38
jeweller 2.13.2
jewellery 9.19.77
Jewess 6.47
Jewish 10.54
Jewry 9.19.68
Jew's harp 3.42
Jezebel 6.14.1
JFK 5.7
jib 10.0
jibberish 10.54.18
jibe 11.12
Jiddah 2.6.5

jiff 10.6
jiffy 9.9.12
jig 10.8
jigger 2.9.5
jiggery-pokery 9.19.16
jiggle 2.37.138
jigsaw 14.13
jihad 1.3
jilbab 1.1
Jilly 9.14.38
jilt 10.22
Jim 10.26
Jimmy 9.15.13
Jimmy Choo 22.14
Jinan 1.21.10
jingle 2.37.144
jingo 19.6.6
jingoism 2.40.48
jingoist 10.53
jingoistic 10.12.80
jink 10.43
jinn 10.31.6
jinni 9.16.18
jinx 10.44
jism 2.40.52
jitterbug 20.7.1
jitters 2.60.7
jittery 9.19.44
jive 11.38
jiver 2.25.14
jo 19.8
Joachim 9.41.2
Joan 19.40
Job 19.22
jobber 2.5.5
jobbing 10.42.13
jobby 9.6.5
Jobcentre 2.22.81
jobless 2.54.35
Jobs 13.1
jobseeker 2.12.10
Jobseeker's
Allowance 2.36
job-share 4.12
job-sharing 10.42.121
jobsworth 7.30.2
Jocelyn 10.31.12
jock 13.10
jockey 9.13.10
Jockey Club 20.0.1
jockey shorts 14.45
jockstrap 1.33.6
jocose 19.45.1
jocular 2.13.24
jocularity 9.22.35
jocund 2.44.2
jodhpurs 2.60.6
Jodie 9.7
Jodrell Bank 1.30.1
Joe 19.8
Joe Bloggs 13.8
Joel 19.34
Joe Public 10.12.16

joey 9.4
jog 13.7
jogger 2.9.8
joggers 2.60.2
jogging 10.42.35
joggle 2.37.139
Johannesburg 7.12.4
john dory 9.19.66
Johns 13.26
Johnson 2.43.134
Johnston 2.43.312
John the Baptist
10.53.22
John Thomas 2.54.57
joie de vivre 2.19.24
join 18.11.1
joiner 2.15
joinery 9.19.21
joining 10.42.92
joint 18.12
jointed 10.2.88
jointly 9.14.92
joint stock 13.10.8
joist 18.15
joke 19.31
joker 2.12.20
jokey 9.13.12
joking 10.42.53
jol 13.13
Jolie 9.14.47
jollification 2.43.158
jollity 9.22.24
jolly 9.14.44
Jolson 2.43.129
jolt 19.36
Jonah 2.15.22
Jonas 2.54.74
Jonathan 2.43.315
Jones 19.43
Joneses 10.62.7
jongleur 7.4
jonquil 10.17.9
Jonson 2.43.134
Joplin 10.31.15
Jordan 2.43.41
Jordanian 2.43.11
Joseph 10.6
Joséphine 9.43
josh 13.37
joshing 10.42.140
Joshua 2.4.1
Josiah 12.0
joss 13.34
joss stick 10.12.77
jostle 2.37.252
jot 13.39
jotter 2.22.49
jottings 10.46.6
joule 22.22
journal 2.37.212
journalese 9.59.4
journalism 2.40.59
journalistic 10.12.82

limpid **10.2.29**
linchpin **10.31.18**
Lincoln **2.43.63**
Lincoln red **6.1.12**
Lincolnshire **2.21**
linctus **2.54.133**
Linda **2.6.23**
Lindbergh **7.12**
linden **2.43.43**
Lindisfarne **3.34**
Lindsay **9.27.10**
line **11.27.3**
lineage **10.11**
lineal **2.37.4**
lineament **2.47.33**
linear **2.1.15**
linebacker **2.12.1**
lined **11.28.3**
line judge **20.9.1**
linen **10.31.17**
line of credit **10.56.5**
line-out **16.16.6**
line printer **2.22.83**
liner **2.15.19**
lines **11.30**
linesman **2.43.105**
lineup **20.40.6**
ling **10.42.58**
linger **2.9.12**
lingerie **9.19.2**
lingering **10.42.117**
lingo **19.6.6**
lingua **2.26**
lingua franca **2.12.24**
lingual **2.37.297**
linguist **10.53.27**
linguistic **10.12.80**
linguistics **10.13.19**
liniment **2.47.33**
lining **10.42.101**
link **10.43.1**
linkage **10.11.4**
linked **10.45**
linkrot **13.39.7**
links **10.44**
linkup **20.40.2**
Linnaean **2.43.12**
Linnaeus **2.54, 2.54.5**
linnet **2.56.29,**
 10.56.25
lino **19.13**
linocut **20.47.2**
linoleum **2.40.5**
linseed **9.29.7**
lint **10.38.1**
lintel **2.37.282**
Linux **20.11**
Linz **10.37**
lion **12.9**
Lionel **2.37.197**
lioness **6.47.3**
lionhearted **10.2.36**
lion-hearted **2.33.20**

lionise **11.42.19**
lion's share **4.12**
lion tamer **2.14.9**
lip **10.47.1**
lipid **10.2.29**
lipoic acid **10.2.32**
lipoprotein **9.43.18**
liposuction **2.43.274**
Lippi **9.18.8**
Lippizaner **2.15.7**
lippy **9.18.8**
lip-read **9.29.6**
lip-reading **10.42.17**
lip salve **1.17**
lip service **10.50.32**
lipstick **10.12.77**
lip-sync **10.43**
Lipton **2.43.310**
liquefaction **2.43.261**
liquefy **11.3.1**
liqueur **15.1.1**
liquid **10.2.95**
liquidate **5.47.12**
liquidated **10.2.40**
liquidation **2.43.149**
liquidator **2.22.11**
liquid-crystal display
 5.8.3
liquidise **11.42.1**
liquidiser **2.27.5**
liquidity **9.22.7**
liquor **2.12.12**
liquorice **10.50.12,**
 10.54.18
lira **2.19.10**
Lisbon **2.43.27**
lisp **10.52**
lissom **2.40.33**
list **10.53.6**
listed **10.2.92**
listed building
 10.42.24
listen **2.43.120**
listenable **2.37.44**
listener **2.15.2**
Lister **2.22.96**
listeria **2.1.25**
listing **10.42.170**
listless **2.54.52**
list price **11.34.2**
listserv **7.32.1**
Liszt **10.53.6**
lit **10.56.19**
litany **9.16.11**
litas **3.43**
lite **11.36.6**
literacy **9.20.9**
literae humaniores
 9.59.10
literal **2.37.236**
literally **9.14.20**
literary **9.19.31**
literate **2.56.38**

literati **9.22.58**
literature **2.24.2**
lithe **11.16**
lithesome **2.40.33**
lithic **10.12.88**
lithium **2.40.1**
lithograph **3.23.3**
lithography **9.9.3**
Lithuania **2.1.12**
Lithuanian **2.43.11**
litigant **2.47.18**
litigate **5.47.18**
litigation **2.43.154**
litigator **2.22.12**
litigious **2.54.29**
litmus **2.54.57**
litmus paper **2.18.3**
litmus test **6.49.10**
litotes **9.59.13**
litre **2.22.28**
litter **2.22.37**
litterbug **20.7.1**
little **2.37.276**
little angel **2.37.146**
little boys' room
 22.25.3
Little Corporal
 2.37.235
little toe **19.18.8**
Littleton **2.43.304**
Littlewood **21.0.6**
littoral **2.37.236**
liturgical **2.37.158**
liturgy **9.12.1**
live (adv, adj) **11.38**
live (verb) **10.61.1**
liveable **2.37.80**
Live Aid **5.21.12**
lived-in **10.31.3**
live-in **10.31.31**
live-in lover **2.25.23**
livelihood **21.0.2**
liveliness **2.54.67**
livelong **13.27.1**
lively **9.14.97**
liven **2.43.324**
liver **2.25.12**
liveried **9.29.6**
liverish **10.54.18**
Liverpool **22.22.5**
Liverpudlian **2.43.6**
liverwurst **7.27**
livery **9.19.56**
livery company
 9.16.10
liveryman **2.43.85**
lives **11.40**
livestock **13.10.8**
livid **10.2.94**
living **10.42.176**
living in clover **2.25.19**
Livingstone **2.43.312**
living wage **5.26**

Livy **9.25.6**
lizard **2.33.26**
Ljubljana **2.15.7**
llama **2.14.6**
Llandaff **1.5**
Llandudno **19.13**
Llewellyn **10.31.11**
Lloyd **18.5.1**
Lloyd George **14.23**
Lloyd's **18.6**
lo **19.11**
load **19.23.2**
loaded **10.2.13**
loading **10.42.14**
loads **19.24**
loadsa **2.27**
loadsamoney **9.16.7**
loadstone **19.40.17**
loaf **19.28**
loafer **2.8.4**
loam **19.38**
loamy **9.15.15**
loan **19.40.5**
loanback **1.10.3**
loanee **9.16.24**
loaner **2.15.23**
loan shark **3.27.6**
loanword **7.10.5**
loath **19.49**
loathe **19.25**
loathed **19.26**
loathing **10.42.31**
loathsome **2.40.33**
lob **13.0**
lobby **9.6.5**
lobbying **10.42.3**
lobbyist **10.53.1**
lobe **19.22**
lobelia **2.1.6**
lobola **2.13**
lobotomise **11.42.16**
lobotomy **9.15.7**
lobster **2.22.89**
lobster newburg **7.12**
local **2.37.185**
locale **3.30**
localisation **2.43.225**
localise **11.42.4**
localised **11.43.1**
locality **9.22.14**
locally **9.14.12**
locate **5.47.19**
located **10.2.42**
location **2.43.155**
locative **10.61.18**
loch **13.10.3, 13.44**
Loch Lomond **2.44.9**
Loch Ness **6.47.3**
Loch Ness monster
 2.22.107
Loch Tay **5.15**
lock **13.10.3**
Locke **13.10.3**

lover 2.25.23
lover boy 18.1
loveseat 9.52.11
lovesick 10.12.53
love story 9.19.67
loveworthy 9.8.1
lovey 9.25.7
lovey-dovey 9.25.7
loving 10.42.176
loving cup 20.40.2
loving kindness
2.54.77
lovingly 9.14.75
low 19.11
lowborn 14.35.1
low-bred 6.1.13
lowbrow 16.5
low-budget 10.56.8
low-cal 1.13.1
Low Church 7.31
low-cost 13.36.1
low-cut 20.47.2
low-definition
2.43.243
low-density 9.22.49
lowdown 16.10.2
Lowe 19.11
Lowell 15.7
lower 2.3.3, 17.1
lowest 2.55
Lowestoft 13.6
low-fat 1.41.2
low frequency 9.20.36
low-hanging fruit
22.34.10
low-key 9.13.12
lowland 1.22.3
lowlands 2.50.1
low-level 2.37.292
lowlife 11.17.1
lowlights 11.37.1
lowly 9.14.47
low-lying 10.42.7
low-maintenance
2.45.18
low-necked 6.12.6
lowpaid 5.21.7
low-pitched 10.60
low point 18.12
low-pressure 2.21.3
low-price 11.34.2
low profile 11.22.2
low-quality 9.22.24
low-resolution
2.43.257
low-rise 11.42.21
Lowry 9.19.69
low-slung 20.36.1
low spirits 10.57.1
low-tech 6.10.6
low technology
9.12.13
low tide 11.14.26

low water 2.22.53
low-water mark 3.27.4
lox 13.11
loyal 2.37.15
loyalist 10.53.7
loyalty 9.22.79
Loyola 2.13.18
lozenge 10.33
LP 9.18
L plate 5.47.39
LSD 9.7
Luanda 2.6.18
lube 22.16
lubricant 2.47.26
lubricate 5.47.26
lubricator 2.22.13
lubricious 2.54.124
Luca 2.12.23
Lucan 2.43.63
Lucas 2.54.33
Lucerne 7.20.2
lucid 10.2.31
Lucifer 2.8.2
luck 20.10.2
luckily 9.14.38
luckless 2.54.45
Lucknow 16.0
lucky 9.13.14
lucrative 10.61.24
lucre 2.12.23
Lucretia 2.21
Lucretius 2.54.116
Lucullus 2.54.35
Lucy 9.20.22
Luddite 11.36.3
ludicrous 2.54.96
Ludmila 2.13.9
ludo 19.4.4
luff 20.4.2
lug 20.7.2
Lugano 19.13.1
luge 22.42
luggage 10.11.3
luggage van 1.21.16
lughole 19.34.3
lugubrious 2.54.9
Luigi 9.12.19
Luke 22.21
lukewarm 14.33
lull 20.14
lullaby 11.2
Lulu 22.6
lumbago 19.6.2
lumbar 2.5.12
lumbar puncture
2.24.6
lumber 2.5.12
lumbering 10.42.114
lumberjack 1.10.8
lumen 10.31.16
luminary 9.19.28
luminescence 2.45.29
luminosity 9.22.46

luminous 2.54.72
lummox 2.36
lump 20.26.2
lumpectomy 9.15.8
lumpen 2.43.108
lumpish 10.54.16
lumpy 9.18.14
Luna 2.15.25
lunacy 9.20.7
lunar 2.15.25
lunar eclipse 10.48
lunatic 10.12.63
lunch 20.34
lunchbox 13.11.1
luncheon 2.43.316
lunchtime 11.25.3
lung 20.36.1
lunge 20.31
lungi 9.10.7
Lupercalia 2.1.7
lupin 10.31.18
lupine 10.31.18
lupus 2.54.93
lurch 7.31
lure 15.1
Lurex 6.11.5
lurgy 9.10
lurid 10.2.30
lurk 7.14
Lusaka 2.12.4
luscious 2.54.116
lush 20.45.1
lusophone 19.40.3
lust 20.44.4
lustful 2.37.133
lustily 9.14.42
lustiness 2.54.69
lustral 2.37.246
lustration 2.43.205
lustre 2.22.105
lustreless 2.54.37
lustrous 2.54.112
lusty 9.22.89
lute 22.34.7
lutetium 2.40.37, 8.0
Luther 2.23
Lutheran 2.43.110
Luton 2.43.288
Lutyens 2.51
luv 20.51.1
luvvie 9.25.7
Luxembourg 7.12.2
Luxemburg 7.12.2
luxuriance 2.45.3
luxuriant 2.47.4
luxuriate 5.47.4
luxuries 9.59.10
luxurious 2.54.13
luxury 9.19.2
lycée 5.13
Lyceum 2.40.17
lychee 9.24, 9.24.3
lychgate 5.47.14

Lycra 2.19.18
Lydia 2.1.3
Lydian 2.43.5
lying 10.42.7
lying-in 10.31
Lymington 2.43.308
lymph 10.28
lymphatic 10.12.55
lymph node 19.23.4
lymphocyte 11.36.20
lymphoma 2.14.16
lynch 10.39
lynch law 14.8
lynchpin 10.31.18
lynx 10.44
Lyons 13.28
Lyra 2.19
lyre 12.2
lyrebird 7.10.2
lyric 10.12.42
lyrical 2.37.169
lyricism 2.40.81
lyricist 10.53.21
lyssa 2.20.7
m8 5.47.40
MA 5.9
ma 3.10
ma'am 1.18, 3.31
Mab 1.1
Mabel 2.37.87
Mabo 19.3
Mac 1.10.12
mac 1.10.12
macabre 2.19.15
macadam 2.40.21
macadamia 2.1.9
macarena 2.15.9
macaroni 9.16.25
macaroon 22.27.7
MacArthur 2.23
Macau 16.3
macaw 14.7
Macbeth 6.53
Maccabees 9.59.1
macchiato 19.18.2
MacDiarmid 10.2.27
MacDonald 2.38.6
mace 5.45
macebearer 2.19.8
Macedonia 2.1.16
macerate 5.47.56
macerated 10.2.52
MacGregor 2.9
Mach 1.47
machete 9.22.60
Machiavelli 9.14.33
Machiavellian 2.43.6
machination 2.43.182
machinations 2.51.3
machine 9.43.17
machine-made 5.21.5
machinery 9.19.27
machine shop 13.31.7

291

mallrat 1.41.8
Malmö 19.12
malnourished 10.55.4
malnutrition 2.43.244
Malo 19.11.3
malodorous 2.54.98
Malory 9.19.18
maloti 9.22.71
malpractice 10.50.24
malt 14.31
Malta 2.22.76, 2.22.77
malted 10.2.80
Maltese 9.59.13
Maltese cross 13.34.7
Malthus 2.54.134
maltose 19.45.3
maltreat 9.52.9
maltreatment 2.47.60
Malvern Hills 10.25
malware 4.15
mam 1.18
mama 2.14.1, 3.10
mamba 2.5.9
mambo 19.3.1
Mameluke 22.21
Mamet 10.56.21
mamma 2.14.1, 3.10
mammal 2.37.191
Mammalia 2.1.7
Mamma Mia 2.1.9
mammary 9.19.20
mammary gland 1.22.3
mammogram 1.18.7
mammography 9.9.7
mammology 9.12.10
Mammon 2.43.80
mammoth 2.58.2
mammy 9.15.1
man 1.21.4
manacle 2.37.149
manacles 2.39.4
manage 10.11.10
manageable 2.37.34
managed 10.34
management 2.47.45
manager 2.10.4
manageress 6.47.4
managerial 2.37.8
managing director
  2.22.71
mañana 2.15.7
Manassas 2.54.114
manat 1.41
man-at-arms 3.33
manatee 9.22.27
Manaus 16.14
manchego 19.6.2
Manchester 2.22.94,
  2.22.96
Manchuria 2.1.19
Mancunian 2.43.10
mandala 2.13.2
mandarin 10.31.21

mandate 5.47.11
mandated 10.2.40
mandatory 9.19.36
Mandela 2.13.4, 2.13.5
Mandelstam 1.18
mandible 2.37.92
mandir 8.1
mandolin 10.31.12
mandrake 5.27.6
Mandy 9.7.20
mane 5.35.6
man-eater 2.22.30
man-eating 10.42.155
man Friday 5.3
manful 2.37.128
manfully 9.14.9
manga 2.9.11
manganese 9.59.8
mange 5.37
manger 2.10.8
mangetout 22.13
mangle 2.37.142
mangled 2.38.4
mango 19.6.5
mangonel 6.14.5
mangrove 19.51.1
mangy 9.12.21
manhandle 2.37.119
Manhattan 2.43.289
manhood 21.0.2
man-hour 17.0
manhunt 20.33.1
mania 2.1.13
maniac 1.10.2
maniacal 2.37.147
manic 10.12.31
manic-depressive
  10.61.5
Manichaeism 2.40.46
manicotti 9.22.68
manicure 15.1.1
manicured 15.6
manicurist 10.53.19
manifest 6.49.1
manifestation 2.43.219
manifestly 9.14.95
manifesto 19.18.11
manifold 19.35.1
manikin 10.31.9
Manila 2.13.9
Manilow 19.11.6
man in the street
  9.52.10
manioc 13.10
maniple 2.37.225
manipulate 5.47.37
manipulation 2.43.172
manipulative 10.61.20
manipulator 2.22.15
Manitoba 2.5.6
manitou 22.13
Manju 22.0
mankind 11.28.2

manky 9.13.18
Manley 9.14.71
manly 9.14.71
man-made 5.21.5
Mann 1.21.4
manna 2.15.1
manned 1.22
mannequin 10.31.9
manner 2.15.1
mannered 2.33.13
mannerism 2.40.78
mannerly 9.14.15
manners 2.60.5
Manning 10.42.93
mannish 10.54.15
manoeuvrable 2.37.54
manoeuvre 2.25.24
manoeuvring
  10.42.120
man-of-war 14.17
manometer 2.22.39
manor 2.15.1
manor house 16.14.2
Manor Park 3.27.5
manpower 17.2
manqué 5.7
mansard 2.33, 3.21.7
manse 1.23
Mansell 2.37.255
manservant 2.47.94
mansion 2.43.279
Mansion House
  16.14.6
man-sized 11.43.5
manslaughter 2.22.51
Manson 2.43.132
mantel 2.37.283
mantelpiece 9.49.3
mantelshelf 6.16.1
manticore 14.7
mantilla 2.13.12
mantis 10.50.29
mantissa 2.20.7
mantle 2.37.283
mantra 2.19.20
mantua 2.4.1
manual 15.7
manually 9.14.5
manufacture 2.24.4
manufacturer 2.19.1
manufacturing
  10.42.113
manumission 2.43.241
manumit 10.56.21
manure 15.1
manuscript 10.49.1
Manx 1.31
many 9.16.14
many-sided 10.2.9
Manzanilla 2.13.9
Maoism 2.40.45
Maoist 10.53
Maori 9.19.69

map 1.33
maple 2.37.222
maple syrup 2.52.3
Maputo 19.18
Maquis 9.13.1
mar 3.10
marabou 22.1
marabout 22.1
maraca 2.12.2
Maracaibo 19.3
maracas 2.60.3
maraschino 19.13.3
maraschino cherry
  9.19.60
Marat 3.13
marathon 2.43.315
maraud 14.19.8
marauder 2.6.8
marauding 10.42.20
marble 2.37.23
marbled 2.38.1
marbles 2.39.1
marbling 10.42.60
marcasite 11.36.20
March 3.52
marcher 2.24
Marches 10.62.5
March hare 4.4
marching band 1.22.1
marching orders 2.60.1
marchioness 6.47.3
march-past 3.47.4
Marconi 9.16.23
Marco Polo 19.11
Marcos 13.34
Mardi Gras 3.13
mare 4.8
Margaret 2.56.32,
  2.56.34
margarine 9.43.10
margarita 2.22.32
Margasirsa 2.20
marge 3.26
margin 10.31.6
marginal 2.37.215
marginalia 2.1.7
marginalise 11.42.9
marginally 9.14.15
marguerite 9.52.7
Maria 2.1.21
mariachi 9.24.2
Mariana Islands 2.50.2
Marie Antoinette
  6.51.5
marigold 19.35.2
marijuana 2.15.7
Marilyn 10.31.13
marimba 2.5
marina 2.15.14
marinade 5.21.6
marinate 5.47.47
marinated 10.2.49
marine 9.43.11

mattress 2.54.111
maturation 2.43.192
mature 15.1.2
matured 15.6
maturity 9.22.38
maty 9.22.59
matzo 2.20.18
Maud 14.19
maudlin 10.31.11
Maugham 14.33
Maui 9.0
maul 14.27
maulvi 9.25
maunder 2.6.17
Maundy Thursday 5.3.6
Maupassant 3.41, 13.28
Maureen 9.43.9
Mauriac 1.10
Mauritania 2.1.12
Mauritius 2.54.124
mausoleum 2.40.5
mauve 19.51
maven 2.43.320
maverick 10.12.44
mavis 10.50.31
maw 14.9
mawkish 10.54.8
Mawlid al-Nabi 9.6.2
max 1.11
maxi 9.20.23
maxilla 2.13.8
maxillary 9.19.19
maxim 10.26
maximal 2.37.192
Maximilian 2.43.8
maximise 11.42.17
maximum 2.40.25
Maxwell 2.37.296, 6.14.11
may 5.9
maybe 9.6.3
May Day 5.3
mayday 5.3
Mayfair 4.3
mayfly 11.5.2
mayhem 6.25.3
mayn't 2.47.24
mayo 19.1
mayonnaise 5.54
mayor 4.8
mayoralty 9.22.79
mayoress 6.47.4
maypole 19.34.4
Maytime 11.25.3
Mazarin 10.31.21
maze 5.54
MBA 5.1
MBE 9.2
Mbeki 9.13.5
McAdam 2.40.21
MCAT 1.41.4

McBride 11.14.14
McCarthy 9.23
McCarthyism 2.40.47
McColgan 2.43.46
McConnell 2.37.195
McCormack 1.10.12
McCoy 18.2
McCrae 5.12
McEnroe 19.15
McEwen 2.43
McGovern 2.43.326
McGrath 3.51
McKenna 2.15.10
McKenzie 9.27.10
McKinley 9.14.71
McLaren 2.43.111
McLeish 9.51
McNamara 2.19.6
MD 9.7
MDF 6.4
me 9.15
mea culpa 2.18
mead 9.29
meadow 19.4
meadowlark 3.27.2
meadowy 9.4
meagre 2.9.4
meal 9.38.3
mealie 9.14.37
mealtime 11.25.5
mealworm 7.18.4
mealy 9.14.37
mealybug 20.7.1
mealy-mouthed 16.8, 16.20
mean 9.43.7
meander 2.6.18
meandering 10.42.115
meanie 9.16.16
meaning 10.42.99
meaningful 2.37.121
meaningless 2.54.35
mean-minded 10.2.21
meanness 2.54.82
means 9.46
meant 6.34.1
meantime 11.25.6
meanwhile 11.22.9
Meares 8.14
measles 2.39
measly 9.14.101
measurable 2.37.51
measure 2.29
measured 2.33.27
measureless 2.54.37
measurement 2.47.33
measures 2.60
meat 9.52.6
meatball 14.27.2
meathead 6.1.9
meat loaf 19.28
meaty 9.22.62
Mecca 2.12.8

Meccano 19.13.1
mechanic 10.12.31
mechanical 2.37.166
mechanics 10.13.6
mechanise 11.42.19
mechanised 11.43.2
mechanism 2.40.72
mechanistic 10.12.84
Med 6.1
medal 2.37.107
medallion 2.43.6
medallist 10.53.7
meddle 2.37.107
meddlesome 2.40.35
meddling 10.42.79
Medea 2.1.3
Medellín 9.43
medevac 1.10
media 2.1.3
medial 2.37.3
median 2.43.3
median strip 10.47.5
mediate 5.47.2
mediation 2.43.140
mediator 2.22.10
medic 10.12.6
Medicaid 5.21.1
medical 2.37.156
medical corps 14.7
medical school 22.22.4
medicament 2.47.33
Medicare 4.6
medication 2.43.157
Medici 9.24
medicinal 2.37.197
medicine 2.43.114
medick 10.12.6
medieval 2.37.293
medievalism 2.40.55
Medina 2.15.12
mediocre 2.12.20
mediocrity 9.22.32
meditate 5.47.64
meditation 2.43.209
meditative 10.61.31
Mediterranean 2.43.11
Mediterranean Sea 9.20.30
medium 2.40.2
medley 9.14.56
Médoc 13.10.1
medulla 2.13.20
Medusa 2.20.12
meed 9.29
meek 9.36
Meena 2.15.12
meerkat 1.41.4
meerschaum 14.33
meet 9.52.6
meeting 10.42.155
meeting house 16.14.1
meeting place 5.45.4
meg 6.6

mega 2.9
megabit 10.56.2
megabucks 20.11
megabyte 11.36.2
megacycle 2.37.184
megadeath 6.53
Megadeth 6.53
megadose 19.45
megahertz 7.29
megalith 10.58
megalithic 10.12.88
megalomania 2.1.13
megalomaniac 1.10.2
megalopolis 10.50.8
Megan 2.43.46
megaphone 19.40.3
megapixel 2.37.254
megastar 3.15.1
megastore 14.15.1
megaton 20.29.5
megawatt 13.39.9
megrim 10.26.3
meiosis 10.50.20
meishi 9.21
Meissen 2.43.123
meitnerium 2.40.15
Mekong 13.27
Mel 6.14.3
mela 3.9
melamine 9.43.7
melancholia 2.1.6
melancholic 10.12.19
melancholy 9.14.12
Melanesia 2.1.33, 2.30
Melanesian 2.43.333
melange 3.59
Melanie 9.16.6
melanin 10.31.17
melanoma 2.14.16
melatonin 10.31.17
Melba 2.5
Melba toast 19.46
Melbourne 2.43.27
Melbourne Cup 20.40.2
Melchizedek 6.10.2
meld 6.15
melee 5.8
melioration 2.43.193
Melissa 2.20.7
mellifluous 2.54.17
Mellors 2.60
mellow 19.11.4
melodic 10.12.7
melodious 2.54.2
melodrama 2.14.8
melodramatic 10.12.58
melody 9.7.2
melon 2.43.76
melt 6.19
meltage 10.11.22
meltdown 16.10.5
melting 10.42.167

Munster 2.22.107
Münster 2.22.107
muon 13.22
muppet 10.56.26
mural 2.37.244
murder 2.6
murderer 2.19.1
murderess 6.47.4
murderous 2.54.98
Murdo 19.4
Murdoch 13.10.1
murk 7.14
murky 9.13.6
murmur 2.14
Murphy 9.9
Murray 9.19.70
Muscadet 5.3.1
Muscat 1.41.4
muscatel 6.14.10
muscle 2.37.253
musclebound 16.11.1
muscleman 1.21.7
muscovado 19.4.2
Muscovite 11.36
muscovy 9.25
muscular 2.13.24
muscular dystrophy
9.9.10
muscularity 9.22.35
musculature 2.24.2
muse 22.40.1
museum 2.40.19
mush 20.45
Musharraf 1.5.1
mushroom 22.25.3
mushroom cloud
16.6.1
musical 2.37.183
musical director
2.22.71
musicality 9.22.14
musically 9.14.66
music hall 14.27.6
musician 2.43.248
musicianship 10.47.10
music master 2.22.93
musicology 9.12.9
music school 22.22.4
music stand 1.22.7
musk 20.43
muskellunge 20.31
musket 10.56.17
musketeer 8.10
musketry 9.19.81
muskrat 1.41.8
musky 9.13.22
Muslim 2.40.25
muslin 10.31.11
muso 19.21
muss 20.42
mussel 2.37.253
Mussolini 9.16.17
Mussorgsky 9.13.22

must (verb) 2.55
must (noun, verb)
20.44
mustache 1.39
mustachio 19.2.4
mustang 1.28
mustard 2.33.22
mustard gas 1.36.1
mustard plaster
2.22.91
mustard seed 9.29.7
muster 2.22.103
mustn't 2.47.82
musty 9.22.89
Muswell Hill 10.17.3
mutable 2.37.71
mutagen 2.43.53
mutant 2.47.88
mutate 5.47.63
mutation 2.43.208
mutawaa 3.18
mute 22.34.5
muted 10.2.68
muti 9.22.74
mutilate 5.47.31
mutilated 10.2.45
mutilation 2.43.168
mutineer 8.6
mutinous 2.54.71
mutiny 9.16.11
mutt 20.47
mutter 2.22.56
muttered 2.33.21
mutton 2.43.302
muttonbird 7.10.1
muttonchops 13.32
mutual 2.37.21
mutualise 11.42.6
mutualism 2.40.57
mutuality 9.22.13
mutually 9.14.5
muumuu 22.7
Muzak 1.10.20
muzzle 2.37.305
muzzy 9.27.7
MVP 9.18.7
mwah mwah 3.18.2
my 11.0
myalgia 2.10.6
Myanmar 3.10
mycelium 2.40.6
Mycenae 9.16.16
mycology 9.12.9
mycotoxin 10.31.23
myelin 10.31.11
myeloma 2.14.16
My Fair Lady 9.7.6
mynah 2.15.18
mynah bird 7.10.2
myopia 2.1.18
myopic 10.12.40
myriad 2.33
Myron 2.43.110

myrrh 7.0
myrtle 2.37.275
myself 6.16
Mysore 14.13
mysterious 2.54.11
mystery 9.19.52
mystery play 5.8.3
mystery tour 15.5
mystic 10.12.83
mystical 2.37.182
mysticism 2.40.83
mystification 2.43.162
mystified 11.14.7
mystify 11.3.9
mystique 9.36.6
myth 10.58
mythic 10.12.88
mythical 2.37.155,
10.16
mythological 2.37.159
mythologise 11.42.2
mythology 9.12.18
mythomaniac 1.10.2
Mytilene 9.16.17
myxomatosis 10.50.20
'n' 2.43
NAAFI 9.9.1
naan 1.21.10, 3.34
nab 1.1
nabob 13.0
Nabokov 13.5.2
Nabucco 19.10
nacho 19.19
nachos 19.52
nacre 2.12.5
nada 2.6.1
Nadia 2.1.3
nadir 8.1
naevus 2.54.136
naff 1.5
nag 1.6
naga 2.9.2
Nagasaki 9.13.3
nagging 10.42.34
Nagoya 2.2
Nagpur 15.3
nah 3.11
naiad 1.3
nail 5.30.5
nail-biter 2.22.46
nailbrush 20.45.3
nail file 11.22.2
nail polish 10.54.10
Naipaul 14.27.8
naira 2.19
Nairobi 9.6.6
naive 9.56
naively 9.14.97
naivety 9.22.51
naked 10.2.25
naked eye 11.0
nakfa 2.8
namaste 5.15.1

namby-pamby 9.6.9
name 5.33.4
name-calling 10.42.75
namecheck 6.10.7
named 5.34
name day 5.3
name-dropping
10.42.110
namegiver 2.25.11
nameless 2.54.47
namely 9.14.70
nameplate 5.47.39
namesake 5.27
Namibia 2.1.1
Namibian 2.43.2
nan 1.21.10, 3.34
nancy 9.20.28
NAND 1.22
nanny 9.16.1
nanny goat 19.47.3
nannying 10.42.2
nanny state 5.47.65
nanometre 2.22.29
nanopublishing
10.42.142
nanosecond 2.44.3
nanotechnology
9.12.13
Nantes 3.38
Nantucket 2.56.9
Naomi 9.15.15
nap 1.33.3
napalm 3.31
Napa Valley 9.14.2
nape 5.42
naphthalene 9.43.6
Napier 2.1.17
napkin 10.31.7
Naples 2.39.6
Napoleon 2.43.6
Napoleonic code
19.23.1
nappy 9.18.1
narc 3.27
narcissism 2.40.81
narcissist 10.53.21
narcissistic 10.12.80
Narcissus 2.54.114
narcolepsy 9.20.37
narcotherapy 9.18.5
narcotic 10.12.71
narcotics 10.13.17
nark 3.27
narked 3.29
Narnia 2.1.11
narrate 5.47.54
narration 2.43.198
narrative 10.61.24
narrator 2.22.18
narrow 19.15.1
narrowband 1.22.1
narrowboat 19.47.1
narrowcast 3.47.2

NIMBY 9.6.9
Nimrod 13.2.3
Nina 2.15.12
nincompoop 22.29
nine 11.27.12
ninefold 19.35.1
ninepins 10.41
nineteen 9.43.20
nineteenth 9.45
nineties 9.59.15
ninetieth 2.58.1
nine-to-five 11.38.2
ninety 9.22.80
Nineveh 2.25.1
Ninian 2.43.12
ninja 2.10.9
ninny 9.16.18
niobium 2.40.1
nip 10.47.3
nipper 2.18.8
nipple 2.37.225
Nippon 13.22.10
nippy 9.18.8
nirvana 2.15.7
Nisan 3.34
Nissen hut 20.47
nit 10.56.23
nite 11.36.14
nitpick 10.12.39
nitpicking 10.42.49
nitrate 2.56.32, 5.47.60
nitre 2.22.46
nitric acid 10.2.32
nitrify 11.3.6
nitrogen 2.43.53
nitroglycerine
   10.31.21
nitrous oxide 11.14.24
nitty-gritty 9.22.63
nitwit 10.56.36
nix 10.13.6
Nixon 2.43.128
no 19.13
Noah 2.3
Noah's ark 3.27
nob 13.0.1
no-ball 14.27.1
nobble 2.37.97
Nobel 6.14.1
nobelium 2.40.6
Nobel Prize 11.42.28
Nob Hill 10.17.3
noble 2.37.98
noble gas 1.36.1
nobleman 2.43.97
noble savage 10.11.26
noblesse oblige 9.61
noblewoman 2.43.90
nobly 9.14.50
nobody 9.7.14
no claims bonus
   2.54.74
nocturnal 2.37.213

nocturne 7.20.3
nod 13.2
nodal 2.37.105
nodding donkey
   9.13.20
noddle 2.37.113
node 19.23.4
nodule 22.22.2
Noel 6.14
noes 19.52.2
no-frills 10.25
noggin 10.31.5
no-go 19.6.4
no-holds-barred 3.21.1
no-hoper 2.18.13
noir 3.18.3
noise 18.17
noiseless 2.54.35
noisome 2.40.33
noisy 9.27
Nolan 2.43.78
nomad 1.3.4
nomadic 10.12.6
no-man's-land 1.22.3
nom de guerre 4.0
nom de plume 22.25.2
nomen 6.29.2
nomenclature 2.24
nominal 2.37.218
nominalise 11.42.9
nominally 9.14.15
nominal value 22.4.6
nominate 5.47.46
nomination 2.43.186
nominative 10.61.23
nominee 9.16.19
nomology 9.12.11
nomothetic 10.12.67
nonacceptance 2.45.33
nonagenarian 2.43.17
nonaggression
   2.43.228
nonaggressive 10.61.4
nonagon 13.22.4
nonalcoholic 10.12.20
nonaligned 11.28.3
nonappearance 2.45.23
nonbank 1.30.1
nonbeliever 2.25.10
nonbusiness 2.54.92
noncausal 2.37.299
nonce 13.24
nonchalance 2.45.15
nonchalant 2.47.28
noncombatant 2.47.88
noncommissioned
   officer 2.20.8
noncommittal
   2.37.276
noncompatibility
   9.22.22
noncompletion
   2.43.234

noncompliant 12.11
non compos mentis
   10.50.29
nonconformer 2.14.15
nonconformist
   10.53.10
nonconformity 9.22.25
noncontributory
   9.19.46
nonconvertible 2.37.65
noncooperation
   2.43.200
noncustodial 2.37.3
nondelivery 9.19.56
nondescript 10.49.1
nondigital 2.37.276
nondurable 2.37.56
none 20.29
nonentity 9.22.50
Nones 19.43
nonessential 2.37.269
nonesuch 20.49
nonetheless 6.47.1
nonevent 6.34.6
nonexecutive director
   2.22.71
nonexistence 2.45.38
nonexistent 2.47.91
nonexternal 2.37.213
nonfat 1.41.2
nonfiction 2.43.273
nonflammable 2.37.42
nonfunctional
   2.37.209
nonintervention
   2.43.283
noninvasive 10.61.3
nonjudgmental
   2.37.286
nonliable 2.37.96
nonmember 2.5.11
non-negotiable
   2.37.61, 2.37.90
non-nuclear 2.1.6
no-no 19.13.5
nonobservance 2.45.39
no-nonsense 2.45.28
nonpareil 2.37, 5.30.6
nonpartisan 1.21.17
nonperson 2.43.118
nonphysical 2.37.183
nonplus 20.42.2
nonplussed 20.44.4
nonprofessional
   2.37.206
non-profit-making
   10.42.44
nonproliferation
   2.43.193
nonrecoverable
   2.37.54
nonrepudiation
   2.43.140

nonrestrictive 10.61.46
nonreturnable 2.37.48
nonrigid 10.2.24
nonsense 2.45.28
nonsensical 2.37.173
non sequitur 2.22.44
nonslip 10.47.2
nonsmoker 2.12.20
nonsmoking 10.42.54
nonspecific 10.12.11
nonstandard 2.33.3
nonstarter 2.22.8
nonsterile 11.22.4
nonstick 10.12.77
nonstop 13.31.9
nontraditional
   2.37.207
nontransferable
   2.37.50
non-U 22.4.9
nonunion 2.43.62
nonverbal 2.37.89
nonviolence 2.45.15
nonviolent 2.47.27
nonvolatile 11.22.6
noodle 2.37.116
nook 21.4
nookie 9.13.15
noon 22.27
noonday 5.3.4
noontime 11.25.6
noose 22.31
nope 19.44
nor 14.10
Nora 2.19.11
Nordic 10.12.6
Norfolk 2.35
norm 14.33
Norma 2.14.14
normal 2.37.193
normalcy 9.20.26
normalise 11.42.8
normality 9.22.15
normally 9.14.14
Norman 2.43.86
Norman Conquest
   6.49.14
Normandy 9.7.19
normative 10.61.21
Norris 10.50.12
Norse 14.42
Norseman 2.43.98
north 14.46
Northam 2.40
Northamptonshire
   2.21
northbound 16.11.1
North Carolina 2.15.19
North Dakota 2.22.55
northeast 9.50
northeaster 2.22.95
northeastern 2.43.312

past 3.47.4
pasta 2.22.90
paste 5.46.1
pasteboard 14.19.4
pastel 2.37.287
pastern 7.20.4
Pasternak 1.10.13
paste-up 20.40.11
Pasteur 7.6
pasteurise 11.42.22
pasteurised 11.43.4
pasticcio 19.2.5
pastiche 9.51
pastille 2.37.287
pastime 11.25.7
pastis 9.49
past master 2.22.93
pastor 2.22.91
pastoral 2.37.236
pastrami 9.15.9
pastry 9.19.88
pastrycook 21.4.4
pasturage 10.11.15
pasture 2.24.10
pastureland 2.44.5
pasty (adj) 9.22.87
pasty (noun) 9.22.85
pat 1.41.7
pataca 2.12.4
Patagonia 2.1.16
patch 1.44
patched 1.45
patchouli 9.14.48,
 9.14.49
patchwork 7.14.2
patchy 9.24.1
pate 5.47.50
pâté 5.15
pâté de foie gras 3.13
patella 2.13.7
patent 2.47.88
patented 10.2.82
patently 9.14.94
pater 2.22.9
paterfamilias 1.36
paternal 2.37.213
paternalism 2.40.59
paternity 9.22.28
paternity test 6.49.10
paternoster 2.22.100
Paterson 2.43.114
path 3.51.2
pathetic 10.12.67
pathfinder 2.6.24
pathogen 2.43.53
pathogenic 10.12.32
pathological 2.37.159
pathologist 10.53.4
pathology 9.12.18
pathos 13.34.8
pathway 5.17
patience 2.45
patient 2.47.86

patiently 9.14.93
patina 2.15.16
patio 19.2
Patna 2.15.26
patois 3.18.4
patrial 2.37.13
patriarch 3.27
patriarchal 2.37.152
patriarchy 9.13.2
patrician 2.43.245
patricide 11.14.21
Patrick 10.12.50
patrilineal 2.37.4
patrimonial 2.37.4
patrimony 9.16.9
patriot 2.56.2
patriotism 2.40.86
patrol 19.34.7
patrolman 2.43.79
patron 2.43.110
patronage 10.11.11
patronise 11.42.19
patronising 10.42.188
patron saint 5.40
patronymic 10.12.26
patsy 9.20.39
Patten 2.43.289
patter 2.22.1
pattern 2.43.289
patterned 2.44.14
patterning 10.42.96
Patterson 2.43.114
Patton 2.43.289
patty 9.22.1
paucity 9.22.39
Pauillac 1.10.1
Paul 14.27.8
Pauling 10.42.75
paunch 14.39
paunchy 9.24.4
pauper 2.18
pauperise 11.42.26
pauperism 2.40.78
Pausa 2.27
pause 14.48
Pavarotti 9.22.68
pave 5.51
pavement 2.47.64
paver 2.25.4
pavilion 2.43.8
paving 10.42.177
Pavlov 13.5
pavlova 2.25.1, 2.25.19
Pavlovian 2.43.25
paw 14.11
pawky 9.13.11
pawn 14.35.4
pawnbroker 2.12.20
Pawnee 9.16.21
pawnshop 13.31.7
pawpaw 14.11
pax 1.11
Pax Americana 2.15.8

Paxman 2.43.98
Pax Romana 2.15.7
Paxton 2.43.314
pax vobiscum 2.40.24
pay 5.11
payable 2.37.26
pay-as-you-go 19.6
payback 1.10.3
payday 5.3
PAYE 9.3
payee 9.1
payer 2.0
payload 19.23.2
paymaster 2.22.93
payment 2.47.35
payoff 13.5
payola 2.13.18
pay-per-view 22.4.13
payphone 19.40.2
payrise 11.42.21
payroll 19.34.5
payslip 10.47.2
payware 4.15
Paz 1.36, 1.48
PC 9.20.17
PDA 5.1
pdq 22.4.4
PE 9.2
pea 9.18
Peabody 9.7.14
peabrain 5.35.10
peace 9.49.3
peaceable 2.37.57
Peace Corps 14.7.1
peaceful 2.37.129
peacekeeper 2.18.6
peacekeeping
 10.42.107
peace-lover 2.25.23
peace-loving
 10.42.176
peacemaker 2.12.6
peacemaking 10.42.44
peace pipe 11.31.1
peace talks 14.25
peacetime 11.25.7
peach 9.55
peach melba 2.5
peachy 9.24
peacock 13.10.2
peafowl 16.9.1
peahen 6.29
peak 9.36.3
Peak District 10.14.3
peaked 9.37
peak season 2.43.329
peaky 9.13.7
peal 9.38.5
peanut 20.47.3
peanut butter 2.22.56
peanut gallery 9.19.18
peanuts 20.48
pear 4.10

Pearce 8.13
pearl 7.16
Pearl Harbor 2.5.1
pearly 9.14.35
Pearly Gates 5.48
pear-shaped 5.44
Pearson 2.43.113
Peary 9.19.62
peasant 2.47.97
peasantry 9.19.85
pease pudding
 10.42.22
peashooter 2.22.61
pea soup 22.29
peasouper 2.18.15
peat 9.52
peat bog 13.7
peaty 9.22.62
pebble 2.37.23
pebbledash 1.39.1
pebbly 9.14.6
pecan 1.21.1, 2.43.67
pecan pie 11.7
peccadillo 19.11.6
peccavi 9.25.1
peck 6.10.4
pecker 2.12.8
Peckham 2.40.24
pecking order 2.6.8
peckish 10.54.8
Pecksniff 10.6
Pecksniffery 9.19.12
Pecksniffian 2.43.1
pecorino 19.13.4
pecs 6.11.4
pectin 10.31.24
pectoral 2.37.238
peculiar 2.1.6
peculiarly 9.14.4
pecuniary 9.19.3
pedagogical 2.37.158
pedagogue 13.7.2
pedagogy 9.12.20
pedal 2.37.108
pedalled 2.38.2
pedalling 10.42.61
pedalo 19.11.2
pedant 2.47.7
pedantic 10.12.74
pedantically 9.14.69
pedantry 9.19.85
peddle 2.37.108
pedestal 2.37.287
pedestrian 2.43.15
pedestrianise 11.42.19
pedicure 15.1.1
pedicurist 10.53.19
pedigree 9.19.75
pediment 2.47.38
pedlar 2.13.28
pedometer 2.22.39
peduncle 2.37.187
pee 9.18

pillarbox red **6.1.12**
pillar of society **9.22.66**
Pillars of Hercules **9.59.3**
pillary **9.19.17**
pillbox **13.11.1**
pillion **2.43.59**
pillock **2.35.1**
pillory **9.19.19**
pillow **19.11.6**
pillowcase **5.45.3**
pillow talk **14.24.3**
pilot **2.56.17**
pilotage **10.11.22**
pilot fish **10.54.6**
pilot light **11.36.12**
Pilsner **2.15, 2.15.2**
Piltdown Man **1.21.4**
pimento **19.18.10**
pimp **10.29**
pimpernel **6.14.5**
pimple **2.37.229**
pimply **9.14.79**
pin **10.31.18**
pina colada **2.6.1**
piña colada **2.6.1**
pinafore **14.3.1**
piñata **2.22.4**
pinball **14.27.1**
pince-nez **5.10**
pincer **2.20.15**
pinch **10.39**
pinchbeck **6.10.1**
pinch hitter **2.22.33**
pincushion **2.43.136**
Pindar **2.6.23**
pine **11.27.13**
pineapple **2.37.223**
pine cone **19.40.4**
pine marten **2.43.291**
pinery **9.19.29**
ping **10.42.104**
Ping-Pong **13.27**
pinhead **6.1.8**
pinion **2.43.61**
pinkie **9.13.19**
pinking shears **8.14**
pinkish **10.54.8**
pink lady **9.7.6**
Pink Panther **2.23.1**
pink slip **10.47.2**
pinky **9.13.19**
pinna **2.15.16**
pinnacle **2.37.149**
PIN number **2.5.12**
pinny **9.16.18**
Pinocchio **19.2**
Pinochet **5.14**
pinochle **2.37.147, 2.37.186**
pinpoint **18.12**
pinprick **10.12.48**

pins and needles **2.39**
pinstripe **11.31.2**
pint **11.29**
pintable **2.37.88**
Pinter **2.22.82**
pinto bean **9.43.1**
pint-sized **11.43.5**
pin-up **20.40.6**
pinwheel **9.38.8**
Pinyin **10.31**
pinyon **13.22.5**
pioneer **8.6**
pioneering **10.42.125**
pious **12.12**
pip **10.47**
pipe **11.31.1**
pipe band **1.22.1**
pipe cleaner **2.15.13**
pipe dream **9.41.3**
pipeline **11.27.3**
piper **2.18.9**
pipette **6.51**
pipework **7.14.2**
piping **10.42.109**
pipit **10.56.27**
Pippa **2.18.8**
pippin **10.31.18**
pips **10.48**
pipsqueak **9.36.7**
piquancy **9.20.27**
piquant **2.47.25**
pique **9.36.3**
piqué **5.7**
piqued **9.37**
piquet **5.7**
piracy **9.20.8**
Piraeus **2.54.9**
piranha **2.15.7**
pirate **2.56.32**
piratical **2.37.175**
pirouette **6.51.1**
Pisa **2.27.4**
Pisano **19.13.1**
piscatorial **2.37.12**
Pisces **9.59.12**
piscicultural **2.37.240**
piscine **11.27.15**
piss **10.50.11**
Pissarro **19.15**
pissed **10.53.15**
pisshead **6.1.4**
pissoir **3.18**
pisspot **13.39.6**
piss-take **5.27.10**
pistachio **19.2.4**
piste **9.50**
pistil **10.17.7**
pistol **2.37.287**
pistol-whip **10.47.15**
piston **2.43.312**
pit **10.56.26**
pitapat **1.41.7**
Pitcairn Island **2.44.6**

pitch **10.59**
pitch-black **1.10.11**
pitch-dark **3.27**
pitched **10.60**
pitcher **2.24.3**
pitchfork **14.24**
pitch pipe **11.31.1**
piteous **2.54.15**
pitfall **14.27.4**
pith **10.58**
pithead **6.1.9**
pith helmet **10.56.21**
pithy **9.23**
pitiable **2.37.90**
pitiful **2.37.124**
pitiless **2.54.39**
pit lane **5.35.4**
Pitlochry **9.19.76**
pitman **2.43.101**
piton **13.22.16**
pit stop **13.31.9**
Pitt **10.56.26**
pitta **2.22.31, 2.22.41**
pittance **2.45.34**
pitted **10.2.59**
pitter-patter **2.22.1**
Pittsburgh **7.12.4**
pituitary gland **1.22.3**
pity **9.22.63**
pitying **10.42.2**
Pius **12.12**
pivot **2.56.41**
pivotal **2.37.270**
pix **10.13.8**
pixel **2.37.254**
pixelated **10.2.44**
pixie **9.20.24**
Pizarro **19.15**
pizza **2.20.18**
pizza face **5.45.2**
pizzazz **1.48**
pizzeria **2.1.21**
pizzicato **19.18.2**
PJs **5.54**
pj's **5.54**
placard **3.21.4**
placate **5.47.21**
placatory **9.19.43**
place **5.45.4**
placebo **19.3**
place kick **10.12.15**
placemat **1.41.6**
placement **2.47.55**
place name **5.33.4**
placenta **2.22.81**
placid **10.2.32**
plagiarise **11.42.22**
plagiarism **2.40.78**
plagiarist **10.53.17**
plague **5.25**
plaice **5.45.4**
plaid **1.3.3**
Plaid Cymru **9.19**

plain **5.35.5**
plainchant **3.38**
plain Jane **5.35**
plainly **9.14.71**
plainness **2.54.82**
plain sailing **10.42.68**
plainsong **13.27.4**
plain-speaking **10.42.48**
plain-spoken **2.43.73**
plaintiff **10.6.3**
plaintive **10.61.49**
plait **1.41.5**
plaited **10.2.34**
plan **1.21.3**
planar **3.11**
Planck **1.30.2**
plane **5.35.5**
planeload **19.23.2**
planer **2.15.9**
planet **10.56.24**
planetarium **2.40.14**
planetary **9.19.41**
planetoid **18.5**
plangent **2.47.23**
plank **1.30.2**
planking **10.42.55**
plankton **2.43.288**
planktonic **10.12.38**
planner **2.15.1**
planning **10.42.93**
plant **3.38.1**
planta genista **2.22.97**
plantain **10.31.27**
plantation **2.43.215**
planter **2.22.78**
plaque **1.10.10, 3.27.2**
plasma **2.14**
plaster **2.22.91**
plasterboard **14.19.2**
plaster cast **3.47.2**
plastered **2.33.22**
plasterer **2.19.5**
plaster of Paris **10.50.12**
plasterwork **7.14.3**
plastic **10.12.79**
plastic bullet **10.56.19**
plasticine **9.43.15**
plasticity **9.22.45**
plastic surgeon **2.43.54**
plastic surgery **9.19.15**
plastid **10.2.90**
plat du jour **15.0**
plate **5.47.39**
plateau **19.18.1**
plateful **21.7.2**
platelayer **2.01.5**
platelet **2.56.22**
platform **14.33.3**
Plath **1.43**
plating **10.42.148**
platinum **2.40.27**

purvey 5.16
purveyor 2.0
purview 22.4.13
pus 20.42
Pusan 1.21
push 21.13
push-button 2.43.302
pushcar 3.8
pushcart 3.49.3
pushchair 4.14
pushdown 16.10.1
pusher 2.21
Pushkin 10.31.7
pushover 2.25.16
push-up 20.40.10
pushy 9.21
pusillanimous 2.54.60
puss 21.12
pussy 9.20
pussycat 1.41.4
pussyfoot 21.14
pussyfooter 2.22.58
pustule 22.22.1
put 21.14.1
putative 10.61.30
putdown 16.10.5
Putin 10.31.26
put-in 10.31.24
Putonghua 3.18
putrefaction 2.43.261
putrefy 11.3.6
putrescent 2.47.84
putrid 10.2.30
putsch 21.16
putt 20.47
putter 2.22.56
putting 10.42.143
putto 19.18
putty 9.22.72
put-upon 13.22.11
puzzle 2.37.305
puzzled 2.38.12
puzzlement 2.47.47
puzzler 2.13.2
puzzling 10.42.59
PVC 9.20.17
Pygmalion 2.43.7
pygmy 9.15
pyjamas 2.60.4
pylon 2.43.75
Pyongyang 1.28
pyorrhoea 2.1.19
pyracantha 2.23
pyramid 10.2.27
pyre 12.3
Pyrenees 9.59.8
pyrethrum 2.40.29
Pyrex 6.11.5
pyrites 9.59.13
pyrogenic 10.12.32
pyromania 2.1.13
pyromaniac 1.10.2
pyrotechnics 10.13.6

Pyrrhic victory 9.19.47
Pythagoras 2.54.97
Pythagorean 2.43.15
Pythia 2.1
python 2.43.315
Pythonesque 6.48
pyx 10.13.8
Q & A 5.3.4
Qatar 2.22.57, 3.15
QC 9.20.22
q.t. 9.22.75
qua 5.17
quack 1.10.19
quackery 9.19.16
quackish 10.54.8
quacksalver 2.25.25
quackster 2.22.106
quad 13.2.4
quadrangle 2.37.142
quadrant 2.47.74
quadraphonic
  10.12.35
quadriceps 6.44
quadricycle 2.37.184
quadrilateral 2.37.237
quadrillion 2.43.8
quadriplegia 2.10
quadriplegic 10.12.13
quadrophonic
  10.12.35
quadruped 6.1.11
quadrupedal 2.37.109
quadruple 2.37.228
quadruplet 2.56.21
quaestor 2.22.95
quaff 13.5
quagmire 12.0
quahog 13.7.3
Quaid 5.21.13
quail 5.30.11
quaint 5.40
quake 5.27.11
Quaker 2.12.5
qualification 2.43.158
qualified 11.14.3
qualifier 12.1.1
qualify 11.3.3
qualitative 10.61.31
quality 9.22.24
qualm 3.31
qualms 3.33
quandary 9.19.10
quango 19.6.5
quangocracy 9.20.10
Quant 13.25
quanta 2.22.78
quantifiable 2.37.95
quantifier 12.1.1
quantify 11.3.8
quantitative 10.61.31
quantity 9.22.50
quantum 2.40.38
quantum leap 9.47

quantum physics
  10.13.20
quarantine 9.43.21
quark 3.27
quarrel 2.37.243
quarrelled 2.38.8
quarrelling 10.42.59
quarrelsome 2.40.35
quarrelsomeness
  2.54.81
quarry 9.19.65
quart 14.44
quarter 2.22.54
quarterback 1.10.4
quarter day 5.3.2
quarterdeck 6.10.2
quarterfinal 2.37.219
quarter horse 14.42.2
quarterly 9.14.26
quartermaster 2.22.93
quarters 2.60.8
quarter sessions 2.51.2
quarterstaff 3.23.4
quartet 6.51.13
quartier 5.1.2
quartile 11.22.6
quarto 19.18
quartz 14.45
quasar 3.19
quash 13.37.1
quasi 9.20.13
quatercentenary
  9.19.27
Quatermass 1.36.3
Quaternary 9.19.21
quatrain 5.35.11
quaver 2.25.5
quay 9.13
Quayle 5.30.11
quayside 11.14.19
queasiness 2.54.70
queasy 9.27.3
Quebec 6.10.1
Quechua 2.26
queen 9.43.24
queenly 9.14.74
queen mother 2.7.4
Queens 9.46
Queen's Bench 6.35
Queensberry rules
  22.24
Queen's Counsel
  2.37.257
Queen's English
  10.54.12
Queen's evidence
  2.45.6
queen-size 11.42.29
Queensland 1.22.3,
  2.44.4
Queen's Messenger
  2.10.7
queer 8.0

quell 6.14.11
quench 6.35
quenelle 6.14.4
Quentin 10.31.27
querulous 2.54.35
query 9.19.63
quest 6.49.14
quester 2.22.94
question 2.43.317
questionable 2.37.44
questioner 2.15.2
questioning 10.42.94
question mark 3.27.4
question master
  2.22.93
questionnaire 4.9
question time 11.25.6
quetzal 2.37.247
queue 22.4.4
queue-jump 20.26.1
quibble 2.37.92
quibbling 10.42.60
quiche 9.51
quick 10.12.90
quicken 2.43.68
quickening 10.42.95
quick-footed 10.2.66
quickie 9.13.8
quicklime 11.25.1
quickly 9.14.66
quicksand 1.22
quicksilver 2.25.25
quickstep 6.43.1
quick-tempered
  2.33.16
quick-thinking
  10.42.57
quick-witted 10.2.59
quick-wittedly 9.14.59
quick-wittedness
  2.54.76
quid 10.2.95
quiddity 9.22.7
quid pro quo 19.0
quiescence 2.45.29
quiescent 2.47.83
quiet 12.13
quieten 2.43.290
quietism 2.40.85
quietly 9.14.86
quietness 2.54.88
quietude 22.17.4
quietus 2.54.129
quiff 10.6
quill 10.17.9
quilt 10.22
quilted 10.2.79
quilting 10.42.167
quince 10.36
Quincy 9.20.27
quinine 9.43.8
quinquereme 9.41.3
quintal 2.37.282

quintessence 2.45.29
quintessential
2.37.269
quintet 6.51.13
quintuple 2.37.228
quintuplet 2.56.21
quip 10.47.15
quire 12.6.1
quirk 7.14.2
quirkiness 2.54.65
quirky 9.13.6
quisling 10.42.83
quit 10.56.37
quite 11.36.22
Quito 19.18.5
quits 10.57
quittance 2.45.34
quitter 2.22.44
quiver 2.25.11
quixotic 10.12.71
quiz 10.62.6
quizmaster 2.22.93
quiz show 19.17
quizzical 2.37.183
quod 13.2.4
quod erat
demonstrandum
2.40.22
quondam 1.18.1,
2.40.20
quorate 5.47.51
Quorn 14.35.7
quorum 2.40.30
quota 2.22.55
quotable 2.37.70
quotation 2.43.211
quotation mark 3.27.4
quote 19.47
quoth 19.49
quotidian 2.43.5
quotient 2.47.86
Qur'an 3.34.1
Qwerty 9.22.61
R & B 9.6.10
R & D 9.7.19
Rabat 3.49.1
rabbi 11.2
rabbinical 2.37.166
rabbit 10.56.3
rabbit food 22.17.1
rabble 2.37.24
rabble-rouser 2.27.8
rabble-rousing
10.42.190
Rabelaisian 2.43.26
Rabi 9.6.2
rabid 10.2.2
rabies 9.59.1
Rabin 9.43.1
raccoon 22.27.4
race 5.45.7
race card 3.21.4
racecourse 14.42.3

racegoer 2.3.2
racehorse 14.42.2
raceme 9.41.6
racer 2.20.2
racetrack 1.10.16
rachel 2.37
Rachmaninov 13.5.3
racial 2.37.260
racialism 2.40.62
racially 9.14.24
Racine 9.43.14
racing 10.42.135
racism 2.40.80
racist 10.53.20
rack 1.10.15
racket 10.56.11
racketeer 8.10
racketeering 10.42.123
rackets 10.57
racking 10.42.42
rack-rent 6.34.3
raconteur 7.6
racquet 10.56.11
racquetball 14.27.2
racquets 10.57
racy 9.20.14
rad 1.3.6
RADA 2.6.1
radar 3.3
radar trap 1.33.5
Radcliffe 10.6.1
raddle 2.37.106
raddled 2.38.2
radial 2.37.3
radian 2.43.4
radiance 2.45.2
radiant 2.47.1
radiate 2.56.1, 5.47.2
radiation 2.43.140
radiator 2.22.10
radical 2.37.156
radicalise 11.42.4
radicalism 2.40.55
radicchio 19.2.5
radicle 2.37.156
radii 11.1
radio 19.2.1
radioactive 10.61.41
radioactivity 9.22.54
radio astronomy 9.15.5
radiobiology 9.12.7
radio-controlled 19.35
radiogram 1.18.8
radiograph 1.5.2,
3.23.3
radiography 9.9.4
radiology 9.12.6
radiometer 2.22.39
radiophonic 10.12.35
radio play 5.8.3
radiotherapy 9.18.5
radish 10.54.3
radium 2.40.3

radius 2.54.2
radon 13.22.2
RAF 6.4
raffia 2.1.4
raffish 10.54.5
raffle 2.37.121
Raffles 2.39
raft 3.24
rafter 2.22.63
rafting 10.42.165
rag 1.6.3
raga 2.9.2
ragamuffin 10.31.4
ragbag 1.6.1
rage 5.26.3
ragga 2.9.1
ragged 10.2.23
raggedy 9.7.11
raging 10.42.37
raglan 2.43.75
ragout 22.0
rags 1.8
ragtag 1.6.4
ragtime 11.25.3
rag trade 5.21.10
ragweed 9.29.8
ragwort 7.28
rai 11.8
raid 5.21.8
raider 2.6.2
rail 5.30.6
railcar 3.8
railcard 3.21.4
railhead 6.1.4
railing 10.42.68
raillery 9.19.17
railpass 3.43.3
railroad 19.23.5
railway 5.17
raiment 2.47.35
rain 5.35.8
rainbow 19.3
rain check 6.10.7
raincoat 19.47.4
raindrop 13.31.6
raindrops 13.32
rainfall 14.27.3
rainforest 10.53.18
rain gauge 5.26.1
rainmaker 2.12.6
rainproof 22.19.1
rainstorm 14.33.4
rainwater 2.22.53
rainy 9.16.13
raise 5.54.2
raised 5.55
raised bed 6.1.1
raisin 2.43.328
raising agent 2.47.20
raison d'être 2.19.22
raita 2.22.48
Raj 3.26
Rajab 1.1

rajah 2.10.1
Rajasthan 3.34.2
Rajasthani 9.16.12
rake 5.27.6
rake-off 13.5.2
rakish 10.54.8
Raleigh 9.14.29,
9.14.45
rallentando 19.4.6
rally 9.14.1
ram 1.18.5
Rama 2.14.7
Ramadan 3.34
Rambert 4.2
ramble 2.37.101
rambler 2.13.27
rambling 10.42.78
ramblings 10.46.3
Rambo 19.3.1
Ramboesque 6.48
rambunctious 2.54.126
ramekin 10.31.9
ramification 2.43.158
ramp 1.20
rampage 5.26.2
rampant 2.47.73
rampart 3.49.5
ram-raid 5.21.8
ramrod 13.2.3
Ramsay 9.27.9
Ramsgate 5.47.14
ramshackle 2.37.148
ran 1.21.13
ranch 3.39
rancher 2.24
ranchero 19.15.2
rancid 10.2.31
rancorous 2.54.100
rancour 2.12.24
rand 1.22.6
Randolph 13.14
random 2.40.22
random-access 6.47.10
randomise 11.42.15
randomly 9.14.70
R and R 3.3
randy 9.7.20
rang 1.28.3
rangatira 2.19.10
range 5.37.1
ranger 2.10.8
Rangoon 22.27.1
rangy 9.12.21
rani 9.16.12
rank 1.30.3
ranked 1.32
Rankin 10.31.7
ranking 10.42.55
rankle 2.37.187
ransack 1.10.17
ransom 2.40.36
rant 1.25
Raoul 22.22

Richmond 2.44.9
richness 2.54.62
Richter scale 5.30.3
ricin 10.31.22
rick 10.12.42
rickets 10.57
rickshaw 14.14
Ricky 9.13.8
ricochet 5.14
ricotta 2.22.49
rictus 2.54.133
rid 10.2.30
riddance 2.45.6
ridden 2.43.38
riddle 2.37.110
riddled 2.38.2
ride 11.14.14
rider 2.6.6
ridge 10.11.12
ridicule 22.22.3
ridiculous 2.54.40
ridiculously 9.14.83
riding boot 22.34.1
riding jacket 10.56.12
riding school 22.22.4
Riefenstahl 3.30.3
riel 2.37.6
Riesling 10.42.83
rife 11.17
riff 10.6.2
riffle 2.37.123
riffraff 1.5.1
rifle 2.37.121
rifleman 2.43.97
rift 10.7.2
rift valley 9.14.2
rig 10.8.1
Riga 2.9.4
rigatoni 9.16.23
Rigg 10.8.1
rigging 10.42.33
right 11.36.16
right-click 10.12.21
righteous 2.54.135
rightful 2.37.132
right-hand 1.22.2
right-hander 2.6.18
Right Honourable
  2.37.52
rightist 10.53.22
rightly 9.14.90
right-minded 10.2.21
righto 19.18
rights 11.37
right-size 11.42.29
right-thinking
  10.42.57
rightward 2.33.25
rightwards 2.34.1
right-wing 10.42.184
rigid 10.2.24
rigidity 9.22.7
rigmarole 19.34.6

rigor mortis 10.50.24
rigorous 2.54.97
rigour 2.9.7
rile 11.22.4
Riley 9.14.43
Rilke 2.12
rill 10.17.5
rillettes 6.52
rim 10.26.2
Rimbaud 19.3.1
rime 11.25.2
rimless 2.54.46
rind 11.28
ring 10.42.112
ringer 2.17
ringette 6.51
ringgit 10.56.7
ringing 10.42.103
ringleader 2.6.3
ringlet 2.56.12
ringmaster 2.22.93
ring-pull 21.7
ringside 11.14.17
ringtone 19.40.14
ringworm 7.18.4
rink 10.43.2
rinky-dink 10.43
rinse 10.36
Rio 19.2.3
Rio de Janeiro 19.15.3
Rio Grande 1.22.6, 9.7
riot 12.13
rioting 10.42.144
riotous 2.54.129
RIP 9.18
rip 10.47.4
ripcord 14.19.5
ripe 11.31.2
ripen 2.43.108
rip-off 13.5
riposte 13.36
ripper 2.18.8
ripping 10.42.108
ripple 2.37.225
rip-roaring 10.42.127
riptide 11.14.26
Rip van Winkle
  2.37.188
RISC 10.51.2
rise 11.42.21
risen 2.43.330
riser 2.27.5
risible 2.37.83
rising 10.42.188
rising damp 1.20
Rising Sun 20.29.4
risk 10.51.2
risk-free 9.19.74
risk-taking 10.42.46
risky 9.13.23
risotto 19.18.6
risqué 5.7
rissole 19.34.8

Rita 2.22.32
rite 11.36.16
rites 11.37
ritual 2.37.21
ritualised 11.43.1
ritualism 2.40.57
ritualistic 10.12.82
ritzy 9.20.40
rival 2.37.295
rivalry 9.19.77
riven 2.43.323
river 2.25.13
Rivera 3.13
riverbank 1.30.1
riverbed 6.1.2
riverfront 20.33.2
Rivers 2.60
riverscape 5.42.1
riverside 11.14.18
rivet 10.56.35
riveting 10.42.156
Riviera 2.19.7, 2.19.9
rivulet 2.56.19
Riyadh 1.3, 3.21
riyal 3.30
RNA 5.10
RNLI 11.5
road 19.23.5
roadblock 13.10.4
roadhouse 16.14.3
roadie 9.7
road map 1.33
roadrunner 2.15.24
roadshow 19.17
roadside 11.14.23
roadster 2.22.89
road-train 5.35.11
roadway 5.17.4
roadwork 7.14.5
roadworks 7.15
roadworthy 9.8.1
roam 19.38.3
roaming 10.42.84
roan 19.40.11
roar 14.12
roaring 10.42.127
Roaring Twenties
  9.59.15
roast 19.46
roasting 10.42.172
rob 13.0
robber 2.5.5
robber baron 2.43.111
robbery 9.19.8
Robbins 10.41
robe 19.22.2
Robert 2.56.5
Roberts 2.57
Robertson 2.43.135
Robert the Bruce
  22.31.6
Robeson 2.43.124
Robespierre 4.5

robin 10.31.2
Robinson 2.43.133
robot 13.39
robotic 10.12.71
robotics 10.13.17
Robson 2.43.124
robust 20.44.1
robustness 2.54.88
Rochester 2.22.96
rock 13.10.7
rock cake 5.27.1
rock climbing 10.42.84
Rockefeller 2.13.5
rocker 2.12.17
rockery 9.19.16
rocket 10.56.16
rocketry 9.19.83
Rockies 10.62
Rockingham 2.40.28
rocklike 11.19.1
rock'n'roll 19.34.5
Rock of Ages 10.62.1
rock salt 14.31.2
rock steady 9.7.7
rockumentary 9.19.51
Rockwell 2.37.296
rocky 9.13.10
Rocky Mountains
  10.41.2
rococo 19.10.4
rod 13.2.3
rode 19.23.5
rodent 2.47.7
rodeo 19.1, 19.2.1
Rodeo Drive 11.38.4
Rodgers 2.60
Rodin 1.29
Rodney 9.16
roe 19.15
Roedean 9.43.2
Roentgen 2.43.46
roger 2.10.5
Rogers 2.60
rogue 19.29
roguery 9.19.13
rogues' gallery 9.19.18
rogue state 5.47.65
roguish 10.54.7
Rohypnol 13.13.1
roil 18.8
roister 2.22.101
Roland 2.44.4
role 19.34.5
role-playing 10.42.1
Rolex 6.11.2
Rolf 13.14
Rolfing 10.42.32
roll 19.34.5
rollback 1.10.6
rollbar 3.2
roller 2.13.19
rollerball 14.27.1
Rollerblade 5.21.4

rollick 10.12.19
rollicking 10.42.49
rolling 10.42.76
rolling stock 13.10.8
rollmop 13.31
roll-neck 6.10.3
Rollo 19.11.7
rollout 16.16.5
rollover 2.25.19
Rolls 19.37
Rolls-Royce 18.14
roll-up 20.40.5
Rolodex 6.11.1
roly-poly 9.14.47
Rom 19.38.3
romaine 5.35.6
romaji 9.12
Roman 2.43.87
Roman Catholic
 10.12.16
romance 1.23
Roman Empire 12.3
Romanesque 6.48
Romani 9.16.7
Romania 2.1.13
Romanian 2.43.11
romanticise 11.42.31
Romanticism 2.40.83
Romany 9.16.7
Rome 19.38.3
romeo 19.2
Rommel 2.37.190
Romney 9.16
romp 13.19
rompers 2.60.6
Romulus 2.54.42
ROMvelope 19.44.2
Ron 13.22.12
Ronald 2.38.6
Ronaldo 19.4
Ronan 2.43.106
rondavel 2.37.290
rondeau 19.4.5
roo 22.10
roo bar 3.2
rood 22.17.9
roof 22.19
roofer 2.8
roofing 10.42.32
roof rack 1.10.15
rooftop 13.31.8
rooibos 13.34.1
rook 21.4.6
rookery 9.19.16
rookie 9.13.15
room 22.25.3
roomful 21.7.1
roomie 9.15.18
roommate 5.47.40
roomy 9.15.18
Roosevelt 6.19
roost 22.32
rooster 2.22.89

root 22.34.9
root-and-branch 3.39
rooted 10.2.67
rootle 2.37.281
rootless 2.54.52
rootstock 13.10.8
ropable 2.37.49
rope 19.44.3
ropy 9.18.10
rort 14.44.7
Rory 9.19.66
Ros 13.45
Rosamund 2.44.9
rosary 9.19.57
rose 19.52.7
rosé 5.18
roseate 2.56.1
Rose Bowl 19.34.2
rosebud 20.2
rosehip 10.47
rosemary 9.19.20
rosery 9.19.57
Rosetta stone 19.40.16
rosette 6.51
rosewood 21.0.6
Rosh Hashanah 2.15.7
Rosicrucian 2.43.136
Ross 13.34.6
Rossetti 9.22.60
Rossini 9.16.16
roster 2.22.100
Rostock 13.10.8
Rostov 13.43
rostrum 2.40.32
rosy 9.27.6
rosy-cheeked 9.37
rot 13.39.7
rota 2.22.55
rotary 9.19.34
rotate 5.47.63
rotation 2.43.211
rotational 2.37.204
rotator 2.22.20
rotatory 9.19.43
rote 19.47.8
Roth 13.41.2
Rothko 19.10
roti 9.22.71
rotor 2.22.55
rotten 2.43.300, 13.21
rotter 2.22.50
Rotterdam 1.18.1
rotting 10.42.160
rottweiler 2.13.13
rotund 20.30
rotunda 2.6.27
rotundity 9.22.6
Rouault 19.0
rouble 2.37.23
roué 5.0
Rouen 3.41
rouge 22.42
rough 20.4.3

roughage 10.11
rough-and-tumble
 2.37.104
roughcast 3.47.2
roughen 2.43.45
rough-hewn 22.27.2
roughhouse 16.14.1
roughly 9.14.62
roughneck 6.10.3
roughness 2.54.62
roughshod 13.2
roulette 6.51.4
round 16.11.5
roundabout 16.16.1
roundel 2.37.117
rounders 2.60.1
Roundhead 6.1.6
roundhouse 16.14.3
roundly 9.14.60
Round Table 2.37.88
Roundtree 9.19.80
round trip 10.47.4
round-up 20.40.1
roundworm 7.18.4
rouse 16.21.1
rousing 10.42.190
Rousseau 19.16
roust 16.15
roustabout 16.16.1
rout 16.16.8
route 22.34.9
router 2.22.59
routine 9.43.18
routinely 9.14.74
Routledge 10.11.5
roux 22.10
rove 19.51.1
Rover 2.25.16
roving 10.42.176
rowan 2.43
rowboat 19.47.1
rowdy 9.7.15
rower 2.3.4
rowing 10.42.11
rowing boat 19.47.1
Rowling 10.42.58
rowlock 13.10.3
Rowntree 9.19.84
Roxana 2.15.7
royal 2.37.15
Royal Academy 9.15.2
Royal Air Force
 14.42.1
Royal Ballet 5.8
Royal Commission
 2.43.242
royal flush 20.45.1
Royal Highness
 2.54.73
royalist 10.53.7
royally 9.14.3
Royal Mail 5.30.4
Royal Marines 9.46

Royal Navy 9.25.2
royalties 9.59.13
royalty 9.22.79
RSPCA 5.1
RSVP 9.18.7
rub 20.0.2
rubber 2.5.7
rubber bullet 10.56.19
rubberneck 6.10.3
rubber-stamp 1.20
rubbery 9.19.7
rubbish 10.54.1
rubbish dump 20.26
rubbishy 9.21.2
rubble 2.37.99
rubdown 16.10.1
rube 22.16
rubefacient 2.47.86
rubella 2.13.5
Rubens 2.51
Rubicon 2.43.68
rubicund 2.44.2
rubicundity 9.22.6
rubidium 2.40.2
Rubinstein 11.27.18
rubric 10.12.47
ruby 9.6
ruby wedding 10.42.16
RUC 9.20.22
ruck 20.10
rucksack 1.10.17
ruckus 2.54.31
ructions 2.51.2
rudder 2.6.12
rudderless 2.54.38
ruddiness 2.54.66
ruddy 9.7.16
rude 22.17.9
rudeness 2.54.62
rudiment 2.47.38
rudimental 2.37.286
rudimentary 9.19.51
rudiments 2.46
Rudolf 13.14
rue 22.10
rueful 2.37.121
ruff 20.4.3
ruffian 2.43.1
ruffle 2.37.125
rufiyaa 3.0
rug 20.7.3
rugby 9.6
Rugby Union 2.43.62
rugged 10.2.23
rugger 2.9.10
Ruhr 15.0
ruin 10.31.1
ruination 2.43.182
ruined 10.32
ruinous 2.54.71
ruins 10.41
rule 22.22.6
rulebook 21.4.1

silent 2.47.27
Silenus 2.54.67
Silesia 2.1.27, 2.1.33
silhouette 6.51.1
silhouetted 10.2.33
silica 2.12.12
silicate 5.47.24
silicon 2.43.69
silicon chip 10.47.14
silicone 19.40.4
Silicon Valley 9.14.2
silk 10.19
silken 2.43.63
silkworm 7.18.4
silky 9.13.17
sill 10.17
silliness 2.54.67
silly 9.14.38
silo 19.11
silt 10.22
silty 9.22.78
Silurian 2.43.22
silvan 2.43.319
silver 2.25.25
silverfish 10.54.5
silver lining 10.42.101
silver medal 2.37.107
silversmith 10.58.1
Silverstone 19.40.16
silvertail 5.30.8
silver-tongued 20.37
silverware 4.15.1
silver wedding
    10.42.16
silvery 9.19.54
Silvester 2.22.94
Silvia 2.1.30
silvicultural 2.37.240
Simenon 13.28
Simferopol 2.37.222
simian 2.43.9
similar 2.13.9
similarity 9.22.34
similarly 9.14.13
simile 9.14.14
simmer 2.14.12
Simmonds 2.50
Simon 2.43.79
Simone 19.40.8
Simons 2.51.1
simony 9.16.7
simpatico 19.10.3
simper 2.18.16
simpering 10.42.113
simple 2.37.229
simple fraction
    2.43.262
simple-minded 2.33.2
simpleton 2.43.304
simplicity 9.22.44
simplification
    2.43.158
simplistic 10.12.81

simply 9.14.79
Simpson 2.43.113
simulacrum 2.40.31
simulate 5.47.36
simulated 10.2.46
simulation 2.43.171
simulator 2.22.15
simulcast 3.47.2
simultaneity 9.22.3
simultaneous 2.54.6
sin 10.31.22
Sinatra 2.19.21
since 10.36
sincere 8.8
sincerely 9.14.36
sincerity 9.22.36
Sinclair 4.7
sine 11.27.15
Sinead 5.21.6
sinecure 15.1.1
sine die 9.3
sine qua non 13.22.9
sinew 22.4.9
sinewy 9.5.1
sinful 2.37.128
sing 10.42.132
singable 2.37.25
singalong 13.27.2
Singapore 14.11
Singaporean 2.43.21
Singapore sling
    10.42.82
singe 10.33
singer 2.17
Singh 10.42.132
Singhalese 9.59.4
single 2.37.144
single-decker 2.12.8
single-mindedness
    2.54.76
single parent 2.47.77
singles 2.39.3
singlet 2.56.12
singleton 2.43.304
single-use 22.31.1
singly 9.14.64
Sing Sing 10.42.132
singsong 13.27.4
Singspiel 9.38.5
singular 2.13.23
singularity 9.22.35
singularly 9.14.13
Sinhalese 9.59.4
sinister 2.22.98
sink 10.43
sinker 2.12.25
sinking 10.42.56
sink-or-swim 10.26
sinless 2.54.48
sinner 2.15.16
Sinope 9.18.10
Sintu 22.13.1
sinuous 2.54.18

sinus 2.54.73
sinusitis 10.50.25
Siobhan 14.35
Sioux 22.11
sip 10.47
siphon 2.43.45
sir 2.20
sire 12.0
siree 9.19
siren 2.43.110
Sirens 2.51
siren song 13.27.4
Sirius 2.54.9
sirloin 18.11
sirloin steak 5.27.10
sirocco 19.10
sis 10.50.13
sisal 2.37.247
Sisley 9.14.101
sissy 9.20
sister 2.22.99
sisterhood 21.0.3
sister-in-law 14.8.2
siSwati 9.22.56
Sisyphean 2.43.1
sit 10.56.32
Sita 3.15
sitar 3.15
sitcom 13.18.2
site 11.36.19
sitter 2.22.43
sitting 10.42.156
sitting target 10.56.7
sitting tenant 2.47.68
situate 5.47.9
situated 10.2.39
situation 2.43.146
situational 2.37.202
sit-up 20.40.11
Sitwell 6.14.11
Sivan 2.43.323, 3.34
six 10.13.11
sixfold 19.35.1
six-pack 1.10.14
sixpence 2.45
sixteen 9.43.22
sixteenth 9.45
sixth-form college
    10.11.7
sixth sense 6.33.3
sixties 9.59.13
sixtieth 2.58.1
sixty 9.22.85
size 11.42.29
sizeable 2.37.85
sizzle 2.37.303
sizzling 10.42.83
sjambok 13.10
ska 3.8
skate 5.47.28
skateboard 14.19.4
skating 10.42.147

skean-dhu 22.2
skedaddle 2.37.106
skein 5.35.3
skeletal 2.37.276
skeleton 2.43.297
sketch 6.54
sketchbook 21.4.1
sketchy 9.24
skew 22.4.5
skewed 22.17.2
skewer 2.4.1
skewwhiff 10.6
ski 9.13.22
ski boot 22.34.1
skid 10.2.25
skier 2.1.5
skiff 10.6
skiffle 2.37.123
skiing 10.42.2
ski jacket 10.56.12
ski jump 20.26.1
skilful 2.37.127
ski lift 10.7.1
skilled 10.18
skillet 10.56.20
skim 10.26
skimming 10.42.84
skimp 10.29
skimpy 9.18.13
skin 10.31.10
skincare 4.6
skin diving 10.42.182
skinflint 10.38.1
skinful 21.7.1
skinhead 6.1.8
skink 10.43
skinless 2.54.48
Skinner 2.15.16
skinny 9.16.18
skinny-dip 10.47
skinny-dipping
    10.42.108
skint 10.38
skip 10.47
skipjack 1.10.8
skipper 2.18.8
skirl 7.16
skirmish 10.54.13
skirmishing 10.42.142
skirt 7.28.1
skirting 10.42.154
skit 10.56.17
skitter 2.22.33
skittish 10.54.19
skittle 2.37.276
skittles 2.39.7
skive 11.38
skivvies 9.59
skivvy 9.25.6
Skopje 9.0
skulk 20.17
skull 20.14.1

skull and crossbones
19.43.1
skullcap 1.33.1
skunk 20.38
sky 11.0
skycap 1.33.1
skydive 11.38.1
skydiving 10.42.182
sky-high 11.4
skyjack 1.10.8
skyjacking 10.42.41
skylark 3.27.2
skylight 11.36.6
skyline 11.27.3
Skype 11.31
skyrocket 10.56.16
skyscraper 2.18.2
skysurfing 10.42.32
skyward 2.33.25
skywards 2.34.1
skywriting 10.42.158
slab 1.1.2
slack 1.10.10
slacken 2.43.64
slacker 2.12.1
slacks 1.11.2
Slade 5.21.2
slag 1.6.2
slake 5.27.3
slaked lime 11.25.1
slalom 2.40.25
slam 1.18.4
slam dunk 20.38
slammer 2.14.1
slander 2.6.19
slanderous 2.54.98
slang 1.28.2
slanging match 1.44
slangy 9.17
slant 3.38
slanted 10.2.83
slap 1.33.2
slapdash 1.39.1
slaphead 6.1.4
slapper 2.18.1
slapstick 10.12.77
slap-up 20.40.7
slash 1.39.2
slash-and-burn 7.20.1
slasher 2.21.1
slat 1.41.5
slate 5.47.29
Slater 2.22.14
slather 2.7
slatted 10.2.34
slattern 2.43.289
slatternly 9.14.72
slaughter 2.22.51
slaughtered 2.33.18
slaughterhouse 16.14.2
Slav 3.54
slave 5.51.1
slave-driver 2.25.15

slaver 2.25, 2.25.4
slavery 9.19.55
Slavic 10.12.89
slavish 10.54.20
Slavonic 10.12.34
slaw 14.8
slay 5.8
slaying 10.42.1
sleaze 9.59.3
sleazebag 1.6.1
sleaziness 2.54.70
sleazy 9.27.3
sled 6.1.10
sledge 6.9.1
sledgehammer 2.14.2
sledging 10.42.36
sleek 9.36.1
sleep 9.47.1
sleeper 2.18.5
sleepiness 2.54.68
sleeping 10.42.106
Sleeping Beauty
9.22.75
sleeping sickness
2.54.78
sleepless 2.54.50
sleep-out 16.16.7
sleepover 2.25.16
sleepwalk 14.24.4
sleepwalking 10.42.52
sleepwear 4.15
sleepy 9.18.7
sleepyhead 6.1.4
sleet 9.52.4
sleeve 9.56.1
sleeveless 2.54.56
sleigh 5.8
sleight 11.36.6
slender 2.6.21
slept 6.45
sleuth 22.36
S level 2.37.292
slew 22.6
slice 11.34
slick 10.12.16
slicker 2.12.12
slid 10.2.26
slide 11.14.10
slide rule 22.22.6
slight 11.36.6
slighting 10.42.158
slightly 9.14.90
slim 10.26
slime 11.25.1
slimeball 14.27.1
slimline 11.27.9
slimming 10.42.84
slimy 9.15.14
sling 10.42.82
slingback 1.10.3
slingshot 13.39.8
slink 10.43.1
slinky 9.13.19

slip 10.47.2
slipknot 13.39.4
slippage 10.11
slipper 2.18.8
slipperiness 2.54.65
slippery 9.19.30
slippy 9.18.8
slipshod 13.2
slipstream 9.41.5
slip-up 20.40.7
slipway 5.17
slit 10.56.19
slither 27.3
slithery 9.19.11
sliver 2.25.12
slivovitz 10.57
Sloane 19.40.5
slob 13.0
slobber 2.5.5
slobbery 9.19.8
sloe 19.11
sloe gin 10.31.6
slog 13.7.4
slogan 2.43.51
sloganeering
10.42.125
sloop 22.29.1
slop 13.31.2
slope 19.44.2
sloppy 9.18.9
slops 13.32
slosh 13.37
sloshed 13.38
slot 13.39.2
sloth 19.49
slothful 2.37.134
slouch 16.19
slough (noun) 16.4
slough (verb) 20.4.2
Slovak 1.10
Slovakia 2.1.5
Slovene 9.43.23
Slovenia 2.1.14
slovenly 9.14.71
slow 19.11
slowcoach 19.50
slowdown 16.10.2
slowly 9.14.47
slow march 3.52
slowness 2.54.74
slowworm 7.18.4
sludge 20.9
slug 20.7.2
sluggard 2.33.6
sluggardly 9.14.57
sluggish 10.54.7
sluice 22.31.5
slum 20.24
slumber 2.5.12
slumlord 14.19.7
slummy 9.15.16
slump 20.26.2
slung 20.36.1

slur 7.4
slurp 7.25
slurry 9.19.70
slush 20.45.1
slut 20.47
sluttish 10.54.19
sly 11.5
slyly 9.14.43
slyness 2.54.73
smack 1.10.12
smacker 2.12.1
small 14.27
small ads 1.4
small arms 3.33
smallest 2.55
small game 5.33.1
smallholder 2.6.16
smallholding 10.42.25
smallish 10.54.9
small potatoes 19.52
smallpox 13.11.4
small print 10.38.3
smalls 14.32
small-scale 5.30.3
small talk 14.24.3
small-time 11.25.5
smarmy 9.15.9
smart 3.49.4
smart aleck 10.12.17
smarten 2.43.291
smartish 10.54.19
smarts 3.50
smartypants 1.24
smash 1.39.3
smash-and-grab 1.1.3
smashed 1.40
smasher 2.21.1
smash hit 10.56
smashing 10.42.141
smash-up 20.40.10
smattering 10.42.119
smear 8.5
smell 6.14.3
smellies 9.59.3
smelling salts 14.30
smelly 9.14.33
smelt 6.19
smelter 2.22.75
Smetana 2.15.5
smidgen 2.43.56
smiley 9.14.43
smirk 7.14
smite 11.36.13
smith 10.58.1
smithereens 9.46
smithy 9.8
smitten 2.43.296
smock 13.10
smocking 10.42.51
smog 13.7
smoke 19.31
smoked 19.33
smoke-free 9.19.74

smoke hood 21.0.2
smokeless 2.54.45
smoker 12.22.20
smoke screen 9.43.13
smokestack 1.10.18
smoking 10.42.53
smoky 9.13.12
Smoky Mountains
10.41.2
smooch 22.37
smooth 22.18
smoothie 9.8
smoothly 9.14
smoothness 2.54.62
smooth-talking
10.42.52
smoothy 9.8
smorgasbord 14.19.1
smote 19.47.6
smother 2.7.4
smoulder 2.6.15
smouldering 10.42.115
SMS 6.47.2
smudge 20.9
smug 20.7
smuggle 2.37.140
smuggler 2.13.2
smuggling 10.42.62
smugness 2.54.62
smut 20.47
Smuts 11.37, 20.48
smutty 9.22.72
snack 1.10.13
snacks 1.11
snaffle 2.37.121
snag 1.6
snail 5.30.5
snail-like 11.19.1
snail's pace 5.45.5
snake 5.27.5
snakebite 11.36.1
snake oil 18.8
snakeskin 10.31.10
snaky 9.13.4
snap 1.33.3
snapback 1.10.3
snapdragon 2.43.47
snapper 2.18.1
snappish 10.54.16
snappy 9.18.1
snapshot 13.39.8
snare 4.9
snarl 3.30
snarl-up 20.40.5
snatch 1.44
snazzily 9.14.28
snazzy 9.27
sneak 9.36.2
sneaker 2.12.10
sneaking 10.42.48
sneaky 9.13.7
sneer 8.6
sneering 10.42.124

sneeze 9.59.7
snick 10.12.30
snicker 2.12.13
snide 11.14.12
sniff 10.6
sniffer 2.8.2
sniffle 2.37.123
sniffy 9.9.12
snifter 2.22.64
snigger 2.9.5
snip 10.47.3
snipe 11.31
sniper 2.18.9
sniping 10.42.109
snippet 10.56.27
snippy 9.18.8
snitch 10.59
snivel 2.37.294
snivelling 10.42.67
snob 13.0.1
snobbery 9.19.8
snobbish 10.54.1
snobby 9.6.5
snog 13.7
snook 22.21
snooker 2.12.23
snoop 22.29
snooping 10.42.104
snoopy 9.18.12
snoot 22.34
snooty 9.22.74
snooze 22.40
snore 14.10
snorkel 2.37.147
snorkelled 2.38.5
snorkelling 10.42.63
snort 14.44.2
snot 13.39.4
snotty 9.22.68
snout 16.16.6
snow 19.13
snowball 14.27.1
snowball effect 6.12.1
snowbell 6.14.1
snowbird 7.10.1
snowblower 2.3.3
snowboard 14.19.1
snowboarding
10.42.21
snowbound 16.11.1
snow-capped 1.35
Snowdon 2.43.30
Snowdonia National
Park 3.27.5
snowdrift 10.7.2
snowdrop 13.31.6
snowfall 14.27.3
snowfield 9.39.1
snowflake 5.27.3
snow leopard 2.33.15
snow line 11.27.6
snowman 1.21.4
snowmobile 9.38.1

snow pea 9.18.10
snowplough 16.4
snowshoe 22.12
snowstorm 14.33.4
snow-white 11.36.22
snowy 9.4
snub 20.0
snub-nosed 19.53
snuck 20.10
snuff 20.4
snuffbox 13.11.1
snuffer 2.8.5
snuffle 2.37.125
snug 20.7
snuggle 2.37.140
so 19.16
soak 19.31
soaked 19.33
soaking 10.42.53
so-and-so 19.16
soapbox 13.11.1
soapflakes 5.28
soapstone 19.40.16
soapsuds 20.3
soapy 9.18.10
soar 14.13
soaring 10.42.127
sob 13.0
sober 2.5.6
sobering 10.42.114
sobriety 9.22.67
sobriquet 5.7
sob story 9.19.67
so-called 14.28
soccer 2.12.17
Socceroos 22.40.3
sociable 2.37.61
social 2.37.264
social circle 2.37.154
socialisation 2.43.225
socialise 11.42.12
socialism 2.40.62
socialist 10.53.7
socialistic 10.12.82
socialite 11.36.7
sociality 9.22.11
socially 9.14.24
social science 12.10.1
social services 10.62.4
social welfare 4.3
societal 2.37.270
society 9.22.66
sociocultural 2.37.240
sociolect 6.12.3
sociology 9.12.5
sociopath 1.43
sociopolitical 2.37.178
sock 13.10
socket 10.56.15
socking 10.42.51
Socrates 9.59.14
Socratic 10.12.62
Socraticism 2.40.83

sod 13.2
soda 2.6.11
sodden 2.43.40
sodding 10.42.14
sodium 2.40.2
sodomite 11.36.13
sodomy 9.15.2
Sod's Law 14.8
sofa 2.8.4
Sofia 2.1.4
soft 13.6
softback 1.10.7
softball 14.27.2
soft-boiled 18.9
soft-core 14.7
soft drink 10.43.2
soften 2.43.45
softener 2.15.2
soft focus 2.54.32
soft fruit 22.34.10
soft-hearted 2.33.20
soft-heartedness
2.54.76
softie 9.22.76
softly 9.14.86
softly-softly 9.14.86
softness 2.54.88
soft palate 2.56.13
soft-pedal 2.37.108
soft sell 6.14.8
soft-soaping 10.42.104
soft-spoken 2.43.73
soft spot 13.39.6
soft top 13.31.8
software 4.15.4
softy 9.22.76
soggy 9.10.4
soh 19.16
soiree 5.12
sojourn 2.43.52, 7.20
soke 19.31
sol 13.13.2
solace 2.54.35
solar 2.13.18
solar cycle 2.37.184
solar eclipse 10.48
solarium 2.40.14
solar panel 2.37.196
solar plexus 2.54.115
sold 19.35.5
solder 2.6
soldering iron 12.9
soldier 2.10.6
soldiering 10.42.113
soldierly 9.14.3
soldiery 9.19.14
sold-out 16.16.2
sole 19.34.8
solecism 2.40.82
solely 9.14.47
solemn 2.40.25
solemnise 11.42.18
solemnity 9.22.26

solemnly 9.14.70
solicit 10.56.33
solicitation 2.43.209
soliciting 10.42.156
solicitor 2.22.43
Solicitor General
2.37.234
solicitous 2.54.132
solicitousness 2.54.83
solicitude 22.17.5
solid 10.2.26
solidarity 9.22.33
solidify 11.3.2
solidly 9.14.58
solidus 2.54.24
soliloquy 9.26.1
solipsism 2.40.80
solipsistic 10.12.80
solitaire 4.13
solitary 9.19.38
solitude 22.17.5
solo 19.11
soloist 10.53
Solomon 2.43.81
Solon 13.22.7
solstice 10.50.30
Solti 9.22.78
soluble 2.37.100
solute 22.34.2
solution 2.43.257
solvable 2.37.80
solve 13.15
solvency 9.20.29
solvent 2.47.93
Solzhenitsyn 10.31.22
som 19.38
Somali 9.14.30
Somalia 2.1.6
Somaliland 1.22.5
somatic 10.12.56
sombre 2.5
sombrero 19.15.2
some 2.40.33
somebody 9.7.2, 9.7.14
someday 5.3
somehow 16.2
someone 20.29.6
someplace 5.45.4
somersault 14.31.2
Somerset 6.51.10
something 10.42.174
sometime 11.25.3
sometimes 11.26
someway 5.17
somewhat 13.39.9
somewhere 4.15
Somme 13.18
somnambulism
2.40.54
somnambulist 10.53.6
somnolent 2.47.28
Somnus 2.54.81
son 20.29.4

sonar 3.11
sonata 2.22.4
Sondheim 11.25
son et lumière 4.1
song 13.27.4
song and dance 3.37.1
songbird 7.10.1
songbook 21.4.1
Song of Solomon
2.43.81
songster 2.22.108
songwriter 2.22.48
Sonia 2.11.1
sonic 10.12.37
sonic boom 22.25
son-in-law 14.8.2
sonnet 10.56.23
sonny 9.16.26
sonority 9.22.37
sonorous 2.54.102
soon 22.27.8
sooner 2.15.25
soot 21.14
soothe 22.18
soothing 10.42.31
soothsayer 2.0
sooty 9.22.73
sop 13.31
Sophie 9.9
sophism 2.40.51
sophist 10.53
sophistic 10.12.80
sophisticate 5.47.27
sophistication
2.43.156
sophistry 9.19.89
Sophocles 9.59.5
sophomore 14.9.1
soporific 10.12.10
sopping 10.42.110
soppy 9.18.9
soprano 19.13.1
sorbet 5.2
sorbitol 13.13
sorcerer 2.19.1
sorceress 6.47.4
sorcery 9.19.32
sordid 10.2.11
sore 14.13
sorely 9.14.45
soreness 2.54.62
sore spot 13.39.6
sore throat 19.47.8
sorghum 2.40
Soroptimist 10.53.11
sorority 9.22.37
sorrel 2.37.243
sorrow 19.15.4
sorrowful 2.37.121
sorry 9.19.65
sortation 2.43.208
sorted 10.2.64
sortie 9.22.69

SOS 6.47
sot 13.39
Sotheby's 9.59.1
sotto voce 9.24
sou 22.11
soufflé 5.8
sough 16.0
sought-after 2.22.63
souk 22.21
soul 19.34.8
soul-destroying 10.42
soulful 2.37.127
soulless 2.54.35
soulmate 5.47.42
soul-searching
10.42.175
sound 16.11.8
soundbite 11.36.1
sounddesk 6.48
sound effect 6.12.1
sounding 10.42.30
soundless 2.54.44
soundly 9.14.60
soundness 2.54.77
soundproof 22.19.1
soundtrack 1.10.16
Souness 2.54.62
soup 22.29
soupçon 13.22.14
souped-up 20.40.1
soupy 9.18.12
sour 17.0
source 14.42.4
sour cream 9.41.4
sourdough 19.4
sour grapes 5.43
sourly 9.14
sourpuss 21.12
souse 16.14
soused 16.15
soutane 3.34.2
south 16.18
Southampton 2.43.311
southbound 16.11.1
South Carolina 2.15.19
southeast 9.50
southeastern 2.43.312
southerly 9.14.8
southern 2.43.44
Southern Cross
13.34.7
southerner 2.15.2
southern lights 11.37.1
southernmost 19.46.1
Southfields 9.40
South Kensington
2.43.308
southpaw 14.11
south pole 19.34.4
southward 2.33.25
southwards 2.34.1
southwest 6.49.13
southwester 2.22.94

southwestern 2.43.313
souvenir 8.6
sou'wester 2.22.94
sovereign 10.31.20
sovereignty 9.22.83
soviet 2.56.1
Soviet Union 2.43.62
sow (noun) 16.0
sow (verb) 19.16
Soweto 19.18.4
sown 19.40
soy 18.0
soya 2.2
soybean 9.43.1
Soyinka 2.12.25
soy sauce 14.42.4
sozzled 2.38.12
spa 3.12.1
space 5.45.6
spacecraft 3.24.2
spaced 5.46.1
spaceflight 11.36.9
space heater 2.22.26
Space Invaders 2.60.1
spaceman 1.21.8
spaceship 10.47.6
space shuttle 2.37.280
space station 2.43.218
spacesuit 22.34.11
space-time 11.25.7
spacewalk 14.24.4
spacewoman 2.43.91
spacey 9.20.14
spacial 2.37.260
spacing 10.42.134
spacious 2.54.117
spade 5.21.7
spadework 7.14.5
spaghetti 9.22.60
spaghetti junction
2.43.277
spaghettini 9.16.16
spaghetti Western
2.43.313
spake 5.27
spam 1.18
spamming 10.42.85
span 1.21.12
Spandex 6.11.1
spangle 2.37.142
spangled 2.38.4
Spanglish 10.54.12
Spaniard 2.33.7
spaniel 2.37
Spanish 10.54.15
spank 1.30
spanking 10.42.55
spanner 2.15.1
spar 3.12.1
spare 4.10
spare wheel 9.38.8
sparing 10.42.122
spark 3.27.5

taxman 1.21.8
taxonomic 10.12.28
taxonomical 2.37.165
taxonomy 9.15.4
taxpayer 2.0
tayberry 9.19.7
Taylor 2.13.4
TB 9.6.4
Tbilisi 9.20.17
T-bone 19.40.1
T-bone steak 5.27.10
T-cell 6.14.8
tchai 11.0
Tchaikovsky 9.13.22
tea 9.22
teabag 1.6.1
tea break 5.27.7
tea caddy 9.7.1
teacake 5.27.2
teach 9.55
teachable 2.37.79
teacher 2.24
teacher's pet 6.51
tea chest 6.49.11
teach-in 10.31.30
teaching 10.42.175
teacup 20.40.2
tea dance 3.37.1
teahouse 16.14.1
teak 9.36.6
teakettle 2.37.273
teal 9.38
tea lady 9.7.6
tea leaf 9.32.1
tea leaves 9.58
team 9.41.7
teammate 5.47.40
team spirit 10.56.31
teamster 2.22.89
teamwork 7.14.2
tea party 9.22.57
teapot 13.39.5
tear 4.13, 8.10
tearable 2.37.55
tearaway 5.17.1
teardrop 13.31.6
tear duct 20.12
tearful 2.37.121
tear gas 1.36.1
teargas 1.36.1
tearjerker 2.12
tear-off 13.5.4
tearoom 22.25.3
tears 8.14
teary 9.19.62
tease 9.59.13
teasel 2.37.302
teaser 2.27.4
teasing 10.42.186
teaspoon 22.27.6
teat 9.52
teatime 11.25.3
tea towel 17.4

teazle 2.37.302
Tebbitt 10.56.2
Tebet 6.51.14
tech 6.10.6
techie 9.13.5
technetium 2.40.1
technical 2.37.166
technicality 9.22.14
technician 2.43.243
Technicolor 2.13.20
technikon 13.22.6
technique 9.36.2
techno 19.13
technobabble 2.37.24
technocracy 9.20.10
technocrat 1.41.9
technocratic 10.12.62
technological 2.37.159
technologically
  9.14.66
technologist 10.53.4
technology 9.12.13
technophobe 19.22.1
technophobia 2.1.2
technospeak 9.36.4
techy 9.24
tectonic 10.12.38
Ted 6.1
teddy 9.7.7
Te Deum 2.40
tedious 2.54.2
tedium 2.40.2
tee 9.22
tee-hee 9.11
teem 9.41.7
teeming 10.42.87
teen 9.43.18
teenage 5.26
teenaged 5.38
teenager 2.10.2
teens 9.46
teensy-weensy 9.27.10
teeny 9.16.16
teenybopper 2.18.10
Tees 9.59.13
teeter 2.22.26
teeter-totter 2.22.49
teeth 9.54
teethe 9.31
teething troubles
  2.39.1
teetotal 2.37.270
teetotalism 2.40.63
teetotaller 2.13.2
TEFL 2.37.121
Teflon 13.22.7
Tegan 2.43.46
Tehran 3.34.1
tekkie 9.13.5
Tel Aviv 9.56
Tel Aviv-Yafo 19.5
telco 19.10
telebanking 10.42.55

telecast 3.47.2
telecommunication
  2.43.156
telecommunications
  2.51.3
telecommute 22.34.5
telecommuter 2.22.60
telecomputing
  10.42.163
teleconference 2.45.24
teleconferencing
  10.42.138
telecottage 10.11.23
teledensity 9.22.49
telefilm 10.20
telegenic 10.12.32
telegram 1.18.6
telegraph 3.23.3
telegraphic 10.12.9
telegraphy 9.9.2
telekinesis 10.50.18
telekinetic 10.12.66
Telemann 1.21.5
telemark 3.27.4
telemarketing
  10.42.156
telematics 10.13.14
telemetry 9.19.82
telenovela 2.13.5
teleology 9.12.5
telepathic 10.12.87
telepathy 9.23.1
téléphérique 9.36.5
telephone 19.40.3
telephone exchange
  5.37
telephonic 10.12.35
telephonist 10.53.13
telephony 9.16.3
teleplay 5.8.3
teleport 14.44.4
teleportation 2.43.210
teleprinter 2.22.83
teleprocessing
  10.42.136
teleprompt 13.20
Teleprompter 2.22.86
telesales 5.32
telescope 19.44.1
telescopic 10.12.41
teleshopping
  10.42.110
teletext 6.13.1
telethon 13.22
televangelist 10.53.7
televise 11.42.36
television 2.43.336
televisual 2.37.16
teleworker 2.12.9
teleworking 10.42.47
telex 6.11.2
Telford 2.33.5
tell 6.14.10

teller 2.13.7
telling 10.42.70
telling-off 13.5
telltale 5.30.8
tellurian 2.43.22
tellurium 2.40.13
telly 9.14.33
Telnet 6.51.5
temblor 2.13.27
temerity 9.22.36
temp 6.26
temper 2.18.16
tempera 2.19.4
temperament 2.47.33
temperamental
  2.37.286
temperance 2.45.23
temperate 2.56.37
temperature 2.24.3
tempered 2.33.16
tempest 10.53.15
tempestuous 2.54.21
template 2.56.21,
  5.47.39
temple 2.37.229
temporal 2.37.235
temporarily 9.14.22
temporary 9.19.31
temporise 11.42.26
tempt 6.27
temptation 2.43.208
tempter 2.22.86
tempting 10.42.169
temptress 2.54.111
tempura 2.19
tempus fugit 10.56.8
ten 6.29
tenable 2.37.43
tenacious 2.54.118
tenaciously 9.14.84
tenacity 9.22.40
tenancy 9.20.33
tenant 2.47.68
tenantry 9.19.85
tench 6.35
Ten Commandments
  2.46
tend 6.30.9
tendency 9.20.31
tendentious 2.54.127
tender 2.6.22
tenderfoot 21.14
tenderhearted 10.2.36
tender-hearted 2.33.20
tenderise 11.42.22
tenderloin 18.11
tenderness 2.54.63
tendinitis 10.50.25
tendon 2.43.43
tendril 2.37.230
tenement 2.47.33
tenet 10.56.23
tenfold 19.35.1

thermodynamics 10.13.4
thermographic 10.12.9
thermometer 2.22.39
thermonuclear 2.1.6
thermoplastic 10.12.79
Thermopylae 9.14.18
Thermos 2.54.57
thermosphere 8.2
thermostat 1.41.10
thesaurus 2.54.109
these 9.59
Theseus 2.54.14
thesis 10.50.18
Thesmophoria 2.1.26
thespian 2.43.14
Thespis 10.50.11
Thessalonians 2.51
Thessaloníki 9.13.7
Thessaly 9.14.23
theta 2.22.26
Thetis 10.50.24
thews 22.40.1
they 5.0
they'd 5.21
they'll 5.30
they're 4.0
they've 5.51
thiamine 9.43.7
thick 10.12.87
thicken 2.43.68
thickened 2.44.2
thickener 2.15.2
thicket 10.56.14
thickhead 6.1.7
thickheaded 10.2.7
thickly 9.14.66
thickness 2.54.78
thicko 19.10.3
thickset 6.51.10
thick-skinned 10.32
thief 9.32
Thierry 9.19.59
thieve 9.56
thievery 9.19.54
thieving 10.42.176
thigh 11.0
thighbone 19.40.1
thigh-high 11.4
thigh-highs 11.42
thimble 2.37.103
thimbleful 21.7.1
thin 10.31.29
thine 11.27
thin end of the wedge 6.9
thing 10.42.174
thingamajig 10.8
things 10.46
thingumabob 13.0
thingummy 9.15.2
thingy 9.17.1
thin ice 11.34

thinkable 2.37.37
thinker 2.12.25
thinking 10.42.57
think-tank 1.30
thinly 9.14.71
thinned 10.32
thinner 2.15.16
thinning 10.42.100
thin-skinned 10.32
third 7.10
third age 5.26
third-class 3.43.2
thirdly 9.14.56
third party 9.22.57
third-rate 5.47.51
Third Reich 11.41
Third World 7.17
thirst 7.27
thirstily 9.14.42
thirsty 9.22.85
thirteen 9.43.18
thirteenth 9.45
thirtieth 2.58.1
thirty 9.22.61
thirtysomething 10.42.174
this 10.50
thistle 2.37.251
thistledown 16.10.1
thither 2.7.3
tho' 19.0
Thomas 2.54.57
Thompson 2.43.113
Thomson 2.43.130
thong 13.27
Thor 14.0
Thora 2.19.11
thoracic 10.12.53
thorax 1.11.3
thorium 2.40.16
thorn 14.35.6
thorny 9.16.21
thorough 2.19.14
thoroughbred 6.1.13
thoroughfare 4.3
thoroughgoing 10.42.9
thoroughly 9.14.19
Thorpe 14.40
those 19.52
thou 16.0
though 19.0
thought 14.44.9
thoughtful 2.37.130
thoughtfully 9.14.10
thoughtfulness 2.54.80
thoughtless 2.54.52
thoughtlessness 2.54.85
thought-provoking 10.42.53
thoughts 14.45
thousand 2.44.15
thousandfold 19.35.1

thousands 2.50
thousandth 2.48
Thracian 2.43.192
thraldom 2.40.20
thrall 14.27.9
thrash 1.39.4
thrashing 10.42.141
thrash metal 2.37.274
thread 6.1.12
threadbare 4.2
threads 6.3
threat 6.51.8
threaten 2.43.288
threatened 2.44.14
threatening 10.42.96
three 9.19.91
three cheers 8.14
three-dimensional 2.37.211
threefold 19.35.1
three-legged race 5.45.7
three-line whip 10.47.15
three-master 2.22.93
threepence 2.45, 2.45.21
three-ply 11.5.3
three Rs 3.58
threescore 14.7.1
three-sided 10.2.9
threesome 2.40.33
three-way 5.17.3
three-wheeler 2.13.8
threnodic 10.12.7
threnody 9.7.3
thresh 6.50
thresher 2.21.3
thresher shark 3.27.6
threshold 19.35.3
threw 22.10.6
thrice 11.34.1
thrift 10.7.2
thrifty 9.22.77
thrill 10.17.5
thrilled 10.18
thriller 2.13.11
thrilling 10.42.73
thrive 11.38.3
thriven 2.43.324
thriving 10.42.181
thro' 22.10.6
throat 19.47.8
throaty 9.22.71
throb 13.0
throbbing 10.42.13
throe 19.15.9
throes 19.52.7
thrombosis 10.50.20
thrombus 2.54.23
throne 19.40.13
throng 13.27.3
throttle 2.37.278

through 22.10.6
throughout 16.16
throughput 21.14.1
throughway 5.17
throve 19.51.1
throw 19.15.9
throwaway 5.17.1
throwback 1.10.3
thrown 19.40.13
thru 22.10.6
thrum 20.24.2
thrush 20.45.2
thrust 20.44.5
thruster 2.22.103
thruway 5.17
thud 20.2
thug 20.7
thuggish 10.54.7
thulium 2.40.5
thumb 20.24
Thumbelina 2.15.13
thumbnail 5.30.5
thumbnail sketch 6.54
thumbprint 10.38.3
thumbscrew 22.10.4
thumbtack 1.10.18
thump 20.26
thumping 10.42.111
thunder 2.6.27
thunderbolt 19.36
thunderclap 1.33.2
thundercloud 16.6.1
thundering 10.42.115
thunderous 2.54.98
thunderstorm 14.33.4
thunderstruck 20.10.4
thundery 9.19.10
thurible 2.37.92
Thursday 5.3.6
thus 20.42
thwack 1.10.19
thwart 14.44
thy 11.0
thyme 11.25.3
thyroid 18.5.3
thyroid gland 1.22.3
thyroxine 9.43.14
thyself 6.16
ti 9.22
Tia 2.1.29
tiara 2.19.6
Tiber 2.5.4
Tiberias 2.54.11
Tiberius 2.54.11
Tibet 6.51.2
Tibetan 2.43.288
tibia 2.1.1
tic 10.12.54
tick 10.12.54
ticker 2.12.15
ticker tape 5.42.3
ticketing 10.42.156
ticket price 11.34.2

weightlifting **10.42.165**
Weightwatchers **2.60**
weight-watching **10.42.175**
weighty **9.22.59**
weir **8.0**
weird **8.11**
weirdo **19.4**
weird sister **2.22.99**
Welch **6.20**
welcome **2.40.24**
welcome page **5.26.2**
welcoming **10.42.84**
weld **6.15**
welder **2.6**
welfare **4.3**
welfare state **5.47.65**
welfarism **2.40.78**
well **6.14.11**
we'll **9.38.8**
well-advised **11.43.6**
well-aimed **5.34**
well-appointed **10.2.88**
well-balanced **2.49**
well-behaved **5.52**
well-being **10.42.3**
wellbeing **10.42.3**
wellborn **14.35.1**
well-bred **6.1.13**
well-built **10.22.1**
well-chosen **2.43.327**
well-connected **10.2.74**
well-defined **11.28.1**
well-disposed **19.53.4**
well-done **20.29.1**
well-dressed **6.49.7**
well-drilled **10.18**
well-earned **7.21**
well-endowed **16.6**
Welles **6.24**
Wellesley **9.14.101**
well-established **10.55.1**
well-fed **6.1.3**
well-formed **14.34**
well-founded **10.2.22**
well-groomed **22.26**
well-heeled **9.39**
well-honed **19.41**
wellie **9.14.33**
well-informed **14.34**
wellington **2.43.309**
well-intentioned **2.44.13**
well-kept **6.45**
well-known **19.40.9**
well-liked **11.21**
well-lubricated **10.2.43**
well-made **5.21.5**
well-mannered **2.33.13**

well-matched **1.45**
well-meaning **10.42.99**
wellness **2.54.79**
well-nigh **11.6**
well-off **13.5**
well-oiled **18.9**
well-prepared **4.16.2**
well-preserved **7.33**
well-proportioned **2.44.11**
well-provided **10.2.10**
well-read **6.1.12**
well-reasoned **2.44.15**
Wells **6.24**
well-spoken **2.43.73**
wellspring **10.42.130**
well-stocked **13.12**
well-suited **10.2.67**
well-thought-of **2.59**
well-thought-out **16.16.9**
well-to-do **22.2**
well-trained **5.36.1**
well-tried **11.14.16**
well-turned **7.21**
well-upholstered **2.33.22**
well-used **22.41**
well-versed **7.27**
well-wisher **2.21.4**
well-woman **2.43.88**
well-worn **14.35.7**
welly **9.14.33**
Welsh Guard **3.21.2**
Welshman **2.43.100**
Welsh rarebit **10.56.2**
Welshwoman **2.43.88**
welt **6.19**
welter **2.22.75**
welterweight **5.47.70**
Wembley **9.14.55**
Wenceslas **2.54.51**
wench **6.35**
wenching **10.42.175**
wend **6.30**
Wendy house **16.14.1**
Wensleydale **5.30.1**
went **6.34.7**
Wentworth **7.30.2**
wept **6.45**
were **7.0**
we're **8.0**
weren't **7.23**
werewolf **21.8**
wergild **10.18**
wert **7.28**
Weser **2.27.2**
Wesley **9.14.101**
Wesleyan **2.43.6**
Wessex **10.13.11**
west **6.49.13**
westbound **16.11.1**

West End **6.30.10**
western **2.43.313**
westerner **2.15.5**
Western Front **20.33.2**
westernise **11.42.19**
westernised **11.43.2**
Western Isles **11.24**
westernmost **19.46.1**
West Ham **1.18**
Westminster **2.22.107**
Westmoreland **2.44.4**
Weston **2.43.313**
Weston-super-Mare **4.8**
Westphalia **2.1.7**
westward **2.33.25**
westwards **2.34.1**
wet **6.51.15**
wetback **1.10.7**
wet blanket **10.56.10**
wet fish **10.54.6**
wet fly **11.5.2**
wetland **1.22.3**
wetlands **2.50**
wet-look **21.4.5**
wetness **2.54.88**
wet nurse **7.26**
wetsuit **22.34.12**
wetware **4.15.4**
we've **9.56**
Wexford **2.33.5**
whack **1.10.19**
whacked **1.12**
whacking **10.42.41**
whacky **9.13.1**
whale **5.30.11**
whalebone **19.40.1**
whaleboned **19.41**
whaler **2.13.4**
whale shark **3.27.6**
whaling **10.42.68**
wham **1.18**
whammy **9.15.1**
wharf **14.21**
Wharton **2.43.301**
what **13.39.9**
whatchamacallit **10.56.19**
whatever **2.25.6**
whatnot **13.39.4**
what's **13.40**
whatsername **5.33.4**
whatsisname **5.33.4**
whatsit **10.56.32**
whatsoever **2.25.7**
wheat **9.52.14**
wheaten **2.43.294**
wheatfield **9.39.1**
wheatgerm **7.18**
wheatgrass **3.43.5**
wheatish **10.54.19**
wheatmeal **9.38.3**
whee **9.26**

wheedle **2.37.109**
wheedling **10.42.61**
wheel **9.38.8**
wheelbarrow **19.15.1**
wheelbase **5.45.1**
wheelchair **4.14**
wheel clamp **1.20.2**
Wheeler **2.13.8**
wheeler-dealer **2.13.8**
wheelhouse **16.14.5**
wheelie **9.14.37**
wheelie bin **10.31.2**
wheel lock **13.10.3**
wheelwright **11.36.16**
wheeze **9.59.17**
wheezy **9.27.3**
Wheldon **2.43.30**
whelp **6.18**
when **6.29**
whence **6.33**
whenever **2.25.6**
whensoever **2.25.7**
where **4.15**
whereabouts **16.17**
whereas **1.48**
whereat **1.41.8**
whereby **11.2**
wherefore **14.3**
wherein **10.31.20**
whereof **13.43.1**
whereon **13.22.12**
wheresoever **2.25.7**
whereto **22.13**
whereupon **13.22.11**
wherever **2.25.6**
wherewithal **14.27**
whet **6.51.15**
whether **2.7.2**
whetstone **19.40.16**
whew **22.4.2**
whey **5.17**
which **10.59.1**
whichever **2.25.6**
Whicker **2.12.11**
whiff **10.6**
whiffle **2.37.123**
whiffy **9.9.12**
Whig **10.8.2**
while **11.22.9**
whim **10.26**
whimper **2.18.16**
whimsical **2.37.183**
whimsicality **9.22.14**
whimsy **9.27.9**
whine **11.27.20**
whiner **2.15.18**
whinge **10.33**
whinger **2.10.9**
whining **10.42.101**
whinny **9.16.18**
whiny **9.16.20**
whip **10.47.15**
whipcord **14.19.5**

zippered **2.33**
zippy **9.18.8**
zip-up **20.40.7**
zircon **13.22.6**
zirconium **2.40.12**
zit **10.56.38**
zither **2.7.3**
Z-list **10.53.6**
zloty **9.22.68**
zodiac **1.10.1**
Zoe **9.4**
Zog **13.7**

Zola **2.13.18**
zombie **9.6.9**
zonal **2.37.220**
zone **19.40.19**
zoned **19.41**
zoning **10.42.92**
zoo **22.15**
zoogeography **9.9.4**
zoography **9.9.3**
zookeeper **2.18.6**
zoological **2.37.159**
zoologist **10.53.4**

zoology **9.12.4**
zoom **22.25**
zoomorphic **10.12.12**
zoonomy **9.15.4**
zoopathology **9.12.18**
zoophile **11.22.2**
zoophilic **10.12.18**
zoophobic **10.12.5**
zootherapy **9.18.5**
zootomy **9.15.7**
zoot suit **22.34.12**
Zoroaster **2.22.90**

Zoroastrianism **2.40.69**
Zulu **22.6**
Zululand **1.22.3**
Zurich **10.12.42**
zwieback **1.10.3**
zydeco **19.10.2**
zygomatic **10.12.56**
zygote **19.47.3**